First published by Jacana Media (Pty) Ltd in 2024
10 Orange Street
Sunnyside
Auckland Park 2092
South Africa
+2711 628 3200
www.jacana.co.za

Khumisho Moguerane, 2024
All rights reserved.

ISBN 978-1-4314-3277-6

Cover design by publicide
Editing by Colin Bundy
Proofreading by Lara Jacob
Set in Ehrhardt MT Std 10.5/14pt
Printed and bound by CTP Printers
Job no. 004149

See a complete list of Jacana titles at www.jacana.co.za

Morafe

Person, family and nation in colonial Bechuanaland, 1880s to 1950s

Khumisho Moguerane

Praise for *Morafe*

'Magisterial, elegant and shimmering with insight on every page, this captivating book traces the story of a renowned southern African family, the Molemas. Epic and intimate, *Morafe* presents a compelling and unexpected cast of characters confronting ethical questions of personhood on a rapidly changing frontier. 'The deft narrative traces the fealties and fault lines within and between families, kin, friends and neighbours, showing how these private dramas had public consequences and shaped larger developments in the sub-continent. A magnificent achievement that changes much of what we think we know about southern African history.'

Isabel Hofmeyr, Professor Emeritus at WiSER, Wits University, and Distinguished Scholar in Residence at New York University

'*Morafe* is the saga of South Africa's formative years as it has not been told before, a luminous, sprawling tale of ambition, injustice, love, bitterness, and tragedy. 'Making full use of several cachés of family letters as well as other archives, Khumisho Moguerane tells how "sons inherited the ambitions of their fathers" in the late nineteenth century but were denied "the means to realise them" in subsequent decades. *Morafe* is scholarly and fine-grained yet written with brio and flair. The story starts in the world of the partnered royal "Barolong" courts, Molema and Montshiwa, under whom Africans and some white men chose to live as subjects, and builds outward, via the successes, loves, divisions and gendered conflicts of a generation of black leaders under siege, including the founders of the African National Congress. It is about people's relentless pursuit of citizenship, through the years of their collective betrayal by the state. '*Morafe* offers a cosmopolitan account rooted in the soil. It opens a vista onto southern Africa's past that is needed most desperately right now – there is nothing else like it!'

Paul S. Landau, author of *Spear: Mandela and the Revolutionaries* and Professor of History at the University of Maryland in College Park

For my parents, Rasegai and Chumile Moguerane

Contents

Acknowledgements	ix
Note on orthography	xiii
Preface	xv
Introduction	1
Fathers/Moreness	41
Family/Placement	89
Sons/Homecoming	267
Conclusion	387
Notes	409
Index	457

Acknowledgements

THE MOLEMAS HAVE THEIR own dedicated and rigorous historian, Galefele Molema, who has meticulously preserved his family papers. He has been interpreting his family's past for longer than my own inquiry. He participated in the making of this book with care and open-mindedness. Without his private records, and his involvement in following the trail of his ancestry, it would have been impossible to write this book. I would like to express my sincere gratitude to him.

I owe the greatest intellectual debt to William Beinart, who devoted many hours supervising my doctoral dissertation at the University of Oxford whence this book draws. Over the years, he has supported every undertaking I pursue, and from the beginning dared me fully to possess my own unique voice as a historian. The late Colin Murray helped to 'break me in' as a historian through his deep care, humour and conversation. Although this book makes very little direct reference to these two historians' work, their writing inspired it to a great extent, especially in how they present the countryside as though it were the centre of every world, and rural lives the epicentres of history.

I owe an immeasurable debt to Professor Leloba Molema and Mrs Mmaditshepe Mercy Molema, both of whom invited me to share their homes when I was doing research in Gaborone, Botswana and in Mafikeng, South Africa respectively. Other members of the Molema family, including Mr Batho Molema, committed time sharing memories of their lives and parents with me, and did so with such a degree of candour and reflexivity that I can still hear and recite from memory some of the remarkable turns of phrase.

I am also indebted to Colin Bundy, firstly for his highly influential work on the southern African countryside, but also because as one of the examiners of my doctoral project at the University of Oxford and editor of this book, he has shared with me a great deal about the art of writing history. I consider it a great privilege to have had him as editor of this book and wish to thank him very much for consistently supporting me and my intellectual projects.

Janis Grobbelaar and Charles Puttergill worked tirelessly to cultivate my sociological imagination. I am grateful for their support and confidence in my abilities. I wish to thank Jan-Georg Deutsch for his support and for convening a weekly afternoon seminar at St Cross College in Oxford. My colleagues, all of them doctoral students and committed Africanists, were stimulating, funny and extremely generous. Jonny Steinberg also convened an equally stimulating weekly seminar at the Centre for African Studies at Oxford.

It is difficult to put into words my gratitude to the University of Johannesburg for its continuing support of my intellectual project. I would like to thank my colleagues at its History Department for many greatly enriching exchanges over the years that have shaped my thinking. Stephen Sparks was the very first reader of the completed manuscript. I wish to express my sincere thanks to him for that undertaking. I owe many thanks to Gerald Groenewald for walking many journeys of intellectual inquiry with me over the years, but especially, as far as this book is concerned, for presenting me with the gift of the Afrikaans novelist Karel Schoeman, who helped me grapple with the experiences of the other side of the colonial frontier – white settlers, and their own struggles of immigration, land and power in the South African countryside. I thank Rafael Winkler for very stimulating conversations on Martin Heidegger. I owe Bongani Ngqulunga a great debt for the three months that I spent at the Johannesburg Institute for Advanced Study at the same university during which time I worked on the more theoretical aspects of this book. The Faculty of Humanities at the University of Johannesburg made possible a year-long writing fellowship during which time I wrote this book. I wish to thank Alex Broadbent and Kammila Naidoo for making that opportunity possible. The former vice-chancellor of the University of Johannesburg, Tshilidzi Marwala, deserves very special acknowledgement for his committed support.

The Molemas' archives involved so many records and people that no single book can do it justice, nor can any single author hope to access and analyse every document. It would have been impossible to complete this book without Brian Willan's two excellent biographies of Solomon Plaatje. I also relied on the unpublished work of Jane Starfield who covers an astonishing volume of archival material about the Molopo Reserve. I wish to thank Keith

Breckenridge for commenting extensively on an article that contained the preliminary conceptual framework towards this book. I also wish to thank Johan Fourie for providing crucial material on interpreting economic lives in early twentieth-century South Africa. I would like to thank the two anonymous readers of the manuscript for very useful commentary.

I thank Bridget Impey for embracing this book from the very beginning, and her team at Jacana Media for publishing it. I am very grateful to Lara Jacob for agreeing to take on the laborious task of proofreading with grace and enthusiasm.

It is impossible to mention by name every single person who supported me throughout this very lengthy journey. I am grateful to my many layers of family: the Moguerane, Kwinana, Gcabashe, Kongisa, Mohlakeng, Boshoff, Heffernan, Malan, Goodgall, Letlabika and Skwatsha families. I wish to express my sincere thanks especially to Anne Heffernan, Sheila Goodgall. Lerato Mogoatlhe, Charles Puttergill, Luana and Dione Malan, Anina Boshoff, Pumla Moguerane, Makatleho Mohlakeng, Lesedi Dibakwane, Sonwabile Mnwana, Nonhlanhla Sebola, Gugulethu Mthembu, Pamela Ngoako and Verah Matola.

It is impossible to exaggerate how much I learnt from the countless, often spirited conversations between ordinary women and men that I have heard in my parents' home over the years. Their lives and stories, their disagreements, their assessment of their own history and social situation, probably shaped my reading of the literature and my understanding of the archive more than any other interpretive lens. This is one of the many reasons I am especially grateful to my family and our home.

I could not have written this book without the love and support of my siblings, Sekhoane and Itumeleng Moguerane, my nephew Lesego Moguerane and my niece Mandisa Kwinana. I was able to write this book in my home in Johannesburg during the lockdowns of Covid-19 because my nephew, Lesego Moguerane, had taken on the sole responsibility of caring for my elderly mother in Maseru, Lesotho. I am grateful to him.

Finally, I owe the very possibility of my unique orientation in the world to my father, the late Rasegai Moguerane, and my mother, Chumile Moguerane. They mediated my first experience of 'moreness', which set me on a course to undertake new ventures with courage. They worked tirelessly to make my 'placement' in the world secure. In their hopes of who I could become, they allowed me many freedoms to shape my own 'homecoming'. These are aspects of being and belonging that I explore in this book, both in a setting of family life and of forging a country. This book is dedicated to them.

Note on orthography

AT THE TIME DURING which these Molemas lived, there was not yet a standardised orthography for the vernacular language I write as 'Sechuana', that was then spoken primarily by people who were coming into a consciousness of themselves as 'Bechuana'. The spelling 'Secoana' and 'Becoana' was also common but there were also other ways of representing the same term intelligibly. I use 'Sechuana' and 'Bechuana' because I am concerned here with the territories that were formally known as 'Bechuanaland' and I wish to convey some congruence between the language, the people and the territory. However, I endeavoured to be faithful to the historical characters' own preference of spelling where their words appear in quotes. I do the same when I quote the work of other scholars. Today, the words 'Setswana' and 'Batswana' are used but this is a more mid-to-late twentieth-century convention, which is still observed today. Finally, especially amongst the Barolong, the letter 'f' is silent and sounds as the letter 'h' in pronunciation. It has become a recent post-apartheid convention to dispense with the 'f' and replace it with 'h'. However here I relied on the convention that stands in the archive that is still followed by many first-language speakers of the language today. This to write the 'f' and pronounce it as 'h'. Hence, the town I present here as 'Mafikeng' now appears in South Africa as 'Mahikeng'. Moreover, I use the spelling 'Mafikeng' to refer to the main town of the Molopo Reserve and 'Mafeking' to refer to the neigbouring town of mainly European settlement adjacent to the reserve. This is the spelling of these towns that appears in the archive. The title of this book is *Morafe* and is properly pronounced 'Morahe'.

Morafe

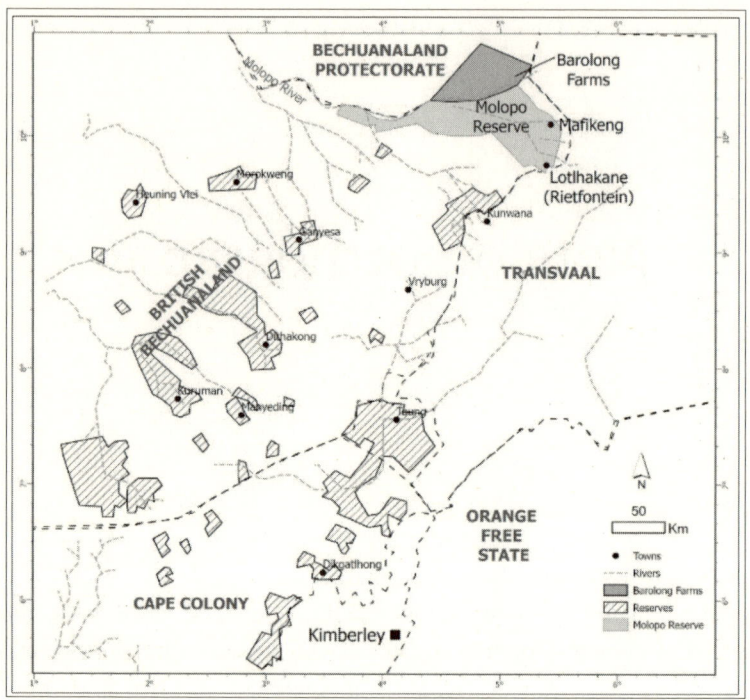

Figure 1: Molopo Reserve and Barolong Farms, 1885

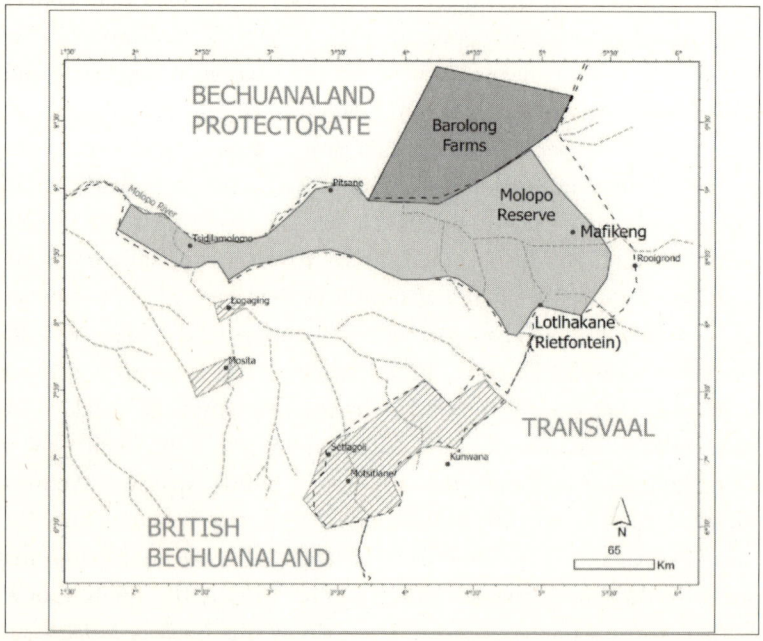

Figure 2: Reserves of British Bechuanaland, 1885. Source: GISP, Lutendo Zwedzi

Preface

IN WRITING THIS BOOK, my intention was not only an immersion in the extraordinarily rich archive and writings of the Molemas, but also to foreground a distinctive theoretical approach by focusing on Sechuana concepts such as *botho* and *morafe* through an interdisciplinary perspective. It is important that southern African scholars explore new general approaches to critical issues in our history, and that we attempt to make these approaches explicit in order to stimulate debate and further rethinking. In the Introduction, I weave together a broader statement of this approach, together with an outline of the Molemas' family history, and a description of the archival sources. While I believe that this is an important and innovative contribution, I realise that some of the theoretical material may appear dense to readers who are essentially looking for a more narrative history. Those readers can read only the first portion of the Introduction, up to and including the section 'British imperialism, African agency and the Molemas' and then move on to the beginning of the first chapter. These readers may also wish to omit the Conclusion, which also contains theoretical elements.

Introduction

THIS IS A HISTORY OF HOW two generations of one family, the Molemas, influenced the arrangements of British rule in Bechuanaland from the 1880s to the 1950s. At the heart of the book are Silas Molema, a pious Methodist convert, chief, businessman and landowner, and three of his children – his nephew Sebopioa, whom he raised as a son, his son Modiri and his daughter Harriet. His sons, Sebopioa and Modiri, travelled abroad to America and Scotland to study law and medicine respectively. The two aspired to be among the leading men of their generation. Their sister pursued her own professional ambitions as a schoolteacher. She came to occupy roles that men would ordinarily perform but were finding increasingly difficult to do under British rule in the early decades of the twentieth century. There is a fifth protagonist, in many ways a member of the family. He is Solomon Plaatje, whose career as a newspaper man, writer and politician is well known. Less familiar is how his career's early genesis lay in his deep attachment to the Molemas. Indeed, a central vein that runs through this story is Silas Molema's aspiration to make and grow a family in ways that transcended both blood affiliation and the boundaries of his own homestead. Around these Molemas swirl other lives, those of siblings, cousins, spouses, children, uncles, many friends and allies who shared the life stories recounted here and belonged to the family. There were also hundreds of ordinary householders, men and women of diverse skin colour and dialects living on the Molemas' farmlands, many of them tenants, whose lives and futures remained entangled with the family's own moral and political sensibilities.

Hence, although this book is a family history, it is also a study of the colonial world in which the Molemas lived. It is a story of people living along a frontier where racial and political identities had not yet become fixed, and how they attempted to live and belong together as the *morafe*. The word *morafe* was and continues to be variously translated today as 'nation', 'tribe' or 'people' but essentially it delineates an ethical boundary outside of which an individual has no capacity for personhood or *botho*. Silas Molema's family, especially in their roles as chiefs of their Barolong, landowners and active members of key political movements, shaped the moral hierarchies, obligations, reciprocities and other everyday procedures that confirmed being in the *morafe*. The *morafe* was at the centre of the ideas and beliefs that animated the Molemas in public and private domains. It informed their sense of honour in their private affairs and the political and social orders they hoped to see established in Bechuanaland. Hence, in telling the Molemas' history across two generations, this book also reconstructs the larger story of a frontier society's struggle to forge and remain connected to the *morafe* and the changes that these intertwined family dynamics and moral struggles together brought about. It is a history that bridges boundaries as it explores the struggles for personhood that shaped what became the countries of South Africa and Botswana.

Britain annexed Bechuanaland in 1885 as two territories, stacked one on top of the other and separated by the Molopo River. The first, British Bechuanaland, encompassed the North West and Northern Cape provinces of today's South Africa, while the second, the Bechuanaland Protectorate, became today's Botswana. The book argues that the Molemas, a chiefly and educated family of the Barolong, were central protagonists in how South Africa and Botswana emerged as two separate and independent nation states. For many decades after 1885, it was not a foregone conclusion that the political boundary between these two territories would be permanent. Instead, where the border should be if it ought to be there at all, and what such a boundary would mean politically, were not questions people considered seriously to affect their lives or movements. Indeed, these were issues they would have disagreed about had it been then necessary to consider the matter. In the experience of many ordinary families along this frontier, the border functioned mainly as a trade and livestock boundary. It had no real relevance for people, for property or for a sense of political identity. In fact, for educated and Protestant hereditary rulers of Bechuanaland like the Molemas and their fellow founding generation of the South African Native National Congress (SANNC) in the early twentieth century, whose members came from both sides of the Molopo River, the nation state was not an attractive way to consolidate a people's nationhood.

The age of European empire on the African continent, as it was in many other parts of the world, was also a fertile window for political experimentation. Empire was not only important in the circulation of competing ideas about nationhood but more critically in how it enabled the 'reconceptualisation of sovereignty' in a context where internationalism emerged as a strong ideal from the late nineteenth century.[1] Following Britain's annexation of Bechuanaland in 1885, the Molemas emerged as a senior ruling family over a territory that was effectively an autonomous chiefly jurisdiction *within* the British Empire. Britain allowed itself very little involvement in the territories and generally left the people to rule themselves. The territory was also a cross-border polity straddling British Bechuanaland and the Bechuanaland Protectorate. The Molopo River ran through it, dividing the territory almost equally between what would emerge as the Republic of South Africa and Botswana in the latter half of the twentieth century. This chieftaincy was not the only one to claim such recognition and autonomy in the British Empire, but its unique situation as a cross-border polity would in later years lend it an intriguing set of historical dynamics as far as the meaning and the experience of the border were concerned.

Although the Molemas emerged as amongst the most significant, probably the most successful, chiefs and landlords on both sides of the border, they were not the paramount rulers of the domain they controlled. The Ratshidi Barolong were under the *de facto* rule of a junior house – the Molemas – that had excelled in establishing the kinds of Protestant 'ecclesiastical statehoods' that characterised the successful decades of reassembling states after the wars and famines of the 1820s.[2] The senior house – the Montsioas – nevertheless hung on, never yielding, and thus precipitated a peculiar symbiosis of shared power between two houses that needed each other, presented a formidable united front against common foes, married each other, and yet remained bitterly at war. Empire created possibilities that were especially advantageous for the Molemas in the family feud. They were educated and forward-looking, ready and able to connect themselves and their educated followers to the global arena of 'progress' and internationalism that were shaping ideals of political freedom and culture.[3]

Ideals of 'progress' profoundly shaped understandings of political authority amongst literate frontier people who were coming into a conception of themselves as the 'Bechuana'. They were embracing 'progress' not as a European aspiration they were adapting to their environment, but rather as a domestic ideal that had its origins in local arenas of practice that predated European settlement. Thus, empire became the frame of political authority and global connections that embroiled 'progress' in contestations about tradition and honour amongst literate communities. It situated debates about the political and cultural requirements of an ethical, reputable life, which as this book argues, are the fundamental existential concerns underpinning all conceptions of nationhood.

However, as arrangements of empire changed in southern Africa, so too did the Molemas' own conceptions of nationhood across two generations. This book is about how family matters, meaning the drama of the intimate hierarchies of affection and privilege in Silas Molema's family, shaped understandings of nationhood along this frontier and by so doing, impinged most directly on how and why the nation state became the dominant model of organising nationhood from the 1950s along this frontier. It is not that the nation state was completely absent from conceptions of nationhood in the earlier period but rather that it remained on the margins of political organisations like the SANNC and especially political platforms in the Bechuanaland Protectorate where hereditary chiefs played leading roles. Amongst the thicker strands that weave the story of the nation state in this setting, are the Molemas' attempts to uphold the original terms of British annexation when colonial governments later determined to do away with them after the South African War (1899–1902). Such autonomous chiefly jurisdictions not only presented serious obstacles to colonial administrators' intention to break up and segregate frontier households of so-called *métissage* and mixed racial colouring, which were typical along frontiers of European settlement on the continent and elsewhere.[4] Chiefly and patriarchal power also mediated a grid of rents and dependencies that effectively locked thousands of landless households out of these reserves. The Molemas' life stories in this unsettled political frontier are all threads that fed the spindle, private lives crisscrossing with dramatic public agendas: their generational conflicts, the disappointment of children never fully free to pursue aspirations too far beyond the legacy of a powerful and propertied chiefly home, and yet the same children's awe of their father and their desire never to fall short of his confidence in them.

The Molemas' residence still stands on the southern banks of the Molopo River in Mafikeng, the capital of the North West Province of South Africa. Mafikeng owes its founding to Isaac Molema, who established it in the mid-nineteenth century as a centre of Methodism and literacy. Isaac Molema was Silas Molema's father. He may have been a man of 'brown' or 'black' skin colour but these categories were not then known or important along this frontier of 'mixed living' and *métissage,* other than as a common description for skin colour with no definitive influence on cultural life or social status. This book shows how these categories emerged as standard classifications denoting race only from the early twentieth century, certainly in the hinterlands beyond the Orange River, but even then it would take a while before 'black' and 'white' could hold fixed social meanings. There also existed a wide array of regional identifications in a frontier situation where there was not yet a solid conception of a 'South Africa' or a 'Botswana'. The territorial reach of both spheres, and to whom they belonged, remained unsettled into the very late twentieth century. The story of the Molemas' changing fortunes across two generations, and of how they reproduced some of their legacy in new veins of influence, is part of the making of these categories and of how they gained legitimacy in political discourse.

Remarkably, this book is the first telling of this story. Nevertheless, Silas Molema (b. 1852) and his son Modiri (b. 1891) appear faintly on the margins of writings on empire and nationalism in South Africa. They appear in John Comaroff and Jean Comaroff's two pioneering ethnographical volumes, *Of Revelation and Revolution*, as the foremost members of a literate class of Protestants from the mid-nineteenth to the early twentieth centuries in Bechuanaland, set apart from their kin and neighbours by a way of life that resembled that of the middle classes in Britain and in the Cape.[5] Jane Starfield has reconstructed a detailed biography of three generations of Molema men – Isaac, Silas and Modiri Molema. However, as this book outlines, biology was not the only delineation of family.[6] Silas Molema had accepted his nephew, Sebopioa (b. 1881), as a son in his household. He had also invited and welcomed Solomon Plaatje (b. 1876) to play some of the critical roles that only a son could play, making Plaatje as it were a member of the family. Brian Willan has written two excellent biographies of Plaatje, who was certainly one of the early twentieth century's most gifted writers and intellectuals.[7] On the other hand, Sebopioa and Harriet (b. 1896) are almost completely absent in the literature. These were not Silas Molema's only children but these four became mature adults during his lifetime, and thus became embroiled in the dynamics of generation and gender that shaped the political history of this northern frontier.

British imperialism, African agency and the Molemas

Britain's involvement in Bechuanaland was a fragile and hasty project, orchestrated by an imperial government then strongly opposed to burdening itself with political control over territories it nevertheless needed in order to secure regional dominance. It preferred to secure its dominance through informal means by forging collaboration with diverse agents on the ground rather than formal territorial control.[8] The actual arrangement of imperial control in Bechuanaland confirms that though it needed these vast territories to retain Britain's dominance in southern Africa, the Imperial Office was careful not to burden itself with matters of governance in the region. Britain's early attempt to cede the territories to others no sooner than it had acquired them, reveals an empire that at best proceeded without any coherent strategy of what to do after achieving its immediate goals.[9] The 'scramble' for Bechuanaland proved very chaotic in its practical implementation, which reminds us that Britain's conquest of new African territories at this time, including Bechuanaland, was less a reflection of imperial strength and volition and more of her extreme vulnerability in world affairs following the crisis it had created in Egypt in 1884. Before this crisis, Britain had resisted the lobbying of missionaries like John Mackenzie and chiefs along and across the Molopo River to annex Bechuanaland and stop the blood bath of frontier warfare over land.[10] Afterwards, Britain went ahead without hesitation, pursuing the annexation largely to militate against the emerging regional dominance of a German and Afrikaner alliance in southern Africa. Britain's primary collaborators from 1885 were chiefs, many of them literate and Protestant.

There are alternative accounts of this colonisation, which place more emphasis on Britain's interest in the burgeoning gold mining industry and in the resistance that Bechuanaland chiefdoms waged against European conquest. This literature foregrounds resistance to, rather than collaboration with, empire as the dominant orientation of colonial subjects, and also situates imperial expansion in the material advantages Bechuanaland had to offer both Britain herself and the thousands of settlers making homes in southern Africa.[11] My intention is not to reopen this debate but rather to highlight the fragilities of empire that made it possible for families like the Molemas to amass great wealth and influence in a colonial situation. Educated chiefs often upheld a crucial distinction between settlers, especially settler governments, and the British Empire. They resisted the authority of settler governments on the grounds that these governments only satisfied settler avarice, but they embraced Britain as a benevolent and moral authority.

Of course, the Molemas and others were never privy to Britain's intentions in the annexation of their territories. In fact, neither were historians until the archive of the Imperial Office became available more than half a century later. Thus, chiefs took it for granted that their colonisation was due to theirs and sympathetic missionaries' lobbying to colonise Bechuanaland and quash the frontier wars that were devastating their chiefdoms. More importantly, as this book relates, chiefs believed that British colonisation was an answered prayer. The Molemas and their supporters were pious men and charted historical events on a cartography of faith. They understood Britain's annexation of their territories not as conquest but as divine intervention to rescue them from the loss of life and land amidst very bloody frontier wars.

Moreover, even as they were courting British protection against settler aggression, chiefs had in mind to pursue a political purpose of their own. In inviting British rule and signing themselves up as the foremost collaborators in the region, these educated Protestant hereditary chiefs negotiated and then enjoyed unusual terms of autonomy in the British Empire from the late nineteenth century. In contrast to the policy in the Cape and Natal colonies, initially the reserves of British Bechuanaland and the Bechuanaland Protectorate were not Crown Lands. They belonged to their inhabitants. Another departure from accepted policy was that Britain recognised hereditary chiefs and refrained from interfering with any matters of governance by chiefs. British officials recognised the paramount chiefs and headmen amongst the rungs of ruling families. Succession in these positions followed existing customs. Chiefs had secure imperial protection and essentially ruled themselves with a guarantee that Britain would protect their territories. It was a perfect environment for productive agrarian life, especially grain farming and cattle ranching. After many decades of unrest the wars were over. People settled down, married and had children. Displaced families returned but there were also many more immigrants coming from many parts of the world looking for land, work and connection to other people. Men transporting goods in their own wagons did particularly well as did traders and probably builders, but this was the situation largely in the northern territories along the Molopo River, where the cluster of Barolong reserves were, and also across the Molopo in the Protectorate. The wars had devastated the southern chiefdoms nearer the diamond fields, like the Batlhaping. For southern chiefdoms, British annexation felt like the final crush of conquest.[12]

Frontier living is volatile and uncertain, but there was no reason to suspect that the northern chiefs' advantageous position in this imperial dispensation would not last. There is evidence of deep trust between Barolong chiefs and British officials in Bechuanaland, of friendship and even mutual affection. Much depended on these relationships. We see in fact that senior bureaucrats of the colonial government allowed themselves to be led by the decisions of their junior counterparts on the ground, who in turn worked with chiefs. Bechuanaland remained an informal affair for some time, even after Britain ceded British Bechuanaland to the Cape Colony in 1895. In the town centres of the Barolong reserves, the 'stadts' as locals referred to them, day-to-day business relied on entanglements of trust and mutual dependence across the colour bar. Regional identities were strong and celebrated the spirit of self-reliance in the harsh, undependable climate prone to protracted droughts. Even when the discourse of race as skin colour was becoming more trenchant, here perhaps there was too much at stake. People were too vulnerable to afford the personal satisfactions of prejudice when deciding where to live and with whom to work and survive. Barolong chiefs with ambition and education were at the top of the social and political ladder. The reserved lands were effectively theirs, and they – not European settlers – were the British Empire's most favoured subjects. In fact, life was often extremely hard for European settlers, both Dutch and English-speaking, especially for their womenfolk. One or two such women, barely literate, have left hints of their own strategies and hardships in a world of often-absent men who were away earning wages in the mines and on the railways.

The turning point was the South African War (1899–1902). It was the first pivotal development that changed the official arrangements of the British Empire on both sides of the Molopo River. For both 'Boer' and 'British', it was a costly and protracted war that forced compromises towards a Union of South Africa. The two British colonies, the Cape and Natal, and the two Boer Republics, the Transvaal and the Orange Free State, were to become a single British dominion. By then, British Bechuanaland made up a large proportion of the Cape's landmass but the continuing terms of annexation that British officials had negotiated with chiefs in 1885 meant that the Cape government, and later the Union government also, had no jurisdiction over thousands of frontier households living in these reserves. Settler governments' own intention after the war was managing the permanent settlement of a European diaspora that had accepted this African landscape as home, and yet these governments could not entirely subdue the populations of indigenous peoples and other earlier colonisers that overwhelmingly outnumbered it. It quickly became apparent that the relatively autonomous chiefly jurisdictions of Bechuanaland presented grave challenges to settler governments' segregationist and other colonial projects, and to the ambitious colonial administrators eager to experiment and leave a personal stamp of their own bureaucratic innovation in the region.

Silas Molema wanted to retain the existing arrangements of British rule after the South African War. His children had to grow up in his struggle. It inspired them, enraged them, limited and yet broadened their horizons. Their father's political struggle was a crucial resource in inducting his offspring into adulthood and, more than that, was what he had in hand to create opportunities of love and attachment to them. A great deal of his mostly landed wealth depended on the outcome of this battle but in any case, his piety and sense of destiny and vocation drove him on. The land he owned, the care of that land, the guardianship of its people, the concern to make it a hub of 'progress' was, in his understanding, all about family, but it also made family matters very difficult. For instance, these struggles and aspirations made love and marriage a complicated arrangement, as was any decision about education, professional life and place of residence.

The children loved their father with exceptional devotion, with a keenness to please him and with deep admiration. They dreaded mediocrity. Their aspirations outran an ordinary commonplace life. The stakes of personal honour were very high. Yet, the desires of love and honour do not always converge harmoniously, at least not everybody agreed about where and how such orientations to the world should come together. Inevitably, there also developed rifts, distance and immense pain in the course of making family and holding it together. Generational conflict emerged here, within these intimate entanglements, long before it articulated through public institutions and political tensions. In African society, as historian John Iliffe writes, contestations about honour are the coalface of generational conflict and as such, a driving force of the continent's political discourse and mobilisation.[13] The Molemas' story lays bare the private disappointments between lovers, between parents and children, between neighbours and friends that underpin generational conflict. In this instance, generational conflict had extraordinary political consequences. Thus, in so far as histories of race, power and nationhood in Bechuanaland affected the making of the nation state in South Africa and Botswana, this is a book about how 'the family functions for society'.[14]

Everyday practice and vernacular categories: Botho and morafe in the Molemas' archive

There is a way of doing informed by social 'rules', which is not to say everyone does the same thing. Rather rules are formal abstractions of myriad tactics and manoeuvres of everyday strategies. Rules are to practice what a map is to a native of a place who has experience with the topography. Unless something extraordinary happens, he does not consult the map but rather proceeds along the 'beaten tracks', along the routes he personally knows to work. Sometimes he experiments, tries a different route or carves a new path on the landscape.[15] The more one grows and develops into a native of the terrain and becomes one with it, the more enhanced the capacity to experiment and to innovate on the hoof. The rule holds the same purpose as a map for the foreigner, who has not had the experience of knowing a social landscape from diverse routes of socialisation: mimicry, children's games, stories, schooling, observing the lives of others and all manner of feeling and learning that inculcates the social environment into a sense of what counts as normal, rational and right. Often the outsider does not possess the advantage of language, a 'mother tongue' that also functions to acclimatise mind and body to its historical dispensation. The outsider, especially the anthropologist, learns social rules as a compendium of 'laws and customs' mostly from the revered members of the society. The natives of the place may never formally learn the idioms and decrees of how to live, the names of the streets as it were, but in doing their walking in the place they know well, they know the strategies of everyday life that earn someone the recognition of his familiars, 'there's a *real* man, *really* a man.'[16]

This understanding of practice will be familiar to readers of Pierre Bourdieu whose insights, especially in his widely known earlier work, *The Logic of Practice*, have shaped the terms of my analysis and my engagement with the archive.[17] In line with this thinking, when families are navigating unexpected situations with uncertain outcomes, they make their rational decisions according to historical understandings of what is 'natural' in the world. In a later work, *Distinction*, Bourdieu observes that people sink into a crisis of 'moral unworthiness' when they no longer have the means or opportunity to make decisions according to their 'natural' role in the world.[18] He also observes that when some people march out of step with existing intuitive feelings of what works and is right, others around them experience a moral anxiety. This is an important observation but unfortunately Bourdieu stops here, without providing answers to some key questions. Why is practice essentially concerned with moral lives? When a moral crisis develops at the limits of practice, that is to say at that point in time where the existing social infrastructure of practice collapses, how do people go on? Or rather *can* they just go on? What happens next?

These questions of moral negotiations matter for a historian of a European frontier like southern Africa, which was characterised by war, conquest, displacement, mass immigration and the 'cultural wars' of faith and technology that disturbed the ordinary cause of how people lived. In

Bechuanaland, the social infrastructure of practice changed many times, typically quickly and suddenly, often within one generation. In this situation, historians' challenge is not only to understand change. We have to explore how it happens that instead of the expected innovation on the hoof, natives of a place find themselves so uncertain about the routine order of practice that they are left wringing their hands, clutching at 'rules', deeply unsettled that there is no longer a moral centre. In other words, how do people reach a consensus on the moral limits of innovation? Yet, how is it that under the same circumstances some people thrive in the seeming chaos, as though they were old hands in a familiar game? I am interested particularly in the human experience of time during these moments of transition and its historical consequences.

Thus, apart from the addition of a further quarter century to the analysis, my consideration of the questions of time, practice and moral negotiations is the significant difference between this book and the doctoral dissertation where I first began the analysis. In the dissertation, I was mostly interested in the historical challenges and opportunities to transfer wealth and status from one generation to another and the bearing family lives had on these transactions. Here I pay very close attention to people's moral response to arenas of practice that were, in their experience, changing very quickly. Amongst the central questions that emerge is whether and how fathers and children managed not to become estranged when the same strategies that a few decades before had conferred honour were suddenly no longer possible. How are new moral universes constituted, and what is the utility of time in the process? Is it inevitable that at least for a moment 'things fall apart'? For that reason, this book is at its core a detailed study of social practice.

I had the advantage of an excellent archive, most dense in connection with practices of landholding, formal education, employment, political office and marriage. These were the most dominant 'multiple lines of play' that the Molemas pursued to establish themselves as a family of standing in the world. The main archival depository for Silas Molema and his family is the Silas Molema-Solomon Plaatje Papers at the University of the Witwatersrand in Johannesburg. The archive is unusual as a depository of a large number of documents produced by colonial subjects in their own hand at this time. The documents are in English and Sechuana although there are a few records in Dutch. The archive contains hundreds of letters but also photographs, private journals, scrap books, lease agreements and hundreds of receipts, invoices and promissory notes that span a period well over fifty years from the late 1880s. There are other extensive records elsewhere: Sebopioa

Molema's private family collection in Mafikeng, Modiri Molema's papers at the School of Oriental and African Studies in London and Rhodes House in Oxford, as well as many files in the government archives of Botswana and South Africa. Significantly, the Molemas' private archives include records of their chiefly bureaucracy. Silas and Sebopioa Molema were rulers, scribes and fastidious administrators – writing in copy, receiving replies and filing away. Local colonial officials, some friendly and some not so, also wrote extensively about the people they attempted to rule with detailed, sometimes verbatim transcripts of public meetings, filled with names and voices of ordinary people.

The archive revealed an everyday vernacular category that mediated practice in Bechuanaland and in Molemas' family life. The word is *botho*, which translates directly into *personhood*. The vernacular name for a solidarity of personhood in Bechuanaland was, and continues, to be the *morafe*, (pl. *merafe*), hence the name of this book. I explore what this vernacular category of personhood meant as a category of practice by scrutinising the events and moral discourses that emerged when, as so often happened along this colonial frontier, people could not, or would no longer follow, the tried and tested ways. This is when people spoke of the decline, even the end, of personhood. I conclude that personhood is not merely a vernacular category, but a key moral variable. I propose that personhood is what human beings create together through everyday practice, and that we cannot confirm our belonging to a quintessentially human existence without possessing this unique social substrate. Thus, the imperatives of personhood are not only moral, but have an existential bearing that makes us profoundly dependent on one another. This is precisely why practice is a moral arena. In my view, the existential debt of the substantiation and confirmation of personhood that we each receive from another, and therefore owe to one another through practice, is the critical experience of subjectivity that the sociology of practice and the social sciences have not yet seriously considered. The Molemas' archive reveals that it was through their attempt, in fact their insistence to remain persons, *batho*, despite highly unstable fields of practice, that the Molemas had the most striking influence on the political map of southern Africa. I propose further that in so doing, the Molemas' lives suggest an intersection between the moral, vernacular category of 'personhood', *botho*, and the analytical category historians refer to as the 'nation'. This is by no means a simple relationship. The elements that link these two categories, 'personhood' and 'nationhood' are the related themes of being, time and narrative.

Everyday lives, self and personhood

The distinguishing characteristic of human existence that makes it distinct from that of any other entity is found *'at first and for the most part* – in its average *everydayness'*.[19] Everyday action is a meaningful relationship with things. Martin Heidegger refers to this 'intricate context of meaning' as the 'world', which is where all existence reveals itself. The world is 'the open space where beings reveal themselves in sundry ways, coming out of concealment into their "truth" and withdrawing again into obscurity'.[20] Heidegger's world is historical. All human existence inherits the past as the only possession at hand to navigate the present 'now' and inform our orientation to the future. Our unique existence as human beings, '*dasein*', is precisely this preoccupation with ourselves in time, which is our creative ability to stretch our minds back into the past to retrieve material – strategies, ideas, norms, imaginations and so on – that can help us assemble an idea of the future. We live, as it were, ahead of ourselves, with the past not behind us, but ahead of us. No other entities in the world have this capacity. Only we have the evolutionary advantage of this 'self-reflexive consciousness', which is how Siri Hustvedt describes the neurological ductility of the human brain to remember oneself in the past and to imagine the same in the future.[21] Without this capacity, we would have no capacity for 'care', a word by which Heidegger means a uniquely human concern with the question of our existence. No other entity has the same concern.

One of the key and early foundations upon which Heidegger constructed his theoretical premise is Karl Jasper's argument that the situations that reveal 'what man is' are the 'limit situations', meaning experiences of crisis, like a serious accident, death or a personal crisis.[22] If 'limit situations' are where existence or being reveals itself, then it follows that instances where everyday practice breaks down are fertile with the possibility of apprehending our quintessentially human existence. This is why for the phenomenologist, the apprehension of oneself is possible only when something disrupts the everyday routines of our lives. Death is one and the most radical of such moments. To die is to experience ultimate aloneness. Death is an experience that is impossible to share with another. Hence, death is a 'limit situation' that mediates the apprehension of each our own singularity.

As a modern academic discipline, history makes very little room for the conception of a real 'self'. As historian Barbara Taylor observes, history has inherited the general understanding of 'self' as 'bourgeois fiction' whose 'invention' or 'making' requires debunking or deconstruction. She notes that especially after the poststructuralist turn, historians have tended to deny the place of a 'self' in the study of social change. '[W]e are told', she writes, 'there is no subjectivity, only social phenomena that produce the effects of it.'[23] Bourdieu for instance rejects the validity of both a self and consequently biography. His sense of subjectivity is only the 'disposition' that practice fashions, which it personifies and inculcates into every individual 'habitus'. Instead of a 'self', he argues, there is a 'biographical illusion', a compilation of the narratives that make sense of the disordered accidents and strategies of everyday life under a single, common name, like Silas.[24] This book is not the place to debate the 'death of the subject', only to suggest – as does Taylor – that biography, as a genre of historical writing, begs some reconsideration of this question before we slam shut the coffin's lid.

In this book, biography illuminates the experience of 'social death', the dearth of personhood, at the 'limit situation' where practice, the very social infrastructure of personhood, is suddenly too thin and inadequate to confirm a quintessentially human existence. The Molemas' rich archive of practice reveals experiences at the terrible precipices where practice breaks down. In the anxieties around the dissolution of personhood that ensued, their archive enables an inquiry into how practice mediates our daily grappling with the dilemmas of existence and therefore mediates the apprehension of each our own self in time. I argue that the outcome of these instances of 'dying' is always uncertain but that one highly successful pathway to resolve such a crisis of personhood is what I refer to as the 'practices of nationalism'.

Furthermore, I argue that these practices of nationalism always entail more than one vision of how to reconstitute anew or revitalise a weakening solidarity of personhood. In essence, I propose that whether benign or lethal, whether relying on a reformist agenda or a groundswell of rebellion, whether modern or ancient, practices of nationalism are always an orientation of everyday life because they are essentially involved and concerned with how everyday practice facilitates our mutual recognition as persons, as quintessentially human – not thoughts, not animals or trees, not merely something alive, standing erect on two feet but not actually, authentically, human. I argue that everyday practice operates like an assembly line to manufacture and confirm a quintessentially human existence. Practice is the factory floor where we each constitute a self but through the mirror of another.

In theory, practices of nationalism are always in motion because even in the most stable societies, practice is always in flux. However, practices of nationalism in fact indicate that there is a moral hierarchy to practice. Not all strategies carry the same moral currency in place and time. Practices of nationalism emerge more forcefully, more visibly, and with more historical significance when specifically those repertoires of practice that make and confirm personhood are no longer continuing with the same rigour but new ones do not yet have sufficient moral consensus of legitimacy, or do not yet really exist. These scenarios of moral anxiety, these experiences of a fleeting, insubstantial sense of personhood, precipitate diverse and multiple visions of how to reconstitute a solidarity of personhood. The modern nation state appears in this analysis as only one configuration of such a solidarity of personhood, which is why, contrary to the prevailing status quo in the literature of empire and nationalism, the nation state should not stand for the analytical meaning of the 'nation'. It is only a type and, in this instance, a very late entrant to the competing visions of the future the people of colonial Bechuanaland imagined for themselves. A type cannot have the whole weight of a concept attached to it. Moreover, the political dimension of practices of nationalism, meaning the point of these struggles that involve the state and state institutions, is not where the struggles of personhood begin. These struggles begin in the hierarchies of intimate lives, in homesteads and families, in marriages and other intricate attachments where we forge ties with others with whom we have no biological ties. The coalface of practices of nationalism is the intimate entanglement of oneself and another. It is the same place where the struggles of personhood articulate.

In her novel, *The Blazing World*, Siri Hustvedt sketches this reciprocal 'synthesis' of self as a substance we create together, oneself and another. Making oneself is an assiduous daily labour but what we are essentially making, the product of our efforts, is another, who exists as an experience that substantiates and confirms oneself and lives as a mirror to reflect it.

> ... S wakes up one morning and is somewhat different. Some crucial aspect of herself has gone missing, her me-ness, her essence, her soul has fled her body... She begins to suspect her upstairs neighbour O... She finds out everything she can about O, whom she has never met, her favourite movies, books, shopping habits, but every new clue tells her nothing. Then S decides to build a monument to her lost self. She works hard every night after work and finally she finishes 'the Thing'. We don't really know what the Thing looks like, but it is some kind of body with writing and images on it. S invites O for dinner. O arrives, looks at the Thing, and says, Oh it's me.[25]

In other words, being oneself is accomplished through recognising one's own 'me-ness' in the work of another. 'What I'm afraid of is not being a person anymore, of not being able to do anything, of not meaning anything', one character says in Karel Schoeman's novel, *Promised Land*.[26] Her dread is a lifetime locked in a small life, unrecognised in the circles of respectable existence as a person.

> ... if you're no longer regarded a person, you yourself begin to forget that you are a person. You lose your pride and your dignity, the only thing that matters is to survive; you crawl and twist and debase yourself at the word of command – oh, I've seen it in my own parents, and I am afraid, I'm so afraid of regenerating like that, more than I fear old age, or illness or poverty.[27]

The dilemma, as she recognises, is that one cannot save oneself. Another's appropriate behaviour is critical to one's own care. It requires some labouring by another to become oneself. She cannot be a person unless another of these upper classes collaborates and confirms their being both of that world. It is a two-way street of mutual recognition.

I am interested in this composition of self that 'we create between us' everyday under ordinary circumstances, especially with intimates and familiar others, the self that emerges in the 'zone between people'.[28] I consider personhood a critical composition of this self and not its whole substance. I understand the 'limit situations' where crises of personhood emerge as instances of the unravelling of this self, of becoming undone, of a truncating existence, where someone left undone the work of making another. The reciprocal labours of recognising, effectively manufacturing another, are unfinished. This is what I consider the people of Bechuanaland to have been talking about when they feared, dreaded, fled and fought hard against the dearth of personhood. In fact, as we shall see later, they had a word for this work of personhood, *tiro*. They pointed an accusing finger at those who stood aloof and indifferent without completing it and thus diminished and eventually exterminated the solidarity of personhood, the *morafe*. The dearth of personhood, or ceasing to *be* in the ethical universe of personhood, is what the people of Bechuanaland, as I relate in this book, fought tooth and nail to resist. It was a struggle waged to inspire and permanently turn the behaviour of another, whosoever it was, who was doing his or her own thing, abstaining from the moral obligations of making persons. The struggle to resist social death shaped people's experience of empire and influenced whether they embraced it or accepted it as a moral ill. What mattered was preserving the capacity to be seen, even under the most difficult circumstances so that, 'however bad might be our plight, we had not sunk to such a depth as to be unworthy of attention at all'.[29]

Historian John Lonsdale shows that establishing a home of one's own was how the Kikuyu of eastern Africa constituted themselves as a single 'moral ethnicity' albeit with different political nuclei.[30] To put it differently, land shortages were the 'limit situation' that halted practice. Lonsdale argues that by preventing many householders from landholding, colonial conquest stymied this route to manhood. Nationalist politics became the available repertoire of practice towards the same end. Lonsdale makes clear that there are always contestations over the requirements of what he refers to as 'civic virtue'. The social category I call 'personhood' has of course to do with the mutual recognition of 'civic virtue'. It takes one to recognise another of one's own type, including a 'man' for instance. My use of 'personhood' rather than 'civic virtue' is not primarily because it is a vernacular category in Bechuanaland's archive. Rather, my intention is to foreground the aforementioned dynamics of being and existence into the analysis and, in so doing, make 'self' fundamental to the study of nationalism.

Furthermore, in foregrounding the crisis of personhood in these historiographical debates, I intend to show how a society attempts to negotiate its way out of such a 'limit situation' by assembling a new social infrastructure of personhood. While the Kikuyu waged a struggle to get their lands back, there are other possibilities of assembling a new order of moral practice. Indeed, the extraordinary characteristic of Lonsdale's Kikuyu is that their countryside adhered very tenaciously to precolonial ways of life. He describes the differences in practice between urban and rural life that emerged along this European frontier. Young Kikuyu men 'soon learnt to wear trousers, the uniform of western decency when job hunting ... [but] returning migrants ... unwilling to offend elders, took off trousers and threw on the blankets thought proper for "common men"'.[31] In contrast, a growing number of elders in colonial Bechuanaland wore trousers and much else of European dress. When many of these elderly men were each establishing an independent homestead, they were often inspired by late Victorian architecture. The Plaatjes, the Molemas and many educated frontier families like them would have loathed the labels such as 'black Victorians' or 'black Englishmen' that historians would later attach to them in light of their everyday tastes and lifestyles. Appropriately, such labels received one of the earliest rebuttals from anthropologist Bernard Magubane.[32]

Jean Comaroff and John Comaroff offer the first analysis of the twin concepts of *Sechuana* and *Sekhoa*. Their aim is to analyse everyday practice as a way to explore 'consciousness' in a colonial setting where typically archives do not contain the narratives of colonial subjects themselves. They understand narratives as a 'a genre of storytelling and history-making; one in which past and present are condensed into linear, realist accounts that make claims to authority and public currency, impute cause and agency, and so assent their own truth value'.[33] They are referring to people's retelling of their own history. They argue that *Sechuana* and *Sekhoa* had become two competing reifications of a fluid and mutable cultural matrix since contact with nonconformist Protestant missionaries and that the Molemas aimed to institutionalise the 'power and knowledge' of *Sekhoa*, a reification of westernisation, and shunned *Sechuana*, which is what the traditionalists embraced.[34] The Comaroffs are interested in nationalism, in the 'revolution' that follows educated and Christianised classes' revelation of the 'Word' in a colonial context. The Comaroffs do not however take into account the human experience of time, which in fact facilitated how the Molemas actually understood themselves not as the people of *Sekhoa* but as traditionalists. They consistently embraced *Sechuana*. Through narrative repertoires of 'reawakening' and these very important twin concepts, *Sechuana* and *Sekhoa*, two generations of these educated Protestant families found an infinitely pliable language for remembering new things as old and inventing old ones as new. They understood the new frontier ensemble of their repertoires of personhood as the *morafe* of 'long ago'.

Our everyday experience of time is not always as something quantitative that we count and measure. Time is also a creative opportunity to travel elsewhere in our minds, to the past or to the future, and in so doing change our orientation of being in this world. This work of the mind – pause, reflection, recollection, imagination, all of which is essentially social also because it relies on language, is a lever to modify our orientation to our own existence. Paul Ricoeur dedicated a lifetime of scholarship explaining how, as a linguistic technique of relating the past, the present and the future, narrative enables these manipulations of time.[35] Stories are part of our instruments to care, to grapple with and manipulate time, and thereby orientate ourselves differently in the present. The capacity for storytelling is a potential agency to acquire a different orientation to our own history, to *be* different, to come into a new consciousness of the meaning of the world, to be 'born again' as it were, to be 'reawakened' into a vision of what we now see we had been all along 'at the beginning'. Hence narratives of religion, with their emphasis on salvation and rebirth, make explicit the fundamental principles about how human beings grapple with the peculiarity and fragilities of their existence. Religious narratives of salvation usually have an implicit 'time zero', an untarnished 'long ago' before the 'fall', followed by a journey of recovering what was lost. Narratives make the experience of time uneven and cyclic rather than linear. They lengthen and amplify the duration and significance of some moments and also alter the chronology of events.

Jan Vansina advocates using 'words as history' and retrieving 'the past from language' such that a genealogy of language reflects paths of historical evolution.[36] For Vansina, words are like a series of etchings. Each new print loses more of the detail yet retains the essence of the original image, with possibilities for innovation if the artist works the etching further. He shows convincingly that frontiers of contact do not alter people's existing 'tradition'. Rather, people borrow practices from newcomers in order to preserve existing institutions. In this process, 'novel foreign practices [are] justified in terms of the old tradition'.[37] He argues further that in the equatorial forests of Africa, the great disruption to tradition happened at the instance of European conquest, which 'prevented the tradition from inventing new strategies to cope with a new situation'.[38] The customs and institutions that the colonial government imposed, coupled to how conquest helped the coloniser prove himself as superior, challenged the cognitive reality of existing traditions. Although the language of the forest people remained, 'the equatorial tradition died in the 1920s'.[39] The people became 'cultural schizophrenics', holding concepts and cognitive meanings with no basis in everyday life.[40]

Such understandings of colonial life as 'nervous states' are indeed apt.[41] However, while a landscape of 'cultural schizophrenia' is theoretically possible, it is existentially not really plausible. The capacity of narrative that mediates the human experience of time is precisely society's attempt to make a way past the 'limit situation' of practice and circumvent such unravelling. I am suggesting, *pace* Vansina, that the struggles of personhood are precisely avenues through which colonial subjects escape or at least attempt to keep such states of mind at bay. Without these struggles, there would be no hope of reconstituting a sense of ordinariness, of *everydayness*, after fields of practice collapse. There would no longer really be 'culture' along the colonial frontier. In other words, there would be no degree of 'nativeness' that allows frontier peoples such a familiarity with their environment that they can at least still talk of having an 'everyday life'. If so, European empire would only have been one horrid, protracted moment of annihilation. Chinua Achebe's *Things Fall Apart* is the story of a man that experienced the frontier of European expansion in this manner, unable to recognise himself or his past in the new everyday practices of Christianity and power in his village.

He kills himself but others like his son found new opportunities of virtue and belonging.[42] Where there is 'cultural schizophrenia', there is no survival. Thus, Achebe correctly charts both existentially plausible alternatives – either the indigenous people succumb to the mental states of social death and fail to *be* or, like the man's son, they assemble new moral worlds.

Indeed, the historical narratives of colonial lives, like the memories associated with them, do not deny the sore hardships, violence and death along these frontiers, yet they also often suggest that people did create meaningful lives for themselves. We have reflected in these histories also the striking sense of ordinariness that life assumed: mundane rhythms of work and family, aspirations of flourish, attainment of pleasure.[43] We know that the European empire was exceptionally disruptive of institutional life in Africa. Nevertheless, as I am suggesting below, the human experience of time lends us agency to retrieve and reassemble a sense of stable continuity at these 'limit situations' of chaos and disruption when familiar social worlds collapse. It is due to this capacity that we can select material from the new, unexpected circumstance we had neither foreseen nor wanted and reinterpret it as a desirable inheritance of our past. We can also reject as foreign the very things we had once embraced but can no longer possess due to changing circumstances.

This is essentially what the narratives of 'reawakening' enable. They are human agency to manipulate time, especially in a colonial setting where people are confronting an arbitrary and diminishing social order. Practices of nationalism rest on this foundation of *being in time* like a tunnel through the dark uncanny seasons where the moral repertoires by which we used to recognise one another as persons are no longer possible. It does not mean we shall reach a sure destination, but we are in fact experimenting with possibilities. These everyday struggles are an attempt to establish a new paradigm of practice, which is not to say they are always successful in meeting their ends. The aim of such practices is to propose, debate and legitimate new 'rules' of practice and elaborate the institutional support necessary to uphold them. In this manner, people can preserve their place within the moral sphere of personhood. They can make the new order ordinary, unsurprising, as something that continues from 'long ago' and which they had anticipated would come. The 'origin' lies ahead of them as a resource to shape and imagine the future but also as a desire finally fulfilled. Practices of nationalism are how people use political means to intervene in crisis of personhood. They court states, state-like institutions or powerful individuals who can exert control on such institutions to help strengthen fragile or newly reconstituted repertoires of personhood. States can help to bolster the new infrastructure of personhood.

These struggles for personhood were the coalface of generational conflict in colonial Bechuanaland as people attempted to preserve their position in a solidarity of personhood by making and remaking their *morafe*, but even within a single generation there was no necessary consensus of what the 'true' *morafe* was, or who the persons at the 'origin' were. How did the *morafe* of 'long ago' live? Who was included in its solidarity of personhood? Hence, at any given instance of these struggles, there was more than one vision of the *morafe*. Men and elders, for instance, could hold a conception of the *morafe* that women and the youth rejected, although there were sometimes such strong areas of overlap between the emerging *merafe* that they could all throw their energies into a mutual struggle. Some points of disagreement were put aside as the united struggle took precedence but sometimes competition between the solidarities of personhood was uncompromising and very rife.

Even where these struggles are successful, their outcome requires time to stabilise, the one resource colonial society rarely possessed. A generation would still be engulfed in one moment of such practices of nationalism, vigorously debating competing visions of moral practice, when another crisis of personhood unfolded, from arbitrary changes in colonial policy and shifting understandings of race and skin colour to drought and unprecedented population growth. How could one generation learn to be available to make and facilitate their elders' personhood if the older generations' socialising institutions were on the precipice of collapse at the very moment of their making, families included? In Bechuanaland, every generation seemed to be engulfed in a new crisis of personhood, saying it is abandoning *Sekhoa* and 'reawakening' to *Sechuana*, and finding new political allies to support the vision of society they claimed was how things were 'long ago'.

Everyday lives, nationhood and personhood

The historian's task is to disentangle these various *merafes*' strands of meaning even as they were in the making, under contestation and interpretation, at the same time. This presents difficulties of interpretation for the historian. In this particular archive, the word *morafe* always has at least four possible translations in English: the '*nation*', the '*tribe*', the '*people*', the '*race*', and with no consistency as to which English concept refers to which meaning of the *morafe*. One can very easily make the mistake that all practices of nationalism had the same end in mind. Most pertinently, one can make the mistake that people always knew precisely the form of state or arrangement of political life that supported the *morafe* of their ideals beforehand. In fact, the interesting historical moments are those where people more or less settle on a conception of the *morafe* of their aspirations and then only later find a name for it. In this colonial context, sometimes in ways more explicit and with greater emphasis than others, they attached the name '*nation*' to the many different infrastructures of personhood they were attempting to assemble or strengthen. Indeed, the earliest records in the Molemas' archive are dense with the words the '*nation*', the '*tribe*', the '*people*' both as linguistic translations for the *morafe*, an endlessly malleable category delineating the solidarity of personhood, and as placeholders for the wide range of possibilities they hoped to achieve.

Thus, as Terence Ranger noted in 1993, few words are as misleading in Africa's colonial archive as the English word 'nation'. In his words, the reference to the nation in the continent's archive is like 'a series of empty boxes with bounded walls but without contents'.[44] Ranger comes to this conclusion after undergoing interesting turns of revision and interpretation. His view is a revision of his thesis in 1984, *The Invention of Tradition*, which he formulated with Eric Hobsbawm.[45] In the revision, Ranger conceded that there were some limits to 'invention'. He explained that the nation, in this instance the 'nation state', had little chance of success and legitimacy, unless it allowed people to *preserve* the sense of themselves that existing 'tradition' made possible. In fact, the 1993 statement was less a revision and more a revival of Ranger's earlier interpretation. In an essay published in 1968, he accurately predicted that the challenge for mass nationalism and the establishment of the nation state in postcolonial East and Central Africa was 'how to increase effective scale without destroying African communalist values more successfully than the primary resistance leaders or the millenarian cults'.[46] Otherwise, the argument continues, regionalist interests in defence of these 'communalist values' will compromise the legitimacy of the 'national', countrywide unitary movement. Hence where the nation state fails, he observes, the 'new society is conceived of as a gigantic village made up of thousands of small villages in which the people find their own authenticity'.[47]

Authenticity – an interesting word. What does it mean? I understand 'authenticity' as a collective feeling that we have preserved our position in the moral worlds of personhood despite obvious changes in our circumstances. We feel that our lives have not deviated from a 'truth' that is 'eternal' about those repertoires of everyday life that make a life of reputation. We remain *really* people, undiminished, still set apart from nature. The key word here is 'feeling', meaning experience, personal moral conviction and a prevailing consensus with others. People come to an agreement that while everyday practice is no longer what it was even a generation or more ago, all that happened is no more than useful innovation and the 'communalist values' of the past remain intact, and that they have preserved their existence in them. This is not an atavistic sensibility that denies change and clings on to a past long dried up. Rather it is a process of welcoming and embracing a different order by reinterpreting its new elements as a moral inheritance passed down to the present. This is not a sensibility that denies conflict or pretends that there has been no violence or bloodshed in the making of the present world. Rather people consider this present world as their destiny and as such, worth the pain, sacrifice and the daily work of personhood required to sustain it.

In this regard, Ranger's observation suggests that mass nationalism failed to facilitate this manner of *being in time,* which when successful, conveys the new democratic and other practices in the fundamentally new world as preserving people's position in an unchangeable ethical universe of personhood. Despite the narrative of 'reawakening', the nation state failed the test of 'feeling' like a true 'destiny'. Instead, colonialism's crises of personhood tended to deepen, including due to a severe scarcity of resources to support new repertoires of personhood. People retreated to their regionalist attachments and there explored, debated and experimented with new ways of making personhood. There seems to be no end to the urgency of 'reawakening' again and again. Hence, historians should do more with histories of nationalism than reveal these mythologies and their consequences in contestations of power. Rather, we should appreciate the existential currencies created by these capacities to experience and manipulate time, especially in a colonial world where the rate of change was often astonishing and existing practices of personhood, as we shall see here, tended not to survive. In this spirit, this book raises the question of whether and if so when and why the nation state became commensurate with the ideals of personhood that the *morafe* represented in colonial Bechuanaland, and for whom this coupling between the '*morafe*' and 'nation state' made sense.

The Molemas understood their divine calling as guiding others towards the routes of everyday life that amplified personhood. They considered themselves responsible for revealing the true repertoires of moral practice that made *morafe* precisely by *living* by them. They considered the 'true' ways of the *morafe* to come by special revelation to those people tasked by God to carry a special grace, 'charisma', and so save the *morafe* from a crisis of personhood. Charismatic authority places the onus upon the aspiring leader to prove himself by his daily endeavours, in how he lives and helps others to live. 'If they recognise him', as Max Weber explains, 'he is their master – so long as he knows how to maintain recognition through "proving" himself.'[48] In this instance, the leader has to prove that he has the knowledge to facilitate his and others' 'fullness' of life, precisely the kind of 'moreness' and fattening of the 'soul' that Emile Durkheim argues promotes moral communities.[49] To reframe in Durkheim's language, the Molemas believed that they had divine revelation of what was required to be in the 'sacred' realm of personhood and not in the 'profane', inconsequential order of mere things – trees, dreams, animals. To their followers, like Solomon Plaatje, the Molemas could be 'saviours', figures of conscience, able to lead the moral struggle to preserve personhood in times when they felt the *morafe* was diminishing. The Molemas could be 'fathers', assembling the *morafe* into a house of vigour, nourishment and pride.

The crisis of personhood, as we shall see, rouses despairing narratives about how others' absence from their appropriate roles in practice diminished personhood. People's own narratives suggest that another's moral life is a necessity in the process of our own care. One's own care, the intricate processes towards the apprehension of oneself, is essentially the labour of another. If the temporal dimensions of narrative provide a capacity for care, then our historiographical focus on personhood should be on the stories people told about others' rectitude and the effect of another's behavior on the apprehension of oneself. In this book, I pay careful attention to the 'mood' of these narratives. In crude terms, the 'answer' to the question of our existence, that is to say the apprehension of self in everydayness, comes to us in a 'mood' – another of the many foundational terms in Heidegger's conception of our unique existential capacity in the world. Moods are those feelings that press upon us, that overwhelm us or those that we welcome and allow to cheer and lift us up. The 'dull weight of things' in boredom, the fullness of 'blessing' and 'abundance' that characterises joy, the empty 'nothingness' of anxiety that makes things feel helplessly out of reach, like drowning, are all moods through which we experience being in the world.[50]

Many of the narratives in this book are of anxiety, often experienced by men pointing a blaming finger at others whose voices often do not appear in the archive: women and youth. Men understood women and the youth to be responsible for the 'unbearable lightness of being' unfolding along the frontier.[51] In a family, the accusation is voiced by an intimate and loved other – a parent, a child, a spouse. This book relates how these private moments in the Molemas' lives, including guarded family secrets, had profoundly public consequences, not because others knew or spoke about them, but because the individuals concerned made critical decisions to the course of their lives during these anxious times, which in turn impinged significantly on the political history of the region. At least in my interpretation as a biographer, sometimes the mood of anxiety can be paralyzing. It washes over individuals and they retreat into the backbenches of their own lives, not moving forward, not making decisions, letting time shape and whittle life whatever way, until one day they say they experience a 'reawakening' and find confidence to act on the world around them. At other times, anxiety is the actual spark of 'reawakening' and mediates ways of being in the world that were before then absent or only partial. The book reconstructs how these private dramas helped stack the odds towards the competing practices of nationalism that made and remade *morafe* and thereby shaped the political history of what would emerge as Botswana and South Africa in the mid-twentieth century.

By way of conclusion, we can consider the question that Benedict Anderson asked, which is why practices of nationalism create such strong affinities that people are willing to die for the 'homeland?'[52] In reply, I would begin by paying attention to the dilemma that the apprehension of oneself requires the indispensable availability and labour of another in intimate, familiar arenas of everyday practice. Nationalism is one way, perhaps one of history's most favoured ways, of enforcing the minimum degree of another's availability in the reciprocal labours of personhood. Hence, as George Mosse and others argue, nationalism is typically concerned with the private questions of gender, intimate hierarchies and sexuality.[53] In Bechuanaland, practices of nationalism were men's strategies to attach more securely to another, especially women and young people, who seemed not to be taking seriously their moral responsibility to be available for the new practices of making manhood that were under transformation. These new frontier practices aimed to facilitate new routines of mutual recognition that would make a *morafe* along the cultural hybridity of a then mixed frontier. But they required women and the youth to take up their appropriate place in the hierarchies of gender, seniority and generation and thus manufacture, day by day, the currency of personhood, especially manhood in this instance. Without these efforts, men were largely invisible, anxious and ashamed. I tell the story in three sections, each one exploring the three articulations of personhood I have identified in the archive, which I then named in the most meaningful way I could determine as *moreness*, *placement* and *homecoming*.

Fathers/Moreness: Silas Molema, Solomon Plaatje and the morafe

The first part of the book called 'Fathers' handles 'moreness', which it derives from Emile Durkheim's conception of a 'soul'.[54] In short, 'moreness' refers to that consequence of social interaction, of doing together, which lends an individual a sense of control over nature. It emboldens and injects a daring into an individual personality. One example is what Durkheim describes as the 'effervescence' people generate together in a religious gathering. One feels larger, more confident that he or she has more substance and capacity than his or her circumstance. Here the book is concerned with Silas Molema's generation. It reconstructs Silas Molema's success during the first two decades of British rule. At the beginning of the twentieth century, he and Solomon Plaatje embraced the British Empire as the political home for the *morafe* of the 'Bechuana', which was 'reawakening' to its foundations of 'progress' from 'long ago'. The words 'Bechuana', '*Sekhoa*' and '*Sechuana*' already existed at the time but especially in *Koranta ea Becoana*, a newspaper under the editorship of Solomon Plaatje and owned by Silas Molema, these words acquire new meanings as does the *morafe*. Educated men were anxious that the younger generation, especially women, must embrace *Sechuana* and reject *Sekhoa*, meaning everyday behaviour that, as they put it, compromised personhood, *botho*, and diminished the *morafe*.

The story of the 'rise and fall' of the African peasantry in southern Africa is widely known, of how new influences of racial discrimination from the late nineteenth century stymied the momentum of these literate and educated peasant householders to advance into, or secure their position as, a class of propertied families educating their children into the possibilities of white-collar professions available at the time. This first segment of the book relays how Silas Molema navigated this moment with fortitude and ingenuity but also the family dynamics and decisions that affected his experience. We also meet his educated chiefly friends, especially those in the Bechuanaland Protectorate. They are deeply anxious about the dimming light of chiefly authority in the countryside, not only as a result of migration and other possibilities of cultural practice. The crisis was also due to the inability of educated men to provide for their families and sponsor the aspirations of the very conception of *Sechuana* their strategies of distinction had created along the frontier, which were schooling, property, white-collar aspirations and the tastes of dress, architecture, cuisine and so on that resembled middle-class life in Europe. What was a father, what was a man, a husband, if he could not make provision for these things any longer? Or was the problem some misunderstanding of the meaning of the things themselves?

Koranta became a gathering to debate, confirm and circulate instruction about the repertories of practice from 'long ago' that would return personhood to people's daily relationships. These practices were mainly formal schooling, respect for chiefly and patriarchal authority and residence in the countryside. The thinking was that schooling would educate the young about *Sechuana* and thereby make proper persons. Schooling was the bedrock of the *morafe* that these educated men wished to assemble. In its focus here on Solomon Plaatje's editorial choices and writings about the *morafe*, especially those in Sechuana, and on his understanding of the Molemas' place in the *morafe*'s future, the book makes apparent Plaatje's own conception of race and skin colour, which took personhood, *botho*, as a grounding concept to outline the meaning of blackness, *boncho*. This matters because it connects Bechuanaland to a broader, global intellectual tradition that was coming into its own by the early twentieth century, where black intellectuals were penning their own theoretical schemes on race. As such, Silas Molema played a critical role in providing Plaatje the opportunity to be part of a transatlantic conversation on race and skin colour that involved intellectuals like W.E.B du Bois and Booker T. Washington. Although his Sechuana editorials in *Koranta* have not hitherto received any scholarly attention, these writings provide rich glimpses of what, had he written it, could have become Plaatje's theory of race. The newspaper, in its deep concern about diminishing personhood, was also his cry for help against the emerging colonial conditions that withered a writer's life, including genteel poverty.

In exploring the practices of nationalism amongst educated men who were proclaiming themselves as the *morafe* of 'Bechuana', I describe why and how this *morafe* had to nurture the British connection to realise who it was from 'long ago'. Empire was a moral authority that, according to the likes of Plaatje and Molema, guaranteed every subject *morafe* equal protections and opportunity to determine and achieve its own path of 'progress' and become great, regardless of its geographical location or skin colour. They considered themselves as an autonomous and self-determining *morafe* within the British Empire. This understanding inspired their remarkable conceptions of the state that coupled chieftaincy to a liberal parliamentary system, all within a global federation of the British Empire. This permutation of power seems contradictory and makes little sense when we look back at it from a standpoint of our early twenty-first century.

There are other paradoxes. Plaatje invested much energy in the project of writing about this form of state as appropriate for an exclusively black personhood and yet the platforms he had available to read and write emerged from his and especially Silas Molema's relationship with Caucasian professionals, business people and friends. These networks helped to establish and sustain *Koranta ea Becoana*. An interesting relationship that comes to the fore is Silas Molema's friendship with the lawyer, Spencer Minchin, who undoubtedly stuck closer than a brother during Molema's time of trouble. Their relationship is the first glimmer of intimacy across the colour line that coexists with the very violent and aggressive acts of race and racial discrimination that were plunging frontier people of African ancestry into a crisis of personhood. In other words, deep, intimate attachments across the colour line coexisted with and facilitated understandings of difference and segregation along the frontier. The *morafe* of this educated generation was premised on understandings of the unique personhood of black peoples, but included a wide mix of frontier peoples, was both local and global, steeped in chiefly hierarchies and yet strikingly liberal and boldly cosmopolitan.

Family/Placement: Property, intimacy and moral hierarchies on the land

'Family' is the book's second instalment. It is the longest segment because it involves five protagonists and their relationships with one another. It also has a sixth character who never speaks for herself but is undoubtedly the most powerful – the land. As far as the understanding of personhood is concerned, this segment handles 'placement'. The word emerges as a translation of the word *peo* in the archive, meaning that land over which each member of the *morafe* enjoyed and negotiated collective and private rights and privileges of ownership. 'Family' provides a close interrogation of the negotiations of placement on Silas Molema's landholdings, which illuminates how placement facilitated a moral orientation to living with others on the land. Men made manhood by sharing land as common property in ways that nevertheless guaranteed secure, private entitlements on the land.

On this foundation I adopt the word 'placement' to refer to the existential dimension of personhood more generally. Placement situates an individual in a realm of care and interdependence with others and by so doing, paradoxically makes possible strong feelings of ownership over one's own environment and destiny. In fact, placement is a pendulum of negotiations between the free capacities of mutual dependence and independent action. Placement is a reciprocal negotiation of every human relationship, one expressing both our need each to chart our own course and yet to remain grounded in a realm of care. These everyday negotiations are historical and typically gendered and hierarchical, vexed with the human impulses towards control and manipulating others whose freedom contradicts our own interests. Yet, placement also reveals our capacity for selflessness and compassion to seek the care of another more than our own freedom. Personhood is a continuous negotiation because giving up too much or taking too much compromise virtue, and therefore each have limited existential dividends, hence the narratives we see here are precisely around the limits of care and of freedom.

Many of the common sayings on the land were statements like, 'The land belongs to nobody'; 'The chiefs owns the land for all of us'; 'The land is free!' Nevertheless, there were many capillaries of extraction through landholding in colonial Bechuanaland that were channeling aid and resources primarily to chiefs, but also to a host of senior patriarchs and colonial 'headmen' by the early twentieth century. Ordinary householders yielded a range of labours and services to them, including the annual service to till chiefs' lands, *pacha*, but throughout the year, young men especially, were also variably available to perform other duties. Silas Molema had access to young men that he could call upon to work for him or for his tenants but he could not entirely control them. Commoners had private claims of their own on these lands but they could also not prevent their chiefs' cattle from drinking freely from their wells in the same way that sons could not refuse working for their fathers, who controlled their labour and increasingly their cash earnings. How do we understand these relationships?

The aim of settlement amongst such Bantu-speaking agropastoralists, as Jan Vansina describes, is to establish 'the House' as an institution that incorporates and naturalises new colonisers of the land through various strategies of making family.[55] These strategies include forming blood ties through marriage for instance, but mostly rely on constructing social genealogies of attachment. Like all families, 'the House' is a hierarchical institution. It has senior and junior houses, commoners and families of high rank. In Bechuanaland, this institution of 'the House' assembles the *morafe* through unequal, filial-like relationships to share the land based not on biological ancestry but by entering a moral consensus about how to live with virtue on the land. Placement enlarged the *morafe* in this manner, swelling its numbers in a setting where, according to John Iliffe, a long history of low demographic densities on the continent privileged fertility and strategies to grow the population as practices of honour.[56] In this manner, placement also incorporated European settlers onto the land as new members of 'the House' of the *morafe*. By the time we come across them in this book after 1885, quite a sizable number of Europeans, large enough to solicit the concern of the colonial government, as we shall see, were living in the Barolong reserves, but also on chiefs' private lands outside the reserves. Some were married to and had children with local women. Others were traders, artisans and professionals requiring herders, domestic servants and so on to flourish on the land.

According to E.P. Thompson, once it had established itself as a way of life in the European metropolises, private property unfolded irrevocably along every European frontier across the globe. He argues that the persistence of the rule, 'the land is ours, not mine' on the English commons, was such that though 'relationships in most villages were already monetarised and subjected to market imperatives long before the act of enclosure struck', the moral sensibility of the commons remained.[57] Thompson argues that before the legal institutionalisation of private property, these monetary exchanges, commercialisation and extensive enclosure reflected everyday sensibilities that accepted unequal privileges on the land as natural, but nevertheless did not derive from the institution of private property. In other words, the exchange of rents and money were not a disavowal of the moral consensus that everyone had a right to land. Thompson describes the evolution of the legal apparatus of private property that finally broke up the moral consensus, thereby excluding and dispossessing thousands of their place on the land. In the age of empire, he writes, '[t]he concept of exclusive property in land was a norm to which other practices must be adjusted, was now extending across the whole globe, like a coinage reducing all things to a common measure'.[58] He describes a 'hardening and concretion of the notion of property which could be rented, sold or willed', which brutally broke down the moral consensus that 'the land is ours, not mine'.[59] This may have been so in England, but not in colonial Bechuanaland.

On his landholdings, Silas Molema was a 'father' to his 'sons' and 'children' who all belonged in his 'House', people of many skin colours coming from different places, all living on his lands. In this way, he provided care and sustenance and, when times became difficult, compassion and forbearance, even when they could not return his 'gift' and fulfil their obligations on the land. Moreover, the land imposed the need for cooperation. It was prone to protracted droughts and the groundwater lay quite a distance from the surface. The work of making the land productive was backbreaking and the yields were uncertain. People had to work together to survive and had to belong together all the more deeply to flourish. Otherwise, it was almost impossible to establish a secure independent home of one's own on the land, without which one lacked the moral recognition of adulthood. Rather than adhering to principles of 'private property', Europeans were assimilating into the moral and civilising practices of these northern Bantu-speaking peoples. They sustained themselves through and as a part of a moral consensus of Bantu-speaking societies that without a home of one's own, one remained a child dependent on others in a realm of care, incapable of the agency to control nature and circumstance enough to establish an independent home.

In this way, Europeans had entered into the reciprocal transactions of 'the House'. Receiving placement was an acknowledgement of the need for another man's care both in sharing the land and in recognising the recipient's status as an adult. At the same time, the recipient was also the giver through the services, monies and rents he gave up to a man like Silas Molema, for transactions of care are reciprocal, and decent good men yield them freely to preserve the manhood of another man. Otherwise, the giver empties himself to another and cannot himself remain a man. A man who earned the respect of his counterparts was not so neglectful of his obligation to share and care for another man that his lands only benefitted his own interests, but neither was he so childlike in the understanding of his personal interests that everybody else's interests hindered his capacity to prove his adulthood by establishing and sustaining a home of his own and to enrich himself. In Bechuanaland, the same applied to women who could hold land, including as an inheritance to bring into their husbands' home at the time of marriage. One could do with one's placement as one desired – letting, selling, exchanging, buying, essentially commodifying the land to create wealth but these free, private entitlements coexisted with moral obligations of mutual dependence on the land.

European settlement, literacy and a monetarised economy further facilitated institutions of private contract upon a moral infrastructure that already encouraged and esteemed the capacity for private ownership. In other words, the tenets of exclusive private ownership already existed along what would become the colonial frontier before the arrival of Europeans. E.P. Thompson's conceptualisation as noted earlier is therefore, in this regard, not correct. Moreover, to the extent that it was strengthened by the European empire, the institution of private property did not wash away the moral consensus that 'the land is ours, not mine' along the colonial frontier. The European empire was not the first instance of exclusive private entitlements on the land. In fact, this private orientation to the land was part of the moral bedrock upon which literate landholders, many of them chiefs but also others who could read and write, formally entered into leasing and other contracts on the landscape – letting, buying and selling.

Here too we need to bear in mind the workings of being, time and narrative. This moral consensus depended on negotiations of intimacy that made the family of 'the House'. In one moment, two parties could be to each other as a chief is to his subject on the land, as father and son, but in another moment the same parties could operate on strict terms of contractual obligations, as landlord and tenant. We owe this ductility to the possibilities in time that narrative allows. In the stories that people create about their relationships on the land, they are recasting the past and also shortening or lengthening its proximity to the present. They are creating for themselves ports of agency to achieve key moments of decision-making, where 'from now on' they are no longer bound to what they no longer perceive to be 'true' or 'natural' or even how things were 'at the beginning'.[60] In these narratives, we see for instance sons who later reinterpret their service to a father as tenancy and as down payment on property, as much as we perceive how two strangers who initially enter a legal contract as landlord and tenant can in time renegotiate such terms of partnership that they become family.

In this regard, I devote a lot of time to the relationship between Silas Molema and his European tenant Phoebus Fincham. Are they partners in business? Are they friends who care about each other, each giving more than what the other legally expects? Or are they simply men of different skin colours who can never come together other than as simply landlord and tenant along a frontier where race was becoming a fact of life? This is not the only relationship where agreements shift between the zone of intimate caring between brothers and that of obligations between landlords and tenants. Such negotiations have a broader significance. A large stratum of people can wish to change their experience of placement. The most fascinating narratives are where people no longer recognise the 'fathers' of 'the House'. In the language of the frontier, they are keeping the land yet 'cutting away', which is to say they are ascribing the gift of the land to the benevolence of 'fathers' in another 'House'. The contestations over land and belonging, over terms and degrees of intimacy on the land, reveal how people can embrace each other to survive the hardships of frontier living, but also how easy it is for things to change, for erstwhile familiars to push one another off the land and end more than two or three generations of ties on the land.

The cost of intimacy could be too high to pay – costs of time, of behaving a certain way, often of sharing material and human resources one was not keen to surrender. The moral dilemma is precisely how much to surrender to someone else – how much land, how much time, how much labour and for how long. People could prefer contractual agreements, which regulated and made the terms of reciprocity explicit. As a strategy of everyday life, placement was not a judicial principle that people necessarily policed, but it could pose considerable anxiety. There was no strict conformity to a 'custom, maxim, proverb, or formula'; no statement that captures how people lived. It was rather a 'saying about a man that, "there's a *real* man, *really* a man"'.[61]

On the land, the *morafe* was therefore a web of contestations and daily negotiations of intimacy. The effect of these moral negotiations, these capillaries of reciprocal transactions, was that the land was both free and not free. In fact, land could be a most expensive, unaffordable transaction. An immigrant could not just make his way into placement. He had to subscribe to a way of life and 'pay up' in the demands of time and resources that forging and maintaining favourable intimacies required. These negotiations shaped gender, marriage and sexuality given that these practices of placement were key to negotiating both freedom and dependence on the land. So it was that despite narratives to the contrary, the land was not free for all – certainly not the autonomous Barolong reserves along the Molopo River, which had become frontiers of mixed skin colour and *métissage* through the institutions of placement. Chiefs were proud that their lands had retained a moral integrity precisely because they were *not* 'common lands'. They intended to keep them that way.

Neither were the Barolong reserves Crown Lands. Hence, these transactions of placement soon presented an enormous challenge to the settler government that emerged after the South African War. The only available path for peace after the war broke out was for Britain to establish a dominion in southern Africa, the Union of South Africa, in which skin colour determined opportunity and political rights. After the war, British rule began the aggressive process of creating two judicial and property jurisdictions: a sphere of representative political institutions and private property for those it would classify as 'white' and one of chieftaincy and common property in the reserves it determined to make 'black'. The way forward was to delineate and fix reserves for the exclusive occupation of the 'black' population. Moreover, these had to be territories on which the colonial government had the jurisdiction to control the movement of people and allocate land. In a setting of severe land shortages, colonial administrators were also ensuring that Europeans' social reproduction sustained itself where their population would never overtake that of existing African societies. There could be no Union of South Africa without former British Bechuanaland territories, whose landmass was vast. The trouble was these reserves were effectively independent and locked out thousands of people who did not belong to the nebulous compositions of *merafe* on the land.

From the very onset of 'reconstruction' towards the new British dominion, the colonial government had to confront this serious challenge to segregation and racial ordering along the Molopo. In Natal for instance, the wars of conquest had brought existing polities to their knees and turned them into 'locations', meaning the land was entirely the property of the Crown, governed through headmen the British appointed. In the hinterlands of Bechuanaland, literacy and Christianity had strengthened chiefly institutions. Placement facilitated manhood and womanhood through crisscrossing chains of 'landlord–tenant', 'chief–subject', 'patron–client' and 'father–son' transactions that shaped the structure and experience of chieftaincy. Land passed down a hierarchy of patriarchal authority, from the paramount chief to his chiefly relations, then to various rungs of senior patriarchs, then to household heads and finally to sons and daughters. Each node of land transfer was simultaneously also a point of judicial authority. At the lowest level, patriarchs could settle family disputes whilst the court of the paramount chief was the highest authority with no recourse to appeal. Placement was the same relationship that also disciplined and punished, restricting land use within the acceptable negotiations of personhood.

In the struggle between various colonial governments and chiefs' determination to uphold the initial terms of British rule in British Bechuanaland, there emerged a particular regime of race and segregation on these lands. Silas Molema was at the forefront of the struggle to defend the autonomy of the Barolong reserves. The struggles were a combination of litigation and political strategy through the SANNC. I argue that the lengthy litigation impinged directly on the set of interests and manoeuvres that culminated in the passage of the Natives Land Act in 1913 – a story hitherto unobserved by historians. I argue further that the Natives Land Act of 1913 was a cornerstone instalment towards territorial segregation in South Africa. The Natives Land Act was intended to demarcate and fix the geographical boundaries of countryside the colonial government wished to *make* 'black' in a context of racial fluidity in the early twentieth century. The Act effectively installed the colonial government as the 'Supreme chief' and principal landlord in the territory the Act defined as 'Scheduled Areas'. This enabled the colonial state to intervene in African reserves directly as a sphere of 'native administration'. However, it would be a mistake to understand this outcome as evidence of a powerful colonial state having its way on the land.

On the contrary, in 'Family', the book illuminates the fragilities of empire in this region, of a colonial government that failed fully to achieve these segregationist ends despite the coercive powers at its disposal. The reason for this failure was precisely that reserves were not free, but rather intricate and essentially hierarchical moral economies that facilitated personhood on the land.

The Natives Land Act of 1913 also failed, dismally in fact, to attenuate chiefly power and loosen property relations from chiefly and patriarchal authority. More importantly, when the land eventually became free of these institutions, the process was not due primarily to colonial law or legislation. Rather, the new dispensation resulted from contestations over placement and their role in reconfiguring the relationship between chieftaincy and property. Ultimately, what successfully opened up these reserves were popular struggles that aimed to preserve personhood at a time when land was very scarce and food shortages very severe. In response, ordinary householders established their own practical repertoires of 'reawakening' to the *morafe* of 'long ago' on the land. By the end of these practices of nationalism, ordinary people, mostly men, came to acquire land (a plot to erect a homestead, fields and access to grazing lands) *freely* such that the experience of property on these commons was effectively 'private property', entirely removed from the labyrinth of reciprocal obligations that existed before. A household head did not have to pay in rents and services. His practice of everyday life had no bearing on his claim to his property.

Such struggles from below helped to turn territories controlled by chiefs, where access to land was unequal, into areas dominated by forms of homestead-based tenure, free of rents and tributes. It took over a quarter of a century for the colonial government to transform the reserves into 'commons'. The homestead head enjoyed autonomy on his property, letting and selling as he wished, constrained only by the intimate hierarchies of family life and its own moral expectations. The land had become common to a *morafe* that was more inclusive than the negotiations of personhood that had before then mediated settlement but also, now the *morafe* was exclusively 'black'. For some, the *morafe* had breathed its last. For others, new possibilities of autonomy and caring for others had at last begun after years of landlessness and a peripatetic existence. Now they had a home. I argue that the pattern of landholding that emerged shaped the Native Administration Act of 1927.

The making of this legislation is a story of how ordinary people themselves embraced racial difference. This was less a calculation of interest and more a moral response to the very dilemmas of personhood that colonial rule precipitated. It reveals that chieftaincy can coincide with a range of property relations and prove remarkably malleable under the changing circumstances of moral life. The outcome of these contestations over authority in these reserves established a template for a relationship between property and citizenship that became a bedrock for new conceptions of identity in these reserves, which relied less on loyalty to a 'tribal' chief and more on affiliation to a hybrid institution that coupled an increasingly symbolic 'tribal' bureaucracy under chiefs to the ever growing, indispensable government bureaucracy of the Native Commissioner. As a result, the 'white' Native Commissioner, not a 'black' chief, applied 'customary law' to scenarios as diverse as marriage and inheritance to a population that was 'blackening'. It is a bizarre paradox in the making of race and segregation in early twentieth-century South Africa that chieftaincy remained the mixed frontier institution that settler governments had wished to do away with, only now it had white bureaucrats as active and overworked 'Supreme Chiefs' of the reserves. Mahmood Mamdani argues that through the person of a chief, colonialism in the reserves of South Africa produced a 'decentralised despotism' where 'the authority of the chief fused in a single person all moments of power: judicial, legislative, executive and administrative'.[62] I identify a different process, which involved to a greater extent, the refashioning of citizenship and relations on the land from below. The era that Mamdani describes did dawn but almost three decades later.

These struggles for autonomy and land were the background to Silas Molema's children's upbringing and early adulthood. They impinged on children's own 'placement' in their home, influencing their experience of care and autonomy. Thus the land and struggles over it shaped how two generations, especially fathers and children, understood themselves. They influenced children's consideration of how much of their time, labour and choices had to be devoted to the care of the *morafe*, to the obligation of their own home, and how much was the preserve of their own freedom. At the same time, not only landholding, but also other strategies that the older generation considered virtuous were becoming a thinning field of practice. In these struggles, where the desire for autonomy, personal and otherwise, coincided with the imperatives to survive a system of racial discrimination that was becoming more rigid, there emerged new contestations about *Sekhoa* and *Sechuana*. The younger people created and navigated new waves of 'reawakening'. They were assembling new fortifications of personhood in the new alignments of family, work and public leadership. These many rearrangements of institutional life were not only a consequence of a racialising colonial setting, but also of how these constraints affected dynamics of living together as families.

Sons/Homecoming: *The Molemas and the politics of the nation state*

If 'moreness' is the social precipitate that injects one with confidence that nature is within one's own mastery, and 'placement' is the negotiation of intimacy that articulates simultaneous capacities for autonomy and dependence on others, then 'homecoming' is the journey of fabricating the story that confirms the moral uprightness of the repertoires of everyday life that constitute these two positions. The moment of 'reawakening' marks a point of 'arrival' to the destiny from 'long ago'. However, 'the good story' is not out there, readily available for our picking. Not just any story will do. It has to be based on 'a dynamic, provisional and intersubjective' truth given that 'we can only know and understand ourselves fully through others – through the way we experience others and ourselves in relation to others, and the way others experience us'.[63] Our story of 'homecoming' is constituted in and through our engagement with familiars – neighbours, friends, workmates, family, lovers.

Hence, even when the public narratives of 'reawakening' to the *morafe* involve dozens or thousands of people, as we shall see in colonial Bechuanaland, these stories have traction as a resolution of intimate, very private, moral entanglements. Moreover, we come to the appropriate narrative of 'reawakening' in the political sphere much like the psychoanalyst and the patient do, through a repeated retelling of our happenings until we settle on an enabling 'truth' that allows a route past the impasse of despair. The story is not the 'truth' of what happened, nor the strict story of the events of our lives. Instead we take our liberties with the plot, switching heroes and villains, shortening and lengthening time between events. Much trial and error precede 'the good story'.

The last segment of the book, 'Sons', is about the second generation of the Molemas' journeys of 'homecoming', which shaped their involvement in the SANNC and in the Native Advisory Council (NAC) of the Bechuanaland Protectorate. These also shaped the story of southern Africa's relationship to colonialism on both sides of the Molopo River. By the middle of the twentieth century, educated members of these forums, including those the historiography refers to as 'nationalists', could not agree on a moral vision for the future. This is despite the fact that they wanted to reverse the dispossession and constraints of power that characterised British and Anglophone colonialism. On both sides of the border, chiefly and patriarchal power remained locked in a struggle to entrench its appropriate practices of personhood. Contestations about *Sekhoa* and *Sechuana* were rife.

Even into the 1940s, the question of whether there was or should be a political border between the Union of South Africa and the Bechuanaland Protectorate remained unresolved. There was still very strong support for the kinds of independent reserves that had characterised the Barolong reserves. The war over these territories was not yet over. In fact, this struggle was only entering another phase in the Bechuanaland Protectorate where British rule had also done away with earlier terms of colonisation that had guaranteed chiefs' autonomy over their own reserves. In the Protectorate, this paved the way for chieftaincy and the nation state later to become entwined for many generations in what would be 'Botswana', a name that emerged from the fierce contestation about *Sekhoa* and *Sechuana* in the NAC. The discipline of anthropology, especially the person and scholarship of Isaac Schapera, also shaped these contestations.

The circumstances and outcome of the Second World War introduced the word 'nationalism' into the lexicon of political discourse in ways that quickened the flashpoint of persisting generational conflict about the requirements of personhood. I show that Sebopioa and especially Modiri Molema navigated these questions not as political matters in the first instance, but as part of their private dilemmas about what and how much of their own personal freedom was theirs to own, not belonging to the fathers, the family and the *morafe*. They entered these discussions also as a way to confront whether their origin – the chieftaincy, their esteemed family name, their *morafe* – had properly facilitated their own personal aspirations, their own weight of esteem and their own desire for happiness. We see in their stories of 'reawakening' how the drama of family matters finds resolution in the politics of the generational conflict that shaped both the NAC and the SANNC. The latter had by then acquired the name African National Congress (ANC). By this time, the two had become mature men, elders in fact, in the eyes of the younger generation.

I argue that Modiri Molema was the crucial bridge between the generations, without whose manoeuvres and mediations, Congress would not have embraced the meaning of 'nationalism' as an independent nation state. It might still have happened at some point of course, but not as early as the years leading towards the Defiance Campaign of 1952. Following the Afrikaner nationalists' victory in 1948, apartheid seemed to offer precisely what the older generation had won and lost: autonomous chiefly jurisdictions reliant on chiefly and patriarchal authority. Apartheid would do away with the hybrid chiefly jurisdiction of the previous British and Anglophone dispensations in the reserves that had made white Native Commissioners the

Supreme Chiefs of the reserves. Why would senior men, in Bechuanaland at least, not take this opportunity to have the apartheid state as a willing ally in their struggles of manhood? For some elderly men, this was an opportunity to reassemble those institutions of personhood that they felt women and young men had abandoned. In fact, as the younger men in the ANC recognised, many in this older generation considered the ANC a platform to reestablish and preserve severely weakened institutions of patriarchal authority in the regional constituencies they represented. I argue that Modiri Molema, by making himself the critical hinge between elders like himself and younger men, was the single point of influence that tilted the balance of forces strongly towards Congress' embrace of mass nationalism and the nation state. We cannot know what would have happened had he, or any of the other members of his family, held different views or chosen different paths, but can only tell their story.

Fathers/Moreness

I

THE TRADITION OF AGROPASTORAL Bantu-speaking people of southern Africa, like their relations elsewhere on the continent, was to settle on the land in layers.[1] Time nativised new settlers. It brought them closer and closer to the land where the most 'native', meaning the earliest living colonisers of the land enjoyed the greatest position of esteem. Hereditary rulers, 'did not so much "rise" above their neighbours as they were, so to speak, "levitated" upwards' as more immigrants arrived, layer after layer, letting time and new settlement push them up the hierarchy of nativeness.[2] The land was not free, at least not in the manner that common sayings and folklore suggest. There were various subscriptions of services, rents, tributes and taxes but the actual experience of settlement affected how people felt about these payments, whether they recognised them as extraction or whether these exactions were invisible, merging smoothly into the rhythm of the natural world as volition and common sense. New settlers tended to pay the highest rents and taxes unless they conquered the land by force and, in that case, immediately encrusted themselves as the apex of the settlement.

Either way, newcomers made their technologies, dialects and other elements of cultural practice available for incorporation into existing ways of doing. In pushing newcomers deeper into the land and spreading their own genome through the population, new settlers' way of life helped to innovate upon cultural practice that was already established along the frontier. In their assimilation into the land and its people, newcomers' way of life also merged into the conversation about which repertoires of cultural life could manufacture 'personhood' such that one occupied an existence in the world that is separate from the natural environment of 'things', like rocks and microbes and plants, insects, animals and thoughts. Personhood is what human beings together manufacture through moral practices of everyday life, hence people must decide, though they typically never fully agree, on what those practices are that raise us above the common essence of 'things', into subjects of esteem that can discriminate between mundane routines and sacred, moral practices.

Morafe

In the hinterlands north of the Orange River, the community of persons (*batho*) was the *morafe* (p. *merafe*). In theory, any newcomer could settle on the land and live on it, seeing that every human being is capable of work and reproduction, but the basis for incorporation into the *morafe* was whether the new settlers were 'persons' or *batho*. In other words, did their repertoires of practice include the essential routines that marked them ultimately to 'be like us', to be persons too, although they might have looked different, sometimes spoke a different language, sought the favour of other gods, and yet demonstrated a familiar way of life that matched the existing institutions along the frontier. In other words, could they count as one with the *morafe*?

People spoke of everyday practice, routines like marriage or tilling the ground or herding animals, as work or *tiro*. This is labour not concerned with accumulation but rather with making oneself as a civic entity. In this cosmology, 'an individual not only produces for himself but actually produces his entitlement to be a social person'.[3] This 'process of social creativity [is] continuous', the unceasing 'work of social life', deriving from 'a vision of the world in which the construction of the person, the accumulation of wealth and rank, and the protection of an autonomous identity were indivisible aspects of social practice'.[4] In the 1920s, ethnographer Tom Brown, writing of the people along these northern hinterlands then known as Bechuanaland, observed that an incapacity to do this work, even though one still ate and breathed, was tantamount to dying. This was the case when a 'man's relatives notice that his whole nature is changed, that the light of the mind is darkened and character has deteriorated so that it may be said that the real manhood is dead, though the body still lives'.[5] They reckon that 'though the body lives and moves it is only a grave, a place where something has died or been killed'.[6] This is the extreme case, but manufacturing personhood together with others is a negotiation of degrees. People desire a proximate association, 'doing together' with others who demonstrate the fullest capacity of life, and distance themselves from those who compromise their position in the existential realm of personhood.

We need not reach into the past to see an iteration of this orientation to the world. We can consider the common practice of exchanging a greeting continuing in these hinterlands today to see the reciprocal transaction of confirming a quintessentially human existence at play, one person to another. In their earliest years, children learn to speak also by learning how to greet their family and others, and thereby also learn, very early on, the 'truth' of things.

'*Dumela*!' (Agree! / Bear witness!) '*Ee*!' (I do!)
'*Le kae?*' (How (much) are you?)
'*Re teng*!' (We are present! / We exist!)
'*Le rona re teng!*' (We too are present! / We too exist!)

Hence, the yellow-skinned people, who were indigenous to the region, commonly known as the San, were mostly not in the *morafe*. The Bantu-speaking people considered them a species apart. When we meet these societies in the 1880s, chiefs and men of high reputation mostly kept them as servants at the cattle posts. They were 'MaSarwa', not worthy of the esteem afforded the prefix 'Ba...' that denoted other persons. They did not, at least in the opinion of others, possess the status of personhood because they were nomads, they never sank roots in the land, and therefore could not participate in one of the central practices that made manhood, which was establishing an independent homestead. Hence, despite being the most indigenous people on the land, the very first layer of settlement, the populations of the San and their other nomadic associations did not fully acquire the status of nativeness among the new Bantu-speaking colonisers of the land. When nomadic life became more difficult, especially after the penetration of European settlers beyond the Orange River, some incorporated into the *morafe*, at times acquiring rank and reputation, but the contestations about whether or not they too were fully persons never completely dissipated.

As with any wave of new migration, the encounter between Europeans, almost always Caucasians, and Bantu-speaking peoples was a 'long conversation' of mutual intrigue, distrust and experimentation to find common ground and to jostle for moral authority on the land, each 'endowed alike with their own history, their own culture, their own intentions'.[7] Yet there had been more than a century of entanglement between the two sets of settlers along the coastal regions of the Cape and Natal. The first Europeans to cross the Orange River only did so towards the close of the eighteenth century, accompanied by 'brown' people. The histories of violent warring and conquest into the hinterlands of southern Africa coincided with that of frontier alliances and practices of mutual dependency and intimacy. At the same time, the settled agropastoral populations of the northern hinterlands beyond the Orange were not an isolated, sedentary population. For instance, although it had fragmented by the eighteenth century, the Barolong kingdom had risen to prominence after 1600. Its trading activities reached the southern coastline of Delagoa.[8] Hence, by the time Europeans crossed the Orange, some reportage of their ways and disposition had already reached these northern kingdoms. Agropastoralists had been travelling in all directions beyond their own territories for centuries.

Like many other Bantu-speaking agropastoral societies on the continent, these mainly agropastoral society considered proving the capacity to multiply in number a matter of honour.[9] It prized women for their fertility but also encouraged other routes of reproduction. Adults established such a status of maturity by not only each establishing independent homesteads of their own, but also by adding to these homesteads, turning each home into an incubator of personhood.[10] The home was rarely only a biological unit but rather an amalgamation of people according to intricate rules of adoption and alliance. This incorporationist strategy increased the *morafe* through a similar political tradition of adding people. Immigration made 'the House' out of the *morafe*, using amalgamations and alliances to make kin of people who had little or sometimes no genetic similarity.[11] Thus, oral tradition and archeological evidence suggests that on the eve of Europeans' arrival across the Orange, the Barolong were actually a member of a twin-polity, paired into one 'House', apparently as a junior brother to the Bahurutse.[12] Within and across that unit, were likely many other alliances and associations. Together all these groups represented a *morafe* but at the same time, there was segmentation, many *merafe*, each delineating the 'landed-polity, living together'. Each 'circumcised their youths together, imprinted a recognisable culture among their elite and created a pattern of belonging for its citizens to emulate'.[13]

The political arrangements were amorphous, with a tendency towards strong chiefly bureaucracies by the mid-nineteenth century, but also other localised arrangements of power and claims of nativeness. In some ways, it was difficult to delineate where the *morafe* started and ended as new groups coalesced around their own ethical repertoires of moral life. On the whole, making 'the House' of reputation was *tiro*, the unceasing work of strengthening and adding to the solidarity of personhood, which was taking place at the same time as individuals were also establishing, growing and multiplying independent homesteads. These moral practices mediated settlement, and despite the possibility of many nuclei of political power, it was this consensus on what made a man and what made a woman, that delineated the *morafe*. The Barolongs' demographic and political dominance was a product of this political tradition and hence their chiefdoms would have been of mixed peoples. The heart of incorporation nevertheless was not just numerical or demographical dominance although that mattered greatly. The point was to forge the *morafe* as a solidarity of personhood. From the viewpoint of the settled frontier populations of the late eighteenth century, the arriving Europeans, with their pale skin and curious ways could prove or fail to prove themselves as persons. If in fact they were accepted as persons, then the *morafe* could reproduce itself through them and raise itself to greater esteem. The prestige of a *morafe*, like the esteem of a household, lay in numbers, but most importantly in moral reputation. The 'long conversation' was also about making this moral assessment.

In 1861, European writer and traveller, Petrus Borcherds, regarded the entire population of 'highveld farmers' across the Orange as 'Barrowlows', but the frontier had already incorporated some 'high status Bushmen' in a situation of worsening land shortages.[14] Another popular encapsulation was the term 'Bitjuana', 'Bootschuana', 'Becwana' or 'Booshuanna' before being standardised as 'Bechuana' or 'Becoana'.[15] The present orthography spells it as 'Batswana'. The nineteenth-century encapsulation was a reference to the similarity of the *morafe* in its plural articulation on the land, deriving from the phrase '*ba coana*', meaning 'to be alike' but the same phrase also referred to a process of 'cutting away', one out of another. The incidents of cleaving and separating, of signifying difference and similarity at the same time, were both elements of assembling the *morafe* and of negotiating personhood.

The frontier quickly acquired the name 'Bechuanaland' with diverse permutations of spelling. The vernacular concept '*Sechuana*' emerged as a frontier word referring to the fluid, continuously debated cultural matrix that fulfilled the ethical requirements of personhood. Those who lived outside the universe of personhood were '*Makhoa*', whose repertories of practice, '*Sekhoa*', could be attractive, sometimes even helpful innovations, but insufficient to assemble and demonstrate personhood.[16] Yet, like all frontier peoples, the people of this region lived highly syncretic lives, borrowing words and ways from one another, newcomers and other places of their travel, to assemble a range of cultural repertoires, each permutation competing for recognition as '*Sechuana*'. These cultural reifications, '*Sechuana*' and '*Sekhoa*', emerged in the 'long conversation' with Europeans, but the boundary between *Sechuana* and *Sekhoa* did not strictly coincide with skin colour, nor did it coincide with cultural repertoires and institutions of 'Westernisation'. The *morafe* was growing as a mixed assortment of skin colour, and an increasing *métis* population, debating amongst themselves about which of the many innovations of practice preserved or compromised 'tradition', *Sechuana*. In this new setting, how could they properly facilitate *tiro*, each be the stage of mutual recognition for another, person to person, and together assemble a *morafe*, a strong solidarity of personhood?

Morafe

II

From around the 1840s, Isaac Molema was presenting himself and his family as a model of how literacy and Protestant piety, alongside other innovations like irrigation techniques, Victorian dress and proficiency in Dutch or English, fulfilled the moral requirements of personhood. He took these practices to bolster rather than compromise *Sechuana*. Isaac Molema had converted to Christianity through the Wesleyan Methodist Missionary Society (WMMS) despite his elders' fierce objections. He became and lived as a Methodist.[17] This happened sometime in the aftermath of the wars and famines of the 1820s and 1830s during which his family had fled from the banks of the Molopo River, along with thousands of others, towards the Orange River, and set up refuge at Thaba Nchu. He had a half-brother, Montsioa, who did not convert and never learnt how to read and write. He was younger than Isaac Molema, but had recognition as belonging to a senior house. Thus, the younger brother became the heir of the claims on land and people that their father enjoyed as the most senior patriarch in their lineage, and as the recognised founder of the *morafe* that had grown around him, both on the lands they had abandoned up north and on the new lands he had acquired during the years of exile. When the brothers made their way home from about the 1840s and settled with their followers at a place called Rietfontein or Lotlhakane, their father was dead, and their following was a larger and more mixed *morafe* than the displaced population they once were.

Molema was one of an early cohort of young men of influence who became the first teachers and evangelists from the mid-nineteenth century.[18] They were spreading the Gospel to their own kin and families and becoming the first catechists and schoolmasters to their growing following. They drew their followers together under the Old Testament model of a 'peculiar people' who understood themselves as divinely placed on their own territory in order to fulfil a divine destiny.[19] Thus in time, Protestantism helped to distil the amorphous constellation of overlapping lineages and settlements of the *merafe* into fewer identifiable nodes of chiefly authority, like the 'Bangoaketse' in Serowe, the Batlhaping in Kuruman or the Barolong in Mafikeng. These were typically 'ecclesiastical statehoods' or 'realms of the Word' where rulers drew from the Bible and conversations with missionary societies to synthesise 'learning' or '*thuto*' as a loose ideological motif that shaped everyday practice throughout the polity and served as an 'index' for political belonging.[20] They used their interpretation of the Bible to induct their following into a new understanding of moral order. This is how they established new centres of political and moral authority in the aftermath of the dislocation of earlier decades. The European missionaries they invited had to accept that teachers like Molema were independent spiritual fathers of the flock, sanctioning what was right and wrong. There emerged fierce debate about whether polygamy, rainmaking, circumcision, paying homage to ancestors and so on were unproblematic moral practices redeemed by salvation or outright heathen, but the fathers of the *morafe*, not the missionaries, shaped those decisions.

Isaac Molema's story is now well known. In about 1857, Molema moved from Rietfontein and established a settlement of his own at Mafikeng, some distance away, with a few followers, all Methodists. He had moved away from his brother but although he had created an alternative moral centre from the life at Rietfontein, he did not quite succeed in establishing an independent chieftaincy of his own. Perhaps he had failed in that purpose or perhaps it was never his intention, but when his following grew, tensions with Montsioa's paramount house exploded. About a decade later 'hundreds' were flocking to his new village, Mafikeng, and learning how to read and write and unwilling to participate in the rituals Montsioa orchestrated – hunting, reed dancing, sowing 'the garden of rain'. Montsioa had his own literate followers, who dispatched a complaint to the Wesleyan Missionary Society that 'Molema stood as teacher of the tribe in my place', and had 'set up a chieftaincy of his own...' 'These Christians', he continued, 'are obeying the Book more than the King, ultimately the tribe will split and perish.'[21]

In other words, for Montsioa it was not the instruction of 'the Book', but rather the word of 'the King', that lent moral force to the practices that made 'persons'. He was remonstrating against what he feared was a rapid precipitation of anomie where anyone could pull his own moral cart in the direction he or she saw fit.[22] Christians thinned the assembly of persons. They did not gather for his work as the first 'father', as the source that brought the rain, as the first seed to have cracked open in the ground. He had germinated their very sustenance. He was the rainmaker. His fields were first to go under the plough – the most useful technology of Europeans that he had embraced, because his work, *tiro*, was to incubate life in the earth and into the homestead, but the Christians would not recognise him. Further, the Christians were mostly monogamous. They rarely aimed for the teeming homesteads of many women and many children that added weight to manhood by making more life, more people, more hands to make food and grow herds. The Christians also held their sons back from circumcision and yet transferred to them land

and cattle and all the benefits of manhood without proof of their worthiness. It seemed to him that the Christians never grew up.

For patriarchs like Montsioa, there was nothing wrong with innovation, with learning Dutch and English. He did not see anything wrong with literacy. He himself used a church bell at his court, wore Victorian dress, and even allowed prayers. All was acceptable as long as it did not undermine or take the place of the proper work of personhood, *tiro*. Those repertories of practices, he felt, had to persist, come what may. Many of his followers – certainly not all – shunned schooling but readily embraced the plough. Some of them erected 'square houses' with bricks and mortar or embellished their round mud huts with some element of the fashionable new architecture depending on taste and money, but did not fail to circumcise their sons. Some of Montsioa's sons were literate but married more than one woman. Even at Molema's Mafikeng, the lines demarcating Christianity were not straight rulings. Molemas, though pious Methodists, continued with the tradition of the levirate, giving their daughters away to the unconverted yet monogamous sons of Montsioa and other relatives.

Hence, at both centres of chiefly power, the conversation about what measure of innovation so diverted from tradition, *Sechuana*, that it compromised the *morafe* was loud and divisive enough to destabilise both centres. It was admirable to be innovative, to find creative routes to get ahead, to complete the journey to manhood and womanhood as soon as possible, but shameful to be seen to be using the new ways as a shortcut because one lacked the capacity for the long, moral haul required to prove maturity. Yet, at the same time, the consensus of what made shame and honour was wearing extremely thin.

III

There occurred in 1877 an event that took place relatively quickly but never remained in the past. It continued to appear as many oral reiterations of an ever-changing plot and altered characterisation of the protagonists. The certainty is that in 1877, the Rapulana Barolong, lineage and close kin of Montsioa's Ratshidi Barolong, forged an alliance with Boer mercenaries to sack Rietfontein.[23] They successfully dislodged Montsioa, who then fled to his brother's Methodist hub in Mafikeng. In years to come, men who were seniors at the time would tell the story before colonial magistrates. Men aspiring to influence would tell it to women and children as an inspiration for the work of religious devotion to raise their *morafe* to its own destiny on the land. Nevertheless, the accounts of what had happened were not consistent and contradicted one another. This single event, involving a few thousand people at the most, and particularly the traditions of storytelling that emerged from it, would feed into contestations about *Sechuana* and *Sekhoa*, and present no small series of challenges to the British Empire and its settler governments. It would prove just how fragile the imperial enterprise in these northern hinterlands was.

About five years after the sacking of Rietfontein in 1881, Isaac Molema welcomed his grandson, Joshua Molema's first son, into the world. Whenever the baby stretched his little legs, one of his feet reached a noticeable distance beyond the other. His father praised God and named him Sebopioa, which means a work of creation that inspired wonder in its uniqueness and perfection. The son with uneven feet would need a cane to pull himself erect to walk. He grew up when people were still talking about the event that had forced his grandfather, Isaac Molema, to surrender his stronghold of Mafikeng to Montsioa. It was not so much the event itself, but more the many crisscrossing narrations of what happened and what it meant, more who told the story and who was listening, that eventually gave that moment its significance in his lifetime. The sacking of Rietfontein was a relatively small happening in the turbulent history of this frontier, but its narrative repertoires would later affect tens of thousands more than four decades later, when the frontier south of the Molopo River was closing into the racialised grid of power that was becoming South Africa.

IV

Indeed, new or returning settlers did not always peaceably assimilate into existing repertoires of life on the land. Often, their intention was to conquer and dominate. Sometimes the moral subscriptions to be nativised onto the land were unaffordable. Some could not pay and others did not want to do so. The frontier along both sides of the Molopo River again turned violent and bloody into the second half of the nineteenth century. European mercenaries, both Dutch- and English-speaking, fought on different sides of warring chieftaincies as they attacked rival settlements and raided cattle.[24] War against mutual enemies brought the two brothers, Molema and Montsioa, and their families together, but the feud between their families was an extensive and complicated rift. There were times when loyalty and ties between the families ran very deep, especially when a father-in-law loved his son's or daughter's spouse, or when the arranged marriage was happy and flourished. Now together at Mafikeng after 1877, the Molemas and the Montsioas armed themselves and their followers with the help of missionaries to defend their stronghold, but the family feud held a lethal potential to destroy this necessary unity.

In the meantime, missionaries like John Mackenzie were lobbying the British government to intervene in the disaster and bring peace to Bechuanaland by annexing the territory as a protectorate.[25] Along the Molopo, a thin presence of Cape troops maintained some limited semblance of order and mediated tentative terms of peace between the warring Barolong groups and their European allies but had little power to enforce armistices. The chiefdoms closer to the Diamond Fields had succumbed to these mixed alliances of conquest, but the northern chiefdoms along and beyond the Molopo, including the lineages of the Barolong, were still on their feet although divided and fragile. Life carried on during wartime and people along the Molopo remained on the lands they still had. They ploughed and reaped and sold grain to the Diamond Fields in Kimberley. This is why wagon riding was such a lucrative enterprise although the war was bad for business. It closed off the transport route. 'What am I to do with my corn if I cannot take it to sell,' Montsioa wrote to the British Captain Henry Nourse in 1881, 'I grow corn for the markets for money.'[26] Mafikeng's resistance was starting to break.[27] Boer settlers established independent republics, Goshen and Stellaland, west of the Transvaal Republic on the territories Montsioa held. Montsioa publicly declared 'spiritual freedom' in an effort to draw WMMS missionaries to Mafikeng as allies in the war. He declared Methodism the official religion in his kingdom.[28]

Isaac Molema's literate sons became indispensable to the security of Montsioa's rule after their father's death in 1881.[29] The paramount chief also had very strong support from Stephen Lefenya, his literate and devoted son-in-law. Israel, Joshua and Silas Molema and Stephen Lefenya were the scribes and senior councillors in the chiefly bureaucracy. They armed themselves and sought alliances to keep Mafikeng from collapse as the war continued. In the meantime, the missionary lobby for Britain's annexation of Bechuanaland intensified but the British government, especially under William Gladstone, did not support the political incorporation of distant territories and preferred to maintain their geopolitical influence in southern Africa and elsewhere through informal collaborations. Gladstone's administration (1880–1885) was especially mindful not to finance the empire through the British taxpayer. There were also settler lobbies who wanted the British government to declare suzerainty on the lands they had conquered or had designs to possess. The lobbies had no success. From the middle of 1883, the probability of British annexation was even more unlikely because Britain was finding it impossible to dislodge her troops from Egypt following a quick military victory against the Egyptian government. Another involvement in 'colonial wars' was not politically prudent.

Nevertheless, two years later, Britain annexed Bechuanaland, acquiring a colossal swathe of territory that extended from the Orange River, shouldering the Transvaal Republic's western boundary and then crossing and extending beyond the Molopo River. What is today Botswana was annexed as the Bechuanaland Protectorate and the territory south of the Molopo River became British Bechuanaland. The reason for this change of mind was the diplomatic arrival of Otto van Bismarck along the southwestern coast of Africa. Bismarck approved the annexation of German South West Africa in 1884 and its status as a German possession was confirmed months later by the Conference of Berlin. Bismarck had sought an alliance with Paul Kruger, the president of the Transvaal Republic, to establish a railway line joining the Transvaal to German South West Africa. He was hoping to become the most dominant political influence in southern Africa. Britain's response was to make Bechuanaland a strategic buffer between its two opponents' territories.[30] Britain's colonisation of Bechuanaland was largely forced and reluctant hence, apart from maintaining its overall dominance over the region, it had no accompanying plan for actually governing the territories. It forced Goshen and Stellaland (the short-lived Boer Republics west of the Transvaal) to surrender but did not have a plan to establish and maintain a permanent peace between the warring chieftaincies, leaving this task to Sidney Shippard, who became Resident Commissioner for the Bechuanaland Protectorate and Chief Magistrate and President of the Land Commission for British Bechuanaland. His task was to settle all land disputes and delineate the boundaries of the new reserves in Bechuanaland. The objective was to purchase British loyalty out of a population which Britain had no desire to rule permanently.

Shippard negotiated extensively with the cohort of literate chiefs, who were proficient in English, in an attempt to settle the frontier down to peace as quickly and as inexpensively as possible. At the Barolong territories along the Molopo, he created as many reserves as the number of key warring Barolong clans he could identify, namely the Ratshidi, the Rapulana and the Ratlou. He installed the then recognised paramount chief of each clan as ruler of a reserve, relying also on his interpretation of how chieftaincy worked in African societies. These reserves acquired reference as the 'Barolong territories' but they were not the only reserves in British Bechuanaland. Most significantly, Shippard avoided displacing and moving populations. He did not interfere with the living arrangements he found on the ground, certainly not in the manner Britain typically categorised and separated people it intended to rule into neat categories of 'racial' and 'tribal' types on the land. The Land Commission 'refrained from defining boundaries between tribes or section of tribes considering the reserves available for all natives no matter of what nationality'.[31] The population of each reserve was a mixed bag of skin colour, dialect and cultural practice. He drew the boundary lines and marked the boundaries of each of the Barolong reserves by surrounding them with private farms, which he sold at auctions to whomever could afford them regardless of the buyer's skin colour.

Significantly, Shippard also departed from another policy of reservation already in practice in the neighbouring Cape Colony. After negotiations with chiefs, he excluded the reserves of British Bechuanaland from the Native Locations Act of 1884. This legislation classified reserves as Crown Lands under the ownership and control of the government. The land belonged to the government and it enjoyed the sole right to make decisions about landholding, settlement and governance in these 'locations'. The government determined who could or could not reside in the locations. In contrast, the reserves of British Bechuanaland did not become Crown Lands. Rather, they belonged to their inhabitants.[32] For this reason, the populations of British Bechuanaland did not pay Hut Tax, certainly not in the 'Barolong territories'. Another important departure from accepted practice in the Cape was that the British government committed not only to recognise hereditary chiefs but also to intervene as little as possible in the structures and decisions of governance by chiefs. The Barolong territories were autonomous and chiefly jurisdictions within the British Empire. Moreover, rather than replacing them with its own chosen headman as was the policy in the Cape and Natal colonies, the British government rewarded the hereditary paramount chiefs with an annual pension.[33] A handful of their kin and councillors also drew salaries as junior chiefs. The questions of property and governance on these 'tribal lands' were for chiefs alone to resolve.

When it came to negotiations with Montsioa, which Shippard conducted through the chief's educated councillors, Shippard was also considerably obliging. He made Montsioa the paramount chief of the Barolong of the Ratshidi lineage. Theirs was the Molopo Native Reserve, roughly 660 square miles.[34] Mafikeng remained the capital stadt and remains part of the capital city of the North West province in South Africa today. Shippard situated Rietfontein within the boundaries of the Molopo Reserve. He surrounded the cluster of new Barolong reserves with private property 'subject to redeemable quitrent' as a barrier against settler encroachment.[35] A number of chiefly notables bought some of these farms. Some also secured title deeds for property in the reserves. Though he denied Montsioa jurisdiction over lands he claimed west of Mafikeng, Shippard compensated him with a further 432 square miles of farmland north of the Molopo River in the Bechuanaland Protectorate, which acquired the name 'Barolong Farms'. These were neither Crown Lands nor a reserve but constituted an independent, private, self-governing domain.[36] Thus these negotiated settlements situated these Barolong in three separate jurisdictions simultaneously – the relatively autonomous Molopo Reserve, the independent territories of Barolong Farms and freehold farms beyond the reserves.

Almost a decade after annexing the territories, Britain decided to cede British Bechuanaland to the Cape Colony and the Bechuanaland Protectorate to Cecil John Rhodes, then Prime Minister of the Cape Colony. Rhodes had already placed southern Rhodesia under his British South Africa Company, which would now assume control over the Bechuanaland Protectorate. Montsioa sent a petition to the Queen through the Governor General that 'we from the very first objected to be under the Cape Government' and that 'we were told that we should always remain under the Imperial Government'.

> You will know us, we are not strangers, we have been your children since 1885… We are sorry you have taken our land from us and given it to the Cape Government, we do not know their ways and laws… The Cape government have the power to take away the … land you gave us in the land settlement of 1886 – there are many people and the land is very little, the land is our life – Help us… Instead of remaining on the present Native reserve we may be forced into locations. Instead of administering our Native laws as is now done according to our Native customs we shall find ourselves under restrictions which will be made law and which we shall not be able to understand. We shall be without leaders by having no voice in the framing of any laws… Barolong are much astonished and full of sorrow because we have heard that the [?] government wants to give away our country in the Protectorate to the Charter Company, we mean the British South Africa Charter Company…My people are increasing very fast and are filling the land… We build houses, we plough many gardens, we sow lots of mealies, kaffir corn, wheat and forage, our people go to work in the Gold Fields. Why do you want to throw us away! Our word is 'No! No!'[37]

In response to Montsioa's and other protectorate chiefs' protestations, as we shall see, Britain agreed that the British South Africa Company would have no jurisdiction over reserves and the Barolong Farms in the Bechuanaland Protectorate. Thereafter, Sidney Shippard entered into another round of negotiations with Montsioa about his reserve in British Bechuanaland. Montsioa agreed that he would not object to the Molopo Reserve's annexation into the Cape Colony on condition that the Cape government would not revoke or attenuate the terms of annexation that he and Shippard had previously agreed on in 1885. Shippard agreed that the policies of the Cape Colony would not apply to the Molopo Reserve and other Barolong reserves.

Thus, the reserves of former British Bechuanaland, again as we shall see, remained largely self-governing chiefly jurisdictions whose hereditary rulers were nevertheless now on the Cape government's payroll. At the same time, annexation to the Cape Colony meant the literate and propertied chiefs now qualified to vote under the Cape's liberal franchise. They were straddling two forms of government seamlessly as rulers of relatively autonomous chiefly jurisdictions in the Barolong territories and as a constituency with representation in the Cape's House of Assembly on equal terms as any other voter in the Cape. The chiefs' pious Protestant councillors would not take credit for their win as due to luck or their own shrewd cunning. Instead, they praised God for giving them victory over an enemy too strong for them – the dispensation of company rule and the Cape government. 'The Barolongs love God,' Stephen Lefenya said. 'He fought with them against their enemies and they have seen that all power is with God, so they love Him and want to serve Him.'[38]

V

Isaac Molema's most enterprising son was the youngest, Silas Molema, whom he sent to Healdtown, a Methodist institute in the Eastern Cape to train as a teacher. Silas graduated with a third-class certificate in 1877 and returned home to build a school in Mafikeng in 1879. When his father died in 1882, Silas took over the congregation. In eight years, he had grown it from 279 to 1200 members.[39] The building doubled up as a school. In 1885, when the British took over the territory, Silas Molema was a preacher, schoolmaster and the most trusted administrator in the chiefly bureaucracy and, by the 1880s, an important and very wealthy man. His wife, Molalanyane, was apparently of 'Griqua' descent. In an old photograph, her cheekbones are high and her skin appears pale.[40] Today, one of her great-granddaughters has the remarkable combination of striking blue eyes and brown skin.

Molalanyane was probably a family member. She and her husband most likely either knew or had heard about each other from their parents or other family members as children, or young adults, before their arranged marriage. She wrote and read, perhaps more comfortably in Sechuana than she did in English or Dutch. Her letters to her husband were short, a few sentences in vernacular to transmit a message or report a death. She would write to him when she was temporarily away at their countryside residence at Madibespruit whilst he remained at their late-Victorian town residence in Mafikeng. The Molemas' town residence stood at the far end of a semi-circle of more modest brick houses all overlooking the Molopo River, although inspired by the same late-Victorian style. The Molema brothers lived a short distance from one another along this semi-circle. This would become 'Molema Square'. Children walked a few feet from their own front door to the home of their cousins. Molalanyane oversaw the care of her home and laboured to attend to herself. The ribbon, lace, camphor and scent from Whiteley, Walker & Co. were for her.[41]

Silas Molema's first child was a daughter. Seleje was born in 1888. Her father would have been at least thirty-two years old, a relatively late age to have children at the time. Perhaps the war delayed conception or perhaps the couple struggled, but custom did not rely on biology alone. There was more than one route to swell a homestead with persons. The levirate, informal rules of 'adopting' and 'borrowing' children and women conceiving for their childless relations were all ways of populating a homestead. This may be how Sebopioa grew up a child in the household of his uncle, Silas. He would have been accustomed to walking a few feet from his own home to his uncle's house as the little person the couple could send about and dote upon. He became Seleje's older brother and such a favourite with his uncle that he bestowed on him alone the privileges and affection he did not extend to his other nephews or nieces.

The boy's biological father, Joshua, encouraged the attachment. Joshua was not as enterprising as the younger Silas, at least not in the wherewithal to make money, nor was he as educated. He admired his younger brother, was very proud of him, and wanted his son to rise and tower above his environment like his uncle did as a man of reputation. Sebopioa thus had two fathers, 'the fathers' as he grew to refer to them, neither more important to him than the other, but his strongest admiration was for the younger father, who was in any case, his primary provider who freely offered him a life of comfort and privilege. There was 'French coffee' and golden syrup and an opportunity to attend Lovedale Missionary Institute in the Eastern Cape without worries about fees and the cost of books and rail fare. Sebopioa did not see the unravelling of his father's money and enterprise because it was initially slow and scarcely visible. He also was not a witness to it because he was schooling away from home. In his absence, first the jam and the chicory left the breakfast table and then the visits to clothing shops stopped, until finally the welt was separating from the skin of the children's boots.

VI

The best years of Silas Molema's life were his thirties and early forties, which is to say the years of British rule before the South African War broke out in 1899. This does not mean they were easy years but he was doing well and growing a family. His line of business was transport. He owned probably the largest fleet of wagons and carts in Bechuanaland.[42] The British administrative centre in colonial Bechuanaland was Mafeking, a town of mainly European settlement that adjoined the western border of the Molopo Reserve. The Molemas did some of their shopping here but there were many other centres of trade across the border in the Bechuanaland Protectorate. The invoices of the Molemas' household purchases from the late 1880s have coffee, tea and chicory as staple purchases. Poor families rarely enjoyed these beverages.[43] The Molemas' list of purchases were long but they never included alcohol.[44]

Modiri was born in 1891, just as his father's transport business was expanding. At the age of seven, he met Solomon Plaatje who had come from Kimberley to take up work in Mafeking and stayed at the Molemas' homestead. Plaatje was then twenty-two and an interpreter at the Resident Magistrate's court. He made a very strong impression on the young man, 'touched [his] heart in an unforgettable way'.[45] Modiri marvelled at the lightness of Plaatje's complexion. 'He was even whiter than the light-skinned Molemas of Mafikeng or the Moswetes of Khunwane, the lightest among all the other Barolong'.[46] At Plaatje's own mother's house they called him 'Tsoeunyane', that is 'the whitish one'. Others thought Plaatje was 'neither European nor an African but a Griqua'. His in-laws disapprovingly thought their daughter had married 'a Hottentot or a San'.[47]

Modiri was also spellbound by Plaatje's polyglot genius and by how quickly and extensively he read – Shakespeare, Dumas, Ruskin and Keats, a 'walking library'.[48] Plaatje consumed current affairs ferociously, both local and overseas newspapers. He was born at Pniel, on a farm that belonged to Lutheran church ministers near Kimberley and had arrived in Mafikeng with news and information about many different parts of the world, and with the intention to travel. On the other hand, the seven-year-old's father had a quiet, sedentary authority as an extension of the rock that had founded the chieftaincy at Mafikeng. Silas Molema had always to be here, an immovable rock living and ruling. Plaatje was like a sediment of this rock that rolled about and yet retained the characteristics of its origins. The little boy was drawn to the momentum of this motion. He was intrigued by the unknown possibilities of the traveller who yields to the road, especially those of the mind and imagination, but retained a faithfulness to this countryside as though he had never left home.

In the meantime, the transport business grew. In 1890, Molema spent £125 on a brand new wagon. Less than a year later, he exchanged fourteen oxen for two new carts.[49] Molemas bought blankets, shawls, jackets, hats, shirts and trousers in addition to coffee, tea, sugar, powdered milk, cordial and golden syrup.[50] The transport business was susceptible to unexpected lulls because it depended on the market of grain. Concentrated investment in wagons and carts in times of boom could easily prove an over-investment a few months down the line if grain yields were low. In the spring of 1892, the Molemas had to purchase mealies, indicating a scarcity of grain.[51] They tightened their spending considerably and relied on credit from traders and small loans to survive a clearly difficult patch.[52] The autumn of 1894, from May until June, brought a bumper harvest.[53] Grain was again in circulation. Business soon picked up. The following year agents like Musson Brother commissioned Molema's wagons and carts to carry grain as far as Vryburg and to Palapje and Molepolole in the Bechuanaland Protectorate. To transport a single load of about 1600lb from Mafikeng to Palapje cost about £48.[54] Takings of £50 a year were enough to purchase some land and pay quitrent.[55] Molema hired men to drive oxen for as many as nine wagons at a time.[56] Many wagons' destination was the Diamond Fields in Kimberley. Buyers purchased mealies, sorghum – known as 'kaffir corn' – wheat and forage.[57]

The tide of good fortune quickly receded. In April 1896, rinderpest crossed the Molopo from the north. The deadly disease killed tens of thousands of cattle. Riders had to abandon their wagons along the roads as their oxen died.[58] Very quickly, donkeys replaced oxen in front of carts and wagons. Molema's advantage was his longstanding relationships with big general dealers. Whiteley, Walker & Co. was a ready creditor and advanced him £190 in December of 1896.[59] This seems to have gone towards the purchase of 38 donkeys.[60] He also borrowed another £190 from C. de Clarke in February of the following year.[61] The scarcity of oxen and his quick ability to convert to donkeys made him one of the few functioning wagon transporters. He expanded his business further. In that very year of rinderpest, Molema's second daughter, Harriet, was born.

The amount of money that Molema had in hand to spend to respond to rinderpest, or could otherwise readily solicit from creditors who trusted him to pay, suggests that he was a relatively affluent man. As comparison, the highest paid civil servant in the colonial administration in Mafeking in 1897 was Civil Commissioner and Resident Magistrate G.J. Boyes, who earned £550 a year.[62] By the end of 1897, Whiteley, Walker & Co. alone owed Molema £900 for transport services.[63] In the meantime, he had accumulated a debt of over £520 across Whiteley, Walker & Co.'s counter. He could take home only the difference. Building up his enterprise through the switch from oxen to donkeys had been costly but his household expenditure had also bulked up considerably. The Molemas were spending a lot, mostly at Whiteley, Walker & Co. on credit, against the wagons' potential earnings from the wholesaler that year. Perhaps Molema was making some purchases in order to resell those goods elsewhere.

Between May and November 1897, the household enjoyed luxuries like 'French coffee' when many were still reeling from the cattle plague. They bought jam, fruit salts, coffee, chicory, tea, sugar as well as blankets, aprons, a tablecloth and a sunshade. There was also new clothing, including a suit, ties, a jacket and a cap that were probably for Sebopioa as he proceeded to Lovedale Missionary Institute. In comparison, Joshua Molema's account at Whiteley, Walker & Co. only amounted to £3-17-6 over the same period.[64] In the younger Molema's household, a considerable amount of expenditure was going on, but perhaps it was not extraordinary, only a life they knew well and had been living a long while. Besides, Silas Molema was exerting himself, working hard to expand his business. He continued to take every opportunity to purchase cheap donkeys.[65] Unfortunately, the days of successful wagon transporters were already numbered.

In 1890, the Cape government started to construct a railway line from the north of Griqualand West to Mafikeng, intending that it would extend all the way north into Rhodesia. It was still necessary to hire wagons to transport goods from stadts like Mafikeng, Rietfontein and others into the town of Mafeking but these were short journeys.[66] Large wholesalers like

Whiteley, Walker & Co. would have been the first to take advantage of rail service to transport goods over long distances. At the same time, the Cape administration was taking a new interest in the European settlers whose impoverishment and fragile livelihoods reflected economic disparities in the settler community. These emerged in official parlance as the 'poor white' problem, but the label is misleading. Settlers had not yet unified around a consciousness of 'whiteness'. Differences in skin pigmentation were obvious, but they did not neatly consolidate into the social fact of 'race'. There was not yet agreement about what 'white', for example, meant. A growing number of these 'poor whites' were taking up cart-driving. They pushed transport prices down to compete with 'brown' and 'black' wagon transporters.[67] Still, the ox-wagon had a competitive advantage over rail because the transporter and merchant depended on one another through the credit cycles that Molema's accounts reflect. To break the attachment, the government offered large traders incentives to dissolve such arrangements.[68] Whiteley, Walker & Co. did not hire Molema's transport services in 1898. Instead, he transported goods for Loosely & McLaren General Merchants, a smaller wholesaler.[69]

The other expense was school fees. At the beginning of 1898, there were at least four young Molemas at Lovedale, including Sebopioa and Seleje. There was also Officer Molema, the son of Molema's late brother, Israel. Silas Molema paid for all of them.[70] Until Loosely & McLaren paid him for transport services rendered at the end of the year, he found himself with very little money in hand and relied on rents from his tenants.[71] By September, Sebopioa and Officer's fees were in arrears. Lovedale warned that 'all boys whose fees are not paid by the end of this month cannot be allowed to attend classes beyond this date'.[72] He had to ask for an advance of payment from Loosely & McLaren.[73] The severity of his financial trouble was now in full presentation. His savings at Standard Bank were exhausted. So little remained that his attorney, Spencer Minchin, notified him that there was no provision for a small bill of £1-1-10.[74] At the end of 1898 his earnings from Loosely & McLaren were just under £320 but due to credit he had taken earlier in the year, he took home a little under £130. Spending in the household appears to have spiralled out of control considering the bill accrued at Whiteley, Walker & Co. for over £400. Joshua's spending at the same store over the same period was just under £35.[75] Amongst the first business transactions early in January 1899 was a loan from the attorney J.W de Kock for £97.[76] It mostly went to school fees.[77] When De Kock called in his loan in April, Molema had nothing.[78] Returns from wagon services to Loosely & McLaren amounted only to about £18.[79] Molema had overstretched himself in his business and the family was spending too much. His prospects were bleak, and he teetered on the verge of bankruptcy.

In October 1899, the mostly European town of Mafeking fell under siege. Mafikeng, the stadt in the Molopo Reserve, was the boundary that sheltered the European town's residences and business district from Boer commandos. Chiefs and their subjects had to defend themselves and their property. Hence, across the handful of Barolong reserves along the Molopo River, hereditary rulers refused to accept the South African War as a 'white man's war', which is how the British administrations and Boer Republics described it. Silas Molema and others also saw the siege as a war against their empire, to which they felt an attachment forged by providence. They defended themselves against Boer fighters and marauders who took advantage of war conditions. The stadt's population was about five thousand. On the holding called Kromdraai in the reserve, which was under Molema's control, the Boers burnt down two large houses, each of three rooms. They destroyed a stable for six horses. They carried away building material, including almost 80 large sheets of iron, 9 to 10 feet long, half of which were new, 18 rolls of barbed wire, and 30 bags of lime. Most of this property probably belonged to tenants on Kromdraai. The war also destroyed the iron house, which had been the Mafeking Market House before Molema bought it in 1898. Molema lost eight ploughs, five of them brand new, a 'good' wagon, three wheelbarrows and a new saddle. Raiders razed two fields of sorghum and fruit trees to the ground and took away eight bags of wheat and four of oats.[80] The war worsened the financial disaster unfolding on the home front.

Children's fees at Lovedale were outstanding.[81] In fact, there were food shortages in the reserves. There was too little money even to chip away at the debt accumulated the previous year.[82] It helped a little that British troops needed carts and wagons to transport supplies. The rate of hire was low, about £1 a day per wagon, but as many as 30 wagons were necessary at one time to carry arms and supplies between various camps.[83] Molema invested in more wagons and carts. He bid for them at auctions.[84] More generally auctioneers, especially Dennison & Cranswick, soon replaced wholesalers like Whiteley, Walker & Co. as a place for domestic purchases, which is why it is difficult to explain the elaborate purchases at Whiteley, Walker & Co. at the end of October 1900, including a suit, ribbon, lace, camphor and scent. They amounted to over £72 and brought the outstanding balance to over £550.[85]

The family could not afford such indulgent slips from thrift, not during the war, and not when children's fees at Lovedale were in arrears.[86] School fees were in fact rising. According to Lovedale's principal, the increase in fees at the end of 1900 was 'absolutely necessary' due to a steep rise in food costs but also a 'greatly increased requirement of Native Education'.[87] By the end of 1900, Molema's account at Standard Bank had a negative balance of over £210.[88] In the New Year, whatever small amount the transport business and tenants' rents brought, bought cows and calves at Dennison & Cranswick auctioneers.[89] Molema was now borrowing money from friends in town. The creditors noose was narrowing around his neck. Minchin paid £100 into the account at Whiteley, Walker & Co., but even then almost £400 was outstanding.[90] Two months into 1901 the wholesaler complained that Molema had 'made not the slightest attempt to reduce the account' for many months.[91] A month later, Lovedale's headmaster also sent a letter that Lovedale was 'under very great expense' to run a boarding school with 'a large amount of fees still unpaid'.[92] At about this time, Molema received £617 as war compensation from the Cape government.[93] He paid school fees and parts of his major debts, including at Whiteley, Walker & Co.[94] Auctions remained the place to purchase clothing and other items. The family still rang up debt at Whiteley, Walker & Co. – jam, lemon squash, tobacco, trousers and shawls.[95] The amount he received from the government was significant. As comparison, the highest paid civil servant in the colonial administration in Mafeking in 1902 was Civil Commissioner and Resident Magistrate, Charles Bell, who earned £650 a year.[96]

Molema was short of money but not of credit. As a businessman, he had a great capacity for risk. In 1901, he became the first person of colour to own a newspaper in southern Africa. This was *Koranta ea Becoana*. If it became a success, it would pay the initial investors and make some money. However, this was not why he took the risk. His political power had risen as his liquidity declined. In 1896, after Montsioa died, his son Wessels Montsioa, became the paramount chief, but Molema's literate following saw no hope of moving forward with a polygamous, barely literate man who enjoyed his drink and who spent money only on himself. Solomon Plaatje and others were on the lookout for a different calibre of leadership, and none was more attractive than Silas Molema.

Even his children's precociousness, ambition and claim to distinction set them apart like eager branded stock. Modiri Molema was ten years old. He was observant and pondered the worlds of the fathers. He saw that his father was also a traveller, indeed a determined one. His father carried himself to many places by virtue of his moral reputation, not by rail and not through the ordinary rituals and ceremonies of departure. At home, the family was adjusting to privation and learning to do without familiar comforts. Modiri was already a boy playing and herding and schooling in Mafikeng when the money troubles had crept up on them, and with them his many little doubts about whether home was the place to keep his treasured things and stave off loss.

VII

Initiation rituals inducted children, boys and girls, into adulthood. For boys, the ritual of cutting emboldened them and proved them to one another as ready to abandon their childlike existence and enter into repertoires of practice that belonged solely to men – landholding, marriage, a voice in the Kgotla, all of the freedom to become fathers, elders, grandfathers. They anticipated that the forces of nature, especially thunder, would confirm their transition. Initiation transported them 'out of the purely profane world' of uninspired ordinariness and childlike pleasures 'into the circle of sacred things', where they are able to participate in ritual ceremonies that displayed the signs and emblems of their *morafe*.[97] Hence, at the end of the ritual the male initiate razed his hut, threw a brand new covering on his shoulders, and left the little person he used to be behind him. 'He was born again in a new form.'[98] Initiates' first responsibility as adults, as entities with autonomy, was to be with kin and neighbours to celebrate their transition. They provided opportunity for the *morafe* to gather in the eloquent celebrations of song, dance and oration. Their proof of maturity facilitated a togetherness that made a lifting of the 'soul', created feelings of 'heart', 'life' and 'consciousness' that knitted them all together in a moment of 'effervescence'.[99] Its effect was to embolden every individual; 'in moral harmony with his neighbour, he gains new confidence, courage and boldness in action', feels more than a single entity but like something unquantifiable, experiences a 'moreness', becomes someone powerful enough to have control over the course of life and nature.[100] The first celebration of autonomy was in solidarity with others in orchestrated rhythms of activity. The lesson was clear. Adulthood is an indissoluble attachment to others.

Being without others is not personhood, only an existence like that of the Cyclops in the Homeric songs. His cave is neat and well ordered, but can never be a home. He is 'all outward power, a wild man, ignorant of civility'.[101] He has the morphology of human life, yet his concern is only with himself, having no 'muster and no meeting, no consultation or old tribal ways, but each one dwells in his own mountain cave … indifferent to what the others do'.[102] Without the 'moreness' that derives from practice, from doing together with others, he has no control over nature, surviving on what lives or grows by itself, ignorant of how to make the ground yield, ever at the mercy of nature like a wild thing. This is what chiefly and patriarchal power feared was beginning to happen to their youth at the beginning of the twentieth century. The young seemed to be shrinking into little people of narrow interests, concerned with only themselves as they took up new opportunities of the frontier, mainly paid work, fast transportation to far off places and formal schooling.

Even as the twentieth century began, there was not yet a moral consensus on the utility of literacy, the proper way to make and spend money, or the appropriate orientations to the land and its customs of life. The contestation was about establishing the boundary beyond which new innovations along the frontier that coincided with Europeans' migration and their way of doing corrugated the cultural matrix of 'tradition', *Sechuana*, to the effect that the *morafe* thinned away, starved of the substance of personhood. Contributors to the newspaper *Mahoko a Becwana* (1883–1896), which was established and run by the London Missionary Society, debated these questions.[103] In the early twentieth century, newspapers in the vernacular were 'textual assemblies', much like the Kgotla, the court where men came together.[104] In *Mahoko a Becwana*, literate men were debating whether or not they were still adhering to the old ways: 'You should know that you are not following either *Secwana* or even *Sekhoa*; you are just in the middle', one writer put it in 1891, 'I don't know Becwana, what we are, because we are not doing the practices of either *Secwana* or *Sekhoa*. For how long are you going to be undecided?'[105] By then, as the newspaper indicated, the *morafe* had a name, 'Bechuana', loosely the people of Bechuanaland but it was not a *morafe* yet unless its people properly calibrated its moral compass and followed it.

At the beginning of the new century, there had emerged conditions in the countryside that seriously worsened these anxieties. Men found that women and young people were not as available for the routine roles that confirmed manhood as before. Women were no longer co-labourers on the factory floor of personhood that made men. Women's role, as men understood tradition, was submission and dependence. This is how women and their children facilitated and recognised manhood, by carrying out their roles of childhood and womanhood in dependence and subservience. Women's demonstration of their own autonomy as adults had always been a delicate negotiation with patriarchy, but what women could do and become independently of men along this frontier introduced deep instability. By the beginning of the twentieth century, educated women could also become teachers or nurses. They could become wage earners and breadwinners. They wrote, read and travelled. They even sailed abroad. They were at liberty to have dreams and aspirations and pursue them independently of men. Even without an education, women and young men could leave the countryside, abandon husbands and fathers to find work and form new attachments. They could afford to spend money they had earned themselves. They could also choose to pass their days as they wished, unaffected by men's understanding of piety or morality because they had money in hand, even if they did not have land of their own.

Men's anxieties did not recede with time. Instead, they intensified. For years to come, this generation of men's rallying cry to remake the colonial world was also an attempt to rehabilitate women and young people, and to gain an upper hand in the gender wars and generational conflicts that were taking place in their own homes. In the meantime, chiefs were also decrying the decline of their prestige. 'Remember', Sebele Sechele, paramount chief of the Bakoena in Molepolole wrote to Silas Molema in 1904, 'now we are people of the whites' (*batho ba makhoa*).[106] Sechele's wife, Macholohelo, had prevented him from taking his lover of over twenty years as a second wife even though, he claimed, his attachment to the woman had the consent of 'Mhiko [the woman's husband] and my wife Macholohelo, and Bakoena, knowing the work (*tiro*), as it is our custom [to] work like this and my wife was quite happy'. The relationship began before his arranged marriage. If Macholohelo had initially consented, she was drawing the line at becoming one of two recognised wives. Sechele's own councillors, who like him were Christians, agreed with her and had been voicing their disapproval for a long time. In 1890, his councillors had insisted that Sechele stand with his wife, Macholohelo, to consecrate their marriage at the church 'so that your children could eat of your youth', meaning the government would recognise them as legitimate heirs. Sechele refused seeing 'it is of no use [because] I am *Mochuana* and have taken out bride price (*bogadi*)'. His councillors had insisted that 'bride price is nothing when it comes to white things (*mo makgooeng*)'. For three weeks, Sechele explained, the church announced the wedding so that 'if anyone knows any obstacle he should speak and they said nothing [,] knowing I love this woman' – his lover.

> That is why I ask if there is any sense for one to buy a horse with an eye gouged out and seeing it [,] and then return it because it has an eye gouged out? Is it right to buy a coat with a tear and seeing it [,] to [later] return it?[107]

He had not anticipated there would be obstacles to the second marriage because as far as he understood his position, his Christian wife had consented to take him as he was, partial in his attachment to her, but by the time he made the decision to marry, Macholohelo had designed a strategy to defend her right. It appears that she approached the colonial government, where she and her husband's councillors presented the challenges a second marriage presented, given the question of succession.[108] Mhiko's wife was probably also mother to the paramount chiefs' children who, as the councillors understood, would then be free to put forward a claim for their father's position when he died. The government indicated that Sechele was free to marry again, as many times as he pleased, but if so then it would recognise the chieftaincy to have remained at the home of his Christian marriage. He would have to leave his position. Sechele called a Kgotla to gather support and make a case for his work, *tiro*, to continue. Other paramount chiefs attended, including Bathoen of the Bangoaketse at Kanye in the Bechuanaland Protectorate. Bathoen could not believe that the private lives of chiefs had become a subject of public hearings. Outside the court, commoners had composed songs reciting the private affairs of chiefly patriarchs that were open secrets but never discussed in public. Commoners also performed none of the customary rituals that marked a paramount chief's visit to another chiefdom. Bathoen was horrified that the Kgotla handled Sechele as it would any other man, as if he were common, like anyone else.

> Bakoena did not even come to greet me … Then I saw a *morafe* that does not love its source [or Master] (*monga ona*) Bakoena speak as they wish to their Chief, as do the Bangoaketse and Barolong … They insulted their chief…[109]

The line between inherited privilege and earned entitlements was no longer clear. Customarily, a father confirmed his son's status of manhood by allotting him a portion of his land. A young man earned this independent status over time through his submission to his father's authority. He yielded his earnings and labour to him until his father released him to hold a part of the land in his own right, hence a prodigal child compromised his ease of qualification to manhood. Fathers subdivided land among sons and daughters when they married or reached maturity. In 1901, Paul Seabetse presented to the Resident Magistrate that his father could not revoke the allotment he had allocated him 'since my father bought the farm the quitrent has been paid by my father with money earned by me'.[110]

> I practically paid the whole of the quitrent. I gave all my earnings to my father. I used to make more than £50 a year. I was riding transport with my own wagon and with wagons belonging to my father and brother. The last time I gave my father anything was just before the war, when I gave him some money and 7 bags of kaffir-corn. I claim the land I occupy on the ground that my father gave it to me and I paid the quitrent ... I contributed towards purchase of the farm.[111]

Silas Molema, Stephen Lefenya and others had to give evidence in such cases, advising the Resident Magistrate about the 'Barolong customs' but it was a shock that a young man, thirty-eight years old, would haul his father before a colonial court when chiefs would not settle the matter in his favour. Lefenya said that allotments by a father to his son can be revoked at will by the father and without compensation. The magistrate gave judgment in favour of the son. It was an unnerving precedent for patriarchal authority. At every point where land transfer was possible – from father to son, from heads of wards to adult men, from senior chiefs like Molema to ward leaders, and from the paramount chief himself to his senior relatives and favourites, the man who held the land heard cases and could discipline his subordinates. Now, young people were relying on the market to access land and on the legal entitlements of private property to keep it. They were purchasing their manhood with hard cash, not through earning the mutual recognition of older men. Young men's capacity for freedom and agency on the land, for control over nature, was now dependent on their discipline to guard their time, labour and money, each working for himself, and not on the 'moreness' of shared routine and ceremonial rites of passage. In paying for the land in cash, they were essentially getting it for free, having paid none of the subscriptions due to others on the land. Even if young men were going through the rite of initiation – and some Christians also did so, they were attending the rite without internalising the lesson, like reciting catechism without true conversion.

Solomon Plaatje, like other educated men, was also worried about the seemingly declining virtues of the young. The moral flaw of Mafikeng's young women, he thought, was idleness. They did not keep themselves productively occupied. This is why fourteen-year-old Emang Marumoloa, impressed him. During the war, she did his domestic chores. He wrote that she 'already knows not only how to cook, but also how to economise with the scanty groceries and preserves everything with skill and forethought'.[112] The spell of domestic service, he hoped, 'made her unused to the ceremonious "squatting"' of young women of her generation which he abhorred. Others saw other moral shortcomings amongst women and the young – indeed, the list of transgressions was long. It was men's talk of everyday. One way of rehabilitating them into *Sechuana*, in other words into the shared routines of work, *tiro*, was by force, especially by constraining movement so that young men and women remained in one place. They would have to earn their freedom through the existing repertoires of personhood that supported chiefly and patriarchal power. When Badirile Montsioa became chief in 1903, he was concerned about 'the bad girls & small boys who acquainted themselves to go up to town without any work at all'.[113] He promised the Cape police that such a 'bad girl or rascal boy' would be 'severely punished'. Chiefs would watch them 'during the day & the whole evening'.

Silas Molema launched *Koranta ea Becoana* during this moment of alarm among educated men in 1901. The newspaper advanced schooling as a strategy to discipline the young, train them into *Sechuana* and preserve the *morafe*. To the literate and those who aspired to literacy, *Koranta* was a sign revealing itself as a sacred symbol amidst an unsettled moral environment. It was finally a message from the *morafe*'s own ethical universe from 'long ago'. It was a long-awaited message transmitted from *morafe*'s antiquity to their own present reality about who they really were. This orientation to vernacular newspapers was not unique to the region. For decades, speakers of literary vernaculars in southern Africa understood their newspapers as a physical manifestation of a distinct masculine authority, representing the ethical universe of all those called to the assembly of the newspaper. Thus, literacy was in itself a moral practice. It facilitated the gathering of men. Of course, women read too and some of the reportage in the newspapers was about them, but as a textual assembly, as a place to converse about the *morafe* to whom the newspaper was communicating, how it ought to live and its proper orientation to the past, these newspapers were the place where men alone assembled.

In 1862, in the first issue of *Indaba*, its editor Tiyo Soga – one of the earliest African newspapermen in the eastern Cape – wrote about the 'national newspaper' as a 'beautiful vessel for preserving the stories, fables, the legends, customs, anecdotes, and history of the tribes'.[114] Soga encouraged readers to collect issues of the journal 'and at the end of the year make a bound volume of them'. *Indaba* was not merely a depository against forgetting, but also a messenger that narrated the collective memories, identities and histories of its readers through 'stories, fables, the legends, customs, anecdotes, and history of the tribes'. They did not and could not know their past without its instruction. Soga encouraged heads of households to bring *Indaba* into their homes to learn from it, and then transfer their knowledge to their families. Soga described *Indaba* as a 'traveller' to whom the patriarch offers hospitality as he reads its contents aloud to his family. Another editor, Tengo Jabavu, of *Imvo Zabantsundu*, also in the eastern Cape, wrote to Silas Molema that these vernacular newspapers were the expression of being a *morafe*, in his words, '*kolu ea bomororafe*'.[115] In one direct translation, the newspaper stands for 'the sound of being a *morafe*', yet this is not just any sound. Another rendering would be that the newspaper is 'the Adam's apple of being a *morafe*', the expression of the *morafe*'s manhood and maturity. The newspaper made manifest the existence of the *morafe* not as a fledgling entity toddling like a child, but as a man speaking and instructing, a prophet with a revelation of truth.

Koranta inspired the same feeling under Solomon Plaatje's editorship. One reader described *Koranta* as a 'risen light', a 'rising star' that made known 'the fortunes of the wise man'.[116] It was also a 'big school' directing the big *morafe* of 'Bechuana' and its constituting small *merafe* like the Barolong, Bakoena and so on towards its roots.[117] Rev. J. Monyatsi described 'knowledge' in *Koranta* as the 'old ways of wisdom' and the 'old ways of prosperity'.[118] This Wesleyan minister was, according to Plaatje, a man most knowledgeable about the past and an 'interpreter of custom'.[119] Monyatsi was 'the greatest Mochuana amongst all Bechuana, both dead and alive'. The newspaper's editorials, letters to the editor and some of its reportage wove together men's conversation on literacy as the cornerstone practice of personhood. Although anxious about the behaviour of women and young people, the mood of conversation was hopeful that a return to the 'old ways' was now at last at hand. Literacy was the bedrock of *tiro* because it revealed the circle of people that connected together to make the *morafe*. Rev. Joel D. Goronyane, a landowner in Thaba Nchu and a committed educationalist, exhorted Barolong that:

> You also today have the *Koranta*, in your own language of Serolong. By taking it, you would be honouring your origin (root), as all other people honour theirs; by not taking it, you are weakening it, and hence weakening yourself. If you honour it you honour yourself ... That is the ambition of being a *morafe*, that each and every one does according to his origin, and if it is not there to make it, to make it so that it can become, because if people do not have their origin, they would not be persons (*batho*) but rats.[120]

Many people's roots in Bechuanaland were actually relatively recent, including the migrant Caucasian population from Europe and other parts of the world who were living in the reserves and on surrounding farms, along with a growing *métis* population that embedded Europe's and even Asia's gene pool into the land. Other settlers had been on the continent a longer time, following generations of migration into the interior, including other dark-skinned Bantu-speakers moving in from various coastal areas. All of these could be proficient in the dialects that were standardising into Sechuana. Goronyane was suggesting that a literary vernacular was the essential foundation for personhood. A literary vernacular was the redeeming quality that forged a civic existence on the frontier, making the otherwise small, wild, undifferentiated mass of living organisms, the 'rats', into a solidarity of mutual recognition, person to person, the Barolong. The written vernacular was the *morafe*'s signifier, its source and 'origin'. Reading the newspaper was like a weekly, maybe even daily, ritual of initiation. The choice Goronyane was encouraging the mixed people of the frontier to make was for each to appear before the assembly of the many in *Koranta*. This is how each abandoned youthful ignorance and became mature, by receiving literacy and written Sechuana as the sacred, age-old symbol of the *morafe* from long ago. In other words, literacy began with the *morafe* in antiquity as a civilising practice. *Koranta ea Becoana* made men.

The newspaper's printing press was in Mafikeng. The distribution of its one to two thousand copies per issue was impressive. One man of Bahurutse stock born in Linokang, Mika Segaloe, wrote that he had left Bechuanaland in 1896 to 'look for education' and managed to lay his hands on the newspaper at Wilberforce University, Ohio in 1902.[121] However, most of the readership was closer to home. The newspaper circulated in large metropoles like Johannesburg, Kimberley and Bloemfontein, but also in smaller towns like Winburg, Kroonstad, Thaba Nchu and Vryburg. Agents also sold it amongst farming communities in Kraaipan, Modder River and Matloasane. These were Sechuana-speakers in the reserves, the thousands of sharecroppers on private farms beyond the reserves, those living and working in the cities – practically every corner of the world where readers recognised *Koranta* as their own assembly and themselves, therefore, as Bechuana. *Koranta* also published long lists of the men from the Barolong reserves on the mines.[122] Those who could read were to read to others who were not literate. They too had to be brought into the *morafe*. Like all symbols that fashion and delineate a moral community, *Koranta* made apparent that 'the senses, the body, in short everything that individualises, is antagonistic to personhood'.[123]

Plaatje explained many times that initiation rites, including young men's circumcision, was not the orifice that birthed the *morafe*. Instead *Koranta ea Becoana* was precisely the proper totemic emblem around which young men ordinarily assembled at initiation school. It gathered them together into collective repertoires of reading together, learning together, writing together, especially in the sacred proficiency of their vernacular and new literary language, Sechuana. Hence, formal schooling, both *Koranta*'s editor and readership agreed, was the only initiation necessary to entrench the lesson of personhood. Schooling taught young people, boys and girls, to align their desires with moral practices that built collective esteem. Proper schooling would inculcate those moral values that brought the *morafe* together as a practice that 'provokes collective feelings of respect'.[124] Success that exalted the individual alone without lending to others feelings of pride and dignity was not *Sechuana*. It compromised personhood, it thinned the 'moreness' necessary for each to feel and accomplish more than is possible on his or her own. This is why readers esteemed Silas Molema. He was not advancing by himself but lending his accomplishments to the benefit of others' own feelings of esteem. He gave them a newspaper. 'Is there a Mochuana', Frank Tebogo said of him, 'that can give birth to such a heavy yoke and that amidst hunger and drought, working for the *morafe* though his own children experience shortage. Oh readers!'[125]

Most of these sentiments were in Sechuana but the Bechuana were not Plaatje's only audience. He also wrote in English to address the pertinent political questions of the time. Some of his editorials in English grappled with whether there was a peculiar essence to skin pigmentation and whether it affected how people lived together. W.E.B. Du Bois, writing at the same time in America, was grappling with the same question in *The Souls of Black Folk*. Was there a 'soul' to blackness of such moral depth that it made people of this colouring peculiar, or was their uniqueness an effect only of their history? Plaatje was attempting to put forward a persuasive answer to this pressing political question. His answer shaped his understanding of the moral ethos formal schooling was to inculcate in young minds. The problem with the times, he suggested, was that disparate communities of personhood along the frontier did not each live according to what was proper to themselves. What he called the *Bancho*, the 'Blacks', were a unique solidarity of personhood and therefore had a unique moral orientation. The German missionaries of his childhood may have introduced him to the conversation in German literature and philosophy that in knowing the foreigner, a society gains a revelation of its own uniqueness.[126]

Plaatje suggested likewise that a mixed frontier is an opportunity for the *Bancho* to comprehend their own unique orientation in their time. The practice most proper to the *Bancho*, he wrote, was an attachment to the land. Agrarian life was how the *Bancho* performed the work of personhood, *tiro*. A proper education, he wrote in one editorial, prepared black children for 'labour through dignity and contentment'.[127] He assured 'Bechuana' that proper schooling would not make their boys 'fear cattle' because such labour, as *tiro*, was the *Bancho*'s natural disposition.[128] In fact, schooling was precisely the course of action that would guarantee that their children, despite their dark complexion, did not become 'white' or *Makhoa*. Schooling should produce 'good black men and not attempt to make impossible white men out of good black men, and thereby waste excellent new material'.[129] That is why schools had an obligation to encourage racial segregation along appropriate lines. Schooling should not be a temptation away from *Sechuana*, away from advancing in life through the rhythms of home and life on the land, towards aspirations that were foreign to one's own proper orientation in life.

> It is of great sadness that Bechuana say they are teaching children, hence they have stopped teaching them the important work of Sechuana, saying now they are educated, they must reach for stars. These stars are that which have killed the *morafe*. Try to help your children to ready themselves with the things they can achieve in their mother's households ... If you skill yourselves well to work with your hands, you will find yourself doing well. Then whilst whites are becoming magistrates and judges, you eat the land and of its fat.[130]

Rather than a 'proletariat of professors' what was needed was 'a labouring class thoroughly and well educated' although it was accepted that 'some ... will naturally occupy positions as clerks and professional men'.[131] Skin colour was not sufficient qualification to 'blackness'. A choice of vocation was an ethical consideration, as was the place of such vocation. The countryside was the proper location for the *Bancho* to remain within their proper existential orientation in the world. Blackness was a moral imperative, not a colouring merely skin-deep.

In the meantime, competition for land was rife. There was already an understanding of 'whiteness' in settler society that associated it with self-mastery on the land, despite the fact that many such farmers depended on the expertise and labour of sharecroppers whose skin colour was largely black and brown.[132] In an editorial in English that appeared twice in *Koranta*, in

Morafe

September of 1902 and December of 1904, Plaatje addressed the rhetoric that identified 'whiteness' as the qualifier for landholding, reducing others merely to the status of workers, not possessors of the land. He made the distinction between 'social' and 'political' equality between the races under an epigram from the Old Testament's Song of Songs 1: 5–6, which begins with the expression 'I am black but comely...'. The song, though he did not transcribe the rest of the verse continues: 'My mother's children were angry with me/ they made me keeper of their vineyards/ but my own vineyards I have not kept.' The black sheep of the family, interestingly a woman, toils away for others with no claim to, and investment in, her own inheritance. It is a song about hierarchy and prejudice between siblings, which conveniently for Plaatje, presents the scarred, exploited sibling as black but, in her consciousness of her skin colour, as also unashamed. Indeed, as Plaatje would write at greater length later, frontier homelands were mixed homesteads – black, brown and white were living together as familiars, as 'brothers' working the land together. It was the reality of farm life on the hinterlands. It would not work to break up the family, but the white brother had turned slave master and was refusing to pay his black sibling his 'just dues'.[133] In the meantime, the darker sibling had developed a consciousness of his own worthiness, being 'black but comely', and wished to attend to the land as her own inheritance just like her white brother, and alongside him.

> We do not hanker after social equality with the white man. If anyone tells you that we do so, he is a lunatic, and should be put in chains. We do not care for your parlour, nor is it our wish to lounge on couches in your drawing-rooms. The renegade Kaffir who desires to court and marry your daughters is a perfect danger to his race, for if his yearnings were realised we would be hurrying on the path to the inauguration of a generation of half-castes, and the total obliteration of our race and colour, both of which are very dear to us. For this reason we advise every black man to avoid social contact with the whites, and the other race to keep strictly within their boundaries.[134]

Across the boundaries of skin colour, he warned, sexual intimacy had a perverse, animal-like instinct as it was outside the ethical universe of personhood. It was not *tiro*. Yet, seeing that 'blackness' was itself not merely skin colour but rather a moral ethos of practice and location, the Caucasian or Asian, whatever colour of person, could be of the *Bancho*, like the 'white Morolong', Sergeant Abrams, whom Plaatje wrote about in his war diary.[135]

Abrams had gained 'the profound respect of all the Barolongs' during the siege. He had fought side by side with them from the beginning, and they thought of him as one of 'only two good and brave Englishmen in the world'.[136] He visited them in the stadt when they were injured. He was one of them, nativised by the land and its people and hence, despite his skin colour, they made his name into Sechuana as 'Aberamo'.[137] In fact, he was very likely to have been the 'S. Abrams' who leased a plot from Molema after the war and lived in the reserve.[138] There was 'social equality', living together and working the land together. What indeed would prevent such a 'native' Morolong of high reputation from marrying amongst Barolong who were his own people?

Just over a decade before, a young chief wrote approvingly in the *Mahoko a Becwana* that education offered 'a life other than holding a spade, or holding horses for a wagon, or herding'.[139] This was in 1886. He was writing approvingly of white-collar work although by then, if his intention had been to raise the prestige of white-collar work as an achievement to be proud of, such employment was already becoming scarce. Even though literacy rates were still low – over ninety-three per cent of Africans in the Cape were illiterate in 1904, many were taking strides to access some level of education.[140] Available schools were struggling to keep up with the demand for education. In January of 1902, Lovedale had to turn pupils away.[141] More importantly, while 17 per cent (17,040) of Africans in the towns could read and write, so could 16 per cent of the rural Africans (36,193) in the far more heavily populated reserves and farms.[142] In other words, the countryside was absorbing the educated demographic, not the urban areas. There would not have been sufficient employment opportunities to satisfy the demand in the reserves. At the same time, the agrarian market was more directly discriminating against an African peasantry.[143] The main effect of not having expendable money was not being able to let or purchase independent property in town or establish a profitable agrarian enterprise in the countryside. Many educated black men were not able to provide for and sponsor the aspiration of their women, children and others who also wanted a formal education or, at the least, the life associated with it.

Koranta was advocating for formal schooling, but there were obstacles to literacy as a route to manhood precisely because white-collar jobs were scarce. Silas Molema's nephew, Joseph, remained poor and unemployed despite his schooling and proficiency in English. In 1899, he begged his uncle to find him work in Mafikeng or in Kuruman. 'I have nothing to do,' he wrote, 'so I think I shall have to starve when I got my hands and feet.'[144] Some parents kept their children away from school for this reason. They thought the children would return home, educated and ambitious, and waste away with nothing to do, not having learnt to eke a living from the land. They sent their children off to the mountain for initiation, smeared their skins with red ochre when they returned and gave them allotments on the land and some of the cattle they had been herding as young boys. Others wished to be included into the routines of literacy, agreed that it was a moral virtue, but could not afford the risks to survival. The latter families would have to navigate the choice between honour and staying alive. Indeed, chiefs were finding it very difficult to pay their debts.[145] Genteel poverty hung about notables' doors.

Plaatje was not unaware of these dilemmas. His message was that the esteem of personhood though formal schooling was not, and had never been, behind the desk holding a pen, but rather behind the plough splitting the ground or following the animals to pasture. An educated man on the land would have no need for the jobs that were in any case not available. He would employ himself profitably on the land and create the kind of agrarian industry profitable to the *morafe*.

> It is not proper that a person takes a child to learning and hopes that the child will forsake his origins and become white … If all people, [both] whites and Bechuana, become lawyers, and the sorghum lacks a ploughman, can the *morafe* survive?[146]

The future was flourishing agrarian towns. A sheep farmer would learn how to read the fluctuations in wool prices and negotiate his trade accordingly.[147] Others could run dairies and produce milk, cheese and butter or own a profitable enterprise weaving baskets or sowing blankets. For Plaatje, the carpenter was the 'greatest figure in history'.[148] Although he felt that he was pointing the *morafe* to it roots, his vision had more immediate influences in the present. He had grown up on a farm at Pniel, close to the Vaal River. German missionaries had bought land and let it to a mixed population of peasant householders, taught them to read and write, introduced them to the plough and encouraged them towards various crafts, including woodwork.[149] His other influence was Booker T. Washington, with his ideas of self-improvement through industrial training, including carpentry, weaving baskets, sewing shoes and blankets, gardening and cookery and so on. Washington's speeches and activities at his Tuskegee Negro Conference were familiar inserts in *Koranta*.

Some readers shared this vision of thriving agrarian towns. Peter Kawa, a resident of the eastern Cape proposed that the 'masses be taught to make bricks, tables, dishes, wagons, shoes and above all let them be thoroughly acquainted with their spades and ploughs'.[150] He added that 'those Native lads who are able, should be taught the higher branches of study for minds are not all alike', and that 'giant intellects' must 'have by any means what is generally termed Higher Education'. Plaatje's ideas however were not quite congruent with aptitude and meritocracy in this sense. Schooling was important to everyone, but more for its moral education than merely curriculum. Plaatje argued that there should be no special curriculum for the black population at a time when missionary schools were directing this demographic towards 'industrial training'. He wanted a 'general education', including a proper mastery of the English language. He reasoned that the moral effects of proper schooling would make clear that not everyone had a vocation as a teacher, clerk, a lawyer or other such white-collar work.

The future lay in 'progress' in the countryside. The word was '*coelopele*', to move forward, to advance, but in fact Plaatje understood 'progress' as a return to the virtuous disposition of the *morafe*'s ancestry on the land. As one editorial argued, young Bechuanas' schooling should 'encourage and increase the work of their forefathers with knowledge much greater than that of their parents, especially farming'.[151] An excellent education returned young people to the land and discouraged them from aspirations beyond their station in life. It also emphasised the natural hierarchies of everyday life. In one editorial Plaatje expressed regret that if schools taught principles of social equality, then parents should 'think twice' before sending children there, because 'even amongst ourselves not every black man is his countryman's equal' and hence, not all Africans could vote.[152]

And yet, Plaatje was by no means the kind of patriarch who prevented women from gaining an education and excelling in their professions. He even supported women's right to vote. His consternation was only that education should not erase a consciousness of a moral hierarchy. Education should not foster individualism, should not create the impression that anyone could become anything he or she wanted to be, and should certainly not throw the accepted rhythm of everyday practice out of kilter, pitting subordinates above figures of authority. When people forgot customs of 'long ago', he wrote, it was no longer possible to distinguish between 'age and youth, man and woman, master and servant, king and *morafe*'.[153] Schooling would have a 'taming' effect on women and make young men, especially chiefs, respectful of their fathers and the ways of the past, which were the ways of 'progress'. As editor, Plaatje took every opportunity to emphasise the special reverence the 'Bechuana' everywhere owed to their chiefs. For instance, when Chief Moroka of Thaba Nchu visited Bloemfontein in 1902, *Koranta* reported that a large crowd came to greet him. Though 'pleased at their love', the chief said, he hoped they had asked their employers for leave to meet him because 'as the Book says a servant is not greater than his master'.[154]

Under Plaatje's editorship, the newspaper's reportage gave voice to educated men's understanding of the moral effects of proper schooling, especially on young women. A new teacher, Mr A. Moletsane, arrived in Thaba Nchu from Kimberley to take up a post at Moroka Institute in 1902. He delivered a passionate address at his welcome reception, reprimanding parents that did not school their girls, instead 'letting them do as they wished – to run rampantly wild, and to act according to their wills'.[155] The year before in 1901, a visiting son of a chief preached a sermon at the Wesleyan church in Mafikeng, which appeared in *Koranta* the following week. He directed his message to women and read from Amos 4: 1, 'Hear this word you women of Bashan ... who oppress the poor, who crush the needy, who say to their husbands, Bring and let us drink!'.[156] Older women 'of days gone by and now aged', he preached, had raised men 'whose names were respectable amongst whites'. Sadly, when it was time to marry, these men took uneducated women as wives. Now their wives lured their husbands to drink. Aged mothers of old, he explained, though they were never 'exposed to the light' of schooling, knew well the way of the past *(bogolo-golo)*, which encouraged excellent virtues that today's younger women could now learn at school. Did the 'princes' not know that brides as virtuous as the mothers of old had 'left their villages for Morija, Lovedale, and Lesseyton to attend school?' Proper schooling would quell a girl's 'wild' independent spirit and culture a quiet distinction to grace domestic life with dependability, cleanliness and order.

At the same time, there was no way back to the old ways of *Sechuana* without schooling, which is why an uneducated chief was the end of the *morafe*. In his editorials, Plaatje castigated Wessels as a leader from a household of 'whites' (*Makhoa*).[157] Wessels Montsioa's conspicuous consumption and insatiable palate for strong drink were pleasures that did not sponsor anyone else's attempts to 'progress', to move forward, especially when the war and its aftermaths had worsened food shortages and overall lack in the countryside. Wessels was like a solitary ship docked on an island, yielding nothing of its cargo. He was not a source, not a proper 'origin', not heavy with the promise of rain, not adding his own capacities to others' work, *tiro*. He did nothing for anyone else and was unavailable for the reciprocal routines that created 'moreness'. He was a diminishing force. *Sekhoa* was this reckless self-obsession. In the meantime, as Plaatje wrote, Silas Molema's children, especially Sebopioa, had already been inducted into service to others by their good education.[158] The young man was already his father's scribe in the chiefly bureaucracy whilst Badirile Montsioa, Wessel's brother and heir to the paramountcy, performed no such roles. Badirile's response to this slight, also published in *Koranta*, was that in fact the Molemas were the chief architects of *Sekhoa*. Was it not *Sekhoa* that Silas and Joshua Molema received government salaries for serving the chieftaincy?[159] They were paid workers, not a river freely flooding its banks to nourish the *morafe*.

Educated men did not want uneducated chiefs. Another of *Koranta*'s correspondents in Kanye in the Bechuanaland Protectorate celebrated Bathoen as 'a chief of yesterday's heart', so 'praiseworthy' that rain fell continually on his *morafe*.[160] Education lent his kingdom respect for piety and hierarchy and established an orderly, efficient bureaucracy. 'At church', the reporter said, 'he [Bathoen] enters first along with his wife and children, followed by his sub-chiefs also there to praise Jehovah of War in the temple.' He continued that 'the church is beautiful, built in the English style' with Bangoaketse crammed full in it. As impressive, in the writer's view, was Bathoen's innovative use of educated men in his bureaucracy. Such wisdom made of the paramount chief a 'true Judge'. Bathoen was reported to have 'an Office in the centre, one with clerks and secretaries all schooled at Lovedale; how the *morafe* respects the judgements of the government of its Master'.[161] An unschooled mind could not possibly help anyone get ahead, and many more people wished to get ahead through schooling.

In February 1903, Lovedale Missionary Institute turned back about 200 African children, citing a severe shortage of space.[162] An editorial commented that 'Bechuana' boys and girls attending schools in the Cape 'show that our *morafe* like other *merafe* is beginning to awaken from sleep', despite the reluctance of some chiefs to educate their children.

> We have some chiefs, that when the *morafe* sends children to school, surround themselves with their children, and they remain behind. ... They must understand that children that are educated today shall have great mysteries revealed to them… After they are educated, when we die and leave them behind, and instruct them to honour their chiefs (just like we honour our chiefs), they will refuse, saying how can they, being educated, honour woolly heads. Shall anybody disagree? Blame would rest with the Chiefs... Owing to them, today's princes will grow up knowing nothing.[163]

Besides, in the history of educated African families, the countryside was not the periphery, but the centre of 'progress' and culture. This is where the twin institutions of school and church first appeared. Uneducated chiefs would compromise what was possible for these towns and villages as landscapes of culture. Pixley Seme, writing in 1906 from the University of Columbia in the United States of America, pronounced the future of his native Zululand in Natal as 'the seat of science and religion, reflecting the glory of the rising sun from the spires of [its] churches and universities'.[164] Seme would return home and nurse the connections he had made abroad with intellectuals like Alain Locke, alongside his desire to travel abroad and reconnect with them again.[165] Another Natalian, John Dube, was of similar sensibility. Like Plaatje, he considered Booker T. Washington a kindred spirit. Dube's model for his Ohlange Institute was Washington's Tuskegee. Dube travelled abroad to raise money for his educational project and also to meet with likeminded people and exchange ideas. In later years, the three men – Plaatje, Seme and Dube – would find common ground ideologically and in their vision for the future. They cultivated partnerships abroad, had a sense of the world beyond their shores, but they were also very loyal chiefly subjects. The object of global connectedness was to foster and showcase local 'progress' or, as Seme understood it, the 'regeneration of Africa'.[166] The continent's return to its great past meant establishing printing presses, schools, technology and the entire infrastructure that marked 'progress' everywhere else in the world. For such men, chieftaincy was a facilitator of cosmopolitanism. Educated chiefs, or at least chiefs who understood the importance of learning, would be prepared to sponsor such developments. They would pay for newspapers like *Koranta ea Becoana*, build schools, roads and hospitals, and sponsor literary projects.

The educated sought to be kingmakers in favour of chiefly domains that would not turn out as far-flung colonial outposts disconnected from the world. This was especially important for a writer like Plaatje. 'Born in a half-savage country, out of date', is how Ezra Pound described the experience of a writer imprisoned in the provincialism of a colonial world too small to match his ambition, his work remaining unknown in the metropolitan circles of culture.[167] These men aimed to invite and retain a particular kind of imperial citizenship that would link remote villages, even ones on the fringes of the Kalahari Desert, to the world. The British Empire had to play its role in creating the 'moreness' that emboldened and enabled the Bechuana to take their place on the world stage. She had to recognise them as equal to her people in the metropolis, as different, but no less deserving of the rights and entitlements that were the staple practice of the metropole's political culture. In his diary, Plaatje wrote that the *Mafeking Mail*, the newspaper of English-speaking settlers in the northern districts, regarded 'the Native as a mere creature'.[168] He identified Britain as unlike settlers and their governments. Britain was the sovereign doing the work of personhood on Bechuana, making persons of the diverse populations of the world and connecting them to the single frame of 'progress'. As a writer in this kind of empire, Plaatje could have an audience as wide as the international connections he had across the world, and an identity as a literary man operating, not in a colonial periphery, but from Bechuanaland as one of many centres of 'progress' in the world.

The exercise of drawing others into new repertoires of practice by urging them to a 'reawakening' to a 'truth' from 'long ago' – in this instance through literacy, was essentially like religious practice. Plaatje was making converts, as were all the other readers who wrote about the state and requirement of *botho*. Their experience of the newspaper as a 'sign' of the *morafe*'s ethical universe from the 'origin', elevated *Koranta* beyond the functions of a newspaper to inform and facilitate a textual assembly of 'Bechuana'. *Koranta* became something of a prophetic text, especially where it brought Biblical scripture into arguments about the *morafe*'s appropriate practices of everyday life and of course the social hierarchies that mediate them. As such a text, it had major contributors like Plaatje himself and minor personalities whose opinions he chose to publish. Plaatje wrote prolifically about the empire and positioned himself as an imperial citizen but other writers' concerns were local. This *morafe* of the literate was a river of many currents, with a strong consensus around chiefly and patriarchal power and enthusiasm for chiefly support for 'progress', but no other reader wrote about Britain or desirable forms of government beyond chieftaincy. The discourse of empire was Plaatje's thinking. He was pronouncing the 'Bechuana' and also projecting them beyond the contours of the region as subjects of a global Britain, and not of the 'South Africa' that the *Mafeking Mail* and other settler newspapers were touting after the war.

In such a settler dominion, owning a newspaper was a practice of whiteness. The *Bechuanaland News* thought Silas Molema was too big for his britches and that the venture would surely fail. The editor advised *Koranta*'s proprietor to 'take the matter philosophically and reflect that after all they have but followed the example of many and many a white man in "this South Africa of ours" as the politicians call it'.[169] Settlers with a consciousness of 'whiteness' wanted a domain where skin colour determined property and political rights. This was 'South Africa', whether as a British dominion or an independent settler republic. After the war, it was clear that settlers were going to have their 'South Africa' as a unification of the two British colonies – Natal and the Cape, and the Boer Republics – the Transvaal and Orange Free State, but how would the *morafe*, with its complicated synthesis of political authority feature in the new dispensation? Plaatje wrote in many editorials that the *Bancho* had to have a political claim in this new dispensation equal to that of their white counterparts. There was to be no different set of qualifiers although it was not as straightforward as that, and a reader of today's sensibility may perceive some striking ambiguities in the permutation of political authority that Plaatje was proposing for the 'Bechuana'.

In the first instance, chieftaincy would coexist with direct representation on the Cape Colony's liberal franchise that allowed educated, propertied men to vote. Whilst some chieftaincies enjoyed official recognition from the colonial government, many were small, informal evanescent negotiations of patronage and settlement through which people of different skin colour secured land and constituted their practices of personhood. As a frontier institution, chieftaincy was not a monopoly of black peoples alone, certainly not in the northern hinterlands. It was a mixed pot of belonging and also constantly in flux. Where were the limits of the chiefly order, both in terms of territory and the reach of its subjects? If *Koranta*'s vision materialised, if chiefly subjects schooled themselves, owned property and therefore qualified to vote, what would be the hierarchy of government, what would be the manner to straddle the two categories of political affiliation? Specifically, where would Britain fit in the equation? For example, would the Imperial government continue to protect the autonomous standing of reserves in former British Bechuanaland from the Union government's jurisdiction even though the educated and propertied from these reserves voted in the Cape Colony? Plaatje and his educated readers did not ask these questions. They did not experience these political positions as irreconcilable. Instead, they made a home in between the apparent incongruities.[170] Moreover, they were living at a time of political experimentation around empire and sovereignty. There was still time to imagine and try out different possibilities. The frontier had not yet closed. The urgent imperative was to come to a consensus around personhood.

Indeed, *Koranta* was not the only platform of assembly trying to induct people of the frontier into *Sechuana*. In April 1903, Plaatje wrote disapprovingly that 'the Barolong have revived the ancient circumcision rites'.[171] He blamed 'the sons of Montsioa' for embracing 'a custom the uselessness of which was discerned by their fathers'. These sons had 'not done their duty.' In contrast, when Sebopioa Molema graduated from Lovedale in 1902, *Koranta* saw in him 'great promise of a learned man much needed by many *merafe* of *Bancho* across the world, especially Bechuana.'[172] A higher education, according to Plaatje, would 'give him a great personhood (*botho yo bo golo*) that would cover his *morafe* like the cloud that leads other *merafe* of renown'. Here was the promise of a cloud that would not withhold the rain. Sebopioa would be the figure of destiny, like the Lord of the Israelites who led them from Egypt to Canaan in a cloud by day. On 7 July 1904, Sebopioa sailed on the *Gascon Castle* to what he called 'this great negro University where young men from different parts of the globe gather for the cause of higher and sound education'.[173] This was Wilberforce University in the United States of America, where he became one of the first Africans to read law.[174] In 1905, Modiri started school at the Wesleyan missionary institute, Healdtown.[175] Away from home, each would confront the dilemma of manhood: how much of himself does a man offer only to himself to keep, and how much time, effort and desire is due to another? In this one sense at least, *Koranta* was right. Schooling was a journey of moral negotiations.

VIII

By mid-1902 *Koranta ea Becoana* was being published only irregularly and in August 1902 a new Sechuana/English version of the newspaper came out. Publication was regular after that until the end of 1904. Despite their enthusiasm, readers could not keep up the payments for their subscriptions. Apparently, Silas Molema's rivals started to mock him but Joshua Molema was sure that God would vindicate his brother. He wrote a letter to the naysayers.

> Lately you say who will print *Koranta*? [You] are one with no understanding ... when God destroys the earth, with whom shall He begin, and who shall He save, and who shall He leave to keep educating others? That is how I see your question. Repent, and live in the ways of God, learn righteousness, lest He strikes you with a curse.[176]

Indeed, if it were not for the conviction that *Koranta* was an element of God's providential plan for the *morafe*, the newspaper would not have survived for as long as it did. Silas Molema, Solomon Plaatje and the people who worked for them did not see *Koranta* merely as a business or day job. It was the very work of God. Every penny, every hour they invested in it, had a reward in their piety more important than in material compensation. Financial remuneration for the proprietor, its editor and the rest of the printing staff was very lean and often absent but they carried the hardships of working sans pay. After 1904, the newspaper appeared very irregularly but it survived for five more years. The few last issues were in 1909. Molema put up a brave fight and the staff supported him though it was impossible to finance the newspaper. His transport business had largely collapsed. *Koranta* sank him into a deeper pit of debt.

At the centre of these negotiations for credit was his friend and attorney, Spencer Minchin. Without Minchin's help, Molema's financial ruin would have been far quicker, *Koranta* would have closed shop much earlier, and Molema would have lost a lot more of his personal property to the venture. *Koranta* was not the beginning of the problem. It catalysed its severity. Molema had two small freehold properties in the reserve and a very large private farm, Vryhof, elsewhere yet it is still astonishing just how many Europeans were willing to lend him money. He never made Vryhof surety for his loans. The gain of this property was not what the creditors would hope to receive should he default on payment. In fact, mostly they found that he had nothing to surrender to the courts when he could not pay – at least not anything they wanted.

Molema kept trying to sustain his transport business. He bought at least two more carts at the end 1902, seemingly from riders disposing of them.[177] His source of income throughout this year was mainly rents from tenants like John Kay and a J. Robinson and also small loans for which he signed promissory notes.[178] In 1903, he borrowed money from the attorney, J.W. de Kock to the sum of more than £180.[179] The law firm, De Kock and De Kock, also processed an additional loan from the wholesaler Kemp & Co.[180] All these amounted to well over £250. Other loans were smaller and indicative of his growing desperation and ruin, like the £8 borrowed from farmer and trader E. Fincham in September and £5 borrowed from Grant & Pennycook General Merchants.[181]

By July 1904, he was trying to liquidate his newspaper. Spencer Minchin devised a plan through which *Koranta* could kick-start a cash flow by registering as a Limited Liability Company. Readers could purchase one share at a value of £1.[182] Molema urged his friends and chiefs in the Protectorate to buy shares. He appealed to them to save *Koranta* not as a private enterprise but as a newspaper that belonged to all Bechuana.[183] His friend Bathoen, it seems either resented that other chiefs had already received Molema's plea for donations and the purchase of shares before he did, or that Molema had dared to go at the venture alone in the first place. His feelings nevertheless relay that in just three years, *Koranta* had succeeded as 'the work', *tiro*, of all the '*merafe* of Setswana'.¹⁸⁴

> Your words about *Koranta* have arrived. Gaboutlelwe and Chief Lengkwane have spoken what you have sent them to say. Even the letter has said everything. We, as Bangoaketse are very saddened, very much, about the deed you have done to us. Do Barolong of Tawana [Molema's clan name] have work (*tiro*) that they wish to do with all the *merafe* of Setswana? And you told all of your *merafe*, Bahuruthsi, Barolong of Seleka and Batlhaping and all the *merafe* after you all came together per your agreement. You heard when someone said that he knows others, Bangoaketse there, do not forget them. Do not speak and do such a thing Barolong of Tawana and Makaba. Ah what great pain! Now that we have heard Morolong what can we say, do as usual according to your seats of position and status! Had you not sat on them, this would be my work, I would be alone in it.¹⁸⁵

Nevertheless, Bathoen made a contribution of £100. He was also not the only chief to contribute but it is not clear how much the others raised. They forwarded all their payments directly to Minchin's office. Chief Israel Moiloa of the Bahurutse loaned Molema about £169.¹⁸⁶

As he sent his £100, Bathoen complained that 'Here we see great illnesses, Bangoaketse are dying of many diseases, flu and stomach sickness'.¹⁸⁷ It was a time of hardship in the countryside – starvation, drought, dying animals. It had been going on for some years. According to Chief Sekhoma's secretary in 1898, the paramount chief was 'very very sick, so sick he almost died'.¹⁸⁸ He described 'much distress as many people are very sick … many are dying in these parts'. He wrote that 'we see poverty, we have no sorghum, only locusts and the sun, not even enough to feed a bird'. Then he asked for prayer, 'Please continue to remember us.' Sekhoma had no more cattle. He asked Molema to purchase two head of cattle for him on credit but his fortunes had still not fully turned by the time Mafeking fell under siege. When Molema asked him for horses and cattle to help the war effort, Sekhoma could only offer one calf.¹⁸⁹ Molema's friends were not in a position to help. In September of 1904 *Koranta* had only issued 60 shares.¹⁹⁰

By this time, Molema's transport business was turning some returns but not nearly enough. A wagon trip of six days earned him only £22.¹⁹¹ In July of 1904, he became indebted to Charles Wenham for £650, and bound thirty head of mixed cattle and all of *Koranta*'s printing machinery as surety.¹⁹²

Two months later, he would have to sell the 30 head of oxen for £290 to meet Wenham's bond premium and pay school fees.[193] Two weeks later, he returned to Wenham to borrow a further £300 and bound a hundred cattle and six mules.[194] Throughout 1904, Chinese immigrants rented Molema's 'garden' in the reserve. Their rents kept him with a small but steady cash flow for the most basic needs.[195] Minchin agreed to advance him about £250 at the end of October 1904. Molema bound his freehold property in the reserve as mortgage.[196] By February of the following year, he had not managed to make a single payment towards the loan. Minchin made him sign a promissory note that he would settle the amount in three months, 'by that time I trust a large number of the subscriptions will have been paid up'.[197] As the middle of April approached, Minchin had grown discouraged. They were making almost no progress with subscriptions. Minchin urged Molema to pass a second bond over his erf because 'as from what I can see the subscriptions due for the paper will not be paid for an indefinite time'.[198] Molema passed a second bond over his mortgage through Standard Bank.[199]

The staff at *Koranta*'s printing office proceeded to work without pay. They were committed and hopeful. 'The work is going on with great difficulty as it was very bad with me,' Jacob Moses reported to Molema, 'but even so God will help us.'[200] Edward Fincham had sent summons for the £8 Molema had borrowed two years before. Plaatje pitched in what he could towards *Koranta*'s debt.[201] Rents continued to trickle in – barely enough to feed a family, definitely not enough to chip away at the enormous debt.[202] Minchin began to act more aggressively to retrieve the money he had borrowed Molema and to save his friend. On 8 January 1906 he approached George Whales, the owner of the *Mafeking Mail*, who had printed *Koranta*'s first 13 issues, to take over the newspaper again. According to Whales, Minchin's suggestion was only one of 'so many varied methods … proposed by so many people' with regard to how he (Whales) might bail *Koranta* out.[203] He insisted that 'the only line' on which he could consider any proposal was if Molema as proprietor tabled a proposal himself. On the same day, Molema tabled his proposal but it was not what Whales wanted. Whales wanted to own *Koranta*. He proposed that 'the natives who intended forming a Limited Company' could purchase £1000 in the form of shares in his Northern Newspapers Co and Molema could own shares worth £50 'for the goodwill'.[204] Molema refused to surrender *Koranta* to an empire of settler newspapers. Plaatje would also not agree to work for Whales and surrender his editorial independence.

Five days later, Molema borrowed £200 from a Mrs Murray. He bound the printing site and all the machinery to guarantee payment.[205] This may have gone towards Wenham's loan, which bound much of his stock. In August of the same year, Standard Bank issued a letter of demand after he failed to pay his instalments.[206] Mrs Murray called up her bond two months later.[207] He could not prevent the inevitable. The printing press went under auction but even that was unlikely to help because potential buyers were offering the 'lowest price for house, land and plant'.[208] He would lose the press and remain in debt. In one potential buyer's estimation, the 'large piece of machinery' was worth nothing, as 'it would take quite as much to put in order as it is worth.' The whole property would fetch 'very little'.[209] Molema held back and did not sell. His creditors were dismayed. At the beginning of October, Minchin, acting as Mrs Murray's attorney, threatened to take possession of the plant.[210] A month later, he demanded that Molema hand over the key to the printing plant.[211] Molema had an alternative proposal that Badirile Montsioa, who had succeeded his brother, Wessels, could purchase the property.[212] In December of 1906, the Sheriff attached the property for the mortgage at Standard Bank.[213]

Minchin was the creditors' attorney and he had not managed to save his own money. The creditors were on the other side of the railway track, in the white town of Mafeking, but he lived in the stadt and was Molema's friend and neighbour. He was still trying to save him. He started talks with Badirile Montsioa, which were promising but in January 1907 the deal fell through probably due to something to do with the family feud. Minchin was furious that Molema felt at liberty to walk away when this was the only available rope, however unpleasant, to pull him and everybody else out of the hole. He had understood why *Koranta* could not be surrendered to Whales but this time there was no excuse. He filed to take possession of the printing plant immediately.[214] Wenham was willing to accept four head of cattle for the outstanding £41-3-7 on his loan. Mrs Murray and Standard Bank awaited the liquidation of Molema's property and printing plant.[215] Nevertheless, when the time came to bring the property under the hammer, Minchin stalled. He was still looking for a way out that would redeem all the debt and not throw *Koranta* away like something he was discarding. People had built it from the ground, from nothing, risking everything. Minchin was mindful of what it meant. If it were to end, which was inevitable, he wished the closure to free the proprietor and not humiliate him.

Minchin went back to Whales to arrange a provisional sale of the land and printing plant to prevent 'the necessity of a sale by the court'.[216] For £1037-11-9 Whales wanted more than the printing plant. He wanted a contract to own the full copyright but even that was too great a compromise for the editor. 'Plaatje has not been near me again', Whales anxiously wrote to Molema, pressing that 'I left it to the Barolongs to decide. They must decide at once'.[217] The choice he offered was between saving the newspaper on his terms, which would probably mean dispensing with Plaatje as editor, or not accepting his help at all. Whales saw that Molema was not in a position to bargain. However, Whales too became insolvent in 1907.[218] Molema once again approached Minchin for another loan and this time Minchin refused.[219] Minchin went around again to Badirile Montsioa and offered him the plant and Molema's property for £1050. There would be a cash payment of £150 (which would settle another loan to a Mr Heath) and a bond of £900. In this way, 'paper, plant and erf' could all be the property of Barolong.[220] The deal again did not go through. Local newspapers announced that all the property would go under the hammer on 28 March 1908, but Minchin would still not let *Koranta* go down in that manner – a public auction that would see a buyer take all for close to nothing. It would satisfy sneering white settlers and leave his friend still entangled to creditors. On the day of the auction he privately offered, perhaps on behalf of someone else, to purchase everything himself for £600.[221] It appears he negotiated with the creditors to write off £380-13-7 of the debt. There was still an amount of £105-12-6 outstanding that Molema could chip away at slowly.

Molema's brother, Joshua, and his nephew, Rev. Molema Moshoela together contributed £15-18-11. Mrs Molema never forgot how the Moshoelas' stood by them. The amount did not matter, only that they tried to shoulder the burden. The times were very hard. Every single pound, every little bit yielded to assist another, held the implication of sacrifice in the reciprocal repertoires of personhood that made 'moreness'. If the inventories of deceased notables in the next generation are anything to go by, their parents had not left them much or if they did, the children could not stretch it to cover the cost of living into the mid-twentieth century. For instance, at his death in 1938, Dichukudu Richard Marumoloa, a little older than Modiri Molema, left nineteen mixed cattle and some small stock, although he did own three double ploughs, a planter, twenty-four yokes, a harrow and a wagon. In his one-roomed house, he left a single bed and its mattress, a rug, two pillows, a sheet, a sofa, four table chairs, a wicker chair, a table, a folding chair frame, a skin-mat, five tea cups, a teapot, four saucers, two table knives, two forks, an enamel plate, two tablespoons and seven teaspoons and one bathtub.[222] He was twice divorced and at the most only in his mid- to late-thirties. There was another scourge killing the crop of young, educated men – very heavy drinking.

Family/Placement

I

SILAS MOLEMA'S LANDHOLDING and prime estate, Mabete, was one of forty-one farms of roughly equal size that constituted the Barolong Farms.[1] The block of farmland was on the northern bank of the Molopo River in the Bechuanaland Protectorate, leaning against the western border of the Transvaal. Barolong Farms' landmass was 432 square miles, which is larger than some sovereign republics and city-states today. It had fertile soil, some natural sources of water and good ranching and hunting veld. Barolong Farms emerged from the negotiated settlement of annexation between Britain and the handful of rulers that had withstood settler conquest and frontier wars in Bechuanaland. Twenty-five farms belonged to senior chiefs, including Silas and Joshua Molema, who each held one. Nine belonged to headmen of large wards who were probably more distant relations and five belonged not to individuals but wards. The notables did not hold private title deeds on the farms because British officials thought they were not 'ready' for private tenure. Rather, they possessed 'certificates of occupation' according to which legal occupants paid an annual quitrent of £1-10-0 to the paramount chief, although each farm was the personal property of the lessee. He could transfer it to his son and it could remain a family holding indefinitely. The occupant could not be absent from the farm for more than 12 consecutive months. The British agreed to recognise Barolong Farms as an independent jurisdiction entirely under the ownership and government of the Ratshidi-Rolong chieftaincy.

Pitsane Siding was on Mabete. Further, with two natural pans, Mabete was a prime site. About a third of the property lay east of the railway to Rhodesia. The railway continued north-westerly towards a patch of private farms, Lobatse, which adjoined Mabete. The landowners at Lobatse were mostly white farmers and traders. Mail between Mafeking and the Protectorate lands came by rail twice daily. The land was fertile, favouring trade in cattle and beef, and the climate was not too arid apart from the times of drought. Those close to the line of rail could also sell milk. The main challenge for ranchers was that the Transvaal government regulated imports on their way to the Rand's mining towns where there was money to be made. The Transvaal was protecting its own beef industries.[2] The Protectorate's administration, on the other hand, did nothing for its farmers, merely looking after the territory on a shoestring budget. The domestic revenue was thin, even after the administration started to collect Hut Tax from the reserves. In 1895, the British government placed the territory under the rule of Cecil Rhodes' British South Africa Company until the infamous Jameson Raid. The British administration took over the ropes of the Protectorate once again with the same half-heartedness, the same wish to give it up to a willing taker as they had done with British Bechuanaland when they ceded it to the Cape Colony in 1895. Protectorate farmers were battling it out on their own under a distant, indifferent administration. Nevertheless, the farmers on the south side of the border also felt the same way, that they were as far removed from the colonial government's realm of concern as their distance and isolation from the port cities and coastal towns.

Barolong Farms was the northern portion of the cross-border polity. The southern portion was the Molopo Reserve, 660 square miles, south of the Molopo River. The reserves of British Bechuanaland were not Crown Lands. They belonged to the populations that lived on them. The British government agreed to recognise them as chiefly jurisdictions and not to interfere with their institutions of rule. The political capital of the cross-border chieftaincy was Mafikeng in the Molopo Reserve where notables resided, but Barolong Farms was by no means of 'marginal status' as a polity, contrary to one anthropologist's observations a century later.[3] The farms were the aorta of chiefs' private accumulation but there were other arteries. There is no real memory of Mabete among the Molemas today but some family members have come across references to it in family records. In addition, Silas Molema also had a private farm called Vryhof south of the river outside the Molopo Reserve. Vryhof was over three square miles. In the Molopo Reserve, he had a further two freehold properties. He had at least three much larger landholdings or wards in the reserve. Their names were Kromdraai, Tantinyane and also Madibespruit where he had a country house. There is no memory of the three landholdings in the family. Nobody knows where the farms were or what happened to them.

II

By the late 1890s 'Mabete Hill' had acquired a reputation as a profitable trading spot.[4] A European tenant, mostly Dutch-speaking, R. Transfeldt operated from the farm as a general merchant and importer selling produce, karosses, game horns and 'native curios'. The landlord, Silas Molema, had agreed not to allow any other tenant to trade on the farm but in January of 1899, Edgar Lee, a tenant on the adjoining farm put up a store on the boundary between Mabete and his farm.[5] Molema ordered Lee to pull the building down but he refused. Mabete had no fence, like all the other forty-one farms. Lee insisted that his store was not on Mabete but on his own rented portion. Transfeldt was confident of Molema's scope of influence, with 'no doubt your *Raad* [court or council] will pass decision in your favour'.[6] For some months the stalemate continued until Transfeldt called a surveyor to establish Mabete's boundaries and withheld six months' rent from Molema to defray his costs, 'therefore there is no money due to you just yet ... I am sorry that you lose money over the whole affair, but I lost money too ... you better claim from Mafeking chief or Edgar Lee'.[7] Transfeldt also hired the lawyer, Spencer Minchin, to defend his claim. He did not stay on after his contract expired. Competition on his doorstep quickly overwhelmed him but more than that, Transfeldt did not possess a suitable disposition for this frontier. Early on, at the very first point of altercation, he played his cards strictly by the stipulations of his contract and relied on the courts to enforce it. He won the legal standoff but lost the prime spot of trade adjoining a siding. We have no more mention of him in the extensive archive of landholding, tenancy and trade in the Protectorate.

The men who typically stuck it out on the land relied on judicial law as the court of last resort, depending rather on decency and the reciprocal obligations of care between men as the moral law that established business. Landlords and tenants approached leasing agreements as a framework for negotiation between 'friends', even 'brothers', who were partners, together establishing a successful enterprise, especially if both parties were ambitious, each wanting to get ahead. Those tenant families who could stay on any one farm for generations became like the landlord's 'family'. A decent good man, a moral landlord, did not throw out his 'family' the minute it could not fulfil the obligations of his contract, nor did such a man, if a tenant, walk away immediately when the landlord could not uphold his end of the leasing agreement. A family clubbed together against all odds, including the hostilities of nature like droughts, cattle diseases and locusts and against anyone who risked the well-being of any one member of the family. The negotiations that went into making family between landlord and tenant were a strategy for both to survive on the land, especially when the tenant had more time, knowledge and experience to make the land productive. Where the symbiosis most closely approximated family life, landlord and tenant had become indispensable to each other or sometimes the relationship had long ago cooled, the points of synergy and mutual benefit had long ago weakened, and the attachment had now acquired the obligations of duty. Either way, it is never easy to break up a family.

The oral histories of sharecropping in the Transvaal and in the Orange Free State provide a well-known record of intimate forms of clustering together on the land, where people of different skin colour together made a home on the farms.[8] Around the 1890s, the majority of the landowners there were Caucasians, many speaking Dutch and its nativised variant that was becoming Afrikaans. Their sharecroppers were 'black' and 'brown' and typically literate. The landscape was of mutual dependency and acculturation. White landowners had farms but they depended on black sharecroppers to work the tough terrain. Sharecroppers were a self-confident and aspirant class, able to negotiate their own terms, and not too readily exploitable by their landlords. Decades later, some of these sharecroppers and most remarkably their grandchildren, could still remember which of these landlords were decent men and which were cruel and abhorrent. Sharecroppers' wives and daughters often worked in the homes of the landowners as washerwomen, cooks, kitchen servants and other kinds of domestic help, but they also raised the children of the landowners with as much care and affection as they did their own.[9] Black and brown women provided friendship and adult company to wives in a countryside setting where the next farm was often a considerable distance away. Even in the middle of the twentieth century, the end of boyhood for 'white' Afrikaans-speaking boys on the farms meant splitting the peer attachment to 'black' and 'coloured' boys with whom they had explored the veld, learnt the rudimentary skills of farm work and played.

Such terms of sharecropping were a favourable arrangement for the wealthier absentee landowner but not so for the small farmer. He had to surrender at least part of his farm to his sharecroppers and allow them control to work as they wished, often with their own stock. If he were to go at it alone, as some farmers did in the Karoo for instance, the farmer and his sons would have to work the land themselves. They seldom had sufficient manpower, animals and experience. Even if they worked the land themselves, the farmhouse still attracted and needed various attachments, like farmhands, herders, trekkers, seasonal harvesters and so on. Women also added layers of helpers in the house who did not always have independent quarters of residence and made room for themselves at the margins of the house. These 'mixed' households required intricate negotiations of intimacy, especially when skin colour was slowly percolating as a caste along the frontier. The South African 'farm novel' exploits the imminent explosions that physical exhaustion, sexual desire and a dread about an unpredictable future created amongst people who had to live together as a family does even when the rifts between tenants and landlords, or between servants and masters, ran as deep as they could between members of the landowner's own family. Even then, despite whatever might compel them to separate, these households held together, often isolated by the great distance between farms and farmhouses. Here lived 'the white man and the Bushman, the master's son and the servant, who survived the long dark of the winter's night, together in their shelter, at last to see daylight again'.[10] They were inescapably dependent on one another.

The protagonist of the 'farm novel' is the settler who loves the land or learns to love it. It is the story of settlers' encounter with the interior's unpredictable temperament, the exertions the land imposes on the people who work it and try to tame it to their bidding. The land, unlike its people, is honest endless yards of open savannah. It is dangerous but penetrable, with nothing to hide. The land discriminates between men with brutality. Its hardships are like an essential test of temperament, the land's own selection of its own species of people. The land makes natives of the immigrants who stay. They are no longer like the families who first arrived on the ships. They even speak a new language, new words – *koppies*, *boers*, *basters*, *sjamboks*. This land is distinctly not Europe, certainly not in the interior. It is brown and stubborn, lush only in short bursts of a few months, but satisfying when at last it yields the harvest. The land invites the settler with its strangeness and unfamiliar beauty. It inspires possession. The disenchantment with the old world, with Europe and all its ways, sneaks upon him like a loss of innocence. The land absorbs all the deposit of the settler's history. He becomes what the landscape and its people have made of him. His children may travel abroad but only to touch the shores of a life they might otherwise have lived had they withheld themselves and not attached to their birthplace. This settler yields neither to the fantasy of the colonial traveller nor to the ambition to command and enslave in a labour colony. Instead, he finds a situation where he proves his manhood, earns the respect of his neighbour, and confirms his civility by demonstrating such a mastery of the land that he establishes a home of its own. In Bechuanaland, the earlier settlers he found living on the land called this opportunity to prove manhood on the land, placement or *peo*.

Every landless settler was a wanderer. He had no roots in a terrain he wished to possess as intimately as he had assimilated it into his consciousness.

Even in the Europe of his ancestry, the vagabond had no reputation, was only a 'skipper of some tramp that crawled from one port to the next, jam full of chaffering hands, a tallier of cargoes, itching for gold', good for hustling and surviving but with no training in the practices of civility.[11] In southern Africa, the wanderer had even less of a reputation. The settler needed a place of dwelling in order to exorcise his association with a wild thing of the frontier, a 'vagabond Hollander', a 'runaway Englishman' or any one of the peripatetic people of the ships going from place to place in the colonies, or a marauder who lived by the gun and only for profiteering.[12] Unless he raised his own homestead, the Bantu-speaking peoples he found growing grain and raising cattle on the land, the people amongst whom he now lived, looked upon him as a child. If he was already advanced in years, they spoke about him as though he were already dead. Without a homestead of his own, his child was barely human because the women had nowhere to bury the umbilical cord. Instead they threw it away as though an animal had given birth.

Often, these black and brown and yellow people were his kin and family. He married among them and learnt their language. He bartered and traded, worked the land and hunted with them. His children were the mixed in-between colour of their parents. He did not consider himself distinctly 'white' – not yet, and even if he called himself by that name, it was not as a marker of superiority. In the lands that had become the Barolong reserves, this settler had already found placement in the ward of the chief or senior patriarch who had offered it to him. He had accepted his placement or *peo* as a gift of care and recognition that he too was a person and a man. He returned it with a gift of his own. Every year, he joined his neighbours to plough his patron's lands and when the harvest came, he returned to reap the fields for him. This was *pacha*. The settler was head of his own household and the master of his domain, with the authority to make the law and enforce discipline in his homestead and the pleasure to transfer placement to each of his children, biological and otherwise, when they had matured to adulthood. Thus, the settler's personhood depended on being of the *morafe*.

The settler sowed his seed in the ground but not before the most esteemed person on the land announced the season to go into the fields. The settler had to wait for the 'father' of his *morafe*, that man from whom all other men acquired their primary recognition, to call on the rain. The settler's patron, the head of the ward who had allotted him placement, stood as a representative of this supreme 'Father' of their 'House'. The head of the ward summoned all the men of his ward to the Kgotla to hear cases and to contribute their views of what would be a fair resolution. If the case found no resolution, it went on to a higher Kgotla under the authority of a more senior patriarch who had charge of this and other wards as his placement. As a case became more difficult and serious, it ascended the rungs of patriarchal authority until it came before this most esteemed person of the entire realm, the 'Father' of all the *morafe*, who was most closely associated with the mythical founders of the settlement to whom everyone owed their placement. It means there were many layers of judicial authority between every homestead head's own court and the highest Kgotla. Each of these courts was autonomous and yet never entirely independent, in the same manner that every adult's independent entitlement to property was unquestionable, and yet the land was not something one possessed without the obligation to share it. These chiefly and patriarchal hierarchies of placement made judicial authority and landholding inseparable.

Immediately after Britain colonised Bechuanaland in 1885 and stilled the frontier warfare, more European settlers flocked to the north looking for land to establish themselves. Their landlessness and impoverishment would soon become a priority of the colonial government in the early decades of the following century. In the neighbouring Transvaal, there had already developed an exclusive oligarchy of landholding under Paul Kruger's government but even without it, the land could in any case not accommodate the dual pressure of population growth and immigration. Competition for land was rife. It had been going on for a long time, even before European penetration. However, conquest by the newcomers worsened tensions. Conquest had always been a possibility, but led by the military prowess of European colonists, the scale of displacement was vast. Nevertheless, in the newly British territories of Bechuanaland, colonial officials gave black, hereditary chiefs advantage over the white settler. Chiefs like Molema held the reserves and had benefitted from land auctions that Sidney Shippard had facilitated, whilst the European settler had no special privileges. If he was Dutch-Afrikaans, a Boer, he might have lost his farm in the republics that Britain had dismantled.

Britain had delineated the boundaries of the reserves of Bechuanaland and had established each one as the autonomous property of its inhabitants. The English word 'chief' had come to describe the patriarchs who presided over the Kgotlas, transferring land and adjudicating cases. These entitlements were hereditary with a recognisable hierarchy of ruling families where 'brothers' often competed for seniority. In the Molopo Reserve, the ruling families included the Molemas, Montsioas, Motshegares and Gaboutloeloes, each with their favourites and followers whom they assembled on the land like an extended family. These were not essentially ties of blood. The transfer of land and authority involved convoluted strategies of family, both adoption and estrangement as well as birth. The result was a 'House' of fluid boundaries and hierarchy. Britain fixed the computation of seniority and power it found in place. In 1885 the Montsioas were at the apex of the hierarchy and were the heads of the paramount Kgotla. The British recognised them as 'paramount chiefs' and their senior relations along a hierarchy of wards and jurisdictions. The Molemas, Motshegares, Gaboutloeloes and others were all heads of their own wards. The British paid a salary to the top and middle rungs of chiefly authority, each according to its place in a hierarchy that had been developing from the early nineteenth century. Chiefly bureaucracies acquired a nomenclature of position and status – 'paramount chief', 'chief', 'sub-chief' and 'headman' although the titles were not used consistently and were often interchangeable, like 'chief' and 'headman'.

In this new colonial dispensation, there was more than one way that Africa conferred civility upon the settler but all of them operated through the same institution of placement, which enabled otherwise landless Europeans to live in a ward on their allocated plot of land. Placement was a wide permutation of practice. It allowed many different possibilities of owning and using the land but only one 'rule' applied consistently. This was, in a word, decency. The ethos of adulthood was the freedom both to prosper, meaning to keep increasing in wealth and people, and also to help others achieve the same goal. This was how one grew in moral standing and it presented a dilemma. How much was one to give towards one's own flourish and how much was one to yield to the flourish of another? The land was the most important raw material in negotiating this dilemma of moral standing. The many possibilities of arranging placement on the land emerged from how men and women tried to broker this paradox. This is how Africans' own moral concern to live on the land with virtue mediated the strategies that started many European settlers on their own course to manhood on Silas Molema's lands in the Molopo Reserve, on Mabete on the Barolong Farms, and also on his private farm Vryhof, beyond the reserve. These arrangements of placement, *peo*, that he offered were more than about survival and accumulation. They were reciprocal transactions to make and amplify manhood on a terrain that was difficult to work entirely on one's own.

As placement, arrangements on the land were the free exercise of every adult man's private entitlement to let, sell and exchange his land but placement was, at the same time, an opportunity for every adult man to demonstrate his capacity to care, to spread his arms wide as provider, nourisher and source.

Women too could buy, sell, inherit and exchange land although the only courts they attended were within the hierarchies of the extended homestead. Nevertheless, most placement holders were men. The pendulum swung between enforcing the rights of private entitlements and the responsibilities of distributing the infrastructure of manhood. This is why men did not just haul each other before the courts for infringements of contracts but spoke to each other, constantly shifting the understanding of mutual benefit. The land was an opportunity to prove decency. Litigious personalities like Transfeldt tended to hurt themselves. In seeking and continuing their attachment to the land in the new Barolong reserves from 1885, European settlers were entering and holding onto this realm of moral negotiations. Either way it was not necessarily foreign to them. Even before British rule, had not many of them already become 'Afrikander', native to the ways of the land?

However, there were already strong influences, religious and otherwise, that were encouraging the European settler trekking into the British territories to think of himself as a person apart from his neighbour, to wish to privilege his skin colour and not his moral induction onto the land, as an entitlement to possess it. At the same time, whatever their skin colour, families wanted to succeed and make more money. The land, at the end of the day, could simply be a resource to exploit. Besides, the moral gauge of decency was not standard. There was no single measure of what made for a fair reciprocal transaction of placement. Indeed an outsider observing these landscapes from the 1880s, would record a range of rents, taxes, subscriptions, labours, tributes and services on the land that spread like a network of capillaries mainly to supply the upper rungs of chiefly and patriarchal authority. Yet, in their own words, people spoke about the land as a free gift, their inheritance as children of the 'House' and members of the *morafe*.

Silas Molema's record of placement was extensive, including to European settlers. In 1891, P. Crause built a three-roomed house with 'walls of brick and a roof of iron' as rent on Molema's property in the Molopo Reserve.[13] Harry Roland Wright hired 1000 morgen on Kromdraai in 1901. He had to build a five-roomed house and a kitchen to the value of £350 over five years. He also had to build a stable for four horses and a cart house together worth £100 during the same period. His obligations also included repairing the fences, unclogging and extending the water furrows and cultivating fruit trees.[14] In lieu of rent, the Wrights were to build 'a dwelling house for four rooms … the outside measurement to be 32ft by 30ft – hip roof and rooms to be sealed by calico'.[15] Once a family had established the stipulated infrastructure they would typically renew their contract and stay on paying rent in cash or expand on their establishment. One tenant was 'most heartily' thankful that his contract was renewed and another had to put up a new windmill.[16] Some families passed their leases onto their sons.

There were other arrangements. In 1898, J.J. Paynter hired a 'portion of ground' in the Molopo Reserve for about £17 per annum for a period of five years.[17] O. Nell hired a 'small two roomed house and a piece of ground for ploughing' for £20 per year in 1899.[18] John Kay paid first £30 per annum and then £35 for lodging and a field.[19] J.J. van Rooyen ploughed Molema's field on Tantinyane in the reserve in 1898.[20] 'Half of all produce' passed on to Molema, who had supplied both seed and oxen. In 1912, P.F. Meintjies was another sharecropper in the reserve.[21] A man recorded as 'European' and 'Philip's son' leased 'an enclosed garden in which stands a house of four rooms' in 1908.[22] He could use both house and garden 'free of charge' and had to plant at least thirty fruit trees every month and 'make a dam on the other garden of mine with (sic) his own expense and plough for me when helped by my man'. Chaeng Hon, Ly Wing and 'Mr Yokehon' were Chinese immigrants who seem to have reached Mafikeng after the South African War. From 1903 they each paid cash rents to Molema to 'hire a garden'.[23] There was also a destitute labourer simply described on a contract as 'John Ludick Coloured Man'. This man of 'mixed race' was a labour tenant on Molema's plot in the reserve on strikingly reciprocal terms:

> ... he ploughs my garden and helped by my man, he takes care of it and in time of reaping he reaps it helped by my people and he must plant fruit trees in the garden and other trees. My oxen are to plough for him a piece of garden within the same enclosure. He pays no rent, and I pay him nothing. I can remove him from my house and garden if I am not satisfied with his conduct given a month's notice, on the other hand he is at liberty to give me a month's notice and leave me.[24]

III

In the years immediately preceding Unification and especially afterwards, English-speaking settlers understood themselves as brave and enterprising pioneers who tamed the Kalahari through culture and agriculture. The 'Northerners', as they called themselves, disparaged settlers of their own skin colour from low-lying coastal parts of the Cape Colony as weak and lethargic yet disproportionately favoured by Cape politicians. This is where the word

'Northerner' came from. They resented the alliance of English and Dutch-speaking political circles in the Cape parliament in Cape Town. In February 1910, Mafeking's Northerners listened to an address by their representative in the Cape House of Assembly, J.W. de Kock, who fanned the flames of their resentment.[25] He stated that the 'Northern people' were suffering under a 'curse' because the previous Cape government was interested only in developing coastal areas 'whilst the rest of the country could go to the devil'. According to De Kock, not only were Cape politicians at the beck and call of 'farmers of the Western Province' who were 'looked upon as experts and possessed of boundless practical experience'. They also neglected farmers of the interior, the very Northerners who 'did the hard work'. The Northerners were only 'a doormat to serve the parts and the ambitions of Cape politicians', he proclaimed, but this was all to end with the installation of a new Union government:

> From the 1st of June [1910] there would be a new order of things and greater issues ... the inland portions of the country would stand together. The Northern people would have a cricket innings such as had never been in the history of this Colony ... Coast legislation had milked them dry, but fortunately on the 1st of June a new order of things would come about. The day of reckoning is at hand.[26]

At the same time, Northerners aimed to stimulate their regional market and curb their dependency on goods from the coast, particularly British imports. In Mafeking, the slogan went 'practice what you preach and support local industries'. Women of the Mafeking branch of the South African National Union (SANU) pledged to buy only 'colonial made articles' whenever 'the price and quality warrant it'.[27] SANU was a farmers' organisation with strong republican sentiments. Local storekeepers stocked and exhibited local goods, including wares and furniture. The push for these local industries focused mainly on cattle ranching. Many members of SANU were livestock farmers. The dairy industry had just been kick-started and these farmers felt that rail was unaffordable, especially given that the system and distribution of railways favoured coastal areas.[28] To them Unification meant extension of the railways and more focused support for the industries of agriculture in the hinterlands. 'Union will, we are hoping, remove many of the drawbacks which at present hamper the interior.'[29] The 'Northern men', in De Kock's words, aimed to turn the dry and arid Bechuanaland into a story of economic success so that 'they would make those noblemen down there at Cape Town, realise that there was something to be said for the pioneer and the developer, who had always been called upon to pay the piper'.[30]

Hence the Northerners spent the years of postwar Reconstruction lobbying the government to invest in the interior by improving the rail system. They were also experimenting with new techniques of cattle ranching and 'dry farming', a method of cultivation in areas where rainfall was less than 20 inches a year. It meant that dry regions could produce reliable crops at low cost. These scientific ideas on ploughing and harrowing the 'deserts' to grow wheat and maize went hand in hand with calls to 'build up a mighty and prosperous nation' for the exclusive benefit of a 'white' population, which necessitated extensive and urgent government intervention.[31] Union settlers were seeking to purchase lands close to the railway. Land prices were very high. In the Cape, a morgen of land close to the railway sold for twelve times more than lands further away because farmers along a line could sell both beef and milk.[32]

The *Mafeking Mail* became the mouthpiece for the Northerner. As a newspaper for the Northerner, the *Mafeking Mail* sought to serve 'white' readers, deploying the term unambiguously to refer to a skin colour that naturally confirmed a higher order of civilisation. More accurately, the newspaper was one platform for the consolidation of whiteness. In reality, the hardships of life in an interior neglected by the government placed too many Northerners in a situation that compromised their place at the apex of a hierarchy of race they wished to see established on the land. A large number of white men were landless. The *Mafeking Mail* was an important voice for these white tenants, those wanderers without land of their own. It explicitly took the side of the tenants as underdogs in the disputes with landlords that appeared before the courts. In a landmark case in January 1910, a court released the tenant, Nills Frederick Murman, from the obligation to carry out the costs of repairing a windmill on Cloverly, the farm of his landlord, Spencer Minchin.[33] Minchin was Silas Molema's attorney, whose own residence was in the Molopo Reserve. Murman had withheld his rent after spending over £68 to repair the windmill. He won the case on appeal in the High Court of Griqualand. The court ruled that Murman could continue to withhold his rent until he had compensated himself for the repairs even though the contract stipulated that the tenant, never the landlord, carried out such repairs, no matter how costly, while the landlord still claimed his rent in full.

There was never mention of a landlord like Silas Molema in the *Mafeking Mail* for he was not a white man. In fact, the commonplace scenarios of black landlords exploiting white tenants subverted the 'natural' order, especially under prevalent conditions where the terms of leasing typically privileged the landlords. This is why Northerners, including through their newspaper, took every opportunity to press the Cape and later the Union government very hard to intervene in the north and give the white landless farmer land of his own to prove his manhood, rather than leave him humiliated as a black landowner's underdog. In the reserves, chiefs were leading lives of distinction, letting the land to whites and never turning the soil with their own hands, whilst accumulating houses, almost living as though they were Europe's landed gentry, and doing so on the muscle of a white tenantry. A strategy of atrophy was necessary.

IV

In January 1904, Chief Badirile Montsioa received notification from the Superintendent of Natives, W.J. Mahony, that a Dog Tax ought to have been collected in the Molopo Reserve in December of the previous year.[34] The Divisional Council of Mafeking had imposed the tax of five shillings for every dog over three months every year. According to Mahony, the death of the previous paramount chief, Wessels Montsioa, at the end of the previous year had made it impossible for his office to collect the tax. Badirile Montsioa was about thirty years old when he succeeded his brother, Wessels. At Wessels Montsioa's installation in 1896, the Civil Commissioner in Mafeking, George Boyes, had reminded the Cape government to comply with the 'special conditions' under which it had incorporated the Molopo Reserve into the Cape Colony. According to this 'treaty', the reserve was an autonomous chiefly jurisdiction. The government could not interfere in its institutions of hereditary rule. As Boyes recommended to the Undersecretary of Native Affairs in Cape Town, '[t]here are many strong reasons which I could place before you showing the advisability of appointing a Chief as successor to the late Montsioa, but think that Sir Sydney Shippard's pledge is conclusive and any deviation from that promise would be a breach of faith'.[35] The Resident Magistrate, Graham Green, had the same advice for his superiors in Cape Town in 1911 when he submitted the name of Wessels' successor. Badirile Montsioa, he wrote, was a 'fairly educated man of sober habits, and in my opinion a fit and proper person to be chief'.[36]

This imposition of Dog Tax was not for the common reasons the Cape government typically imposed such a tax on reserves, which were curtailing hunting in areas the government and some conservationists wished to preserve or appeasing farmers who felt dogs preyed on their livestock.[37] The Divisional Council of Mafeking was a regional arm of the representative government in the Cape's northern districts beyond Griqualand. The Dog Tax was a test of whether, and a mechanism to ensure that, this local government had jurisdiction over all the reserves of former British Bechuanaland in the new postwar dispensation of British rule. From 1902, the Cape and Natal colonies and the two Boer Republics, the Transvaal and the Orange Free State, embarked on 'Reconstruction' to become the four provinces of a single British dominion. The Union of South Africa would come into being on 31 May 1910 and unless the Divisional Council of Mafeking could prove that the Molopo Reserve was under its jurisdiction, this and every other reserve of former British Bechuanaland would be beyond the jurisdiction of the Union government.

In 1886, a year after annexation, Sidney Shippard's Land Commission had established the reserves of British Bechuanaland.[38] When the Divisional Council for the Division of Mafeking was established the following year, the proclamation (No. 29 B.B. of 1887) did not include the reserves of British Bechuanaland in any of its districts. In fact, the proclamation made it expressly clear that 'the said Divisional Council should have no jurisdiction over native reserves'. Two years later, another proclamation (No. 62 B.B. of 1889) confirmed the autonomous status of these reserves again by appointing a board of trustees that treated the reserves as a 'legal estate'. The board of each reserve would carry out the ordinary functions that Divisional Councils typically undertook, like the building of roads and bridges. However, the Molopo Reserve had no such boards of trustees appointed. It is possible that although the proclamation made provision for these boards, none were established for the reserves of former British Bechuanaland. The war would have been one reason why this was the case but in any case, the establishment of the boards would have entrenched the legal status of the reserves.

In 1892, Shippard had nevertheless imposed Hut Tax on the reserves of British Bechuanaland for the first time (Proclamation No. 33 B.B. of 1892). Britain wished to relieve herself of the financial costs of keeping the peace and securing the borders of the reserves in these territories. In collecting Hut Tax, Shippard was shifting the financial responsibility of this undertaking to the inhabitants of the reserves themselves. They would fund the imperial arrangement that guaranteed their autonomy. When Britain eventually ceded Bechuanaland to the Cape Colony in 1895, the agreement with chiefs was that the legal and political status of the reserves would remain unaltered. The terms of annexation (British Bechuanaland Annexation Act of 1895) stipulated unambiguously that the initial terms of annexation in 1885 remained in place and 'shall not be deemed to be abolished by the passing of this Act'.[39] The Cape government had no powers to promulgate any new proclamations over the reserves. In fact, the reserves had to be 'returned' to their inhabitants for their own use as stipulated by the Land Commission of 1886.

The proclamation of the agreement that Sidney Shippard signed with Montsioa was also unambiguous in its stipulation that 'the present jurisdiction of Native Chiefs over their own people be preserved' as set out in the very first proclamation of annexation in 1885.[40] In other words, the laws and policies of reservation in the Cape Colony would not apply in the Molopo Reserve but remarkably, hereditary chiefs would receive an annual pension from the Cape government. Montsioa would receive £300 every year and his successors would each similarly receive £150 every year. Should the Cape government wish to apply its policies in the reserves, it would first have to pass 'special legislation' that confirms the approval of the British government. Hence, the Native Locations Act of 1884 by which the Cape government had full jurisdiction of reserves as territories belonging to the Crown did not apply to the reserves of former British Bechuanaland, which Britain had ceded to the Cape Colony. 'This', Shippard apparently said to Silas Molema after signing the agreement, 'is your charter'.[41] Hence, the situation at the onset of 'Reconstruction' was that the Divisional Council of Mafeking and the Cape government had no jurisdiction in the Barolong reserves. From 1902, in preparation for Union, the Cape government was now attempting to undo the arrangements of British rule in former British Bechuanaland.

This is why Badirile Montsioa refused to collect Dog Tax in the Molopo Reserve. If he paid, then the Divisional Council of Mafeking and by association the Cape government had jurisdiction in his reserve. As he put it, 'we do not agree with this matter' because when the Cape took over British Bechuanaland 'we were assured that the laws and regulations with which we have been governed will not be changed'.[42] He added, 'so it is very hard for us to pay for our dogs'. Badirile drafted his responses in his own hand before Silas Molema and Solomon Plaatje rewrote and polished them for the audience of the colonial administration. Green attempted unsuccessfully to sell the Divisional Council of Mafeking as a 'local government' onto which Barolong chiefs could nominate representatives, and that the Dog Tax could be used to improve roads in the stadt. The paramount chief still refused:

> ... about having our Representative in the District Councils of Mafeking ... I saw that we do not need one ...we also have our own Council in the stadt which has nothing to do with the Divisional Council. We therefore strongly object to dog tax in our reserve.[43]

Badirile Montsioa appeared before the Resident Magistrate on 17 August 1904 for failing to pay tax on one dog.[44] He was found guilty and fined £1 or 14 days' imprisonment with hard labour. On appeal, the Supreme Court in Cape Town quashed the conviction on 14 November 1904. His attorneys argued that the Molopo Reserve did not fall within any of the districts set forth and described in the legislation for annexation to the Cape (No. 432 of 1896). The chieftaincy had presented its suit as against both the Divisional Council of Mafeking and the Prime Minister of the Cape Colony. On 9 March 1905, the *Mafeking Mail* reported that the Divisional Council of Mafeking had 'resolved that an application be made to the government to issue a new proclamation that would incorporate the reserve within the districts for local government purposes'.[45] The following day Badirile Montsioa sent a letter to the Resident Magistrate that the report 'greatly troubled me and my Councillors'. He was adamant that the rulers of the Molopo Reserve did not and could never allow any external statutory body to have a say in the governance of the reserve:

> Matters of 'local government' in the reserve have since the Annexation of our territory been under the jurisdiction of the paramount chief, and in the hands of his Chief and Headmen, and I see no reason why any Council should encroach on these our rights and privileges... As a nation we do not know this council, in the past we had no dealings with it and we do not wish to have any at the present or in the future... We do not wish for any local authority or for any officials to come between the Government and us...[46]

The 'Government' to which he was referring was Britain, according to the original settlement of 1885, and not any settler authority.

In 1905, the opinion of one Cape official whose identity is not clear was that the 'special conditions' applying in the Molopo Reserve did not exempt it from the Native Locations Act of 1884. He argued that the Location Act had in fact been applying in British Bechuanaland all along, albeit in an attenuated version.[47] He reasoned that without the Location Act, Sidney Shippard would not have been able to collect Hut Tax in the territory from 1896. Since the government of British Bechuanaland could only have collected Hut Tax on Crown Lands, the success of its Hut Tax collection was evidence that the reserves had all along actually been each a 'location', meaning Crown Lands, and belonged to the British government, and not territory belonging to the people living on it. This memorandum does not mention Dog Tax but relays the actual reasons why it was critical that the Divisional Council prove its jurisdiction in the Molopo Reserve. The Dog Tax did not matter. Its collection was a test to confirm that the Native Locations Act of 1884 actually applied to the reserves of former British Bechuanaland, as it applied to any other reserve in the Cape. If the reserves were 'locations' and therefore Crown property, then the Cape government had jurisdiction to decide what happened in the reserves, specifically who could lawfully reside there. The memorandum's concern was the question of who could reside in the reserve. Any 'European' and anyone 'not Native' were expressly undesirable unless they were traders with special permission to be in the reserves.

> ... if the question should arise in a clearer form in the future proceedings the Supreme Court would (notwithstanding the appeal case of Montsioa) hold that the Locations Act of 1884 ... does apply to Native Reserves in British Bechuanaland, and that persons who are European and not Native cannot get lawful authority from a Chief to reside or remain within such a Reserve...it is for the benefit and protection of the Natives themselves that intruders, not approved of by the Government should not find a footing in the reserve. If such people are once established it may become difficult if not impossible to dislodge them.[48]

On 21 May 1906, the Cape government passed Proclamations No. 173 and 174 that declared the Molopo Reserve as within the Mafeking Division and hence under the jurisdiction of the Divisional Council of Mafeking, which once again imposed Dog Tax on the reserve on 16 October 1908.[49] In January 1909, the tax collector arrived in the stadt to find that Badirile Montsioa had not collected a single penny. On 29 August 1909, the Secretary of the Divisional Council, Thomas Alfred, sent him a letter of demand for five shillings for his own dog. Alfred later called on Badirile and found a 'big red dog' in his office. When he asked Badirile 'if he had a dog of his own', he 'replied in the affirmative', and then 'declined to pay the tax'. Badirile appeared before the Resident Magistrate again on 8 March 1910 and argued that the Molopo Reserve belonged to him 'in trust for the people of the tribe who occupy and use it in subordination to him under 'tribal' tenure'.⁵⁰ Therefore, he argued, in announcing the two new Proclamations, the government was acting beyond its powers – in legal jargon, *'ultra vires'*. The only way to promulgate the proclamations was therefore an Act of Parliament. The Resident Magistrate again found him guilty. On 29 April 1910, Badirile Montsioa filed another appeal in the Supreme Court of Cape Town.⁵¹ Litigation was very expensive. The chieftaincy could not afford further legal counsel and did not push for the hearing.

V

Sebopioa Molema was one of the handful of Africans to read law at Wilberforce University in Ohio in 1904.⁵² Graduates of missionary boarding schools like him felt hamstrung by the very limited opportunities available at home. One could be an interpreter, a clerk, a teacher, perhaps a newspaperman but very little else. As one headman described to the South African Native Affairs Commission in 1904, there were already 'too many of the schoolteachers and they cannot get work'.⁵³ America was an opportunity for a 'wider education'. Over one hundred and fifty African émigrés entered the American educational system between 1894 and 1914. Stephen Lefenya's grandson, George Montsioa, was one of them. He left for America in 1902.⁵⁴ In March of 1904 alone, eighteen Africans passed through Cape Town en route to America.⁵⁵ The African Methodist Episcopal Church supported about half of such students in America and many of them, like Sebopioa, ended up at Wilberforce.⁵⁶

In May 1904, the church's resident bishop, Rev L. J. Coppin, and his wife visited Mafikeng.⁵⁷ His reception was at the Masonic Hall. The crowd responded with loud cheers when he described the mission of his church. They were listening, in Solomon Plaatje's words, to 'a new thing' and 'very strange', which was a 'church religious denomination managed exclusively by coloured people' without any supervision beyond themselves.⁵⁸ Coppin was only one of the African-American evangelists scouring the South African countryside for promising young black people to spread the message of 'upliftment'. He received Sebopioa Molema in Philadelphia early in August 1904 and arranged for him to start his preparatory studies in law.⁵⁹

The letter of introduction that Sebopioa held in hand for Coppin came from Silas Molema. Joshua, his biological father, had declined to write because he felt he was only 'good enough to bask in the sun and let his beard grow'.⁶⁰ The further Sebopioa went with his schooling, the more unfamiliar

Joshua became with the landscape of aspiration his son desired. He retreated and let his younger brother take charge, but for the son, the dilemmas and uncertainties of plural filial attachments were inevitable. Sebopioa worried about being presumptuous and asking for too much when Silas Molema had already given him all that a son could expect from a father. Yet as a son, surely he could express his needs and wishes? He was unsure. Once, soon after the siege of Mafeking, Silas Molema arranged for his daughter Seleje's travel to Cape Town where she would spend her Christmas holiday but made no such arrangements for Sebopioa to leave Lovedale with her.[61] Seleje pressed him to write to their father and ask to return home. He was too afraid to write but she reasoned with him that a son always made his wishes known to his father. A father cannot grant a wish that his son has not expressed. He was relieved that he, not his father, was to blame.

> My sister [Seleje] asked me to write to you and request to come home (for our holidays). I was afraid many times [but] I discovered that a child must ask his father (which is reasonable).[62]

The journey to Wilberforce had started with a trip from Mafikeng to Cape Town where Sebopioa had waited to board his ship. He had visited Zonnebloem College but had been little impressed with the school because 'the general health of the place is bad for upcountry people'.[63] He had felt ill at ease with the city and that being so 'close to town [,] one was liable to get bad companies'. He had observed the liquor, the 'coloured boys' with their poor English from a distance and made no friends. He wrote to his father, who may have sent him to Zonnebloem to gauge whether Modiri could matriculate from there rather than Lovedale, that the school was not an option. As soon as he arrived in Ohio, he sent an account of his journey to *Koranta* to 'be of interest to some people who are pleased with the prosperity of human beings'.[64] In 1904 the largest contingent of black South Africans, twenty in all, were at Wilberforce.[65]

In 1906, Sebopioa graduated from his preparatory training and joined the collegiate division of the university. He was one of only three black South Africans who did not opt for qualifications in education and theology.[66] Whatever the qualification, a university education set them apart and granted them an elevated status in society, home and abroad, albeit Wilberforce's glow was like an early twilight. Its best days were behind it. W.E.B. Du Bois identified the signs of decline as soon as he took up a teaching post at the university in 1894.[67] The university's financial resources had dwindled and the annual $3,500 it received from the AME was not sufficient to offer an education that matched Wilberforce's reputation. There was no proper library until 1903. The large majority of students were in the preparatory and not the collegiate division. Until 1939, no white institution recognised its qualifications and the reason, according to Du Bois, was not racial prejudice. 'In Europe', Du Bois commented in 1940, 'such an institution would not be allowed to confer degrees at all'. Nevertheless, the university enjoyed the support of its neighbouring black middle-classes. Teachers like Du Bois had enormous gravitas and were formidable role models. The daily routine, as in many other 'black colleges', was monastic and gruelling.[68] Nevertheless, regardless of the reputation of the institution or the calibre of its qualifications, any graduate who wished to practice law in territories under British rule required a second qualification from Britain.

By 1909, Sebopioa's funds were dwindling, which was not an unusual problem for many African university students. He had to ask for help from the Freedmen's Aid Society 'several times' in 1909 whilst he was pursuing his studies.[69] He also raised funds to support himself by entertaining crowds as 'a pleasing speaker, a good singer' who 'plays music thru [sic] the nose'.[70] He gave at least two lectures in 1910. One was 'an unusual and sensational lecture' on 'The Africans and their Customs', during which he told an audience at a Baptist Church about 'how many wives they marry in Africa and about the honeymoon'. A similar lecture followed a few months later at a Presbyterian Young People's Society programme. He fortunately found work at an attorney's firm, I.L. Purcell, in Jacksonville, Florida, but remained enrolled at the university. All this he took in his stride. He had also met beautiful, elegant Nora, who returned his love and wanted to settle down with him after they completed their studies at Wilberforce.

Yet, all this time, he was suffering. He had not received a single letter from his father or Seleje since he had arrived in America, only letters from Joshua, the subsidiary father, and a few others. There was no explanation although he often questioned and blamed himself. He felt abandoned and grieved his loss very deeply over the years. A letter finally came in October 1910.[71] His father was asking him to leave America, travel to England and take up work the fathers had arranged for him at a law firm in London. The idea made sense because an American qualification would in any case not allow him to practice in the now Union of South Africa, which was a British dominion. He would be moving on to a necessary apprenticeship in Britain and there find opportunity perhaps to study further, but it meant not giving himself a chance to complete the journey he had started at Wilberforce.

He had already spent six years at Wilberforce and even if he had not yet completed his studies, the path ahead was shorter than what lay behind. He knew he would have had to return home at some point, and that was in any case his plan and intention, but if he followed through with his father's plan, he would have to leave immediately and cut ties with his law firm without notice. He would have to separate from Nora without warning, and without time to merge the attachments of his new world with the home to which he would be returning. There were clear advantages to leaving – starting a life and career in London, gaining a qualification that would help him to practice at home, but now in Ohio, he had the advantage of a city and a university and people that he knew well.

In the end, he chose his father, the path that gave the two of them a chance. If he remained in America, it would be as though he were punishing his father for his absence of six years. The wound would never heal. Across the Atlantic, there would be no way for them to turn again towards each other. He would be 'cutting himself away' from his most important attachment. He wanted to mend, not remain like a man with an injured knee, limping, yet refusing crutches. He needed to leave for London to prove that he remained his father's son.

> As stated in your letter, I could not help but have all sorts of strange feelings, when failing to hear from you, but was never tempted to entertain the idea that father loved me the less by reason of such long and continuous silence. I am free to admit that as a son, I feel clear in my conscience that I have played my part and did all that was and is my duty to do by writing to you. Once I was faced to feel that I had become an unknown quantity in my father's own house ... Indeed this is enough to cause one to have perturbation of mind, but my love to parents has not been changed nor even shaken.[72]

Moreover his father needed him. The instruction to proceed to London was a show of trust. It was an invitation into the world of mature adulthood to handle the affairs of their *morafe*. The letter had mentioned the 'boundary dispute' that confronted the Barolong. The apprenticeship in London put him on a path to become their lawyer. He immediately prepared 'to suspend my law studies in America and proceed to England' all 'pursuant to the decision of fathers Joshua, Silas, Messrs. Plaatje and Mbelle'. Isaiah Bud-Mbelle was Plaatje's brother-in-law and the first African to pass the Cape Civil Service examination.[73] He reminded 'the fathers' nevertheless of the desires and aspirations of the life, his life, that in this one decision, they were now taking into their hands.

> My aim in life is a very high one, in short my ideals are as high as the stars and shall never stop until I have accomplished all that is possible ...The sons of Molema should be leaders among the Bechuana just as our grandfather was the instigator of civilisation to the Barolong, so his grandchildren should perfect those fundamental principles that he had ... I hope you will keep on improving the conditions of our people till we shall come, when we, young people, with all the advantages before us hope to do better and start where you have left.[74]

When he arrived in London, he learnt that the government of the Union had denied him the required approval to work. The new Resident Magistrate in Mafeking, E.C. Welsh had written an unfavourable character report blaming the Molemas for 'all the pretentious claims which the Barolong have from time to time presented to the Government'.[75] Welsh was making the Molemas pay for their refusal to submit the Molopo Reserve to the jurisdiction of the Mafeking Divisional Council and to his own authority to intervene in the reserve. At the same time, Welsh was also a colonial officer in far-flung Bechuanaland, a region which British and Cape officials did not regard as a reputable place of work. The last thing he wanted to do was recommend a young man for a career in London. Most likely, racial prejudice provided quick resolution to envy. The decision not to grant Sebopioa leave to work in Britain had already been made by the time the fathers' letter reached Ohio, but the fathers had not waited to make sure the coast was clear before Sebopioa packed up and disembarked in London. When he arrived there, he found he had no work. He had to sail home to Mafikeng.

He arrived at about the same time that Pixley ka Isaka Seme and his own cousin, George Montsioa, were also returning from abroad. News of the trio's return appeared on the same page of *Tsala ea Becoana* but the other two men's university qualification appeared next to their names. Plaatje's editorial decision was to place all three together on one page to make it clear to them, and to the readers, that the three were of the same league, and also to state publicly that Sebopioa Molema's journey was not over yet. He wrote that Sebopioa had 'studied considerably', that 'the cattle had returned to the kraal, and milking pails shall overflow'.[76] This 'follower of Jesus Christ' would return to England to study further. Sebopioa's own intention was not to stay home but to return to Britain and complete his studies. Hence, he did not attempt to seek employment as a clerk or interpreter, nor did he pursue another line of training.

He found that a lot had changed after more than six years of absence. His family of wealth and reputation was considerably poorer. Plaatje was no longer in Mafikeng and the Molopo Reserve faced a new threat of conquest. A dreadful drought was approaching its third year. The paramount chief in the reserve, Badirile Montsioa drank heavily and was not a man who could orchestrate a defence of the reserve's autonomy. The reserve was also in a bad way through drought and destitution. The fathers were ageing and tired. He could not walk away immediately, not yet. He stayed to offer his youthful energies to support the fathers and also to pause and come to terms with the unexpected truncation of his life in America. He stayed in the reserve because turning his mind to something else would mean he had given up on the dream to sail back to England – and that he could not do.

The politics of Union were also shaping new forms of political organisation along the lines of 'blackness', which appealed to a young man who had spent six years at Wilberforce. Pixley Seme had issued a call for the South African Native National Congress. His motivation was 'a general desire for progress, and co-operation' that would unite all 'natives' to reject 'all those things which poison the springs of our national life', including the 'divisions' and 'jealousies' between ethnic enclaves.[77] 'We are one people'. He explained that Congress would be 'the only effective means whereby [we] shall be able to make [our] grievances properly known and considered both by the government and by the people of South Africa at large'. There was at the same time a certain disposition of chieftaincy that went with this 'general desire for progress' – literacy, efficient administration and a strong defence of the rights of the population of the reserves in the face of land shortages, a steep burden of taxation and the lack of a political voice in the new dominion.

Badirile Montsioa succumbed to heavy drinking and died, aged only thirty-five, on 4 April 1911.[78] Sebopioa became the official 'National Secretary' of the Molopo Reserve and the right-hand man to the regent who succeeded Badirile Montsioa, an elderly man by the name of Lekoko Marumoloa, who took up the surname 'Montsioa' during his regency. Sebopioa did not sign his own name to the mass of neat typescript of correspondence he produced as the 'National Secretary'. Only here and there did he print his own initials below the regent's signature. All his service was in the name of Lekoko Montsioa. Sebopioa travelled to Cape Town, Lovedale, Middledrift and King Williamstown in the spring of 1911 as the new face of Mafikeng's chieftaincy.[79] He also travelled across the border to the Bechuanaland

Morafe

Protectorate to urge its chiefs to attend the launch of Congress or send representatives to Bloemfontein on their behalf.[80]

He also turned his attention to the burden of rural householders that could hardly feed themselves in the drought. During and after the war, British officials were finding it difficult 'to meet demand for Transport natives from [the] Cape Colony'.[81] Peasant households were working the land as keen suppliers and contractors for grain and other produce.[82] A decade later, many of these householders were destitute. When Sebopioa wrote to the General Manager of De Beers to employ some of the men in the reserve, he replied that the mine already had 'more natives than they can find work for'.[83] Sebopioa also wrote numerous petitions to Welsh's office to lessen the burden of taxation, including licenses to gather firewood in specified forests and woodlands. Women paid at least six shillings a bundle.[84] There was also a labour tax. Welsh demanded men to fence railway tracks and to maintain any such infrastructure going through the reserve.[85] In the autumn of 1913, Sebopioa noted that taxation caused 'such unrest among my people'.[86] It is not clear whether the reserve complied.

It was a lot of work, in addition to lending a leading hand in the litigation over the 'boundary dispute', which had not gone away. 'The fathers', as he called them, had promised to pay Sebopioa £7 per month for his work as National Secretary. They had not done so. He confronted them in December 1913. 'The Barolongs are a strange nation.'[87] How could they claim the chieftaincy had no money to pay him whilst 'lots of money has passed from my hands to be sent to your lawyers?' He presented that he had been 'working for the Barolong as a *morafe*', for 'the Chief of Barolong' and for 'my fathers as a son'. He begged to 'resign and [go to] work as a[n] [ordinary] member of Barolong, as fathers, brothers and others are doing, before you make me resign on account of being insolvent'. That same December he had become indebted to someone and promised to pay with a sheep.[88] He had no money. The fathers pledged to try harder but they had little available even for themselves. He wanted a portion of the money they had raised for the litigation, but they asked him to wait until the storm was over. In the meantime, they hastened to make available to him the infrastructure of manhood.

His first reward was a bride. He married his cousin, Emang Marumoloa, Lekoko's daughter, the same young woman whom Plaatje had praised for her housekeeping skills. The property she brought to the Molemas as her possession from her father's house was the ward 'Signal Hill'. The fathers made and recognised Sebopioa as chief at Signal Hill. This high-ranking placement was also the fathers' strategy to defend this ward on the northern outskirts of the reserve against Boer encroachment, which remained a threat. There was then no returning to Nora, although she had written. There is one letter with a photograph. She stands tall and beaming behind her father. 'This is photo of my mamma, papa. Three brothers and I.'[89] He could not have told her of the traditions of arranged marriage in his family but then, far away in Ohio, in the circles of students and professionals, a different future had been possible. A marriage of choice was possible for a man who remained abroad for an extended time. He could have married and returned with her to Mafikeng but instead he had arrived home by himself and over thirty years old. 'The fathers' gave him the best bride they had to offer.

He also gained a father in the elderly Lekoko, who relied on him to be more than a son-in-law or a 'National Secretary'. Sebopioa became the son the regent could never have in his own and only son, Dichukudu Richard Marumoloa. He went by the name 'Dick'. The principal of Healdtown Missionary Institution, Rev. James Henderson, reported that Dick's conduct at the College Division was 'not giving satisfaction'.[90] Later on, Dick deserted and came home to Mafikeng without his father's consent. His father felt 'greatly humiliated' but Sebopioa kept trying to find a place for him elsewhere. Sebopioa, not Dick, would sit by the old man in his sick bed to take down his last words and wait with him to die.[91]

VI

When the Union of South Africa came into being, *Koranta ea Becoana* had not appeared for over two years. In February 1910 the editor of *Imvo Zabantsundu*, Tengo Jabavu, wrote to Silas Molema in Sechuana that he was 'very sorry to see that in today's great matters, of the unification of all the colonies of South Africa, Becoana are the only *morafe* without the voice of *bomorafe* (*kodu ea bomorafe*)'.[92] Jabavu offered 25 shares of his newspaper to any ten Bechuana men 'who possess a spirit of progress of their own as the *morafe* of Becoana (*moea oa coelopele eabo e le morafe oa Becoana)*' so that Becoana too would have a voice, like the Xhosa, the Zulu, Basotho and whites'. Soon afterwards, Jabavu and Co. became the first registered proprietors of *Tsala ea Becoana*. Plaatje moved to Kimberley to work as its editor. The financers were Barolong, chiefly landowners in Thaba Nchu in the Orange Free State.[93] A newspaper had become more than a textual manifestation of a *morafe* standing for the authority of its moral universe. Newspapers were also a *morafe*'s expression of its interests and political opinions in the new Union of South Africa. In the Cape, they could influence the African vote.

Editors and newspaper audiences understood that their skin colour was the basis of colonial discrimination but their sense of being 'black', being the *Bancho* as Plaatje put it, was not a uniform grid of experience. The regional histories of empire in southern Africa were not the same. For instance, Natal had experienced a long and violent history of colonisation with considerable loss of life at the hands of the British. After the Bhambatha rebellion of 1906, British officials had banished the paramount chiefs, reduced the borders of their territory and reinforced their template of 'customary law' under their choice of chiefs.[94] In Bechuanaland on the other hand, hereditary chiefs like Silas Molema made a clear distinction between Britain and settler governments. They embraced the former and rejected the latter. Sidney Shippard had secured for them terms of autonomy that guaranteed them control over their own territories and governance. Barolong along the Molopo had almost no experience of the colonial imposition of 'customary law' in their reserves. Hence, educated black people of 'progress' did not all want the same thing, or conceive of an identical future, because their colonial histories were not uniform. Their newspapers allowed their different blocs of interest to make themselves heard.

This variegated colonial experience was the background to the characteristics of early-twentieth-century politics among black educated classes in the territory becoming the Union of South Africa. Not only did they understand that the effects and experience of colonial rule on their territories was not uniform, they also recognised and protected the very regional and other differences that their newspapers represented, or at least the newspapers some of them still aspired to have. Their political strategy was to assemble a platform of cooperation where they could together bolster support for one another's various and particular struggles. Their aim was to work together so that each regional block could achieve its own ends. Their conceptions of both race and government in a colonial setting made ample room for this regional pluralism. They aimed to achieve each their region's own ideal of 'progress', fair processes of representation in the Union government and crucially, the right to land.

It was not an easy negotiation. Although there were many overlaps in their thinking, there were also strong differences in the separate visions they were developing for their regional locations. There was conflict and a great deal of falling out, but they continued to work together in and outside the assembly of cooperation that they named the South African Native National Congress

(SANNC). The Congress represented both support for particular interests, like the Barolong's struggle to retain the independence of their territories from the Union government's jurisdiction, and also collective mobilisation around issues that affected them all. In fact, the word 'national' was yet to refer only to the people within the boundaries of the Union – everybody came, including the Swazi and Basutoland territories and representations from the chiefdoms of the Bechuanaland Protectorate. Congress was the place to represent and thereby confirm and gain recognition for peculiar, often chiefly, regional interests and identities.

This pluralism is the backdrop to Plaatje's career as a man of Congress, a newspaperman and a writer of various genres. His writing took its tone from experiences and ideas that were precipitating a 'black' consciousness as his politics similarly expressed the joint struggle to defend black peoples' property and political rights. However, his sense of vocation also germinated along the points of departure from this feeling of sameness or 'blackness' that he and many others had embraced and yet were still grappling with, still attempting to settle into, especially where the frontier remained open. Union found Bechuanaland still 'mixed' and its reserves not quite conquered. Plaatje's regional constituency was in that manner unique. Often his frustration was that while the people of Bechuanaland held this unique and privileged opportunity in the configuration of empire, they did very little to maintain their position or mature into the fullest expression of their unique *morafe*. He expected the people of his homeland, the people his newspapers referred to as 'Bechuana', to support the work he intended for their benefit. His sacrifice for their newspaper – debt, effort, time away from his family – was for them. His chief role in Congress was to protect their particular interests. As a writer, he worked to establish their cultural and literary prestige. In all these ways he aimed to amplify their reputation. Often he saddled himself with other work just to get by and feed his family. Nonetheless, his vocation was of a writer. For the sake of that craft, he would in any case have dared to take the risks of penury.

The SANNC was not his first countrywide political platform. He and Silas Molema had become founding members of the South African Native Convention on 24 March 1910 in Bloemfontein.[95] Molema had accepted a nomination as vice-president, with John Dube as his counterpart. Dube had close attachments to the paramount house of Zululand in Natal. Dube and Plaatje struck an immediate rapport. Plaatje admired Booker T. Washington but Dube had travelled to America and had actually met the man. Dube and his wife had modelled their Ohlange Institute after Washington's

Tuskegee. Plaatje and Dube would meet likeminded Pixley ka Isaka Seme, under whose direction the earlier Convention became the SANNC on 8 January 1912, which also launched in Bloemfontein. The Congress was constituted of a House of Chiefs (elected from at least three provinces and all the Protectorates) and a larger house of ordinary members. Plaatje was its first General Secretary. Seme's main attachment in the countryside was to the Swazi queen. Plaatje had already written about Seme's education and entry to the bar in Johannesburg in *Tsala ea Becoana* and had published and honoured Seme's call to mute the divisions that separated black people by establishing a forum to unite them. Concerns with chieftaincy had made a trio of synergy out of Plaatje, Dube and Seme in the Congress.[96] They were committed to reviving 'progress' in its original home, the countryside, with all its complicated moral hierarchies. They did not think of their aspiration to 'progress' as playing 'catch up' to the rest of the world or as merely following in the template of the worlds abroad. The countryside was their landscape of virtue, their centre, their metropolis and their connection to the world.

By the end of its first year, *Tsala* already teetered towards financial collapse. Rev. Joel D. Goronyane pleaded with Silas Molema to pour 'your heart and soul in the work' and collect subscriptions 'as the only solution to relieve us from the present embarrassment'.[97] This was in the winter of 1911. The difficulty with sustaining Bechuana's newspapers, *Tsala* and *Koranta* before it, quite apart from the unnegotiable terms of independence that prevented Plaatje from accepting financial help from European businesses and individuals, and the difficulty of getting a sufficient number of paid-up subscriptions, was his disdain for patent medicaments. Newspapers like *Imvo* drew about 90 per cent of their advertising revenue from companies like Graham Remedies that sold a wide range of medicinal substances, including herbs and other compounds of 'traditional' medicine. Plaatje refused to advertise for these 'enterprising quack medicine canvassers' with the notable exception of Dr Williams Pink Pills, which used educated African personalities as the faces of their advertising columns.[98] He kept on going with threadbare resources and sinking in debt. The early months of 1911 were terrible for Plaatje.

His home remained Mafikeng where he held placement. There were many others like him in Kimberley, Cape Town, Durban, Johannesburg and other port and industrial cities. No matter how far they might travel because of work or any other circumstance, a home in the countryside was a desirable place of return. In Mafikeng, Plaatje rented a plot and he intended to keep paying his 'house rent' from Kimberley. If he had built the house on the plot himself, he would have already spent considerable money on the house, its surrounds and farm infrastructure, just as many European settlers were doing on the lands they leased. He owned stock, which needed water and may have made some investment in boreholes and so on. His most distressing concern was not keeping up with rent payments and losing his placement. It seems he had let the property to his brother Monnapula Plaatje in his absence and the rent was due to Joshua Molema, who had taken up a sizeable loan to help Plaatje start up working on *Tsala*, but the rent was not forthcoming from Monnapula.[99] Joshua had received summons and was jolting in panic.

Plaatje's strategy was to work hard and earn something to throw into the debts and collect from his own debtors, the chief Gaboutloeloe and his own brother Monnapula, who both owed subscriptions for *Koranta* for four months.[100] He also took up additional work writing freelance articles for the *Pretoria News*.[101] 'I work day and night just to have something at the end of every month to pay up these things.'[102] He was also selling insurance.[103] Someone else, one Rosenberg, owed him money for a 'bakkies pump'. This too could go to Joshua Molema if Rosenberg paid up. His other debtor in Mafikeng was the Reverend George Rolland, the Wesleyan Church superintendent recently arrived in Mafikeng, who was letting either Plaatje's house or fields. If all the monies from these debtors could go on to Joshua Molema, he would hopefully hold the lawyers with their summons at bay. In the meantime, he had to let Joshua Molema sell four head of his cattle. He wrote to Silas Molema and asked him to do the rounds and collect, and to calm his brother, Joshua, down. For weeks, Plaatje heard nothing from Silas Molema. He kept writing him letters of alarm.

> I am still writing with a saddened heart because I do not know anything (A) about the four cattle that Chief Joshua took. (B) about the money for rent from ministers. (C) about money for newspapers from Mr Gaboutloeloe. (D) Promissory note for the pump …That is why I am troubling you like this. Please be patient with me. Those four 'incomes' are the ones we are depending on but now that you are away from us, I thought I would hear from you but you are so quiet. Monnapula has written to tell me that Rev. Rolland hasn't got my money. I expected to hear about all this from you because you are the people who have to find the money and ask Teacher Sampson (Steward) because the money is urgently needed.[104]

He was getting out of debt, he wrote, but in 'thin measures', a tiny amount at a time though he was confident that 'by the middle of the year I will be free'.

If only Joshua Molema would 'carry the burden of my cross with patience, I will work for him'. Joshua Molema was threatening to impound more stock but the cattle he was referring to were not Plaatje's own. They belonged to a relation, a widow on his father's side of the family. If he lost the cattle, he would face the accusation that he had 'swallowed the cattle', that 'he had killed my aunt' and he would 'be taken by [the lawyer] De Kock, and my sun would have set'.[105] The ground would open under his feet. The report would go to the church, who would instruct De Kock to sue, which would begin the immediate unravelling of the web of personal trust and monies that kept *Tsala* afloat.

In the meantime, he pressed on. He was hopeful and committed to the course of *Tsala ea Becoana*. He trusted the yield of his own unrelenting labour. *Tsala* still had some committed readers who recognised it as the sign of the *morafe*'s proper moral orientation and its expression. For these readers, a *morafe* was only as strong as it appeared in its vernacular newspaper. Piet Fomatsohle in Mafikeng criticised young readers' contribution to the newspaper because their letters and inserts were about sport and concerts and not about the 'progress of the *morafe*'.[106] He urged them towards industrial works, including the manufacture of wagons, carpentry and shoemaking. He tried to impress upon them their responsibility to sustain *Tsala* as paying subscribers and, as important, to recognise and come to a knowledge of themselves as a *morafe* through it:

> Our friends, Barolong, Batlhaping, Bakoena, Bakgatla, Batlokoa, Balete, Bahurutse, Bamangoato, pay attention to keep your paper *Tsala ea Becoana*. Know that when it is said *Tsala ea Becoana*, it is meant the peoples (*dichaba*) whose names I have written; keep your paper so that it does not die. Welcome it and pay for it as it is printed with money and show other *merafe* that yes, you are paying it attention.[107]

One E. Tshongwana was alarmed by the poor quality of the Education Department's matriculation paper for Sechuana. He identified himself as a Mpondo in Alice in the Eastern Cape. 'Bechuana ought to be ashamed of themselves', Plaatje responded, 'because the language is theirs and the paper is theirs, but it is the Nguni-speakers who say something'.[108] He added that 'we do not know when Bechuana will stir from their great sleep'. The tone was desperate. The volume of letters to the editor was a great deal smaller than that of *Koranta*, hence readers like Fomatsohle worried that there were no longer many devotees to the newspaper as a revelation of the *morafe*'s sign and moral universe.

Plaatje kept at it relentlessly, worked hard, travelled away from his family to raise funds and to represent the chieftaincy in all the forums of Congress, especially at the meetings with officials of the Union government in Cape Town. This is where he would present the Barolong's case, maintaining that the rights and guarantees they had negotiated with Britain remained in place despite Unification. Barolong chiefs made no provision for his travel, let alone a basic stipend. In April 1912, after Congress sent its first deputation to the Minister of Native Affairs, John Dube recognised Plaatje as Chief Lekoko's 'special representative' in the Congress and parted with £21 to cover Plaatje's costs of travel.[109] (Dube later claimed the money from Barolong chiefs in Mafikeng.)

Plaatje could not sustain the newspaper into the second half of 1912. He had to seek other partnerships to start up another similar venture. The Nguni-speaking educated classes of various urban districts, especially in Kimberley, collected money for the Bechuana to purchase a printing machine in August 1912.[110] The newspaper he was starting up was to be called *Tsala ea Batho*, the Friend of the People. The deal almost fell through because Pixley Seme attempted to persuade Elka Cele, an executive member of Congress, not to lend Plaatje the money. Plaatje attributed Seme's action to a hostile *'Setebele'* spirit, an undesirable disposition like *Sekhoa* that likewise opposed personhood or *botho*.[111] However, John Dube, paradoxically another of the 'Matabele' helped him to keep the arrangement, borrow the money and buy the machinery. It was not always easy to hold hands across the divides of regional colonial histories and the different, sometimes contradictory, visions they inspired.

Seme probably had a different paper in mind, particularly his own *Abantu-Batho* that he was starting up, which he intended as a mouthpiece of the black 'races' as opposed to vernacular newspapers with regional interests. *Tsala ea Batho* was going to be only in 'Serolong, Sepedi and English'.[112] Plaatje described it as a 'Union between the Barolong and Bapedi people'.[113] Seme may have objected to a newspaper whose starting capital came from an Nguni-speaker and yet the editor could not conceive of an Nguni language as a third vernacular in the newspaper. Were 'the Matabele' only good enough for money and not for the textual assembly where the vernaculars of Sechuana and related dialects met? On the one hand, Jabavu and Dube wanted to lend a hand to the Bechuana to stand on their own, independently, as a *morafe* of reputation through their own newspaper. Also, Seme perhaps thought vernacular newspapers were perpetuating a moral outlook that maintained regional differences that divided a *morafe* that he, Seme, understood simply as *Batho*. This is not to say that Seme himself was not concerned with the reputation of his own regional centre in the countryside. He aimed to use the resources of the Swazi queen to finance *Abantu-Batho*, a paper that would be like a mouthpiece of Congress and accommodate as many vernaculars as possible. *Abantu-Batho* would bolster the Swazi's moral reputation, seeing their queen had yielded all her capacity to make all black peoples a demographic of moral reputation, one people with their own newspaper.

Clearly, there was no consensus on how the 'moreness' of personhood should operate between the representatives of the countryside's regional interests. Land shortages were making these contestations more urgent. The routine processes of making the *morafe* on the land were continuing through the various moral repertoires of incorporation and exclusion. From the late nineteenth century, conquest and land shortage were an incentive for many people's lobbies that the colonial government recognise them as a *morafe*. A newspaper that represented the literary vernacular of such a *morafe* would help such a claim. A literary vernacular coalesced various settlements and populations by standardising their related dialects, whilst a newspaper publication in this vernacular language confirmed that there was indeed such a *morafe*. Hence, the politics of newspaper publishing also emerged from these pressures. The sense of 'Africanism' or 'pan-Africanism' did not, and could not, do away with regional and vernacular identities. It muted them in some contexts, whilst in others, especially contestations on the land, these localised feelings of place, chieftaincy and language flared up.

The word 'Matebele' emerged during the early nineteenth century as a colloquial reference to the Ndebele armies that were flattening the countryside in warfare as they moved north. They had crushed the people who were already known as Barolong and had forced Silas Molema's father, Isaac, to flee south to Thaba Nchu. The prefix 'Ma' indicated to the native speakers that these were not people but entities without moral virtue – displacing thousands of people, razing their fields, swallowing up the land like an insatiable cannibal. The memory of the past continued in living memory. It raised suspicions when people worked together across those historical divides. Nevertheless, Plaatje used the word casually most of the time. The Matebele were the word he used for the Nguni-speakers, many of whom belonged in his intimate circle. He had, for instance, married one. Plaatje had an exceptional capacity to connect with people across very deep divides. He also understood that others were not like him. He had to resist pressure from his family when he married Elizabeth M'belle. He could also anticipate that these prejudices could threaten a newspaper venture.

Family/Placement

It was not mainly that prejudice festered from the injuries of the past, but he feared that chiefs would find it unthinkable to bring the 'Matebele' into the realm of sacred things like a newspaper, just as a family would oppose a marriage that compromised their moral standing. The *Bancho* had its own convoluted pecking order according to everyday stereotypes and competition for reputation.

There were concerts of fundraising and celebration planned for the day the first issue of *Tsala ea Batho* would come out. They were to be held in Krugersdorp, Nancefield, Johannesburg, Pretoria, Klerksdorp and Kimberley on the day. The purpose of the concerts was to 'find money as a working capital to pay the workers for a start' and to 'impress upon the people through these concerts to support their combined newspaper'.[114] Plaatje urged Molema to encourage Chief Lekoko that

> ... while these concerts are organised that Barolong should not be left behind. That is why I suggested to them that they should do something for themselves because it is said that God helps those who help themselves. Please help me by encouraging the chief to do something even if it is a smaller concert so that it will be read that Mafikeng also took part. It must not appear that the chief of Barolong does not like unity...[115]

In the meantime, he had to travel to the Transvaal to procure the machinery.[116] He put the machinery on the train but could not afford to pay for it, then travelled further down to Thaba Nchu in the hope of finding money, only to find that there was nobody to help. Then he put himself on the train with no money to pay, even for his own fare, in the hope that his wife would pay when he arrived. He felt let down by the Barolong who so far, he felt, had not lifted a finger to help him.

> There are many things that disappoint me. What tore my heart was when sympathetic Matebele bought us the machinery for £200 and I realised that the Becoana are unable to collect even small monies and start their own newspaper. Even the scheme for concerts was arranged by Mr Msimang. People are aiding us! It makes one sometimes feel that there is no good in all this striving for the rights of the Becoana people.[117]

He had been absent from home for three months. 'I have heard very little from home and it is so hard to go and arrive there after three months without a penny. It would not be so shameful if the train money had been paid for'.[118]

He kept at his toil, as he described to Silas Molema. He was 'working double shift – day and night.'[119] There was a lot of trouble with the business. He begged Molema to plead with Chief Lekoko to invest some of the capital from the chieftaincy's own coffers into *Tsala*. If Lekoko would lend him some money, he would consider him a shareholder.[120]

The year was approaching an end. Things were getting more desperate. He pleaded for a loan of £100 from Barolong.[121] 'I don't know why Becoana do not care for the things that uplift the *morafe*'.[122] Had they helped *Koranta*, he thought, things would have worked out very differently. At the very least, they could have purchased the machinery from Minchin.[123] He started 1913 in complete despair. 'Please plead with him for me', he continued to press Silas Molema to speak to Lekoko, otherwise his debts would ruin *Tsala*, 'a work of such promise'.[124] After all, this same chief was sending Plaatje, Silas and Sebopioa Molema to Cape Town to meet with the authorities about the dispute over the government's jurisdiction in the reserve. 'We will try everything we can for the Barolong'.[125] Four months into the year and still no luck and not a word from the Barolong paramount chief. Plaatje kept writing to Molema. 'I am begging you to please ask Chief Lekoko to hurry up!'[126] He was hard pressed. 'Please plead with him for me, Sir.' The debt was too deep, too wide to be covered by his exertions. He kicked hard and pushed forward to stay afloat but he also had a family in Kimberley to maintain. His family then included Silas Molema's children, Modiri and Harriet Molema, who were staying in his home. After all, this is what it also meant to be a man, to prove one's free capacity to care for others.

VII

In 1910 the firm of attorneys, De Kock and De Kock, asked the former Resident Magistrate and Civil Commissioner of Mafeking, Graham Green, to explain why he had had jurisdiction to adjudicate a certain dispute in the Molopo Reserve seeing that six years ago when he had heard the case, as the Barolong chiefs claimed, the reserves of former British Bechuanaland were not, and never came, under the Cape government's jurisdiction.[127] In that particular case, the paramount Barolong chiefs, Badirile Montsioa of the Ratshidi Barolong of the Molopo Reserve and Phoi of the Ratlou Barolong of the neighbouring Setlagodi Reserve, had each claimed to have jurisdiction over a certain population of the Molopo Reserve. Green had ruled in favour of Badirile Montsioa. How Green had had jurisdiction to rule in that dispute mattered in the present 'boundary dispute' between Barolong chiefs in the Molopo Reserve and the Divisional Council of Mafeking. Chiefs were still maintaining their position that the Divisional Council of Mafeking, the Cape government and the soon-to-be established Union government, had no authority to intervene in their reserve. The Divisional Council argued that if the Cape government had never obtained jurisdiction to intervene in the Molopo Reserve, then Green would not have had the authority to adjudicate a dispute between chiefs in the reserve. Instead, the Barolong would have settled the matter in their own Kgotla. Green explained that his authority to adjudicate the matter had stemmed from the Native Locations Act of 1884.

> I contend that under the Regulations Promulgated under the provisions of the 29th section of Act No 37 of 1884 [The Native Locations Act of 1884], I had power to locate the people in any part of the Native Reserve that I consider most beneficial for the whole. I take it that under Section 7 of the Native Locations Act No 37. of 1884, the Natives Reserves in Bechuanaland fell under the Act at the time of Annexation … except where the Location Act clashed with any of the provisions of Bechuanaland Proclamations then in force… The Government were constantly endeavouring to enforce the Location Act Regulations, and did to a great extent, and the people accepted them, as also they did the special Hut Tax imposed under Section 16 Act 33 of 1892, which was only applicable to locations and Crown Lands and was practically a part of the Act of 1884.[128]

The legitimacy of the government's present claim that it had always had jurisdiction in the reserve depended on such testimony. Any previous case where Barolong chiefs had accepted any court ruling or colonial law under the Cape government after 1895 proved the reserve was actually already a 'location' and therefore the property of the government. Badirile Montsioa's successor, the regent Lekoko Montsioa, understood that involving colonial officials, especially one as adversarial as the new Resident Magistrate, E.C. Welsh, in the disputes between Barolong chiefs gave the government ammunition in the 'boundary dispute' against the Union government. Therefore, when a similar dispute over land emerged between him and men claiming to represent the paramount chief of the Rapulana Barolong, Lekoko determined not to breathe a word to the colonial authorities about the turbulence that was brewing in his reserve at Rietfontein. He feared he would risk excavating an archive of his predecessor's unsuspecting submission to the Cape government that would now compromise his present case against the Union government in the Supreme Court of Appeal in Cape Town.

Rietfontein was on the eastern boundary of the Molopo Reserve. Its name was also Lotlhokane, although people commonly referred to it as Rietfontein. This settlement, at the eastern edge of the reserve, adjoined the Transvaal Province. A fence separated the two provinces of the Cape and Transvaal. According to Z.K. Matthew's account in 1945:

> About 1874, some of the Rapulana crossed the Transvaal boundary and moved over into Tshidi territory, to Lotlhakane (Rietfontein) in the Cape, where they settled, it is said, with the permission of Chief Montshiwa [Montsioa], who was then at Sehuba, not far from Lotlhakane. For a few years the Rapulana and the Tshidi lived together in peace in this land of their forefathers, but about 1880 Montshiwa became dissatisfied with the attitude of the Rapulana who apparently refused to acknowledge that they were subject to his jurisdiction, although they lived within what he regarded as his territory. Montshiwa accordingly made an attack on the Rapulana and drove them out of Lotlhakane across the Transvaal boundary to Polfontein where the main body of the Rapulana had remained. At Polfontein a counter-attack was organised. With the help of the Ratlou under Moshwete and some European freebooters the Rapulana returned to attack Montshiwa and eventually they succeeded in dislodging him from Dithakong (Sehuba). Hard pressed, he withdrew to Mafikeng... Eventually in 1882 the parties agreed to a settlement of the dispute. Under this settlement Montshiwa lost to the Transvaal much territory which he had formerly claimed as his own. The land obtained by the Whites under this treaty was named Goshen.[129]

Now in 1910, as far as the Ratshidi nobility was concerned, Rietfontein was again theirs and the Rapulana resided there as recipients of their placement. They reasoned that the land belonged to them because they, the Ratshidi, were earlier colonisers of the land and therefore its chiefs, but also because the Land Commission of 1886 had allocated Montsioa territorial jurisdiction across the entire Molopo Reserve, which included Rietfontein. The Rapulana believed, on the contrary, that the land belonged to the Rapulana chief, Machabi, and was theirs as spoil because they had won the war against Montsioa in 1882. Moreover, as far as the Rapulana were concerned, although it was in the Molopo Reserve, Rietfontein was an independent domain whose autonomy had received unambiguous confirmation from a ruling by the former Resident Magistrate and Civil Commissioner of the Mafeking District, C.G.H. Bell, in 1898. The instigator at Rietfontein was a man called Seiso Modise.

Rietfontein was only one in a cluster of boundary disputes between Barolong chiefs in the 1910s, but the timing and the strategies that the Rapulana chiefs pursued threatened to jeopardise the legal approach the Ratshidi were relying on to defend the autonomy of the Molopo Reserve from the Union government. The Rapulana were basing their claim on a court ruling made by a Cape official in the reserve after former British Bechuanaland had become part of the Cape Colony. Nevertheless, Solomon Plaatje's feeling was that chiefs had friends in the Native Affairs Department who were of a very different political timber from the new Resident Magistrate, Welsh, who 'looked down on Barolong'.[130] He was right, for the most part. Edward Dower, the first Secretary of the Native Affairs in the Union government, was ready to negotiate up to a point and set himself to steer the course of engagement away from litigation by engaging personally with Barolong chiefs.

Dower received a petition from chiefs in January 1911, which was a complaint that the cost of legal representation was very high and hindered Africans from accessing the courts. Since Badirile Montsioa had filed an appeal in the Appellate Division of the Supreme Court after the lower court had ruled against him, nothing had happened. It was now more than six months, and the case was still not yet on the roll. Dower construed that litigation was not a route the chieftaincy could afford to pursue easily. He wrote to Badirile Montsioa that 'the fault lies with the Natives themselves who are fond of litigation and often place themselves in the hands of legal practitioners' rather than rely on sympathetic colonial officials to resolve problems.[131] The petition raised numerous other concerns, including pass laws, the fact that Africans could not purchase land in the Orange Free State, and the 'lack of attention and civility on the part of Railway officers'.

Dower was determined to ensure that the Union government have full jurisdiction to intervene in the Molopo and other reserves and indeed had plans of his own for the reserves. Only he wanted to handle the matter his way, without giving in to the Northerners' pressure to act quickly and to do so in their way. Early in May, 1911 Daniel Wessels, a parliamentary representative for Bechuanaland districts in the House of Assembly, raised a question in the House whether the Minister of Native Affairs would commit to 'abolish or restrain the jurisdiction of native chiefs in Bechuanaland, and to establish the reserve as part of a District Council'.[132] Wessels also pressed the Minister of Native Affairs, Henry Burton, to discuss 'abolishing the conditions preventing the Union government exercising the right of alienating any portion of the Native Reserve in Bechuanaland' with the imperial government (during his official visit to England). Northerners were pushing the government to pass whatever legislation was necessary to give it immediate jurisdiction to intervene in the reserves of Bechuanaland. On 8 May 1911, the *Mafeking Mail* reported that in response to Wessels the minister had implied 'taking away the power of the Bechuana chiefs' as an option.[133]

The newspaper report plunged the chiefs in the Molopo Reserve into panic. They wrote to W.P. Schreiner, former Cape Prime Minister and well-known defender of the Cape's liberal tradition, seeking his advice.[134] They reminded Schreiner of his invitation to them that 'if [there is ever] any question we did not understand re government action, that we were to communicate with you at once.' They asked Schreiner whether it would be prudent to send a petition directly to the imperial government 'so that the Union government would not put away the conditions, which exist between us re our land and the imperial government'. They also implored Schreiner to 'write to us on this matter at once, because our hearts are very sore on it ... there is danger of our imperial Father being asked to break confidence with us'.[135] Schreiner advised that they should rather send a petition to the Native Affairs Department. Reverends Amos Burnett and George Weavind, two European missionaries, delivered the petition on 5 June 1911.[136]

The scribe was Sebopioa Molema but Plaatje had had to 'make a flying trip' from Kimberley to Mafikeng to offer advice and add his eloquence to the document.[137] The new regent, Lekoko Montsioa, could read and write but he had little or no proficiency in English. This time, Dower's reply was in hand-written Sechuana, in contrast to the chieftaincy's own English typescript.[138] Dower outlined his vision to transform the reserve into a robust chiefly jurisdiction. He suggested that Lekoko need not fear because rather than attenuating his independent chiefly power, the Union government only sought to strengthen its foundations by cutting chieftaincy loose from the subversions of European settlement, jurisprudence and institutions, so that what was left was pure *Sechuana* – 'tradition' proper. Dower assured Lekoko that 'nothing would be done that can break the agreement between the government and Barolong'. The reserve could continue as per the negotiated settlement beyond the jurisdiction of a Divisional Council. All that the government intended was a 'law' that would apply not only to Mafikeng but to other parts of Bechuanaland too. This law would rectify the 'confusion' about the relationship between reserves and Divisional Councils. All chiefs had to do was recognise and accept the powers of the Union government to implement such a law in the reserve.

> There are parts of Bechuanaland where land was allocated to *Bancho* prior to Annexation. The status (*boemo*) of blacks (*Bancho*) in these areas has to be rectified by law, for which the government requires the cooperation of chiefs. The status of whites and traders that have been given a place in the reserve is not fully satisfactory and some of them want matters to be put right with regard to their houses and their [infrastructural] improvements (*go aga ga bone*). Their status must be properly discussed and settled, so that there are no people in the *morafe* that are disadvantaged, and also that the white clerics and traders can acquire suitable conditions [of residence].[139]

Without such a law, he warned, 'there can only be a continuation of the difficulties of courts and legal expenses.' The law would ensure that Divisional Councils stay out of chiefly jurisdictions as the reserves would be strictly spheres of 'tradition'.

The law would also make sure that the judicial system in these reserves is rational and fair and therefore on par with the European system. This law would establish a centralisation of chiefly powers under one paramount Kgotla, rather than the dispersed rung of chiefs and senior men trying cases, which Dower argued only bred confusion. 'Would Barolong', he asked, 'not be acting wisely if they found a way through which the Paramount's court can be formally recognised, [like the Resident Magistrate's court] so that it can settle local disputes?' In such a setting, the law would make provision for the paramount Kgotla to operate through the 'customs of *Sechuana*' (*mekhwa ea Bechuana*), but it would have to be the only court that presided over disputes and therefore also handled placement on the land in the reserve. There was no place for 'whites' in these territories. In fact, Dower was suggesting that whites' placement in the reserves was what was causing the ongoing dispute with the Mafeking Divisional Council in the first place. These settlers did not belong in a domain of tradition but required a different judicial and property dispensation, more so given the houses and other developments they were putting up in the reserves. If there were no such residents in the reserves, then the reach of the Council into the reserves would be unnecessary.

There was another reason why Dower was keen to negotiate. He was taking seriously advice that the Native Affairs Department had received from its legal counsel that a strategy by the government to bring the matter to trial came 'with the possibility of losing it'.[140] This notwithstanding, the Minister of Justice, General Barry Hertzog, whose department was responsible for the defence, insisted that the Native Affairs Department should place the case on the roll. However, Herzog was not really pressing for a court appearance. He was placing pressure on Burton's department to act swiftly and find a solution. If Burton did not act and the Barolong brought the case to court and won, the Union government would have egg on its face. The so-called 'liberals', the 'friends of the natives', would suffer a humiliation that would compromise the fragile coalitions with conservatives like Hertzog himself. In October 1911, Burton was certain that Lekoko would compromise and that he 'appears to be doing his best to carry out his duties in harmony with the Government' hence 'it does not appear desirable to stir up feeling in the Reserve'.[141] Moreover, Burton was of the opinion that 'the suit has apparently been abandoned by the Natives'. It was now well over a year and half and the Barolong chiefs had still not brought the matter to trial.

Hertzog wanted the government to resolve the matter decisively. At the end of that month, Hertzog asked Burton to confirm whether the course to avoid court action was 'a matter of policy' by the Native Administration Department.[142] Burton maintained the position that to let sleeping dogs lie was politically expedient because 'the Natives in the Reserve are settling down under the new Chief Lekoko' and hence 'it is desirable to avoid as far as possible any action which may have the effect of reviving the dispute'.[143] 'It is advisable', Hertzog responded, 'to have this case removed from the roll of pending cases as not to have it hanging over the Government's head indefinitely' and 'absolution be asked for with costs'. Only thereafter would his department consider waiving its claim to costs against Chief Lekoko as per the ruling of the lower court against the chief.[144] The two ministers met for a verbal interview and Hertzog agreed to let the matter stand in abeyance but only 'until the end of the financial year, namely 31 March next'.[145]

Dower travelled to Mafikeng on 12 January 1912 to gather information on landholding in the reserve.[146] He met with Chief Lekoko and instructed him to 'furnish a list of all the squatters on the Molopo Reserve with full details and particulars of leases or other conditions or agreements under which they are residing thereon'.[147] Lekoko did nothing. On 24 January 1912, Dower addressed a circular letter to all magistrates and commissioners in the Transvaal and the Orange Free State asking for comments on introducing a squatter's bill in the reserves.[148] He then forwarded a draft of a new policy to Mafikeng in March 1912.[149] According to this new 'law', the paramount chief's court was the only court that the government would recognise in the reserve, operating strictly under 'customary law'. Nevertheless, there were protocols that regulated how the paramount chief imposed fines in his Kgotla and that provided routes of appeal to a Native Court under the jurisdiction of a Native Commissioner – which was the same as a Resident Magistrate in Bechuanaland. The Native Commissioner could review the judgements of this paramount Kgotla. However, the Kgotla only had jurisdiction over civil cases and even then only if the fine was below a certain threshold and over minor criminal cases. Serious offences like rape, culpable homicide and witchcraft were under the jurisdiction of the Native Commissioner's court, which also operated under customary law like its *Sechuana* counterpart in the reserve.

This was the policy of 'native administration' and it was not going to augment the authority of the paramount chief. Instead, the Kgotla of the paramount chief would be secondary to the court of a Native Commissioner. Chiefs were furious that they would preside over cases of significantly inferior status and dismayed that there were routes of appeal beyond the paramount Kgotla. They were even more enraged that, apart from the paramount chief, they would lose their powers altogether. The centralisation of chiefly power to one Kgotla left chiefs like Molema out in the cold. It shed chiefs from the institutions of placement that facilitated how they presided over cases. It dispossessed them of the swathes of land they controlled. Moreover, because there already existed routes of appeal to the rulings of the local Resident Magistrate in Mafeking, higher Native Courts beyond the Mafeking District would hear the appeals against the paramount Kgotla, as well as the appeals to all the cases over which the Kgotla no longer had to adjudicate. The chiefs' reply pointed out that

> the Mafeking District is bounded on the South by the Vryburg District, on the East by the Lichtenburg District of the Transvaal Province and on the North by the Bechuanaland Protectorate. Leaving the Bechuanaland Protectorate out of consideration as not within the Union, the Council protests against the policy of allowing cases to be tried outside their own District at, possibly, considerable expenses to the litigants and by a magistrate to whom the Barolong laws and custom are, in all probability completely unknown. The Council further submit that should there be a right of Appeal in cases involving more than a certain amount from the Magistrate to a Higher Court of Appeal in all cases even when they exceed the jurisdiction of the Magistrate in his own Court would not be fair to the Barolong people.[150]

In effect, 'native administration' meant that a hierarchy of Native Commissioners in and beyond Bechuanaland would have jurisdiction in every reserve of Bechuanaland. The whole bureaucracy of the colonial government would practically intervene directly even in the smallest decisions of the paramount Kgotla.

It was a blow, but chiefs had long seen the writing on the wall. They were almost prepared as they had been raising money to bring the appeal to trial. A month before, chiefs had called a large public gathering where they instructed every household in the reserve to contribute towards the cost of litigation against Dog Tax, although this is not how they put it to Welsh.[151] They said they were handling the 'large indebtedness' incurred by the chieftaincy during Badirile Montsioa's tenure. In the words of the paramount chief, 'the nation unanimously agreed that each and every member of the Barolong Nation should willingly contribute an ox or cow'. There was, not surprisingly, resistance at Rietfontein where chiefs' messengers seized 'any ox or cow (or equivalent thereto) for the purpose aforesaid'. In fact the only reason Lekoko Montsioa was informing Welsh was because he anticipated that the Rietfontein instigators would use the seizures as evidence against the Ratshidi in the ensuing dispute, thereby involving the colonial government in a matter that Lekoko intended to resolve himself. The seizures, he explained to Welsh, were 'our law and custom', only that the 'former residents of Rietfontein' were 'causing trouble to my messengers'.[152]

Nevertheless, the colonial government by then already knew about the tensions at Rietfontein. The Rapulana chiefs' strategy was to involve the government in the dispute where and when such involvement suited their claim. By the beginning of January 1912, Sebopioa Molema had already communicated to the Native Affairs Department, through the attorney Spencer Minchin, that only Lekoko Montsioa had the independent jurisdiction to govern and intervene in the allocation of land at Rietfontein.[153] At the beginning of 1912, the Native Affairs Department had received complaints that Paul Montsioa was evicting certain householders off the land at Rietfontein. In the meantime, the Native Affairs Department was still trying to steer Lekoko away from pushing ahead with the litigation in the Supreme Court of Appeal. Dower was hopeful that chiefs would be amenable to the laws of 'native administration' that he was designing and besides, he was sure they would not afford to take their objections to the highest court of the land. In response to Lekoko's insistence that he, as paramount chief, had autonomy and power to act in the conflict at Rietfontein, Dower did not contest his claim of independent jurisdiction in the Molopo Reserve but rather placed emphasis on its limits.[154] '[T]he Government,' Dower wrote, 'wishes him to understand that it does not recognise any rights as being vested in him under section thirty-one of British Bechuanaland Proclamation No. 2 of 1885 to despoil law-abiding Natives residents on the Native Reserves in British Bechuanaland.'[155] He referred to the ruling by C.G.H. Bell in 1898 that upheld the Rapulana's claim to Rietfontein. The matter, as far as Dower was concerned, would end there. Lekoko said and did nothing while Paul Montsioa's men in Rietfonten did not yield the lands they had appropriated.

Plaatje travelled to Cape Town in April 1912 as a member of the first deputation of the SANNC to meet with various ministers. According to the President of Congress, John Dube, Plaatje had 'made a good stand on behalf of the maintenance of the Bechuanaland chieftainship' in Mafikeng and especially the 'combatting of location laws'.[156] In April 1912, the chieftaincy sent another petition to the Resident Magistrate following yet another attempt by the Divisional Council of Mafeking to impose Dog Tax on the reserve. A tax collector 'had already entered upon his duties'.[157] Welsh forwarded the petition to the Native Affairs Department. A few days later, on 1 May 1912, police officers arrived in the reserve visiting cattle-posts and counting stock.[158] A week later Silas and Sebopioa Molema travelled with Plaatje and Paul Montsioa 'to discuss a matter about collection of Dog Tax and other matters in the Native Reserve' with cabinet ministers.[159] Following this meeting, Dower again pressed Lekoko for a list of all the whites in the reserve, along with full details of their leases. This time Lekoko complied but added the important detail that 'in every such agreement, no one has the right to remove any improvements he shall have made on such gardens'.[160] Chiefs were bracing themselves for the worst.

After a cabinet reshuffle in June of 1912, Burton relinquished his portfolio and became the Minister of Railways and Harbours. Hertzog became the new Minister of Native Affairs.[161] The chieftaincy sent another petition to the Native Affairs Department in July of 1912.[162] On 12 August 1912 Welsh confirmed that all 'rents accruing from stands occupied by traders and others' in the Bechuanaland reserves 'must be paid into Revenue', which meant they could no longer be pocketed by chiefly landlords.[163] The government denied the chiefs' plea that the rents on their lands go into the chieftaincy's coffers. The following day, on 13 August 1912, the Secretary for Justice, J. Roos, advised the Divisional Council of Mafeking that as far as the appeal was concerned, 'the Government has decided not to press for judgement against the plaintiff ... and to pay its own costs if the plaintiff withdraws the case'. The government was confident that this was the close of the matter.

This would have been the end of the government's intervention in the reserve if chiefly landlords had given up the fight, which they did not. On 23

September 1912 the chieftaincy requested W.P. Schreiner to represent it in the appeal case 'given the good work you have done for natives'.[164] Hence, the Justice Department was stunned by receipt of fresh summons on 7 January 1913 when it had been certain the government had pegged its designs on the reserve permanently. The new Secretary for Justice, Charles Pienaar, wrote a 'very urgent' note to the Native Affairs Department, requesting it to 'return ... all the papers and blue books relating to the case which were sent to you ... 31 October 1911'. 'The case having now resumed,' he continued, 'these papers are urgently required.' The parties were to appear before the Supreme Court on 29 January 1913.[165]

The following month tensions again flared up at Rietfontein. The Ratshidi had still not surrendered the lands they had appropriated from the Rapulana nine months before. Seiso Modise wanted these properties back because in his account, they were placements from George Motuba, a representative of the Rapulana paramount chief at Rietfontein and not Paul Montsioa. The new Acting Secretary of the Native Affairs Department, Edward Barrett, received the complaints and was as measured in his reply as his predecessor had been. He instructed Lekoko 'to deliver up possession of the lands in question' and 'not to disturb or interfere with George Motuba and the other Natives residing at Rietfontein as long as they conduct themselves in a lawful manner'.[166] The Department was not directly contesting Lekoko Marumoloa's claim that he had jurisdiction to act in Rietfontein. Rather it was directing him towards an interpretation of that power as limited, as no more than maintaining law and order. 'The claim of George Motuba to be recognised as chief', Barrett continued, 'cannot, however, be entertained'. Still, Lekoko did nothing. Immediately after drawing in the harvest in early summer, Paul Montsioa 'again started ploughing the lands which he held within the area'. When the Superintendent of Natives, H.J. Frost, called on his house, his family told him he was at the cattle posts.[167] The Ratshidi chiefs were ignoring the government even though the Department recognised them, and not the Rapulana, as holding jurisdiction in Rietfontein.

In November 1912, Henry Burton, now as Minister of Railways, opened a railway line in Mafikeng. The government had not issued the chieftaincy an invitation to attend the ceremony. Sebopioa Molema staged a coup at the event. *Tsala* reported that 'though their chief had not been officially notified, still as sensible people [chiefs] forced their way to the platform to greet the Hon. Minister, for they thought it their duty as humble members of the British Nation to show some signs of courtesy to a Cabinet Minister'.[168] The embarrassed officials, right there and then agreed Lekoko would have

Burton's audience at the courthouse the following Monday, which bought chiefs some time with a minister they still considered a 'friend' as the hearing of their case in the Supreme Court in Cape Town drew near. Afterwards, Sebopioa showed Burton around certain improvements in the stadt and read a speech that described how the railway line 'connects our small town with the gold-fields of Transvaal and the metropolis of the Union of South Africa.' He added that 'our little town' was turning into a 'Junction City', and 'the Mafeking market will be much improved'.[169] Another month later, Hertzog was no longer the Minister of Native Affairs. The Prime Minister, Louis Botha had effectively dismissed him from cabinet in December 1912. Hertzog's radicalism alarmed Botha, especially Hertzog's republicanism that questioned whether settlers loyal to Britain could also be loyal to the Union.[170] Jacobus W. Sauer, a liberal politician and another 'friend of the Natives' replaced him.

On 22 January 1913, Silas and Sebopioa Molema and Solomon Plaatje arrived in Cape Town at the residence of James Molebaloa to seek an attorney to work with Schreiner and attend the Supreme Court hearing.[171] At home in Mafikeng, Lekoko attended a meeting with Welsh to discuss the 'matter of the eviction of the whitish ones'. The word he used, '*bashoeunyana*', interestingly, would have included someone of Solomon Plaatje's complexion. Two days later, the discussion became official. On 24 January 1913, Sauer introduced a squatter's bill in the reserves. None of the 'whitish ones' could remain in the reserve without the government's permission. He also confirmed the system of a single paramount Kgotla that operated alongside a higher Native Court under a Native Commissioner, both of them adjudicating cases through customary law. Sauer had implemented the policy of 'native administration' in the reserve.

Sauer's was the third of three consecutive interventions in the Molopo Reserve by Ministers of Native Affairs Department. Burton gave the chieftaincy an early draft of the policy of 'native administration' and instructions to issue a list of the 'squatters' who held leases in the reserve. Hertzog instructed that all 'rents accruing from stands occupied by traders and others' in the reserve 'must be paid into Revenue' and refused to direct any of these monies to the chieftaincy's own coffers. Finally, Sauer had declared everyone whose complexion leaned to 'whiteness' as 'squatters', including those that might not have appeared on the list of 'squatters'. The consistent element across all three ministers' approaches was the intention to transform the Molopo Reserve into a place for 'Natives', people it was classifying officially as 'black' and to consider them to be living on the property of the

Union government, which was therefore free to decide on who could lawfully reside in these locations and on how they should be governed.

If the upcoming ruling of the Supreme Court of Appeal on 29 January 1913 upheld the lower court's judgment, then the government did not require an Act of parliament to intervene in the reserve. It had acquired its aims. If Sauer could make his 'squatter's bill' hold in the Molopo Reserve, then all the reserves of British Bechuanaland were similarly subject to the jurisdiction of the colonial government. The government would have jurisdiction to intervene in the reserves as a separate domain of property and political rights, a realm of 'tradition' or *Sechuana*. If the Union government was the supreme landlord of such Crown Lands, then it could lawfully enforce its rulings even on disputes such as the matter at Rietfontein. If Sauer's policy against 'squatting' held, then he would have won quietly and decisively without the trouble and politics of promulgating an Act of parliament. He would have established that the Union government had jurisdictions over these reserves as 'locations' exclusively for the settlement of a 'black' population.

Four days later, when Lekoko's deputation in Cape Town informed him that they had secured a meeting with some government officials, he urged them not to tell the government anything about the 'boundary' disputes at Rietfontein.

> … say nothing about the matter of Phitsane, of John Mosibi, and of Lotlhakane [Rietfontein]. Discuss only that you seek an attorney and ask what is really the prerogative (*thata*) of the chief over his people because the new laws truly have done away with the laws of the chief to rule his people so that if he gives a ruling they can erase the ruling of the person to whom they belong … This government has its ear to the ground so that when you speak of it, it may do you much harm. Today the laws that expel the whitish ones from here at home [stadt] and the farms and those with contracts was announced… I am alone here at home.[172]

He wrote to them again the next day to emphasise the need not to mention the boundary disputes. He knew that his deputation, which included Plaatje, still had confidence in the government, at least in those personalities with whom they had some rapport. Lekoko worried that the deputation might yield to the temptation to trust one or other official. He waited, alone and troubled, worried that the flare up at Rietfontein put any chance of victory in jeopardy. He forbade Silas Molema and the rest of the delegation from talking about it, even if the government itself brought it up.

I plead with you that when you meet with the Government, do not say anything about the matter of the Rapulana, or of Disana or Phitsane. The matter of Lotlhakane [Rietfontein] is for discussion here. You can only discuss the matter of the dogs.[173]

If the court did not rule in his favour, he understood, it would all be over. He would have absolutely no say at Rietfontein or anywhere else where his opponents were claiming territory. He would have no jurisdiction in the Molopo Reserve and would be at the mercy of the government. He would have to accept the diminution of his judicial powers and be the lowest judicial authority in a hierarchy of 'Native Courts' where white Native Commissioners would use laws of *Sechuana* to review his decisions on appeal. He would also have to accept Sauer's 'anti-squatting' policy in the reserve and the sudden, heavy haemorrhage of white rents it would make permanent. Lastly, the Northerners would celebrate their victory over them and humiliate them. In fact, some white tenants who had been living among Barolong for some generations were now striving to throw them off like a horse, long broken in, that suddenly bucks at old routine. These intimacies had bonded families together for generations in the reserves and chiefs had determined never to surrender the reins.

VIII

In the Bechuanaland Protectorate, Phoebus Fincham approached his 'old friend', Silas Molema, to let a portion of his farm, Mabete, in the Bechuanaland Protectorate. This was at the beginning of March in 1911. He also proposed that should Molema be willing to let the land, as landlord he 'must also agree to sink a well'.[174] Just a year earlier, 'Fincham's Grocery Store' in Mafeking had ceased to appear on the advertisement pages of the *Mafeking Mail*.[175] At the beginning of 1910, this grocery store advertised the sale of 'Early Rose' seed potatoes.[176] The Finchams ran a number of trading enterprises. A.W and A.E. Fincham owned Fincham's Ironmongery Stores in Mafeking. They sold wire, timber, paint, ploughs and other farming implements, crockery, glassware and kitchenware. The pair appear to have taken over Phoebus Fincham's grocery store whilst he operated a general dealer in Ramatlabana in the Bechuanaland Protectorate. The pair also owned another shop at Vryburg where there was a large saltpan. According to a widely publicised murder trial that involved them, the Fincham family were landowners in their own right.[177]

Phoebus Fincham probably came from trading and farming stock but was less successful than his relatives, or perhaps his move from the Union, across the border to the Protectorate, had to do with the murder or its trial and the aftermath of souring relationships. The sum of his ambition when he approached Molema was to operate 'a little shop' at Pitsani Siding on Mabete.[178] Molema agreed to let the land but refused to sink the well. Fincham was a Northerner. He could possibly have crossed the Molopo River into the Bechuanaland Protectorate with the early stream of settlers expecting that very soon the privilege of 'whiteness' would apply in the Protectorate as it was beginning to do in the Union of South Africa. The High Commissioner, Lord Selborne, had announced in 1910 that the Bechuanaland Protectorate would become part of the Union 'in the natural course of things'.[179] The stratum of landless white immigrants included Dutch-Afrikaans speakers. The pressure on the land in the northern districts was intense and yet some of the most fertile portions just north of the Molopo River, the Barolong Farms, a portion of about 432 square miles, belonged to about three dozen men. On Mabete, landlord and tenant entered the agreement as two men, Silas and Phoebus, two individuals tied to each other by the terms of their contract, but they each would have recognised that just some kilometres south of Mabete, in the Union, the very agreement they were entering into was at risk of criminalisation. Their relationship lasted for some sixteen years. During this time, Fincham wrote to Molema frequently about the happenings on the farm, sometimes twice a day.

Fincham thought of himself as a general manager operating an enterprise on Mabete for an absentee proprietor. He saw himself as a partner, an 'old friend', as someone familiar, not as a tenant doing what he should do. At the same time, he presented himself to Molema as something of a boon to him, as someone who was offering him possibilities beyond the usual profits of tenantry. Molema was in that sense, he thought, lucky and should respond with gratitude, which included helping with the enormous work and expenditure of starting up and remaining on Mabete. Moreover, Molema's best interest, as Fincham saw things, would be to surrender control of the farm to him entirely and give up the entitlements of proprietorship. This was after all how Molema treated the peasant householders on placement on Mabete. He left them alone to do as they wished although they gave him, as far as Fincham could see, nothing in return. Above all else, being in control allowed Fincham a peace of mind. He hated the uncertainty that was inevitable when somebody else was in charge. He found unpredictability unnerving. If he were simply a 'tenant', that meant conceding to dependence, to the terms and whims of the landlord that shaped the contract. Lack of freedom gave him even lesser control over an unknowable future. His dilemma was how to be his own master, the director of his own fate, even when he did not have a farm of his own.

It had taken some months to move from Ramatlabana to Barolong Farms but by the middle of May 1912, he was hard at work on Mabete. He had already built a house and put up buildings for his store. However, he could not find water within his portion of Mabete. He had to dig elsewhere on the farm. These districts were in the middle of a very harsh drought. 'Man, I am working hard,' he told Molema, 'and you must help me [as] the stones are very hard in the well and the water is little.'[180] According to the general template of such contracts, sinking wells was the obligation of the tenant, but as many Northerner tenants thought, the contract obligations that tied them to the land were exacting even if the landowner was another Northerner. Absentee landlords gained impressive farming infrastructure – farmhouses and fences, boreholes and windmills. On the other hand, the tenant would walk away with nothing when he left the farm. He would have broken the farm in so to speak, made it habitable, but unless he remained long enough at least to transfer his contract to his children, he worked only for the landlord.

During the same week when Fincham was sinking the well, Molema bought a little sorghum from a trader, an L. Irving, on credit.[181] He was in no position to help anyone. He owed money everywhere, including to some of his tenants. He had borrowed money from a Chinese immigrant on a leasing agreement in the reserve and a white tenant on Vryhof.[182] Lovedale had sued him for unpaid fees.[183] He was also indebted to Sundel Gordon, owner of 'Gordon and Sons Butchers and General Cattle Dealers' in Mafeking. He had borrowed money from him at the beginning of February 1911. In addition to just over £88 owed to Gordon in unpaid accounts and cash loans, he had also taken a further £75 as a bond from the same trader in March of 1912.[184] He had bound eight donkeys and five slaughter cattle. Transport was the only business he knew but now it was no longer profitable. He was not alone though. The drought had dried up many livelihoods, although he had been sinking in debt for years before then. He had to keep on borrowing as a way to keep going and to prevent the drought from swallowing him completely. He could not pay Irving when the debt for sorghum was due.

The winter of 1912 was the worst of it. He had to turn to his nephew, the Rev. Joshua Moshoela to send grain from Klerksdorp, in the Orange Free State. 'Here people are reaping,' he read in the reply, 'but I do not like to buy the whites' sorghum because it is not ripe, they reap it green, and so I will buy from the Bechuana, who are still reaping but I do not know how many bags we shall find.'[185] At the beginning of July, Molema received four bags from Klerksdorp, only he did not have money to pay for carriage.[186] About ten days later, another ten bags came. This time, his nephew had paid for carriage so 'you are to pay nothing'.[187] For another two weeks, his nephew kept looking for more grain. It was possible to purchase grain on credit at the trading stores but his nephew, as always, desired to save him completely. 'I saw the little shillings I had left, and I do not want to take up debt for you.'[188] If Molema had a few shillings, his nephew suggested, he could send them and he would return the money in the next letter. He had none. Three weeks later in mid-August, he received seventeen more bags, including one bag for another family. Again, he did not have to pay for carriage.[189] Two weeks later, the price of sorghum had gone up to 15 shillings, from 13/3, his nephew explained, 'and I do not think I will find any sorghum because I have no money, truly I am saddened by this'.[190] A month later, Molema received twenty more bags of grain with an apology that he would have to pay for carriage. 'You will pay it that side Morolong. If I had money, I would have paid it, but I am short off it.'[191] This is how the Molemas made it through the winter of 1912. Joshua Moshoela had exerted himself to save him, just as he had attempted to do during *Koranta*'s money troubles.

The rain finally came in the summer and with it an expectation of a good harvest. There were many more tenants looking for land, which worried Fincham. His agreement with Molema protected him from trading competition on Mabete, but there could be competitors along Mabete's boundaries with a neighbouring farm. It was better to find a suitable neighbouring tenant, and recommend him to that landowner, than to risk landing up with a man who threatened his trade. He also collected a fee for playing the middleman. In July 1912, he recommended a suitable tenant to the regent Lekoko Montsioa on his farm, Pitsane Photlokwe, which adjoined Mabete on the south. This was N.J. Crosby. He presented Crosby as a 'friend' who was 'not a Dutchman but a man like myself', a 'good man' who could sink a 'good well' and build a 'good decent house' on the farm.[192] The said Crosby was a brick-maker.[193] For four months, he heard nothing from Molema about Crosby or anything else he wished to discuss. So he chided him, 'you must know it is bad policy to a businessman not to answer letters'.[194] He was nevertheless desperate, pleading with Molema to make sure Lekoko 'must please say yes and not no.' Crosby started up on the neighbouring farm as he had hoped, although his relief was short-lived. Next he heard that Dirk

Immelman intended to rent another one of Lekoko Montsioa's farms, Sarra Kop, also on the boundary with Mabete. He wrote to Molema,

> ... now I believe that farm belongs to my friend Chief Lekoko and I also know that Immelman will have to get the chief's permission to put up a shop there and I think it is not right that another shop should be so close to me [because] either one of the two shops will not make a living [.] I trust that you will use your influence and not allow another shop so close to mine and please keep this confidential and protect your friend.[195]

That very month, at the beginning of March 1913, Ben Burger, a Dutch-Afrikaner, arrived on Mabete. Like Fincham, he would make the usual 'improvements' on the land and pay a monthly rent in cash. He leased the portion of Mabete on which Fincham had sunk a well.

Fincham was unhappy but Burger was not a trader. There was nothing to prevent Molema from taking him on as a tenant. Besides, Molema agreed to share the cost of a new borehole with him to compensate him for the well and allowed him to water stock at one of the two natural pans where the peasant householders on the farm watered their stock. It was not enough for him nevertheless. He wanted Burger to understand that he, Fincham, was the farm's overseer and the most senior authority on the farm. At the end of two months, he collected Burger's rent, £1 for two months, dispatched it to Molema and asked him to write a receipt. The next morning he heard, probably from Burger, that another man wished to let a portion of Mabete. He wrote to Molema a 'confidential' note, that it was better to 'refer him to me' and that 'don't on no a/c [account] close with him before you see me first & I will explain to you'.[196] This was James Higgs, who was in the meantime urging Molema to meet as early as possible 'and be ready to fix up agreement and don't disappoint me'.[197] By the end of April, Higgs had also started on the farm, sinking a well, but had to dig deeper than he had anticipated. 'My well is 50ft already and is very hard [and] it cost me a lot for blasting.'

The Land Commission of 1885 had not allowed the 'occupants' of the farms to fence their allotments. In 1911, Molema had prohibited shooting game on Mabete although tenants like Fincham, Burger and Higgs could hunt. He also prohibited people from cutting brushwood to make cattle-kraals without his permission.[198] During the autumn of 1913, Fincham reported to Molema that 'there are too many cattle and sheep drinking at our pan', and that 'there is only one plan for us', which was to 'fence the pan in' and to 'put on a gate'.[199] He suggested that Molema supply seven rolls of barbed wire and he (Fincham) would contribute poles and find labour. As the fence went up around the pan, Molema issued another notice prohibiting shooting game on the farm. Fincham pinned it to the door of his store. Meanwhile, the most senior placement holder on Mabete was a man by the name of Setlhako Mancho. Molema referred to him as 'my headman on the farm'. Mancho knew nothing about putting up a fence around the pan and heard about the reinstated ban on hunting from Fincham, and not from Molema, his chief.[200]

In the winter of 1913, now two years into his contract, Fincham was confident in the partnership. He wrote to Molema about Mabete as 'our farm.' He was in very good spirits. He felt he was in charge. Molema rarely answered his letters. Fincham let veld to 'old Mr Nel' to graze 400 sheep on Mabete for a fee.[201] He also suggested to Molema that there was 'too little water' and that they should share the costs of a new borehole.[202] The best news was that Lekoko Marumoloa had allowed Dirk Immelman no trading rights on his neighbouring Sarra Kop. Fincham was grateful for Molema's help and assured him that he would safeguard both of their best interests on Mabete.

> … you acted wisely & I thank you again [.] You must bear in mind that in our agreement it clearly states that no one will be allowed to trade on this farm and I think you & Chief Lekoko will protect me & not even grant a license at Sarra or anywhere else within 24 miles of this place as if you do I will loose [sic] a lot of my customers & it will mean that all my improvements that I have made on your farm will be of no value to you or me. I think the Immelmans are a mean lot of people as the country is big enough & plenty of room for all without one another cutting each others [sic] necks off.[203]

Fincham however had not anticipated illicit trade. A few days after Immelman failed to procure trading rights on Sarra Kop, one or other trader started to operate there without a trading license.[204] It could have been Immelman. There was a lot of traffic around the place after the rains of 1912. There followed a bumper harvest. The harvest had returned wagon riders to the roads, transporting sorghum and maize even into the towns of the Transvaal.[205] The government was also ready to collect Hut Tax, which it had not managed to do for some years.[206] Life was waking up from a sad, bare spell.

IX

Modiri Molema understood very early on that his father's fortunes were declining in the years leading up to the South African War. As a young boy, he knew they were a respectable family but of limited means. The shopping sprees of his early childhood were gone. His father purchased their clothes at auctions and at their tea table the jam, the cordial and the chicory had all disappeared. When he had to move on from the school in the stadt to boarding school, his father could not afford to send him and Harriet to Lovedale where Sebopioa and Seleje had attended school. He went off to Healdtown Missionary Institute, the second-best option. For two years, 1909 and 1910, his school fees went unpaid. The headmaster, Rev. Richard Hornabrook harangued him.[207]

In handling his situation, he came to accept that he could not trust his father to rescue him, not timeously anyway, not without the risk of help arriving too late. He also understood that his father kept him at school by sacrificing many other things, including the hopes and aspirations of his siblings. He felt gratitude but at any moment, he feared, the whole enterprise of his schooling would collapse. Any day he could sink. He felt gratitude and distrust together. His father was the single hero to whom he owed everything but as the same time he was also the most unreliable sponsor of his aspirations. He felt the same about home. The place of his origin was both cradle and snare together. His family name inspired him, convinced him he was born into greatness, yet that very high calling is what, as far as he could see, had depleted his father, being responsible for doing everything for everyone – building a school, making provisions, funding a newspaper. Home was a knot of feelings, love woven into disappointment.

His father could often not afford the rail fare to bring him home for school holidays. He became comfortable making a home in other people's homes and turning his precocious eye to the lives of strangers. The homestead of a Barolong chief, his father's house, had become only one point in his constellation of belonging. From childhood, he had been gathering influences beyond his father and meeting figures of equal, perhaps even greater gravitas, with very different vocational ambitions, like Plaatje, who seemed to bring all the corners of the world within reach through his books, the people he knew, and the largeness of his own personality. Plaatje was a big person – bigger than the mission station, Pniel, where he was born, bigger than Mafikeng. Plaatje inspired wonder and curiosity and a desire to stretch one's wings.

Modiri's own father was also a great man, well respected and ambitious, yet he was a sedentary authority who did not have any desire to be elsewhere but with the chieftaincy in Mafikeng. Chieftaincy was a bureaucracy tied to a place because the tributaries quickly dried up without their source. It was like raising a child that never learnt to be and walk by itself. Chieftaincy was a lifetime of care.

In the winter holidays of 1908, he stayed at the residence of Rev. Walter Rubusana in East London. His father could not pay for rail from Healdtown to Mafikeng. Rubusana was an ordained minister of the Congregational Church. In 1909, he became the president of the new South African Native Convention and soon embarked on an illustrious career as a politician in the Cape parliament where he was the first and only African to sit on the provincial council from 1910, representing Thembuland. Rubusana also wrote and published books in his vernacular language of isiXhosa.[208] By then Modiri was seventeen and elated to have met the man. Rubusana provided a living model of a professional life that revered chieftaincy without making it the all-consuming centre of 'progress'. He could not be at home because his father could not arrange for it, yet here he was at seventeen, already embarking on a journey of dissociation from home. He felt grateful to be in someone else's home to gain some practice, a little exposure, at another way of cultivating a meaningful vocation – books, life in the city, a professional career, travel abroad. All this and yet Rubusana remained rooted in the countryside of his youth in his sensibility and in his service to its chiefly authorities. Rubusana was somewhat like Plaatje or rather, he presented another possibility of a countryside cosmopolitanism. 'Oh father,' he wrote home, 'I owe them as many thanks as you do'.[209] He was grateful for much more than hospitality.

At boarding school, he sought ways to plug the holes of his father's delays in payments, and to protect himself by becoming more independent, always learning how to be free of his father's financial care and counsel. He applied for and won a scholarship of £20 so that he could proceed to Lovedale at the beginning of 1910.[210] In October of the same year, his father confirmed that 'the way planned for me' was to become a medical doctor yet it was difficult to imagine how it was all going to be paid for.[211] Lovedale was the only institution that trained students who wished to 'matriculate' with a senior certificate to apply for a university degree in Britain or America. His father had chosen his vocation for him, but in winning the scholarship and proceeding to Lovedale, he had forged the path for himself. His father had named the career and was willing to fund it, likely in the same alarming inconsistency that could sink the ship very early on. As soon as he won the scholarship, he stayed away from home more consciously. He made himself dispensable and unnecessary to the rhythm of life in Mafikeng. He was leaving his father a decreasing margin of responsibility and enlarging his own capacity for managing himself. That spring break, he wrote to his father that 'I do not suppose you will want me very much at home since I was there last December'.[212]

He was seeking to be in a position to board the ship to Britain as soon as money was available from whichever source it would come. These were complicated life strategies. His father would have to fund his university tuition, yet he would himself lead his father along this path. He would prove his status of adulthood and claim its freedoms by demonstrating a mastery of the responsibilities that a father typically handled for his son. Concerning the Lovedale scholarship, he had written down 'the general principles and circumstances, under which one may be recommended for the bursary' to the last exhausting detail, 'explain[ing] this to you Rra [father] because I know that Mr Moikangoa did not explain it to you clearly'.[213] His teacher, Mr Moikangoa had said he would communicate all to his father, whatever for, when he himself was in the adults' league?[214] Then he failed the matriculation examination in 1910. He did not despair or blame himself. In fact, as he explained to his father, it was brave of him to have sat the examination in the first place because the Education Department had confirmed his enrolment into the examination too late for him to prepare adequately.[215] However, he could not return to Lovedale without a scholarship.

The first medical superintendent of Victoria Hospital at Lovedale, Dr Neil Macvicar offered him a way out, which at the same time rescued him from the harassment of his former principal at Healdtown, Rev. Richard Hornabrook, who kept pushing him to pay up the tuition fees he owed there. The principal of Lovedale, James Henderson, agreed to exempt him from afternoons of industrial training at Lovedale to work in a hospital every day from 3 to 5 o'clock, a full day on Saturdays and until lunch on Sunday. In return, Macvicar would settle all the outstanding fees at Healdtown. Modiri agreed without hesitation and wrote home to inform his father after the fact.

> On the closing day I met Mr Henderson and Dr Macvicar. I entered into arrangements with them to the following effect. Father dear, you will pardon me for not consulting you beforehand but I thought you would approve of it as [being] ok[ay] ... I dont [sic] know if I have made myself clear, but if not Rra, I shall have much pleasure in explaining anything that you do not understand.[216]

At the very commencement of his work with Macvicar, he had warned his father, 'further *Rra*, I shall not be able to go home ... [as] this gives me a shorter holiday than other scholars'.[217] He would remain in Lovedale to continue his work at Victoria Hospital over school holidays and then spend Christmas at the residence of a James Molebaloa at Ndabeni Location in Cape Town.

His father's money troubles meant he was safe from summons to come home although it did not mean his father saw him as an adult who would be careful not to ruin himself. His father was displeased about the trip to Cape Town and worried that he would become lost in the city like Dick Marumoloa, the regent's son. If so, the two would not be the only young men from chiefly households to have succumbed to the peer temptations of unsupervised independence in the port city – drink, spending the money they had in hand, idling time away. The city was trouble. This was the opinion of the fathers. Modiri was indignant that his father had believed the rumours that he and Marumoloa were friends spending time together. Instead of the maturing man, his father saw a teenager and worried about bad peer influences.

> Rra, I do not know how to answer your letter because I feel that it does not do me justice. It is quite natural that I should defend myself in the charge made against me but Rra, all I ask is that you should not believe that report until you have a sure proof.[218]

Macvicar wanted him to take up work formally with an apprenticeship at the hospital in March 1912. He refused because this was not what he had agreed to do. As he explained to his father, 'that would greatly interfere with my school work'.[219] Apart from the experience, Macvicar gave him no other compensation and reneged on his promise to settle the debt at Healdtown. Matriculating students sat for the Senior Certificate examination in November. His father instructed him to return home to Mafikeng thereafter. 'Yes,' he agreed, 'I have also a mind to go home in December.'[220] 'Perhaps,' he suggested, 'I may leave just after then if I find it necessary.' 'But,' he added, 'I am not decided yet on that point.' The examination period would be over by the end of November but Lovedale closed two weeks after that. Pupils could remain on the premises until then. He needed that time to make arrangements that would prevent that journey to Mafikeng. He had no prospects there and his father had no money. If he returned home, he would have to accept some chiefly responsibilities with no pay. Sebopioa had been in that position for two years. What if he too went home and never left?

He had to delay his departure for as long as he could to give James Molebaloa enough time to write to his father in Mafikeng, let him know that he had found him work at Graham Remedies Co. and assure the chief that Modiri was welcome to stay with him and his family in Cape Town. He urged Molebaloa to write immediately and gave it a few days before he wrote again to his father, this time asking him for permission to remain in Cape Town. 'The post is in one of the Medical Companies and I believe the pay is reasonable.'[221] Graham Remedies Co. was hardly a 'Medical Company'. It was a company that sold patent medicaments and James Molebaloa's place of employment. Still, that was better than going home, which he felt would be a waste of time. 'I have been wondering what I shall be doing next year and also all the time till you send me across.' He would 'not like to stay, doing nothing, during that time'. He wanted to earn money. 'To be frank Papa, I think it will be a great advantage to me.' He would be prepared to visit home for a short time 'if necessary' before starting work. 'I write Papa dear, to give you my view of the matter as I think you would like to know it.'

His father agreed.[222] He also instructed him to apply for a teaching post at Tiger Kloof Native Institution and then travel home to Mafikeng after his examinations before he started work in Cape Town.[223] Tiger Kloof was about 100 miles from Mafikeng near Vryburg. He matriculated successfully but Tiger Kloof turned him down, 'so I immediately turned my eyes to something else'.[224] He was not going home. 'You see Papa, I have made up my mind to get some employment this next year.' In two days, it would be New Year. 'It may not be possible to get a good post from the very start but great things have small beginnings.' He helped to write and edit brochures at Graham Remedies Co. In the meantime, Molebaloa's house was turning into a home of familiars. His cousin, Theo Gaboutloeloe, was also spending the holidays there. Molebaloa had asked him to stay with them, probably to look for work.[225] Solomon Plaatje had come to visit with Mr J. Motshumi, the principal of Lyndhurst Public School in Kimberley.[226]

He, on the other hand, had not been home for over two years, during which time the household was twice visited by death, losing a baby and an older woman. 'But you know Rra these incidents come almost as a reproach to me that I should have gone home to be present and mourn the deceased with you.'[227] Perhaps he felt 'almost' guilty but mostly lonely, as he explained, after his cousin's departure back to Mafikeng. His father wrote that he disapproved of such a long absence from home, which included three

Morafe

Christmas holidays. He replied that he could not abandon his work when he was so deep in debt to Healdtown and Lovedale.

> As for your second letter, I must say I am prepared to go home any time when it is necessary. Besides the fact that I long to see the people, there are many things I would like to have explained to me in connection with my education and starting life. Somehow I always want to hear something myself. The letter[s] never satisfy me and consequently I never write about them. But Rra, I am very anxious to have Mr Henderson's account settled before I leave Cape Town. These small debts never make me feel quite free and happy until they are squared off. I promised to get it paid before the end of May and if I stay here till then I reckon that I shall manage it. But of course, this cannot confine me here. Even if you call me home tomorrow I shall be ready to respond to [the] call as long as there is provision made for Mr Henderson's account to be payed [sic] in due time.[228]

His father said there was a doctor in Mafikeng who was willing to take him on as an apprentice but there were no details. He suspected that it was a slapdash arrangement that would leave him stuck in Mafikeng. He had to check. 'I wonder could they communicate with me.' No letter arrived from the doctor and his father did not write on the subject again. Instead, he received a letter from Plaatje in April that he should come up to Kimberley to fill an open post at Lyndhurst Public School. He had already met the principal of the school, Mr Motshumi, when he visited Molebaloa's home with Plaatje. 'I hope you will find nothing to displease you in the step I have taken father.'[229] Henderson was now demanding payment from his father for the debt at Lovedale. He wrote to his father that come what may, at the end of May when the debt was due, Henderson 'will get every farthing of it.'[230] His first salary at Lyndhurst would pay for his long outstanding high school tuition. He had thus independently financed the last four years of his schooling himself.

The months went by. He realised that his father was no longer saying anything about him going home, but he was also not saying anything about the next step of a university education abroad. He could never raise the money to travel abroad by himself. He had to ask his father. He had claimed his freedom. He had proved his independence. He had paid his own way. Nevertheless, sailing to Britain required money that only his father could raise. He needed his father to care for him. Only then, could he securely establish his independence. He had to bring himself into alignment with the proper workings of placement in his father's house despite the risks. He would have to toe the line, demonstrate that he was still a child and would not acquire independence on his own terms. He could not independently make himself a medical doctor and an educated man of the world. He could not pave his own way to adulthood. He would have to return home. This time, when his father beckoned him homeward, he complied. Besides, it was safe because he would have to return to Kimberley to teach after the school holidays.

In Mafikeng, he found a bumper harvest and an obliging father. He would have to press him again as soon as he returned to Kimberley to 'make definite arrangements', but the determination was that he would leave for university the following year.[231] At home, he took every trouble to make house calls to relatives and family friends. Once he accompanied family guests on their way to Kunana, another stadt about 80 kilometres from Mafikeng.[232] They took a train from Mafikeng to Kraaipan. There was a further 10 kilometres by wagon to go but nobody arrived at the station to pick them up. He had to use 'all the persuasive faculty at my command' to convince a Jewish merchant to give them room in his wagon, 'an old jickery thing' and decided to ride with them all the way to Kunana. He revelled in telling the story to his father. He had somewhat forgotten the scenes of the countryside, the wagons, the rough, isolated terrain between the stadts, the characters that made for a good laugh. 'When you come to imagine that I, a native of these parts – (*ngoana oa hae*) could scarcely see any people I knew.' He had returned, finally he was home and of the place. He had come up on the surface of his dread at last and was happy – also, as it happened, in love.

X

During the early years of Union, many Dutch-Afrikaner farmers in the Orange Free State and the Transvaal were landlords over thousands of sharecroppers, many of whom came from neighbouring Bechuanaland. Sharecroppers brought their dispositions of placement, *peo*, to these farmlands. It was a position of dependency in relation to the landowner that also facilitated autonomy and respectable manhood. These men were a confident, aspirant stratum. They were often Christianised and educated and wanted firm, secure roots on the land. Sharecroppers refused any other terms of tenancy other than 'sowing on the halves'. The landowner surrendered his lands to the sharecropper, and received half of the yield. With independent access to land, sharecroppers typically sowed their own seed and controlled their own family labour on the farm. The oxen that bore the plough were their own. 'The real master', one J.A. Jorissen from the eastern Free State wrote in the *Farmers Weekly*, 'is the native', who is 'independent' and refuses to avail his services for money or any other alternative contract.[233] 'The only course he is agreeable to is to sow on the half, whether the owner likes it or not, he has to submit.' Sharecroppers would not accept a situation of dependency with no freedom. They refused to become common labourers. Unless landowners in the Transvaal and Orange Free State surrendered to these terms, they had no labour to work the lands. These terms of sharecropping were unsatisfactory for landowners because they compromised their positions in a universe of virtue where demonstrating mastery over the land confirmed white manhood.

After General Barry Hertzog lost his cabinet position in December 1912, he turned to the countryside with populist aplomb. His ejection from the cabinet had not suppressed his opposition to British dominion, his republicanism or the Afrikaner nationalism he had devoted himself to mobilise. The expulsion had given him a platform of unrestrained expression and other radicals, especially the white farmers demanding a 'squatter's bill', became his constituency and their number grew. In parliament, his position was that of the 'small group of zealots, predominantly from the Orange Free State' that were agitating for a 'squatter's bill' on their territories.[234] Such legislation would classify the black demographic on the farmlands as 'squatters' unless they remained on the land as labourers. This would immediately criminalise sharecropping and force the thousands of such people of colour to accept terms as labour tenants on the land. They would no longer be 'sowing on the halves' on white-owned land. They would be working as labourers on terms that the white 'Master' would dictate.

Nevertheless, when parliament opened on 24 January 1913, the Governor-General said nothing in his speech about any plans to introduce national legislation on the 'native question'. The press observed that the government was not intending to move on the said legislation. J.W. Sauer, as Minister of the Native Affairs Department, would not bend to pressure to introduce legislation against 'black squatters' or against the purchase of land by the same demographic. On 28 January 1913, he made it clear to parliament that he could not promise introducing such legislation that year. However, by 11 February, the minister had suddenly changed his mind.[235] On 28 February Sauer's response to a motion for a 'squatter bill' from the conservatives was an announcement of his own that the government would in fact be legislating a Bill concerning 'Natives'.[236] The press and members of cabinet took for granted that Sauer changed his mind to buy in 'Hertzog agitators' who could sink the government at a time when the alliances of 'Union' in the cabinet were very fragile. Indeed, some conservatives saw the Bill as a concession especially to them.[237]

In fact, Sauer had learnt that the Supreme Court of Appeal had reserved its judgment on whether the government had jurisdiction to intervene in the Molopo Reserve, and therefore any other reserve in the vast territory of former British Bechuanaland, then north of the Cape Province in the Union. The Supreme Court of Appeal had heard the matter on 29 January 1913. If the court found that Proclamations No 173 and 174 to include the Molopo Reserve in the Mafeking Division were *ultra vires*, it meant the 'squatters' bill' he had introduced in the Molopo Reserve to confirm the government's jurisdiction to intervene there, and extract everyone who was not 'black' from the reserve, was unlawful. A judgment reserved was as good as a judgment lost. It meant the reserve was not within the government's jurisdiction.

In the meantime, as he too awaited the court's judgment, the chiefs' advocate, W.P. Schreiner, understood at that stage that the consequences of a judicial victory for him and the Barolong chiefs held dire consequences for other black peoples. He almost hoped, it seems, that he had lost and if so, that chiefs would let the matter drop and hold their peace. He decided that if he had lost and chiefs decided to keep fighting, he would not make himself available to represent them. He instructed the attorney on the case to write to the Barolong chiefs and urge them not to take further steps if the court ruled in the government's favour because otherwise, the government would have no option but to promulgate legislation that would 'fall very heavily on the people'.[238]

> In the event of judgment being in favour of the Government, a point which Mr Schreiner earnestly discussed with me, if we may be allowed to offer you our [..] would say to the Barolong we sympathise [with] them [...] We feel how the matter according [...] their view point affects them and how sore [...] will be, but we say that it would be best [to] bow to the inevitable and not to take the matter further for apart from the further very great expense, the Government have [sic] now not the old Cape government to deal with. They have another mixed lot of interests in the present Government and they do not show, as this case is evidence enough, the same sympathy for the Natives as the old Government. So by moving further it is possible that further legislation may be passed which might fall very heavily on the people which otherwise they will escape and such rights as they still have would be respected, for without good and

substantial reasons the Government dare not move and if the Barolong were to take action we advise against [it as] the Government might use it as an excuse. I trust you will not consider I am going out of my way in tendering you this advice which as I have said, Mr Schreiner approves of, but I think by now you realised that I have all along had your interests thoroughly at heart and that it is solely given with that view.[239]

Schreiner was correct. If the Union government wished to intervene in the reserves of British Bechuanaland, it required an Act of Parliament to bring these reserves under the Crown's jurisdiction. It is only then that the government would have jurisdiction to effect 'native administration' or any other policy in these northern reserves. On 28 February 1913, Sauer indicated that a Bill was forthcoming which would 'see that no native purchased land from a European, and that no European purchased land from a Native'.[240] On 4 March, the department notified the Surveyor General in Cape Town that it would use data on African areas 'in the schedule to a Bill'.[241]

In the meantime, the court had appointed a commission of inquiry to take evidence from Rev. George Weavind, Edgar Rowland, Silas Molema, Stephen Lefenya and Lekoko Montsioa on 10 June 1913. They all defended the chiefs' right to place whomsoever they wished on their land.[242] Sebopioa Molema was the translator in the proceedings. Eighty-year-old Stephen Lefenya argued that the Divisional Council of Mafikeng could not possibly have jurisdiction over the reserve because 'the Barolongs have not been conquered by anyone'. He continued that before the treaty of annexation, the paramount chief held the land 'and gave it out to different people with the advice of councillors', and that this was an 'old custom and it is still carried on today' without government interference. The Dog Tax, he concluded, was 'a new law that we don't know'. Edgar Rowland said 'there are no locations other than the one belonging to the [European] town'. In his view, the entire Cape Colony was Crown Lands, owned by the Cape then Union government, but not the reserves of Bechuanaland. All the 'natives', he said, lived in 'stadts' and they 'never called them locations, only stadts'. This meant that the Divisional Councils had no jurisdiction over this population. Silas Molema started his testimony by explaining that he had been Chief Montsioa's advisor upon his return from Healdtown Missionary Institute to relay his technical understanding of the agreement between Sidney Shippard and his great-uncle in 1895.

> Lekoko Montsioa is the Paramount Chief of Barolongs. Lekoko owns the land in the Reserve. He holds it for the people. In 1895 negotiations were going on for annexation to the Cape Government. I acted as interpreter. I remember the obtaining of the letter of August 1895. Montsioa had [heard] that the Cape government ill-treated natives, and he wanted assurances on this point. Sir Sidney Shippard said, here is your Charter, and handed him the letter.[243]

On 9 June 1913, the government passed the Natives Land Act of 1913. This Act had two stated provisions. The first provision demarcated a 'Schedule of Native Areas', which included all of the African reserves that were already in existence (between 7 and 8 per cent of South Africa's land mass).[244] Africans could not purchase land outside the Scheduled Areas but neither could whites purchase land within them. The second provision was an anti-squatting legislation prohibiting Africans from occupying white areas unless employed by whites. This included black sharecroppers on white-owned farms in the former Boer Republics, the Transvaal and the Orange Free State. This legislation listed all three reserves in the Mafeking District in the Schedule Areas – the Setlagodi, Mosita and Molopo Reserves. The Barolong territories were now under the jurisdiction of the Union of South Africa through an Act of Parliament. The government had lawful jurisdiction to intervene in this Schedule of Native Areas as territories specifically for 'Natives' only, meaning 'member[s] of an aboriginal race or tribe of Africa' in the words of the Act. The discriminating variable was skin colour.

Thus, the Natives Land Act of 1913 was the cornerstone instalment of territorial segregation in the making of South Africa at the time when ideals of 'whiteness' were emerging at the coalface of mixed living, *métissage* and acculturation along the northern frontier. The peculiarity here was not the fact of reservation, of fixing a particular territorial sphere for the sole habitation of a specific demographic based on skin colour or 'tribe'. That had been British policy all across the continent. Moreover, as was the case everywhere else, reservation went beyond merely mapping on the land the differential grid of property and political rights that separated 'black' and 'white' as social categories the colonial government aimed to make normative. As a policy that emerged not from the radical lobby groups fuelled by incendiary personalities like Hertzog, the Natives Land Act of 1913 intended to address very unique concerns of governance in a settler colony. It was necessary to set aside land for Europeans to keep reproducing themselves and their institutions, given that they were a numerical minority.

Hence, the government had to delineate land exclusively for the use of the population it classified as 'black'. These had to be territories on which the colonial government had the jurisdiction to control the movement of people and allocate land. In Natal for instance, the wars of conquest had brought existing polities to their knees and turned them into 'locations', entirely the property of the Crown, governed through headmen the British appointed. The specific difficulty the settler government faced was that this was not the case everywhere, especially not into the hinterlands of Bechuanaland where literacy and Christianity had strengthened chiefly institutions, and almost two decades of British rule had safeguarded their autonomy.

Black landlordism over a white tenantry may have been a unique feature of the Barolong polities along the Molopo, but there may have been other areas, especially in the earlier decades of the twentieth century, where black landlords exploited whites. For Northerners, black landlordism over whites presented an abhorrent permutation of the pattern of mixed living on African-owned land, but for the colonial government these institutions of placement also presented stumbling blocks to the distribution of land, certainly in the reserves of Bechuanaland. Property was a moral negotiation on the land in these northern reserves, with no fixed rules, only intricate strategies of freedom and dependency and ambiguous, constantly shifting meanings of rents and services, all as moral purchases of adulthood. For those 'black' people who wished to make land productive without these negotiations of intimacy and dues of obligations to others, or who could not afford the transactions of tributes and other rents, sharecropping on white-owned farms was a better prospect. Thus, territorial segregation was impossible where African polities still preserved the institutions of landlordism that characterised the forms of chiefly and patriarchal power that agropastoralism had acquired by the time of European settlement in the interior. Placement incorporated new settlers onto the land, but was available only for householders who wished, and could afford, to participate in the reciprocal transactions of personhood on the land. They excluded everyone else, whatever their skin colour, who did not subscribe into the moral and material infrastructures of chiefly and patriarchal power on the land.

The Union was not the only colonial government that understood the challenge that patronage and tribute presented in such territories, despite people's narrative of communal landholding. These institutions of landlordism made it immensely difficult to carve up African society into neat ethnic or racial enclaves precisely because they hindered the free settlement of people on 'communal' lands. There was nevertheless a way out, as the

British were learning to do in the Uganda Protectorate, which it had acquired at the same time as it colonised Bechuanaland. The solution was to appoint a salaried headman of a different 'tribe' as the paramount chief of any such reserve, and to secure his term of office through a salary and colonial law, and not through the various forms of subscriptions on the land and popular consent.[245] The formula freed the livelihood of this ruler from the moral and social negotiations of placement. It reduced placement to an economic transaction, which took place only at the apex of a centralised chieftaincy. The appointed ruler would receive payment from the government for hearing some cases and implementing colonial policy while opening up the reserve to anyone and everyone of the 'race' or 'tribe', according to the government's system of classification. This paramount chief's position depended only on the government's recognition and not on the hierarchies of moral subscription on the land.

This was indeed the model of 'Native Administration' that Edward Dower had designed, only rather than appointing a chief of a different 'tribe' to rule over a reserve, a white Native Commissioner would accomplish the same task. The white Native Commissioners would be the supreme chiefs and landlords of the reserves, thus reducing hereditary chiefs to a subsidiary, partly supporting, partly redundant position. As Dower had explained to Lekoko, each reserve would have one chief – and one chief only, whose judgments about placement or any of the minor cases under his jurisdiction would have direct routes of appeal to the office of the Native Commissioner. The only trouble then had been that the Native Affairs Department had no jurisdiction to interfere in the reserves of former British Bechuanaland.

Nevertheless, although it had all of the elements of policies of reservation under British rule, the Natives Land Act of 1913 had a peculiarity, which is that even though the government was already aggressively pursuing territorial segregation on the ground, including through a 'squatter's policy' like Sauer's in the Molopo Reserve, it was extremely reluctant to promulgate a countrywide legislation towards this same end. In other words, the Union government was reluctant to promulgate legislation which was commonplace in territories of British rule. The legislation came about because in their struggle to keep their small reserve of 660 square miles beyond the jurisdiction of the Union government, Barolong chiefs had prevailed against the Union government in the highest court of the land. Thus, their litigation impinged directly on the set of interests and manoeuvres that culminated in the passage of the Natives Land Act of 1913. Their struggle made it necessary for the government finally to conquer the reserves of former British Bechuanaland through legislation, and thereby grant the settler government full jurisdiction over these thousands of frontier people for the first time.

Indeed, when the Supreme Court of Appeal handed down its judgment on 7 August 1913, both judges considered it to have been beyond the government's powers to issue Proclamations No 173 and 174 to include the Molopo Reserve without an Act of parliament to that effect. Without the Natives Land Act of 1913, Sauer's 'squatter's bill' in the Molopo Reserve would have been unlawful. The *Cape Times* carried the judgment verbatim.[246] The government's legal counsel urged the Justice Department that they 'strongly advise appeal'. The appeal took place on 14 November 1913 in Bloemfontein where the Supreme Court, certainly in the light of the new Land Act, made a ruling in the government's favour.[247] The litigation forced a legislative solution to the 'special conditions' applying in Bechuanaland. It also sounded an alarm that there could be other unplanned, variegated arrangements of British rule on the ground that would present serious challenges to the project of territorial segregation.

The Natives Land Act allowed the Union government free reign to establish 'native administration' in the reserves of Bechuanaland and throughout the 'Schedule of Native Areas'. The government vigorously policed the legislation in the new 'schedule' of 'native lands', especially in the northern reserves. The police evicted everyone who did not match the classification of 'black' from the Molopo Reserve, including people of so-called 'mixed race'. They acted swiftly to extract any trace or resemblance of 'white' even if it meant tearing down deep affinities in the reserve or splitting up families. Nevertheless, some resisted the government's basis of racial categorisation and tried to remain in the reserves. The fair-skinned H. Buchman, probably a son or other descendant of the German mason who had settled in the area in 1863 refused to leave. The Resident Magistrate was willing to make an exception 'provided he is a genuine Griqua', but Sebopioa Molema 'was not prepared to certify his being a genuine Griqua' because Buchman's father had paid several cattle for his Morolong wife 'to comply with the Sechuana custom', which made him a Morolong.[248]

> As to Mr H. Buchman's recognition of the Barolong Chief's authority there is no question about that. He is born and raised among us and he knows of no other custom than that of Barolong. I hope Sir, that although I am not prepared to testify to his being a genuine Griqua still as a Government Representative you will find your way clear to grant him permission to live with us. We consider him to be a member of the Barolong Nation.

> The only power that can cut off his only and former identification and citizenship as a Morolong is vested in the Government.[249]

However, Dower had underestimated the resilience of indigenous institutions and the resistance of human beings, in this case chiefs, to the loss of power. Yet perhaps he had understood just how powerful these institutions are, and how vociferous the resistance would be to a policy that undermined the judicial and moral authority of many senior men. The policy of 'native administration' shed chiefly landlords like Molema from the routine institutions of rule and effectively dispossessed them of their landholdings and people. Thus, Dower had attempted to buy the paramount chief in at the expense of all other men. The paramount chief would, he had thought, choose 'native administration' as an interpretation of *Sechuana* that swept away the rungs of chiefs, courts and senior men that coexisted and therefore competed with the paramount court. As it turned out, the government would realise later that paradoxically, the sudden and extreme demographic pressure in the reserves in the wake of the Natives Land Act of 1913 actually strengthened and ramified institutions of landlordism in these reserves, never mind that the government now actually owned the reserves. The negotiations of placement continued to lock out the very 'Natives' from white-owned farms that the legislation intended to establish in the 'Schedule of Native Areas.' The reserves had immediately become 'black', but chiefly power dug its heels in.

Erstwhile sharecroppers had no place to go. They remained shut out of the reserves by the moral and other reciprocal transactions of placement at the same time as they were also prohibited from remaining on white-owned lands as sharecroppers. Almost immediately, many of these sharecroppers drifted back to the now officially 'white' farmlands although they were no longer the same robust communities. The legislation gave landowners an advantage over their sharecroppers because their practice was unlawful. Sharecroppers could either agree to the landlord's new terms of labour tenancy or leave his farm with all their stock and belongings. J.G. Keyter in Ficksburg in the Free State wrote that 'when the boy had his whole piece of ground to sow and was given a half of the crops, he was not a servant but a partner – a master'.[250] After the promulgation of the bill, 'you draw the line under the new law' and immediately, 'you draw the line on your farm and say, "you can sow this for yourself", he is your servant'. In the words of Timothy Keegan, 'things were never quite the same again'.[251] Sharecroppers' earlier confidence 'to build schools, carve desks and hire teachers' belonged to a frontier of opportunity that had shut overnight. Their situation was extreme dependence. The land

Morafe

was no longer theirs to work, no longer an expression of ingenuity on the free terms of manhood.

The Union government did not police the second provision of the legislation. What would be the point? Observers in the Transvaal had noted that the bill 'stimulated trekking on an extensive scale from various parts of the southwestern districts [and] many natives, with their families and stock had crossed over into Bechuanaland'.[252] However, the reserves of Bechuanaland, to which sharecroppers initially flocked, were shut through expensive moral transactions. In the meantime, the boundary disputes between chiefs in the reserves, including at Rietfontein, continued. In their conflicts over land, chiefs carried on like elephants at war, unconcerned about the rulings and directives of the government. They rammed against each other and locked tusks in their brawl, but the grasses under their feet were ordinary people. In and outside the reserves, ordinary people were struggling to maintain their autonomy in the face of the growing power of chiefs on the land. The crisis of personhood, particularly manhood, was deepening.

XI

In the late 1880s, a white tenant, J.W. Hall, rented a portion of Silas Molema's landholding known as Kromdraai, west of Mafikeng. He paid £25 every year.[253] He is likely to have been Charles Hall's father as tenancy agreements often passed down generations. The older man had bound himself to carry out building work on Kromdraai and to extend a water furrow and bring it onto the farm at the cost of £14. He was also to plant and cultivate fruit trees and a vineyard. In 1905, the younger Hall and Richard Rowland, together signed a six-year contract to 'make a larger & good dam' on the same lands. In return, they could live on the 'enclosed' garden for six years 'free of charge'.[254] Molema also required that they 'keep the Barolong laws and customs on the farm'. The Halls had been on the farm for a long time, more than twenty years.

The Rowlands too had been in the reserve a long time. Edgar Rowland was one of the four witnesses that signed 'the treaty between Montsioa, his sons and councillors and the Imperial Government in 1884'.[255] Montsioa wrote that 'I give the queen to rule in my country over white men and black men'. Edgar Rowland, a white man, was the fourth most important councillor in the paramount Kgotla after Israel and Joshua Molema and Stephen Lefenya.[256] He was probably Richard Rowland's father or an older brother. If so, father and son leased the farm 'Matusing' three miles west of the stadt in the reserve in 1905.[257] The agreement leased the farm to the two men, as well as 'their heirs and assigns' for a period of six years. Their obligation was '… to build – as full and absolute remuneration for the six years lease of the said farm – one four roomed house outside measurements to be 30 ft by 30 ft … roof and room to be ceiled [meaning ceilinged] with calico'. Silas Molema, as the lessor of Matusing, would provide the bricks but the Rowlands would have to pay for them by planting fifty fruit trees on the farm.

In the same year, Richard Rowland made himself party to a third leasing agreement. He hired one hundred morgen on the same farm, Kromdraai, where he already had a partnership with Charles Hall.[258] He enclosed the portion with a wire fence but on the southern border was a stone wall that marked Silas Molema's own property. He bound himself to build 'a dwelling house of four (4) rooms during the second year, the outside measurement to be 32 ft by 30 ft. – hip roof and rooms to be ceiled [meaning ceilinged] by calico'. Again, Molema would provide bricks on condition that Rowland plants fifty fruit trees on the property. In addition, Rowland would '… maintain and repair all existing fences and shall keep open all water furrows'. He would also 'cultivate the said lands in husband like manner'. In keeping with all Barolong customs, Rowland had right of grazing on the farm and all other grazing lands in the reserve.

By 1911, Richard Rowland had crossed north into the Bechuanaland Protectorate. Charles Hall and Silas Molema were on good terms, helping one another, respectful, but not intimate. In a letter of 1911, the tenant addressed his 'dear Chief Molema'.[259] He needed to have his wagon repaired but anthrax restrictions prevented oxen from outlying farms from entering town, not even to tow wagons to a blacksmith. He only had two donkeys. 'Could you kindly lend me 7 donkeys for a few days, if so I would like them to go down to Kromdraai this afternoon?' He was grateful and certain Molema would come through, and 'yours very truly, Chas Hall'.[260] Molema did not let him down. These were more than relationships of tenancy. They were families living together on placement, sharing land. The drought was stretching into its fourth year by 1911, and then a fifth year, and still another year. Tenants still had to pay up. A white tenant may once have felt gratitude for the generosity of the man that shared his lands, but by then the Northerner spirit was claiming skin colour and not moral negotiation, as the basis for landholding and entitlements on the land.

As soon as the Minister of Native Affairs, J.W. Sauer, introduced his anti-squatting policy in the reserve on 20 January 1913, Hall and all other whites in the reserve became 'squatters' overnight and could not lawfully reside there without the government's special permission. On 2 February the Resident Magistrate of Mafikeng, E.C. Welsh, informed Hall that all rents due to Molema were to go instead to the Cape government.[261] The government adopted Hall's contract and he could remain on Kromdraai until his lease expired, in effect, another three years. As Welsh explained to Hall, 'you must however clearly understand that the Natives have no right to lease any portion of the Reserves' because the lands belonged to the government. In March of 1913, Hall sent Welsh's letter 'which explains itself' to Molema and further asserted that 'I must therefore pay the Government and not to you'.[262] The government had not freed him from rent, but rather from his attachment to a black landlord, until his lease expired.

Molema could get absolutely nothing from Charles Hall and threatened to evict him, as 'you did not carry on your part according to the agreement', but Hall made himself subject to no such laws.[263] He pulled down the kraal he had built on the farm and re-sold the stones in the town. He pocketed the proceeds. He also sold the sand and kept the money.[264] He let his cattle graze on Molema's trees and fields and those of other placement holders on the farm. Molema could do nothing to bring about Hall's eviction, nor could he force Hall to pay for anything. Hall wrote to Molema in May 1914, 'will you please understand once and for all, that there is no agreement of any kind existing between you and me'.[265] One morning in April of 1915, Molema wrote to Hall that

> I have the honour to inform you that on Tuesday ... your cattle did great damage on my garden and I went and spoke to your foreman the white man and he promised me that he will pay the 13/- within 3 days time and now he is not willing to pay and I hear that he is leaving today for good. So I want you to know because I want to summon him. Please reply to bearer Sir.[266]

In a scribble underneath Molema's letter, Hall replied that 'you had better give me the full details of the matter, as to what and where the damage was done, and if my cattle have done any damage, I as the master am responsible, not my servant'.[267] He was not saying he would investigate, or that he would hold his man on the farm responsible. He was reminding Molema once again that he, erstwhile tenant, now lived on the farm as its 'Master'. The Natives Land Act had undermined black landlords' power over white tenants. Those categories, 'black' and 'white', were no longer merely a reference to skin colour. They were a reference to a hierarchy of opportunity and political power.

Nevertheless, some of the deep connections across the colour line survived. In April 1913, former white tenant and erstwhile councillor, Edgar Rowland, testified on the side of the chiefs in their litigation against the government. 'I know all the customs of the Barolongs'. He said that 'the land is held by the chief for his people' and that the 'tribesmen' had 'tenure' as 'allotments of land by the chief'.[268] This was the common language of placement and he had received his own private entitlement to the land through it. The Rowlands' ties to the Molemas were a shared negotiation of manhood. The two families remained attached throughout the long drought until the harvest in the autumn of 1913. Silas Molema's people reaped his fields in the reserve but many people had nothing because they would not have had seed to sow. Molema saved 40 bags of 'good corn' for Richard Rowland who was in Lobatse in the Bechuanaland Protectorate.[269]

Rowland was now a private landowner on a plot of his own. The hard work of tenant farming and the relationships he had cultivated in the Molopo Reserve over the previous years had paid off. Silas Molema had given him and his family their very first break on the land. Molema had planted him and had nourished him into the independence he now enjoyed. He had reciprocated this free gift by giving his time and toil to establish Molema's farm. When the drought had ended, Rowland saw the good yields of his friend, and reminded him of the nature of their relationship. The two of them were tied to each other as a face to its own reflection, man to man. Rowland thought there is no better opportunity to prove manhood than adversity – drought, suffering, isolation.

> I am exceedingly pleased you have at last had a little luck. We had a hard time of it together for six years. So, I hope we have nothing but good times for the future. I have long ago seen how your words to me about too much wealth or good luck not being good for a man – taken in a manly way bad luck makes a man a real man. I think cruel as the experiences we both had to go through were we are both today the better for it. I will always be proud to think that instead of giving in we made a fight for it and won unaided.[270]

XII

On the first anniversary of the Natives Land Act, Solomon Plaatje praised Silas Molema's property, Mabete, in the Bechuanaland Protectorate as 'a farm more developed than any other farm in this region, with the largest dam from the Madibe River having just been completed'.[271] The editorial appeared in *Tsala ea Batho*. He wrote that Molema had no competition, 'with grain and hay that can fill villages'. He also mentioned the large dams on the properties of Joshua Molema and another relation, Joseph Tawana. About two months later Silas, his son Sebopioa and the regent Chief Lekoko visited the Barolong Farms to inspect 'improvements'. Plaatje's report applauded the tough handedness with which Molema and his cousin, an R. Taoana, handled tenants who did not fulfil their contractual obligations. Molema had won a suit against such a tenant who subsequently had to pay £80. Plaatje praised 'the works of whites' on these notables' farms in the Bechuanaland Protectorate where 'a person lets to a white and a white can let to a black just as they like'.[272]

Reading these editorials, nobody could have guessed Plaatje's own distress. He had just lost his property at the hands of chiefs across the border in the Molopo Reserve. The arrangements of collecting debts to pay his 'house rent' in Mafikeng that he had been attempting to handle remotely did not work, until finally the senior chief in the ward withdrew his placement, including the house, and allotted it to someone else. It was a nightmare, the worst of the tragic outcomes he had dreaded. He learnt of it in the second week of May 1913, just when he was due to travel to a meeting with the Minister of Native Affairs, J.W. Sauer, to represent Barolong chiefs as a member of the SANNC.[273] He did not go because, as he wrote to Silas Molema, he did not have money for railage but really, he lacked the strength. He was shocked and angry and he was grieving. He wrote to Silas Molema that 'as I had no means to go our affairs were not represented' and then described his tale of 'such sorrows as the wrenching of heart of finance that I find myself in'.[274]

> Maduo [Ncoa] has given away my field and the site of my house to Mr Ephraim Molema and he says he is confiscating my house on his lands. Ncoa has spoken before to Chief Joshua Molema and the late Mrs Palo Molema and the sons of Monnaoapula [Plaatje's brother] that he had given me placement on a farm, (*fa a mpeile tshimo*), how can he renege just like that. When he evicts me, need he only speak to Monnaoapula and say nothing to me? Monnapula is pressing me for a reply. I do not know what to say.[275]

On the eve of the promulgation of the Natives Land Act, none understood better than Plaatje that the very reserves that the Native Affairs Department wished to legislate into a 'Schedule of Native Areas' were not available for such use. As things stood, the transactions of rents and services were even more costly, especially after a long drought. New people, including erstwhile sharecroppers coming into the reserve could push the negotiations of placement towards more expensive transactions, jeopardising the position of a 'small man' like him who wanted to continue letting property in the reserve but could not, for instance, compete with sharecroppers who may have had deeper pockets. He was experiencing the effects of an increasingly impoverished and increasingly desperate chiefly hierarchy, which saw advantage in exploiting the new influx of destitute sharecroppers, who nevertheless had a lot of stock and extensive experience working the land. Chiefs were claiming the right to give and take away placement at will as a customary imperative. They were squeezing the 'small man' into smaller pieces of land – that is if they allowed him to remain at all, and were taking up cash and other rents from the highest bidders. The suffering and dire material circumstance in the reserves left no room for common decency and just enough for the raw instinct of survival.

Indeed, senior chiefs were in dire straits, especially Silas Molema. When the Natives Land Act took effect on 20 June 1913, it also dispossessed private property holders in the reserves of their property. Silas Molema and any others who held freehold property in the reserve lost it overnight. It was no longer theirs and the property of the Crown. These landowners no longer had these properties available for mortgage. They had now severely limited access to credit. On private farms outside the 'Schedule of Native Areas', the government prevented blacks from letting more than ten morgen of land to whites. On senior chiefs' landholdings in the reserves, like Silas Molema's placement at Kromdraai and Madibespruit, chiefs no longer had white tenants to put up farming infrastructure. Silas Molema's country house was on Madibespruit. His wife and children spent a lot of time there. This was also where he held funerals, celebrations and public feasts. The cost of maintaining the water supply on the holding had ordinarily fallen on white tenants, but after their expulsion, Molema had to shoulder the burden. Later in 1913, he hired his white tenant on Vryhof, a Stephanus van Jaarsveld, to undertake the work at a cost of £260 and could not pay. In 1914, the sheriff attached a 'cart, 2 horses, 20 goats, 1 plough and a number of sheets of gal [galvanised] iron, also furniture and other effects' as guarantee on a promissory note.[276] Molema was to pay the amount owed at 8 per cent interest at £50 per month for six months.

Immediately after its promulgation, Plaatje travelled through the countryside of the Transvaal and the Orange Free State on a bicycle to document the consequences of the Natives Land Act. He travelled to London in 1914 with a delegation of the SANNC, which intended to make representations in Britain against the Act. Their hope was that the opinion of British voters would compel the British government to rescind the legislation. The Barolong in Mafikeng tasked Plaatje to remind the Secretary of State for Colonies of the 'special conditions' of their reserves' annexation into the Cape in 1895. If the delegation succeeded and the Union government repealed the legislation then, at the very least, the question of the autonomy of the Barolong territories would once again be in the courts. Plaatje was also to present these concerns to the Aborigines' Protection Society, the Native Races Committee, the Wesleyan Missionary Society and 'all the Christian people in England'.[277] Sebopioa Molema attempted to generate as much financial and moral support as possible from other chiefs in Bechuanaland for the trip, both in the Union and across the border, and invited them to sign a petition.[278]

The delegation enjoyed a warm reception in Britain, but its plea was of no consequence though Plaatje kept up the fight. He remained in London to write his book, *Native Life in South Africa*, which he published there in 1916. He wrote that the idea of a 'Schedule of Native Areas' made no sense because how could 'natives', or anyone for that matter, buy lands in the reserves which were absolutely *not* common areas, but jurisdictions where people settled and lived according to the peculiar prescriptions of their own 'clans'.[279] In his understanding, these reserves were neither open to the sharecroppers evicted from what had become 'white' farmlands nor were they 'common' property for everyone, including chiefs, to dispose of as though they were freehold property – an instance that his own eviction from the Molopo Reserve represented. The only way landholding in these areas could be that of common areas, he pointed out, was if these areas were classified anew as territories of private property, which required that the 'clan' disband or cease to exist. Until then, those 'who had grown up among white people', meaning those whose sensibility was not congruent to the reciprocal practices of clan life, should have the right to purchase land outside these areas. In other words, cultural sensibility, not skin pigmentation, should be the basis for territorial segregation.

> ... what are these Scheduled Native Areas? They are the native locations which were reserved for the exclusive use of certain native clans. They are inalienable and cannot be bought or sold, yet the Act says that in these 'Scheduled Native Areas', natives only may buy land. The areas being inalienable, not even members of the clans, for whose benefit the locations are held in trust, can buy land therein. The areas could only be sold if the whole clan rebelled; in that case the location would be confiscated. But as long as the clans of the location remain loyal to the government, nobody can buy land within these areas – let alone a native outsider who had grown up among white people and done all his farming on white man's land.[280]

He was proposing that the privatisation of the reserves, meaning a process to break up the association between a reserve and one or other specific cultural order, would be necessary if these jurisdictions of 'custom' were to become open to all black peoples. Then the land would be common to all, cut up into as many private holdings as there were private landowners, each under the exclusive control of the landowner.

However, as Plaatje described, 'exclud[ing] the arid tracts of Bechuanaland', the reserves were locations that had 'been granted on such a small scale that each of them became so overcrowded that much of the population had to go out and settle on the farms of white farmers through lack of space in the locations'.[281] In other words, white-owned farms, and not reserves, were many ordinary black people's actual home where they belonged to reciprocal transactions of intimacy that were unique to these farmlands. The white-owned farm was a landscape of placement for its own clan, with its own mores. In his travels, Plaatje recorded the attachment between the white Dutch-Afrikaner farmer's wife and the black sharecropper's wife and daughters. The women shared the very intimate spaces of the farmhouse, nurturing and raising white children. Now, white men were breaking up their ties to black families that had lived on their lands for decades. When the black women servants said the farms were 'no longer a home to us', Plaatje observed, there was often a farmer's wife who refused to break up the synergies of her mixed domestic life.[282] Plaatje recognised the white woman's response as moral and probably the most successful resistance to the displacements of the Natives Land Act of 1913. The white farmer's wife was unwilling to cut off the steady coloured hands that loved and cared for her children.

XIII

Silas Molema had never met the perfect stranger who was living with Modiri in Maitland Location, otherwise known as Ndabeni, in Cape Town, until he travelled there for the hearing at the Supreme Court of Appeal in January 1913. He had learnt about James Molebaloa's childhood and earlier life in a letter that relayed Molebaloa's early experience as a sharecropper living amongst whites in the countryside.[283] Molebaloa understood his life as a double injury. The first and early injury was landlessness, which he described in the letter to Molema. The other was the theft of his vocation. He would write about the second injury when he had finally redeemed both aspirations in a memoir more than two decades later. He wrote of the perpetrators as one category, *makhoa*, meaning whites. Whether they were Dutch-Afrikaner or English, they were guilty of the same crime of his disenfranchisement, first on the farmlands that his family had worked for decades, and then in a church he had served faithfully throughout his youth and early adulthood. As he described in the letter, he was not dispirited. He had become wiser and now entrusted his recognition as a person to other persons, *batho*, which were black people, and to them exclusively. The terms, '*makhoa*' and '*batho*' were an explicit reference to skin colour that at the same time indicated a position within the ethical position of personhood. He thought the proper placement for personhood lay only, and exclusively, with black people. Whites robbed, injured and diminished.

His father had died a sharecropper on the farm of a white Dutch-Afrikaner.[284] He wrote that 'we were born amongst the Boers all of us, just brought up in the wild, even we did not know people (*batho*), only that we are Barolong of the Ratshidi'. His family's most proximate attachments on the land were not people of colour who looked like them. His father worked hard on the land, poured himself into it and shared the grain 'on the halves' with the landowner. They were just working to feed themselves, never really flourishing. In the 1890s, Molebaloa was travelling between various Methodist circuits in Bechuanaland as a lay preacher and an interpreter for European missionaries with whom he travelled.[285] He had felt a calling to the pulpit when he was fourteen, had passed his examinations as a local preacher aged 16 and became an officially recognised 'evangelist' when he turned eighteen. In 1899, he attended Kilnerton Training College and formally qualified for induction in the Methodist church but when the war broke out, the Wesleyan Missionary Society postponed his installation. After the war ended, the Society would still not ordain him despite his qualification and his feeling that he had earned his keep.

After Molebaloa's father died in 1900, he left the farm because he 'could not agree with the manner of residing amongst whites (*makhoa*) while there were other Bechuana'.[286] He left to work the land for black landlords where he would care for the landlord and the landlord would care for him, where his placement would be his own property, and his autonomy a moral entitlement to manhood. He went to Dithakoaneng in the Batlhaping territories. 'As for my siblings, they have no thought of removing to the land of Secoana, only to squat on white farms, but I parted ways with my late father to offer myself to Batlhaping because I wanted to give myself to other Bechoana rather than give myself to whites.' His siblings had 'still not built anything'. They also 'have no thought of going to the lands of Secoana, only to squat on the farms of the whites'. His father had not left them a home.

Soon after the war, his wife's health had deteriorated. It was mental illness. He took her to an asylum on Robben Island, some fourteen kilometres off the coast of Cape Town, which is why he left Dithakoaneng and ended up in a Cape Town location where he still lived. When he moved to the Cape, his cattle died. His goats disappeared during the war. 'I have not a cow today or even a goat.' He gave up his placement in Dithakoaneng and started to build a life in Cape Town. His wife died in 1905 after she contracted tuberculosis on Robben Island. Life in a location was temporary and lived on borrowed ground. He was making ends meet as an itinerant peddler of patent medicaments by Graham Remedies Co. His current situation of depending entirely on the whites, *makhoa*, at Graham Remedies Co. for his survival distressed him.

He had never overcome the injury, the betrayal of the clerical fathers and the sight of his biological father dying old and wearied without a home of his own. At this age, now in a second marriage with children, he expected nothing from white settler society. He looked elsewhere to be seen. He needed care, and he said so unashamedly. He asked Molema for the kind of mutual dependency another adult man from the countryside would instantly recognise. Reading the letter, Molema understood that Molebaloa was not asking for a free ride. He was looking to work, but to work with moral urgency, to be helped to become someone, to be prevented from wasting his exertions on survival, and to be given a chance to prove himself. Molebaloa wanted to extricate himself from white employment and to return to the land to some degree. He was asking for a father whom he could serve so as to 'eat from my own people just like I eat from the whites here.'[287] He wanted to make a fresh start on the land. Besides, whites were not dependable. 'As for me, Morolong, when I have nothing, I will not be ashamed to eat from he that has something, truly, truly, sir. As for me, I think it is well to eat from your own people than to eat from whites.'[288] Whites as a species, he was suggesting, did not grow people. They shrunk them, swallowed them up, and erased them. He was seeking a fruitful situation – placement, in all the freedom it allowed a man to care for himself and for others.

Molema offered him placement. He did not only give him an allotment on the land but also opportunity. Molema wrote to him that he had a home in Mafikeng and that 'the best of all would be visiting first & to look around the place'.[289] Molebaloa also suggested to Molema that he relay to Graham Remedies Co. that 'a man like me visiting home should take the almanacs with & distribute them through the country'. Later on, Molema received Molebaloa in Mafikeng and helped him to travel to Dithakoaneng and across the border to Kanye, Gaborone and other places to sell the medicaments of Graham Remedies Co. and to distribute the 'almanacs' which would 'work out very good for their firm'[290] Molema was spreading his covering over Molebaloa and resuscitating the capacities of manhood and maturity he had lost in the injuries of youth. After all, this perfect stranger had already made himself family, looking after his son.

From then on, Molebaloa joined the stream of white-collar migrants in the reserve, coming and going between city and countryside, no different from the migrant labourers that spent long months in the mines away from home. Even if he let his placement or left it in someone else's care, Molebaloa had independent, secure roots on the land. He had a home of his own to stage the pedigree of a quintessentially human existence. He had a doorpost whence he emerged to dominate nature. He had a place of return and a domain of freedom to be his own man. He had an anchorage of care for his dependents. He was prepared for an unknowable future. He would not meet death, like his father, in the 'wild'. Twice married, with children, but only now a man. A return to the reserves was one circuit in a larger odyssey to proper 'origins' that educated black men were staging in their minds and in their associations. Men like Molebaloa were retreating, 'cutting themselves away' from the mixed frontier intimacies that had established schools, churches, farming enterprises and political alliances, but now tied aspiration solely to skin colour.

As an educated chief, Molema understood his place in black educated men's journeys of 'return' to personhood. He was the rainmaker, not simply by rite of birth, but by proving himself assiduously in the most moral undertaking of growing people.²⁹¹ In these years after Union, the indictment against black dishonour at whites' hands was growing louder. It was mediating a black exodus from erstwhile mixed frontier institutions. Africans felt there was little recognition for black merit. White institutions treated them as though they were no more than children, always needing to learn, ever requiring supervision. There was a lot more than rage involved here. There was hope and the energising optimism of a new vision to assemble all black people together as a solidarity of reputation. If black people were to redeem their esteem, then they would have to lift themselves up and build their confidence through their own institutions.

In the independent African churches, blacks allowed one another titles like 'Rev' and 'Bishop' that European missionary societies had denied them. They appeared in their vestments every Sunday in their own churches as the apex of the clerical hierarchy and graced their walls with certificates and photographs of achievement. Churches were a ready platform to demonstrate black persons' free capacity to offer one another a redemptive grace of care and recognition, and not only because there were so many qualified preachers who could not move forward with ordination. More importantly, the church had been offering them the arsenals of moral strategies that made possible a radical departure from a situation of social death. Christianity had equipped them to access the existential possibilities of 'reawakening'. It had taught them how to break up with the deficits and dissatisfactions of the present and reach for a better future that already existed through their faith, like the 'Kingdom'. The gospel had trained many, many thousands of frontier peoples that it was not necessary to remain helpless in fruitless ground. One only had only to encounter a new 'truth', not a new material circumstance, and create a new reality through the works of faith.²⁹² Hundreds of black Christianised men were now severing their ties with the barrenness of frontier attachments and freeing themselves to turn to one another for care.

In February 1913, Molema received a letter from Cornelius Maseloanyana, a young educated man at the Robinson Deep Gold Mining Company in Johannesburg.²⁹³ He was a congregant of the Wesleyan church in Mafikeng and someone with a qualification and aspirations for ordination as a minister. He was asking Molema for a testimonial to submit for his ordination in an independent church because 'I do not want being a reverend to pass me by as it did in the Wesleyan church'.²⁹⁴ Maseloanyane was joining a new independent congregation, the African Holy Catholic Church. His father however would not approve and would not yield his son's certificate of membership in the Methodist Church.²⁹⁵ When Molema wrote to relay the father's feelings to the son, the latter would rather face his father's disapproval than remain Wesleyan. 'As for life,' he wrote, 'I have lived with my spirit in great, great pain, so much so that if I do not find work, I must become a beggar, because I truly do not want to return to the Wesleyan church because it has caused me pain and has greatly weakened my spirit.'[296] He would either serve an independent church or withdraw from church life altogether. 'If I do not find work, I will rather do the things of the world.'

Molema prepared and sent a testimonial to the Rev J.D. Masigo, who led the African Holy Catholic Church. He sent him a good report of Maseloanyane's conduct in the Wesleyan church. Significantly, he also included his own declaration of support to the movement of black independent churches. 'The reason I am writing Reverend, is that I too love the black congregations of my own people and their progress although I alone am still in white congregations.'[297] The Reverend replied that

> whites are selfish amongst us blacks, like when they say, oh really, even that small black can lead his own congregation, yet even so, God is still standing with us. Please, my master, let the church be accepted by you, our chiefs, and all will be well when our chiefs welcome the work of God … We are facing hardship from whites. Our own laugh at us, saying the African Holy Catholic Church is not a church because it has no whites. The only churches are those that whites recognise.[298]

A month later, at the beginning of 1914, Cornelius Maseloanyane was serving as an ordained reverend of African Holy Catholic Church in Klerksdorp.[299] He wrote to Molema that this was a church 'of blacks own country', which had 'granted him work in the fullest capacity' and has 'appended Rev. to my name'. Molema continued writing to Mosigo.

> Dear Reverend, I wish to say may you grow. May the great Lord help your congregation with his most miraculous aids and help all the congregations with only his help. I wish to say may you grow as the only way that the congregation for us blacks will be under the care and leadership of our black reverends. May you grow. The only place where we too can praise the accomplishments of blacks in their congregations and elsewhere.[300]

Similar churches were making their appearance in the northern districts, including the Zion Gospel African Church under Senior Bishop J.N.R. Mosaka. When Mosaka visited Mafikeng around August 1914, he felt that

Molema had 'handled me like a child that you have known for a long time'.[301]

> I still say that the Zion Gospel African Church should work among the *morafe* of my homeland through you, my faithful chiefs, and as for me, I am preparing to come and speak to the Barolong and I have a lot to achieve… This church is not mine, it belongs to the black *morafe*. I am merely a shepherd that works for the black *morafe*. I expose how the black spirit is bound and the black body is bound. Also, please know my lord, that the work of someone like me is very great. My delay is not due to sitting doing nothing. The work is just beginning … I do all the critical work of taking the work to places under (1) the government of the whites (2) the chiefs of our black people.[302]

Within a few months, Mosaka had planted a church in Mafikeng. Cornelius Maseloanyana defected to this church and returned home.[303] Molema wrote to Mosigo about the young man's breach of trust but he wrote mainly to express his solidarity with the new independent movement.

> It is still all my desire, and all my prayer that you may grow. The only way our congregation as blacks can all be governed and led by their own black people, and they all become exclusively under their government and leadership. All of the denominations, hence I say, beloved reverend, the Barolong here in Mafikeng, are being begged and marked by many ministers of many churches, whites and blacks, to be allowed to teach here in the land of Morolong. Anyway now the Barolong are of the mind that they must allow a large denomination to come here, a true congregation and strong in the works of God and in the works of helping their *morafe*. Barolong love distinction, they love their blackness, and they do not forget those who can be of help in their *morafe*… You know I told you that I am a Wesleyan and that black congregations are what I love and honour greatly and pray that you may grow and become strong.[304]

Especially after the catastrophe of the Natives Land Act of 1913, the independent churches in the northern countryside gained momentum from those black sharecroppers who left the traditions of Anglicanism, Methodism and Presbyterianism behind. Having no home or desire to be in the reserves, they drifted back to white farms in the Transvaal and Orange Free State to confront new terms of dependency and paternalism, but they created new forums of mutual recognition through the independent churches, even as they were drifting unattached from place to place, transient in places that were not securely their own. For hundreds, the legislation had begun the long night of existential death. As Rev. Joel Goronyane put it in 1921, blacks had become things, pounds of flesh, which others used up at will and then discarded.[305]

> In this government, we blacks (*Bancho*) are like a piece of meat on a hob, and whilst it is cooking, the cooks remove now and then a piece to eat as it boils, and so on; it seems that finally it is to be dished out and completely finished off.[306]

In the meantime, Molema was contributing Sechuana hymns to enlarge the Methodist hymnbook.[307] The invitation came early in 1913. Molema contributed no less than ten original compositions and five transpositions of existing hymns from English to Sechuana. In one original composition on the death of Christ, he imagined a coming time of hope and restoration. 'I will eat the tree of life/ I will walk with God/ I will see friends/ Generations long gone/ We will hold hands/ We will praise God together.'[308] In another, he prayed for unity, all the people of the world, a congregation of mixed colour and creed. 'May your word increase/ Among all people (*ditshabeng*) of the world/ The knowledge of you increase/ Among many, many nations (*merafing*)/ Your Kingdom come/ One common agreement/ Of men and angels/ May love abound.'[309] The hymnbook had a supplementary section with five hymns of lament 'for the *morafe*'. Molema's composition is one of them. It is a prayer with the message of the independent churches, that Africans would know and recognise one another in solidarity, working and waiting for the day of their redemption. 'Jesus, a sun of righteousness/ Light among us/ On the land of Africa… Teach our children/To know one another/They are weak/ They are dishonoured … We beg for freedom/ From the prison of the guilty.'[310]

XIV

In May of 1914, Silas Molema appeared as a witness in a case against his uncle, Tantinyane Motshegare, who was then seventy years old.[311] Motshegare's teenage niece, had died allegedly at his hands a few days after he had given her a lashing. The elderly man had raised this niece, 'the child Pueng', who was then nineteen years old. Just before her death, he had suspected that she was either stealing from him or, more likely, associating with a man who was giving her money or buying her clothes like the new shoes and a headscarf he had noticed. The case was heard by the Resident Magistrate. The paramount Kgotla no longer had jurisdiction to hear such cases.

Motshegare said he had only 'punished the girl, as he would punish his own child', for stealing money from his handkerchief whilst he was sleeping. His witnesses were her other uncles who had held her prostate on the ground, with the upper part of her body bare, whilst he administered the lashes. They testified that she was fit enough afterwards to serve them coffee. As for the 'broken rib, a severe wound on the lower part of the body, which might have been caused by a kick, and weals on the upper part of the body and neck', Motshegare said she was most likely assaulted by a young man, because later on that same day she had run away to that man's hut. A few days later, according to Motshegare's testimony, he found his niece outside the door exhausted and suffering from her injuries, from which she had later died.

What concerned the magistrate, as far as the reportage in *Tsala ea Batho* relayed verbatim, was not whether the chief was guilty of murder. but rather why he had not brought the case of theft before him instead of taking matters into his own hands. Silas Molema testified that according to *Sechuana* custom, a man disciplined his own child. Motshegare's sentence was nine months in prison, which he was to serve in Cape Town. Molema wrote to James Molebaloa to ask him to keep an eye on the elderly man. Molema's view was that his uncle was only guilty of *Sekhoa*. His uncle still lived in the past where men of his age and status held authority.

> I know he was as a chiefly Morolong son ought to be, but he understood nothing of the whites (*makhoa*) as we their workers and messengers [,] that know whiteness (*sekhoa*) and [its] servitude do.[312]

XV

The harvest of 1913 made a big difference in Silas Molema's financial affairs – or rather, it provided new opportunities to start things up again after the losses he had suffered to the drought. In the spring of that year, he was preparing to send his son to university abroad to train as a medical doctor and replenishing his stock. He sold forty bags of 'kaffir corn' to Richard Rowland and another 128 bags to another trader, a Mr Amos.[313] He bought eleven big oxen, eleven medium oxen, six small oxen and two bulls for £149.[314] He paid for it all in cash and bought a wagon on credit.[315] He still had creditors – but had at least paid the £1 he had borrowed from a man who could not write and made a mark for his name.[316] Although he had promised Fincham to share the cost of fencing around the pan and digging a borehole on Mabete, he could not pay his £86-6-3 when it was time to split the bill. At the end of October, he paid Fincham only £2 and signed a promissory note for the rest.[317] At the end of the month, he made no provision for the promissory note at the bank, asked Fincham for more time, and requested him not to involve attorneys.[318] By the end of the year, Molema had not paid a single penny towards the debt.

Fincham felt that Molema was putting his own interests first and had left him alone to drown in the expenses on the farm. He started to withhold the rent that he was collecting from Burger, £1-10-0 a month, against the money Molema owed him.

> I asked you to help me & you treat me as if I am nothing. I must have some money from you. You asked me not to let you wash down the river when your promissory note falls due … if you could have helped me now in time of need I could return the complement to you but you don't even try to help me you agreed to pay half the expense & now I ask you to help me & you simply sit down & leave it all to me.[319]

Early in 1914, Fincham approached Spencer Minchin to summon Molema to provide for his promissory note.[320] He told Molema outright that he longer considered him a 'big man & a friend' because such a man would not let him 'drown' and would 'let me keep my name with the bank'.[321] He also informed him that from that point onward he would be like any ordinary tenant and offer nothing beyond his contractual obligations. He would not ward off trespassers or collect money from farmers who grazed on Mabete unless Molema paid him a fee as 'I have enough work to do myself'.[322] They faced one another in court on 10 March 1914, but Minchin negotiated a settlement. Fincham offered that as a friend, 'I am not cross with you' but as far as the debt is concerned 'it is a matter of business'. He demanded that Molema pay at least £30 in cash at the beginning of April.[323]

Circumstance somewhat contrived to save Molema in the sense that Fincham needed him. Ben Burger could not continue on the farm. Unless a farmer also traded, it was impossible to stay on. Burger had already put up a house. It was impossible to recover at least some of the costs unless another tenant bought him out. Fincham offered to buy him out for £70 and pass on the contract to his brother-in-law, Dickerson, who then worked on the railways. Tenants often preferred to rent adjoining portions of a farm with relations so that they could share water and pasture.³²⁴ Fincham approached Molema to vouch for Dickerson as 'not a rich man' but a 'good man' who would carry out good improvements on the farm. He desperately needed Molema to agree. Burger, though a 'Dutchman', had not been so bad after all. He had not traded, even at the cost of his survival on the farm, but Fincham had had to watch him very closely, having learnt that his contract to be the sole trader on Mabete did not protect him from illicit trade.

Indeed, to replace Burger, he needed a new neighbour tenant he could trust. Nevertheless, this was not all. He had sunk the well on Burger's site at great expense. He wanted it back. That well had been his first undertaking on Mabete, digging very deep because the country had not had rain. He wanted a tenant who would allow him use of that well. He had not given it up. Dickerson was family, which made it easy to negotiate shared resources. Above all else, he wanted less uncertainty and more control. He desired the autonomy to plan ahead, some stability at least to be able to anticipate what would happen next. If he could not stop the constant movement on the farm, he wanted power to make decisions about it. He asked Molema for recognition as Mabete's official overseer. That would give him better control, he said, to take care of his friend.

> I have also placed to your account 10/- which I charged Rowland of Kanye [for grazing] and 10/- I charged Nel for grazing and water from the pan. So you see I am looking after you, and if you are agreeable I would be pleased if you will give me more power to act on your behalf here and then I can show people that I am master here and acting for you & will collect all the moneys I can for you from this farm.³²⁵

He found it impossible to wait through the uncertainty so he sold Burger's right on the farm to Dickerson for £70. He wrote to Molema after the fact, in May 1914.

> I want you to approve of this as it is a good man & will still improve the property [.] [Y]ou must not be afraid [because] in the end the building is yours all the same and you hold out your right to water your cattle @ [sic] the well just the same as when Burger was there [.] [A]ll that Mr Dickerson wants is a proper lease to be drawn up for 5 years. This of course we can talk about when you come[.] [W]e will always meet one another as we are old friends & will not squabble over nothing.³²⁶

Molema had allowed him some right to handle his affairs on Mabete, although it was far short of the 'overseer' role he had requested. He had the right to charge or impound the stock of 'any white man' who grazes his stock on the farm or otherwise to impound the stock if he refused to pay.[327] It was not nearly enough freedom, but it was enough that Molema had also approved of the arrangement with Dickerson. Molema agreed that his own animals would no longer drink at the well, and so Fincham arranged to share the well with with his brother-in-law. He was reclaiming his well. Molema also agreed that he and Fincham would have exclusive access to one of the two natural pans on Mabete. The arrangement worked well for Fincham. He was settling down to the business of farming and trading. He was close enough to his brother-in-law to prevent him from trading. He welcomed the stability, the sense of having some control, but it did not last very long.

Molema was signing up more tenants and had diversified the terms of tenancy so he could tap a more consistent flow of cash rents rather than only infrastructural developments. Fincham reproached him for 'letting more ground to other people, strangers whom we don't know', and wanted Molema to protect his interests because 'I think as I am your first tenant and have already made improvements to the value of over £700-0-0 on this farm that you must protect me & assist me for any grazing rights'.[328] In June 1914, just a month after Dickerson started up, Molema was urging J. van Rensburg to make up his mind about whether he would hire a portion of Mabete as 'there are many people who want me to lease this farm to them'.[329] He and Van Rensburg were in a business partnership, but apparently not quite of a lawful kind. The 'anti-squatting' regulations of the Natives Land Act of 1913 made it difficult for white traders to sell grain in the reserves of the Cape Province across the border. Van Rensburg had provided Molema with 300 bags of sorghum to sell for him in the stadt. Fincham remonstrated that Van Rensburg brings only 'troubles and complications' but Molema took him on anyway.[330] The contract stipulated that van Rensburg would build a house of five rooms on the farm.[331]

The new tenant was not a small farmer. He was a successful Dutch-Afrikaner who, unlike Dickerson and Burger before him, would not find Fincham daunting to defy. Fincham knew this and was already seeing his end. The exercise of protecting himself on Mabete was like scooping the ocean back with a spoon. He wrote to Molema that 'my heart is sore today as I see troubles in store for all of us here'.[332] In August, Van Rensburg started to sell mealies from his front door.[333] The reality was that without trade, it was impossible for these tenants to survive on the farm. This is why Burger had left.

Elsewhere on the farm, things were not going well for James Higgs either. He too had had to quit and leave 'in a hurry'.[334] He was taking up paid work in Potchefstroom in October 1914. He had been on the farm for only eighteen months of his five-year contract. Higgs begged Molema to reimburse at least part of his spending on the farm 'as you are an honest man'.[335] He pleaded with him, 'please have pity on me and give me say only £10 of all the expense which I had. I can tell you that my family have to sup without meat now for 2 or 3 weeks.' Molema never had spare change. Instead, he had become more desperate in his pursuit of rents. He took on G. Beukes as a new tenant and Dickerson's new neighbour. He allowed Beukes use of the second natural pan on the farm.

Fincham was furious. The location of Beukes' new well would drain water from the one on Dickerson's property.[336] Both Beukes and Van Rensburg were watering their stock at the well on Dickerson's portion but refusing to pay. They said they were paying Molema. Fincham and Dickerson then decided to formalise their agreement with Molema through an attorney because Molema was 'causing & have been the cause of a lot of trouble here between the white people … You agree with one man this way & the other that way & you are causing rows & unpleasantness'.[337] It was unnerving, having so small a margin of control. If farming and trading on Mabete were like a game, it seemed to him it had no rules and yet any one mistake could displace him. Where would he go, seeing he had no place of return.

In the meantime, ordinary householders on Mabete no longer had access to the two natural pans, one being for the exclusive use of Molema and Beukes and the other for the exclusive use of Fincham and Molema. In September 1914, a herder took his animals to drink at Dickerson's well. The 'Native Mongolish', Dickerson wrote to Molema, 'though very respectful about it he cannot see that he should pay'.[338] Dickerson also wanted Molema to provide '3 boys for white man's wages' to help him to dig deeper into the ground for water. Dickerson did deepen the well but like James Higgs and Ben Burger before him, he too could not keep up the venture. He took up paid work at Blanc Witkop Mine in Zeerust where high-grade fluorspar had been recently discovered.[339] He had been on the farm a mere four months but could not remain unless he supplemented his income with a wage. He left Mrs Dickerson in charge. Fincham was besides himself. Whosoever bought Dickerson out would gain exclusive right to the well, the very right he had frozen in a contract through the attorneys. The contract still had four more years to run.

A few months later, Fincham returned to Spencer Minchin to issue

Molema with fresh summons for the £58-1-0 he owed him.³⁴⁰ Molema received these on Christmas Eve. Three months later, in March of 1915, Molema wrote to Fincham, asking him to consolidate his debt at £100 by lending him another £30.³⁴¹ Fincham did not entirely refuse. He thought he could use the opportunity to manage the situation of Dickerson's very possible departure. He wanted to keep his well.

> All owe me money & no one pays me so how can I help you. I am indeed sorry for you ... Now a line about Dickerson. I hear he wants to sell his right ... if you can manage it you ought to try & keep the place for us as it is the only water we can depend on & a new man may be nasty & do us out of water.³⁴²

Fincham then learnt that Beukes wanted to lease Dickerson's portion so that his children could move into Dickerson's cottage to be closer to the primary school on the farm. Fincham had raised funds to establish the school for white children.³⁴³ He suggested to Molema that Beukes should only rent the house and pay for monthly lodgings, while he would take over Dickerson's 'right' to the well and grazing grounds. Then 'when I see my way clear', Fincham explained, he would take over Dickerson's lease entirely.³⁴⁴ He would not give up his well. He also tried to force the arrangement by pressing Spencer Minchin to proceed with collecting from Molema. He discovered that Minchin was choosing sides – and not the side of the paying client. Minchin arranged that Molema would pay £2 a month. It would not even be payment in cash. Fincham would have to collect rents on the farm until they had cleared the debt with interest.³⁴⁵ 'Mr Minchin and you know that you owe and are not playing the game, you owe money and you never pay anything off.'³⁴⁶

Fincham had only hard words to fling at Molema, and he hoped that they would sting. 'You seem to have a lot of trouble [and] work, don't you earn anything by it.'³⁴⁷ He wrote to Molema that people were cutting the fence around their pan. Instead of stopping them, he had decided to use the wires and poles for something else.³⁴⁸ Molema had paid nothing towards the cost of fencing in any case. 'I am quite sure you can make some money from the water in the pans. It is no use you asking me to do this or that as I can't leave my shop & go and stand [at] the pan & look after other peoples [sic] cattle'.³⁴⁹ The reality was he had tried to get the local herders to pay and they had refused. They also refused to provide any labour when Fincham ordered them to help make fodder as their cattle trampled the grass on the way to the pan.³⁵⁰ Fincham showed Molema's headman on the farm, Setlhako Mancho, a notice from Molema that forbade anyone watering animals at the pan but Mancho merely 'went home and said nothing to me'.³⁵¹

Molema wanted Dickerson's family to remove from the farm as soon as possible. Dickerson received a scathing note from Molema for not paying rent, not planting fruit trees, and not 'improving the place as much as you can'.³⁵² Dickerson took a train to Mafikeng to talk to Molema face to face 'rather than have everything settled through a letter'.³⁵³ He wanted to explain all his improvements on the cottage and the well, and to plead for a little more time to remove his family. He was working on the mines, where would they go? Molema was not at home to listen. Dickerson waited for him but eventually returned to the farm, leaving an account of all the work he had carried out over the course of his very brief stay on the farm. At the very least, he was hoping Molema would understand that he was not slacking off, waiting for someone to buy him out. He was begging for compassion. Survival on the farm was difficult.

At the beginning of June, Molema transferred Dickerson's whole lease to Beukes, although Beukes was still having difficulty finding the money to pay.³⁵⁴ Fincham had not given up on the quest to gain some measure of control over the constant changes on the farm, including increasingly defiant trespassers. These matters unnerved him. They made his own roots on the land fragile. He had also not given up on his well. He asked Molema for power of attorney to make all decisions on the farm. In turn, he promised to handle the entire farm as a joint enterprise for both him and Molema. He would sell water, charge fees for grazing, manage the other tenants, and collect their rents. This legal authority would let him deal decisively with trespassers watering their stock in the pan. There were Basotho on his portion, who answered to Mancho and 'will not listen to me [and] as a matter of fact my agreement with you does not give me the power to interfere with them, all that I can say is that you are losing money every day in this matter'.³⁵⁵

He sweetened the proposal with a demonstration of its benefits to the landlord. He prepared two leasing agreements. The first agreement was for a family called Sanger to build another cottage of three rooms across the railway. That way, like the Beukes, they would move closer to the school. They would pay 5 shillings a month for the stand whilst building the cottage. Another unnamed tenant would build a cottage of three rooms as a school near that cottage, this time for 'coloured children'. He would also pay 5 shilling per month.³⁵⁶ Molema agreed on both leasing agreements but did not grant Fincham power of attorney.³⁵⁷ Fincham could only hope to get his hands on the money to take over Dickerson's contract before Beukes could raise the same.[358] The year was nearing its end, and Dickerson had still not left his site.

In November a farmer by the name of Van Wyk arrived on the farm. He helped Beukes to buy Dickerson out of his lease. Nevertheless, only four months later, Beukes was already behind on his rent of one pound a month on the site. He had to 'beg' Molema to 'wait a little longer as I am hard up just now but I shall make a plan'[359] Fincham offered to hire Beukes as his itinerant trader in other parts of the Bechuanaland Protectorate. Beukes decided to make his own money selling hides and skins from his own front door. Fincham wrote to Molema that Beukes 'is doing me a lot of harm here and with a vile tongue' and subsequently he, Fincham, was 'losing a lot of customers'. He wanted Molema to kick him off the farm and he would find a replacement tenant, but 'not a Dutchman again [.] I will get an Englishman this time.'[360] In the meantime, the other 'Dutchman' on the farm, Van Rensburg, had taken steps to make his trading lawful by obtaining a trading license but not for cattle. Fincham objected. He submitted his complaint to the Protectorate government, but the government replied that it 'was not aware that the Protectorate had granted you exclusive privilege'.[361] First, Molema would not defend the terms of their agreement and now the government had also shrugged its shoulders and looked away.

Fincham started to harass Beukes. He demanded control of the well that he had sunk 'with my own money'.[362] He threatened to take legal action. Fincham knew the threat was empty because Beukes had inherited his exclusive ownership of the well through the very rigid contract that Fincham himself and Dickerson had drawn up through their attorney.[363] He travelled to Mafikeng to see Molema in July 1916. They had a 'long conversation' but he returned to Mabete dissatisfied.[364] Three months later, Molema wrote to him that he, as landlord, would speak to Beukes to allow him, Fincham, some water from the well. Fincham did not wait. He immediately sent his herders to the well with a note. His intention was to show Beukes that he, Fincham, had won the fight, but Beukes wrote in Dutch that 'I give no water ... unless Molema tells me so himself'. Fincham's stock drank, but he had to pay.[365] The same afternoon, Fincham saw men carrying about thirty skins to Beukes' place.[366] Ten days before that he had watched some of his own customers follow the same path to Beukes' door.[367] He wrote to Molema in alarm that Beukes was 'driving a business on this farm'. He was prepared to beg. He pleaded desperately with Molema to evict Beukes, whom he said was 'the only trouble' between he and Molema. Were they not like brothers? Without Beukes, surely 'we can settle'.[368]

Molema did nothing. Things had now gotten out of hand. Fincham returned to Spencer Minchin to ask him to arbitrate between him and Molema.[369] He also made an appointment to see the Resident Commissioner in Mafeking the following month.[370] He returned from the meeting satisfied. The Resident Commissioner had listened and had promised to act decisively to force Molema to honour their contract and allow no other trader on the farm. He warned Molema:

> … you have now completely broken our friendship & I shall only expect you to carry out our agreement …don't think I am finished with the authorities yet [.] [Y]ou will hear more … I don't require any answer to this [.] [T]reat it as usual.[371]

Molema did 'treat it as usual' and did nothing. The following day Setlhako Mancho offered two men placement on Mabete. They paid their rents to Molema in cash. They appear to have been 'brown' men. Fincham threatened to graze his stock over their fields. He warned Molema to expect trouble from the Resident Commissioner. 'I want you to be very careful to carry out our agreement in future.'[372] Molema still did nothing. Beukes was still trading. Beukes was still refusing to let him near the well. It was clear to Fincham that the Resident Commissioner had not done as he had promised. The only route left open was again to plead with Molema as a 'brother' and an old, dear friend.

> My heart is bleeding over this matter if I consider that I should have course to have to go to law and be bad friends with my dearest friend I had before Beukes came here and why should our written agreement be broken through an outsider [.] [M]ay God grant and strengthen you to put this matter right soon. [I am] yours as ever so soon as our agreement in fulfilled.[373]

This time, Molema replied, because Fincham had mentioned God. It meant Fincham was accusing him of moral corruption. It implied that he, Molema, was a swindler, a man without decency. He agreed that something had indeed broken between them, but not because of Beukes. It had broken long before their squabble over the water in the well and the other men on the farm. In fact, he suggested to Fincham, what was between them had never been a true friendship because he was a black man, and Fincham had always thought he was a fool, not a partner. Yes, Fincham liked to call him 'brother' and his 'friend', but these were empty words, especially from a Christian who did not have the good conscience to treat a black brother as an equal. In fact, he wanted Fincham to know that he was no fool at all. He had seen through all his pretenses, but had looked past these offences because God's commandment was love and forgiveness.

> Sir, I am so greatly moved by your letter ... in ... which you said may God grant that our friendship not be broken by a stranger, and outsider that I have thought [about] it deeply when you said in your letter [:] I think you think that I am a fool kaffer who do [sic] not see thing[s] in the light of business ... Surely you think you must think I am a fool but [because] I want to be in peace with my very dear friend Mr Fincham to give him all the chance I can, not through my foolishness. I am getting letters nearly every day from the attorneys demanding this and that in favour of Mr Fincham. This troubles me much. Dear Sir, imagine say I might [have] died and you are still alive, and my son comes in, and goes through all the correspondence which passed between us of late years [.] [D]o you think he will give you any more chance. [A]s to myself I am alright we are old friends; just nearly like brothers, although one white and the other a black man, still we are talking together and not with bad spirit but as brothers in the same family.[374]

It was not possible to ignore the feeling of the young people in one's dealing with whites. He had to think about his son. The younger generation was accusing their elders of being too conciliatory with whites, instead of abandoning constitutionalism and adopting a stance of militancy. This stance had its first big, public explosion in the riots in the Witwatersrand from 1918. It involved the younger, educated men in the Transvaal National Congress, including the lawyer Pixley Seme, whom he knew.

Next, Molema addressed Fincham's suggestion that he was placing more people on the farm for the sake of money, like a common extortionist, with no other rationale than to enrich himself. He clarified that in fact he was operating from a position of common decency. He had allowed two men who had nowhere else to go a place on his farm to plough and feed their animals, instead of turning them away just because they could not afford to lease a farm as Fincham was doing. He had felt compassion for them and charged them only a little money. This was placement, to give another man a chance, not some cheap moneymaking scheme.

> ... you say it has come to your notice that I have let certain lands for ploughing purpose to Subganger and Antony ... I never let any place to [them] but he, Antony, has been ploughing there ... They have [sic] been placed there by my Foreman, Setlhako Manco, who has a perfect right to place him there at that time ... of course seeing that Antony is using my farm for ploughing purposes and also grazing his stock, it came to my mind that I must charge him, something, not to say that I have let my lands to him.[375]

He made it clear that Fincham was himself on the land due to the same moral duty. Had he, as landlord, been a ruthless rentier, he would handle tenancy on his land quite differently, as purely a rational economic transaction.

Beukes' trade in hides took him even further north. Early in January 1917, he travelled all the way to Lake Ngami to trade. He left his rent unpaid. When Molema demanded payment, Mrs Beukes pleaded with him to 'work mercifully with us to put a few pounds together [.] [P]lease be patient [,] [M]y husband will pay all that we owe when he comes back.'[376] Nearby, Van Rensburg was selling cattle without a license. Even he was having a hard time finishing the five-roomed house he had agreed to build on the farm. He asked Molema to share the cost of the stone and wood. Molema refused that plea for help but suggested that Van Rensburg lend him money.[377] 'If you lend me the sum of £35 and give me four months to pay it without interest, I will then agree to pay you the sum of £45.' He needed the money to pay his attorneys, De Kock and De Kock, who were representing him in a suit that the trader Sundel Gordon had brought against him.[378]

Fincham wanted Van Rensburg gone, but he understood that the courts could not help him. The only path to some measure of control was attaching to the landlord more deeply. Attorneys were an expensive and futile exercise. He had not expected Molema's reply, certainly not to read anything about one being white and the other black. Now he felt ashamed and wanted to smooth things over. He pleaded with Molema that 'if you will only trust me all will be well and no trouble will come [and] may God bless you to put more trust in me'.[379] Besides, Molema said he had forgiven him. In fact, Molema wrote that he had been to the Resident Commissioner, who was apparently satisfied that the two of them had merely been 'disputing like friends in a friendly spirit' over the well.[380] Molema said he had asked the Resident Commissioner to prevent Beukes and Van Rensburg's trade on the farm, but that the official had said the government could not prevent anyone from buying hides or cattle. 'So you can see that I have tried my best for you but

Morafe

could not succeed.' If that was true, then the Protectorate government had again shrugged its shoulders and sent Fincham away, as if he were something they could make disappear.

XVI

Sebopioa Molema handled the trouble still stirring at Rietfontein with his usual administrative efficiency on the regent's behalf. He maintained the line of reply to the government that only Lekoko Montsioa had the jurisdiction to resolve the dispute at the eastern border of the Molopo Reserve. The regent would not accept the government's intervention even when the Native Affairs Department ruled in his favour. After the Superintendent of Natives H. Frost's investigation, the department had concluded that the Rapulanas' complaints at Rietfontein 'are without foundation' and that the 'Government does not intend to interfere in the matter'.[381] This was in early autumn, March 1913. The chieftaincy's response was measured and not celebratory. 'I hope now rest and peace will be restored.'[382] In the chiefs' mind in Mafikeng, this 'rest and peace' would not follow as an outcome of the government's ruling but because the chieftaincy had established its authority at Rietfontein independently.

In the last week of May 1913, the matter at Rietfontein came to the attention of a new Resident Magistrate and Civil Commissioner, R.C. Lloyd. He and Frost rode out to Rietfontein after some householders complained 'concerning the treatment received by them from Headman Paul Montsioa in connection with the lands out there'.[383] The Rapulana instigators, especially George Motuba and Seiso Modise, had taken advantage of the change of guard in the Resident Magistrate's office to press the government to intervene. Lloyd's predecessor had handled the matter remotely. He had not travelled there and, unlike Frost for instance, could not match faces to the names and erf numbers involved in the dispute. Lloyd threw his energies into the dispute. He studied the available official documentation on Rietfontein and called public meetings there to hear the matter. Moreover, people were anticipating a good harvest after a long drought, which likely escalated the dispute beyond chiefs and their agitators to include ordinary householders at Rietfontein. These peasant producers knocked hard on the door of the local colonial government to intervene and protect their fields.

On 29 May 'a large number of Natives' had gathered at Rietfontein to make representations to both Lloyd and Frost.[384] Lloyd took extensive notes, probably working through an interpreter and transcriber, to record the events that both the Rapulana and the Ratshidi presented in support of their claim, but the basis of his ruling was Sidney Shippard's report of the Land Commission of 1886 that had established the reserves. He found the Commission, as the report outlined, 'purposely refrained from defining boundaries between tribes or section[s] of tribes considering the reserves available for all natives no matter of what nationality'.[385] According to that policy, every paramount chief had jurisdiction over the whole population within its borders. That meant Lekoko Montsioa was the paramount chief with jurisdiction over all the Molopo Reserve, regardless of the 'nationality' of the residents under his domain. Nevertheless, Shippard had not entirely stuck to the principle. He had made some exceptions to this policy at Rietfontein.

The principle had made reservation easier and uncomplicated in the new territories of British Bechuanaland, which he understood Britain wished to govern as cheaply as possible, and at a distance. Shippard had worried that when the Land Commission had implemented the policy and turned its back, leaving chiefs with unusually extensive powers over autonomous reserves, there would be vulnerable householders, almost a thousand at Rietfontein, who would almost certainly face immediate dispossession. He had described how the Rapulana chiefs at Rietfontein had 'waited upon me and begged earnestly that they might be allowed to remain in the possession of kraals, cattle posts and land in and around Lotlokana [Rietfontein], occupied by them on behalf of the Chief ... of Polfontein [in the Transvaal] since 1874'.[386] There were about 960 Rapulana in Rietfontein in 1886. He had also been aware that Montsioa had been attempting to drive these families back into the Transvaal, but 'has never up to the present time succeeded in dislodging them'. This is why Shippard made an exception to the principle of 'territorial jurisdiction' in the Molopo Reserve by both giving Montsioa full territorial jurisdiction and right to collect tribute throughout the reserve, including at Rietfontein and, at the same time, also recognising Rietfontein as an independent Rapulana enclave within the Molopo Reserve.

Not only that, Shippard had also built an extra buffer against dispossession by making sure that the settlement at Rietfontein remained connected to the larger polity of the Rapulana at Polfontein in the Transvaal. His usual practice had been to auction private farms along the boundaries of every reserve to prevent new encroachment by settlers and other alliances, yet in the Molopo Reserve, he had departed from the practice. Private farms enclosed the reserve, except along its eastern border at Rietfontein where only a fence

Morafe

separated the reserve from the Transvaal. A fence could move westwards, placing the Molopo Reserve behind Rietfontein should it be necessary for the miniature reserve to break away at the discretion of his government. 'It appears to me that I could not equitably deny to [Rapulana] the privilege [they] sought [and] I say nothing of common humanity in this case.' Shippard had considered this action as stemming from good conscience.[387] Hence, Lloyd's reading of Shippard's report led him to the conclusion that 'the claims of the Rapulana are sound and just … whether or no[t] they first took possession of Lotlakana'.[388]

At the beginning of the meeting, the Rapulana based their claims on their early conquest of Rietfontein.[389] However, most of their claims focused on the present, not the past. They said Paul Montsioa had recently ordered two spans of oxen to one man's field to 'turn over the lands with the mealies as they stood' just as the man was about to reap. For this reason, Seiso Modise said, the Rapulana 'do not acknowledge Paul as our chief – our ruler is George Motuba'. Isaac Lerang said the incident on his fields had happened whilst his son was sick, 'and therefore it shows Paul is not my chief as he oppressed me when I was in trouble'. He wanted the government to act. 'I am applying for assistance from the Government'. The reports emphasised that Paul Montsioa's recent acts of dispossession proved that the Rapulana were a separate people. 'He did this,' Hermanus Phokoanyane explained to Lloyd, 'to show me, that I was not one of his people.' Mancoe Mogani said he paid 'Hut Tax' in the reserve, and yet had to cross the border into the Transvaal to plough. How was it possible to belong to a chief where taxes did not guarantee placement? Ramathiledi Mosekare thought his double payment of taxes, both a 'levy' to Lekoko and Hut Tax to the government, was a moral purchase of their care. 'I am a taxpayer both to the Government and to the Chief.' Hence, he expected to flourish. He would be happy to accept Paul Montsioa as his chief. His only concern was that 'we do not prosper'. He expected to prosper by the hand that collected his taxes. 'People prosper through the chief.'

Lloyd did not refer to these narratives when he recommended that the Native Affairs Department consider Sidney Shippard's report of 1886 and rule in favour of the Rapulana. On the other hand, Joshua Molema was paying very close attention to them. He understood the political repertoire at play. He wrote to his brother Silas, that '[Seiso] says Paul Montsioa must cut himself away from them (*a coe mo go bona*) [;] he is not their chief [as] he took their fields and gave them to Segalo and Rrabodima and Moshoeu and the sons of Mokgojoa'.[390] He recognised the repertories of oration and performance that a tributary population put on display when it wished to disband its attachment to an existing authority. The same repertoire of storytelling took place when chiefs themselves contested genealogies in succession disputes. Lloyd's public meeting had provided a platform to stage such a performance to a large audience, where householders could woo alternative sources of patronage, in this instance, the government and the Rapulana chiefs of the Transvaal.

At the end of June 1913, the Superintendent Frost called yet another public meeting at Rietfontein, but the crowd was smaller, about 200 people.[391] The meeting coincided with the promulgation of the Natives Land Act. The Molopo Reserve, including Rietfontein, had all become Crown Lands, which is probably why Frost, an official who preferred to be hands on and visible on the ground, determined to handle placement on the allotments himself. Perhaps he had confidence of better results in light of the legislation and wished to prevent any further confusion. The paramount chiefs of Mafikeng and Polfontein, Lekoko Montsioa and Monchosi Motlaba both attended. The business of the day was administrative. Frost stated that he 'had not come to address [or] discuss the Rietfontein question in general but only to verify the statement as to the allocation of lands'.[392] He proceeded to the lands in question to map the positions of at least fifty-five 'holders' in the contested lands. Despite all this, Lekoko Montsioa would not yield.

Lekoko main objection, as Sebopioa relayed to Lloyd, was that 'this is a civil matter between my people and according to the power vested in me by the Government, I have the exclusive jurisdiction to decide the matter at my "Kgotla"'.[393] Sebopioa also wrote on the regent's behalf to Rev. George Weavind about the contestation at Rietfontein as a 'son soliciting your fatherly [advice]'.[394] He wrote that 'the new development of the contention is kindled by the would-be-officials of the Government in their capacity as Superintendent of Natives and Inspectors of Native Reserves, who would like to see the native people split up and the power of the Chiefs broken that they may have great and glorious name that they have destroyed us'.[395] The Native Affairs Department, despite Lloyd's feeling that the Rapulana's claim had support in Shippard's report, decided to uphold Shippard's overall principle that lent all paramount chiefs full territorial jurisdiction over their given reserve. It delivered its ruling on 7 January 1915, in favour of Lekoko Montsioa.[396]

The ruling made little difference on the ground. It could not quell chiefs' incessant butting of heads and the popular discontent it created at Rietfontein. The more radical Rapulana agitators wanted Lloyd to 'make a division of the Molopo Reserve' so they could establish themselves on their own land.[397] It appears they invited the Rector of the Anglican Church, Rev. George Robinson, to establish a church in Rietfontein. When Frost requested Lekoko Montsioa to indicate a suitable spot, Sebopioa Molema wrote to refuse because this was 'merely a pretext' to the original dispute.[398] Sejesho Mothibi, one of the leading Rapulana instigators had apparently said, 'Where on earth have you ever seen a people hindered to worship their God by those in authority, asking that instead of worshipping God they must be worshipped? Those in power do not want us to build a church house, they want us to worship on trees.'[399] 'This is a beginning', he had reportedly urged, 'great matters to encounter are ahead.' Sebopioa Molema did not allocate land for the church and that was the end of the matter. The dispute settled at a stalemate. Despite the promulgation of the Natives Land Act of 1913, the government could not force chiefs to comply on lands that were now Crown Lands. The regent withstood pressure through Sebopioa's cool technocratic vigilance to explain his refusals to comply with action by the colonial government.

Sebopioa refusal to recognise the Union government's jurisdiction in the reserve infuriated colonial officials, but at the same time, the office of the Resident Magistrate and Civil Commissioner benefited from Sebopioa's efficiency of administration and tight control of the movement of young people and women. The anxieties about loitering youths and 'wild women' from the decade before continued. Sebopioa had for instance written numerous memoranda to Lloyd's predecessor concerning the 'removal of loiterers from the streets'.[400] The movement of women was under strict surveillance. One woman pretended to be sick for three months, 'acted as a lunatic and was confined to her bed and helpless' only to escape one Sunday when everyone went to church.[401] Sebopioa also appealed to the magistrate to dispatch police to patrol the reserve, 'compelling able bodied males to seek proper employment'.[402] In 1915, he wrote that 'long since we have complained to the government about this class of persons who are under nobody's jurisdiction'.[403] He surrendered those elements of the population that unsettled chiefly and patriarchal power in the reserve to the government.

After the regent's death, the Native Affairs Department agreed to recognise John Montsioa. He was brother to the late Wessels and Badirile Montsioa. The government opted to recognise a hereditary ruler because Lekoko's tenure had been stable with excellent administrative efficiency, unlike those of Wessels and Badirile before him. '[There] was happily some improvement and Government is determined that such improvement shall be at least maintained.'[404] The difference was Sebopioa's service to the fathers.

The government may have also recognised a hereditary ruler because, as the situation at Rietfontein was daily demonstrating, chiefs were able and prepared to fight to do as they wished in the reserves. The new reality of conquest notwithstanding, the colonial project in these northern reserves remained a struggling, incomplete undertaking. However, Sebopioa would not stay to serve a much younger man as he had served the fathers. When he again left the reserve after the regent's death mid-1915, he was still the tall, lean dark figure with a walking stick that had left once years before, but he was not sailing overseas. That ship had sailed.

XVII

Modiri Molema returned to Mafikeng for the Christmas holidays of 1913. He was there to say goodbye before he sailed to Britain the following year. He was finally going to university. Pixley ka Isaka Seme and Dr Abdullah Abdurahman, who was also leader of the anti-segregationist movement, African Political Organisation, had advised him to consider the Universities of Edinburgh and Glasgow, 'but I shall not decide until I see things for myself over at England'.[405] He returned to Kimberley the following year to finalise his affairs and attended a meeting of the SANNC. He was also spending time with a woman he had met in Kimberley. He had decided he would qualify as a medical doctor and return to marry her, but for the time being he introduced her to nobody, made no mention of her at all. He set sail on the *Armadale Castle* for England on 7 March 1914. His letters were cheerful and earnest and full of detail about life, places and people. He was very happy as a storyteller for others' pleasure. He was becoming a writer.

He wrote to his father when he arrived in London, 'I was lonely on the ship, but God was with me.'[406] 'There were very many of us on the ship,' the letter continued, 'but that was nothing as the whites of South Africa see Blacks as kaffirs always.' A ship crammed full of white South Africans was as good as an empty vessel. His solitude was complete, as the water spread under the bow, his 'only friends from Cape Town coming here were letters'. When he disembarked, he had no expectation of the same prejudice. Britain was another country. He considered he would be at home in Britain with friends and a family to embrace him. Disembarking, he felt he was leaving the colonial isolation of South Africa behind on the ship. Surely, there would be people and a home in the British metropolis. There was time and there were possibilities. At the docks in Southampton, he let himself stand still.

> When we landed at Southampton, Southampton people came in to meet their friends and take away their luggage, and I soon found out that I was being left alone, but what is funny about me, I am never anxious about this things [sic]. I am always confident that my God will send someone to help me. And there I stood.[407]

A man, a perfect stranger, 'came and took my luggage to the custom house' and told him what to do and where to go next. Another man came along and got him a cab to the train station. At the train station, yet another man helped him find a train to London and transfer his luggage onto the train. When he arrived at Waterloo, 'a man again the 4th simply came & showed me the way to the cloak Rooms, because you must remember the station[s] are very large out here and platforms many so that one really is quite at a loss which way to go especially when you have so much luggage'. He found accommodation at a boarding house that a 'Christian old lady' kept. 'Now Rra,' he wrote, 'what I call the wonderful works of God is this.'

He said nothing about the colour of their skin – these perfect, nameless strangers. During those first daunting hours, they had shrunk a large unfamiliar metropolis into a place small enough for him to manage freely by himself. Later in the day, he told his father, 'I was able to get about myself' with a 'booklet of the whole plan of London, with streets and everything.' He felt safe and free and surrounded by others who cared. 'That is what God has done for me, and I am sure he shall ever go before me, to make friends for me wherever I may go.' He visited the Rev. Owen Watkins in London who told him 'of the old times in Mafikeng, how the Boers used to trouble the Barolongs, and how he wrote the dispatches to the Imperial Government, which brought General Warren and 1000 soldiers to Mafikeng'. He told him 'quite a lot of things', and that he missed 'his friends'. Watkins also said, 'I love the Molemas'. Those first few encounters in Britain made white racism a peculiarly South African problem, a sensibility of the colony with its narrow, provincial mind-set. 'I have not yet met any difficulties to make me homesick.'

For a change, his father had wired the money on time and had a 'bank draft' ready for him to claim at Standard Bank in London.[408] He had quite a bit of legwork to do before he could settle in, including travelling to Scotland to choose between the Universities of Edinburgh and Glasgow. Seme and others had advised him against choosing a small university like Leeds, where he 'might not be as efficient' as if he received his training from 'some larger university'.[409] He chose Glasgow, even though it would cost a fraction more than Edinburgh would have done. There were many reasons why Glasgow was favourable. 'There are not many South Africans here as in Edinburgh, but the great reason of my coming here is the large hospitals. Glasgow is the second largest town in the British Empire, and thereby its hospitals are only second to those of London which means a great advantage to a medical student as he can get practical training which even Edinburgh University cannot give".[410] It also held the advantage that he could pay fees in instalments, rather than render the lump sum at the beginning of his studies. He estimated that he would have just enough money in hand to afford boarding and lodging for the first year, which was 'what really takes all the money.' He calculated that he required about £50 every year for five years.

He stayed with 'a good Christian family' and felt 'quite comfortable with them', but there were other pockets of home that were emerging around him. 'The Wesleyan Church is my home.' He loved the church. 'I always feel at home there, and some people of God here seem quite interested in me and are trying to show as much kindness to me as they can.' He accepted an invitation to spend one of his vacations at the home of one of his father's old friends, Rev Sharp. Another of his father's friends, Rev. Appelby, introduced him to a Wesleyan minister who invited him for 'teas and so on'. He spent most of his free time in the care of others. Of course, skin colour did not escape him, nor the reversal of the demographic situation. There were very few black people, so few that he settled on a count very quickly.

> There are about 7 coloured students in our university – West Africans and West Indians. The white students are quite a decent lot, and although I had not yet formed friendship with any, I can see that they are by no means prejudiced.[411]

This was the Britain of his experience, not large and unmanageable, but open with opportunity. It seemed not to have any apparent racial strictures. He did not anticipate any. Yet his letters said nothing about Glasgow apart from that it was cold. He lived there but for the most part Glasgow did not claim his attention. His thoughts were on South Africa, on the question of race and skin-colour, as though he had never disembarked at Southampton at all, but had remained on the ship with the taste of white prejudice still present in his mouth, all those people, and not a single companion, only the few letters, the loneliness, and the salt in the air.

He was thinking about the question of solidarity. Colonial life was isolated. Black people had too little support to make their way in the world, living as they each were in the hostility of white prejudice, choked almost to dysfunction by its worsening constraints. At the same time, conflict was inevitable among them, given the small regionalist worlds of the fathers. The question in his mind was how to cultivate their sense of belonging together; how to inspire those feelings of wonder and consolation that would buoy each up above the limitations of racial discrimination, like when the Southampton and London strangers had helped him find his way in their cities. Solidarity created the small miracles of grace, as he had told his father, 'the wonderful works of God'. He set his mind to the task of fashioning this *morafe* amongst the black people of southern Africa. He became the President of the African Races Association (ARA) of Glasgow. He devoted himself to long hours of ethnographical and historical study about the Bantu-speaking societies of this region, the dark-skinned people. He attended classes, completed his clinical attachments and read for examinations, but mostly he applied his mind to the political question of the colonial world. Nevertheless, the *morafe* was a destiny one lived. Its constellation of virtues was not in a book, but almost intuitive to those to whom it revealed itself, to know it intimately, serve it faithfully and love it freely.

In the meantime, he was a university degree away from an arranged marriage. The woman was his first cousin and the eldest daughter of the Rev. Joshua Moshoela in Klerksdorp. Anna Moshoela was his father's way of letting him know that he was very proud of him and that he was worthy of the best pickings in the choice of a spouse. His father would have been familiar with the name of T.D. Mweli Skota, who started out as a clerk in the Crown Mines of Johannesburg, but was building a name for himself as a newspaper man with an influential role in the SANNC. He wanted to marry Skota's daughter, even though the two families of Molema and Moshoela had long ago resolved to exchange the most sacred things – blood, land, loyalty. Yet with each meeting of the ARA, with every new ethnographic insight about the 'Bantu', and with every letter from the woman he loved, he considered that the fathers' plural worlds were crumbling.

XVIII

Not all educated opinion supported chiefs' struggle to maintain the autonomy of the Barolong reserves, especially if it had to pay for it. After the promulgation of the Natives Land Act, the Union government expected chiefs to pay the cost of the litigation. This was just over £400.[412] Writing under a pseudonym, a 'Setumo' wrote to *Tsala ea Batho* that the population of

Barolong should never have agreed to pay for the legal costs of the campaign against Dog Tax. 'Today money is required,' he wrote, 'each man a beast to pay for the Court of the Dogs.'[413] He continued that 'if Barolong had simply made a Court of the *Morafe* like the Zulus in the Transkei, there would have been no Dog Tax'.[414] He meant that money had gone towards the interests of self-serving chiefs, the 'Dogs', rather than to serving the interests of the common people. 'Barolong should have made for themselves roads and other works in their land, and they would have been the owners of such works, and their own managers.' They would also have a printing press of their own. Consider that a woman, Setumo wrote, 'Queen of the Swazi *morafe*' had purchased a printing press for *Abantu-Batho*. As he suggested in another letter, 'a newspaper is the mouth and representative of the black *merafe*', and 'chiefs are the newspapers of the black *merafe*', but Bechuana chiefs, despite being 'wealthy with cattle and money' were not employing 'teachers with certificates in full' who were living unemployed 'in the big villages of the *merafe* of Bechuana'.[415] He counted ten. 'How shocking!'

> The fault lies with the chiefs of the Bechuana who care nothing for education. If it were not for white missionaries there would have been no school. We are thankful to the white missionaries for forcing chiefs to build the schools that exist today. Hence I say, you are the chiefs of the morafe of Bechuana. Wake up from your sleep. Look for teachers in your villages and improve your morafe through education just like the morafe of the Matebele [Zulus] and the Basotho.[416]

Silas Molema's daughter, Harriet Molema, was one of the few teachers employed in the Molopo Reserve, but sometimes she had to go for many months without pay. She had been a teacher since she was around sixteen years old. She had worked very hard to establish herself, although what she made of herself had to grow in the spaces that the men allowed. She was a woman and she did not expect to go where the men in her father's house aspired to be, at university abroad. She understood that the world worked that way, but still, her father had offered her the best that he had available. He doted on her and was fiercely protective of his 'little girl'. He educated her, supported her teaching career, but insisted as much as possible that it all happen in places he considered safe, and none were safer than his own hands, although as she realised very early on, he did not always have the means, especially the material means, necessary to save her from distress. She adored her father. It was not a burden to aim to please him.

She had left Healdtown and proceeded to Emgwadi, a girls' school in the eastern Cape in 1909, where she did her utmost to impress her father with demonstrations of thrift, her small sacrifices for his sake, and her ability to handle money. He had impressed upon her the necessity to mind every penny and to stretch every pound. Even when her father had included a few pennies 'for buying anything I liked' in February of 1909, she paid that amount into her fees and books.[417] She completed her studies at the end of 1910, when Modiri was starting up at Lovedale to matriculate and preparing to go abroad. Her own schooling had ended at Emgwadi after which she had struggled to secure employment as a teacher. Her father had despaired when Lyndhurst Road School in Kimberley turned down her application in March 1911. A Wesleyan missionary school in Pretoria, Kilnerton, was then the only potential opportunity. Her father would have let her go if Kilnerton would take her, but Plaatje had warned that 'Kilnerton is too unhealthy', and that a 'Miss Masoafa came back here through illness, and Miss Klassen just died there'.[418] Instead, Plaatje had offered to take her in and promised to use his influence, especially as a member of the Lyndhurst Road school board, 'to make sure that Harriet could get it although the reply has already been made in the negative'.[419]

Lyndhurst Road School had appointed her in April 1911. Black teachers' earnings were low and not always consistent. Salaries for women teachers were generally around £40 a year.[420] Harriet received her pay at the end of every school term.[421] The school had just under 200 students and only 52 of these were in Standard I to Standard IV. All the rest were in the lower grade, probably still learning how to read and write.[422] She was very young and inexperienced, but she excelled at her teaching. She received a letter of commendation from the Kimberley School Board and an extra cheque at the end of 1912.[423] The board acknowledged her 'good and efficient work' and congratulated her on her 'good example' that trained children 'both educationally and morally, to become good and useful citizens'. She was also a model daughter, conscientious and self-sacrificing. When Modiri wished to go on tour to Cape Town with the Lovedale choir in June 1912, she sent him the £4 he had required.[424] She did not remain in the employ of the Lyndhurst Road School very long. Her father called her home to teach at the school her grandfather had founded when the Department of Education registered it as the Wesleyan Methodist Mission School. She earned £20 a year. Her father had himself worked there.

The principal, Rev. George Rolland had shut down the school early in 1913.[425] The food shortage and devastation from the drought had made it impossible for parents to pay school fees even though the teachers were dedicated and the children still attended school. Every time Rolland had announced the school's closure, the regent Lekoko Montsioa had pleaded for more time until finally there was no more leeway for grace. 'This is my last word on the matter,' Rolland had written, '[as] I have done my best, and have failed.' Sending the children away, he had said, was 'a great sorrow'. The regent had continued to plead for the children, but by August of that year, nobody had found the money to remedy the situation.[426] Rolland had shut down the school for one quarter. Chiefs had then gone about collecting money from parents, or perhaps impounded stock for sale. They had raised about £80 but Rolland could not afford to pay every teacher. Harriet had received nothing. In fact, she had never received her money in full, until finally her father intervened and wrote to Rolland,

> ... it is my duty to put before you the complaints of my daughter Harriet Molema who tells me that she has not been paid in full for four quarters in local contribution the amount which now £20 [,] which sum if not paid this quarter will amount to £25 next quarter. Dear Sir, I know very well that the school children do not pay but the little they pay quarterly ought to be divided among the three or four teachers ... Sir, I do not think that is fair. I think she must always get something from the little which is received quarterly from the children.[427]

Setumo's letters had appeared in *Tsala ea Batho* at around this time, in the winter of 1914. Harriet was not one of the ten teachers, if his count was correct, who had qualifications but were unemployed, but all the same, she was taking home nothing.

It was clear that the reserve needed funds for public works to spend on services and salaries and so on, although that same fund would also have to handle the cost of the litigation. Spencer Minchin prepared the chiefs' proposals to collect three shillings per annum from everyone paying Hut Tax from January of 1915, which they submitted to the Native Affairs Department.[428] The fund would generate sufficient revenue to pay off the debt in a single year. The balance would establish a fund 'to be expended for the benefit of Barolong'. It would be 'applied to the promotion of education of Barolong children and to the payment of deficient salaries of teachers and similar objects'. It would also provide a salary for the National Secretary and the Deputy Tax Collectors and pay for fences and seeds. Chiefs had set about collecting, it seems, well before they had applied for approval, which they nevertheless received.[429] They collected in the reserves and even in the mining compounds.

Migrant labourers at the mines were the primary tax pool for public works because they had a consistent wage. Chiefs and commoners alike, even despite the benefit of an education, lived in the countryside's scarcity, and in growing numbers. Chiefs pinned their hopes on mining wages not only to provide necessities like seeds and perhaps boreholes, but also to sustain those projects of 'progress' in the reserves that an educated constituency cared about – roads, sanitation, certainly schools. The fund gave the paramount chiefs cash in hand at last to sponsor growth like the rainmakers of old. The mineworkers themselves had something to gain. Their women, elderly and children benefited from the services of the tax because they remained in the countryside, even though this was an additional layer of taxation, considering Hut Tax, tributes, rents and other subscriptions on the land. They paid because it guaranteed security of placement in the reserves at a time of severe land shortage, especially if they were 'naturalised Barolong' that had come from outside the reserve. Taxpayers were recognised placement holders. Thus, the school kept running due to the success of the fund and the large number of men working on the mines. Teachers' salaries came from mine wages, including Harriet Molema's earnings.

As Harriet had experienced, to find secure white-collar employment relied heavily on patronage, even for a chiefly woman. She could have withdrawn into the sphere of domestic life. Housewifery would have been a respectable occupation, but it was not an option for the men. Some of her educated male cousins were in fact descending mining shafts with their uneducated subjects in Johannesburg and elsewhere. They clung all the more tightly to their dynastic family names, desperate to hold on to some sense of distinction. The ascriptions of noble birth were the only qualification that could set them apart from the other men. As the young chiefs joined the seasonal pools of migration into mining towns, they exported the chieftaincy into mining compounds by representing the person of the paramount chief in the compounds. Barolong chiefs' presence in the mines provided one of the pillars around which migrant men could establish new local hierarchies in the cities, alongside the renegotiations of gender and masculinity that compensated for the absence of women. Compound managers saw advantage in safeguarding chiefly hierarchy in the mines. They allowed chiefs' sons to take up posts as headmen of their kinsmen, and thus positioned young chiefs to function as group leaders. Harriet's cousin, Officer Molema, who had been at Lovedale with Sebopioa and Seleje, had become a mineworker by 1915.

When he returned to the mines after a visit home, he carried a memorandum from the chieftaincy addressed to the Native Recruiting Cooperation:

> This is to certify that Officer I. Molema is a member of the Barolong Nation at Mafikeng, in the Molopo Reserve. His rank among the Barolong in the said Reserve is that of Headman, and among all Barolong boys employed in your cooperation there is none higher than the said Officer Molema. I commend him to you Sir ... he is now returning to his duties at Knights Deep in your Corporation.[430]

Those junior chiefs languishing in the reserves without any employment sometimes acted as 'messengers' of the chieftaincy and were 'sent to visit several mines for the purpose of seeing all the boys belonging to the Barolong nation'. They could look for men who had left the chieftaincy without permission or those who had to attend trial in the reserves.[431] Thus, on 1 October 1914, chiefs Tiego Tawana, Sebopioa Molema and Botshelonyane collected money for the National Fund from Nourse Mine compound. At that stage, chiefs Officer Molema, Phillip Motshegare and Richard Phetu were recognised Barolong chiefs at the same compound.[432] All these men, at the very least, held qualifications from Lovedale and other respected missionary institutions.

Young educated chiefs' unemployment wrought havoc on the institution of arranged marriage. Parents could sit down to arrange a marriage, but the radius of eligible bachelors was shortening. Chiefly women brought property into their husbands' families, and chiefly men brought cattle to their wives' family kraals. Families protected land and stock by arranging their children's marriages within closed kinship circles. Property rotated between close kin and confirmed family ties, but it was not enough. The expectation was that the young man would be the head of his household, providing for his wife and children. The capacity to care for others in an independent home of one's own was a key marker of manhood. Now lack, unemployment and indebtedness were releasing dozens of unmarried chiefs into penury. They were not available to marry in their younger years and, in the meantime, too often drink and anxiety claimed them in the cities where they were looking for work. It was difficult to guard young women's chastity as they waited for arranged spouses' readiness. People did not pay as much attention to men's sexual behaviour. Nevertheless, children were the most significant offering of good faith between families, which meant young unmarried men could also not afford to do altogether what they wished. They too had to be seen to be leading respectable lives.

This is why James Molebaloa wrote urgently to Silas Molema about Theo Gaboutloeloe, who was still staying with him at Ndabeni Location early in 1913.[433] Theo Gaboutloeloe had arrived during the Christmas holidays of 1912. Molebaloa had found him work, as he had done for Modiri. Gaboutloeloe squandered his pay, played truant and then finally lost his job. This was serious because as far as Molebaloa knew, the young man was due to get married to Molema's daughter. 'The thing that disappointed me about this boy is (1) that he is a Morolong (2) he is a child of truly proper persons (*batho sentlentle*) (3) he was once the secretary of the paramount chief of Barolong (4) he is promised to marry the daughter of Chief S.T. Molema.' Molebaloa urged Molema to make means available to dispatch Theo back to Mafikeng as soon as possible. 'I am letting you know because I know that this would make you ashamed just as I am ashamed'. The only then eligible daughter for marriage in Molema's household was Harriet, and Theo would have been the most promising stalk in a vulnerable crop of chiefly men. Silas Molema had to look elsewhere.

There was John Montsioa, who had just become the paramount chief in the Molopo Reserve. John Montsioa earned £120 a year. It would take Silas Molema, the most senior headman in the reserve, another decade before small increments in his pay allowed him to draw a salary of £16 a year from the Native Affairs Department.[434] John Montsioa had a missionary school education and a secure salary for life. Moreover, his home was a short stroll from Molema's residence. If they married, Harriet would continue to earn her £20 a year at the school. She would be the reserve's 'first wife', and her father would be there, close by, to help her husband and to keep guard over her. In other words, Harriet would marry, but essentially, she would not leave home.

It was as her father wished for his 'little girl'. The world he had assembled around her was good one – a fulfilling professional life, the most prestigious role in the *morafe* that a woman could hold, and an educated husband who would not lack employment. All she had to do was live in his world, which she did, quietly and dutifully as was her fashion, but she observed the tiny creases and cracks that shot up here and there to mar the perfect picture. She responded prudently, evening out and filling in the rifts emerging between her and her husband, and keeping at it, wanting happiness, and at the same time trying to keep the entire reserve from folding over when her husband failed. There were letters of distress to her brother in Glasgow when it was too much, but she was determined to bear it, especially because it was not entirely her husband's fault. Her husband had a mental illness that imposed strain on all his relationships.

John Montsioa could not accommodate the extreme pressure of the paramount chief's position, not at the turbulent juncture when the government was still attempting to impose 'native administration' in the reserve and the protracted tensions at Rietfontein were still simmering on. Even without those additional pressures, the role of a paramount chief was demanding. He had to preside over cases at a time when his subjects could appeal his rulings. He had to control immigration and handle placement, which also meant resolving the many disputes over the limited land. He collected fines and taxes and marshaled men for public works. He also had to coordinate seasons of ploughing, planting and harvesting. There was a lot to do. He did not have a 'National Secretary' – certainly not one of the calibre and sobriety of Sebopioa Molema, who had handled all these duties with efficiency and calm, even while resisting the government's interventions in the reserve. At the same time, his father-in-law, Silas Molema, was himself no longer a young man, even though he tried very hard to assist him. His father-in-law wanted firstly the marriage to work, as did Harriet, but also to keep the chieftaincy from collapsing under the strain of his episodes of illness and hospitalisation. He also had the devotion of his wife, who took care of him, paid his medical bills, and partnered with her father to keep the chieftaincy going, yet he could not contain his violent outbursts. His condition worsened with drink.

It made matters worse that his tenure had not started smoothly. At the beginning, the Native Affairs Department had been happy to recognise John Montsioa, but then reneged for the reason that his two brothers, Wessels and Badirile Montsioa, had not managed the reserve efficiently. At least, this is the reason the department put forward. It appointed Joshua Molema as paramount chief in November 1915, but the consequence was such disgruntlement and division in the reserve that only hostility ruled.[435] Joshua Molema did not have the support of his own brother, Silas, who wanted John Montsioa, his own son-in-law, on the paramount seat. Joshua Molema had never considered the Montsioas legitimate rulers of Mafikeng, which after all, Isaac Molema had founded. The late regent's brother staged some kind of coup by taking over the paramount chief's court. The Molemas, including Silas Molema, stayed away in protest. In fact, as regent, Lekoko Montsioa had only postponed a succession dispute that had erupted after Badirile Montsioa's death. John Montsioa had a challenger, Lotlamoreng Montsioa, a relatively unknown mineworker whose claim, like so many others, relied on very intricate interpretation of genealogy in polygamous households that practised the levirate and allowed various strategies of adoption and 'cutting away'.[436] Lotlamoreng's kingmakers had sent him to school to get a basic education at least, and now he was back in the reserve.

John's uncertainty about his position caused his mental state to unravel quickly. Nonetheless, he was not passive. He sought allies among neighbouring Barolong chiefs to bolster his popular support.[437] In the middle of 1916, Harriet prepared a petition on his behalf to the Prime Minister, Louis Botha.[438] The petition gathered sixty-one signatures of the men of the Kgotla and probably some of the neighbouring chiefs. In the letter, Harriet objected to the government's intervention in the appointment of chiefs that, as she explained, contravened the 1895 agreement with Sidney Shippard. She said her Barolong had not surrendered their status as 'a nation claiming special privileges' in the British Empire.

> We claim to be a nation claiming special privileges given to us by the imperial government and recognised by subsequent governments of this country ... the jurisdiction of the native chiefs is to be preserved... The Barolong take any appointment of a paramount chief by the Government without the assent of the people as an infringement of the jurisdiction of the Native Chiefs over their own people which was promised to them. ... Long before our request to be allowed to come under and enjoy British rule we respected and loved that Government and even before we became British subjects we fought in support of British interests.[439]

After this petition, the government agreed to recognise her husband, but even then, the decision came in February 1917, more than six months later, after much waiting and uncertainty.[440] It meant John's official recognition came when the anxiety and opposition had worn him down. He fell ill that year. Harriet paid his medical bills of over £10.[441]

In the meantime, she kept working at the school. All the teachers in the Molopo Reserve now had consistent pay drawing from the new fund. The chieftaincy even had money in reserve to spare. Neighbouring reserves began to take notice, especially because they too had to pitch in to the cost of the litigation. In June 1917, William Letsapa wrote to Molema to 'discuss the matter of the three shillings', with the suggestion that his Barolong, the Ratlou of the neighbouring Setlagodi reserve, wished to contribute one shilling towards this fund.[442] 'Barolong wish to meet as the council of the Barolong so that when the debt of the Dog Tax [litigation] is settled, we can see what each village [stadt] should receive.'[443] A year later, various Barolong reserves along the Molopo had launched the Barolong Educational and National Council, which had an office at 99 Rissik Street in Mafeking town.[444] The founding meeting was at Kunana on 15 April 1918 where 'all chiefs, headmen of the Barolong People' discussed the fund's constitution as

> to form branch committees for the purpose of enrolling members and collect their fees for the National funds, to make arrangements to purchase all stock from the people and also to discuss the matter to buy their produce generally, to discuss the advisability to have secure land to have as a stock farm for cattle and sheep, to improve the breed of cattle and sheep [and] also to discuss various matters that may be deemed advisable to the general welfare of the people.[445]

Chiefly bureaucracies along the Molopo had money to spend on the populations in the reserves of their district. The fund allowed them to operate as a confederation of Barolong chiefs, exploiting primarily mining wages through the tax to amplify their visibility and make themselves indispensable in the negotiations of agrarian livelihoods. Thus, apart from the opportunity that mine wages lent chiefs to employ and pay themselves in institutions like schools and 'tribal offices' in the reserves, mines and mineworkers became chiefs' critical constituency. Chiefs determined to show these men that they cared by routinely visiting them at the mining compounds. Industrial zones were emerging as places where chiefly and patriarchal power was resuscitating itself, and from there, exporting itself back into the reserves. Chiefs' hold over the agrarian settlements of the reserve had its material basis in the mining compounds. Between 1920 and 1921, the Barolong Educational and National Fund had spent just over £630.[446] It received a boost from new diamond diggings in the reserves from about 1924 by letting the ground.[447] Chiefs spent money not only on paying salaries for 'civil servants' – the secretaries, teachers and even a postman, but also on stationery and a typewriter for their offices. The Great War offered chiefs another opportunity to make themselves visible and indispensable to the empire. They sent men to France and East Africa.[448] The moment was a high tide of chiefly power in the reserves and educated chiefs rode it with confidence.

John Montsioa, at this very moment, felt very vulnerable. He had not sent men to fight. He was not, in his view of himself, playing in the big league. A neighbouring chief ridiculed him that 'your services to King and Empire seem to have ended in the South African War', but he may have had a nervous breakdown, or his father-in-law may have prevented him from doing so. In the meantime, his marriage was breaking down due to his drinking, his violence, and his long absences in the city. Harriet did not once give up, and neither did her father. She kept writing to her brother in Glasgow. It was distressing because it seemed the union could not carry the weight of her efforts. Each intervention seemed to leave the marriage more fragile, less able to withstand her next effort to keep her husband stable, and to keep herself with him. Modiri was intimating she should abandon the mission and walk away, but she worked at it, even more assiduously. It was her way to save herself, her woman's way to find her freedom, to make sure her husband would not consider her an enemy, would remember her consistent devotion, and in time, reward her by peaceably letting her go.

XIX

Sebopioa Molema had been doing the work that kept the chieftaincy going in its ordinary routines for over five years. He had mastered the art of holding the place together and had refused to yield the chiefs' own freedoms to the government. Things had nevertheless changed. There were many more people in the reserve. More of them were making their way to the offices of the Resident Magistrate and Native Commissioner for matters the Kgotla had ordinarily managed. Nevertheless, all the rungs of the chieftaincy kept going, including the intermediary Kgotlas where junior chiefs like the Molemas still heard cases and arranged or denied placement. The years in the reserve had brought him closer to 'the fathers' whom he had served as chief, secretary, messenger, errand runner and son, especially Silas Molema. Their relationship had healed from the years of silence whilst he was abroad. They had worked together side by side to hold at bay the forces that threated to sweep chiefs' power away. Now, he was away from home again, but this time, he had with him the full and dedicated attention of his father, who made sure to reply to his letters without fail. They had mended and become an intimate pair.

In January 1915, he had sent an application for work in the Public Services Commission.[449] The Secretary of the Public Services Commission considered him a well-qualified potential employee but required the usual confidential report from the local Resident Magistrate. Like his predecessor, R.C. Lloyd prepared an unfavourable report. He referred to Sebopioa's relationship to the ruling family, especially his marriage to the regent's daughter. 'In manner,' Lloyd added, 'he is always courteous and respectful', while 'in appearance he is as much as any native [though] he shows pallor more than usual aspect in the bridge of his nose.' The Resident Magistrate was suggesting, again, that Sebopioa Molema was too big for his britches. His conclusion was 'very strong advice' that Sebopioa should not have employment in the Native Affairs Department 'for obvious reasons'. Sebopioa finally found work in the Bechuanaland Protectorate, up at Taung, in August of the same year, which was close enough to Serowe, where he visited his father's 'old friend Chief Khama and Raphosa' who had warmly received him.[450]

He was in the inner circles of chiefly families in the Bechuanaland Protectorate. He wrote to his father about the death of Khama's grandson, Davide, and the process to liquidate his estate, seeing he owed many people and traders.[451] The Bechuanaland Protectorate was a new experience. He wrote a letter that 'dealt at length with the nations of the country' but in some ways it was not quite another country.[452] It was more like shifting his orientation within the single universe of the *morafe* into another constellation. He was interested in how each of the *merafe* compared with any of the other and especially with his own Barolong. 'I am pleased to say that the Bangwato Nation have a very nice church house which will never be excelled by any building to be made by Native Races in S. Africa'.[453] The *morafe* of the 'Bechuana' was like a head with many faces. He studied each one very carefully as he moved between the various chiefly centres – Kanye, Serowe, Maun, and so on.

Still, his father had been very sad to let him go. A few months later, he received his letters with details of all that was going wrong in the reserve since his departure. In November 1915, just over two months after he left home, the other father, Joshua Molema, had accepted his appointment as the acting paramount chief of the Molopo Reserve for two years. Sebopioa first learnt about it in the *Mafeking Mail*.[454] This is when 'the fathers' had their falling out. Joshua took the position, but the younger brother, Silas, insisted that he decline it because the cost of this appointment was too great. The Native Affairs Department had refused to appoint John Montsioa, the candidate that had emerged from the customary succession processes that followed an incumbent's death. This meant the government was meddling in the affairs of the chieftaincy, contrary to the clear stipulation of the 1895 agreement with Sidney Shippard. The appointment would render that 'Charter' null and void, whilst the chieftaincy still considered it binding and, in fact, its basis of resistance against the Natives Land Act and the jurisdiction the legislation allowed the government to impose through policies of 'native administration' in the reserve.

Silas Molema supported John Montsioa, whom the government had at first appointed, but the latter was young, unstable and inexperienced, also embroiled in a succession dispute with Lotlamoreng Montsioa. Sebopioa had not anticipated these troubles when he left. Now he felt his father's grave sadness when he left could have been a premonition. 'I know how you regretted very much when I came up here [;] I think God was speaking to you but now it is too late unless you see your way clear to act as I think.'[455] He was giving advice and consolation from afar. 'I am very sorry that I am very far from you and cannot give you immediate help in the way of advice'. He understood, as his father was suggesting, that what was required, indeed necessary, was for him to pack up and go home. He could not do that. He could not quit paid work – not with a family, and certainly not with his debts. He felt regret that life had not worked out as he had planned, as they had all hoped. His hard work, his commitment to his family, the fathers' investment in his education had not been enough to save him or to help them now. The chieftaincy, the very office that he had considered an inheritance, was imploding from within as the family feuds took unexpected twists, and crumbling from without where the government was chipping away at the chiefs' routine powers in the reserve. Yet, he could not dislodge himself from his current position, being no longer only a son, but husband and father also.

> You have spent thousands of pounds educating me to help you and now is the time. Dear father I shall stop here as I feel very very very (sic) sad when I think how helpless you are in the new nature of things. My thoughts are with you day & night.[456]

It was also actually more than that. He was staying also because the work was proving to be surprisingly satisfying, far from his initial apprehension. He worked as an interpreter, but he also carried out other administrative duties.[457] At the beginning, he took the position because he needed the pay. He would be earning a steady salary, which was a relief, but the nature of the work had been short of his initial aspirations. He had worried that the work would prove insufficiently challenging for a law student of his acumen and that working under officials who would not entrust him with responsibility would become mentally draining. He had also anticipated that it would become physically exhausting. He would have to ride large distances on horseback into the reserves of the Bechuanaland Protectorate to deliver messages, assist in the collection of taxes and help in various police investigations. He only had leave every twelve months of service. If his superiors drove him very hard, he had feared it would be too much for someone with a disability in his legs. He had also dreaded the daily run-ins with colonial officials who, he was sure, would not treat him as an equal. They would speak to him and treat him as one does a child. The colour of his skin would be the cause of daily diminishment, while he himself did not count himself as one with all black people. He was an educated man. He was also a chief, a man of noble birth. His employers would not recognise this distinction, which is why he had asked his father to speak to his 'personal friend', the Resident Commissioner in Mafikeng.

> Tell him that I am your son, I have been brought up in good society [,] that you would be very much pleased if he would see that I am well treated by the officer under which [sic] I am working. The [officer] is said to be a very cruel man, who treats men as dogs. Tell him that I am lame and cannot do much walking over long distances. That I shall do all I can to be obedient to my higher officer.[458]

Now that he had the feel of the new place a few months later, he liked it and he liked the work. He had a good relationship with his superiors, and there was a degree of freedom in the work. He could see a future for himself. He was not a lawyer with overseas qualifications, but he was embracing what was possible.

He worked in the colonial civil service. He had no attachment to Nora, or to Ohio's educated circles. His wife was his cousin, Emang. He missed his wife. He barely knew her when they married and now they were friends, playful with each other, intimate. They called each other 'Charm'. She had proved steady and buoyant through his hard times, a very capable and independent homemaker. In his absence now, he considered her the present chief of Signal Hill. When a delegation of the Bataoana was due to travel to Mafikeng and meet with colonial officials, he provided to her all the details about their mission and asked her to represent him by taking the matter to his father, Silas Molema, the most senior administrator in the chieftaincy.[459] He could have written to his father directly, but instead he told him to expect her with the details. He had not had the bride of his choosing, but he was determined to have a marriage of his own design – a partnership with a woman who had a public voice.

His fathers were attempting to negotiate his transfer across the border to work in Mafikeng because they both felt they each could not do without him.[460] Emang, on the other hand, soldiered on and placed no demands on his availability. She needed no rescue. He would be happy to return to Mafikeng if such transfer could take place, but if he could not remove back to Mafikeng, he wrote to his father – not Silas, but Joshua Molema, 'I would not like her to make a home there'.[461] He wanted her to come across the border to stay with him at least for three months. He was approaching his mid-thirties. There was time enough to make a life with her elsewhere. He intended to keep his employment and build his family life around it in the Protectorate if he had to. He had already acknowledged his feeling that despite his immense efforts he had dropped the family baton. Yet, at the same time, he wanted his father to know that what he had to do in his present job mattered. He was good at it and had the trust of his superiors and the other officials who worked with him.

> I wished I were present and would have done my duty to my people and nation, but in any way I could not have done more than what you have done. I can imagine what difficulty you are having and everything seem [sic] to be against you but God and right is [sic] for you. Today I am going to Mababe with the Dr and we shall have to travel a distance of 100 miles on horseback without water, living on wild game which we shall have to kill on our way. We have received news that murder had been committed there and were going to investigate … "Keep on Father" [.] "Go on Sir" [.] The nation is your[s] by God's design.[462]

This was in the early autumn of 1916. He had been in his work for about nine months. His initial apprehension had turned into confidence. Life was coming together. He spent the winter at Ngamiland, northwest of the Bechuanaland Protectorate. The administrative centre of the district was Maun, where David Livingstone had visited Lake Ngami. This was the territory of the Bataoana. He received a 'long communication' from his father in June 1916, with a request for him to come home, but he declined.[463] His father said he had a plan. He wished there was a way he could return home but he needed certainty.

> Your letter is indeed a good one & I have it with me every time I think of home. How wise are your plans! How good is your speech! I feel I could throw away everything to come home to help you dear Father but I think I shall have to remain here all the while to finish my term as agreed between B.P. Government and myself.[464]

He committed to going home on leave in July of the following year, still a good thirteen months away. Until then, he hoped, 'the Lord will help & keep us till we meet dear father'.[465] In the meantime, the fathers could benefit from some of the advantages of his job in 'this far country'. The Bataoana's Hut Tax season began in September. They would dispose of their cattle at very low prices.[466] 'You cannot miss a chance like this.' He could purchase seventy heifers for just £100 and have someone drive them to Ditlharapeng, which was Joshua's allotment in the Barolong Farms. His father, Silas, wanted the cattle, but by the time the Bataoana were disposing of their stock, he had no money to spare. He said that the deceased Davide Khama in any case owed him £20 and suggested that Sebopioa claim it from his estate, but Sebopioa refused to receive the money directly for fear that his employers would find out.'[467] So I refuse to have anything to do with it.'

Across the border in the Molopo Reserve, a war had ensued between Joshua Molema and John Montsioa. Sebopioa received the news of 'the two systems of Government existing at Mafikeng'.[468] It only ended when the Native Affairs Department finally appointed John Montsioa in 1917. Joshua had had his run at the helm of chiefship, 'for one year and eight months', as he himself counted.[469] This father wanted to marry again, but he had been unwilling to choose a spouse for himself. He had been waiting for the children to decide for him. 'I became old waiting for them ... lest they say that I took their mother's house and gave it to the wrong woman'. Sebopioa was certain there was nobody in Mafikeng that would be 'as good as' his late mother, 'but I believe there are many true women who can be just as good if properly looked for'.[470] However, he did not care about following tradition. He asked for pardon for his 'departure from Secoana laws and customs'.[471] He was speaking frankly. He was convinced that the customs of arranged marriage had been especially costly to him. He had lost his mother two years before, which in his mind was an unnecessary death. His mother's death fitted into a pattern he had been closely observing: an arranged marriage, unhappiness, and finally a woman's early death.

> I know the Bechuana always marry relatives but I myself do not care very much for this selection as they are often the cause of much trouble and often hatred and at last death of so many of our mothers. If in your opinion you can find a Fingo to Mokgalagadi [sic] woman that can be a mother to us please do not be afraid to choose [her]. We want a mother. Father Joshua is old...[472]

He wrote everything out respectfully, earnestly, but he knew he was breaking the rules. He was advocating for people of little status, the women of the people the fathers called the 'Matebele', the 'Makhalakhadi'. To the fathers, these people were a little less than persons, but he was saying they were one with the *morafe*, so much so that their women could become wife to a senior chief of the Barolong.

His audacity was in part also a reflection of the political moment. His immediate environment of the reserves had 'blackened' with the promulgation of the Natives Land Act, not only the colour of people's skin about him, but also a more intimate embrace of the solidarity of blackness in all its hues. However, his association with elements of black consciousness had started much earlier. He had lived at the epicentre of a confident black sensibility, the educated community in and around Wilberforce in Ohio. This was his main disappointment with the Bataoana in the time he had spent living among them in Taung. They had not embraced a proud consciousness of their blackness. The deputation that had travelled to Mafeking, the same deputation about which he had written to Emang, had refused to stay at Moratuoa, Molemas' residence in the stadt, because 'they were sent to Europeans and wanted to be near them', and hence 'did not see anybody or anything'.[473] They had not seen the works of 'progress' in the reserve, like the 'sanitary closets' that black people just like them had built.[474] He thought his father should not take the matter personally for 'as I have already written to you the Batawana are still far behind civilisation'.[475] 'It will take time to make them see simple facts'. The same 'simple facts' should apply to love and trust and marriage.

When he returned from his posting in Ngamiland to Kanye in February 1918, he missed the train, but his employer overlooked his lateness. Instead his employer was very relieved to have him back. 'I am his favourite.'[476] He had in his possession both volumes of John Mackenzie's *Austral Africa: Losing or Ruling it*, which had belonged to his father-in-law, Lekoko Montsioa, 'who had bought them out of his pocket, not out of that of the Tribe' and therefore, he wrote to his father, 'I consider them as mine'. The books were Mackenzie's consideration of whether British interests were best served by 'losing or ruling' every point from the southern tip of the continent to Central Africa. Sebopioa wanted his father to read them because they 'are no more published and unless they can be kept very safely, we may be in want of some valuable information, which cannot be had from any book than from them'. He had a sense of mission that enlarged his work beyond its mere administrative functions. He was earning, he was reading, and he was travelling, with a steady stream of letters from Emang and his father. He felt well in mind and body. He determined not to return to Mafikeng, not even after the death of his mother, Silas Molema's wife, Molalanyane. He reeled in grief, but he stayed where he was. 'God alone knows better.'[477] This season of himself, these quiet hours, he meant to keep.

About five months later, his father, Joshua, became ill.[478] He spent time at Victoria Hospital but without any improvement. The news came with a request from the other father, Silas, for him to return to Mafikeng, 'in case my father does not improve in health'. He had known of his father's grave illness for a long time but had 'been putting it off and off to write' to ask about his health. He finally put on a request for special leave during the first week in August yet it could take some time before he could have leave to return home.[479] 'My mind is not here,' he wrote to the other father, 'I am daily and nightly worrying the life out of myself about the health of my father.' He remained hopeful that Joshua would recover, but he lost him. He buried him in Mafikeng. If there were another offer in Mafeking, he would go home for good. He started to make enquiries from his superior.[480] 'I asked him that if there was a vacancy at Mafeking, I will only be too glad to take it up, as I will be near my small and young brothers.' At the end of his month-long leave, he headed back to work, despite the living father's plea that he stay.

The next letter left him less resolute to remain in the Protectorate. From what he could put together of the events that had transpired, his absence from home was reason for this next loss of life. Whilst he was away, the Spanish flu of 1918 had claimed his younger brother.[481] He himself had been down 'with the Epidemic' for three days, but he had recovered somewhat, until news of the death sapped his strength. 'I am up not well,' he wrote. 'This report made my knees to knock together, my whole hope is very dark and I do not know what will happen.' The flu was ravaging Kanye. The school and churches had closed. Many people were dying.

> The epidemic is very bad here at Kanye and the people are dying daily from 10 to 20 per day... Everybody is ill. It is so very sad here because we have no Doctor and no Chemist in the country. We are shut up in the Desert.[482]

The epidemic was still claiming lives in the reserve with over 500 deaths at the beginning of March 1919.[483] However, he still counted his brother's passing a death that could have been easily avoided. In his brother, the flu had claimed a young life from a recently orphaned household. It had 'cut down' the young man 'as a bud from the flowering tree of life' because nobody had kept an eye on him.[484] In Mafikeng, unlike in the Protectorate, there was help available, at least for people with some means to purchase 'the Medical [kit]', with instructions. Molemas all lived together at 'Molema Square'. Why didn't somebody help his brother? 'I wonder,' he wrote, 'what is the feeling of all the parents at home.' He sent his father the medical kit. 'I hope you will spare nothing to get medicines for the family – there are sheep, goats and what not which God has given you to protect yourself with'. In the meantime, he would start packing up and remove back into the reserve. His absence had caused a loss of life.

His father was growing impatient. He wanted him to return home as a matter of urgency, whilst his employer, the Resident Magistrate at Kanye, would not let him go.[485] He turned the magistrate down, even after he asked him 'very prayerfully' to remain a further three weeks.[486] Nevertheless, he would not allow his father to push him too far. 'I shall stay over to see what arrangements he [the Resident Magistrate at Kanye] has made regarding my application to leave the Service. I did not want to leave and through [sic] [throw] away Mr Dray as if I was being driven away or have done something criminal.' The reason for his father's urgency was that the chieftaincy had another opportunity to reclaim the autonomy of their reserves and to own their lands. Solomon Plaatje feared that they may have already waited too long.

XX

Historians of educated black Natalians observe that 'many of the African national leaders in the twentieth century [have] come from Natal', and also 'a strong tendency on the part of many of these same leaders to hive off and run their own show in the province, where a somewhat different political context' shaped their operation.[487] The personality that has attracted the most attention as an example of this inclination to remove from the centre's 'broadly based *African* nationalism' and participate in the provincial countryside politics of a 'narrowly based Zulu nationalism' is the first president of Congress, John Dube.[488] The 'centre' in these interpretations is a countrywide 'nationalism' and a quintessentially 'modern' sensibility, competing against the rural splinter ethnic nationalisms that distracted from Congress' actual mission. The mobilisation of a rural constituency in support of chiefs in these readings of Dube's political life was a result of crisis. One reading is that Dube was a man of typical 'petty bourgeoisie' pretensions and prejudices, who could not adapt to the new militancy of Congress politics during the violent rebellions of industrial working classes in the mines from 1918.[489] Another is that the revelation of Dube's failings in his marriage cost him the trust of the respectable educated circles during Congress' first deputation to England.[490]

As far as Solomon Plaatje was concerned, the word 'nationalism' stood for something essentially undesirable. His own moral inclination was 'to hive off' into regionalist projects of his own, which amongst other intentions, was to sustain the integrity of chieftaincy in the British Empire. After his return from his first trip to England, Plaatje had in mind to found a Brotherhood movement in Kimberley. In England, he had delivered his public lectures and meetings under the auspices of the Brotherhood movement. The aim of the movement was not only to help men strengthen 'the spiritual part of life', but also to aid in 'social matters', to 'help the downtrodden' by following Christ's example.[491] Plaatje determined then to establish a branch of this society in Kimberley. It was a way to diffuse the alienation of many people's new life in the industrial zones, but he was also responding to the unsettling reality that many mineworkers were educated men who needed an outlet for the cultural life and leisure pastimes the mines could not provide.

The state's efforts at segregation also restricted movement. Many of these men worked in 'compound offices'. These positions did not elevate them much above the ranks of their compound mates and, especially in earlier decades, many worked in underground 'office' jobs that were menial and routine. In Johannesburg, the growth of this educated black demographic in the mines inspired the American missionary and anthropologist Ray Phillips to found the Bantu Men's Social Centre in the city.[492] At the same time, the Industrial and Commercial Union was making strides in the countryside in part for the same reasons.[493] The movement was providing a launching pad for white-collar occupations for its educated organisers. A Brotherhood society allowed a cultural avenue for piety, a forum to think about 'self-improvement' and leisure activities like tea parties that members' thin material circumstances did not allow.

He knew, given his own desperate financial situation, that some of the unskilled and semi-skilled workers who were up in arms in the Rand's revolt had imagined their lives would take a different course in earlier years – that they would retire as teachers, members of the clergy, lawyers, clerks, court officials. He was familiar with the young Barolong men, even chiefly ones like Modiri Molema, who often could not see their way to their aspirations and had first to settle for informal jobs in the hope that something better would come up. Too often nothing did, and a temporary stopgap became all there was to feed and occupy themselves. If they had families, they had to settle for unskilled or semi-skilled work. The growing militancy of the ICU, and the radical tone of the Transvaal's educated classes in Congress, were also the loud explosion of the scenario that he had tried to anticipate as editor of *Koranta ea Becoana*. He had desired to save the educated countryside folk of the destitution many now faced. He had urged them to return to the land with education and innovation, but the Natives Land Act had crushed such aspirations to a pulp.

He was still very involved in collecting the stories of the legislation's aftermath, still very active in the meetings and duties of Congress, and even in this new initiative, a Brotherhood society, he wished to create a holding place that could nurture educated aspiration. The political crisis unfolding in the Transvaal had his class of people at the centre, the educated black men, typical readers of vernacular newspapers, who were now speaking for themselves through the Transvaal wing of Congress, and with the men of very little education with whom they worked in one voice. Lawyers like Pixley Seme had managed to escape the scourge of white-collar unemployment by having professional qualifications from abroad. Black lawyers and medical doctors had relatively secure professional lives and could employ themselves, although black lawyers were constantly under threat of sanction from the Law Societies. They could be struck off the roll. Nevertheless, wartime increases in the cost of living made everyone vulnerable – lawyers and domestic servants, doctors and mineworkers.

Kimberley's branch of the Brotherhood movement would provide a place of conversation, a kind of gathering of hope, where educated black men could rub shoulders with one another. At the same time, the movement he had in mind would display what was possible between black and white in the Cape, the oldest British colony in southern Africa. His intention was also to link up his Brotherhood movement to the international organisation, which would allow him some access to funding and also launch him as a leader of a global movement. The Diamond Fields Men's Own Brotherhood was not going to be just a respectable pastime. It was a serious undertaking for self-advancement. Here again, the local had resonance with global ideas of 'progress', not through mimicry of people overseas but through a creative assertion of local cultural understandings of moral authority, including chiefly and patriarchal hierarchy. Another strand of Plaatje's attraction to the Brotherhood movement was that it demonstrated imperial solidarity. The society was non-denominational and committed to racial equality, especially in its own organisation. In England, he had seen people of colour play as much a role as anyone else in the movement, including as chairpersons and speakers.

He found little time to devote to the project upon his return from England but in January 1918, he approached De Beers mining company to let him have an old tram shed that it was demolishing, so he could use it as a 'place of meeting' of 'all Natives, of any Church or no Church'.[494] The company agreed, but at an annual rental of one shilling, and on condition that the new tenants pay all the rates and taxes of the place, which were almost £30 that year alone. The company also provided £100 for the necessary improvements.[495] He and the mining managers understood the opportunity their partnership presented in the Cape. Plaatje did not support the Transvaal's turn away from constitutional means of protest and representation. The Brotherhood movement would demonstrate that the Cape was a province of peaceful reprieve away from the disruptions of violent protest. De Beers wished to buy black educated classes' peace. As David Harris, De Beers' director pointed out, 'the direction suggested by Plaatje' was 'good policy' because it would help in 'enhancing their (black workers') loyalty to De Beers as a generous employer of labour'.[496] Plaatje's stance was costing him his reputation, seeing 'there is a belief among some of the native population here that I am in the pay of De Beers – employed to keep [me] quiet'.[497]

In the meantime, the First World War had pushed the alliance between 'Boer' and 'Britain' in the Union government to further unravelling, and with it, a more vociferous call for republicanism among some of the new Afrikaners rose. They resented the sacrifices the Union, a dominion, was making for Britain's imperial war. Plaatje supported the war effort. In 1917, he and other members of Congress had agreed to recruit workers for the South African Native Labour Contingent to assist in the war abroad. The Prime Minister, General Louis Botha, had approved although many in his own constituency of Dutch-Afrikaners did not. The rising Afrikaner nationalists took up the cause of resistance against the campaign. Botha held his ground nevertheless and asked Plaatje to support the recruitment effort, which he said, 'would help the native people better than any propaganda work'.[498] The government finally abandoned its efforts to recruit black men for service but the alliance between the 'white races' remained very brittle. Having made a fragile start after the South African War, the alliance continued to wear thin. It could give in under further pressure, which is why Louis Botha and his right-hand man, Jan Smuts, were nervous about the meltdown on the Rand.

The project of Unification was facing opposition from too many fronts. Black militancy and white republicanism all added to the instability and frustration of a divided population surviving a war together. It seemed to Plaatje that the only constituency that could offer the government support was men like himself. The Union officials who wished to continue with British dominion needed new allies who were willing to strengthen the British link, whilst at the same time, supporting the war and shunning violent protest as a political instrument. This is why Plaatje thought that chiefs should strike whilst the iron was hot, when Britain did not yet know how the war would end and could not risk a postwar order without overall control in southern Africa. It was time to bring about more or less what had transpired almost three decades before, for educated chiefs to sit down with British officials and negotiate an arrangement suitable to both parties. The moment was ripe for chiefs to collaborate with Britain, and in that way continue to rule themselves. The Brotherhood movement was already active and, if and where opportunity allowed, it could serve as a platform to bring the parties together. He was also a pious man of deep faith. His hope never diminished. It made for an excellent strategist.

When he learnt that the Governor-General, Lord Buxton, was due to visit Kimberley in August of that year, he wrote to him and asked him to lay the foundation stone of the 'Assembly Hall for Natives at Kimberley – a present from De Beers Company'.[499] The Governor General declined. Plaatje then sought the aid of General Botha to help. Buxton then confirmed that he would come and would be happy to make a speech. Plaatje had secured the presence of Britain's representative to attend the meeting – that was the first and most difficult task. In the advertisement for the hall's opening on 7 August 1918, he stated that Lord Buxton was the 'eyes and ears of King George V'.[500] He requested that in his speech the Governor General should focus on the role of black men in the war, particularly their service in the Cape Corps and the Native Labour Contingent.[501] All that the Bechuana chiefs had to do was attend the celebration and offer to Britain what it then sorely needed – dependable and peaceable allies.

Yet Plaatje was not entirely confident that the Bechuana would perceive the opportunity. He feared that chiefs, especially his own Barolong, could well make light of a potentially momentous occasion. He worked tirelessly to collect as many monetary pledges of support from as many Bechuana chiefs as possible and also from his white friends, which he would read at the launch before the government officials in attendance. He urged Silas Molema to make sure that the chieftaincy send both a representative on the day and make a financial pledge. Three days before the opening, he had received nothing from Mafikeng. Again, he wrote to Molema, 'Please help me to plead with Chief John to send a message of greeting and thanks on Tuesday or Wednesday morning'.[502] He requested at least £25, but he wanted John

Montsioa to top all the other Barolong chiefs with a donation of £50. He also sent along a draft of how John's message should read if he could not be present.

> Sorry cannot personally attend ceremony. [In] your speech please convey to His Excellency Lord Buxton the loyalty of myself and Barolongs to the Imperial and Union Governments also our thanks to Directors of [De Beers] as most of my workmen go to Kimberley.[503]

Still he received nothing. Three days after the event he wrote again, to plead with Molema to plead with John to send a donation so that, at least, his name would appear along with the list of other donors in an edition of the *Diamond Fields Advertiser*, which included Spencer Minchin's donation of £2.[504] He wanted the government to understand that chieftaincy in the Cape Province and other Bechuana districts was the adhesive that held people together peaceably on the ground, that chiefs were educated men of 'progress' and of good, Christian morality and that they had a history of supporting Britain. 'I did not forget to tell the Government about Montsioa and Khama so they both must do something to make things square'. Still nothing.

When the war ended in November 1918, there was again talk in the Congress to send a second deputation to England. The feeling was that the onset of the war had derailed the first deputation's mission by forcing them to come home earlier than they otherwise would have done. Not only Plaatje and other members of Congress, but also the network of supporters he had consolidated in England, thought a lobby of a second delegation to England would convince Britain to intervene in the disenfranchised position that the Union's people of colour found themselves in. This population group had supported Britain's war effort at the cost of their lives and had gained due recognition in a speech made by King George V to members of the Natives Labour Contingent in France in 1917. In December of 1918, Congress held a special meeting to discuss sending this second deputation. Plaatje accepted his election to the committee very reluctantly, with conditions of his own, because, as he wrote to Molema,

> ... since I returned from England, they [Congress] use me with nothing but words in return. I had *Tsala* ruined after I built it on the foundation you had dug at the cost of great impoverishment. If I had not gone to England, *Tsala* would be consoling us, wiping our tears here and there: all that fell by the wayside along with many other very glorious works.

Unless they give ME only, £1000, I am going nowhere – one does not stir the gallbladder twice.⁵⁰⁵

The work of Congress mattered because there was power in joint voices and colonial disenfranchisement affected all black people, but the total financial ruin from the trip to England would have been more palatable if he still had *Tsala*, and the other 'glorious works' – those would have been consolation enough. Congress had raised his political profile, yet in his estimation, it had reduced his effectiveness in the matters he cared about the most. This is why he had declined the nomination to be Congress president in 1917, to prevent the further 'deterioration of my business', and had tendered his resignation as general secretary for the same reasons.⁵⁰⁶ He regretted that in playing such an active role in Congress, he had perhaps put the cart before the horse. He had allowed the fruit of the tree to poison its roots. Congress' mission had compromised the works of his own personal priorities, including his life as a writer.

Many people were pleading with him to go. He yielded primarily because Barolong chiefs asked him to go to represent their issues. Moreover, the Barolong in Mafikeng, were footing the £1000 bill at the very sore cost of their cattle and the little monies they had. The Barolong in Thaba Nchu also added substantial funds to the cost of his travel. He did not see any tension between his efforts to intervene in the regionalist struggle for the Barolong reserves' political autonomy and a uniform political solution that enfranchised blacks on the same terms as whites throughout the Union. The situation of empire held both ideals as plausible and simultaneous futures. Plaatje and many others thought the terms of their imperial placement were still open to negotiation. If black people did not have basic freedoms and could not take for granted a social infrastructure that distributed care, there was no way for them to take charge of their lives and destiny anywhere in the Union, including in the reserves along the Molopo. A unified black coalition with a political voice was critical if there was hope of protecting regional interests and separatist visions of development. The trip to England, as far as he was concerned, proved precisely that the political arrangements of Union were not yet final.

Immediately after the war, the stakes were very high for everyone in the Union, not only black people. General Hertzog was due to make an address at Versailles in France. Hertzog intended to lobby support for South Africa's right to self-determination as an independent sovereign state. The enterprise of Union would collapse if Hertzog could convince his constituency that

British rule would in the end compromise the hierarchy of white privilege. However, senior British officials, including Governor General Lord Buxton, wanted to demonstrate the loyalty and commitment of black British subjects in Europe, which is why he supported Congress delegates' trip to England.

> Lord Buxton said we have full right to see our King, more especially because the Nationalists are going to attempt to destroy our kingship (*bogosi joa rona*) ... we are going to defend it.[507]

The key organiser getting Plaatje ready for his trip was Sebopioa Molema. On the evening of 13 March 1919, Plaatje met Sebopioa and his cousin Tiego Tawana at the train station in Kimberley where they held their hurried meeting.[508] They decided that Lord Buxton's support for them was so strong that there was nothing to fear in divulging the contents of their petition to the Resident Magistrate in Mafeking who wanted to see it. They also decided that in Britain, Plaatje would not present the Barolong as unworthy supplicants on their knees. He would display every marker of their own kingly status as royals ruling a people of reputation.

> We agreed that the mission to England is to show the English that we too are a people [.] It is proper that we collect hides of jackal and [...] and leopard if available as gifts of the kings of Secoana to the [English] dignitaries and other important officials, so that as we make our presentation they should see we are really representing persons indeed.[509]

Sebopioa dispatched the message to Chief Gaisitsioe of Bangoaketse in Kanye, Chief Lenchoe of Mochudi, both in the Bechuanaland Protectorate, and Chief Moiloa of Lohurutse, west of the Transvaal, inviting their donations of money to support Plaatje's trip and blankets to offer as gifts to British dignitaries.[510] In mid-March 1919, Sebopioa attended a meeting of Congress in Bloemfontein so he could represent the Barolong chieftaincy. His aim was also to meet W.Z. Fenyang of Thaba Nchu and coordinate the two centres' joint efforts to send Plaatje to England.[511] The Barolong in Mafikeng applied for a £300 grant from the Barolong Educational and National Fund in order to aid the deputation.[512] Silas Molema also commandeered stock from the people to raise more funds. 'Barolong are gathering the *morafe*'s cattle in large numbers and the *morafe* is simply quiet, not hindering the regiments in any way.'[513] He was not sure about the number of cattle they would get on the Barolong Farms in the Bechuanaland Protectorate 'as the regiments

Morafe

have crossed over there yesterday, but here, the day before yesterday, 208 cattle were gathered and fetched £601-0-0'.⁵¹⁴ There would be at least an initial £900 from Mafikeng alone, and more would come from the Barolong on the Barolong Farms. Sebopioa also dispatched notices to other Bechuana chiefs to invite them to send a representative to England. He wrote to Chief Molaloe Mankuroane of Batlhaping.

> Barolong are resolute in their minds to go and they are making ready to find the shoes to carry them to England… We would be very happy if Batlhaping also can prepare themselves to go to England and speak on their own behalf, so that the oppression that is pressing against us can be relieved by the kingship of England. And the *morafe* of Bangoaketse has also been told to prepare themselves to go, all the peoples of the land that are black are intent to go, and so Motlhaping, even if we personally cannot go – oh Sir let nothing hinder your going. I am confident we can find our way overseas.⁵¹⁵

The deputation did leave for England but its mission failed, despite its enthusiastic reception. British officials were sympathetic overall but were not prepared to challenge the constitution of the Union government just at a time when the view that Britain was compromising on the colour bar could strengthen whites' republican cause. The deputation could not affect the terms of Union. Thus, the Natives Land Act of 1913 was and remained lawful in the Union of South Africa. The Barolong reserves had come irrevocably under conquest.

Another opportunity for Plaatje to edit a paper came along at the beginning of 1912. He would coedit *Umteteli wa Bantu*, meaning 'mouthpiece of the people', with John Dube.⁵¹⁶ A handful of Congress members, including his brother-in-law, Isaiah Bud-Mbelle, had approached the Chamber of Mines to sponsor a newspaper that would offer an alternative voice to *Abantu-Batho*, which was under the control of the more radical Transvaal members of Congress. The Chamber of Mines invited them to set up the initiative under its new Native Recruiting Corporation. The first issue of *Umteteli* appeared in May 1920 and carried both Plaatje and Dube's names. When the other Congress delegates returned to South Africa, Plaatje was making ready to travel to Canada and the United States of America and had travelled to France. In July of the same year, he launched the South African Bantu Brotherhoods Committee in London to 'erect, furnish and maintain meeting halls' for 'Brotherhood and Sisterhood work' in South Africa, and to 'promote Brotherhood amongst the tribes by the printing and circulation of suitable literature in English and the vernacular'.[517] Plaatje's financial situation, especially that of his wife back in Kimberley, was deplorable but the same conviction about his vocation kept him going, in the same manner he had kept going with *Koranta* for seven years without pay. He turned down the editorial position at *Umteteli*. A newspaper funded by the Chamber of Mines imposed limitations on his editorial freedom. Also, he would have had to move to 'that hellhole', Johannesburg, where he had no vote.[518]

All this is what he intended Molema to understand in the letter he wrote to him before he boarded the ship en route to the United States of America. He communicated that he had not given up on their sacred mission. The two deputations to England had not made any difference, but very much could still happen. He wrote to Molema that he was informing Henry Taberer, manager of the Native Recruiting Cooperation, of his withdrawal from *Umteteli*'s editorial pairing. He did not want Molema to give up hope. Their work for the 'Bechuana' – their independent territories, their language, their place of distinction in the world all – remained his commitment. In giving up a much-needed opportunity of salaried work, he was also indicating to the constituency of his homelands that he had not abandoned their struggle. He did not have any particular and definite political vision in mind other than to remain available for conversations and opportunities that could still change the future of southern Africa. Indeed, they were still living along an open frontier, not behind the curve of a defined, unalterable political situation. Hence, it was important that the Bechuana have ready their own mouthpiece. *Umteteli* would not do.

> I will tell Mr Taberer that my people will not allow me to write a paper of mixed languages. They want me to edit a paper in Secoana in the same line as Basotho have one in Sesotho and Matebele have their own. If you stand with me in this, *everything [sic] will come right and we will resuscitate the Tsala again.*[519]

XXI

The Natives Land Act included the Molopo Reserve in the 'Schedule of Native Areas' as Crown Lands held by the Governor-General, but chiefs remained gatekeepers as the population of the reserves swelled. In 1916, Silas Molema appeared before the Beaumont Natives Land Commission, whose aim was to find land for black settlement and define the territorial boundaries that separated the Schedule for Native Areas from the rest of the Union. Molema testified that '...we are now more in number than when the reserve was made' and are 'multiplying every year'. As a consequence, '[we] can only receive some of our people who went to work in the mines and on the farms, but those who went away a long time ago I could not receive back because the land is only big enough for us'.[520] The Natives Land Act prevented chiefly landlords from continuing with the 'white' and 'mixed' tenants that had paid hefty rents in the reserves, but at the same time, it created such competition for land that the capillaries of rents, tributes and services on the land thickened and ramified. There was not enough land but the tradition of absorbing new settlers into the landscape through such subscriptions continued. In the Molopo Reserve, black newcomers, especially sharecroppers, became the new cash cows, especially on the landholdings where the 'anti-squatter's bill' had cost chiefs and other black landlords their white tenants.

In 1919, Molema leased Madibespruit to a group of 'Fingoes and Xosas', who agreed to be 'governed by the Rules and Customs of the Barolong Nation'.[521] They carried out all the labours that people rendered to chiefs under customary law, but also much besides. In addition to paying a Hut Tax of 12 shillings, an annual contribution of 3 shillings to the Barolong Educational and National Fund, and paying 'any special levy made by the Paramount Chief',

> the Fingoes and Xosas aforementioned agree and bind themselves to plough each season one garden of, and for the benefit of Silas Tawana Molema, being a plot of arable land measuring 900 x 400 wherever indicated by the said Silas Molema, and they further bind themselves to cultivate and sow with their own seed, reap and thrash the crop of the said garden at their own expense and deliver the produce to the said Silas Molema ... reside and plough on the premises, and to graze their stock thereon, provided they undertake as they hereby do, to effect improvements on the same building houses, making dams and sinking wells.[522]

The Natives Land Act had allowed the government to take ownership of the 'Schedule of Native Areas' and evict whites and others who were not black from them, but that was not the same thing as opening up these reserves to other black people. Plaatje had already written in *Native Life*, three years before then, that reserves were not available as a catchment area for all black people who desired or needed to settle in them.

Indeed, the government had intended that 'native administration' would remove rents and services from the everyday negotiations of law and property in the reserves. The Schedule of Native Areas was the landscape of 'native administration'. Through this form of governance, white Native Commissioners would grant a black demographic entry into the reserves according to official understandings of race and 'customary' law that did not include subscriptions on the land. The policy made an ornament out of chieftaincy. The paramount chief had little else to do than earn his salary and adjudicate the handful of cases that were still under his jurisdiction. He would not interfere with the real centre of chiefly power – the office of the Native Commissioner, which allocated land and had taken over much of the judicial responsibility that had facilitated placement. Of course, now the government had the jurisdiction to implement its policy in the reserves, but it was not enough to tell chiefs that their reserves were now under 'native administration'. The government was as serious about implementing 'native administration' in the reserves as chiefs in the Barolong reserves were about resisting it. Silas Molema and others were still letting their properties, replacing the 'whitish ones' with unambiguously black tenants.

The government perceived that the Natives Land Act had not sufficiently weakened chiefs' power along the Molopo nor loosed their grip on the land, as though 'native administration' had not been imposed. Acting Secretary of Native Affairs, Edward Barrett, visited the capital stadts of the Barolong reserves in the last weeks of December 1916 and early January 1917 to announce a new policy outlined in the Native Affairs Administration Act of 1917.[523] James Molebaloa may have attended the meeting, seeing he then had placement in the Molopo Reserve. Moreover, Silas Molema and others had stayed at his house when they attended the Supreme Court hearing in Cape Town, hence he understood chiefs' position well enough to compile an illuminating history about this new legislation – both its intentions and chiefs' objections to it.[524] At the meeting, as James Molebaloa recorded, Barrett explained that the Native Affairs Administration Act of 1917 would 'take over' from the Natives Land Act of 1913 as a 'scheme for the creation of common native areas' in the reserves.

Molebaloa prepared a petition on behalf of the 'branches of the [Barolong] nation', which laid out chiefs' objections.[525] The petition explained that through the new proposed legislation, the government would put an end to the administration of justice through the courts, 'shutting the doors of the Supreme Court in the faces of the Native litigants', and instead confer powers upon Native Commissioners. Chiefs had not accepted that the Union government had jurisdiction over the Barolong reserves.

> Sight should not be lost of the fact that these territories were never conquered, but that they were ceded to the British Imperial Authorities by mutual agreement and any scheme for the creation of common native areas should not embrace the Barolong Reserves. The Native Reserves in Bechuanaland are tribal property, set apart for the exclusive use and occupation of the Barolong tribes, and to turn them into a cosmopolitan native area, as it is proposed to do in this Bill, is equal to the confiscation of freehold farms, and a distinct violation of the Annexation Act of 1895, which the owners should resist.[526]

Most importantly, the new legislation would 'take over' from the Natives Land Act without making any provision to increase land the previous legislation made available for black people, which meant Barolong reserves would become a reservoir for 'the natives who have been farming on their own in the South-West districts of the Transvaal ... Free State, and Colonial natives'. 'The petition explained that the difficulty with these sharecroppers, 'unless they were Barolong', was that they 'complicate the peaceful administration of tribal affairs on the Reserve, disorganise the tribal management, and add largely to the responsibilities of the chiefs and their people'. These immigrants were unfamiliar with moral repertoires of respectable citizenship in these reserves. The proposed legislation, 'by locking up the country to such natives, will reduce our Reserves to a dumping ground for the overflowing black population of the industrial centres, some of whom do not tend to make the best of citizens'.

For men like Molema, Plaatje, Molebaloa and Lekoko Marumoloa, manhood meant secure roots in the countryside, where one knew and was known by others along a hierarchy of gender and generation in ways that confirmed and amplified personal esteem. One's neighbours could not be just anybody, but persons (*batho*) who shared a consensus around the moral requirements of personhood, not merely putting the plough to the ground, but demonstrating respect for social hierarchy. It would not do for their reserves to become common areas, free and open to all. The Union government passed but did not implement the Native Administration Act of 1927. Chiefs held their position in the now 'blackened' reserves. The arrangements of placement remained under their control. They continued to reward their favourites and new clients with land, locking out those households for whom they were unwilling to make room.

In the Molopo Reserve, chiefs kept up the stalemate at Rietfontein. Despite now officially owning every square inch of the reserve, the government still could not resolve the dispute. In February 1917, the government recognised both Paul Montsioa and George Motuba as headmen on their payroll at Rietfontein. It was an official strategy to force peace. Paul was paid £12 per annum, twice the amount of George's stipend.[527] In April 1917, Silas Molema, requested the Resident Magistrate to clarify the position of Paul Montsioa at Rietfontein. He was reconciliatory. He agreed with Edward Barrett, now Secretary of the Native Affairs Department, that 'if we continue to quarrel within ourselves about the question of precedence and jurisdiction we shall never be a nation'.[528] The recognition of George Motuba at Rietfontein was too much for John Montsioa's mental instability. In September, he opted to use a show of force to push the stalemate at Rietfontein to resolution. He and some of his men apparently rode to Rietfontein for a 'looting raid' where John Montsioa burnt down the hut of one of the key instigators, Sejesho Mothibi.[529] 'Where was it ever that a Chief enters houses for purposes of looting,' one neighbouring chief asked John Montsioa.[530] 'You persecute this people for the simple reason that they are Bora Rapulana and that you want to restore your tribal headman at Rietfontein.' The violent episode stirred popular anger, even beyond Rietfontein. The Rapulana chiefs finally took the matter to court, naming both the Ratshidi chiefs and the Native Affairs Department as the defendants.[531]

The ruling of this case in the Supreme Court in Cape Town was when the tide finally turned in favour of the Native Affairs Department, but the triumph was actually that of ordinary people in Rietfontein. With the support of the Transvaal chiefs, the Rapulana householders had made representations that they were free from the Ratshidi nobility in Mafikeng because, according to 'custom', 'the Chief's jurisdiction is personal and not territorial'. In other words, the Rapulana had abandoned their claim of Rietfontein as their bounty from conquest that colonial officials, including Sidney Shippard, had recognised. Instead, they presented an argument about *Sechuana*. The court ruled in the Rapulana's favour. The new Resident Magistrate and Civil Commissioner of Mafeking, A. Wilmot, communicated the judgment to the chieftaincy during the last week of December 1920, elaborating that

> the Chief's jurisdiction is personal and not territorial. This means that the chief cannot exercise jurisdiction over any particular area (such as the Molopo Reserve) but only over the natives belonging to his own tribe.[532]

The court had not overruled Sidney Shippard's policy of not 'defining boundaries between tribes or section[s] of tribes considering the reserves available for all natives no matter of what nationality'.[533] It had however departed from the understanding that a chief has jurisdiction over every resident, every homestead, and every placement holder in the territory he ruled.

From that moment on, a chief's subjects everywhere in the reserve were only those who shared his ancestry. This determination of 'tribe', given it is here primarily a biological genealogy, had no litmus test, only the word of the 'tribesman' or 'tribeswoman'. The Rapulana said their ancestry lay in the Transvaal, and therefore, from the moment of the ruling, they owed nothing to the chiefly centre in Mafikeng. They were not alone. The 'Fingoes and Xhosas' on Madibespruit, now had their own chiefs a very great distance away from Mafikeng, and owed their placement to them, not to Silas Molema. Every man and woman in the Molopo Reserve who was or claimed to be of any 'tribe' other than the Ratshidi Barolong became his or her own personal 'chief' on the placement where his or her homestead, grazing lands or fields were. The only authority on these Crown Lands, at last, had become the white Native Commissioner, to whom all these 'foreigners' answered. Neighbouring reserves followed suit. Finally, chiefs' power south of the Molopo River had collapsed. Their rents ceased, choked off by the Supreme Court's ruling in the last instance, but primarily by the popular rage at Rietfontein that had pushed the matter to the highest court in the land.

XXII

According to philosopher Alain Badiou, falling in love has the potential to be an 'Event' – capital 'E', by which he means, an encounter with 'truth' that fundamentally alters one's situation of belonging. One becomes aware at that moment that he or she no longer belongs 'here' but over 'there' in a new experience. The 'Event' is something that happens to us, not something we manipulate through volition. This unexpected shift in the knowledge of oneself is an instance of subjectivity.[534] The question is whether we will determine to rearrange our lives according to the revelation of this truth or fearfully retreat into the comforts of the familiar? On the other hand, Pierre Bourdieu, sociologist and self-pronounced non-philosopher, sees no accident in the unexpected encounter of romantic love. He says all love is an arranged marriage. 'When one loves, there is always an element of loving in another person a different realisation of one's own social destiny.'[535] We 'fall in love' with those who represent and entrench our place of power and interest in the world. There is a mundane, practical, social patterning to desire, where class and status, for instance, mediate choice.

Modiri Molema's situation in love would satisfy both propositions, but eventually she would leave him no choice but to give her up. There is no surviving record of their attachment to each other, which for a long time was only by letter whilst he was in Glasgow. Only one letter, the second of three that he wrote to his father pleading to be allowed to marry her, survives. It states only her surname – 'Skota's daughter' – and not her name. She had grown up in Kimberley. She was not known to the intimate circles of the *morafe* that the fathers recognized. Yet, in her education and ambition, and in the colour of her black skin, she stood to him as the revelation of truth about where he belonged. In her professional ambitions, in her vision of the world and in loving him, he saw that she knew her *morafe* intimately, served it with devotion, and she loved her people freely. With her by his side, he imagined, he would step more boldly into the fathers' shoes. He would demonstrate more accurately the possibilities of the *morafe*'s own peculiar destiny.

His 'revelation' was that the *morafe* was in the moral aspiration of blackness, which manifested itself in the elevated consciousness that Christianity and education had lent to the 'Bantu', the peoples of Africa. The lovers' meeting was of course complete coincidence, though it had a feeling of a fated affinity. Surely an educated black man like himself could only ever be with a black woman like her. All around him in Glasgow, after the war broke out in 1914, he saw many examples of her – strong, self-directed, independent, working women. The war had brought Scotswomen out of their homes to take the place of men who had gone to war. As he described to his mother, women were driving trains and issuing rail tickets. They were running factories that made weaponry, but also learning to shoot and to handle guns because 'they say they want to go to war'.[536] He was conveying to his mother and clarifying for himself, the qualities of the man he wanted to become.

He was interrogating his own relationship with women and paying attention to the cultural influences of his own personality. He was trying to step out of the emotional reticence he had recently identified in himself by learning to express his full range of feeling. His intention was to nourish all the women he loved with a language of tenderness. He had never told his mother before that he loved her, but now he intended to make it a habit. Rev. Holdsworth was encouraging families to love one another with words.

> ... even if people were to forget their mothers, I would never forget you ... You will understand what I mean when I say I have a friend here, a reverend and an Englishmen called Rev Holdsworth ... Every Sunday when we meet at church he asks me "Have you written to your mother?" ... He says parents must tell their children that ["]My child I love you ["] and the children the same. And thus mother – I love you.[537]

He exchanged no letters with the reverend's daughter, Anna Moshoela, to whom a marriage had already been arranged. He carried that situation as a quiet restlessness but no more than that. He had confidence in the future. He hardly received any letters from his father. At most, there was a letter from him once in about six months, but he sustained himself mentally through the ties he had with the women in his life – Harriet, his mother, his bride. Besides, his own letters to his father were always hurried, written as a matter of urgency to ask for money. He had started with just about enough and then quickly ran dry. In the meantime, one of his younger brothers could not attend school until he had completed his sojourn in Glasgow.[538] There was no room for failure or waste of time, even though he was constantly without the financial support necessary for a speedy completion of his studies. The cost of a medical degree at the University of Glasgow was £150 over five years. Upon arrival, he had calculated that boarding and lodging costs would be roughly £52 per year but the Great War drove costs to at least £110 a year.[539] He kept a meticulous calculation of every farthing he spent and sent these records home with the news about his good progress through university. At the end of 1916, he was almost £60 in the red (having already fallen behind on his rent of £1 a week) but his father could only send him £20.[540]

By 1917, the cost of boarding and lodging had doubled. 'If this war does not end soon,' he wrote wryly to Harriet, 'I am afraid it will reduce many people of whom I will be one – to pauperism.'[541] This is what it meant, 'being a poor man's son'.[542] In March 1918, he had to postpone his training at a maternity hospital because he could not afford to travel to England.[543] He had been looking forward to it for months. When the time came, he had no money for rail. He blamed the self-sacrificing world of the fathers that had emptied the family purse on account of Bechuana. He determined at that very moment that as a doctor he would generate an income for himself. Patients would have to pay. He would not follow the path of service that had drained his father, and now placed him and his siblings in material difficulties. There was no question that patients would have to pay.

> I am really quite furious just now over this affair as I had made all arrangements, booked a place for myself in a special maternity hospital, and here at the last moment – no money! Just now I am worth less than nothing – Hopeless condition for a medical student to be in. If '*Bechuana ba rona*' [our Bechuana] think, by any chance that after all this suffering they shall have medical attendance, medical advice and treatment from '*ngoana rona*' [our child] free of charge, I fear me they are laboring under the greatest delusion conceivable.[544]

He was fleeing from the instinct that had depleted his father, and then Sebopioa, and now Harriet, whose ambitions had to be contained in Mafikeng. The same instinct had depleted the breakfast table of his childhood. It had sponsored a newspaper for a readership that did not pay. It had sapped everything to a bare hardship. He asked Harriet to plead with their father for £100 so he could register for his final examinations just twelve months away. He was nervous, 'so far it has been a struggle for life'. He did not know if he would manage to remain a student at the university. It was a miracle that he was still studying. 'It would not have been possible,' he said, 'but for some strange luck, but luck is not a dependable ally.'[545]

Just over a month later, his father wired a message that was not about money. His mother had died.[546] The death was sudden, possibly untreated appendicitis.[547] 'Oh God why, why, why?' He knew that 'grief must hang on everything and every place that mother had been in this life'.[548] Worse than the shock was the loneliness of his collapse, the wheels of his comfortable solitude buckling under his grief. He begged his father to write, 'now there is no mother to write to me, and one to whom I can write'. His sole consolation was that he would break with custom and tend to his mother's grave. In the meantime, the owners of his boarding house had been patient with him for years, but they could no longer wait for him to pay his dues. They were speaking to their lawyer to sue.[549] He considered the owners of the boarding house the best of people, only the war was squeezing them to desperation. He was grieving deeply, but mostly he was very worried about money. There was a lot of anxiety and shame. There was not quite time enough to nurse the wounds of loss. This time, his father came through for him. He received a handsome £100 when he had been pleading for '£50 to £60 at least'.[550] 'I shall now be able to look any man in the face, as I shall have all my debts squared up.' He had not afforded a trip to Manchester to complete his midwifery cases, but now he could finally proceed to St Mary's Hospital over the summer.

About a year after his mother's death, he received news that made him exceedingly happy. Rev. Joshua Moshoela's daughter had married the late regent's son, Dick Marumoloa, in the early months of 1919. Anna Moshoela and Sebopioa Molema had married siblings, Dick and Emang, respectively. The marriage was all technically above board, a marriage between cousins, nothing that would raise any eyebrows. In reality the two families were embarrassed. Modiri learnt from Harriet that apparently Anna had compromised her chastity, and the Rev. Moshoela had insisted on a marriage. Perhaps it was what Anna wanted. Dick was a charming man with an education. He was then the National Secretary of the chieftaincy. He was also a man of leisure who enjoyed company and drink. Perhaps, Anna wanted a quick escape from life in a remote mining town like Klerksdorp. The reasons did not matter. Just as the noose was about to tighten, fate had orchestrated his freedom. He feigned disappointment for Harriet's sake because she took it for granted that he would be crushed, while in fact, he rejoiced. He replied that his 'intentions were honest and honourable', that he had 'intended to ask for Anna's hand in marriage but that Anna's behavior led him 'therefore [to] believe in my conscience that I am not opposing my [late] beloved mother's will, nor my father's by not marrying her'.[551]

After this, there were no letters from his sister, only a 'long silence'.[552] He construed it had to do with the troubles in her marriage. Harriet's position was precisely the loneliness he wished to avoid in a marriage, especially after so many years away living by himself. Three years before he had written to her after more than five months of being unable to go into the streets of Glasgow for lack of money.[553] He had only recently met James Moroka, who had just completed his medical studies at Edinburgh. Moroka was also a Morolong, from Thaba Nchu, and like him, also a son of a senior chiefly family. So he knew people, including through the African Students Association, but he thought even if he had the means available, he would choose to remain shut up in his quarters, slogging away at his studies or working on the book he was writing on the 'Bantu' of southern Africa. Three years before, awake at midnight he had written to Harriet to say that perhaps his isolation was better, because the bustle of people would be too painful a contrast with his 'funny life' – 'staying in apartments and lodgings' being 'away from kith and kin'.[554] Coming across 'happy crowds of people' would only make 'one realize how much "alone" he is', how 'you practically live alone, eat alone, sit alone and so forth alone'.[555] Now, in 1920, he still felt the same way.

He was ready for a lifetime of intimacy. Next would be graduation and then residency, after which he hoped he would sail home to a marriage. His mother had 'broken [his] life by passing'.[556] He regretted that he had not been there 'to sit by her death-bed, to clasp her hand, to kiss her'. He had bid farewell to her at the railway station with the thought that 'I would raise myself to fame' for the sake of her rejoicing, that he would 'do this and that for my mother to make her happy'. In those first few weeks after her death, study had been almost impossible. Her death had sapped his fortitude. He had been ready to surrender to the forces of his financial lack. He had considered leaving the university. Had she only waited for their reunion, for then she would have died happy with him by her side.[557] In her absence, he felt famished of connection. He longed to give himself away like rain falling.

Finally, in April of 1919, he learnt, it was all over.[558] The war had nearly doubled the price of everything and yet, he had made it to graduation. He had completed his studies in less than £600.[559] 'I can safely say that no one else could have lived and got his education on that amount especially during the course of the war.'[560] When graduation came, he went into mourning on account of his mother's absence. He graduated in the month that marked the anniversary of her death, and so his 'joy at finishing mingled with a bitter grief'.[561] He hurried past the day to the next thing. He went to Dublin as a Resident Medical Officer at Hume Street Hospital.[562] He travelled to London to see Solomon Plaatje, who gave him a letter from his father with a surprising proposal, to which he replied.

> I agree with you father when you say I should take a higher degree so that no one may for a moment question my merits and ability when I get home. The idea is a very good one and falls in with my ambition; namely to have the best medical education and medical degree in this country although this means my being kept away from my dear home with all that home means to me, if it is your wish that I continue my studies [here] for a longer time then I am pleased to obey.[563]

The instruction took him aback. He had already made up his mind to stay but had expected that his father would demand he set sail homewards as soon as possible. His father's own choice to do without him, even after five solid years, was not what he had been bracing himself for. Perhaps he had all along been judging his father too harshly. Perhaps, Silas Molema was just as pragmatic and open minded as he was. He was elated that his own father was proving to fall outside the mould of the fathers' world. His father wanted him to thrive and explore the world, to grow and not quickly return to the strongholds of duty and service in Mafikeng without wide experience. It dawned on him that he had the rare benefit of distinguished parents even in the generation of the fathers. Silas Molema was free in his thinking, a man of 'progress,' a solid cut above his contemporaries.

> I think that we, the children of Father and Mother, must thank God greatly for giving us parents like you, who taught us to love them greatly and to love our kin, the grandfathers and the grandmothers and the aunts and so on, and to love our *morafe*. I especially must be grateful for the education that nobody else in our *morafe* has ever gained hitherto. If others had been my parents will we have received such breeding and education and such great love. Father, we your children have been granted distinguished parents although we do not know it as people do not ordinarily appreciate their breeding properly.[564]

The grief in his letters was beginning to lift. Instead, he had praise for his father, with every recollection of home and of his upbringing. Every memory of home carried a new revelation about the great personality that was his father. He stretched that pedigree of distinction upon his consciousness until it folded into the past to include his grandparents.

> You my dear Father have been very good. I am only beginning to properly realise and be truly thankful to you for several things which you have done in the past, and which seemed to my eyes to have no meaning. Today I am thinking how you very often sent us every holiday time to Motlhokaditse and to Kraaipan to see our maternal grandparents. It is now when I cannot see them that I begin to realise the lesson. It is now when I am trembling with fear that I may not see my dear grandfather that I wonder [why] I did not appreciate your practices of sending us to see him years ago. Will you therefore write soon to me![565]

He was preparing to travel to Liverpool for three months to take up his studies in Tropical Medicine at the beginning of 1920. His book, *The Bantu Past and Present*, would be in print by then. He was looking forward to returning home. It was clear to him, that he and his father shared a vision of the future, that they were alike, a source and a tributary flowing in the same direction. The excitement, the anticipation of continuing happiness, all the relief of the end of his financial struggles as he started to work, emboldened him to claim his freedom, as though he were one man standing on many fronts and on many feet, watching all of nature shrink into something he owned. He felt heavy, as more than the sum of his own strength. His family did not belong to the parochial, unimaginative worlds of the fathers. His father was giving him freedom to become the man of his own aspiration, to come and go, and impose his own design upon the world. Hence, he wrote to him about his intention to marry the woman he loved.

He received a most affectionate letter from his father, which also relayed £60 and permission to remain in Britain another eight months, but it was not yet the reply he was waiting for. It seemed his own letter had not yet reached Mafikeng because in his reply, his father was broaching the subject of marriage.[566] Once again, he and his father were of the same mind. 'I understand you Father when you say you do not know who will become my companion in marriage.' He continued: 'I trust that you have [now] received my letter where I have asked you to allow me the woman I have considered.' He was happy to have time to remain abroad, 'I am glad', but he longed to return home. 'I am preparing to do as you wish Father, and I miss you.'

His father's letter was mainly about what he should anticipate finding when he returned home, especially the political dilemmas that were facing the Molopo Reserve. He learnt of the Supreme Court's ruling in the litigation about Rietfontein. In replying, he redirected the focus to the question that most alarmed him about the situation. The strife between the Barolong in the reserve reflected the continuing hostility between members of what, in his mind, ought to be a united people. In such a war between kin there were no winners.

> I have been hearing about how the talks and litigation of the Barolong are proceeding. I have heard that the case about the land between the Ratshidi and the Rapulana has gone in favour of the Rapulana and has taken all the money and hard earnings of the Ratshidi ... Having appealed to the highest courts, we shall have to abide by their judgment. And the news of the chiefship I have heard also. It is very bad news – especially that it has caused divisions amongst the Ratshidi, and ruined the establishment of the place.[567]

His father felt tired and old. He assured him that now that he had graduated, he was ready to offer the *morafe* his devoted service, and to advance the same course of 'progress' that he knew they both espoused.

> It is perhaps impossible for me to fully appreciate these things until I see them for myself and I am very anxious to do so, and especially to be of assistance to you my dear father. I feel that the many misfortunes that have befallen us during the last few years have become a heavy burden upon you, in your increasing age, and I feel sorry to think that I have been and am still so far away, and unable to do anything. I am proud of Brother Sebopioa for all he is doing and for what he stands for. Since I qualified, I have been doing my best to increase my knowledge and to make myself

> proficient in my profession so that I shall be better able to help my people at home. I have several plans, which I want to discuss with you such as beginning.1, a Nursing Home or Hospital, 2, improving the sanitation of the stadt, 3, giving lectures in First Aid to intelligent girls.[568]

When the next letter came, he only then perceived that the bottom had long fallen out of his hope. Had he misread the cues about his father's character and now had to choose between two loves, that of a woman and that of his father? Should he have waited until his return to speak to his father face to face? She had been anticipating all along that he would have to make the choice, which is why she was ready to end it as soon as he said his father had refused him permission to marry her. He asked her for more time. He pleaded desperately with his father. She was unwilling to weather the storm, but he was determined to sway her to stay. He wrote very carefully to his father, that happiness in a marriage was impossible without a pairing of compatible sensibilities. She could not see how they would survive, and not be split up by the war between father and son.

He insisted that, contrary to his father's view, he had not made a choice between his honour and his desire. Nor did he intend to make the question of who he married a test of his love for his family.[569] He was not a child acting rashly, or rebelliously, or losing himself in a chance meeting with her. 'I have looked for such a one.'[570] He asked his father to reconsider.

> I can safely say that no son loves and honours a father more than I love and honour you, and I shall ever be deeply thankful to Providence for such a father, and to you for the excellent and rare education you have given me – education which makes me today one of the foremost men of my race and one of the best educated amongst black and white in South Africa. This alone dear father is in itself sufficient to make me hold you in high esteem, but apart from it, I have a very high sense of filial duty and deep love for you Rra. ... My dear father, I must earnestly and humbly ask you again for your approval. [571]

He stressed that he had been in love with her for seven years. They had been exchanging letters throughout his stay in Glasgow. She was 'an educated and intelligent partner.' His intention had not been to defy tradition. He was nonetheless a man with a great sense of purpose. It was inevitable that his heart would gravitate towards a woman who could support his vision of his future. In fact, his attachment to her had created the very possibility of who he could be in the world. 'Our people have not taken the trouble to educate their children, and they cannot rightly expect their uneducated daughters to have educated husbands.' His vocation depended on it. 'I must have an intelligent partner'. Also, what of the heartbreak he would be causing her if he walked away, especially 'after keeping her waiting all that time, after my asking her to be my wife and after me giving her promise to be my wife.' He had dwelt at length on the question of 'love and education' but this was not the only consideration. 'Honour alone would dictate but one line of action and one duty.'[572]

The next month, in June, his book, *The Bantu Past and Present*, was in print. Plaatje came up to Scotland and they met at Edinburgh. Afterwards he travelled and holidayed in Dublin, still waiting for his father's reply. He had been waiting for two months. His father had not even written to congratulate him on his book, although he would have received the copies. He could no longer tame his anxiety or contain his dread, so he wrote another letter. 'You have not written to me for a long time [and] under the circumstances I don't know whether your silence implied anger or not.'[573] He did not want them to become estranged, yet he could not yield. Now they stood on either side of their divide, each unable to reach across the moral breach between them about the meaning of honour. 'I sincerely hope – especially that I have not hurt your feelings for I would far sooner go through fire and water for your sake than see you in a moment's pain.'. He was arranging to return home 'promptly' although there were 'several things I would like to have done by way of gaining more clinical study and experience'. His book was gaining favorable reviews in the British press. The *London Times* had dedicated a whole column to it and the church periodicals, *The Methodist Times* and the *Methodist Recorder*, were enthusiastic. The publishers wished to produce a 'second and enlarged edition' of *The Bantu Past and Present*. He shared news of his success with his father and waited another three months to hear from him, with the silence gnawing at him.

At last, the reply arrived, and again, his father had refused, but this time more doggedly, with a slew of the sacred words – *morafe*, *Sechuana*, *botho*, but these same words were his defense – *morafe*, *Sechuana*, *botho* – these were his feelings precisely.

You have refused to do as I asked, that you allow me to marry Skota's daughter ... you say the person I want to marry is of another people [*dichaba disele*]. I am not asking for permission to marry a white woman, a *lekgoa* like many men here are doing, some of whom are my friends.

> Father, I am also not asking you to allow me to marry a woman of the Cape (coloured) or a black woman from Nigeria in West Africa, or a black American woman, or just some woman from elsewhere. I am not asking for any of these things. I am only asking you to allow me to marry a woman you know well, who is a child of people who esteem themselves, who have personhood, a person who also has personhood and education and love, a person I have not just met yesterday, a person who has been my best friend from long ago ... You know father, beloved of my heart, I asked this of you, and I asked you with love.[574]

His love for this woman, his experience of their synergy, was enough sign and confirmation that it could be no other way. Only he had no arbitrator to intervene for him in this one paramount crisis of his manhood, being denied choice like a small boy. He would not allow it – that much of himself he would not offer, but she had already given him up. She would hear nothing of going ahead when his family had rejected her. She left, and they ended, but so too, in crucial measure, had he and his father. There they stood, facing each other, each on the opposite sides of the breach, unyielding. He was preparing for his passage to Mafikeng, but he had resolved to leave his father's house.

He replied to his father that his request was 'not of a person who did not love himself' or 'lost himself'.[575] There was nothing in it to 'disgrace our name'. In fact, his father's consent would be a pure example of 'the works of the most esteemed things, the works that make the *morafe* or one people, hence the work of all Blacks'. In other words, the ways of the fathers – and not his choice, compromised honour, especially as he was not asking for 'a great difficult thing'. Surely, to care about one's own son's happiness, 'making the person who loves you most in the world happy', was not shameful – quite the contrary. In fact, he continued, if there was any place where Molemas' great name had to prove its distinction and its commitment to 'progress', it was in the painstaking labour to birth this *morafe* and no other. Moreover, the times were pressing upon the Molemas to occupy their highest calling, as the source, the birthing place, of the *morafe*. 'This is a time of war between the (skin) colours.' There had to be a field marshal 'with education and love enough' to 'unite all the Blacks'. In the hardships of the battlefield, there was a providential grace to bring forth the *morafe*. All that was necessary was a midwife. He felt that calling intensely, and understood surely, 'that is a work of God'. The works of one's own life had to reveal the moral boundaries of this *morafe*, hence he disapproved of the choices of some educated black men around him. If any persons 'love Africa, they should not mix their blood with white blood by marrying whites (*Makhoa*).'

> I am letting you know that it is my desire and my intention that your name as Rre Molema, should not die with the Barolong, or reach only the Bechuana, or only the black people of South Africa. As I see befitting both flesh and thought, my intention is to live for and to work for the freedom and life of all the Blacks (*Bancho*) of the land of Africa. To do so is my intention, to bring ruin to division and hatred between our people, so that I can unite them to become one *morafe* – not just merely small peoples (*dichabanyana*). This is the first work (*tiro*) of persons thirsty for progress…What I am saying is whether I marry her or I do not marry her, I am not giving my life to the Barolong only or to the Bechuana only. I have given it to work for all the Blacks of South Africa and of Africa … A proper life is to live for all of the black *morafe*, the children of Africa.[576]

He had already done a great deal of the work in Scotland by completing the 'ethnographical and historical study of the Native Races of South Africa'.[577] This was the subtitle of *The Bantu Past and Present*. There was not yet a book of such a framing in southern Africa. It brought together all the different coloured peoples of 'South Africa', from the San to his own Bechuana, under one frame as the 'Bantu'. There were no distinctions between 'the Bantu' under the unifying frame of the colour of their skin and the peculiar moral hues appropriate to them. The transformation of empire, both its hardships and the benefits of Christianity, had happened to all of them, such that there was no hierarchy of 'civilization' or 'progress' among them. Moreover his 'South Africa' was not the Union. It was the territories on both sides of the Molopo River. The 'Bantu' were all one. Solomon Plaatje was very impressed with the book, although as his letter to the author showed, he read it through the lenses of the fathers' way of seeing the world.

> My only regret is that this book will excite the jealousies of the very Bantu for whose benefit you have laboured thus unselfishly for the book is BIG. Other tribes will maliciously belittle your efforts while the 200,000 Barolongs will offer you their lip loyalty instead of recommending it to possible buyers.[578]

In the meantime, his own father said nothing, not about the book and nothing more about the marriage. 'My love for you prevents me from marrying a woman you do not approve of, and she too will not allow herself to be my wife against your will.'[579] Nevertheless, he was not yet surrendering. If his father would not yield, then he would not marry at all. 'Personhood (*botho*) and truthfulness and honour dictate that I obey you by not marrying her but also that I do not injure her by marrying another woman.'[580] In January 1921, he made the passage home.[581]

XXIII

The aftermath of John Montsioa's 'looting raid' at Rietfontein was a further handicap to his deteriorating state of mind. The more unable he felt to keep going, the more he absconded from his responsibilities and drank, until he eventually left for Johannesburg in 1918, ostensibly to meet his Barolong subjects as other chiefs were frequently doing. In Johannesburg he borrowed £300 from the British Loan Company for a spree of drinking and conspicuous consumption.[582] When he could not pay, the company threated to sue and have him imprisoned. Pixley Seme, who supported chieftaincy and wished to promote its reputation as an institution of the highest moral authority, wrote to John's father-in-law, Silas Molema.

> It gives me considerable pain that I have to tell you that the Barolong nation is on the point of experiencing a very deep disgrace. The cause of this lies in the attitude and manner of Chief John Montsioa who has disregarded my advice in several matters of great importance... I went at my own expense to Mafeking to tell him that the position was very very serious, – that the people would sue him and sell all his property, the houses, furniture, cattle... I am exceedingly disappointed in John Montsioa and I feel that unless the nation will take hold of his affairs and even the Chieftainship you will go into ruin.[583]

Lotlamoreng Montsioa stepped up to claim the chiefship when his opponent had ruined himself. John had no state of mind for a fight and he had burnt many bridges. The Acting Secretary of the Native Affairs Department, F.S. Malan, called a meeting at the courthouse to resolve the dispute between the two claimants in front of about 800 people. John Montsioa lost his position in November 1919.[584] Silas Molema's attention was on saving Harriet, both her marriage and her reputation, which meant stepping in to assist John Montsioa. More than that, he cared for John Montsioa. His son-in-law had a serious mental illness. The pattern was clear. Whenever his mental state gave in, everything collapsed with it. Any pressure pushed him towards the loss of control and drink. His deposition as paramount chief caused John great suffering, but it also meant he could retire from the pressures of the position

Family/Placement

and pay attention to his health even though such a public humiliation allowed him no reprieve from tortuous thoughts.

Nevertheless, the question of chieftaincy was an open political campaign that never ceased. There was still hope if John could be well. The priority was to get him help and give the marriage a fresh start. Molema arranged for John and Harriet to go Pietersburg, about 540 km northeast of Mafikeng. They travelled after Easter in April 1920 and remained there for some time for John's recuperation. Harriet had to stop teaching. 'We are quite happy', she reported to her father, and that John is 'improving daily' due to the 'change of climate'.[585] Things were looking up in her marriage. Even Modiri in Scotland adopted a more positive line of enquiry around his brother-in-law's health.[586]

John's mind, however, was on nothing but the chieftaincy he had lost. He wrote to his father-in-law, pleading with him to call another public meeting and to petition for his reinstatement.[587] His father-in-law started to gather petitions against the deposition in June 1920. His strategy was to ensure that whatever happened next, John would have something in hand, some domain of his own to rule, even if he could not occupy a position as paramount chief. One solution, given especially that the paramount chief's jurisdiction was no longer 'territorial' but 'personal', was for the Molemas and their followers to 'cut themselves away' from Lotlamoreng Montsioa and his supporters. Failing John's reinstatement as paramount chief, Silas Molema's petition requested that the

> ... Tribe be divided up into different Sections, i.e. Stadts, without any ... [paramount] Chief; each stadt to conduct its own internal affairs under its own Chief Headman [and] settle its own tribal, civil and criminal disputes and trials, the only reference to any outside Court to be to the Magistrate as an Appeal Court in terms of Sections 33 BB Proclamation No 2 of 1885. Should neither of the above be done there is no doubt that in the near future disturbances of a very serious nature, which are now maturing, will materialise.[588]

It was the same separatist claims that the Rapulana instigators had from the beginning been making and had finally won. Silas Molema was merely using the opportunity to redeem the two young lives that needed earnings and a fresh start. Besides, even he did not want to recognise Lotlamoreng Montsioa as his own paramount chief.

Barely three months later, on 1 July, he received a wire from Harriet, 'meet me tonight' at Mafeking's station.[589] Clearly, she had had reason for flight without warning. By the end of the month, John was in hospital in Johannesburg after which he transferred to Pretoria.[590] Now Modiri was pleading more seriously with her to reconsider her situation. He thought it was time she braced herself and walked away, which she could only do, he thought, if she saw the marriage as an error of human judgment, not a fate she could not overturn. The question was whether she was up to the challenge of a new beginning.

> I can never think of you without a severe feeling of regret, dear ... Indeed, my Harriet, it often happens that the very things which present misfortune are our making or at least we rise renewed and re-invigorated and our strength increased from the effect of what seemed to be a catastrophe. But to do so, it is necessary above everything that we be strong, we must have a character [,] a moral strength and a dogged determination. You my little girl have some of those qualities which make up a strong personality. I must pray that you give your qualities a full and free exercise.[591]

After two years, John had still not recovered and the hospital saw no reason to continue treatment in the ward.[592] Another of Plaatje's brothers-in-laws took him in so that he did 'not wander about the streets'.[593]

It may have been during his hospitalisation that Harriet wanted to 'start as a fresh teacher in a fresh school so that I may improve my position with the school'.[594] In her application, she promised to 'do my utmost best to discharge my duties to the satisfaction of the managers and the approval of the inspector' at a new Green Point School' in Kimberley. She continued in dutiful loyalty towards her husband, and towards her father, until eventually, her husband freed her from himself. He filed for divorce in 1925.[595] The separation was peaceful and amicable. Harriet had won her freedom by her exercise of duty. Her father grieved deeply that 'the children have separated'.[596] Shortly after that, John died, which worsened the old man's sorrow. He considered himself to have failed his children, Harriet and John both. He wrote to his nephew, the Reverend Joshua Moshoela that he was seeking answers from God, but Moshoela reproached him for blaming himself. What had his uncle expected from a family that had not accepted the saving grace of God?[597] The reverend said it was simple – drink had claimed yet another prodigal Montsioa.

> To some was given children but those children held nothing of worth to the world. No Father. God is great, it is only that often our hearts

do not have God and we forget that we are sinful ones because we do not entrust our lives to Him. In these times, the person who will survive a little while longer is he who entrusts his life to the care of [spiritual] doctors. Father, the days of prodigality are long gone, then we were not in the light we have today. I know it is liquor that has taken all of these children of Montsioa that I know, except Mokgeeta.

Indeed, many educated fathers were losing hope. Chiefs exchanged reports of sons who were living only for the satisfaction of their own desire. Fathers thought the plague of their son's generation was an unwillingness to do the works of personhood. Young men had abandoned tradition, including the basic virtues of temperance. Plaatje's sons, including his eldest son whom he was preparing for university education at the new Fort Hare University, established in 1916 as the South African Native College, were also struggling under the addictions of liquor.

Nevertheless, fathers had no choice but to pass on the baton, especially to the new generation of chiefs. When Silas Molema asked him a question about land in the Batlhaping reserve, a chiefly councillor L. Monnarora wrote that his people knew 'very little about land' since the death of their old Chief Molale.[598] All they knew were 'whites and their tax, which they demand now standing on their feet and the debt we owe to stores'. Monnarora wished he could return to the past because 'now we remain with a child here, about whom we do not know, but it seems he will not please his *morafe*. He cares about nothing, takes no advice, and has nothing to do with the councillors of the Kgotla'. At Kanye in the Bechuanaland Protectorate, one elderly chief complained to the Resident Magistrate that when he tried to advise the young Sebele on 'native custom', 'the Chief started to scold as if he is not speaking to his father but a wild animal, and that pained us very much because we are his eyes and his ears'.[599] The fathers were retreating from public life into their private troubles, crippled by debt, disappointed by sons.

XXIV

In June 1922, Sebopioa Molema 'left home so abruptly' to take up work in Natal.[600] The province greeted him with an unexpected brunt of white hostility. A black person like himself could not walk about at night or walk on the pavement or enter the town without a certificate of exemption. Natal had a long history of settler colonialism and an established hierarchy of white privilege, which as Sebopioa saw his situation, made no distinction between an 'educated native' like him and a 'Zulu from the wilds'.[601] He worked at Endloveni, a company owned by A.H. Todd, which produced traditional 'African' medicaments from herbs and probably other concoctions. Such remedies yielded healthy profits for black traders with licenses to distribute them, including one Khotso Sethuntsa from Lusikisiki who became a millionaire through the trade.[602] The name of Todd's own brand was *otukululayo*, which he claimed, expelled disease as it loosened the bowels. Sebopioa thought Todd was a 'hard Master' but also a 'father' and 'good advisor' to him.[603] Todd offered to approach Natal officials to issue Sebopioa with an exemption certificate. All Sebopioa had to do was ask his father to collect testimonials from various people whose opinion mattered, including the Resident Commissioners in Mafikeng.[604]

When the Native Affairs Department issued his certificate of exemption a year later, the document was without his voter registration, even though a black man of his education had the right to vote in the Cape province. He was horrified that 'at this later hour in my age I do not want to be left behind when humble votes are being cast by my comrades for the good of my country and my home'.[605] He had left Natal by then to work as a timekeeper for the Afrikander Mine in Klerksdorp. He was satisfied well enough with 'my humble work'. The work was useful to relieve his debt and the financial strain on his family.[606] By 1926, he had managed to 'meet his obligations & debt' and to have a 'good salary'.[607] He also had a peace of mind, and found once again that the rewards of the job were in the opportunities to care for the *morafe*. He had become a resident chief of the industrial zones. He was making a person out of himself in Klerksdorp in the Transvaal. He kept a watchful eye on Barolong immigrants into Klerksdorp from the reserve and helped to place them in surrounding mines. He saw this work as a 'privilege' he conferred on 'children of Molema and Barolong'.[608] He established a network of friends and relationships that could help families find men who had gone missing. He also wrote letters on behalf of families to the Native Commissioner to make inquiries when relations died in Klerksdorp, far from home.

There were many like him in the mining compounds, men with chiefly roots from the countryside, but also new incumbents who derived their positions as chiefs by assembling people together in the industrial zones in order to facilitate claims to land and other resources in the countryside and elsewhere. There were new *merafe* quickly mushrooming in urban towns and cities, carrying the names of the constellations of the countryside

There are no photographs of Silas Molema in the family's voluminous records at the University of the Witwatersrand. His grandson Batho Molema's recollection, of how many of his parents' and grandparents' photographs were destroyed, captures the family's declining fortunes and the deepening generational divide between educated parents and children in Bechuanaland that began in the early 20th century and continued even into his own childhood. This undated photograph of Silas Molema in horse-riding gear is in the private collection of the late Mrs Mercy Molema at Signal Hill, Mafikeng.

Solomon Plaatje remained at the centre of the Molemas' family life and political influence from when he took up a post as a clerk and court interpreter in Mafeking in October 1898. Plaatje served the political and other aspirations that the Molemas had for themselves and the Barolong with as much devotion and sacrifice as Silas Molema expected from all his children.

Sebopioa Molema joined the collegiate division of Wilberforce University, Ohio, in 1906. This is the only photograph of him in the Molemas' papers at the University of the Witwatersrand. An enlarged image of the same hangs in the living room of his daughter-in-law, the late Mrs Mercy Molema, at Signal Hill, Mafikeng. There are no other photographs of Sebopioa Molema at Signal Hill.

This is Modiri Molema, as a young boy, in horse-riding gear. This photograph is undated but continues the studio motif of a figure who poses next to a chair, as in the photograph of his father, also in riding gear. There is a similar photograph of a young girl, presumably Harriet, his sister. There are no comparable photographs of the younger siblings, probably because the family could no longer afford such expenditure.

This photograph is one of many unnamed subjects in the Molemas' family archive, held at the University of the Witwatersrand. She is assumed to be Harriet Molema, though it could also be her older sister, Seleje. There are more than 150 photographs in this archive, although strikingly none of these are of her parents and sisters. Unfortunately, present members of the family are unable to identify the unnamed people in the photographs.

Joshua Molema sits outside his home in Mafikeng. He is the only Molema to have ruled the Molopo Reserve. The colonial government deposed the then paramount chief, John Montsioa, in 1915 and appointed Joshua in his stead. Joshua did not have the support of Silas and Sebopioa Molema, mainly because they resisted any intervention by the colonial government in the political or territorial affairs of the reserve.

Lekoko Montsioa was the regent of the Molopo Reserve from 1911. John Montsioa was still too young to rule for himself. Lekoko was the paramount ruler when the Barolong successfully defended their right to rule their reserves as autonomous territories that did not belong to the colonial government in 1913.

Chief Wessels Montshiwa.

Chief Badirite Montshiwa.

Wessels and Badirile Montsioa were brothers and became paramount rulers of the Molopo Reserve in 1896 and 1903 respectively. Like the more educated Molemas, the Montsioas understood themselves as traditionalists, despite the European dress, styles of architecture, furnishings and other such influences that they and many others had blended into their everyday lives along this frontier.

and establishing new ethical universes of care and freedom in the mining compounds. Making or claiming belonging to new *merafe* and assembling various kinds of chieftaincies was one way people who were typically far from home, with little money and often shut up in routines of institutional life that were mainly not of their making, tried to coalesce around new moral routines that would confirm personhood.

In the meantime, in the countryside where Sebopioa came from, chiefly power was no longer the source of placement on the land after the Supreme Court ruling in favour of the Rapulana in the Molopo Reserve. The hierarchy of chieftaincy was no longer an example of a reputable life. Hundreds of people had 'cut themselves away' from the chiefly centre in Mafikeng. These people and households were under the complete jurisdiction of the Native Commissioner on the lands that the government owned. With every visit home, Sebopioa was becoming more aware, more angered, by the diminution of his authority in his ward, Signal Hill. However, he had not given up his domain, and would not do so just because the government had insisted on it.

Thus, in the winter of 1926, he came to blows with one Pholo Thari who, it appears, had been a member of a work party constructing a dam very near his residence at Signal Hill while he was away in Klerksdorp.[609] Thari chopped down about thirty poles of brushwood and left them floating in the dam, contravening both the regulations of the colonial government to preserve forests and chiefs' authority to authorise the cutting down of forests and extract a license fee. Upon his return from Klerksdorp, Sebopioa found the poles floating in the dam. He charged Thari for contravention of forest regulations but also for 'contempt', in that 'he ignored my presence at Signal Hill as his superior represented by Mrs Emang S.J. Molema'. He did not issue a fine because Emang and others begged for his leniency. He only instructed Thari to remove the poles from the dam and to bring them to Emang. Six weeks later, when he returned from Klerksdorp, the poles were still floating in the dam, now ruined by mould. He had to jump into the dam himself because nobody had seen fit to retrieve them. He removed all thirty poles unaided. Sebopioa fined Thari two oxen, but after much 'praying', Thari managed to bring down the fine to one ox. The record of the case is in Sebopioa's neat typescript, but there is no record of whether Thari paid.

A few months later, in the spring, Sebopioa returned to the reserve to take over his father's position as the most senior headman in the reserve. He would be able to draw an annual salary of £24 from the Native Affairs Department, but before he gave notice to his employers, he wanted a firm 'guarantee' that Lotlamoreng Montsioa will pay him 'wages for services' every month.[610]

Morafe

In the end, his earnings were a steady cash injection, necessary, but never enough. He would have to rely on the land to make ends meet, although not in the manner of collecting returns from sharecroppers and other tenants. He would have to farm, plough the ground and turn the soil with his own hands, which his fathers had never had to do. His chiefly privileges on the land had ended with the broken regime of the fathers' rule.

XXV

In 1918, Phoebus Fincham started to build a stable on Mabete, but the headman named Papename at the quarry on a neighbouring farm refused to let him have stones unless he paid ten shillings per load.[611] Fincham wrote as usual to Molema about 'more trouble to settle'. The quarry, like pans and forests, was common property, but Papename had reminded him that Molema had made people on this neighbouring farm 'pay heavily for the trees they chopped' on Mabete.[612] It was May, winter was beginning, and it was very dry. The reply was long in coming but when it did, Molema was asking to borrow £15, despite the money he already owed.[613] For several years now, Fincham had not been paying his rent to defray that debt. He was unwilling to lend his landlord any more money, especially when Molema hardly intervened to protect him on the farm.[614]

In the spring, Van Rensburg, who was Fincham's undeniable challenger on the farm, left Mabete.[615] Fincham was pleased but not entirely relieved. The departure meant change again and change that he had to try to manage. The new tenant was another Dutch-Afrikaner, by the name of Wolhuter. They did not get along. Wolhuter started to let grazing fields to other farmers looking for land. One day in May 1919, he brought 300 cattle on the farm to graze. Fincham reported to Molema that 'Mr Wolhuter wants to get mostly like the rest of the [D]utch. [T]hey always look for trouble.'[616] Wolhuter impounded any stock that strayed and crossed his boundary, no questions asked. He also traded without a license in cattle, sheep, corn and consumables like coffee from his home, and he was very good at it. He had grain even when supply was scarce. He bartered widely. In September 1919, he sent three bags of mealies to Molema presumably in lieu of rent.[617] Fincham had had enough.

He reported Wolhuter's illicit trade to the Lobatse authorities directly because, as he told Molema, 'I am sick & tired to be always complaining to you.'[618] The court found Wolhuter guilty of selling mealies from his home without a license. 'The question is,' Fincham asked Molema 'what are you going to do about it.'[619] It was Fincham's first decisive victory against trading competition on the farm. For over eight years, he had tried unsuccessfully to protect the privilege stipulated in his contract. Now, at last it seemed the law could do something for a hardworking man. He was busy sinking another well for Molema, his third on the farm, with no compensation for the loss of the first.[620] Molema's reply was that he should talk to Wolhuter and try to reach some agreement with him. Fincham refused because the court victory meant none would 'interfere with me in future'.[621] From now on, he would trade more securely, breathe a little more freely.

> I have told you of this trouble for some time past and you take no action to clear up the dispute. If Wolhuters [sic] action was genuine and only spite and malice I would be agreeable to come to some arrangement but under the present circumstance I will not waive any of my rights. I might also mention that your chief told me yesterday that I could shoot on the whole of this farm if I like. Bring your copies of your agreements with you so that you can show Wolhuter how matters stand. I have written for the last time...[622]

Molema did not enforce the court ruling by disallowing Wolhuter's trade. In February of the following year, about five months later, Fincham's attorneys were now preparing to sue Molema, only by then Wolhuter had acquired a dealer's license and was quitting Mabete to set up a trading store elsewhere.[623] Wolhuter was selling his lease to Gert Pretorius whom Fincham had no doubt would be another impossible 'Dutchman'. He offered to pay £50 for Wolhuter's right and suggested that he and Molema would then share the well on the stand. They would then have 'no more trouble about it.'

Molema desperately needed money but, it happened that at the very moment that he was writing to Fincham to accept his proposal about Wolhuter's stand, the summons from Fincham's attorneys arrived.[624]

> I am sorry to say that when I was just writing to Mr Wolhuter to tell him what you wished me to say a letter came into my hands from your attorney ... challenging me that if I am not doing this and that immediately you were going to take proceedings against me and I was so annoyed by this letter I stopped sending my letter to Mr Wolhuter so as to let your attorney to take steps he intends to take; because I have often told you not to speak with me by the attorneys but we must speak as friend to friend [.] [T]he attorneys are for money [,] not for friendship so you better please yourself with the step you are going to take.[625]

Morafe

If Fincham wanted to discipline him like one did a stubborn mule, then Molema determined to leave him to the futile endeavour of confronting nature alone, unaided.

Molema was then beginning to see his way into a different financial future. His son overseas had completed his studies, which had cost him all of £600, excluding the cost of passage. The worst patch of that difficult situation was when Modiri's landlords were threating to sue. He had had to borrow money from two Jewish traders.[626] He also borrowed money from one Daniel Mokaka, who died in 1919 before Molema had paid back his £18-5-0. His widow and his children had written to him 'Please send us our money we are in need of it.'[627] Now that Modiri had graduated, he had a chance to settle his debts, set straight his financial affairs and keep the other children in school. He was finding new ways of generating income. In July 1920, he paid a subscription fee to join Benefits Limited pyramid scheme.[628] He earned £10 'as salary for the first month', and thereafter 50 per cent commission on each new member he subscribed. He also qualified for a loan of 5 per cent per annum from Benefits Limited. The new decade was promising for many. There were prospectors who thought they could make a fortune digging for diamonds, possibly gold, in the northern districts. The diggings roused the wagon business once again and the market for grain.

Fincham resolved not to say anything more to Molema after that last letter. He took no further legal steps against him, but from that February of 1920, he also withdrew from Molema completely. For one whole year, he did not send Molema a single letter, only the statements that reflected the monthly rents he was withholding to settle the money Molema owed. In the meantime, Wolhuter had changed his mind and had remained on the farm. It troubled Fincham greatly. Wolhuter was trading, and legally too. Fincham survived in his lone, seething quietude until one day, the following February, Wolhuter impounded his animals.[629] It was critical at this juncture to break his silence. A new set of troubles was beginning to brew on the farm. The peasant householders were becoming increasingly hostile. He wanted to fence himself off from them and asked Molema if he could erect such a fence around his portion.[630] There were then 3154 people on Barolong Farms. Only 150 of them were absent migrants.[631] Molema would not allow any portion of the farm to be fenced off. At most, he would allow Fincham to fence only the southern portion of the farm for his and Fincham's 'exclusive use'.[632] Fincham established this 'camp' promptly. It measured about 600 morgen and enclosed one of the two natural pans on the farm.[633] This was in April 1921.

In order to establish this camp, Fincham had forcibly removed at least one household who had set up their homestead there. They were a family that had already been dispossessed of their placement elsewhere and had recently found placement on Mabete. Molema received a note of distress.

> I tell you about Fencham [sic] that while he put up a fence along the farm he removed those of Makepe from there [all the while] knowing he is chasing the ones of Makepe from there and [now] with whom do I remain if these ones of Makepe are removed due to Fencham while he knows [what he is doing]. Chief it grieves [me] very much because [already] Radipetse had taken away their fields and now Fencham is fencing them away from there knowing he is sending them away and I want to know Chief if you have allowed Fencham...[634]

African householders were not the only ones still struggling to secure roots on the land. The Protectorate government had established the European Advisory Council in January 1920 to legitimate the new taxes it was imposing on cattle farming.[635] The forum gave white farmers room to make their representations of what would help their cattle ranching, but this was not the same thing as actual state intervention in their primary dilemma, which was landlessness. Even in their success, big traders like Van Wyk were landless. Nevertheless, that white farmers had some political voice boosted their confidence, especially on Barolong Farms due to the railway line.

In fact, the biggest change on Mabete happened after Molema agreed to transfer the railway strip at Pitsane Siding to the South African Railways (SAR).[636] 'Here is more trouble,' Fincham wrote to Molema in alarm, 'I want you to protect my agreement.' Van Wyk, Wolhuter and N.J. Crosby, who had arrived on the adjoining farm as a bricklayer, negotiated with W.H. Wallis, the District Superintendent of the SAR, to operate as an agency receiving and forwarding goods at Pitsane Siding. Fincham was more worried than he had ever been. The partnership between Van Wyk, Wolhuter and Crosby threatened to shut down Fincham's shop. On the other hand, a small farmer like Beukes who was surviving on bartering and itinerant trade had no hope at all. In May, Beukes left the farm.[637] One Mr Botha had shown interest in the place but he took up tenancy elsewhere.[638] The tenant who replaced Beukes remained on the farm for barely two months. The new trading partnership at the siding made Mabete an unfavourable farm for tenant farmers who had not yet established themselves.

Fincham's daughter had married the year before. Her father wanted to give her and her husband, Orbell, a start-up in the farming and trading enterprise. He also needed a fresh input of capital into his business given the growing competition on the farm and some improving prospects for white farmers. In October of 1921, Fincham and his son-in-law set out to build a silo for green forage. He sent his 'boys' along the familiar route to the quarry on the neighbouring farm where the locals had previously forced Fincham to pay. The locals chased the 'boys' away and threatened to get them arrested.[639] On Mabete, Fincham's relationship with the peasant householders on the farm had deteriorated completely. They had cut up the fence around his camp. Incidents of trespassing had escalated to hostile confrontation, as though they were daring him to act against them and give them a reason to retaliate. In June 1922, Orbell impounded cattle and goats that had 'strayed' to their well. Their owner, a young man called Dota came armed to confront Fincham.

> Then Dota himself arrived at the store armed with a knobkerrie and in a nasty manner demanded to know who had interfered with his cattle… he threatened me with his knobkerrie and told me that the water on the ground did not belong to me, and that he was going to do as he liked.[640]

Molema did nothing, partly because he was considerably busy. Like many others, he sought to make money out of the diggings. 'Times are very hard,' as Fincham had put it earlier that year, 'so things are very bad and tight [and] no money anywhere.'[641] Molema was clearing his debts one at a time, even settling with some very old creditors from a decade before like Stephanus van Jaarsveld, whom he had hired to build a dam at his country home at Madibespruit in the reserve in 1913.[642] The sheriff had impounded Molema's stock and property a year later, but there was still money outstanding. Now in 1922, he was finally paying Van Jaarsveld. He paid with two bulls, one cow, £24 worth of rent on Vryhof that Van Jaarsveld had withheld, iron sheets and at least twenty-eight bags of sorghum.[643] The entire debt was only paid off when the mineral diggings helped the wagon transport and Molema transported corn for Van Jaarsveld, who was still his tenant, and lent him two span of oxen. Molema was also receiving a commission from one J. Oosthuizen for a supply of 'kaffertjies' for labour.[644] The word referred to young black men.

Fincham's focus was to establish Orbell on the farm and launch their joint venture, Fincham & Co. General Dealers, speedily. In August 1922, he asked Molema to take over Beuke's old house and refurbish it into a cottage worth £150 for Orbell.[645] 'I will fence the new house and garden in properly like a white man do [sic] work as you know, all I do I do properly and make good work & it will be a great improvement to your farm.'[646] They would not pay the rent for the cottage while they worked. Fincham wanted to take over Beukes' place because of that very first and best well he had ever sunk on the farm. He was so determined to get it back that he was prepared to sink yet another well elsewhere on the farm to share with Molema.[647] Some months into the New Year, in April 1923, Fincham learnt that Molema was about to lease the eastern portion of the farm, including the two natural pans, to a Dutch-Afrikaner, J. van Zyl.[648] Fincham had enough experience with such tenants to know he would trade, but his court win against Wolhuter, in September 1919, had established a binding legal precedent against competition on the farm. He would not roll over and play dead. The last time he had taken legal action to compel Molema to enforce this court victory on the farm, it had broken their relationship into a silence that took over a year to mend. Nevertheless, he briefed Minchin and Kelly to take action.[649] They were not pursuing the matter aggressively enough and so he acted through De Kock and De Kock.[650] In the meantime, Van Zyl established himself on the farm.

When Fincham finally received a reply from Molema, he read that 'matters between you and I are somewhat complicated'.[651] Molema had reached a conclusion that he owed Fincham no money at all because all the iron, wood, doors and windows of Beukes' old cottage were sufficient to settle everything. Molema also refused to sign the papers to approve the establishment of Fincham & Co. General Dealers because Fincham had gone ahead with these plans, without first asking for his consent. Instead, he wanted rent for Orbell's cottage now that the renovation was complete. Fincham said they should meet because, after all, they were 'old friends'.[652] He would let that matter rest a while, but made it clear that Molema could not expect rent for Orbell's cottage, 'the cottage I built', until he had recovered his costs. 'When the cottage is fully paid for then I think it will be enough time to discuss what rent is to be paid for this place further.' Moreover, if Molema wanted to discuss the matter then he should come to him.[653] He was not prepared to ride to Mafikeng. It was very important to impress upon Orbell the stance that a man running a business on hired ground had to adopt. Otherwise, he and his daughter would not survive there.

Fincham received a reply that Molema as landlord had a 'perfect right' to the new cottage and 'I can let it to whom I like and charge the rent I like'.[654] He wanted his rent from 1 June 1923. He also again refused to sign the papers to do with Fincham & Co. General Dealers. 'I have not done so as I want that all our matters be put right first.' It was clear to Fincham that Molema was on a war path, whilst he himself was worn out by the arrangements of property in these parts that, in his experience, rewarded the owner of the farm and never compensated the hands that worked the land. 'It seems to me that you are a very hard man,' Fincham replied.'[655] He urged Molema to sign the paperwork for Fincham & Co. General Dealers, 'for the simple reason that I am on the verge of bankruptcy on account of having spent too much money on your farm and I was compelled to take in my son-in-law, with the capital he had to bring myself out of difficulties'. He would not plead his case like a guilty supplicant when he was the injured party. He dug his heels in and withheld the rent. Instead, he charged Molema the full cost of Orbell's cottage and paid himself back at £1 a month, starting from 1 June 1923. The total cost was £176-12-3. Meanwhile Orbell had been waiting since the end of 1922 for his father-in-law to establish Fincham & Co. General Dealers as a legal entity. The two of them had been working together without a legal framework that conferred and protected his share of ownership. Orbell would not continue like that for a third year. He left the farm at the beginning of 1924.[656] In Orbell's cottage, Fincham put his clerk, Fitzpatrick Cole. He had lost the opportunity to inject his business with new blood and capital and had to say goodbye to his daughter.

In April 1924, Molema acquired the contract to transport concrete to the new Public Office the government was putting up in Mafeking.[657] In May of the same year, he obtained his own license for digging at the growing Molopo Diggings although he did not manage to establish his own diggings.[658] There were opportunities in the transport business in which he had ample experience. In the autumn of 1924, Richard Wright paid him weekly for the hire of wagons.[659] The oxen were Wright's, only he had no grazing land to keep them. Wright was in the business of carting water, mealies and sorghum to and from the diggings. Molema also supplied the grain for sale. Wright worked very hard. Even when he was ill in the winter, he did not want to give up the enterprise and promised Molema that 'you will not be disappointed with me'.[660] They understood that the new mineral rush, or an anticipation of one, could not last very long. They hoped to continue like this for at least until the rains came.

At the beginning of 1925, the tenant Fincham had placed in Orbell's cottage also left, which meant all of Beukes' old place, including the well he had himself dug and the cottage he had built with Orbell, were up for someone else's cheap hire. 'I hope he is a nice man, is he English or Dutchman?'[661] He had been taking care of the place, for the sake of these works of his hands. He wrote to Molema that the new tenant 'must agree to look after the windmill and pump and keep it in repair and oil some from time to time'. It was the first letter in about a year. Their relationship had broken down. Molema did not reply to him directly but sent Van Wyk to inform Fincham that he could still use Beukes' well. He also gave him time to reap his crop before the new tenant ploughs.[662] It was an olive branch. In April, Fincham ploughed Molema's pumpkin fields at a small cost, 4 shillings.[663] That too was a gesture of goodwill. At the end of the year Fincham brought the people on the farm together for a party. At the beginning of 1926, he sent three photographs of the event to Molema, 'one for yourself, one for Dr Molema and one for Chief L.R. Montsioa'.[664] 'I hope you will like these although if the people had not enjoyed themselves [so much] and were more quiet I would have liked to have sat all of us in the front row but it was impossible to get the people quiet.' Apparently, the people were 'too merry'.

The merrymaking did little to change the reality that the peasant householders on Mabete were not as agreeable as Fincham wished them to be. In fact, these neighbours could be outright hostile. He could not control their movements on the farm nor get them to constrain their animals. The incidents of trespassing on the farm were growing in frequency and violence. The men were goading him, daring him or his son to act. Fincham knew 'they purposely do it to see what I will do'.[665] In late winter of 1927, he left his sons in charge and travelled to Mafikeng. Some men provoked his son. They brought their cattle round to his house and kraal. The younger Finchams acted with some restraint, but it was clear that the battle was just beginning.

> Yesterday, some native cattle were worrying [me?] around here all day, and just after dinner I told the boys to tell the herd[ers] to take the cattle away, and the herd[ers] turned round and said that they let them get round the kraal purposely to see what we will do. I then put them in the kraal, and locked the gate, about 6 o'clock, the owners came, Bles and a couple of others, and defied Tony and I, and simply broke the kraal open and took the cattle out… I am today fencing to camp off the ground down below at the corner of our camp, but won't tackle the work until we have written Molemo [sic] about it. I am today writing Molemo, requesting him to let me know how many cattle he has that are to drink at our well, and if he won't let us know, I will get at it through Minchin & Kelly, and stop the other nigs [sic] from drinking here.[666]

The Finchams were white and extremely vulnerable. They were too tenuously integrated into the routines of everyday reciprocity that many of the other white tenants practised on the land. The very fact that Fincham would only collaborate with white English-speaking men meant he could not enter partnerships with other tenant farmers. Northerners who could enter into agreements with Dutch-Afrikaner men fared much better in the Bechuanaland Protectorate. Although the government was now turning its ear to listen to the concerns of the white farmer on the ground, the Bechuanaland Protectorate was a different country from the situation across the Molopo River, a mere 15 kilometres away. In the Union of South Africa, whiteness was a qualification for property. Silas Molema was trying to establish his own S.T. Molema General Dealer business in the Molopo Reserve during same the winter of 1927. The Divisional Council of Mafeking denied him permission to trade.[667] The council had presented 'no reasons or grounds' for denying him placement.[668] Across the river, the Molemas were black and powerless.

XXVI

Modiri Molema arrived back home from Scotland in early 1921. There was no Sechuana newspaper to publish and celebrate his achievements. That did not matter. He had a very firm sense of vocation and besides, other press outlets at home and abroad had carried the news of his book, *The Bantu Past and Present*. Over a decade before, *Tsala ea Becoana* had highlighted the deplorable situation of health care available to the black population in the Union of South Africa.[669] Black nurses could not find employment in the hospitals, while white nurses refused to attend to black patients. Plaatje had written in outrage about the black population's lack of access to healthcare, especially at a time when communicable diseases like tuberculosis were affecting immigrants from the countryside in emerging cities like Johannesburg. Modiri was the fourth black doctor in the Union, having qualified a year after his best friend and relation James Moroka, but the politics of health, especially nursing, had not changed from the situation of the decade before.

When Plaatje returned from England in mid-November 1923, Modiri had already established his medical practice in Mafikeng. In the meantime, the SANNC had acquired a new name, now the African National Congress (ANC), though it was a considerably weaker organ than the one that had sent the last delegation to England. The organisation had lost some of its foremost provocateurs, like John Dube and Walter Rubusana. Tensions in the

Congress had been high after the Rand strikes of 1918 to 1919. Some of these central leaders had retreated to the regional constituencies whose interests they had been defending through this platform of collective representation in the first place. These transformations in the Congress were happening just when black people were making the new industrial cities places of permanent settlement.

In 1920, the government had announced the Native Affairs Act of 1920, which made provision for the Native Affairs Commission to advise the government on the interests of the black population in ways that would shape policy. The legislation also made provision for district councils that would represent the same demographic. The government would select these representatives, including among chiefs. Many in the Congress considered this form of representation as a gain, although it fell far short of the question of parliamentary representation that two delegations had travelled to England to attempt to secure for black people across the Union. Plaatje had a vote in the Cape, as did Modiri, but for Congress members from the other provinces, this was the closest they had come to representation in the government. Stalwarts of Congress, like Richard Selope Thema, thought the government was at last listening to their appeal, and although Plaatje thought the legislation was not enough, even he had to agree that at least this legislation was not imposing 'additional humiliations' on black peoples.[670]

After the Drought Commission of 1923, treasurer of Congress Selby Msimang circulated an urgent memorandum warning Congress members that the reserves were becoming bare landscapes of denuded forests, soil erosion and severe malnutrition. Msimang's fear was that the 'segregation bogey' would cut educated blacks like himself off from 'contact with civilised influences'. Before then, he urged, 'a beginning should be made now to equip ourselves for the hard life awaiting us in the segregated areas'.[671] He was not asking the black population to resist territorial segregation. Rather, he was urging them to prepare for it, make sure to improve the reserves for themselves before then, and rehabilitate these territories into an infrastructure that people of 'progress' could live in.

Upon his return from England, Plaatje had travelled around the countryside to familiarise himself with rural and agrarian town transformation during the five years of his absence. He was also showing films in bioscopes. His favourite was a film about Booker T. Washington's Tuskegee Institute, but he also showed scenes and people he had visited in Canada and the Unites States. The early vision of thriving agrarian towns he had expressed in *Koranta* two decades before remained with Plaatje, but even he attested to the reality that the countryside was no longer the frontier of 'progress' that it was in his younger years. Nevertheless, the countryside was where he felt most at home as a political actor and as a writer. He was still documenting the effects of the Natives Land Act. In the meantime, the cities were growing, including a blackening Johannesburg. There were educated women, like Charlotte Maxeke, who were advocating for a social infrastructure in the city, including hospitals and healthcare, which could facilitate the making of families and the reproduction of cultural lives. The city was now beginning to hold respectable sentiments of virtue that it had failed to hold for the likes of Sebopioa Molema. The countryside was embracing Johannesburg as a permanent place of settlement. Some countryside families wanted a claim in the possibilities of the city's future. The centre of gravity of educated black politics was shifting to the cities, although some of the leading members of this class, like Selby Msimang and Pixley Seme, had not given up on attempts to make sure their vision of 'progress' in the countryside, with its peculiar regionalist dynamics of chiefly power, survived. The year before, Seme had joined the deputation of the Swazi king to London, which was lobbying the Colonial Office to intervene in the matter of the Swazis' land concession.[672]

In some cities, educated opinion welcomed territorial segregation. In Bloemfontein, educated Sechuana-speakers welcomed the Urban Areas Act No 21 of 1923. The legislation segregated urban residential places and established mechanisms of 'influx control' to restrict the movement of black people into urban areas. According to John Mancoe, the compiler of a directory of educated blacks and 'coloureds' in Bloemfontein in the 1930s, this embrace of urban segregation spread beyond this city.[673] Mancoe noted that 'the general policy of the segregation of Natives in Urban areas was widely accepted' during the passing of this bill. In Bloemfontein, the main complaint against the bill was not segregation, but rather that the 'administration of the laws was haphazard and incomplete' because it did not improve the lot of educated middle-classes who lived in urban squalor. The 'slum areas, liquor dens and hotbeds of crime and vice' remained intact, and the government had made no provision for 'respectable' housing accommodation. In the 1920s, territorial segregation was not a policy that all educated black opinion rejected in its entirety. A sizable number of the black educated classes wished for it not only to be on fair terms, but also to be complete.

In Mafikeng, Modiri thus found himself situated in a place that was quickly becoming a periphery. He had little interest in regionalist struggles. Meanwhile, his book did not generate the sales required to warrant the second edition of the *Bantu Past and Present* that his British publishers had anticipated. In fact, the book hardly stirred conversation back home. Instead, he found that where a consciousness of 'blackness' was strongest, it coincided with territorial and institutional segregation, like black homelands or black independent churches. This was not his position. There was, as far as he was concerned, one united black *morafe*. It was sacred, so much so that sexual intimacy or marriage across the colour line was morally abhorrent, yet at the same time, he thought that territorial and social segregation was a step backwards that compromised the 'progress' of the very *morafe* of the 'Bantu'. In the first place, black people could not afford to give up any square inch of the country, more so when so much of the territory lay in white areas – arable soils, minerals, water, wildlife. Most importantly, though the *morafe* was black, the esteem of the *morafe* lay in its repertoires of personhood, in the moral virtues that made its members tower above other living things, not in the pigmentation of its skin. The capacity to know the *morafe* intimately, to serve it without reservation and to love all its members freely – that was its practice of virtue. Skin colouring was not a straightforward indicator of moral esteem.

His was a complicated position, especially for a young man to articulate on his own, without the concert of respectable educated opinion. The ANC was not a natural home for such views. He also did not have much time for political activism. He was starting up as a medical doctor. His working hours were long and there was a lot of demand for his time. His thoughts were fully occupied, not least with the woman he still loved but could not have. Nevertheless, when there was a platform to do so, he expressed his views. On 9 January 1925, by invitation of one 'Synod Missionary Meeting' he offered his audience a complete statement of his ideas.[674] He stated that the 'foremost political problem of South Africa and of the world in general today is to find a way whereby the different races may live side by side in peace, harmony and goodwill.' It appeared to him that segregation was not only 'a political question' but also one of 'spiritual values and moral issues'. 'It therefore directly touches and challenges that body, the church, with which we naturally associate the highest conception of humanity and morality.' His argument was that racial segregation is the wrong direction for the future firstly because it was impossible for segregation to take place in a fair and just way.

> Now Africans, and we may be sure, Indians also, do not fear or dislike segregation as such. In fact the majority of them would readily welcome it if there was an assurance of fair dealing, Equality of opportunity and

justice with application of the measure. But such assurance is under the present conditions impossible to expect. One of the two races holds the monopoly of power, absolutely, and it is most unlikely that it will waiver an iota of its right – real or imagined or sacrifice a jot of its interest in a settlement, which in reality demands sacrifice of interest on each side.[675]

Yet, quite apart from the question of equity – and indeed even if such equity were possible, segregation was 'a retrogressive step' because it did not follow the 'natural' inclination of historical transformation.[676] 'Humanity moved forward or improves by association not separation, by aggregation and not by segregation, and if this is not yet the time, sure the day will come when the Black and White races will gladly move towards each other.' This was inevitable, he considered, in the situation of South Africa where 'the African and the European are inter-dependent and cannot by any conceivable means be separated from the other'. The Union government's efforts to sever the two demographics, to attempt segregation both 'geographically or economically' was 'quite impossible and what is attempted is bound to be pure half-hearted measure – worse than useless'. The 'political segregation', where there would be a 'native parliament' without legislative powers, the 'industrial segregation' that provided economic opportunity according to the colour bar, as well as 'territorial segregation' through the Natives Land Act, could not deliver what the government and other supporters of segregation promised.

> We are told by the prophets that each race will be able to pursue its ideals and follow its traditions, conserve its institutions, preserve its race purity and develop along its own lines unhampered by the other race. Segregation to be a success needs to be complete. It must be very strictly just and equal. It must be segregation in truth not discrimination. Otherwise those fine words about developing along national lines are, in relation to Africans, mere words.[677]

The 'scheme of segregation', he argued, 'is foredoomed as failure', and even where black people took the lead in assembling their own separatist institutions, they were actually being led by whites because they were responding to white racism. Wherever they were following the segregationist course, they were following the whites' lead. They were surrendering themselves to the impositions of others on their free will. The result was not 'peace and harmony' but rather the creation of segregationist black institutions like 'The Organisation of African Workers for Strikes, [the] foundation of the indigenous African Church' as well as ideas like 'self-determination' and 'cries of Africa for the Africans', which, he felt, left blacks stewing in the backburner of 'progress'. Separatist black institutions were a peril because society fits together, functionally, like the body's organs. Fitting together, not separating, was the evolutionary law of 'progress'.

> Self-preservation is the law of the jungle, by which I conceive that many weaker and innocent animals suffer from the stronger. Wherever it holds sway, the everlasting question is "Can I kill Thee or Canst Thou kill me?" … It is one of the most powerful motives in lower nature, which in man is, or should be tempered by reason, judgement, a sense of Right and spirit of sacrifice.… Can we not conceive and conceiving treat the human race as one family as an unity and as a living organism whose several parts and organs are mutually dependent and cooperate for one common good? We are aware that an injury to any single part or group of cells of a living organ immediately diminishes the efficiency of all the other parts of the organism as a whole.…This is the law of nature and this is a law of invariable sequence. Life is one and its purpose is one.[678]

In other words, black people were indeed a unique moral entity, but they could go nowhere unless they moved with the rest of the community that was all human beings. In fact, as he argued, ideals of segregation were typical of a people that had not yet come into a consciousness of themselves as black people, and therefore, were allowing themselves to follow the short circuit of animal instinct to resolve complicated political problems.

> The law of human progress is not simply the transference of the laws of vegetable and animal evolution to the human sphere. In the one case there is ruthless self-assertion. It is continually 'I for myself, Life exists for me; this brief life is for my pleasure and my ease; give me my rights, stand clear of my way; I want or I will have'. In the other case it is self-negation. In the place of survival of the fittest [and] primitive nature, the moral law ordains the fittest of as many as possible to survive.[679]

This address was one of the few he delivered, perhaps the only one for a long time. He focused on practising medicine. In 1927, white nurses resigned from Victoria hospital after he admitted some of his white private patients there. The nurses objected to taking instructions from a black medical doctor. He took legal action and the nurses had to return to work.[680] This season of his life was a kind of dormancy, as though he was waiting for life to wake up. His relationship with his father, even after a few years back home, was not yet smooth. Richard Rowland reassured him that his father's disappointment with his choice of bride did not mean that he was not proud of him. Rowland also pleaded with him not to cheat himself of companionship by his decision not to marry. Rowland warned, 'see that you do not leave things too late as I have & miss real happiness.'[681]

However, he was not merely refusing to yield to family pressure. He also felt that having lost his first companion, it was impossible to recover the same depth of attachment and synergy of vocation with someone else. At the same time, he had returned home also to flee from loneliness, and that feeling remained. The most accessible company nevertheless were women, including Anna, whose marriage to Dick Marumoloa had dissolved. Anna was not satisfied with a relationship without commitment.[682] She thought he was punishing her for the marriage to Dick Marumoloa, but he told her only that 'it takes a long time to forget or get over some things'. Nonetheless, when she pleaded with him to spare her further humiliation by being with her and not marrying her, he complied.[683] They married in 1926.[684]

XXVII

The Supreme Court ruling of 1920 that chiefly jurisdiction in Bechuanaland is 'personal' and not 'territorial' coincided with pressure on the Native Affairs Department towards 're-establishing its effectiveness', rather than continue as a structure 'overwhelmingly dominated by the prerogative to contain, deflect and defuse conflict'.[685] The Department increasingly sought to monopolise every sphere of government that had to do with 'native affairs'. It therefore resented the establishment in 1920 of the Native Affairs Commission, under Dr C.T. Loram. This commission emerged from the promulgation of the Native Affairs Act in 1920 to support 'indirect statutory forms of black political representation, as the basis of a moderate segregation solution'.[686] The Native Affairs Commission sat in Mafikeng on 6 and 7 April 1923, hearing representations from 'Lotlamoreng [Montsioa], other Chiefs, Counsellors (sic), Headmen and a large number of natives'.[687] In the meeting, Lotlamoreng's supporters presented to the Commission the view

> that legislation should be passed to overrule the decision of the Appellate Division of the Supreme Court ... in as much as:- (a) personal instead of

territorial jurisdiction in the case of Chiefs is not in accord with either Native custom or European practice, is subversive of discipline, leads to difficulty in the management of Reserves and creates friction. (b) the Natives object to the reserves being under the Locations Act of 1884, as this means (i) that the final allocation of land is taken out of the Chief's hands and put into the hands of the Magistrates or other Government officials, and (ii) that the existing allocations will be disturbed.[688]

They reiterated that the government was 'guilty of a breach of faith' in disregarding the terms of annexation, diminishing the rights of the chiefs and claiming to own the land. They objected that

(a) the rights of the chiefs have been taken away and they are told that they are only such in name; (b) the natives are told that the Reserves are not their own land but belong to the Government: and the Natives wish all their original rights restored to them. (iii) that "foreigners" who have settled in the Reserves are not subject to the authority of the chief, ploughing and doing as they like. (iv) that if the Government will not allow Chiefs to have authority over "foreigners" it should remove them from the Reserves and give them land elsewhere.[689]

The spirit of these objections is, most strikingly, against the objectives that the Natives Land Act of 1913 had sought to achieve. That legislation had intended to transfer the land and the people of the reserves from the jurisdiction of chiefs to that of the colonial government. Now belonging to a 'Schedule for Native Areas', the reserves would be landscapes of 'native administration', in other words 'locations', where the settlement and the movement of those whom the legislation classified as 'black' would be mainly under the imperatives of 'native administration'. In this meeting, chiefs were clearly stating that their end had come with the decision of the court in 1920, and not with the Natives Land Act. Apart from 'blackening' these northern reserves, the legislation's effects had been very limited. The actual practical transformation of the Molopo Reserve into a 'location' had followed unexpectedly from the popular rebellion at Rietfontein. This pressure from below had ultimately loosened chiefly power over the people and over the land. From the 1920s, the office of the paramount chief in the reserve became considerably weaker, but as an institution of rule, chieftaincy thrived under the Native Commissioner as the 'Supreme Chief' over every reserve, especially over the people who were not under the paramount chief's personal jurisdiction.

It is significant that the records of this meeting were later attached to the files of the implementation of the Native Administration Act of 1927, which extended the authority of the Native Affairs Department, such that by 1928 the Department 'was potentially more powerful than it had ever been'.[690] F.S. Malan, Deputy Prime Minister but also in charge of the Native Affairs Department, had met the same people in Mafikeng shortly before this. It is most likely that after his own meeting with Lotlamoreng and others, Malan then dispatched the Natives Affairs Commission to hear representations. The shift in power dynamics between chiefs and commoners in the Molopo Reserve was not lost on Malan, Loram and the Native Affairs Commission. As soon as he returned to Pretoria, Loram wrote to the Resident Magistrate in Mafikeng, A. Wilmot, to ask for his opinion on 'a matter I am investigating in which we are both interested viz. the position of the courts of the native Chiefs'.[691]

Wilmot's response was an exhaustive description of 'native administration' in the territories of his jurisdiction, which he felt remained weak. He recommended that there should be courts of appeal for chiefly judgments, 'in the first instance to the court of the Magistrate and thence to the Supreme Court'.[692] He proposed that in civil cases the chiefs' jurisdiction should not exceed debt or damage of £50. Chiefs should not hear criminal cases where the fine would be more that £10. Once this was accomplished, then 'Chiefs should be given jurisdiction over Natives of all tribes residing within their territory, which should be defined and proclaimed' because, as matters stood, '[n]atives, residing in the stadt, who are not of the Chief's tribe, can with impunity disregard the rule to the detriment of good order'.[693] Wilmot wanted to establish more courts of appeal to oversee the paramount chief's courts, limit the latter's jurisdiction to a certain category of cases, and then bring the populations of the reserves back under the jurisdiction of this weakened centre of power to maintain law and order in the reserves.

The Department's reply was that '[t]here can be no question of reversing by legislation' the decision of the court.[694] Chiefs could continue to allocate lands, the Secretary for Native Affairs continued, but 'the final allocation of land should be in the hands of an impartial officer' who would have the 'power to rectify abuse'. This was of the utmost importance to the Native Affairs Department. All of those thousands of black people over whom the paramount chief had no jurisdiction, would be granted right of settlement into the reserves by the Native Commissioner, who would also have a say on their movement in and out of the reserves.

On the eve of the promulgation of the Native Administration Act of 1927,

Wilmot again pleaded with the government to bring the large population of 'foreigners' under the jurisdiction of chiefs and only thereafter promulgate the legislation.[695] There were many 'foreign natives', he explained, over whom chiefs had no 'personal' jurisdiction and who were therefore fully his own responsibility to manage as Resident Magistrate. He explained that 'in many instances' people that were claiming to be 'foreign natives' had in fact 'been granted right of residence, lands and grazing by local chiefs' and that 'whilst it suits them they conform to all laws and customs of the Barolong'. However, as soon as chiefs summoned the same to their Kgotla either to resolve a dispute involving them or to address their infringement of the law, then 'they object to the jurisdiction of the Chiefs on the grounds that they do not belong to their tribes'.[696] He suggested that the government overturn the principle that chiefs' jurisdiction was 'personal' not by arguing that chiefs' jurisdiction was 'territorial', but rather through a legal reclassification of tribal association, such that one became of the 'Barolong' as soon as one found placement in the reserve. The chiefs would not act independently, but alongside the Superintends of Natives in the reserves.

> As owing to the interpretation placed on this provision by the Courts, it has been found that the chiefs have no jurisdiction over a considerable class of natives of other tribes, who have, from time to time, taken up their permanent residence in the Native Reserves in this District and as this interpretation has been the cause of much friction and misunderstanding ... Briefly the proposal is that if a 'foreign' native takes up his domicile in the Native Reserve in the District with the consent of the local chief and the superintendent of natives he should be deemed to have become a member of the tribe of such chief and to be entitled to the same privileges and subject to the same disabilities as an ordinary members of such tribe.[697]

Again, Wilmot's idea could not be entertained. The situation in Bechuanaland had presented the Department with a successful template to open up the reserves to settlement. Chieftaincy was to operate as an institution of 'direct rule' through white Native Commissioners, especially for people who would have no attachment to the 'clan system' that Solomon Plaatje and James Molebaloa described, and who wished to carry on with their independent business on the land without the reciprocal obligations that citizenship in the reserves entailed. These new immigrants, including erstwhile sharecroppers on white-owned farms, were fast becoming the majority in these reserves. They were fully under the jurisdiction of the white Native Commissioner and Resident Magistrate who had the final authority over their right to enter reserves and hold their land. More generally, the entity of 'the Government' (embodied by colonial officials on the ground), as the sole recipient of taxes for large parts of the population, had become the custodian of the infrastructure of personhood. Not only were these white officials the centre of transactions of rents in that they collected Hut Tax and other colonial impositions, they offered placement. They opened up the reserves by allowing as many people into the overcrowded reserves as possible, despite population growth, as long as the new settlers were black. In distributing land, white officials, not traditional chiefs, became 'fathers' in the overpopulated reserves.

This bears repeating because it is, in a nutshell, the spirit of the Native Administration Act of 1927. The 1927 Act made the Native Affairs Department through the Governor General, the 'Supreme Chief of all natives' and allowed this 'Chief' to make and alter laws in the reserves by proclamation rather than a parliamentary process. This is why the Native Affairs Department did not consider the Native Administration Act of 1927 as novel but as the application of proven practical measures and principles drawn from different provinces.[698] It followed processes already apparent on the ground in the Barolong reserves. In fact, as James Molebaloa wrote in 1936, the Native Administration Act of 1927 was not the first time that the Native Affairs Department had tried to introduce legislation towards the same ends. He had earlier laid out his objections to the then proposed Native Affairs Administration Bill of 1917, which the government did not then pass, but had initially intended to 'take over' from the Natives Land Act as a 'scheme for the creation of common native areas' in the reserves.[699]

The Native Administration Department had had a long and frustrating experience with chieftaincy in Bechuanaland as a gatekeeping institution of family and patronage. It knew only too well that limiting chiefs' powers through legislation had for a long time proved inadequate to bring the reserves under the control of the colonial government. Moreover, if power had to be returned to the chiefs, the government would have to depose paramount chiefs in Bechuanaland and replace them with headmen that were not hereditary rulers. No doubt chiefs would resist, especially in the Barolong reserves. It was possible to allow chiefs some powers in territories elsewhere where hereditary rulers had long been dislodged from institutions of rule. In fact, it was ultimately the people, and not the government, that had finally broken the power of chiefs in colonial Bechuanaland. The people, and not the government, had created a path for the institutionalisation of 'native administration' in their reserves. This was not for a love of empire.

Rather 'native administration' was the most readily available and effective strategy for black people in these reserves to preserve their personhood on the land under severe constraints of land shortage in what was emerging as South Africa.

XXVIII

In the 1920s, Silas Molema had entered a new phase of life. He was ageing, but at the same time, he was ready to make a fresh start. He was again starting up at business and had become a father once again. He had remarried. His new wife was Badirile Montsioa's widow, which meant he had married Harriet's husband's sister-in-law. This is how the levirate worked, as did arranged marriage, offering and returning land, cattle and children between blood relatives. The last four of his children from his first marriage were still at school, including Sefetogi and Morara who had remained home whilst Modiri was abroad. He and his first wife had added two younger girls Stella and Margaret to their Seleje and Harriet. In recent years, he had become a father to two more little girls by his new wife. He had given up his duties in the chiefly administration and let Sebopioa take over. He was now primarily husband and father, which was a freedom he had not enjoyed as a young man when the land and its people still belonged to chiefly rulers like him. His aim was to establish a sustainable business to provide for his relatively young family and enjoy the privileges of a patriarch's twilight years at the same time.

He was working hard at clearing his debt. He still did not have sufficient money, although Modiri and Harriet's earnings also helped. In March 1924, his son Sefetogi wrote from Healdtown Missionary Institute

> to tell you that I am going almost barefoot. You know that my only one pair of boots was finished when I left home. Of course, I did not press on this because you promised me that you would send us some money before the end of last month 'February'. Rra, I know quite well that you have no money but being in this condition I absolutely cannot go without making complaints as these.[700]

Modiri sent new clothes to Sefetogi at Healdtown and to Morara at the School of Agriculture. The sizes were wrong. 'We were very much thankful,' Morara wrote to his father, 'though buying clothes for an absent person always proves wrong, but I want you to thank the Dr for us.'[701] The youngest son was also coming into his own in matters of heart and God.

> No doubt you will be very much pleased to learn that I am now a full member of the church of God. Pray for me that God should [make or help] me realise the responsible and most important position I have liked, and that my liking it should not only be to please the world, but be to do the will of God. I am also a member of the 'Young Men's Christian Association' which is carried in the institution and I attend the morning prayers. In spite of all these, I wish I was doing everything according to how God would like me to do. I hope through your prayers, what I wish for will be granted to me.[702]

His boys have always had a more difficult time away from home than the girls due to his money troubles. Only Seleje had proceeded to Lovedale but otherwise he sent his daughters to less expensive institutions than the boys. It made it easier for him to pay their fees timeously and shield them from the anxiety he expected his boys could handle with more resilience, whether at the local boarding schools or at universities overseas. He did not treat the girls and the boys in the same way. He wished to keep his daughters as close to him as possible, and if they had to be away, he made sure his 'little girls' were free of care. Other than that, the same rules applied to them. In his family, there were no lone rangers. There were also no favourites. He felt Modiri had to be made to understand this.

His son's response to the news of the Supreme Court decision of 1920 had hurt him. His letter had offered his father no consolation. He had said he was sorry about all the money spent on the litigation and the divisions between the people but had said absolutely nothing about the crucial things – the loss of land and the loss of people. Then he had shrugged it off, 'we shall have to abide by their judgment'.[703] He had found it impossible to recognise a record of himself, as a father, in his son. Could an apple fall so far from the tree? Not only that, but Modiri was also in Scotland at the time, right at the front door of the British authorities, and it never occurred to him that he could do something. Instead, his letter to him had been all about his plans, his ambitions, that is to say, the desires of his own heart – his hospital, his book, his choice of bride. Who else, if not one's own father, could rehabilitate a young man into the ways of manhood? He had had a duty to rein Modiri in. At the same time, he was very proud of him. Modiri knew how to weather any storm and possessed that pioneering spirit of the Molemas. As Plaatje said, Modiri's achievements, especially his book, proved that the Barolong were a people of reputation.

Whilst I was walking in dismay that Barolong will come to ruin, works like these promise that when a person (*motho*) dies, a person shall remain. Now we do not know what to do with the resentments of the peoples (*dichaba*) when Barolong write books that are read around the world like those of whites, while other *merafe* are still trying to write [basic literacy] but are unable to do so.[704]

Fathers were ageing or dying. In the meantime, the sons had not managed to inherit the erstwhile flourish of the fathers. Between the generations was distrust, disappointment and conflicting interpretations of what had gone wrong. Each generation blamed the other. Was it the fault of the fathers or that of their children? Only a few decades before, the northern countryside was thriving. The educated classes had embraced piety and 'progress' together in the countryside. Fathers were still insisting that this was the only respectable way to live, but even if sons agreed, those routes to manhood were no longer available, especially property.

Their sons, the new generation of black absentee landlords on private farms like Vryhof outside the 'Schedule of Native Areas', could only lawfully let ten morgen to every tenant. It was difficult to turn their farms into profitable farming enterprises because these landholdings had been 'private locations' in former British Bechuanaland since the 1880s. The properties provided secure placement for thousands of people. In the Orange Free State, the 'anti-squatting' regulations of the Natives Land Act had provided landed chiefs with an opportunity to push people off their private farms outside the 'Schedule of Native Areas', but chiefs did not, and could not, take advantage of this clause without losing their entitlement to chieftaincy.[705] There could be no tributaries without a source, no claim to chieftaincy without the capacity to facilitate routes of manhood and womanhood on the land.

As political authority, chieftaincy in the reserves was not a position behind a stately desk. It was not a post in a bureaucracy with a salary, which is what the colonial government intended to make of the institution. Chieftaincy had always pegged itself on the ground through the hierarchies of domestic life, through kinship and cooperation. Property is what allowed chiefs power. They gave placement. Hence, Silas Molema allowed hundreds to remain in their placement at Vryhof. There was no greater honour than to be a father, to be the source of a great number of people's freedom on the land. Hence he had never evicted those hundreds of people in order to set up a farming enterprise. There was no way he could become a commercial farmer. In fact, he had never worked the land with his own hands.

In the Cape Province, the government had been forced not to apply the 'anti-squatting' regulations of the Natives Land Act on private lands outside the Schedule of Native Areas because such application could affect some black voters' qualification to the franchise. The second generation of Mafikeng's black landlords continued to keep white tenants on these private farms, on much smaller margins of land, and on exacting terms. C.R. Hulme hired ten morgen of Ephraim Molema's farm Lotlage in 1923 for five years.[706] The rent was £5 per annum. He also had to 'dig a well on the said farm and find sufficient water therein to water 100 head of cattle per diem'. He also had to 'build a house of six rooms of raw brick with pitched iron roof' and also 'make a dam 10 yards long, the wall of which shall be 7ft high, 14 ft wide at the bottom'. Hulme also had to 'agree not to interfere with the natives now living on the said farm'. He was 'not entitled to any compensation whatsoever in respect of the said improvements or any other improvements'.

This next generation of black landlords also inherited their fathers' farms on the Barolong Farms across the border in the Bechuanaland Protectorate, but they also inherited the fathers' family feuds, which were affecting their control of the land. The paramount chief, Lotlamoreng Montsioa, was worried, for good reason, that his educated age mates did not respect him, and that after the Native Administration Act of 1927, these men would retreat from the centre onto the farms. He started to collect routine rents from his age mates. If they would not pay he seized their oxen and sold them. 'It is clear that he is doing much ruin,' Dick Marumoloa wrote to Silas Molema, I don't feel like keeping quiet this time.[707]

Sons had inherited the ambitions of the fathers but often not the means to realise them. One of the young educated Leteanes, cousins to the Molemas, held a low-ranking white-collar occupation at best. He felt he had little to show for all his learning. Yet, education still mattered greatly to him 'for a present South Africa accommodates no seats or vacancies for ignorant men'.[708] Nevertheless, his was a 'poor lamentable state' of lack. Younger children had to make do with clothes their older siblings handed down. 'Tell my dear to give you my white summer suit, that's your Xmas present, the one that I asked Mrs Julia M. Leinana to wash; trousers, a jacket & its waist coat.' It was the most this Leteane could do for his younger brother. 'Please don't touch the woollen suit. You may use all my boots and shoes that I left, but don't touch anything other than that.'

It would have been more bearable to the fathers if the sap had been dried from their sons' aspirations without discrimination. It would have been a softer tragedy if all their children had failed in the same way, if the last decades had eaten up their children's livelihoods like locusts flattening a field, leaving nothing behind. Instead, the dispensations of race and dispossession had splintered the families along different trajectories of occupation, earnings and status. Educated households were crystallising into a distinct class hierarchy. The family had emerged as the primary site of social differentiation. Some of the kernels had emptied out before the heads were ripe, but some lives stood tall like stalks with fat, heavy spikes in the bright sun.

Modiri was the fourth black medical doctor in the Union of South Africa. He had time, he had earnings, and he had a motorcar. His busy life was punctuated by excursions by motorcar to the countryside for picnics and 'fine moonlit nights' where he 'sang and ate all along the way … and tea flowed like water'.[709] The eldest son, Sebopioa, was confident and resilient even despite his failure to realise his earlier ambitions. He had inherited the father's salaried position as headman in the reserve in 1926. He was also the National Secretary once again. Harriet Molema had moved on to another arranged marriage in Thaba Nchu, and ostensibly, to her life as a teacher. In her father's reserve, women like her were breadwinners, buffering men's inadequate means to feed their families. Emang Molema too had had to take the place of her absent husband at Signal Hill.

Educated chiefly men were absent, working petty, insecure white-collar jobs in the new industrialising zones, as Sebopioa Molema had done. For much of his working life, he was no different than the thousands of mineworkers who were seasonal migrants. Young educated chiefly men were also absent because they were dead – almost all of the paramount household's men in Mafikeng died very young; drink had long ago already claimed their lives. On 6 September 1927 Silas Molema too died. Solomon Plaatje said 'there were no indications', just four weeks before 'that the end was near', a sure testimony that death folds in the helm of one's garments, such that 'in the midst of life we are in death'.[710]

Sons/Homecoming

I

BRITAIN ALMOST RELINQUISHED all of the Bechuanaland Protectorate to Cecil Rhodes' British South Africa Company in 1895. A now popular photograph shows the three Protectorate chiefs who travelled to Britain to raise their objections and alarm at the change of administration. Britain's decision was that the reserves would not fall under Rhodes' control. They would come under the protection of the Crown, but in return chiefs would have to surrender the autonomy of their reserves. Unlike Britain's agreement with the chiefs at the time of annexation in 1885, the terms of the new agreement were under the 1891 Order-in-Council according to which the High Commissioner had sole jurisdiction over such Crown territories.[1] Legislation in these territories would be by proclamation and in line with 'Native Laws' to the extent that these did not interfere with the Crown's jurisdiction. Chiefs could no longer adjudicate cases that had to do with 'treason, sedition, murder or attempted murder, culpable homicide, rape or attempted rape, assault', as well as all 'offences relating to currency, perjury, offences constituted by any Statute in force in the Territory'. Accordingly, seeing that the reserves had become Crown Lands, the government announced a Hut Tax in 1899, fourteen years after it had declared the Bechuanaland Protectorate a British domain, although it only started collecting in 1902. By the close of the 1910s, the administration was collecting its own taxes, no longer relying on the chiefs to collect and surrender the taxes in return for a commission. It received the remittances of migrant labourers directly from the Union mines and deducted the tax.

As historian George Padmore observes, British governance in the Bechuanaland Protectorate was not 'indirect rule' – at best, it was 'semi-indirect rule'.[2] Nevertheless, outside the reserves, colonial rule still felt remote, including on the Barolong Farms. This Barolong territory was an exception to the new state of affairs that prevailed after 1895 in the Bechuanaland Protectorate. Montsioa had not travelled to Britain, but he had petitioned the monarch that 'The Queen's government must not give my people's land in the Protectorate to the Company'.[3] Sidney Shippard agreed that the Barolong Farms remain an independent territory under the ownership and political control of the Barolong chiefs across the border in Mafikeng. The collection of Hut Tax did not make a legal difference to this arrangement, hence J.C. MacGregor, the Resident Commissioner of the Bechuanaland Protectorate in Mafeking, did not initially invite the Barolong chief Lotlamoreng Montsioa to attend or send representatives to the Native Advisory Council he established in 1920. He was imposing an additional tax on the reserves but did not have jurisdiction to intervene in any way on the Barolong Farms. MacGregor was the senior Resident Commissioner of the Bechuanaland Protectorate. He reported to the High Commissioner of the Protectorate, Lord Sydney Buxton. The seat of the High Commissioner was in Cape Town as this office was also that of the Governor-General of South Africa.

MacGregor requested permission from Buxton to establish a 'Protectorate Emergency and Development Fund' for eradication of cattle diseases, education, public health, roads and the general 'betterment of the community as a whole'.[4] His idea was to impose the tax and in turn offer chiefs representation in the structures of government. He intended to follow examples of such 'national funds' elsewhere on the continent, including the Swaziland National Fund. The tax on Europeans' cattle alone, he suggested, could yield no less than £7000, whilst 'native sources' could generate a further £6300. He had in mind a single fund where both Europeans and 'natives' would form one advisory council. 'The Native is heavily taxed as with the Hut Tax and the Customs tariff framed as it is against [him]' while 'The European, on the other hand, pays nothing directly, and the Customs tariff is all in his favour'. 'Most of them [Europeans] are "well to do": some of them are wealthy, and it seems to me only reasonable to expect them to contribute something towards the well-being of the country in which all of them have prospered'. Buxton disapproved of a joint fund. It would be impossible, he said, to reconcile 'the views of a progressive European farmer or trader with those of a native chief or headman'. He paid no attention to MacGregor's attempts to make Europeans, and not the populations in the reserves, pay more tax. Instead, he insisted that the latter surrender half of their revenue for stock eradication into 'General Revenue'.[5]

There were light teething problems, specifically reluctance from the Bangoaketse in Kanye to pay the levy, but on 2 November 1920, they and others attended the first meeting of the Bechuanaland Protectorate Native Advisory Council (NAC) at the so-called 'Gaberones'.[6] Chief Isang Pilane of the Bakhatla in Mochudi expressed appreciation for the forum as a 'national vigilance association and deliberate assembly or council' to 'promote mutual help, a feeling of fellowship and a spirit of brotherhood'. It would 'bring us together into common action as one political people' such that 'racialism and tribal feuds, jealousy and petty quarrels' would not stand in the way of collective advancement, especially education and industry.[7] Tshekedi Khama of the Bamongoato, furthest north in Serowe, refused to join the Council. He said he would attend the meetings only as an 'observer'.[8] He also said he could not cooperate with the southern chiefs because he did not trust them, as they did not cooperate with him in his attempts to stop European liquor entering the Protectorate and to eradicate initiation schools.[9] Further, he reasoned that his population was much larger than that of all the other reserves and therefore he could not commit to follow the Council's decisions. During this first meeting, the delegates had agreed that Lotlamoreng Montsioa should receive an invitation to the gathering.[10] Macgregor forwarded an invitation to Lotlamoreng two weeks before the next meeting but without pressing him, 'you are free to come and not as you like'.[11]

There were then 647 taxpayers on the Barolong Farms.[12] Every paramount chief could nominate a further four men from his reserve as representatives on the council. Sebopioa Molema was a leading representative for the Barolong, as was his brother, Modiri, after he returned from Scotland a medical doctor earlier in that year. Just two months after the second meeting of the council in March 1921, Lotlamoreng Montsioa made a claim for money to help sink a well at the pan on the farm, Korwe Pan, 'for my tribe'.[13] MacGregor recommended the approval of the application to the new High Commissioner of the Bechuanaland Protectorate (and Governor-General of South Africa), Prince Arthur of Connaught. However, MacGregor proceeded with caution because of the status of the Barolong Farms. He wished to avoid a scenario where Barolong notables were claiming public funds for farms that were effectively private. He relayed a reinterpretation of the status of the farms to the High Commissioner. 'Korwe Pan is one of the Barolong Farms lying within the Bechuanaland Protectorate, which were allotted years ago by the applicant's father to members of his family, on the understanding that at their death the ground would revert to the Tribe.' In fact, this was not the case. According to the Land Commission of 1886, the original 'occupants' could transfer their right and certificate of occupation to sons.[14]

The government wished to increase the levy at the beginning of 1922, but a severe drought made collection at the higher value impossible. Tshekedi did not agree to raise the tax. The Resident Magistrate in Bakoenas' territory reported that 'there will be no crops this year' and the prices of cattle were very low hence he could not recommend an increase in taxation.[15] Yet,

Lotlamoreng Montsioa accepted the increase in 1922 but 'owing to such a great depression my people have only agreed to raise the fund to 5/- by paying 2/- more.'[16] In 1924, the new Resident Magistrate, Jules Ellenberger, wished to postpone the introduction of Africander and red Shorthorn bulls cattle in the reserves as 'there has been very little rain – just over an inch since the winter – and the country is really in a very bad state'.[17] Lotlamoreng Montsioa was one of the few chiefs who went ahead. When the Bakoena could not accommodate their Africander bull, Montsioa took it up.[18] There was very little forage. In one instance, an Africander bull died from ingesting a poisonous plant.[19] On the Barolong Farms, chiefs had the benefit of a white tenantry that supplied water for irrigation and livestock even when it was very dry. The Barolong Farms did very well through the proceeds of the fund. Apart from the introduction of pedigree cattle, money also went to teachers' salaries and school furniture.[20]

In March that year, Modiri Molema insisted that the council should take care in the presentation of the minutes because '[t]his Council is the beginning of our Parliament and Minutes printed in pamphlet form are better and easier to handle than typewritten copies'.[21] The reference to a 'parliament' was not naïve. Far from it. The European Advisory Board was placing great pressure on the Protectorate's administration to cede the Bechuanaland Protectorate to the Union. At their meeting of 18 March 1924, chiefs were incensed at what they saw as an attempt by the white settler lobby in the Union to twist the arms of their counterparts across the border. For instance, the Union had announced a new regulation that only cattle weighing more than 800 pounds could cross the Molopo River into the Union. The more difficult it was for white farmers to sell their stock across the border, the more likely they were to support the incorporation of the Protectorate into the Union.

In the Council, concern about the possibility of the Protectorate's incorporation would deepen and continue into the early 1950s.[22] A border that had not greatly mattered that much before 1910, apart from some regulations controlling taking stock across the border (mainly to prevent the crossing of stolen animals), was now the boundary separating chiefs from a dispensation of crude racial ordering that squeezed anyone who was not white into the margins of political power and property holding. The reference to 'Parliament' was a signal that the Protectorate should establish itself as a separate and different British domain, one with fair representation for Africans. Even in these very early meetings, the NAC wanted statutory and legislative powers, and with them, a say in how the administration utilised the general revenue.[23]

Another concern of the Native Advisory Council in its first decade was the administration's use of 'native laws and customs' to adjudicate cases, the very same system that was operating in the Union. In 1928, this was a sore point in the meeting. Chiefs relayed strong dissatisfaction that the High Commissioner 'does not recognise our laws as laws, he does not recognise us as chiefs'. They wanted 'a collection in the form of a book of all native laws and customs'.[24] They were suggesting using such a 'book' for a systematised application of 'native law and custom' across all chiefly courts in the Protectorate. They thought that such a standardised and legally recognised text would make the Kgotlas in the reserves credible and render the 'Native Courts' of the Resident Magistrates unnecessary. The government's position was that there was no 'native law', only 'native custom', which was not written. In the Union, Pilane argued, 'they have a term which places the law and custom together'. By this, he meant 'native administration'. 'In spite of there being this expression that natives should be tried by native law we see that the power of the Chief is greatly diminishing.' In other words, in the Union the government had in fact written down 'native custom' into 'native law' but Native Commissioners, not chiefs, used this 'law' in their 'native courts'. The High Commissioner had 'no objection' to the compilation of the book, just as had happened in Basutoland, yet 'it was not thought expedient to take any official action' by giving the volume 'legal effect by means of proclamation'.[25]

The first decade of meetings closed with a meeting in March 1929 where chiefs' remonstrated against racial discrimination in the Bechuanaland Protectorate.[26] Sebopioa Molema, as spokesperson for chiefs, presented that the 'Council greatly resents the government's regulation that only a select grouping of traders, with licenses, all European, could purchase stock at a set price'. He lambasted 'what we call "monopoly" in our country' and wanted the government to allow a free market in the trade of cattle, open also to buyers outside the Protectorate. 'Our cattle are in good condition and we want to sell them.' The status quo, he suggested, 'is encouraged by the European Advisory Council', a constituency that did not pay Hut Tax, but sold all its merchandise to the Africans. He maintained that the Native Advisory Council was wholly dissatisfied with having a say only in the operation of the Native Fund, and not of the General Revenue. 'The Europeans have representation "practically without taxation" while we are not allowed to advise the Government [on] how to spend the General Revenue although we provide most of it'.[27]

In the same meeting, he explained that the question of race and representation had become urgent given whites' relentless insistence that Britain cede the Protectorate to the Union. Such incorporation would sink the black population of the Protectorate in the same political situation as their South African counterparts, without any platform of representation. As the lobby towards incorporation intensified, chiefs were using the Native Advisory Council to bring resolutions or petitions against it to the Protectorate government.

> There is no place except here where we can express what is in our minds. We are here and you are Governors because you are white people. We consider things and you consider them as white men. We are trying to adopt your way of considering things because you are our teachers. Although there is an European Advisory Council which has to deal with matters concerning Europeans, and a Native Advisory Council which has to deal with matters concerning Natives there are some points where we come together. We are caused [sic] to bring this resolution because of what we read in the newspapers, which are an indication of what the white people think ...They said in the papers that there is no good ruling in this country and that it should be put in another country. [28]

This final meeting followed newspaper reports that intended to stir public opinion, even in Britain, in favour of the Bechuanaland Protectorate's incorporation into the Union. 'The natives are absolutely in the power of their chiefs, a Chief makes them work on his farm or guard his cattle, he levies taxes as he pleases, and the native is without redress for he dares not complain to the Magistrate'.[29] The reporter suggested that incorporation 'is also the desire of the Bechuanaland native', who was begging for release from a backward, tyrannical situation, which was holding the 'pastoral country' back from economic advancement. According to the reports, the African population was saying, 'we work for nothing but were this [the Protectorate] a colony we would receive wages'.

Chiefs were incensed, but they had been enraged for years. In 1926, one Mongoaketse headman had spoken about the situation of chieftaincy in 'modern times' where chiefs had lost even the powers to collect Hut Tax for the government. 'If there are two Chiefs in a tribe who has the power?'[30] This had been the first meeting that Tshekedi had attended, though he had done so as a bystander – listening and observing – not as the regent of the Bamongoato. Though paramount chiefs did not consider the council as their primary channel of contact with the colonial government in this first decade of its operation, they took the platform very seriously as an institution to collaborate and strengthen their position. The meetings helped to stage prestige and to revive their confidence before an audience of colonial officials, their own junior kin and other representatives. The men who would emerge as firebrands in the council were young chiefs – Tshekedi, Pilane and later Bathoen when he joined the council. However, since its early years, frictions had been emerging in the council. In 1924, Modiri Molema had chastised the chiefs for picking out their favourites as representatives on the council whilst the 'best brains' remained in the reserves.[31] 'Many able people are apt to be left out,' he had objected. Nevertheless, as time went on, disagreements did not necessarily stand in the way of working together although in Bathoen's mind, the ink was drying on Modiri Molema's record of unsubtle slights. He loathed the way the doctor addressed paramount chiefs as though they were not his fathers, but juveniles or undiscerning common people, forgetting all the while, it seemed to Bathoen, that Molemas were not rulers, only children, because they belonged to a junior house.

II

When Sebopioa Molema returned to the Molopo Reserve in 1926, Lotlamoreng Montsioa left the reserve to settle across the border on the Barolong Farms.[32] At first, it was not clear that the paramount chief had in fact set up home on his farm 'Good Hope' in the Bechuanaland Protectorate. Sebopioa never thought that anyone, not least the paramount chief, could abandon the town and capital, Mafikeng, for farms that chiefs used 'for cattle posts under the supervision of our servants'. The state of affairs only became clear when he (once again 'Secretary of Barolong'), Dick Marumoloa and especially the paramount chief's favourite, Tiego Tawana, found themselves on a rotating roster as acting paramount authority, whilst he, Lotlamoreng, played truant, 'pretending to be sick, so that he can live in the Protectorate as a farmer than as a chief'. Apparently Lotlamoreng returned to Mafikeng 'three days in two or three weeks', before he returned to Good Hope, where he 'farms in large scale', feeling at liberty to use the servants and cattle of his absent kin, 'and when we in the Union complain to him about this his usurpation of powers, he terms us "Intellectual" people, hard to govern'.[33]

Lotlamoreng was taking advantage of the developments that the Native Fund were encouraging in the Protectorate, but chiefs like Sebopioa were unfamiliar with a sensibility that turned away from the conveniences and infrastructure of town life – the stadt, as the centre of the chieftaincy. Even the old Chief Montsioa always resided in the town centre and political capital, not at the outskirts where the most common people and the servants, often the Basarwa, resided. 'No Barolong chief before Lotlamoreng', as Sebopioa complained to the government, 'ever lived in the Protectorate'.[34] It made even less sense to him that Lotlamoreng would pursue this course because the paramount chief had a better paying government job and a sure salary in the reserve. His own earnings as headman were meagre, although not any worse than the salaries literate black people earned in the strata of occupations available to them, including in the mines. He took Lotlamoreng's decision to remove to country living as evidence that he, Lotlamoreng was different from them, an interloper to the royal family. Indeed, Lotlamoreng was an erstwhile mineworker and a farmer, a man who worked with his hands. His predecessors, even the minimally literate Wessels Montsioa, had all been landlords with tenants; they were actual townspeople. Lotlamoreng was not, in that sense, like the rest of them.

Yet Sebopioa himself found that there was not much to do in the Molopo Reserve anymore. He was aged forty-six when he returned to the reserve in 1926. His aim was providing for his family and steering himself far from the shores of debt where he had once been wrecked in the reserve. The days in the reserve had many unfilled hours. Whilst Lotlamoreng Montsioa was retreating at his farm, Tiego Tawana was taking charge of a small Kgotla responsible for only those people who identified as Barolong of Ratshidi stock. Householders who claimed a different ancestry or chiefly affiliation, even if they were Barolong, were not under the paramount chief's personal jurisdiction.

Sebopioa's only son, Matlho, was away at boarding school. His wife, Emang had always been home, and now he too had time and availability to be home, although with very little money and without active occupation apart from his trumpet. In the early 1930s, some American evangelists of the Seventh Day Adventists were working in Mafikeng. The church catered for the tastes of the educated classes of the countryside. It distributed pamphlets and reading material and even held film shows at the Elite Hall.[35] Emang attended the meetings. When she invited him to come along, he had time to do so and time also to witness her new spiritual flowering. She was making her way towards a decision she would announce in September 1933 that she was 'resigning' from her duties as secretary of the Methodist Women's Prayer Union and as a member of the Wesleyan Church.[36] She had become a devout Seventh Day Adventist. He supported her – very strongly so.

By the time she gave herself for baptism a month later, he was himself emerging from his own journey of darkness. The deterioration of his eyesight had seemed to match the circumstance that then engulfed him. He almost envied her moment of relieving herself of the past and starting again. 'You must now feel like a newborn baby,' he wrote to her from a hospital bed at Kanye Mission Hospital. 'If I were there I might have arranged also to be baptised.'[37] He wrote to her having just recovered his full sight after persisting 'eye troubles' and days under a blindfold, which the doctor removed on the same day as Emang's baptism. Then the doctor, A.N. Tonge, also an Adventist, hurried to attend Emang's ceremony. The hour was auspicious. He had experienced his first encounter with light on his wife's day of a new birth. It was spring. He wrote her letters from his hospital bed. He was bright and relieved, nourishing a lush, hopeful soul, though outside the sun had dried up everything to greys and the Kalahari's hues of rust and browns. As he described it to her, the landscape of the Bechuanaland Protectorate was denuded, with many cattle dead.

By then, he had had no work to return to in the reserve. The recent loss of his employment had been a dark episode in his reputation, which at the time he had thought was impossible to reclaim. Lotlamoreng had fired him as the National Secretary of Barolong that same winter 'on reasons of embezzlement'.[38] According to the notification of his dismal, when Sebopioa started his duties as tax collector for the government in August 1926, he had accepted a payment of £2-10-0 for Hut Tax but had 'kept half the money to himself'. His official record of the payment in the books was only half the sum he had recorded on the receipt he had signed and had handed over to the taxpayer. He had also allegedly received a sum of £1-10-0 from Richard Lyons, a white man, in exchange for permission to operate as a blacksmith in the stadt. Lotlamoreng had assured the Superintendent of Natives that the charges were not false as he was in possession of these receipts as evidence.

Sebopioa had replied to the Native Commissioner in a long letter, explaining that to make a spectacle of dismissing him, Lotlamoreng had called a 'large meeting of Barolong in a most unusual manner'.[39] 'Messengers were sent all over the stadt and to workers in town, trumpets were sounded early in the morning'. Lotlamoreng had announced 'that I his secretary was a thief' to an audience of 500, 'with the aim, to bring me into contempt and to expose me to public hatred and ridicule'. Sebopioa had publicly said he was not guilty. All this, he had written to the Native Commissioner, was because 'the Molema family is hated by their brothers the Montsioa family by reason of the Molemas' status of educational qualification and some acquisition of property coveted by the ruling party as was the case in Naboth's vineyard'. He wrote that the charges were a personal vendetta by an incumbent who 'had not forgotten that when he was installed as chief some thirteen years ago, I was a leader of the opposition and did not recognise him as chief'. Nevertheless, Sebopioa had known that this was more than a political ruse. In fact, his dismissal had taken him by surprise because he had in fact already acknowledged that he was in possession of money that did not belong to him, and had been paying it back piecemeal to the chieftaincy.

Lotlamoreng had hit him where his pilfering had made him vulnerable. Lotlamoreng had not let the matter end after he had confronted him and he, Sebopioa, had admitted that indeed he had made a 'mistake'.[40] It was not enough for Lotlamoreng to retrieve the money. His foe had also been waiting for an opportunity to humiliate him and found the perfect moment to throw down the gauntlet when the chiefs, Tshekedi and Bathoen, two young paramount chiefs of reputation of the Bechuanaland Protectorate, were in the stadt to discuss the business of the Native Advisory Council. This is when Lotlamoreng assembled the unusual Kgotla and brought with him the records to state and substantiate the charges of theft. Quite apart from the obvious catastrophe of a loss of earnings, the records made it impossible to salvage his reputation. Lotlamoreng had announced to hundreds that he, Sebopioa, had fallen. The only way he could then have defended himself and salvage what reputation he had left was to bring to the government's attention the record of ill feeling between the families and thus bring Lotlamoreng's motives in reporting the crime into question. 'It is obvious', he had continued writing to the Native Commissioner, that 'the chief Lotlamoreng has driven me like a dog from the Barolong National Office without a reasonable degree of care and threatened to shoot me dead with his gun'.[41]

This is how it had happened, how he had thrown himself, the man of political convictions so deep that they had cost him his youth, under the bus to save the man that still had to live, raise a son, love a wife and look other men in the eye. There had been no other way to alleviate his shame other than to give up the man he had been. He had had to forsake that son of the fathers who would yield nothing to the authority of a white colonial official. Instead, he had begged to belong to the Native Commissioner. He had had to 'cut himself away' from Lotlamoreng Montsioa and flee from the punishments and humiliation that the paramount Kgotla would undoubtedly impose on him. Public disgrace was after all Lotlamoreng's only intention seeing that he, Sebopioa, was already paying back the money. He had had no choice other than this unmaking of himself, this empting of the drawer of his past in a desperate operation to salvage his reputation. There he had been, the very bulwark of independent chiefly rule, begging to come under the 'customary' jurisdiction of a colonial official.

> I, as a tribal headman of the Barolong may be deemed as now solely and entirely under and responsible to the Native Commissioner… [and that] I shall not be obliged to go to the Chief's Kgotla for any case affecting me brought by any member of the Barolong … and that such cases be tried by the native commissioner in whom I believe to have a fair and impartial hearing. That such cases be tried according to Native Law and Custom.[42]

He had not had a sudden change of mind to embrace a method of colonial government he had spent more than twenty-five years resisting. On the contrary, he had fought the system to the death. He was merely saving himself, simply looking to land on a more honourable shore. He had suggested that 'as an alternative, the Government may be pleased to forward me with letters of exemption relieving me from the operation of Native Law and Custom, measures granted to certain persons elsewhere within the Union of South Africa'. He also argued that Lotlamoreng's 'autocratic powers' were such that he had dismissed him without trial, hence his request that 'for reasons of justice the Government may be pleased to pay me out a round sum equaling salary for six months, to serve as proper and fair notice'.[43]

The next episode of the matter had been yet another spectacle that Sebopioa had not anticipated. The Native Commissioner had not resisted the inclination to use Sebopioa's request to demonstrate that the government was indeed the highest tribal court in the reserve, a court of *Sechuana*. The Native Commissioner had not called the chiefs to his office but had taken his position in the stadt and had held Kgotla as the Supreme Chief of the reserves in order to hear Sebopioa's appeal against the judgment of the paramount Kgotla and thus adjudicate in a matter concerning the judicial system of the Kgotla itself. The case had been, all in all, the perfect hallmark of the Native Administration Act of 1927.

There were two such gatherings, on 21 and 23 July 1933, where Sebopioa had acknowledged wrongdoing.[44] He had explained that he had already paid 25 shillings at the end of one month and another 30 shillings a month later towards the debt. 'I don't deny that I had made a mistake.' He had explained that upon the resumption of his duties in 1926, 'I had just begun to deal with money matters'.[45] He had written out a 'provisional receipt' but had recorded only half the amount on counterfoil. He conceded that he had also accepted money from Richard Lyons but that it was less than £1-10-0 and, he had said, it had been Lotlamoreng who had asked him to take a bribe on his behalf. 'Lyons came to me saying chief wants something from him for being in stadt' and had parted with the money. 'I handed this money to [the] Chief about a year ago', and the 'Chief would not take it at first, but later on he handed to me a receipt for it & he took the money'. The Native Commissioner's recommendation to both parties and to the Secretary of Native Affairs had been that Lotlamoreng should report the matter to the police. Finally, the matter had ended up in the private audience of the Native Commissioner a month later, where Sebopioa 'unreservedly withdrew his letter' of complaint against Lotlamoreng, who had accepted his resignation and had asked that the government pay him in full for the months of July and August.[46]

The trouble with his eyes had either started or worsened around the time of the humiliation but also around that time, in the duration of unfilled hours, there had happened the incident allegedly involving him, his best friend in Francistown in the Bechuanaland Protectorate, John Ratshosa, and a young woman alone in her hut whilst her mother was thatching grass.[47] People had started to talk. 'I personally do not care what they say for no one dare speak openly about us, it is only the idea of evil people who want other people to have bad and evil (sic) against other people.' In addition to the rumours about what had happened with the girl, and the baby she was expecting consequently, as he explained to Ratshosa, were the accusations of 'embezzlement & misappropriating some Public money'.[48] These darker episodes had been a prelude to his stay at Kanye Mission Hospital in September during a year where 'much has happened for and against me'.[49]

The events that were 'for' him, he did not describe, but they had included meeting Dr Tonge, the Adventist who could help with his eyes.[50] He had been excited about leaving for Kanye just as he was immersing himself in the new Adventist faith. It had brought him close to Emang. It had made possible a new kind of seeing. He had ordered a new 'pyjama suit' although he had been entirely unsatisfied with the result. 'The jacket is very small & it is impossible for me to sleep comfortably. There are no buttons on the jacket & yet you promised to put them on. The trousers is not loose enough...'[51] It had felt a little like going on a vacation and escape the shame that made it a mercy not to be able to see properly, to avoid the small shadow of himself in other men's eyes. Before departure, he had helped Emang prepare the letter that severed her from Methodism. His happiest event was the new path of their faith, which had saved his eyes and illuminated his spirit out of the failings of the past.

When he had arrived at Kanye, he had 'eye trouble and pains on the shoulder' but even then he had been confident.[52] 'Do not be afraid of anything,' he had written to his wife, 'but put your trust in God about my recovery.' He then was already tapping life from a new apprehension of himself in blessing, through his faith, even when the world around him was in lack. 'There is no food of any kind here, people are eating cattle like they drink water.' The drought was severe. 'Cattle are dying like flies at Kanye.' He had taken in the sight of catastrophe with compassion, but also relief that his own placement of grace had positioned him on the side of abundance. 'There is no grass from Lobatse to Kanye & Bangoaketse are starving indeed, in Mafikeng conditions are much better'. It had taken about a week before he could undergo the operation.

After the operation, he wrote to Emang on his typewriter even whilst blindfolded, 'there is no food in the country & people are suffering for want of food'.[53] On the day of her baptism, he urged her towards their sense of mission, to use their lives and words to illuminate the Kingdom, the one true origin, which was the source of all virtue. He and Emang had the revelation to make disciples of all the *morafe*. 'I trust you will preach to several others.'[54] He remained in hospital another week. The Adventists' way of life was a practical orientation towards rest, avoiding meats in favour of fresh produce, evangelism, routine study of scripture and fellowship with other Adventists. He was ready for all of it, to fill the time that would otherwise lie empty *before him*. Soon he would be home with his wife. 'Keep my bed ready & warm waiting for my arrival at Mafikeng.'[55]

III

On the farm Vryhof in the Cape, a white tenant farmer was making a count of his stock from the late winter of 1932.[56] His name is unrecorded. Vryhof was the private farm that then belonged to Modiri Molema after the death of his father. The farmer's records are an account of a mission to establish and develop a farming enterprise after he either started or renewed his contract on Vryhof in the late winter of 1932. The tenant counted about 200 cattle at the beginning of August, amongst them fifty-seven oxen. He also had seven horses, fourteen mules and three donkeys. He also had stock on another nearby farm, Kromdraai, or perhaps he had family there, also farmers, and they rotated stock and shared pasture.

The month proceeded as usual for a cattle rancher, with a sale of thirty-five oxen. In that month, he killed one ox. In the new year, business was still very promising. In February, he received more oxen, 'sent away' four but by the end of the month, he had killed two more oxen and ten days later another two. Two weeks later one had died. In nine months, he had lost almost half of the oxen. He was down to thirty-one oxen in May. The deaths and killings were due to foot-and-mouth disease that had crossed the border from then Rhodesia. The strain, according to veterinary experts, was 'a very mild type but terrible in its consequences'.[57]

The farmer's cows started to die during the calving season. He made a similar painstaking record of their demise.[58] At the beginning of August of 1932, he counted seventy-two cows and twenty-eight calves. The cows were calving much faster than they were dying and the calves were surviving. He lost only three cows between August of 1932 and the end of January 1933. However, from March 1933, the cows started to succumb despite his measures to kill an infected cow. He managed to remove at least sixteen calves from Vryhof to Kromdraai in an attempt to save them. In June 1933, he recorded the 'calves without mothers' and the 'calves born dead.' From that same June, the mothers and their young started to die very quickly. He lost thirty-eight cows, one bull and seven calves in seven months.

At the beginning of January 1934, he sent a calf to the 'Dr in Mafeking', his landlord Modiri Molema. The calf was likely in lieu of a late payment of rent, having paid nothing in 1933. Or perhaps he had borrowed money from the landlord. He had been cash-strapped for some time. Two years before, at the end of 1932, he had paid the landlord £1-0-0 but also a debt he had owed to another Petrous for £3-6-0. The rinderpest later that year had started when he had just undertaken the costly work of repairing the farmhouse, which was part of the terms of his contract. He had not yet been on his feet when that hurricane landed. He had already purchased wallpaper, three gallons of paint, wood for railings, white lime, murals, raw linseed oil, three paintbrushes, one and half bags of bone meal and the same quantity of salt. He had managed to sell some fifteen bags of sorghum, twenty-five bags of mealies and one and half bags of dry beans by the end of the year. He had produced the sorghum but not the mealies, which he had bought. Of the thirty-two bags of mealies he had purchased, only two remained for his family. Mark, from whom he had probably borrowed ploughs and other implements, had to be paid with five bags of mealies and five bags of sorghum. The other workers also had to be paid, '1 bag corn for Setlogi; 1 bag mealies for Cark, 2 bags corn for Petrous.'[59]

This unknown man was a farmer with experience and determination but farming the interior was a risky and difficult enterprise. Most importantly, the land did not belong to him. It was still not quite a white man's country. Debt left him a very narrow margin for recovery with close to half of his stock lost and very meagre yields in grain, all amidst a global economy in depression and the drought of 1933. He probably quit the farm early in 1934. This would be how his record book came to be in possession of his black landlord. He would have gone to Modiri Molema in the Molopo Reserve to explain how he had failed to save his oxen, cows and calves from the blisters in their mouths and the fever that claimed their lives.

IV

In 1931, there was both a Resident Magistrate and a Native Commissioner for the reserves in the district of Mafeking but the system of native administration under the Native Administration Act of 1927 was beyond the capacity of the bureaucrats charged to carry it out. They were not coping with the workload of what was in practice *direct* rule over tens of thousands of black people in the reserves. The Native Commissioner reported to the Secretary of Native Affairs that the government had to intervene urgently. He reported that 'the tribes have become accustomed to regard the Government as their upper Chief i.e. to look beyond their chiefs for assistance'.[60] He added however that 'This evolution is only making a start in Bechuanaland and recent legislation which has tended to take away powers from the chiefs is responsible for this change'. In his view, 'Native Administration by Chiefs in Bechuanaland is very poor and checks progress'. 'It will be found,' he added, 'that the following changes are long overdue.'

a. the appointment of a resident native commissioner for Bechuanaland who will originate and lay down policy to be followed in this territory.
b. criminal jurisdiction of chiefs should be taken away as the Kgotla system of fines is obsolete and impoverished the people.
c. the appointment of Assistant Native Commissioners in the place of Superintendents with criminal jurisdiction
d. Land administration to rest in the hands of the Resident Native Commissioner with power to delegate so much of his duties to assistant Native Commissioners as he may deem expedient.

His explanation for this glitch in 'native administration' in Bechuanaland was that 'Government Headmen' were 'minor chiefs', which was a settlement of

British Annexation in 1885 that the colonial government had not undone. Chiefs had considerably less power by the 1930s, and even then only over the people upon whom they had 'personal' jurisdiction, but the government had not replaced them with commoners as 'headmen'. Everywhere else this official had been, hereditary chiefs had no recognition and government appointed headmen. He thought that if the government would finally strip hereditary chiefs of power completely in Bechuanaland and appoint alternative 'headmen' in their position, it would then be possible to transfer some of the responsibilities to maintain law and order in the reserves to these 'headmen'. The 'headmen' would help to adjudicate cases except in criminal cases and, most importantly, in matters related to land. As things stood, he as Native Commissioner and the Resident Magistrates were the 'upper Chiefs' adjudicating all sorts of cases over the many thousands of people over whom chiefs had no 'personal jurisdiction'. Colonial officials needed help, both in the form of assistant Native Commissioners and salaried 'headmen' that could implement 'native law' in the reserves.

In Mafikeng, not only commoners but also Barolong chiefs themselves sought the arbitration of colonial officials to resolve their own disputes over the rules of chieftaincy, rank and seniority in the reserve. These chiefly ranks mattered as they influenced chiefs' chances in competing for the salaried posts of 'headmen', regents and paramount chiefs. In 1936, the Motshegares lodged a complaint with the Native Commissioner that 'Motshegares' sons have always been the superior brothers of the Molemas, and it is only during the present rule of L.K. Montsioa that the Molema sons are supposed to be our superiors'.[61] Lotlamoreng Montsioa could not care less which way the axe fell. 'I have given my decision and if either of the parties is dissatisfied, he has his remedy in the usual way.' Presiding over such disputes was an onerous task and he was busy farming on his 'Good Hope', with little time to preside over a Kgotla with lengthy presentations of contested genealogies. He wrote to the Native Commissioner that

> I do not understand why the matter comes to me as a complaint, and would be glad of some enlightenment. If the parties wish this longstanding dispute to be reopened, I would suggest that a departmental inquiry be held. You yourself know that this question of status has been a bone of contention for years, and I have no intention of allowing the parties to revive it continually for the purpose of making a strife, nor do I see why I should be made a party to the dispute in this manner. If the parties have a grievance the proper channels are there for them to ventilate it. Let them use these channels.[62]

The Native Commissioner had no time available and requested the Resident Magistrate to adjudicate the matter, but the Resident Magistrate declined to do so or to release staff from his office to provide support, because he had himself 'two lengthy appeals' from the Kgotla to handle.[63] 'For myself, my own time is more than fully occupied, (I am myself understaffed and employing temporary clerks), even supposing I was sufficiently experienced in Native Law and Custom.' He recommended that the Native Commissioner and the Civil Native Commissioner, his colleagues in the system of 'native administration', request more assistance that all of them could then share, at least a 'Native Affairs Official' to 'take over a few of the cases' now that the assistant they had all been sharing was being transferred. He warned nevertheless against the temptation to recruit just anybody in their desperation to get relief, as 'should the officer taking his place be inexperienced you will readily understand the acute position that shall obtain'. At the beginning of the century, one man could function as Resident Magistrate and Native Commissioner, but with the wane of chiefly and patriarchal power, the offices of colonial bureaucracy were recruiting new layers of staff to rule the reserves, all white men.

Throughout his tenure from the 1920s, Lotlamoreng Montsioa could not curb new immigration, despite his injunction that people 'must not place foreigners on the lands of the Barolong'.[64] His councillors informed him that people were placing themselves on the land without anyone's permission and were resisting eviction. In a 1936 dispute, one sub-chief, Tiro-ea-Modimo sought to evict 'Hlazo', a nativised immigrant from Natal, to whom he had 'lent a plot' but in 1918 Hlazo had 'gathered all the Zulus from the location to come and farm'. When Tiro-ea-Modimo evicted them, probably shortly after 1920, Hlazo had stated that 'he had no chief', that 'the land belongs to the Government', and 'proceeded to farm and give himself land'. When Hlazo's son returned from 'the whites', he too had apportioned himself a plot and farmed. In 1936, Lotlamoreng Montsioa conceded that he could do nothing. The Native Commissioner's ruling was that all the men make peace and 'shake hands'. Hlazo's case had been dragging on for more than fifteen years, each time with an added twist. Lotlamoreng merely said, 'these matters are very difficult', and sent the claimants back again without judgment. In the 1940s, anthropologist Isaac Schapera counted that only twenty-one of eighty-four different wards in Mafikeng were Barolong settlements. The rest were a mix of Hlubi, Thembu or Sotho, who spoke a different language.[65] They were all 'black', squeezed together on properties of diminishing size, often with no attachment to the chief. In the Molopo Reserve, Lotlamoreng

Montsioa had no land, and not many people. What indeed was there for a paramount chief to do in Mafikeng?

V

Historian Michael Crowder writes at length about Tshekedi Khama's stance against the colonial authorities in the Bechuanaland Protectorate. The most famous incident was when he sentenced a young white man, Phineas McIntosh, to a flogging at his court at Serowe in September 1933.[66] Sebopioa Molema read about the 'great trouble' in the newspapers and reported the incident to his friend, John Ratshosa, who had apparently suffered the same fate some three years or more before in the same court.[67] Sebopioa had received a telegram that 'Tshekedi is deposed until further investigation is conducted.' By then, Tshekedi and the Resident Commissioner of the Bechuanaland Protectorate, Charles Rey, were already at loggerheads. Crowder explains that the war of attrition between the two men almost brought the running of colonial administration to a halt. 'Rey's tendency to ride roughshod over opposition from whatever quarter it came, his arrogance and conviction that he was always right, combined with his basic hostility to the institution of chieftaincy, exacerbated the suspicious side of Tshekedi's character as it did his stubbornness, and made any compromise difficult.'[68] Crowder observes that given the frequency and scale of some of Tshekedi's actions, particularly his resistance to Rey's attempts to regulate and attenuate chiefs' administrative and judicial powers in 1932, it is small wonder that the British never deposed the regent. Crowder explains that the laws of succession and Tshekedi's popularity amongst the Bamongoato meant there was no alternative.

Nevertheless, Tshekedi's strategy in one of the most explosive moments of resistance against the British administration in the Bechuanaland Protectorate invites a reconsideration of whether, in Crowder's words, 'Tshekedi's opposition to the British between 1926 and 1936 is unique in the history of British rule in Africa'. He insists that 'none so consistently challenged his colonial overlords over issues great and small without being deposed'.[69] Tshekedi certainly stole the show at the Native Advisory Council meeting where Rey tabled the two new policies of 'native administration', before dragging the highest levels of the administration in the Union and in England to intervene against Rey's plot to attenuate the powers of the chiefs further.

The Bechuanaland Protectorate Native Administration Proclamation stipulated procedures for 'the election and recognition of future Chiefs, providing for a 'Committee of the Chief's Councillors for him to work with', as well as other various procedures including how chiefs should work with their Kgotla and decide on levies and corporal punishment.[70] The proclamation also outlined the conditions that could lead to chiefs' deposition and the procedures of such an outcome. The second proclamation, the Bechuanaland Protectorate Natives Tribunals Constitution and Jurisdiction Proclamation established 'Native courts and tribunals', their jurisdiction, and routes of appeal to the Resident Magistrates. Both proclamations relied on 'native laws and customs'. Rey's motivation, in his 'secret report' was that 'the interests of 200,000 natives in this territory have been sacrificed for the sake of preserving the personal interests and privileges of half a dozen chiefs'.[71]

In his resistance to the legislation, Tshekedi was not a firebrand operating as a lone ranger. In fact, contrary to Crowder's telling of the story, Tshekedi relied extensively on the advice and experience of other chiefs to stage his resistance. Sebopioa Molema had extensive experience in how to use the courts to resist 'native administration'. The reason why both Tshekedi and the young Bathoen were in Mafikeng when Lotlamoreng fired Sebopioa at the beginning of June 1933 was to discuss and work on amendments for these two Native Administration Proclamations. As Crowder writes, 'The Chiefs had before them the original drafts with the amendments stuck on the relevant paragraphs and written in red ink'.[72] The chiefs had done all that work in the Mafikeng stadt, with the two Molemas and Dick Marumoloa acting on behalf of Lotlamoreng Montsioa. At the meeting, Rey was unwilling to do more than read the amendments, defend his position and leave the proclamations largely unchanged. Hence, on 7 December, Tshekedi and Bathoen sent a petition to the High Commissioner, Sir Herbert Stanley, requesting him to appoint a 'Royal Commission' to investigate the matter and grant them an interview.[73] The following day, Sebopioa wrote to Ratshosa that 'Chiefs Tshekedi & Bathoen were here yesterday and met Barolong with the object of making application to interview the High Commissioner and we sent to His excellency such a request, each Chief to go with 2 men to Cape Town'.[74] At the beginning of January the following year, he wrote again to Ratshosa that

> Sometime during January, the Chiefs at Protectorate received a reply from High Commissioner regarding the desired interview, which I wrote to you about last. The High Commissioner said the Chiefs should put in writing everything they wanted to see him about, complaints and otherwise. That

they must not be afraid to express themselves fully and when he shall have realised such communication he will consider if he could grant them the desired interview. As usual, Chiefs Tshekedi, Bathoen, Lotlamoreng, Dick Lekoko, SJ Molema & Dr Molema spent several nights writing and amending the Draft Proclamation, & we have sent such long letter to His Excellency and are waiting on the reply.[75]

The High Commissioner agreed to a meeting, and Sebopioa Molema reported to Ratshosa that 'The High Commissioner has called Chiefs Tshekedi & others to be at Cape Town on the 23rd.'[76] He added that 'Lotlamoreng is sick as usual & he said Lekoko [Dick Marumoloa] & myself should accompany Chiefs Tshekedi & Bathoen' but that '[on] account of ill-health I did not go but Dr Molema went [in] my place'.

The deputation represented chiefs' objection to Rey's two policies of 'native administration' that would recognise a chief only if he or she had the administration's approval. They objected to Rey's idea that the chief would have to share his powers with a 'Councillors committee'. The Natives Tribunals Proclamation repealed Section 8 of the Proclamation of June 1891, which had delineated the jurisdiction of 'Magistrates Courts' and the 'Native Courts'. The Magistrate's courts would now have the jurisdiction to oversee both the 'Senior' and 'Junior' tribunals that would constitute chiefly courts. The proposed legislation, they argued, prevented a chief from adjudicating the already limited category of cases his Kgotla could hear. He had to adjudicate cases as a member of a Senior Tribunal, which consisted of representatives of the 'tribe' that the government approved. The paramount chief could not decide on a ruling on his own. A government-appointed headman or sub-chief presided over the 'junior' tribunal. The establishment of tribunals would not enlarge the scope of the jurisdiction the chiefs had lost in 1891. In fact, the chiefs would have considerably less powers than those that remained with the chiefs under the Order-in-Council of 1891. 'We have still to learn,' the deputation remarked, 'that our present Magistrates possess any better and superior qualifications over chiefs so as to entitle them to exercise control over native tribes.'[77]

Sebopioa Molema was hopeful. He reported again to Ratshosa that 'Chief Tshekedi & others have returned from Cape Town & say though His Excellency was angry with them … he promised to send their objection to England'.[78] It took another nine to ten months but the proclamations became law in January 1935.[79] Tshekedi resisted the proclamations in his reserve for almost the entire year. He finally submitted the names of his 'Councillors

Committee' only when he had sought legal counsel and was ready for litigation. His counsel argued that the proclamations could not stand because they went against 'Native Laws and Customs', which the Order-in-Council of 1891 had specifically stated would remain in place under the new terms of British 'protection'. Moreover, if they continued, the proclamations would be impracticable, for instance it was not clear how the tribunals would coexist with the Kgotla. However, the most important legal argument against the proclamations was precisely the same as the one the Barolong had utilised to secure their independent jurisdiction from 'native administration' from 1902 until 1913. The Barolong had argued that the government had no jurisdiction to intervene in their reserves and promulgate policies of 'native administration' given the treaty they had signed with Sidney Shippard. For ten years, the Barolong had defeated the colonial government through the courts, arguing that its interventions were *ultra vires*. Similarly, Tshekedi argued the same point based on a verbal treaty with Charles Warren in 1885.

A judge of the South African High Court heard the case in Lobatse in mid-1936. What was the scope of jurisdiction that Britain, in this instance not a dominion government, had over territories under its protection? Did the Crown have the 'unfettered and unlimited power to legislate for the government of and administration of justice among the native tribes in the Bechuanaland Protectorate and [is] this power limited by Treaty or Agreement?'[80] The argument was about the degree of autonomy that colonised peoples retained after the event of annexation. This had been the Barolongs' argument, a view of empire as a negotiation of autonomy, not as a surrender of government and territory to the empire. None amongst the chiefs would have understood the complexity more than Sebopioa Molema, who had not only trained as a lawyer, but had in fact read every line of the argument Schreiner had made to secure their victory. He had listened to every word of testimony and even acted as an interpreter during parts of the Barolong trial.

Sebopioa had also handled matters of rule along these lines when he was the National Secretary and *de facto* chief during the tenure of his father-in-law, Lekoko Montsioa. Daily he had been deciding upon and delineating the boundaries beyond which the Native Affairs Department could not act. Through his neat, respectful typescript, never losing restraint, he had conceded little ground to the Native Affairs Department, certainly not jurisdiction over Rietfontein or the power to evict 'whitish' people who counted themselves as Barolong after the Natives Land Act of 1913. Sebopioa Molema would never lash a white man at court like Tshekedi had done, and yet colonial official s' disapproval of him and their private records of his activities is evidence that they recognised that behind his courtesy and seemingly fawning orations lay a conviction that chiefs retained the right to rule their lands. Hence, in the Union, they denied him every opportunity for employment in the civil service. Sebopioa's intention had been to utilise imperial citizenship towards the freedoms of the *morafe* and not to break the tie with Britain.

At the 1932 meeting that introduced the two 'native administration' proclamations at the Native Advisory Council, which chiefs had studied the day before, Crowder remarked that, 'No other chiefs spoke', except Tshekedi but in fact, the minutes record that Sebopioa Molema did say a few words when Rey asked if anyone wished to say anything. [81] He welcomed Rey back from his leave in England, adding that 'England is the home of the British people and we consider ourselves humble citizens of that government'. He had set the tone of what he considered the terms of engagement – their placement in Britain as a moral government, duty bound to be just. 'I think the people of this earth would be glad to see a man from heaven to tell them about things in heaven.' He was reminding Rey that British justice was the moral basis for its empire. Even Tshekedi would learn the power of the soft politics of restraint.

When he first became the regent of the Bamongoato in 1926, Tshekedi was a student preparing for his matriculation at Fort Hare University. He was concerned about his lack of experience and had initially looked to British administrators for guidance. When he perceived there was nothing there but tutorship and a desire to control him, he ran his own ship, did well sustaining himself and going against the administration's wishes when he did not agree, but not always in ways that could keep him afloat. After McIntosh's flogging, he in fact had found himself deposed and had had to apologise, and thereafter had landed up in hospital with a broken leg but also mental strain.[82] It was precisely the kind of situation Sebopioa Molema considered reckless and not a show of strength. Besides, what was the moral genesis of the British Empire if not also to facilitate chiefs' free rule over their own people and strengthen their autonomy? Colonial officials like Rey, in Sebopioa's mind, much like Union officials, had to be reminded or otherwise inducted into the moral underpinnings of empire. By the mid-1930s, Tshekedi had made himself part of a coalition of other chiefs, regardless of his earlier refusal to join the Native Advisory Council formally or even to collaborate with his peers. He was learning to talk to Britain, to use its judicial systems, to compromise and broker deals that would retain his position as chief.

In the meantime, Modiri Molema was finding his position on the Native Advisory Council necessary but also uncomfortable. He found it difficult to accept that whilst chiefs were working together on the Council, they did so as representing separate 'tribal' enclaves of the Bechuanaland Protectorate, like the 'Barolong', the 'Bakoena', and so on. The Council was like the Congress of 'the fathers', where people were forming coalitions to gain the numbers that could protect each separate, particular interest. Modiri found it frustrating to work with Tshekedi, who had a very strong regional identity as chief of the 'Bamongoato'. He found Tshekedi's earlier refusal to join the Native Advisory Council immature and rather foolish. His feeling was that Tshekedi was not moving ahead with the times, not raising his head beyond the borders of Serowe, much less the borders of the Bechuanaland Protectorate to see examples of what was possible, especially the opportunity to turn the Council into a legislative council, a process which required collaboration between Britain and local leaders. He expressed his frustration to one colonial official. 'Dr Molema said that Tshekedi seemed to him to be incredibly foolish as he would have no friends in England or Africa if it were known that he was not cooperating with or was endeavouring to impede the Government in its business'.[83] It was shortsighted, in Modiri's view, for Tshekedi to 'paddle his own canoe'. Michael Crowder wrote that it took Tshekedi Khama until the 1940s to 'challenge the fundamental British colonial policy of ruling their colonies through the traditional authorities'.[84] In contrast, Modiri Molema had in mind from the first meetings of the Council a legislative body, even a 'parliament'.

As far as resistance to the two proclamations of 'native administration' were concerned, chiefs lost the battle. Charles Rey won his proclamations. The new Secretary of State for the dominions, Malcolm MacDonald, at the inquiry of the court, held that the Crown had unlimited powers to intervene and legislate as it wished. The court allowed Britain to be both player and umpire in the matter. This defeat was serious. However, chiefs had already perceived that their greatest enemy was not Rey, but in fact the repertoires of practice amongst their own people that corroded chiefly and patriarchal power. Chiefs perceived that ordinary people believed the colonial administration had greater capacity to support their welfare and aspirations than chiefs had. The negotiations of the NAC throughout the 1930s illuminate how the debates about government policy, even resistance to Rey's proclamations, served also as a platform of negotiation for chiefs to lobby the colonial government as an ally to preserve 'tradition' or *Sechuana* against new patterns of migration, consumption and sexual lives that threatened chiefly and patriarchal power. Their greatest threat, in their view, was not British officials, it was rather the peril of *Sekhoa* that was corroding their authority slowly and from within. If the government had the legislative and judicial capacity to intervene in the reserves through 'native administration', then this policy was welcome if it would stabilise and strengthen those repertoires of personhood that supported the authority of senior men and chiefs rather than the designs of a new generation of men and women.

Even before Rey's tenure, chiefs had been soliciting the colonial government's help against new cultural tides, some of which they claimed emerged from the Union and were sweeping 'tradition' away. They had already been using the Council's meetings to express alarm and to lobby the government to hold *Sekhoa* at bay in favour of the interpretation of *Sechuana* that they were in fact fighting amongst themselves to define and establish. In 1930, Sebopioa Molema spoke strongly against the system of deferred pay, which remitted a great portion of mineworkers' wages home.[85] Other chiefs preferred the system because it ensured that the men that crossed the border into the Union came back to the reserves of the Protectorate. In fact, Protectorate chiefs were just as eager to export their authority into the industrial zones as the Union chiefs had done. Isang Pilane insisted that an 'officer' from the reserves travel to the Transvaal 'to look after the interests of Protectorate natives in towns'. As another headman explained, 'we would also know where our boys are'. Sebopioa Molema replied that

> I have been free and I like to be free. I have been taught to be free, born in a free country under the British flag. When I work I want to get all my money to do with it as I please, and I want all other people to get their money, not to have it taken from them by force except for Hut Tax. It is through that freedom of having the right use of one's money that one has civilisation. If I go to Johannesburg I can buy anything I cannot acquire here, and I can introduce it into this country as an item of civilisation.[86]

He was the sole dissenter. Modiri Molema did not attend the meeting. The Bakoena had lost 1500 men to the mines in 1935 alone, leaving only 4000 men fit to work, which was only 37 per cent of men in the reserve. Their chief then lamented 'the lack of manpower to cultivate the land and carry on tribal labour' and the resulting food shortage, but also the state of moral decline suffocating the *morafe* to death. Women were without husbands 'and immorality takes place' while young men from the mines, 'if they go every year and for long periods, lose contact with the tribe, and when they come home, they do not care for tribal work and they have no respect for their Chiefs, Headmen or their elders'. 'Something must be done!' Lotlamoreng Montsioa, who rarely spoke, commented that young men with 'nice glasses and new suits' were 'detribalised when they come home, others are bad and have acquired European habits'.

At the same time, unlike Sebopioa who embraced and respected it, Modiri had a perceptible weariness about some elements of chieftaincy. In 1931, as Rey was preparing his proclamations, Modiri Molema proposed a repeal of the Proclamation No 2 of 1923 'which provides that no advocate or attorney may plead in any court of the Protectorate held in any of the Reserves, in any civil case in which the natives are concerned'.[87] He observed that the law already allowed defendants to use the Magistrate's court as a court of appeal after the Kgotla's judgement. He wished also to offer defendants legal representation at that level where 'we want an exposition of European Laws and at the same time native customs'. He knew that chiefs had been outraged at the very idea that there could be a court of 'native laws and customs' higher than that of the paramount chief, but he felt he 'must especially appeal to the Chiefs to be broadminded in considering this issue.'

> I want the chiefs to remember that our idea is to protect the small man in the Protectorate – the man who cannot express himself. If we are broadminded enough, we would not look to protecting ourselves, but protecting our subjects; and if they can engage an attorney, the Chiefs should enable him to do so, and the Government should help ... I appeal to you, Chiefs, that this proclamation is not to the good of the ordinary man in the protectorate, and that taking that broad view of the matter we should repeal it.[88]

Bathoen and Isang, both educated men, objected. 'By a common person,' Isang objected, 'we mean the uneducated man who only knows native law and custom.' Bathoen supported Isang. 'We do not know the white man's laws and we are not able to stand in front of lawyers.' Sebopioa Molema argued for a system of justice fit for every British subject, seeing 'the principles which govern the Protectorate are British principles'.

> We do not mean to force everybody to employ a lawyer, but we want the door open. We speak as small men of the tribe before our Chiefs, and we are not trying to undermine their authority We would further say that the time will come and it is near at hand, when our chiefs should study law

> ... Cannot we have lawyers in the magistrate's court the same as in the Special Court. What is good for the Chief is also good for the small man ... We want to be the same as all British subjects. We want protection for everybody, the small and the great man.[89]

Modiri Molema lost the vote – '39 against, 6 in favour' – and yet he questioned Rey at the same meeting, in fact immediately after the vote, on the 'vague and alarming rumours' about 'the intended proclamations regarding the powers of chiefs ... contemplated to limit the powers of the Chiefs, to curtail their jurisdiction and restrict their privileges'. In other words, the principle applied both ways. He was as critical and objected as strongly to Britain's overreach of its powers over its subjects as he was of chieftaincy's own encroachment on the rights of the same people. As far as chieftaincy was concerned, he perceived how 'native administration' could both allow ordinary people necessary protection against unlimited and arbitrary hereditary exertions, whilst offering the added advantage of creating a single, uniform judicial and legislative system across the entire Protectorate. If 'native administration' could be fair, it could unseat the differential patchwork of traditional authority across the territory, which created different 'tribes'.

He too perceived that 'native administration' was not at all in practice colonial rule through chiefs, but rather allowed the intervention of the colonial government *directly* into the concerns of the common man and woman. Chiefs would welcome 'native administration' if it strengthened chiefly and patriarchal power, but he wanted it as a means to soften ordinary people's experience of chiefly power and indeed to shorten the reach of the paramount Kgotla. Moreover, 'native administration' was a centralised system. If it were under the control of black people themselves, and they were making just laws through the very legislative body he envisioned as the future of the NAC, then 'native administration' could transform chiefly subjects into citizens of a central state, with fair and equal means of representation for all.

He had walked a journey under a moral code that had robbed him of a primary and intimate freedom, to love and to associate at will. This injury lent him a sharp sensitivity to freedom, or rather to the risks of the loss of freedom that could suddenly overtake and overwhelm without any warning at all and without any arbitration. The difficulty was that he did not quite know what arrangement of power would facilitate and protect the placement of his longing. He would only recognise that homecoming when he finally walked through its gates. He only understood that at that time, the *morafe* would come into its own, and a man's virtue would be judged by his personal choices, on whether he possessed the discipline of a well calibrated moral antenna to gauge situations, and not according to a pedigree of inherited status. He lived looking outwards to the rest of the world, learning and observing, to glean insights of what was possible. Other colonies and peoples were experimenting with ideas of democracy, rights and sovereignty. He did not know the answers. He was searching, like a fly angler who casts a line, never knowing what in the end his catch would be, only that he would recognise it instantly by the torque it transmitted through his wrists and body, and be ready to toss it back if not satisfied.

VI

In October 1916, the Resident Commissioner of the Bechuanaland Protectorate, E.C. Garraway, wrote to the High Commissioner, Sydney Buxton, about a transference of rights between two tenants on the Barolong Farms.[90] It happened that a G.L. Elen was ceding his rights to P.M. Fincham on the farm Ramah, which belonged to Stephen Lefenya. 'Apart from the question of leases,' Garraway observed, 'the position with regard to these farms appears very unsatisfactory.' He confirmed that after the issue of the certificates of occupation to the Barolong, the certificates 'were finally registered in the Deed's Office in February, 1898', a status quo with which he disagreed because he considered the territory a 'Native Reserve'. He was also concerned that there was no clear due process to regulate transfer of occupation at the death of an occupant. On the one hand, 'any change of occupation is on the nomination of the Chief', but in practice, 'the certificates follow the native law of succession without regranting by the Chief.' He proposed to 'consult with the Barolong as to the introduction of a simple form of transfer analogous to that contained in Part II of Cape Act No. 25 of 1894'.[91]

Nothing came of the attempt to handle the Barolong Farms under the terms of the Glen Grey Act, which established a system of individual tenure where allotment holders in effect leased land on quitrent from the government. There is no further record of the planned consultation. In 1925, during his tenure as Resident Commissioner, J. Ellenberger asked Lotlamoreng Montsioa whether he would prefer a proclamation of the Barolong Farms as a Native Reserve.[92] Two years later, Ellenberger reported to the High Commissioner, the Earl of Athlone, that the Barolong 'would prefer that these farms be registered in the Deeds Office for the Bechuanaland

Protectorate in the names of those to whom certificates of Occupation were originally given ... or in the names of their heirs'.[93] When the Secretary of State for the Colonies visited the Bechuanaland Protectorate that same year, one of the Barolong gave a speech that included the following:

> The Chief and the people request that these farms be made proper farms, and owners granted title deeds. We however [also] wish them to remain inalienable and the rental be paid to the chief as today. We are, Your Honour, very much suspicious of what may happen. The Bechuanaland Protectorate may at some future time be incorporated to the Union of South Africa. From what we have learnt, the Union authorities would not recognise any certificates of occupation of these 41 farms.[94]

According to Ellenberger, the Secretary of State 'was non-committal'. 'As for the 41 farms they may rest assured that their rights will be protected by the King to the same extent and just as certainly as the rights of every other native in Bechuanaland are protected.' The following year, the next Resident Commissioner, Rowland Daniel, assured Lotlamoreng Montsioa that, as per the sentiment of the Secretary of State, the Barolong's right on the farms were secure.[95] A few weeks later, the registrar of deeds asked Lotlamoreng Montsioa for the names of the original occupiers and a record of any changes in the occupiers since the granting of the farms.[96]

The next Resident Commissioner was Charles Rey. He too took a stab at the problem, but his approach was simply to pronounce his view on the matter as law. After a meeting of the Native Advisory Council in 1931, where the council also discussed prospecting and mining in the Protectorate, the 'representative of the Barolong Tribe raised the point as to whether they should not more properly come under Part V of the Proclamation, i.e. Prospecting and Mining on Private Lands'.[97] They maintained that 'their farms were in the nature of private lands rather than Natives Reserves'. Rey's response left no room for discussion. 'The ownership of the land appears to be tribal and accordingly the so-called 'Barolong Farms' are and always have been regarded and treated as a Native Reserve.' The High Commissioner, H.J. Stanley, agreed that the Barolong Farms should not fall within the category of 'private lands'. He thought he would seek legal counsel as to whether the government could not insert a 'Clause 2' that the term 'native reserve' on Rey's proclamation also included the Barolong Farms.[98] That would be a quick fix. Matters for a while simmered there, but in the meantime, the Barolong chiefs, like the rest of the Council, were resisting

Rey's 'native administration' proclamations of 1932 as an extreme overreach of the Crown's powers and did not consider themselves to be bound by the two proclamations.

In April 1933, Lotlamoreng Montsioa asked for the 'registration of the Barolong Farms', but only three such farms, 'following the instruction and assurances of government letters' after the visit of the Secretary of State.[99] The Registrar of Deeds confirmed that he had noted the names on the Certificate as 'it must be distinctly understood that these certificates are not registrable [sic] by me.'[100] He filed copies for his records and noted the names on the certificates. The chief wrote back to him to ask, 'What Officer of the Bechuanaland Protectorate Government is entitled to have these Certificates registered not only for record purposes but for the proper object of registration at the deeds office?'[101] The reply was that the rights conferring the Certificate of Commission were 'permissive rights only' as otherwise, if the deeds had been 'registrable documents', then the occupants would have been required 'payment of stamp duties and registration fees', which applied to 'land owned by Europeans'.[102]

As Rey prepared for the promulgation of his two Proclamations, the Barolong wrote to 'advance the contention that the provisions generally … did not apply to the 41 Barolong Farms'.[103] They argued their position by supporting the objections that the 'principal Tribes of the Territory' had expressed against 'native administrative', which were that Rey's proclamations 'appear to conflict with native law and custom' and 'that they will be found unworkable'. Yet, they stressed that whilst they agreed with the other chiefs on that point, Barolong had a different contention, which was that their lands were their own, and not a Native Reserve. This is when Rey appended the following clause to the first proclamation: 'The definition of 'tribal areas' in each case shall be amended to include the Territory known as the Barolong Farms described in Schedule B, proclamation No 1 of 1896'.[104] As far as he was concerned, he had settled the matter, and expected it there to end, which it did not.

Lotlamoreng followed the prescriptions of Rey's proclamations after they became law in 1935, yet on the understanding that the Barolong Farms were not a 'Native Reserve'. Otherwise, the Barolong would have had to withdraw from the Council. When Rey was away, the Acting Resident Commissioner, R. Reilly explained that in order for Lotlamoreng to 'function as President of a Senior Tribunal' under the proclamations, he had to be a Chief over a tribal area as defined' in the proclamation.[105] The High Commissioner requested a report from the Dominion's office explaining the position of the

Barolong Farms based on the terms of the annexation of the Bechuanaland Protectorate.[106] The report made clear Britain's reluctance to rule the territory formally and its preference to leave subject populations alone, as far as possible, to manage their own affairs. Lord Milner had decided to create only as many reserves as there were sizeable populations of 'tribes'. He had counted five. Milner 'did not consider it necessary or expedient to formally create reserves' for the Bamalete or the Barolong, on the grounds that 'it was inadvisable to create too large a number of reserves or to attempt to give these Chiefs, who are of decidedly inferior importance ... the same status as will be accorded to the five'. In other words, it would be too much trouble. When the High Commissioner's Order-in-Council in 1909 described 'Crown Land', it had explicitly excluded 'the forty-one farms known as Barolong Farms held by members of the Barolong tribe by virtue of certificates of occupation issued by Chief Montsioa on the 28th March, 1895'.

As comparison, in 1909, the Bamongoato, the largest population within the borders of the territory had a population numbering 87,200 on an area of 39,000 square miles. The Barolong had 3,600 people on 450 square miles. The Bamalete had a population of 4,700 on an area of 178 square miles, while the Batlokoa's population was 3,600 on 56 square miles of land. Yet the same Order-in-Council established the Batlokoa and the Bamalete's lands as 'Native Reserves', which puzzled J.H. Thomas, who was probably the High Commissioner's legal counsel.

> The Barolong are represented like the other six tribes on the Native Advisory Council, and for all practical purposes, their territory appears to be regarded and treated as a Native Reserve. In the circumstances, it is not clear why their status has never been regularised by formally establishing their Reserve by Proclamation.[107]

The policy had no coherent logic. He also felt that 'the position of the Tribe on the Barolong Farms is a more serious matter'. There were thousands of people legally outside the jurisdiction of the colonial government, though they paid Hut Tax and the Native Fund Tax. 'The matter,' he admitted, 'is a complex one, and in view of the fact that a petition on the subject has been received by the Tribe, the time would appear opportune for attempting a solution.' He also noted that 'about 6000 Barolong ... live on the Union side of the Molopo River'. His point was that across the border in the Union, the very same Barolong lived on Crown Lands.

The High Commissioner prepared a draft proclamation that classified the Barolong Farms into a 'Native Reserve' but Rey, surprisingly, had reconsidered his view.[108] He welcomed the draft proclamation, but explained that after a discussion with Modiri Molema, he now reckoned the Barolong understood the legal premise that excluded them from the classification as a 'Native Reserve'. Although the draft proclamation 'would indeed simplify matters', he continued, 'native opinion among the Barolong is strongly averse to this course, and its adoption would undoubtedly give rise to difficulties with the tribe who prefer to regard themselves as 'owners of farms' rather than as members of native reserves.' He was not confident that a draft proclamation would stand in a court of law. In legal jargon, the colonial government would find that every intervention on the territory was *ultra vires*. 'The Barolong,' he stressed to the High Commissioner, 'are legally outside the two Proclamations and are fully alive to this fact.' The Barolong were prepared to yield to the classification of being a 'Native Reserve' only to the extent that his proclamations would have effect on their farms. In return, he would protect the classification of the Barolong Farms as autonomous territory, and not a reserve. Charles Rey and Modiri Molema had struck a deal and Rey left the matter of the Barolong Farms alone.

VII

On 31 May 1928, the Union of South Africa adopted its national flag after two years of wrangling about whether to exclude the Union Jack, as the Minister of the Interior, D.F Malan, was suggesting.[109] The outcome was a compromise. The Union Jack, together with the old flags of the Transvaal and the Orange Free State all appeared side by side upon the flag of Jan van Riebeeck – orange, white and blue. Prime Minister Barry Hertzog's own republicanism had mellowed considerably, and he jettisoned the ideology as he attended the Imperial Conference of 1926, which established the legislative independence of all dominions from Britain. In part, Hertzog's apparently softened political stance was due to the need not to alienate members of the Labour Party, with whom he had entered into a Pact government. Malan's faction of the Nationalist Party watched in dismay.

In an attempt to ramp up the anxieties of white voters in the 1929 election, Hertzog campaigned on the ticket of a 'black peril', a fear that blacks' demographic advantage would drown whites' interests unless the government did something to prevent '*gelykstelling*', meaning equality between black and white.[110] In 1930, the government legislated that all white women older than

21 years could vote and stand for election in South Africa. They did not have to meet a property or education qualification. The government was willing to offer the black population more land, including land available for purchase outside the reserves, but black peoples would have to surrender their franchise rights in the Cape. The Cape's black voters would have to appear on a separate voters' roll to elect seven white representatives in parliament.[111] Hertzog won the 1929 election, with soaring popularity amongst the white population.

The fuel for their loyalty was 'poor whiteism', which no political party in the 1920s and 1930s could afford to ignore. At the beginning of the 1920s, during the postwar depression, more than 20 per cent of active whites had no employment, but Hertzog's postwar legislation for this demographic was paying off – not least the colour bar in semi-skilled jobs. He won the election with a strong majority, enough not to rely on the Labour Party coalition to rule. He was confident that he had achieved an unbreakable unity between whites such that, even outside the republican cause, whites stood together 'in the spirit of a consolidated South African nation'.[112] At the Imperial Conference of 1930, the country secured its constitutional status in the Commonwealth as an equal partner. In the meantime, South Africa's economy had recovered. Its twin primary sectors of 'maize and gold' were strong and robust but in the 1930s the growth of industrial manufacturing outstripped both agriculture and mining. South Africa serviced its industrialisation by establishing an Electricity Supply Commission and the Iron and Steel Industrial Corporation to provide electricity and steel.[113]

Solomon Plaatje observed and commented upon these developments with dismay, although the passions of the writer and linguist, not politics, consumed much of his time. He wrote night and day. There were translations of Shakespeare, political commentaries, Sechuana proverbs, fiction and other writings. From 1925, he turned his mind more attentively to Sechuana orthography, objecting to the extensive changes in spelling that white linguists were putting in place without any consultation with native speakers of the vernacular.[114] Since 1927 Plaatje was also working as a 'Special Missioner' of the Independent Order of True Templars.[115] At a meeting of the Templars in 1931, there was a decision to launch a newspaper, *Our Heritage*, 'to keep us all in touch with each other' but more importantly to spread the Templars' message.[116] Nevertheless, from the very first issue, Plaatje used the paper not only to advocate for temperance, but also for the 'Coloured and Native people' to 'tell the world – and South Africa – just how they fare twenty-one years after Union and how they feel about it'.[117] The newspaper was in

English, Afrikaans and in the Sechuana orthography that he had set himself to improve and preserve. Yet, his desire that the Bechuana have a newspaper of their own had not abated. He could not see how the Bechuana could come together otherwise. They would remain a fragmented and diminished people. They had no knowledge of their own peculiar repertoires of esteem.

> If the Bechuana do not raise themselves, rouse themselves and strengthen themselves to do the work, they will not be able to nurture a newspaper on their own. Because publishing requires massive resources and reserves ... Is it not a disgrace, in this age of enlightenment, to observe how the Bechuana do not know one another? The Bakoena of Sechele do not know the Bakoena of Mma-Nochi and those of Mma-Egamano-a-khale do not know the Bakhatla of MmaMarapyane ... This is a response and a call to the *morafe* of Bechuana. Let us raise ourselves. Let us work together. Let us unite.[118]

Plaatje had begun to think of himself as 'South African', but with strong moral qualms about the term. As he said in an address in Kimberley in June 1931, he found that the fact of a 'South Africa', to which he had been vehemently opposed three decades before, had finally happened and he had no place in it.[119]

> We have learned to think materially in the larger. We have got accustomed to speaking of the Transvaalers, Free Staters, Natalians and Cape Colonists as 'South Africans'. All this is to the good. But does the welding together, in one people as this would imply stand the test of critical examination? I think not... If the Indians, for example, rightly protest at their rights being trampled on, at least they can look back to their own homeland. ... For them there is a way of escape. For the Coloured and Native People of this country – there at once the tragedy and there the cruelty and tenfold injustice – in their own country the elementary rights of citizenship are denied them ... they have nowhere to retreat.[120]

In Plaatje's experience, the 'Coloured and Native people' had exhausted every possible avenue to satisfy the requirements of their recognition as 'South Africans', but the settler government had refused repeatedly to recognise them. They had tried to prove, through their work and peaceful cooperation in the life of the country, that their own umbilical cord lay under the foundations of Unification in 1910, as a newborn's lies under the flooring of the homestead in Bechuanaland. Plaatje no longer desired a turning back of the clock to the former British dispensation before the war and Unification. His undertaking was not to rebuild the ruins of a city that had fallen. He had not anticipated this political dispensation, and had resisted it when it dawned, but for a *morafe* that otherwise had no placement, this South Africa had to be its destiny. The Bechuana therefore had to be 'arriving at a favourite dwelling, one preferred to all lands'.[121] South Africa could be 'the metropolis of all nations', of all the *merafe* of the land, if black peoples could rehabilitate this unplanned, unforeseen situation into 'a town of old'. They could come home to South Africa. 'So massive it was a task to found the new race', to become 'South Africans', that not just any convenient route towards this end would do.

Plaatje insisted that the means of struggling for personhood mattered. The struggle for black people to regain esteem in the world should not unwittingly defeat these very same ends. In the same 1931 Kimberley speech, Plaatje addressed what should happen when people of colour have 'looked and appealed to the Government in vain' and it refuses 'on the anniversary of its 21st birthday', to recognise them.[122] 'Shall we then fight the Government?' There was, he conceded, justifiable cause, but he was not convinced that the outcome would provide future generations of black people with the very home and hope that they sought. Instead, he worried about a total moral vacuum that would emerge in a war for racial equality where any means, including violence, justified the ends. 'We solemnly think the Government is not worth fighting, at least in the way that such challenge will conjure up'.

In taking up arms, black peoples would be dismantling the very moral repertoires that confirmed their esteem and reputation. They would be shrinking themselves to the inhuman size of their opponent. Further, the ensuing war would destroy the already diminished possibilities of adulthood that existed for them, leaving black people with no education, no means to provide for themselves, no capacity to set up independent homesteads. He feared therefore that 'acting red will only bring us the abyss'.[123] The solution was not forcing the state to surrender through violent revolution. It was rather to look beyond the government. He thought there were other centres of care, other institutions and people with resources and goodwill that would recognise and support black people's struggle for freedom.

> Let the enlightened Whites be appealed to. They can be appealed to beyond the seas even. Many helping hands from England and America will, I am sure, be extended to us. But something else we must do. Our Coloured and Native people – their children that is – cannot be forever

denied their right to live as full citizens of a civilised country. Educated they must be. To build their own houses and homes, to make their own furniture and clothing, to grow their own food and to produce the necessaries of a civilised life. Let us wait no longer on the doorsteps of politicians. Let us ourselves be up and doing...[124]

The British Empire had failed him, but Plaatje had not lost faith in internationalism or in the global 'Brotherhood' of goodwill and fair dealing between ordinary men and women, only he did not live long beyond this turn of mind to test this arena of cooperation. A few months later he died on 19 June 1932.

In the same year, the government did away with the qualification that barred many white men from the ballot. All adult whites could vote. Apart from their propertied, educated classes in the Cape – a thin stratum indeed – blacks could not participate in the custom that now marked white adulthood. Nevertheless, this was not enough to help Hertzog as the onset of the Great Depression and the collapse of the economy affected his popularity.[125] In February 1933, Hertzog accepted Jan Smuts' proposal to enter a coalition government. They established the United Party. It did not matter that one was once a staunch Republican and the other had always defended empire to the death. Those were two alternatives towards the same end of making Afrikaners a home at the tip of the continent, either as a Republic or as a secure element in a British dominion of white rule. There was ample room for negotiation. The political future of the Union was not cast in stone. D.F Malan formed his 'Purified' National Party, intent on establishing a primarily Afrikaner Republic. Moreover, the social status of whiteness remained ambiguous. Seventeen per cent of all whites lived in poverty and landlessness remained a dilemma for many of them.[126] The Representation of Natives Act No 12 of 1936 removed all black voters in the Cape from the common roll and placed them on a separate 'native voters roll'. The Natives Trust and Land Act No 18 of 1936 created a Native Trust to find additional land to increase the landmass available for the black occupation in the jurisdiction of 'native administration'. The legislation increased the available land for blacks' occupation to just 13 per cent of the country.

VIII

In Modiri Molema's opinion, Solomon Plaatje died of fatigue. 'He would grow weary of reprimanding, opposing, fighting, and advocating for the rights, liberation and advancement of his people.'[127] Modiri last saw him barely three days before his death. He was 'extremely ill' but in the doctor's opinion, he 'interrupted the recovery process' by walking about ten miles to the railway station to board a train to Johannesburg on a 'cold winter's day in June'. Plaatje had to go to the bank and attend meetings about publishing his books.[128] He collapsed on his way back to the railway station. He died in a city he loathed, Johannesburg, a few days later. The cause of his death and the weight that must have been on his mind until his last breath, left a strong impression on Modiri. He saw Plaatje's passing in his mid-fifties as an early and unnecessary death. His own sister, Harriet, had died in 1929, two years after their father, at only thirty-three years old.[129] These loved ones shared a common thread. They had exerted themselves and spent their lifeblood in the worthy project of making persons of their kin and neighbours, their spouses and children. He admired and reviled this sensibility, this determination to find extreme satisfaction in giving oneself up for others. He lauded it and blamed it all at the same time.

Indeed, the need for commitment like Plaatje's was never greater amongst the country's surplus people who only counted instrumentally as so much labour and liability in the stockbook of South Africa's economic and political enterprise. The black peoples needed a source and a founder, those 'civilising heroes' who would humanise them by removing the yoke from their cheeks. These are men – very seldom women – who later acquire a separate, legendary life as 'mythical beings' that brought others into the quintessentially human sphere of personhood.[130] Before such a hero, Emile Durkheim writes, 'there were no men, but only masses of formless flesh in which the different body parts and even the different individuals were not separated from one another. It is he who has sculptured this raw material and who drew properly human beings out of it'.[131] The 'civilizing hero' is immortalised by storytellers as a man on a difficult journey. He battles his way through many difficulties, but one way or another, destiny always intervenes and he arrives safely home. The 'civilising heroes' are those 'to whom mythology has ascribed a preeminent role in the history of the tribe and has therefore placed above others' as 'the father of men'.[132] These stories mediate struggles to establish placement and live in moreness with others.

Plaatje was an immensely talented storyteller and intellectual. He had the ear of thousands of black peoples who trusted his acumen and listened, or at least considered, his propositions about their 'origin' and the manner of life that was faithful to its reputation. He had the skills and personality to facilitate the conversations on moral life, which is why he wished eagerly for the Bechuana to have a newspaper. At the same time, he had capacity for the monastic discipline to lead the life of 'the father of men'. He also had access to the literary platforms to display himself as such a 'civilising hero', but he was not that way inclined. He did not wish to be credited with the revelation of the *morafe* despite his intricate political visions, his enormous energy and capacity to mobilise others. He did not consider that charismatic role to be his vocation. Instead, he pointed to other men, especially the Molemas, and their manner of life as the moral example to follow towards a life of reputation. He suggested some key ideas about government and political citizens that could preserve and strengthen the moral universes of personhood.

This is not, nevertheless, how Modiri Molema understood Plaatje's motivations and historical significance. Plaatje's life story was amongst a handful of biographies that he produced, some in Sechuana and others in English. He wrote two biographies of Barolong chiefs from the early nineteenth century under the titles *Chief Moroka* and *Montshiwa*. His last work was the life of the Old Testament prophet, Moses.[133] When he wrote about Plaatje, he described him as a Moses of his own time, 'a soldier, a valiant man'.[134] 'Of Plaatje,' he concluded, 'it must truly be said, "Greater love hath no man than this, that a man lay down his life for his friends".'[135] He gave Plaatje a role in history as a 'father of men', but even as he applauded this way of life, he also rejected it because serving the *morafe* was a life of hard exertion. It was Christ-like, an unending sacrifice.

> It might be said that he died of overwork and anxieties over his publishing and finances. He died just as he had lived – in the midst of worries over publishing his work and over lack of finances. And again, as one can say of many others, he died of overwork. Plaatje was born in October 1876 and died on 19 June 1932. He lived a life of fifty-five years, eight months and ten days.[136]

IX

Sebopioa Molema decided on convalescence at Signal Hill after his eye surgery in the spring of 1933, rather than to return to Mafikeng where Emang managed their full-time home. His doctor had counselled him to 'remain quiet for some time & keep away from wind and bright light'.[137] His country home suited his preference 'to keep away from much talk and wind'. 'Today,' he wrote to Emang, 'I am confined to the house and have never been out as the wind has been very strong.' He never really returned to Mafikeng, not to the routines of ordering the days that he was used to doing. He no longer had his paid employment as 'National Secretary' of the Barolong in the Molopo Reserve. There was not much to do in Mafikeng. Signal Hill provided an alternative strategy of living. There was land enough to work, a task he did not consider onerous at all. Seventh Day Adventism encouraged a return to the land, alongside abstaining as much as possible from meat. He was turning to the Adventist diet of mainly grain and fresh produce. He was farming, ploughing the soil and harvesting his crops. It was not the first time he worked the land himself, but during those younger years he had been supplementing his income, forced to work with his hands to survive. This time he was returning to the land piously, with gratitude and supplication, as an example of how others ought to live.

Money was nevertheless something he could scant neglect. He did not have any and he was desperate. He was feeling the pinch of unemployment. He started to collect debts – two bags of sorghum from a man whose cattle had damaged his fields and from the Mafeking Local Council for an allowance for the attendance of a meeting some weeks before.[138] In the meantime, it was very hard work to plough. 'Here our mother', he wrote to Mrs Gaisitsioe in Kanye, 'we are in the serious drought trouble', whilst at the same time, 'the whites have shot our cattle' to curb the spread of foot-and-mouth disease and 'we have no cattle that plough'.[139] However, though the rains were very late, when the clouds finally filled enough to burst, there was 'splendid rain', though for many it had come too late and 'the country still looks bare and without a blade of grass'.[140] He relayed to John Ratshosa in Francistown that 'there is much sickness and deaths at Mafikeng'. He was still better off than his friends who were in the Protectorate. He sent Ratshosa a bag of 'a very trusted strain of seed, which was not very tall and not very short just about 5 ½ foot'. He and Ratshosa were running an 'experiment' with trees.[141] He had long 'created a habit' of smoking Assegai Tobacco.[142] It may have helped as he was ploughing fields in the middle of summer, 'with great difficulty'.[143]

His son wanted to come home from school for Christmas, but under the circumstances, he could not grant that wish. 'One of the reasons why we cannot allow you to come home is because much money say about £4 will be given away to the Railways and you will have nothing with which to buy your clothes and possibly you would not be able to return to Durban for school as it is even hard to get money for school fees.'[144] Matlho would have to 'remain in Durban for your holidays for economic principle'. He would hear nothing of his son's request to change schools from Durban to Johannesburg – 'we regret very much the idea cannot be entertained by us' and had no sympathy with the problem that the young man was 'in bad terms' with the principal. He wanted him to pull up his socks. 'Your spelling is very bad. There is not a letter you write to me where you do not make careless mistakes.' Matlho was in Form II on a course that was preparing him for matriculation. His father wanted him to proceed to university.

The rains continued into the new year, but the damage of the drought and the cattle plague persisted. 'There is much death in Mafikeng.'[145] He was waiting on a very promising harvest. 'We are having plenty of rain & our crops are looking very promising, but locust is playing over the sky, we do not know if we will be save [sic] from damage as young locust is [sic] all over.'[146] In the meantime, he needed money desperately. 'Here we face the great drought of unemployment'.[147] In February of 1934, he started to plough new fields at Signal Hill although land shortages hemmed in his ambitions. There was 'plenty of rain' in the district, but many people could not plough because they had no seed.[148] He started to make inquiries about whether he could get his old job back at the Afrikander Mine as a timekeeper. If there was opportunity, he would need some time as 'my home little duties are still scattered'.[149] He considered himself skilled in 'mining work', as 'Timekeeper & Compound and Induna Management or as a clerk in the ordinary office or a typist'.[150] One firm had written to him with an offer for employment but it was 'far away near Lawrence Marques'. He thought he would take it up if nothing else materialised by the end of February, 'but it is against my will to go very far from my family'.[151] As it turned out, though he was desperate, he was not desperate enough to abandon the purpose he was cultivating at home. February ended and he stayed home. When he received a request to be part of the delegation to Cape Town to meet the High Commissioner about the two proclamations of 'native administration' in the Bechuanaland Protectorate he declined due to 'ill health'.[152]

Apart from the endeavour of working for himself on the land, he did not want to dissociate from the circle of Adventist faith that Emang had grown around their family. Modiri's wife, Anna, and later her two sisters, Hellen and Ella Moshoela, had also left the Methodist Church to become Adventists, despite their father being a Wesleyan reverend. In April 1934, Emang and Anna travelled together to a Seventh Day Adventist Conference in Johannesburg where they would remain for at least a week.[153] Hellen Moshoela would marry Modiri's brother, Sefetogi. Sebopioa helped the women make their travel arrangements and remained behind to watch whether the locust would fall on the crop. He had decided not to use poison, 'against which the whites object for killing the cattle, and they say the sorghum also dies from it'.¹⁵⁴ He observed the 'sorghum is still birthing, some have swollen bellies, we do not yet know whether it is food, but if only God would make it food before the locust sinks its teeth ...'. The locust did come. It forced many people to cut and harvest their grain before it was yet ripe. His crop remained untouched, 'God has protected us', although half of Emang's field had been damaged on one end 'but yet we remain trusting'.¹⁵⁵ He yielded a bumper harvest, 'plenty corn and mealies in our fields', but the market was poor and he could not make money.¹⁵⁶

In the meantime, his son could no longer bear remaining at boarding school during every school holiday. There was just enough money to cover his fees, and no more than that. His son had not come home for the winter holidays, with instructions, 'when you are there try to get some work'.¹⁵⁷ When school reopened, he had nothing to send his son:

> Dear Matlho we have not forgotten you and it is impossible for us to do so, as you are the only boy of our home. It is only through hardship that we have not sent you sufficient money in order that you may purchase your requirements, as at this late stage some or all of them (clothing) must be worn out. However, rest assured that your welfare is in our hearts day and night.¹⁵⁸

His reliance on the land for life was almost complete, with no opportunity of earning beyond what he could fetch with his produce. Yet, though he wanted work, he did not want to uproot himself and leave home, at least not for the forms of employment he had previously readily accepted. He did not want to leave Emang at the point of their deepening intimacy as they explored their new faith together. Still, he looked for work earnestly but close to home. In October of 1934, he wrote to the Civil and Native Commissioner as well as to the Magistrate's Court in Mafeking 'to apply for situation as an interpreter in your court should there be a vacancy'.¹⁵⁹

> Your servant and applicant herein is a sober and capable man to serve the Government faithfully should he be employed ... as regard the Sechuana language I challenge anyone who can do better that your servant. I am acquainted with office work and have the knowledge of legal phraseology.¹⁶⁰

There was a very promising response from the office of the Native Commissioner, even a meeting, but nothing came of it.¹⁶¹ He ended 1934 with a good harvest at Signal Hill.¹⁶² He may have started to sell Assegai Tobacco calendars. He wrote to the company to ask for a batch in the New Year. 'This year's calendars are beautiful and have useful information in business and private life.'¹⁶³ There was, he explained, 'a great demand here' in Mafikeng. 'Moon Phases and Postal Information are indeed very helpful and the beautiful & artistic work above the calendar is indeed a unique advertisement by itself, as well as serving as decoration in our homes.' At last, something emerged that he had a long time ago desired but could never make happen, which was to teach boys to play the trumpet. In March, St Mary's Mission in Mafeking offered him a position as 'Bandmaster'.¹⁶⁴ He would 'teach and supervise the boys' twice a week for one hour for ten shillings a week. The work, when it started, was not permanent, only for less than two months, but he could make something of it. A year later, Sentinel Publishing Company requested him to revise a Sechuana translation of a baptismal booklet. This is how the journey began towards his translation of some Adventist literature into Sechuana, including the *Quarterly Lesson*, some of the hymns in *Kreste mo Kopelong*, and the all-important *God's Answers to Man's Questions*.¹⁶⁵

The constraints of money tightened but his hours were full, all on his terms, every hour made meaningful by how he chose it in freedom. In Cape Town, James Molebaloa had finally become an ordained minister in the Bantu Methodist Church of South Africa in 1935 after many failed attempts to secure such a position in the Methodist Church. Molebaloa had written to him many times, offering to open the salaried doors of ordination for him, but he declined.¹⁶⁶ 'Your writing to me so often (though I never answered) show very plainly that you love me, but you can be assured that I think very dearly of you though often silent.' He wrote to Molebaloa that the Bantu Methodist Church could employ him for secretarial work if they so wished to do. He had cast his net on the side of his new faith and it was straining, full.

> At present I do not belong to any church. But do not be surprised if you hear from me later that I have joined my wife as their faith seems to be founded on Truth as we read it from the scriptures. ... At any event as you seem to be taken up with the Bantu Methodist Movement, I would say you are old enough & sensible enough to make your own choice but whatever you do, do it for the salvation of our own soul, and not of being a Black Man's Movement. ... We must be born again & seek peace with God.¹⁶⁷

X

The Native Advisory Council convened for five days in 1940.[168] The anthropologist, Isaac Schapera, attended the second day of its sitting when his *Handbook of Tswana Law and Custom* was under discussion. Schapera was using the new vernacular orthography. He had carried out his ethnography amongst the Bakhatla at Mochudi. The *Handbook* raised tempers and divided opinions. Some of the animosity from previous tensions amongst chiefs resurfaced and there were some sharp exchanges of words. Modiri Molema's interests often diverted from those of his peers, but never so sharply as during this meeting. At the same time, new intimacies had forged between Tshekedi Khama and the Molemas. After his divorce in 1938, Tshekedi had married Ella Moshoela, the youngest daughter of Reverend Joshua Moshoela, which meant he and Modiri and Modiri's brother, Sefetogi, had married sisters. The three sisters and Sebopioa's wife, Emang, had become inseparable as family and as pious Adventist evangelists. None of this placated Tshekedi's opposition to Modiri's views in this meeting, but the two of them were family, with ties that went beyond the meeting. Things between the two of them could mend. On the other hand, the damage to other relationships in the Council would prove extensive and irreparable. The meeting had proved what the paramount chiefs in the Council had suspected all along, that Modiri Molema cared nothing for chieftaincy, had little regard for chiefs and, despite his chiefly origins, did not wish to be one of them.

The issue at hand was property and customary tenure. The Resident Commissioner, Charles Arden-Clarke, had distributed Schapera's *Handbook* among the delegates beforehand but not, he emphasised, as 'a codification of the laws and customs of the Bechuana'.[169] Rather, he saw it as 'a record of considerable scientific value of the laws and customs obtaining in certain areas of the Protectorate' and as a 'useful guide to administrative and other officers of the Government and to the Native Administrations themselves'. He appreciated that 'your laws and customs are live things' and hence 'subject to change', which meant the *Handbook* was not a finished compilation, although he hoped chiefs would update the volume over the years. Tshekedi appreciated 'the amount of work that has been put into this' yet 'maintained that a study of the Bakhatla could not stand for the 'law' amongst all the 'tribes', and that the opinions of the informers should not imply the standpoint of the 'nations'. The book could stand as no more than a 'guide', which is why he wished to 'cooperate with him [Schapera] in his undertaking'. Bathoen also suggested that Schapera revise the book with fresh input from chiefs.

Speaking after Tshekedi and Bathoen, the two critical and educated young firebrands, Modiri Molema said Schapera had written a 'wonderful book', a 'monument to his name', with mistakes only 'here and there'. He said the details of the *Handbook* would 'reflect our law' with some input from chiefs rather than the extensive revisions with specific attention to 'tribal' peculiarity that Tshekedi and Bathoen, with the overall support of other chiefs, had in mind. Modiri said he was happy precisely with Schapera's effort towards a method of standardisation that made all the 'tribes' uniform as the 'Batswana' – in Schapera's orthography. In his mind, there was only one fundamental error that Schapera had to correct. He said Schapera's error was his interpretation of land tenure. 'Your Honour, I am not a Mokhatla but I have the temerity to challenge the statement here in the note that in the Bakhatla tribe any man may be turned off his land.' 'If that is so,' he continued, 'then the Bakhatla are not Bechuana.'[170]

Schapera began his reply with a reading of this portion of the *Handbook*. 'The Chief may on occasion deprive people even of land they are actually using.' This may happen when these lands are required for 'tribal purposes' such as making boreholes. 'The man thus dispossessed is always given new land elsewhere, but even though he is thus compensated it is obvious that he has no security of tenure.' This lack of security of tenure, according to Schapera, 'more than anything else has militated against improvement of the land such as fencing and attempts at irrigation'. This is the reason why Arden-Clarke was especially interested in the *Handbook*. He wished the Council to consider whether 'the present system of land tenure is entirely satisfactory', and whether the new irrigation schemes that chiefs were putting in place through the Native Fund were interfering with customary tenure. Were people losing homes and fields to make space for the new infrastructure, for example? The chiefs' general response was that the *Handbook* did not hold the answer as there was no standard practice of land tenure common to all 'tribes' of the Protectorate. The paramount chiefs would not accept the idea that there existed a 'Setswana' – again Schapera's orthography – that applied across all polities. Each wished to speak about customary law in his own unique *morafe* as it applied to the land in their reserve, but Modiri Molema argued that security of tenure was in fact 'Setswana' and applied to all 'Batswana' such that even under the most extenuating circumstances 'it is not right that a man should be turned off his land'.

It is not right to say that a chief can turn a man off his land. He cannot expropriate a tribesman's land unless such expropriation is done for the public good, or in cooperation with the owner in the same way as Divisional Councils inspect a field and speak to the owner with a view to arriving at suitable compensation. I think we can be quite clear that the Sechuana law does not contain such an anomaly. It is also quoted here [in the *Handbook*]: 'It is obvious that such man has no security of tenure.' That also is not right. A man who has had land granted to him by the chief has full title to that land, and, generally speaking, that land remains his and his heirs. In fact he has as much security of tenure as if he had bought that land.[171]

His contention was that without such security of tenure, the Bechuana would be an oddity in the universal pattern of landholding anywhere in the world. Schapera, he continued, had made the error of confusing the customs of 'security of tenure' with those of the 'system of tenure', which was quite a different matter. It was the latter, he argued, the 'system of tenure', which stunted improvement on the land and gave ample credence to Arden-Clarke's observation that Bechuana display a 'backwardness' in their agrarian practice. Modiri Molema explained that despite certain and indisputable security of tenure, the system of tenure prevented landholders from implementing rational and 'progressive' methods of farming. These rational practices included fencing and taking independent decisions about when best to plough and sow seed. His explanation was that *Sechuana* carried an ambiguity with regard to landholding, which was that it guaranteed security of tenure, yet retained a system that did not allow landholders freedom to make decisions about property that unambiguously belonged to each one securely and irrevocably.

He was describing the tensions indeed embedded in the practice of placement, in how property was both private and yet communal. This is how the land guaranteed exclusive ownership yet depended on affiliation and obligations to a rung of patriarchal authority, how it belonged entirely and exclusively to the occupant and yet the occupant had no individual powers outside of the rungs of that authority to do with it as he wished. Placement allowed one to establish an autonomous home of one's own, and yet making a home had to do with assembling and incorporating other people. This is why property stood without enclosure.

The hindrances and interferences with progress are due to the system of tenure. I think under essential Bechuana law there should be no

> permanent fence anywhere on the land. For instance, a man may not fence his ploughed lands except during the time of ploughing. Now this restriction naturally militates more than anything else against permanent improvements of lands. You heard this morning or yesterday that we could have done better during the last season if we had taken up progressive ideas on agriculture. What are those ideas? They are contained in turning the soil over in winter, turning it over again and conserving the moisture in the ploughed land. How can you do that if you have no fenced land? The cattle come and trample in your fields. I think that is really the essential drawback. How can you plant trees in land which is not fenced? The cattle of your neighbours will come and make things difficult for you, and under Bechuana law you cannot sue because the land belongs to the tribe and to the Chief, and you cannot expropriate some of it by putting a fence round it.[172]

His feelings on the matter were strong and he had come prepared. He did not hold back when Arden-Clarke, careful not to alarm chiefs with fears of a further attenuation of their powers, interjected to 'correct' him: 'I said the Government has no intention of passing a proclamation.' Modiri pushed even further, asserting the moral need for a legislative curtailment of chiefly powers that would make landholding entirely independent of chiefly authority. He added that such legislative intervention of the colonial government to limit chiefs' powers was actually the good of Rey's proclamations. He said he was glad that Rey's tribunals attenuated chiefs' independent authority.

> I would remind Your Honour and Council of our very strenuous opposition to the Native Administration Proclamation and the Tribunals Proclamation. We were very opposed to them but now we realise, for instance in the Tribunals Proclamation, that there is a lot of gold there and you see quite often it seems that progress has to be almost imposed.[173]

He did not stop there. He made an argument in favour of individual titling, which he wished the colonial government to consider seriously and facilitate, even while he explicitly acknowledged that private titling threatened the longevity of chieftaincy. In his view, the Land Commission under Sidney Shippard had missed the opportunity to resolve the contradictions of placement. Instead, in its attempt to provide partial private title in order to retain a partial form of chieftaincy, the Commission had created the unsatisfactory 'middle way' that was the Barolong Farms. If the Commission had resolved the contradiction, then at least in his view, private titles would

Morafe

have been protected by the colonial government and not the chief. Each landowner would then do with his or her land as he or she wished to do. The 'security of tenure' in *Sechuana* would have continued without the irrational 'system of tenure'. Instead, the Commission had made preserving chieftaincy a priority.

> To be helpful I was going to quote what happened here in 1886. The Land Court of Land Arbitration Board under Sir Sidney Shippard also found that the Barolong and Bechuana system of land tenure was a great hindrance to progress. They suggested that the plots allocated to certain tribesmen should be recognised as individual titles so that these men could fence and improve their holdings, but they had no sooner said so than they realised that the power of the Chief rested on the land. The minute you give individual titles to tribesmen the Chief has no more hold upon them.[174]

He was sparring, one man against a floor of chiefs. He welcomed Schapera's handbook precisely because it muted 'tribal' difference. It extrapolated sameness from the particular 'Bakhatla' to the unifying plural solidarity, the 'Bechuana', as a fact of unadulterated scientific inquiry. He thought that even the grievous error of interpretation around landholding that he believed the anthropologist had committed – the confusion between the 'security of tenure' and the 'system of tenure', had the benefit of confronting the elephant in the room, which was the tyrannical intrusions of chiefly and patriarchal power on individual freedoms. The *Handbook* appeared to him to have the force of remarkable timing, as though conceived for just such a time as this. He said as much, that 'when we consider the insight and the power of interpretation which are evident in this book I say it is a miracle'.[175]

Tshekedi and Bathoen were outraged to put it mildly. Their reply took up the rest of the meeting, missiles of objection against *Sekhoa* as those tendencies that favoured the interests of the individual at the expense of repertories of practice that amplified everyone to the status of personhood. Title deeds, in their view, lay outside the possibilities of placement, morally speaking, because they dismembered the *morafe*. In practical terms, in dissociating property from the judicial and social nodes of family and the Kgotla, individual titling chipped away at the land and shrunk the territory available to incorporate people onto the land. Tshekedi explained there were circumstances that allowed chiefs to remove people from the land, which were subject to the customs of each 'tribe', although he agreed a man could not be removed willy-nilly from lands he had already cultivated. 'I know that instance can be quoted where it has been necessary for such removals to be made. The question of the removal of a man from a property which he occupies is as carefully undertaken by the Chief and tribe as by the Government'. Just like the government, chiefs could compensate such an individual for his investment on the land. 'My opposition to any change in the system is not due to the fact that I fear any change in the Chief's powers, but I fear that the Natives will lose their lands'. 'What Dr Molema referred to', Tshekedi added, 'was title deeds', which would be issued by the government and not the chiefs.

> ... my fear is not that the Chief will lose power over his people, but that Africans will lose their country. If everyone, wherever he settles, were given the title deed of the land, that would mean that that piece of land is taken out of the tribal control and is called "that man's". If that man is in debt for money or goods his creditors come along and take that land because it belongs to him. At present, no such thing can happen.[176]

The meeting adjourned, but the discussion continued the following day without any further input from Modiri Molema. Chiefs debated the question of fencing, of whether or not chiefs could remove a landholder and reallocate his placement elsewhere, and the implications of new technologies for sourcing water on tenure, but all this was within the solid consensus that private title was not and had never been *Sechuana*. Chiefs had turned the NAC into an assembly of contestation about *Sekhoa* and *Sechuana* and, certainly as far as the question of land was concerned, had strengthened the institutions of chieftaincy and patriarchal power. The deliberations ended with a suggestion that Schapera investigate the practices of tenure at various 'tribal' centres. In such an undertaking, chiefs would be his hosts, his informers and his research assistants.

XI

In the Union of South Africa, tensions within the Fusion government culminated in September 1939 as war in Europe appeared imminent. The question of whether the dominion should enter a war saw Hertzog and Smuts take opposing positions. Hertzog's motion that South Africa should declare its neutrality won sixty-seven votes while eighty votes were cast for Smuts' motion that South Africa break diplomatic ties with Germany.[177] The Governor-General denied Hertzog's request to dissolve Parliament and call for an election. Hertzog resigned, and Smuts again became the Union's prime minister. The union between English-speakers and the steadily crystallising society of Afrikaners had always been fragile and reliant on the compromises of the political elite. When that centre failed to hold, the divisions on the ground heightened, even precipitating new radical formations among Afrikaners. Nevertheless, the majority of the men who had volunteered for service once war was declared were Afrikaners motivated as much by the principle to defend democracy as by their poverty and unemployment.[178] The Afrikaners were themselves a house divided. In early 1940, Hertzog and Malan found each other again and formed the Reunited National Party, with Hertzog at the helm, but before the year ended, their reunion had completely collapsed because Hertzog did not approve of a discriminatory constitution that did not place English-speakers on the same footing as their Afrikaner counterparts.[179] By this time, South Africa had been drawn into the war, not least by the Cape's geographical location as an alternative sailing route away from European waters for warships and a place to moor ocean liners for repairs.

In the meantime, all kinds of people were making Johannesburg a habitable city where they could establish families and live permanently, although the government, especially through the pass laws, was making the city as inaccessible to black people as possible unless they were coming temporarily to work. In addition to the commercial sector, warehouses and shopping districts, there were also new residential areas. The large Western Native Township was already home to thousands by 1930, but there were also many slums. The war accelerated industrial manufacture in a rapidly diversifying economy and the demand for black labour grew dramatically. The government battled not only to regulate the influx of people into the city, but also to provide adequate services, especially housing, even for those who had permission to remain in the city. The crisis of housing, alongside conditions of work and sanitation, were fertile ground for a growing movement of civic organisations, who aired their concerns through protest action, like the squatter movements of the 1940s, and through their representatives on the Advisory Boards that the government had established in the 1930s.

The Johannesburg of the early 1940s was the city that received educated men and women from the countryside. Their intention was to make it home, whether out of choice as was the case with the young Nelson Mandela, or out of the misfortune of loss and displacement as happened to Ellen Kuzwayo, whose grandfather was one of the landed Thaba Nchu notables.[180] Johannesburg was becoming the desired home of black professional classes, more so the young men who were graduates of or wished to proceed to Fort Hare University, then the South African Native College. Other attractions too had long pulled Barolong chiefs, like John Montsioa, from the countryside into the city, like leisure, things to buy, company, time away from the suffocating dictates of moral life in the reserves and the allure of urban modernity. Large numbers of women also flocked into the city. Aspiration and destitution, desire and opportunity, brought blacks from all walks of life and places of origin to Johannesburg, and situated them together in locations and shantytowns that the government was finding difficult to map and segregate according to skin colouring. Living spaces were not strictly segregated. Not yet. Households who had more occupational status or financial affluence lacked the physical mobility to hive off into enclaves of their own. Washerwomen, teachers, nurses, liquor brewers, labourers, clerks and writers lived cheek by jowl.

Especially as the war continued, the Johannesburg of the 1940s still held the promise of change. The international discourse during the war promised a postwar dispensation that unshackled people from forms of government that did not have their consent. Life was not easy, but the atmosphere was of hope and possibility. Black politics absorbed these international currents, especially given the involvement of black people in the war effort, while at the same time conditions of work and labour were encouraging trade unionism. The Congress of Non-European Trade Unions had more than 150,000 members in 1945 belonging to over 100 affiliated unions, despite the fact that the government did not recognise black union membership.[181] Johannesburg had been the city where the first black lawyers had coalesced after their training overseas. The distant cousins, best friends and medical doctors James Moroka and Modiri Molema were also establishing and growing adjunct practices in Johannesburg, although their main location of operation remained the countryside.

In 1940, another medical doctor, Dr Alfred Xuma, who had trained in Europe and in the United States of America became the president of the African National Congress. The general assessment of historians is that he resuscitated Congress from a moribund state and was a strong institutional builder.[182] He had increased the membership of Congress to over four thousand by 1945. The Congress had also afforded women full right of membership and had abolished the House of Chiefs. Modiri Molema attended a Congress meeting in 1942 after decades of absence. 'For over two years', he wrote, 'the

African National Congress – its name and content – has been echoing and re-echoing somewhere in the recesses of my grey matter' until such a point that 'these echoes became so persistent and clamant' that he attended the meeting in Bloemfontein on 20 December 1942.[183] He cherished the memories of the meeting of Congress he had attended in Kimberley just before travelling to Scotland in 1914. Even in those early days, he embraced Congress, but not as a united platform to strengthen plural regionalist political geographies of language and chieftaincy. His thinking had been growing where the 'Event' of love had opened the procedure of truth.[184]

In his private life, Modiri had departed even further from the world of the fathers. After Anna Moshoela died in 1937, he had married Lucretia Hommel, a nurse and in the classification of the time a 'Coloured', not quite 'black' and yet not 'white'. He spent his time and money on travel. He once made a pilgrimage to Jerusalem.[185] He possessed the currencies the fathers had lacked – time, leisure and money. His son and daughter, Lesedi and Warada, sat on his lap in his study whilst he worked on his typewriter. He sang in the choir. He replenished his family's breakfast table – chicory, jam, golden syrup. He owned his own clinic and nursing home. He had built an imposing house, Mochosa Estate, on his placement in the reserve. The young lawyer and Congressman, Nelson Mandela, would spend long hours with him here in the early 1950s, 'in the stately and peaceful residence, with all the wild and rugged beauty that surrounds it, an ideal retreat at the end of a busy and strenuous day'.[186] He had strayed from the fathers' ideas, but also from their exhaustion and penury.

What he aimed to possess of the past was the pre-eminence, reputation and confidence of the fathers, not their regionalist agenda. There was little hope for the future of black peoples without these bold attributes of the fathers. This is why his recollection of the Congress meeting of 1914 mattered so deeply to him. That meeting had been very successful, highly anticipated and very well attended. Even the government understood Congress as a very significant platform of action and mobilisation. He had come home from Glasgow to find that Congress had not moved significantly from that understanding of its mission. He had this memory of the 1914 Congress when he finally attended the meeting of 1942. He would also keep returning to these recollections alone at his writing desk for many years to come. He also hoped that Congress had by this time diverged from its early-twentieth-century consensus on political identity. Xuma, like him, had trained abroad and he hoped would be open to the international currents of political thought and ideas precipitated by the war.

Thus, on 20 December 1942, Modiri Molema arrived at the Community Hall a few minutes before 10 in the morning, which was the time the session was due to begin, but to his 'dismay, there was not a soul about; and the Hall was closed, and there was nothing to indicate that some great and exciting event was about to take place'.[187] 'He had seen the agenda beforehand and looked forward to hearing the Mayor's opening address.

> At 10.30, I smoused [sic] about the Hall again. All was still quite. I felt uneasy. Perhaps, after all, the meeting had been a week before, or was postponed for a week later. Or perhaps I was late, and the Congress might be in session, the Hall crowded and the audience entranced by some bewitching operation and I would get no seat and only disturb the proceeding by opening the door and looking for a standing room. Very carefully and quietly, I opened the door. Not a soul. I could almost have laughed at my own chagrin. One more uneasy walk around, and at 11 a.m., fully an hour after the supposed opening, I returned to the Hall.[188]

This time he found a handful of delegates, including Xuma, outside the hall, 'a poor representation for the expected audience of a thousand souls.' They welcomed him warmly 'as a long-lost brother' but the mood was tense.

> Each one seemed determined to hide his fears, and the disappointment written large on his face, at the way things were shaping. Why, the Hall should have been crowded, its approaches swarming with people, and the Mayor should have opened the Congress at 10.a.m, and now it was 11.15.[189]

A few more people did arrive, and at 11.30am Modiri suggested that they begin. The president 'always courteous and open to advice' agreed. The commencement of the session did not ease his apprehension, as 'all eyes kept turning to the entrances'. Everyone was 'on the tip-toe of expectancy'. The Mayor had not arrived to offer 'a usual courtesy that had crystallised into custom'. About seventy people attended, 'dotted haphazardly in a hall holding about 150', a much smaller figure than the 700 to 1000 that he expected. 'I felt there was something wrong, and fixed my eyes on the floor for the most part.' Xuma spoke and 'contrary to his democratic ideas' singled out 'a few so-called "notabilities"' whom he introduced. There were 'a professor, an MP [Member of Parliament] (really an M.R.C.) [Member of Representative Council], and two medicos all from the Cape Province; an Arts graduate, and two medicos from the Free State; a solicitor and an arts graduate from the

Transvaal' despite the fact that they 'seemed to differ in no way externally, from their fellows'. It was only after the provincial secretaries, treasurers and other committees read their reports, 'all somewhat incomplete, jumbled and disordered' that 'my eyes were opened' to the state of affairs.

> The average membership of the Congress in the four provinces of the Union was revealed to be about 253, and the finances were of course, correspondingly low. I could hardly believe my ears and the evidence of my eyes. Then I realised that what had happened to me all these years had happened also to other Africans. The Congress had gradually lost its glamour for about a score of years, and Africans at large had lost faith and interest in it. We been unmindful of our political interests, and so one discriminating and insulting law after another had found its way into the Statute Book without any united African opposition and agitation. We had been fast asleep, and as a corporate organism, we were half-dead.[190]

His impression was that Congress was drowning in organisational dysfunction. He left the meeting in 1942 with a very strong feeling of disappointment. The meeting was nothing like that of the Congress of his youth. In fact, he thought it had turned out to be a deplorable spectacle. His thoughts, as he wrote upon his return from Bloemfontein, went back to the 1914 meeting of Congress he had attended in Kimberley, 'when all the giants of our race were present'. Some of these he named, including Solomon Plaatje, his uncle Joshua Molema, and men whom he had come to know and admire, Walter Rubusana, Pixley Seme and Plaatje's brother-in-law, Isaiah Bud-Mbelle. There were assembled 'Chiefs, commoners, professional men and businessmen from all over the Union and from High Commission Territories'. More than that, a meeting of Congress was not an occasion Union officials and other whites of influence could afford to miss. In his memory, that was a time

> when Edward Dower, the Secretary for Native Affairs – so-called – felt it incumbent upon him to attend as the ear of the Government, to keep the flame of indignation burning low; when the Mayor of Kimberley – Sir E. Oppenheimer – felt it a privilege to address the Congress; when millionaire companies like De Beers entertained the Congress session; when the City Hall of Kimberley was thrown open to welcome and entertain the delegates to Congress; when every African felt it an imperious duty to be represented, and a personal loss to be unable to attend the Congress session; when branches sprouted and blossomed

everywhere in the land, when money flowed fast into the coffers of the Congress; when the grinding provisions of the Natives Land Act were upon us; when Deputations, costing thousands of pounds were elected and sent to England; When, when, when. It is an epic and a pageant.[191]

He thought it an undisputed fact that 'there has been a decline', and that the 'child' the founders had birthed had become 'listless and emaciated, anaemic and ailing'. Yet, he also understood the consoling attractions of nostalgia, and had the reckoning that 'the past is always glorious, and we are too apt to exalt it and hanker after it'. Nevertheless, he held on to the memories of 1914. They encouraged and inspired him. He would use them to give himself direction, to find some way to resuscitate Congress to its past glory. Also, he was doing something else with those thoughts. From 1942, upon returning from a Congress meeting, he would recall those memories to reach across the old breach and reconcile with his father. In writing about the embarrassing state of the present Congress, he brought to mind and applauded the grace and stature of the fathers. The Congress he longed to return to was the one they had made. He was on a journey returning to the fathers, to Silas Molema and Solomon Plaatje. He was going home. Nevertheless, there were elements to congratulate in the present Congress, not least the 'crowning excellence of the President'. He was pleased with the presidential address, 'a masterpiece of thought and composition':

> ... a cool and masterly review, a penetrating and dispassionate analysis of Afro-European affairs, delivered with an appropriate air of scientific detachment and un-emotional, no futile repetitions, no woolly, amorphous, pointless ideas, no more grandiloquence; no spinning, stringing together and slinging of polysyllables; no shouting, no fist shaking and finger drilling; no undue elevation of the voice; just a quiet, sober statement of observations and their deductions and conclusions.[192]

In Xuma, he thought Congress had the kind of leadership he trusted, which meant there was hope. He thought the missing element was the Congress' knowledge of its historic mission, a revelation of its own truth, to which it needed a 'reawakening.' There was also a need to grow the numbers of Congress and make clear that it stood as a microcosm of 'Africa'. For him, the international discourse of the time relayed more clearly the method of birthing this 'Africanism'. Significantly, it also gave the struggle for this moral universe a name, 'nationalism'. He identified with the name as though it was a thing of old, but years before the term had come along, before it stood for a certain arrangement of political power and territory, he had been waiting and desiring to serve as midwife to its moral solidarity for over twenty-five years. He had been living in, arguing for, and determined to model that *morafe* throughout his adult life.

By January 1943, he had also taken inspiration from India's Mahatma Gandhi towards forms of nonviolent protest and civil disobedience.[193]

> There is prodigious strength in the African National Congress. Stupendous forces, which we little dream of, lie in it. It is like Africa herself, so prosaic, and outwardly unattractive at first sight, but rich beyond the dreams of avarice and only awaiting exploitation. The African National Congress is a giant, dormant, asleep. He only needs to stretch his limbs, put out his hand, and take of the luscious fruit, which hangs over ripe and only awaits picking ... We have leaders ... and we Africans must come in our thousands to help rebuild our house, which must not be a mere hovel but an edifice, bigger, stronger and statelier even than the original plan, and worthy of the new Africa that we are. ... What we want then, of each man is extensive recruiting with some self-denial, indefatigable advertising and some sacrifice, all our effort to build up the Congress for Africans ... In short we want Propaganda without and Proper-Gandhi within.[194]

In 1943, Jan Smuts' United Party won the general election. His international role in the war, the rise in employment opportunities and the allies' improving fortunes had turned the electorate in his favour. Smuts' role in the war kept him away from home for weeks, sometimes months at a time, just as the black political scene was becoming more active. The social and political turbulence in the growing cities gave the white electorate and political elite great reason for disquiet, even panic. There were strikes and boycotts in the Witwatersrand. In 1943, people in Alexandra Township responded to an increase in bus fare by commuting on foot, setting off the first in a series of bus boycotts in the 1940s.[195] The number of informal settlements grew, as did squatters' movements fighting for rights to land in the city. Johannesburg was a city in turmoil, but Congress had little involvement in these political activities. Smuts refused to meet with Xuma and feared little political consequence.

In the meantime, Anton Lembede became the first president of the African National Congress Youth League in April 1944. Lembede had arrived in Johannesburg as a young lawyer serving his articles in Seme's law firm. His

'Africanism', which also derived from Garveyism in the 1920s, shaped the manifesto of the Youth League.[196] The manifesto described South Africa's dilemma as a racial war between a white oppressor who prizes a philosophy of individualism and personal gain and a black oppressed who had essentially different values of communalism, but no longer had power nor land to establish those mores. The manifesto also lambasted white trusteeship, urging blacks to look to themselves for their own liberation, which it said would not emerge from the polite constitutional means the Congress was still espousing, but rather from a popular and confrontational militancy.

In the meantime, Modiri Molema was growing more frustrated. It discouraged him that the happenings of 1942 at Congress were not an isolated event. Year after year, he confronted the same scenario. 'You think you must be late, and mistaken about the venue and the date', and then only 'see a likely delegate strolling leisurely towards the hall, then another two or three or four', he was still observing five years later.[197] The funds were not improving. The financial statements were not satisfactory, 'and you feel they could have been better tabulated and better conserved'. The annual review provided little information of how officials had spent money and there was no projection of future expenditure, and 'when you hear whispers and murmurs of unauthorised blank cheques and payment of organisers who only organise themselves and never report, of self-payment of officers, and above all that no accredited accountant passes your accounts, your faith is shaken'.

During the meetings, people drifted in and out, 'some jumping up some jumping down the platform, others entering the side doors'. There was little sense of protocol. 'And you find that you – a nobody – can also sit on the platform unhindered'. The Mayor usually arrived, though this was 'never a certainty' and not 'properly arranged for', and after his departure, what would come next in the presidential address would be, 'a survey of the white man's whips and stings, and the black man's burdens, tears, fears, and sighs, and finally a call to rise again from the dust'. That was, for the most part, all he felt there was to every Congress meeting from 1942. 'Here really the Congress seems to begin and end'. After that, 'very often chaos begins to reign and precious hours are squandered amidst pandemonium and turmoil of surging and seething humanity. The Congress was 'impotent and infantile', a 'failing light on a fading star'.

In the meantime, Jan Smuts was working on the Charter of the United Nations in September 1944. The preamble declared 'faith in fundamental human rights', in the 'better standards of life in larger freedom' and 'international peace and security'.[198] It was adopted in June 1945. At the first meeting of the United Nations General Assembly in London in 1946, India's representatives argued that the treatment of the Indian population in South Africa violated their human rights under the Charter. Smuts' argument that segregation in South Africa was congruent with the Charter did not convince the assembly, which ordered him to align the rights of Indians in South Africa with his document. Modiri Molema was incensed that Congress' disorganisation at that time meant it could not take the opportunity to join forces with Indian opinion.

He studied the minutes of the Congress' 1946 proceedings scrupulously. The Transvaal Congress' administrative performance was dismal. In December 1946, there was worry about financial maladministration in the Transvaal branch.[199] The branch did not relay their share of membership funds to the national office 'but put the money through their bank with the intention to pay the share at some future point'. The Transvaal was 'totally unable' to pay the debt owing to the national office, which placed Congress at the peril of 'financial chaos'. Nevertheless, despite these troubles, in March 1947, Xuma hosted a joint meeting of the African National Congress and the South African Indian Congress.[200] The meeting drafted a joint statement in conformity with the principles of the Charter, including full franchise, recognition of trade unions, freedom of movement, the abolition of pass laws and 'removal of all discriminatory and oppressive legislation from the Union's statute books'.[201]

General Smuts lost the general election of 1948. Dr Malan's Nationalists won on a ticket of 'apartheid', or 'separate development' between the races, although they won by a slim margin and did not win the popular vote. Before the election, Smuts had been sympathetic to the Fagan Commission's report, which had recommended a relaxation of black influx control into urban areas and the encouragement of a stable, black working class in the cities as an efficient response to both the problem of labour and the associated political unrest. Moreover, while Smuts had been confident that his accomplishments during the war would secure another term as prime minister, the continuation of some of the hardships of war, including petrol rations and shortages of meat, focused the electorate's attention on the home turf. Yet Smuts had also anticipated that his support of the Fagan Commission would cost him. It was a difficult decision for his own political career, but though a staunch segregationist, his views and ideas were not always straightforward. He felt his dilemma was that 'by appearing pro-Native' and consequently losing the election he would 'thus hand the Natives over to the other extreme'.[202]

On the black political front, Congress was still struggling to connect with ordinary people's sense of alarm and growing pockets of resistance. In December 1947, an organiser in the Orange Free State, Martha Motlhakoana, wrote to the National Office that the 'African National Congress has made very little progress this year in the OFS Congress'.[203] There was 'very little if no response from the people'. 'It would not be wrong to state,' she continued, 'that the African people are very much interested to know just what Congress is, only that the leaders fail, or cannot or are unwilling to make the average African understand where he is being led to.' In December 1948, the Congress assembled for its annual general meeting in Bloemfontein. Modiri Molema attended the meeting. There were 81 accredited delegates at the meeting.[204] Significantly, the Youth League had taken the opportunity of the Transvaal Congress' extreme disorganisation and absent leadership to take charge of the office. Thus, Oliver Tambo and Walter Sisulu were on the National Executive of the Transvaal Congress.

Xuma's address in the 1948 meeting, according to the minutes, 'ably showed up the multifarious and nefarious injustices of the ruling class and the disabilities under which the African people are placed' but 'without suggesting any particular line of action'.[205] Nevertheless, the resolutions towards a programme of action in response to apartheid revealed the regionalist inclinations of the past. The first resolution was that 'an earnest appeal be made to the members of the Native Representative Council to petition parliament on behalf and in the name of their several constituencies for leave to secede from the Government of the Union of South Africa on the ground of incompatibility of race-relationship'. In other words, the reserves of the 'several constituencies' would sever from the Union and each go their separate way. Although what 'apartheid' meant in practice was not yet clear, one of the earliest impulses for independent 'separate development' emerged from Congress itself. It was an idea similar to Selby Msimang's earlier call in 1924 that 'civilised' black strata prepare the reserves as a place of their own development and retreat to these homelands.[206] A second resolution in the 1948 meeting came from members from Basutoland, Swaziland and the Bechuanaland Protectorate. They intended to organise a petition to Britain 'suing for the extension of her protective wings over the territories' and that 'should Great Britain be unable to grant the petition, approaches be made to any other foreign state to afford and take the African people under its protection'.[207]

In other words, opinion strong enough to table resolutions was strongly regionalist and often also separatist. For some, empire remained an important framework to protect the autonomy of these domains. Congress members who had the numerical strength to carry motions either wished to ensure the permanence of already established vernacular and cultural enclaves or sought to strengthen them where they were fragile. It was an outcome of an enduring Congress tradition. For decades, internationalism itself had supported struggles to develop and strengthen regionalist enclaves, each of whose centre and cultural heritage was in the countryside. Protestantism had shaped their associated literary vernaculars and strengthened their territorial claims.[208] In 1948, Congress was not yet agitating for an independent republic of majority rule even when the new international discourse supporting this form of sovereignty was at its loudest pitch and apartheid was knocking at its doors. Xuma's own directive at the meeting was that Congress pursue works of social welfare. He suggested that 'in order to win the confidence of the people it was necessary to help them in their daily pinpricks', including assisting parents to manage feeding schemes in their communities.[209] 'If we kept in touch with the people, not only would we be able to know their needs but we would also be able to tell the Government the true position: granted enough land, the influx to towns would be checked.'

On the last day of the annual meeting of this critical 1948 meeting, A.P. Mda and V. M. Kwinana moved that the 'Report of the Plan of Action Committee' should take precedence in the discussion.[210] They lost the vote by 43 votes to 14. When the report was tabled, there was such distrust and division that the meeting resolved that when there was finally a 'programme of action' to speak of, the executive should not discuss or make any decisions about it without first circulating it among the delegates. The minutes note that Congress ended without a 'clear lead' only that the National Executive Committee would receive recommendations for the Plan of Action Committee. In frustration, one of the Transvaal delegates, David Bopape urged that, 'The people want a lead from us. We must decide now whether or not we shall give them that lead.' The minutes also reflect that 'Mr Sisulu supported by Dr Molema complained and criticised the procedure of Conference', but Xuma did not think such discussion would serve a good purpose.

Modiri Molema was besides himself as he wrote a 'short review' of the Congress at the end of this meeting. He acknowledged 'a sense of defeat, disappointment and frustration almost verging on despair and disgust'.[211] Congress had ended in disarray, leading to 'laughing and victorious headlines – "The African National Congress breaks up in disorder" in the European daily papers'. It was, in his view, 'a year of Disgrace at Bloemfontein', with the 'Commander in Chief' installing 'general disorder' with 'terrible authority'. As usual, he was dissatisfied with the actual procedure. 'The movers are not bothered to speak to their motions, which are thrown upon the house without any apparent limits or division of time'. He thought the entire meeting was a waste of time, 'which is fritted away in hair-splitting cross-remarks, appeals for order, legalistic squabbles etc.' and with the formation of 'small cliques and committees'. He was astonished that the Congress had not circulated financial statements and 'no ordinary member knows whether the credit balance is three thousand pounds or three farthings'. That there was 'much unsavoury matter in this point of finance' was most distressing to him, perhaps because he was thinking about his own father's newspaper. 'One need, however, only remind his compatriots that Financial mismanagement has been the submerged rock upon which many hopeful ships of African organisation have foundered and come to grief.' Congress was moving further away from the community of reputation he remembered in 1914. The timing of this collapse could not have been worse: blacks had no vote, Malan had won, and the Congress had no plan. 'Of diverse and conflicting opinions and plans of action, say nothing.' He was certain it was time for a complete overhaul – of everything, both delegates and strategy.

> One cannot rid oneself of the feeling that it is up to the more serious-minded Africans to change completely the structure of what seems to be an anaemic, effete, time destroying and verbose organisation, and replace it by, or at least integrate into it, new blood, new values and new orientations. The change must be drastic if it is to be beneficial. It must be of official personnel, of procedure and even of constitution. ... In short, there must be a complete scrapping of everything during these many years of its prolonged adolescence and deferred maturity.[212]

XII

The Bechuanaland Protectorate contributed both men and money towards Britain's war effort during the Second World War. In 1940, the 'Native Tax' increased from 22 to 25 shillings, but Europeans also suffered a steep increase in taxation.[213] The following year, the imperial government announced it was scrapping its annual grant of £16,000 to the Protectorate.[214] Resident Commissioner Charles Arden-Clarke suggested a differential system of taxation to cover the shortfall, 'as much as many of the poorer people might possibly pay' and a lot more from 'certain classes of people who could pay more than that'. For this reason, the government would not impose the tax through the existing 'Native Tax Proclamation' as this made no provision for a differential scale of taxation. Instead, as he explained to chiefs, he was suggesting 'a special "war levy" which you impose upon yourselves for the purposes of the war at the request of the Government'. Chiefs were willing to support collection as, in the words of Tshekedi, 'a thing done by Government' and an 'innovation of Government', and not a tributary levy, which Tshekedi considered to be the prerogative of chiefs alone. The people had to know the difference. 'Will it mean then that Government will impose taxes and also levies; and what scope will be left to the chiefs and tribes for operation?' The 'majority of the council', according to Tshekedi, insisted on 'an additional tax, and payable by every adult' but not a differential scale. Modiri Molema disagreed – forming a minority of one. He said 'the flat rate of tax is almost sanctified by custom', but that 'the more just course would be to make differences in distributing this' according to income. Arden-Clarke was in any case not willing to relent. Chiefs had to yield.

In 1942, they had started the 'African War Levy' as a levy that 'Africans voluntarily imposed on themselves'. At the meeting of the following year, Arden-Clarke considered the differential tax a 'novel scheme' and a 'revolutionary step' that was 'based on the principle of the European income tax' compared to the 'old customary method of collection as a flat rate'.[215] Chiefs were not applauding. The debate in the meeting revealed why a differential system of taxation raised such deep anxieties. The difficulty was that a differential tax individualises. In reality, there was already a convoluted system of differential extraction on the land as there was one of redistribution. Rents, donations, levies, payments, gifts, lending and borrowing were not a one-way exchange. They were reciprocal transactions of autonomy and dependency without a fixed rate or a precise meaning. One of the chiefs presented that 'there are certain premises Dr Molema had not stated'.[216] This chief described a common custom of lending a few head of cattle to a man who had none. The calves would belong to the borrower, and therefore, one man was helping another to create wealth. However, if a man ever sought to return the cattle that he had borrowed, he was in effect 'cutting himself away' from his patron and severing the bond that tied him to his benefactor. It was morally repugnant. How could a 'son' cut himself from the care of his 'father'? The chief wished to know how a system of differential taxation would handle that situation. 'A man may be found to hold 100 head of cattle, whereas his actually owned cattle would be five.' In other words, everyday practice had moral expectations that were already taxing the 'big man' more than the 'small man'.

In the next meeting in 1943, the council addressed a similar situation of differentiation when the new Resident Commissioner, A.D. Forsyth Thompson, revised the 'native administration' proclamations by introducing a clause that exempted people from 'Tribal authorities" depending on their educational qualifications.[217] 'The Council is of opinion,' Bathoen presented, 'that this section, if carried out, would create differences among members of a Tribe from the jurisdiction of that particular Tribal area, and it is not clear what the type of people are who are referred to here'. These 'particular people', he continued, 'would regard the native authorities or Chiefs as fools – in fact, already there is a class of people in the Tribes who think they are very clever and should not fall under the jurisdiction of the Chiefs'. The Council, again with the sole recorded exception of Modiri Molema, wanted to expunge the clause. Modiri explained:

> I rise with some hesitancy and am reluctant to say what I have to say ... I am hesitant because I seem to realise that I am in a very conspicuous minority .. [This] particular Clause [,]I can see nothing but good in it. It is permissive. It gives the High Commissioner powers that he has a right to exercise. ... The Clause is deliberate; it is intelligent; it is intentional. There surely must be a person or persons in Tribes whom the High Commissioner thinks should have protection of some sort, as indicated here. It does not go so far as to say that these names will be separated or divided exclusively from the Tribe, or even that there shall be any differential treatment ...[218]

He argued for some 'safeguards' in case a new generation of chiefs are not 'men of high education and of liberal and catholic views' as men in the meeting. He warned against the possibility of a 'leader who is careless', not of 'liberal mind' who makes distinctions between people, perhaps on account of their greater wealth or better education.

> After all, Sir, the rule by Native authority, although it may be a group of persons, is essentially a personal rule, and it is important, where personalities can come into the relations, to safeguard some people who might be victimised. I am not trying to insinuate, Sir, that there is at present any personal feeling between the Chiefs and any of their tribesmen, but I say we have to make safeguard for the future.[219]

The objections that the rest of the Council raised against him were trenchant.

Morafe

These were firstly that the colonial government had already created routes of appeal to the District Commissioner, and therefore there was no reason to grant the Commissioner more direct access to the population. Secondly, and more importantly, was the moral argument that the clause would not be acceptable to self-respecting persons. The new law, according to Moutloatsi Mpotokoane of the Bamongoato, separated people from one another. In the end, these educated individuals would live isolated from the moral universe of reciprocal responsibilities that made personhood. In a word, it would be as though these individuals no longer existed at all.

> We Africans, whether in the Protectorate or anywhere else – every one of us – have our rights in our community; and we cannot understand how this particular individual who is beng held apart from the rest of us, his tribesmen, is going to carry out the obligations expected of him. We do not know if the individual himself would agree to the idea of being treated apart and would perhaps be willing to sell his rights for the sake of being held apart from his fellow men.[220]

How could the fathers possibly agree to facilitate the death, the 'nothingness', of their children? Mpotokoane further warned against the encroachment of *Sekhoa*, to which he felt the new government policies were adding momentum. Like the earlier assembly of educated chiefs and their followers four decades before in *Koranta ea Becoana*, this later assembly was similarly debating the appropriate role of education in the making of a *morafe* of 'progress'. The point of a formal education ought to be personhood, *botho*, and not 'European-ness', another way of saying, *Sekhoa*. Mpotokoane continued that

> If such an arrangement were made now, I think it would be dangerous to us and get most of us in trouble; I think it would endorse the opinion that is being held by some of our parents for some time, who say that when they have given us a bit of education, we regard ourselves as Europeans... What I am clear on, Your Honour, is, when these people are separated from their people, to what class will they be put – whether to the European class or what class of people, who would be considered between Europeans and Africans?[221]

Tshekedi, himself a Fort Hare University man, although it was still the South African Native College when he was there, also described the great peril of education if it severed individuals from the integrated world of reciprocal obligations. Unless an educated individual aligned himself to others in practice, his placement was a perfect vacuum, undermining the healthy vitality of the *morafe*. His schooling would not only be a misuse of education because it injured others by separating him from them, the educated individual would also be committing an offence against his own soul. In his dissociation from his solidarity of personhood he would become a wandering creature with no home. In a colonial situation, where the government, in his opinion, served mainly the interests of whites, where would such an individual find a realm of care? He would be like a madman, absent to himself, and no longer fully alive. Hence, chiefs had the urgent moral obligation not to sanction such an inhumane law.

> Sir, should the need arise for a man to be held apart from the rest of his Tribe, that man would be regarded as a loss to his Tribe; he cannot help his fellow members of the Tribe. Even when he tries to speak to them, they will tell him: 'No, you are not one of us; you do not lead the sort of life we are leading.' ... If he is a lawyer and had been removed from the jurisdiction of his Chief, he would be a loss to that Chief and would not help him in the trial of cases ... There is this point, too: personally, I have nothing but pity for the man who would ask the Government that he be accorded that treatment. I know nothing about overseas countries, but I know something about this country ... If he is given a status of his own, not being that of an European or an African; he is left to himself.[222]

This complete rejection of his view did not stop Modiri Molema from raising more concerns, this time against the powers that the government seemed to be affording its officials, both its own bureaucrats and chiefs. He objected to the clause that 'no person shall be liable to be sued in any court' if he was under the 'jurisdiction conferred by this Proclamation'. He objected that it gave any such official 'something of a blank cheque' – almost unlimited power to act. As he put it, it gave an 'over-zealous' government official, or one with 'less discretion' allowance to 'overstep' the limits of his duties. As examples, he referred to cases of police brutality in the Union that the African National Congress had criticized and the assault of a white man by the police that had raised D.F. Malan's alarm in parliament. He made a plea for some 'safeguard to protect an allegedly accused or guilty person'. Sebopioa Molema agreed and added that unless it is possible to sue officials, it is impossible to establish 'good faith'.

The meeting of 1943 was from 3 to 14 May, many days of wrangling. Chiefs accepted revisions to Proclamations yet resisted the changes that further undermined 'Tribal Authority' and their sense of the appropriate moral course of everyday life. For instance, they objected ferociously to the idea that a personal will, rather than a sitting of the family and the Kgotla, could decide on the distribution of a deceased's estate. They resisted the further intrusion of the District Commissioner's jurisdiction into the operation of the tribal courts. They refused to allow him to check those records of cases that were still within the jurisdiction of chiefs. The Commissioner would therefore not be able to order retrials, reverse judgments or adjust fines and punishments. Yet, at the same time, chiefs also actively sought the aid of the colonial government to curb social transformations that they did not sanction.

Tshekedi would much rather that the government 'make steps to deal with the control of wages' than encourage a trend towards trade unionism.[223] Young men from his reserve had 'formed themselves into a sort of association', standing up against the colour bar that depressed their wages relative to those of white workers who sometimes had fewer skills. Tshekedi requested the government to fix a minimum wage and so 'forestalling them'. Sebopioa Molema wanted the government to stop militancy in its tracks. 'When a plague is about to break out in the country you generally devise means for preventive measures ... and we ask you to make plans beforehand about this fire which is about to kindle, and that in the absence of Trade Unions amongst us, you be our Trade Union'. Modiri Molema again broke rank. He considered the association 'not only legitimate' but also 'commendable'.

Chiefs could not prevent a deep attenuation of their independent authority, but at least, unlike their counterparts across the border, their negotiations in the Council made sure 'native administration' policies did not summarily write them out of judicial and property relations altogether. In the Union of South Africa, there was hardly anything left for chiefs to do, hence Lotlamoreng Montsioa ruled the Molopo Reserve largely in absentia. In the Bechuanaland Protectorate, chiefs were still there, visible, with a role to play. What they lacked in actual power, they found in the very stage and function of the Native Advisory Council, partly as a platform to display prestige, partly in their attempt to limit the effects of colonial authorities' direct control of their reserves, but primarily in the capacity that the Native Fund gave chiefs to become sponsors of life on the land.

The 'native fund' was assisting to build more schools and to pay teachers' salaries. In 1944, there were 17,180 children enrolled in primary schools in the reserves, 2,631 more than the previous year.[224] From the special breed of cattle and the boreholes that were the initial developments in the reserves from 1920, to the 150 creameries that were exporting butter and second-grade cream by 1930 – an astonishing rise from only a dozen a decade before, the

Protectorate reserves were turning into hubs of agrarian industry. The push from chiefs as far as possible to protect their cattle from discrimination in the export trade gave some more opportunity to black farmers large enough to navigate competition with white cattle ranchers. There were silos raising their grain above the horizon as a buffer against the droughts that could press relentlessly upon the landscape. At the same time, the system of remittances of mine earnings that continued, despite Sebopioa Molema's objections, ensured that thousands of working men spent the bulk of their money in the countryside, not in the cities of their employ, and seasonally returned home to work on the land.

Plaatje had envisioned such thriving agrarian towns in *Koranta ea Becoana* at the beginning of the century. He had however not anticipated that if Britain were to help chiefly and patriarchal power, it would come at a great cost. The colonial administration would whittle down chiefs' powers considerably, even in the Protectorate where the territory answered not to a settler dominion but directly to Britain through the High Commissioner. Nevertheless, it would have pleased him that the Protectorate's reserves were domains of 'progress' precisely along the lines he had advocated. Formal schooling and respect for the hierarchy of chiefly and patriarch authority coexisted and shaped the moral universes of *Sechuana*. Though he would have sneered at the orthography, his imagination of *Botswana*, meaning the way of being in *Sechuana*, was unfolding north of the Molopo River.

From 1944, after the finalisation of a uniform programme of 'native administration', the contestations about *Sechuana* between chiefs and the Resident Commissioner and amongst themselves in the meetings of the NAC quietened down. In essence, given how directly involved the colonial administration had become with everyday life, Britain had become an arbitrator in the moral negotiations of personhood. The government had become a benign mediator in the everyday moral contestations between chief and commoner, men and women, fathers and sons. At the same time, the war had brought the Bechuanaland Protectorate into the vortex of international wartime discourses about forms of acceptable government. The reserves, especially those of the Bamongoato and Bangoaketse, had offered troops, seventy of whom had died between the council meetings of 1943 and 1944.[225] This brought the number of fatalities to 89.

The international discourse, especially the Atlantic Charter of 1941, fostered an understanding that territorial boundaries coincided with a single identity, a so-called 'national' identity, under a single, unitary state. Neither territorial boundaries nor the constitution of the government, according to the Charter, could change without the consent of the people within those territorial boundaries. In the Charter's words, there was no room for 'territorial changes that do not accord with the freely expressed wishes of the peoples'' in a postwar dispensation. The United States of America and Britain, the two allied powers that conceived of the Charter, would also 'respect the right of all people to choose the form of government under which they will live' and would 'wish to see sovereign rights and self-government restored to those who have been forcibly deprived of them'.[226] Hence, in 1944, chiefs' central charge at the meeting of the NAC was the need to transfer the mammoth bureaucracy of 'native administration', which was the hybrid institution of chief and District Commissioner, to Africans themselves. This colonial bureaucracy was in many ways the social infrastructure that supported being a Mochuana or *Botswana*.

The discussion on this delicate matter was not direct, but the question shaped conversation about other items on the agenda, including the use of funds, public services and the matter of incorporation of the Bechuanaland Protectorate into the Union that had not died down. Tshekedi argued for the establishment of Hospital Advisory Boards. 'In these circumstance', where hospitals did not rely on any 'charitable funds or public fees' but belonged to the government or missionaries, 'we, the public, have no say in the management of the hospitals'.[227] When Forsyth Thompson insisted that boards could not interfere with the running of public institutions, Modiri and Tshekedi unusually spoke with one voice. 'Our hospitals,' Tshekedi proceeded, 'have been built for us by the Government; and what I want to point out was that the Government is by no means an individual, but we ourselves form the members of the Government: it represents us.' Modiri agreed with him.

> ... as Chief Tshekedi hinted about Government and the functions of Government, and the composition of Government, we are Government. That suggests, Sir, large implication as to the duties of Government. The increasing consciousness as to the rights of man seems to show that Government is constituted for the people. Government is there to provide education; it is their duty to provide education, and the people are thankful for education. Similarly, Government is there to provide hospitalisation, and while we are thankful for such services, we are thankful for realising that Government is doing no more than its duty.[228]

Forsyth Thompson thought that Africans are not yet ready to rule themselves. 'The principle of indirect rule, I think, as you all know, is that as a people develop they are progressively given greater responsibilities in the functions of government.' He imagined that a future government would be a jurisdiction of chiefs. 'The time will no doubt come when hospitals are established and entirely run by the Tribal Authorities', but not yet. He said he hoped for 'that time', but 'until the people are ready to manage them themselves, all matters on internal discipline and internal organisation must be kept in the hands of the Government.' Modiri Molema was not satisfied. If Britain sought to retain control of the Bechuanaland Protectorate because the territory was 'not ready' to rule itself, then he expected Britain to pay for its 'progress' out of its pocket. In fact, he suggested that Britian had done so little for the Protectorate that the latter may start ruling her own people.

> ... I do not know, Sir, but somewhere in the back of my heart there is some disgruntlement. Year after year we hear of these large grants from the Colonial Office. We see the budgets balanced; therefore it would be incorrect to say we work under deficit, and yet one feels too that we work under very great handicaps. We feel we are struggling. We feel that somehow the Protectorate does not seem to come out of the wood. It is sixty years since we have been under British protection, and in sixty years people outside must wonder what the people in the Protectorate are doing?[229]

The council also took a decision to open the meetings to the public by holding them at each of the reserves in turn. In establishing the new draft constitution and rules of the Council, chiefs also settled on proportional representation of the reserves onto the Council where such members would remain on the council for three years and return only if they won another election. It unnerved Forsyth Thompson that chiefs insisted on the 'election' and not 'appointment' of members: 'You are going to introduce a big principle if you start elections.' Words mattered greatly in anticipation of a postwar dispensation. Chiefs also wanted a salary scale for their employees in the chiefly bureaucracies of the reserves, a kind of 'subsistence allowance', seeing that with all the developments in the reserves, the duties of the staffers were increasing. There was also great disgruntlement, expressed by Tshekedi, that black soldiers only received 14 per cent of the total sum of money Britain afforded returned soldiers, relative to 51 per cent for whites and 16 per cent for 'Asiatics and Coloured'.[230]

At the close of this meeting of 1944, Bathoen concluded the session, as was customary for the chairperson of the chief's council to do. He referred to the recent revival of the lobby to incorporate the Bechuanaland Protectorate into the Union of South Africa. A few days earlier, the South African parliament had held a discussion about the future relations of Britain with her dominions. 'This Council,' Bathoen proceeded, 'respectfully submits that the peoples of the Bechuanaland Protectorate do not desire any change in the Government and wish to reaffirm their continuing loyalty to His Majesty's Government.' Modiri Molema was not satisfied with the phrasing of the objection. He said the Barolong had submitted a different statement through the chairperson of council, and he had a 'suspicion' that the statement was 'purposely left over to the end with the intention of foreclosing any discussion on it'. Chiefs did expect, he explained, that there would be 'renewed agitation in the South African Press' for the incorporation of the Protectorate into that dominion but 'what alarmed us was the assurance of the inevitability, and imminence of, the transfer of the Protectorate to the Union of South Africa'. The Barolong's objection was not merely to the event of the territory's incorporation in the Union, but they were also of the opinion that either way, the government could not take a unilateral discussion. There had to be a process of consultation with the people of the Bechuanaland Protectorate themselves.

> Sir we feel that we are entitled to a consultation. The principles which are embodied in the Atlantic Charter, for instance, seem to make it a moral duty for Governments to consult with their peoples, and that people shall be ruled as they like to be ruled, that is, they will submit to the Government willingly and, Sir, we claim, in terms of those human principles, that we in the Protectorate are also entitled to security and the freedom from want and from fear.[231]

Forsyth-Thompson said Bathoen's and Molema's sentiments were similar, only that the latter 'has gone further by saying that there should be the fullest consultation before any specific action in the matter is taken'. Bathoen's curt reply was that 'what Dr Molema has said Council is not in agreement with'. Indeed, there was serious disagreement between Modiri Molema and other chiefs around precisely the matter of 'consultation'. Chiefs were comfortable with democratisation on their own terms through mechanisms, like the election of members to the NAC and its public hearings, but at this stage, no more than that. As Tshekedi had learnt, it was necessary to cooperate with the colonial government, indeed often to yield considerable power to the administration, if chiefs were to resist forces that had swept them away in the Union. The more they collaborated, paradoxically, the more they could negotiate for British rule that was less direct. They would retain some powers in the evolving edifice of 'Tribal Authority', the hybrid chieftaincy of white District Commissioners and chiefs. Chiefs' battle against *Sekhoa*, their attempt to hold up the repertoires of chiefly and patriarchal power through the muscle of the colonial government, including 'native administration', was still in full swing and just as it seemed they were finally striking a comfortable compromise with the administration, the war and its implications on the understanding of government introduced a new fragility, the idea of rule by the people through democratically elected leaders, somewhat implicit in the stipulation of 'consultation.'

However, the Barolong had nothing to lose from the outcome of a consultation with ordinary people about their political future after the war. The lands of the Barolong were not a reserve. As independent landowners on effectively private lands, all they had to fear was a white supremacist settler government which could dispossess them of their farms. Bathoen insisted that chiefs' final statement of objection to the transfer of the Protectorate to the Union stand without any reference to 'consultation'. 'Our feeling, Your Honour, is embodied in the note which I handed to you and requested that it should be passed on to the higher authorities.' Chiefs were not prepared to have a conversation with ordinary people about how they wished to be ruled. The continuing threats of *Sekhoa* were evidence enough that if the population had a choice, it was likely that those tributaries would run dry. Bathoen would have none of it.

In just under eighteen months, the war had ended, and with it, Modiri Molema's uncertainty about the form of government that preserved the *morafe*. Sovereignty was not only perfectly conceivable outside the empire, such an arrangement was the talk of the day. International sentiment not only described this moral configuration of government, but also gave it a name, the nation state. This meant a *morafe* bounded by its territorial borders, independent, and ruled by popular consensus. That solution to the dearth of personhood had gathered a name and vocabulary as 'nationalism'. His political energies were peaking now, in his mid-fifties. Even then, it was the recollection of his past that motivated him, the deep injuries he had suffered, and the longing to redeem those years and make things right. He was assembling an actual political home for the man he had become, who married for love, spoke his mind, who had room to care for his own soul and freedom. The 1940s were finally his years of homecoming.

In fact, he was increasingly losing patience with his obligation as a senior patriarch, who sometimes had to attend the Kgotla in Mafikeng. He had given himself to other concerns following the war, keeping his eye on the international landscape. The obligations of the chieftaincy in Mafikeng seemed petty, needlessly time consuming and very frustrating, especially because his peers were sloppy with time and organisation.

> I call for Sebopioa & find him with Theo [Gaboutloeloe] to hear that the case is put off without notice. This is very annoying after I have altered my appointments to the request of Tiego [Tawana] to be thus shunted unceremoniously.[232]

Just over two weeks later, he had forgotten about the appointment.

> 10 am. Phone from Theo [Gab] that Madibi case is about to start & can I come? I have several cases and urgent appointments and could possibly leave theirs. I answer 'carry on'. Kgogobi is said to have given me a letter about this case a week `ago. I faintly remember seeing Kgogobi on pavement in front of surgery & it is possible that he did give me a letter but […] I cannot remember.[233]

XIII

In 1942, the Bechuanaland Protectorate's administration, following Charles Arden Clarke's interest in the practice of land tenure in the territory, requested an investigation by Isaac Schapera. In his report, the anthropologist 'preferred to concentrate' on the Barolong Farms, mainly 'upon the special features created by the fact that the land is divided into separate farms held on individual tenure by certain prominent members of the tribe'.[234] He concluded that the farms have 'the history of an unsatisfactory experiment in "individual" land tenure', to the consequence that they are the only 'tribal' area in the territory 'where European squatters are allowed to live and farm, with the consent of both the tribal authorities and the Government'.

This was the first of the 'main problems' Schapera wished to bring to the attention of the colonial government. He pointed out that the Europeans had established 'private farms' of their own on the properties, which led to substantial improvements of the farms because they erected houses and found water, but none of these improvements benefited farm residents 'as a whole'.

Europeans were also cutting off other residents' stock from their 'private farms'. He recommended that the government should no longer permit such letting to Europeans, nor allow Europeans elsewhere to graze their stock on 'areas already reserved for Native occupants'. In the meantime, he further suggested, the government should ensure that all such 'stand rents' accrue into the Tribal Treasury.

Secondly, Schapera considered it contrary to 'custom' that the residents of the farms who were not European tenants on lease agreements were 'Native tenants', paying an annual rent of ten shillings in addition to their Hut Tax. 'It is the principle of the rents which I consider objectionable.'[235] His recommendation was that the government should curb the role of occupants as 'landlords' over their 'tribesmen' by refusing their request to possess title deeds. 'As far as the Administration is concerned, there should be only one reply to this claim: an uncompromising refusal'. Thirdly, he recommended that in abolishing tenantry on the farms, the difficulty of the legal status of the farms will find easy resolution. He advised that 'the Barolong Farms should be given the same legal status as the proclaimed tribal Reserves'.[236]

The administration had attempted no further interventions on the farms since Charles Rey's advice to let the matter rest and not attempt any further to alter the legal status of the Barolong Farms. Even after the incident of Schapera's report, the government still did not act. Only in 1947, when Lotlamoreng Montsioa reported to the administration that he wished to resign from his post due to ill health, did the administration take opportunity to address the matter with the resident peasant population on the farms. From as early as the 1920s, as Schapera's report had noted, there had been some complaints about rents from ordinary householders that had reached the ear of the administration, but the government had no jurisdiction to intervene in the territory. Over two decades later, Schapera's report had given the administration confidence that there was enough disgruntlement on the ground to turn an inquiry into the question of Lotlamoreng's succession into a public referendum on the legal status of the farms.

In the meantime, Lotlamoreng Montsioa had changed his mind about the legal status of the farms. He was no longer in favour of individual titling for the occupants. The rift between him and some of the landowning notables had widened beyond conciliation, and so his own opportunity to secure one or more title deeds for himself was, it appeared to him, less important than the risk of losing his rule over the small propertied class of occupants on the farms. Moreover, after the war, it was clear that the Union and the Bechuanaland Protectorate were emerging as separate countries with different administrative and political spheres. Two very distinct and separate political geographies were emerging. Neither the colonial administration nor he, as the paramount chief, could any more take the border to be so permeable as to be without consequence. Just because he was paramount chief in the Union's Molopo Reserve, did not secure the position of his son as successor on the Barolong Farms. In fact, following his illness, the Protectorate administration reserved the right to choose his successor, as per the practice of 'native administration' because, in order to maintain the status quo on the farms, he had agreed to let Rey's proclamation be in force on Barolong Farms. Lotlamoreng wanted to do whatever was possible, and offer the colonial government whatever it required, to make sure that his son, Kebalepile Montsioa, then a minor, would become paramount chief on the Barolong Farms, not only across the border in the Molopo Reserve.

As per the call of the colonial government, the Kgotla of about one hundred men assembled on Lotlamoreng's farm, Good Hope, at the beginning of January of 1947 to discuss the subject: 'Government says this land cannot be well-served with Government Funds as long as it is called Barolong Farms. This land must be taken as an ordinary tribal land or area.'[237] Most of the occupants of the farms were not present at the meeting, a matter that unsettled some of the participants. Nevertheless, the men present strongly supported the administration's point of view. In the words of one,

> I have found that these farms belong to foreigners because we pay 5/- rent. I do not think the land belongs to the Chief as it is today called Barolong Farms property. I suggest that these farms should be turned into one farm and place it under the administration of the chief.[238]

There was general agreement that Barolong Farms 'should be converted into 'one farm', meaning a reserve, and become like the territories of the Bangoaketse, Bakoena, Bamongoato and so on, 'and that the government abolish 'farm ownership by individuals' and all rents. 'We cannot do anything by ourselves', another householder complained, and 'I wish these farms should be converted into tribal area so that we can make our living freely'.

About two months later, Lotlamoreng applied for two years of sick leave seeing that 'the Chief's proposal to resign was not accepted by his Tribe, who said, "a Chief only dies" and does not abdicate'.[239] It may have been that he was not really ill but wished to step down in order to help his son ascend to the paramount seat on the Barolong Farms whilst he was still alive. The outcome of the meeting would, he hoped, persuade the colonial administration to support his son. Kebalepile Montsioa would be the first chief to rule Barolong Farms as a native reserve. The administration considered the 'weakness, physical and mental of the present chief' reason to consider whether it should create two centres of power an acting chief for Lotlamoreng in the Union, and a regent for Kebalepile in the Protectorate or perhaps a 'separate dynasty' there altogether.[240] Two centres of power would ensure a strong chiefly administration, not one where the paramount chief spends most time with 'the majority of the tribe' in the Union. 'The whole position,' the District Commissioner in Lobatse wrote, 'is further complicated by the need to clarify the status of the Barolong Farms as recommended by Schapera.'

The difficulty of 'two governments' was precisely that it would potentially cut the Barolong Farms away from Mafikeng, thereby afford autonomy to the 'occupants' who would no longer be under the jurisdiction of Mafikeng, which is a situation for which the certificates of occupation made no provision. It would thus be more difficult to alter the status of the farms to that of a reserve. At the same time, the Commissioner thought the sole reason why Lotlamoreng was now supporting the change of the farms' status to a reserve was as a bargaining chip to ensure that his son would succeed him on the territory. The administration did not make a decision, and by going on sick leave for an unspecified time, Lotlamoreng held on to power without abdicating, with Tiego Tawana as acting chief on both sides of the border.[241] He held on for almost a further seven years.

XIV

At the next general meeting of the African National Congress, from 15 to 19 December 1949, again in Bloemfontein, Modiri Molema and Robert Sobukwe were the two delegates from the Cape Province.[242] The proceedings began with a squabble over who were delegates, and why certain names did not appear under the national executive. It was not a promising start but it turned out that the wind was moving in a new direction. Some of the older stalwarts and newer members were tired of the old drill. The Natalian Selby Msimang's response to Xuma's presidential address was that 'the position of the African was so rapidly deteriorating that the time had arrived when the ability of our leadership was to be put on a true test'. Gaur Radebe from the Transvaal pushed the sentiment further. 'Congress stood in dire need of reorientation of a policy and departure from the beaten track of speeches to which he had listened for the past fifteen years.' A.P. Mda, as President

General of the Cape Youth League, 'spoke at length by popular consent on this need for re-orientation of policy'. He said it was 'imperative that Congress, as a National Liberation Movement, should set itself a goal, an ideology towards which every member should strive', and he submitted that this 'can only be found in the doctrine of African Nationalism and the instrument with which to achieve this ideal could be none other than Boycott'. Another of the old guard, Selope Thema, concluded that 'in short we have come to dedicate our lives to the cause of those heroes who fell 100 years ago and to leave as a heritage to our children the fighting spirit of our erstwhile heroes like the Dingaans, Nlambes, Moshoeshoes and Sekukunis'.

The prevailing historiographical consensus understands the 'radicalisation' of Congress after 1949 as a victory of the militant Youth Leagues, especially in the Transvaal, over the 'old guard', including Modiri Molema.[243] In fact, there was a broader push for change, as much from the youth as from a cohort of the 'old guard', chief among them being Modiri Molema. His vision of the future *morafe* and his long embrace of militant but passive resistance coincided with that of the younger members. Especially among the stalwarts that were agitating for change, the push for a reorientation of strategy came from a realisation that Congress, throughout all four provinces, had been overtaken by events on the ground.[244] For instance, in the Cape, there had been unrest at Lovedale Training College, which had to shut down. In the Transvaal, there had been disturbances at Krugersdorp and Randfontein, where some protesters had died. In Natal, the government had carried out evictions at some of the rural districts, which led people to negotiate their own strategies of resistance. There were riots in Durban in 1949. In the Orange Free State, Congress had completely lost competence when its president abandoned his branch and moved to another district.

On the morning of the 16 December 1949, Xuma arrived late, and upon his arrival the delegates pressed him to lead their march to the Market Square where he would read a public statement but, before then, the meeting would consider the statement before adopting it. There was a 'long discussion' because, as one delegate from Basutoland, Ntsu Mokhehle explained, the statement Xuma had planned to deliver 'did not properly reflect the African point of view, the whole approach did not evince the spirit of the African'. The conference worked on the 'Programme of Action' collectively, accepting it only once it had been 'thoroughly scrutinised paragraph by paragraph and amendments made'. The minutes note that four people took the lead in drafting the programme, Walter Sisulu, a young Transvaaler, and three doctors – Modiri Molema, James Moroka and James Njongwe. Congress also adopted the following critical resolution, 'that only those people who signified their willingness to carry out this Programme should be elected into the incoming executive.' The new committee included some of the old veterans – including four medical doctors, Modiri Molema, James Moroka, Roseberry Bokwe and Xuma, who stayed on in the executive, and new blood – the Cape's A.P. Mda and James Njongwe, and the two Transvaalers Oliver Tambo and Walter Sisulu. James Njongwe was younger than his fellow medics, and in 1945 was one of the first two Africans to graduate in medicine at the University of the Witwatersrand, where he became politically active as a student.

The situation was clear enough for the new generation. The disarray of Congress at the provincial level, certainly in the Transvaal, had partly created a leadership vacuum which the new generation could fill. However, if their programme was to go forward, it was not enough for them to be in the national executive. The members on the ground had to be willing to carry out the programme, otherwise it would remain a victory only in the books. The younger firebrands understood that they could either light their torch on the flame of willing, likeminded patriarchs – and of these there were not many – or otherwise shine brilliantly on the stage of Congress meetings with impressive speeches but enjoy no collaboration from branches thereafter. Patriarchs did not yield to the instructions of youngsters. Indeed, it would soon become apparent that the main reason Drs Modiri Molema and James Moroka received votes from the Bechuana delegates to serve on the National Executive was less due to support of their ideas and more because of their position as accomplished Bechuana notables. Age, chiefly and patriarchal power, education and profession, region and language – these were the political currencies that still mattered profoundly for elections on the floor of Congress.

Indeed, days before the election, the Youth League had still not found a candidate who would both support the Programme of Action and possess the professional and other credentials to replace Xuma. Available accounts of what transpired offer no clarity as to how and why Dr James Moroka's name came up. Moroka had never been a vocal member of Congress, and in fact, does not appear in the minutes during Congress' discussions. The younger radical members understood that they needed an 'elder' on their side if the radical programme was to go forward. An elderly medical doctor would have been a reasonably obvious choice, but they would not have known whether they could trust Moroka unless someone else could vouchsafe that he was a secure pair of hands and would not sabotage the 'Programme of Action'.

Modiri Molema was Moroka's distant relation and his best friend. They had met in Scotland where they were both at medical school. At the same time, as the minutes of Congress the year before suggests, there had been a proximity of thought and good rapport between Modiri Molema and Walter Sisulu as well as with James Njongwe. Modiri Molema was the bridge of trust between Moroka and the new Congress men with a radical agenda. James Moroka became the new President General of Congress and Walter Sisulu its General Secretary.

The other important ingredient towards success was money. The educated black classes had been struggling to make ends meet for decades. A radical programme of action that required an enlargement of membership and boycotts required an executive that could travel across the country to visit branches and turn up as keynote speakers in gatherings. The medical doctors had cars, could foot their own travel expenses, and – unlike Solomon Plaatje – did not have to wait for the Congress or a helpful bystander to provide the cost of railage.[245] The medics could fund the running costs of their portfolios. In fact, the financial situation of Congress was catastrophic. In 1948, the acting treasurer had not circulated the financial records because there had been no audit. The following year, the audit reflected a deficit of £219 and Congress had to cover it from a reserve bank account with about half as much. The functioning account of Congress had no more than £20.[246] Few things frustrated Modiri Molema more than poor management of one's own finances, either as an individual or as an organisation. He volunteered for the role of treasurer.

The new executive started up on the work immediately. On 4 January, Sisulu sent out an invitation for the first meeting of the working committee, and specifically asked Molema to do all he could to attend the meeting, 'in order that the administration should be straightened up'.[247] That meeting, held in Johannesburg, seems to have gone well. At the end of the following month, A.M. Kathrada of the Defend Free Speech Convention invited Molema to speak at the launch of its manifesto in Johannesburg at the end of March following the banning of the president of the Transvaal Indian Congress[248]. 'Even organisations like ours,' Kathrada wrote, 'will come under a similar ban if the government is allowed to have its way.' The launch of the manifesto was a joint collaboration between the African National Congress, the Transvaal Indian Congress, the African People's Organisation and the Johannesburg district of the Communist Party. Modiri Molema seems to have declined the invitation but he did send a message of support.[249] Following that successful launch, Sisulu sent out an invitation for the first meeting of the Working Committee of the Programme of Action, again in Johannesburg early in April. 'My dear Dr Molema', he wrote, confirming the details of their telephonic conversation 'wherein I informed you the Affairs of Congress require immediate attention'.[250] 'In view of the Defend Free Speech Convention, the Country is anxiously waiting for a lead from the ANC.' Molema may have failed to attend the meeting, but if so he had sent an apology for his absence, but Moroka had simply failed to respond to invitations and was a no show. Sisulu was furious, and dispatched a 'petition to Moroka',

> ... [We] do hereby express our disappointment and disapproval at the absence of the President General, the chairman on the working committee, at this meeting ... Having regard to the importance and urgency of matters awaiting deliberation and decisions of the Working Committee we hereby petition the chairman to attend a meeting of the Working Committee.[251]

He sent Molema another invitation with the petition enclosed.[252] 'The petition speaks for itself ... It is my sincere hope and desire that you will attend this very important meeting.'

It could be that the professional commitments of the two doctors who both lived some considerable distance from Johannesburg were getting in the way of the duties of their political office, especially Moroka, who had been roped in at the last minute, and may have not expected the degree of travel required. The two were not young men and were the only medics in the executive who were also members of the Working Committee. It is telling nevertheless that Moroka then called his own meeting, insisting that it should be either in Bloemfontein or in Thaba Nchu.[253] The elders, he was suggesting, could not be routinely travelling to the youngsters in Johannesburg. Moroka held the meeting at his home in mid-May, where the Working Committee launched 'a campaign for a national day of mourning' as protest against the 'Unlawful Organisation Bill', which was the Suppression of Communism Act of 1950 and the Group Areas Act of 1950. The latter was an attempt to eradicate residential zones of mixed colour and establish segregated areas in urban areas. The Transvaal's Youth League considered this day 'the birth of a new era'.[254] Its rhetoric of black unity or Africanism derived from a memory of frontier wars when Europeans first arrived in southern Africa.

> The protest is to us a manifestation of all those divine stirrings of discontent

of the African people since the 6th of April 1652 onward – through the period of the so-called Kaffir Wars, the days of the Dingana [sic], through the days of Moshoeshoe, through the days of Sekhukhuni against the Grondwet, through the days of the Treaty of Vereeniging, through the days of the White Union Pact of 1910... What is more significant to us is that for the first time since 1652, African National leaders are going to stage SIMULTANEOUSLY a forceful opposition to our oppressors. If Nakana, Dingana [sic], Khama and Sekhukhuni had defended their country jointly, Africa would have been saved for posterity.[255]

The Transvaal Youth League's brand of Africanism looked within the borders of the Union for inspiration. Its conception of self-determination was not the language of the United National Charter that, for instance, was shaping Modiri Molema's conception of the form of sovereignty and democracy a unitary African *morafe* should achieve. As the head of the task team for 'propaganda', Sisulu oversaw the founding and publication of the newsletter or 'journal', *Lodestar*, as 'the official organ of the African National Congress Youth League'.[256] One of the earliest editions stated that the Congress and its vision are 'not an exotic plant like the Communist Party or the Trotskyite group'. Rather Congress 'is deeply rooted in the soil and is bound, with tender care and love, to bloom and bring forth fruit. It is somewhat unfortunate that the "tender care and love" that we refer to have not been forthcoming in sufficiently large quantity, and consequently the "blossoming" and the "bringing forth fruit" have been delayed.' If the Congress was a foreign element, 'a plant imported from abroad', it would have 'succumbed to the storms and droughts of the South African political climate'.

In May, Sisulu sent out a memo announcing that on 26 June, 1950 'the African people should refrain from going to work and regard this day as a day of mourning for all those Africans who lost their lives in the struggle of liberation'.[257] Modiri Molema set up a national 'finance committee' to raise funds 'in terms of our Programme of Action'.[258] Congress required an estimated £75,000 in total, with an amount of £7,000 required initially.[259] On 11 June, Moroka sent out a statement calling for a 'stayaway' across all races on 26 June.[260] 'I am perfectly satisfied,' Sisulu wrote afterwards, 'that as a political strike, Monday June 26, was an outstanding success.'[261] The planning and eventual 'success' led to greater cooperation between Congress and other organisations, including the South African Indian Congress and the 'Non-European Trade Unions', and the Communist Party, which had been declared an illegal organisation under the Suppression of Communism Act. Walter Sisulu and Yusuf Cachalia were joint secretaries of this joint working committee. Nelson Mandela was in charge of its office. Congress established provincial, district and local coordinating committees 'throughout the country'. After the Thaba Nchu meeting, according to Sisulu, 'young men and women spontaneously came forward and freely placed their services at the disposal of the National Executive'. Thereafter, he wrote, it was necessary to respond to the question 'what next?' The joint committee issued a lengthy report on the question. Fundraising was key, but 'political action cannot be suspended until all the required amount has been found'.[262] The other important imperative was 'mass membership'. Next would be a campaign of civil disobedience.

> We recommend that the basis of political struggle be Civil Disobedience based on Non-Co-Operation and Non-Violence. In our opinion such a struggle cannot fall under the provisions of the Suppression of Communist Act, because it is not Communist propaganda or activity, but it is in fact based on the teachings of Jesus Christ. Christianity is a State Religion in South Africa and the principles of Civil Disobedience based on Non-Violence are identical with the ethos of Christianity, and therefore cannot be regarded as a foreign ideology. This form of struggle is in fact a product of South Africa, which was practiced by Mahatma Ghandi [sic] against the oppressive laws of the country; and is acknowledged by the world generally and by South Africans particularly. Count Leo Tolstoy, the great Christian, approved and appraised such a struggle from the very beginning.[263]

The report continued with the argument that 'Political freedom is meaningless without economic freedom'. To this effect, 'all economic, industrial, social and other activities must be centralised in settlements to be established throughout the country in cities, towns, villages, farms, released and trust areas in the territories of African chiefs and in other areas where Africans can own land'. The inspiration was that of the early 'Christian missionary stations' in South Africa, and in the Middle East, 'the establishment of Jewish settlements which carried out farming and industrial projects' as well as the establishment of 'Ashrams' in India. 'We suggest that the settlements be established throughout the country where (a) an industrial program be put into operation; factories for hosiery, safety pins, furniture, clothing, footwear etc., etc., and a "home industry" scale be introduced; (b) farming – vegetables, fruit, poultry – be established and encouraged; (c) educational, political and moral training be given'. One of the key functions of these settlements would be to 'sustain all political workers and they would be relieved of their economic anxiety'. In other words, there was still no clear vision of how the future would look after the 'success' of these political struggles. The idea of 'settlements' was one avenue of experimentation. In his notes on the report, Modiri Molema indicated that he supported the idea of 'settlements' and included 'flowers' as another industry that they could pursue.

In mid-July 1950, the leadership of the joint forum of resistance, including Molema, Moroka, Matthews and Msimang, as well as Cachalia and President of the African Mine Workers Union, JB Marks, spoke at a 'freedom rally' to condemn the City Council of Johannesburg's decision to ban 'peaceful meetings' in its municipal areas.[264] Molema's responsibility as treasurer was raising money given these dire straits of economic hardship that dedicated political activists were facing. At the beginning of July, he circulated a plea to 'all lovers of justice, liberty and fair play'.[265]

> In view of the menace that has arisen in the African, Coloured and Indians' struggle for Liberty, and the challenge to our manhood contained in the recent Acts of Parliament, there is an urgent and immediate need for £30,000 to carry on our struggle for Existence and Liberty. On behalf of the Coordinating Committee of the African National Congress, the African Peoples' Organisations and the South African Indian Congress, I appeal to all Non-Europeans and to all liberal minded people of South Africa for Donations and Contribution towards this Liberation Fund - £30, 000.[266]

He himself donated £250. 'This is a very good step for you my dear Doctor,' A.W. George Champion, President of the Natal Congress wrote to him.[267] Yet raising money was only one of Molema's responsibilities, which though a mammoth task, was a straightforward responsibility.

The more difficult task of his position was holding at bay senior leaders like Champion and others who were not committed to either the strategy of the new executive, the Programme of Action, or the idea of 'nationalism' that was informing it. The likes of Champion considered Molema to be like them, an elder and patriarch who thought like them, and in whom they could confide and raise their alarm while, in the meantime, the question of segregation remained unsettled. Some of Congress' most important senior leaders wrote to Molema to express what he represented to them, which was a hope to preserve the former sentiments of Congress. The new executive had no sooner taken up office than Doyle Modiakgotla, general secretary of the Cape Congress in Kimberley, invited Moroka and Molema to a 'great reception' where they would also be 'a few European liberals' present.[268] Other Bechuana from the Free State would also attend including Professor Z.K. Matthews, a Bamongoato by birth and, as an anthropologist, an enthusiast of Barolong history, and Dr Roseberry Bokwe. Matthews and Bokwe were also the Cape provincial president and treasurer respectively. There would also be attendants from the Bloemfontein branch, a considerable distance from Kimberley, and the Orange Free State executive, as well as 'the chiefs of Taungs', another Bechuanaland chieftaincy. In other words, all the foremost leaders representing the Bechuana's regionalist strongholds would be there. 'For your information,' Modiakgotla wrote, 'there are also those who ... watch or wait for your failures but have prejudged and predicted that Congress in the hands of Bechuana will fail'. He added that 'it is mostly this prediction which prompted to intensify the organisation and to invite you to come and bless our work.'

Molema and Moroka's visit left these Bechuana inspired to extend the reach of Congress and, two months later, Modiakgotla was preparing to travel across the northern countryside 'for the purpose of rousing our people and getting them to join the Congress'.[269] Modiakgotla asked Molema for funds to travel and organise people, lamenting that

> Our failure to have a strong delegation simply means that we are going to swallow the dictations of the extremist element – the so-called Youth League with their senseless boycott resolutions. ... Is the prophecy of those who hate us becoming true? They have told us here that Batswana people are like babies. They cry for leadership and as soon as they get it they do not know what to do with it. These people are right. We must start right at home to clean our own houses before we go too far afield. Our chiefs must be organised.[270]

In other words, the Sechuana-speaking strongholds of the Orange Free State and the northern Cape had leaders like Modiakgotla who sought to organise chiefs to garner support for Congress in the reserves, but this as an attempt to bolster Bechuana's prestige. They were trying to assist Molema and Moroka in a situation where other members understood the presence of the Youth League and its insistence on a shift in strategy as evidence of the Bechuana's weakness, seeing that Congress was, in their view, falling apart under an executive led by two Bechuana elders who, if they were mature leaders, would not be allowing young city boys to control them. The new strategy of Congress was, in their view, a spectre of embarrassment. Leaders like Modiakgotla understood themselves to be trying to save face. They saw themselves as helping Moroka and Molema, and thereby upholding the good name of the Bechuana. At the same time, their strategy of organising was not a plan to galvanise every woman and man into action. They were going to focus specifically on Bechuana by persuading their chiefly leaders to support Congress. Meanwhile, Congress members typically voted for leaders of their own vernacular constituency and were not as happy to roll up their sleeves to work under a Mochuana president. Modiri Molema did not agree to fund Modiakgotla's trip. These Bechuana had backed the wrong horse.

Selby Msimang, as Provincial Secretary of Congress in Natal, sent Molema a lengthy response to his call for funds. 'I regret that I am not in a position to meet your most depressing appeal for funds.'[271] Natal's President, George Champion, had not yet set a date for a meeting of the provincial executive since the general annual Congress in Bloemfontein in December, and it was already August of the following year. Msimang had circulated an annual report, 1949–1950, among the provincial leadership, with the financial statement, but the documents were 'merely noted and nothing further was said about them' despite 'an amount so big which is owing to me'. Msimang had been funding some of the initiatives himself. 'I have been unable to do anything more effective and I fear the report for this year will be almost nil'.

Msimang was disparaging of the Natal province's performance. Its Congress had 'an absence of militant policy'. The branches had no direction and there was an 'absolute lack of team-work by the members of the Executive Committee' just at the time 'when great upheavals take place throughout the country'. Msimang was a committed stalwart who wanted to pull the cart in the direction of the national executive, which if it were to happen, would be sufficient reimbursement for his money. 'The deficit shown in the accounts represents the amount I am out of pocket of, which can be reimbursed if all members of the Executive Committee could play their part and pull their full weight in the national cause.' He agreed with a more militant strategy. Yet he had not moved on from his understanding that segregation, where the black population would develop itself separately on progressive agrarian lines was the answer to the country's political situation.

> When our people are being driven from pillar to post, there lies a country (Maputoland) [present-day Mozambique] rich in cotton and sugarcane which as a race we could agitate for its conversion into an African area

and open for immediate occupation. We cannot think about these things until we have a mammoth fund at our disposal which would be the force behind any representation we make to the Government.[272]

At the same time, the President of the Natal Congress, Champion, about whom Msimang had bitterly complained, was also writing to Molema. Champion was not surprised, he said, at Msimang's report. 'The Circular letter would be alarming to one who does not know the facts.'[273] Champion felt he had warned the Congress at Bloemfontein of what was sure to happen if it allowed the Youth League any room. He thought the radical programme was the reason it was very difficult to get his provincial members out on the streets organising people. Instead, he explained, Congress had disregarded his warning, surrendered itself into the hands of young, reckless militants, and now Msimang and others were surprised that other provincial leaders had abandoned Congress and walked away just as ordinary people were looking for leadership.

> To me, it becomes a fulfilment of the warning I gave you at the Conference in Bloemfontein last year. I was deliberately misunderstood and the Students from Fort Hare were allowed to have their own way. The new branch known as the Youth League was given all the ropes to hang whomsoever they hated. You will remember my appeal to the Congress. That this was a Voluntary Organisation of Good-Will: That Experience must count a great deal. That as far as I am concerned things were moving to a precipice. I have never seen a Congress of years organised by old people to be given to the care of Students to run it. Men who are full of book education – theorists, who have just mastered the studies of Karl Marx, Gandhi and the rest of the reformers and want to step into their shoes without taking the trouble to study the local conditions, disregarding advices [sic] from well and tried officers.[274]

In the meantime, the Youth League in Natal had stepped into the leadership vacuum, alongside the chiefs whom Msimang had indicated had 'had an awakening and now want dynamic leadership'.[275] The province's Youth League had been 'very busy throughout the year and has tackled vigorously the introduction of passes for women'.[276]

On the one hand, Modiri Molema allowed himself to be the ear that listened to his contemporaries dissenting cries of discontent but on the other hand controlled the tight purse that quietly stymied their strategies against the Programme of Action before they matured. He made it difficult for dissenters to mobilise by not funding their mission but only those efforts in line with the resolution of the national executive committee and the working committee for the Programme of Action. In its report at the annual conference in December 1950, the Executive Committee supported the Youth League and celebrated boycotts and protests. The report made Congress' vision and strategy bold, uncompromising and unambiguous. 'The Programme of Action indicated a definite form of struggle for the African people and reflected a new attitude towards the oppressor and demanded the National Independence of the African people as a nation.'[277] The mission of Congress, at least the executive and its supporters, was the nation state. Any other agendas were officially off the table.

Molema also raised the monthly subscription fee for membership.[278] Early the following year, he sent out an invitation for members to pledge donating money to Congress.

> The African National Congress is a spear-head of the African people's attack against white domination. It is the only organisation which with your support can and is going to bring down the oppressor. In 1949, the A.N.C. adopted a Programme of Action. Note that the Programme entails action. Support the ANC by donating to our National Fighting Fund and thus help to bring the day of our freedom nearer. If you love freedom, if you love your children, if you love your country, you have only one choice – to support the African National Congress.[279]

He was seeking out people to entrust with the responsibility to raise funds. He nominated a D. Twala in Johannesburg, with a hope that 'you will not only accept but be also a live member by which I mean a live wire'.[280] He warned him that the 'finances of the ANC are in a distressing situation'. The Cachalia brothers were willing to make films available for viewing, 'a thing like "Jim comes to Jo'burg"'. The other fundraising option was a 'Zulu dance'.

At around this time, Modiri Molema gave an address to the South African Institute of Race Relations for which he drew heavily from the earlier speech he had offered to a synod meeting in 1925. The Institute had asked him to speak on 'The Present and Future Political Representation of the African'.[281] He began this address with the establishment and dissolution of the Cape's liberal franchise, which had not discriminated on the basis of skin colour. Thereafter he launched into a discussion about 'segregation and parallelism', which he rejected as firmly as he did the idea of 'trusteeship' that locks black people in a permanent position of dependence. He also rejected the representative councils, which were not the same thing as the black populations' full participation in the parliamentary system. He warned both European and African against a 'mistaken survivalism', where each assumes that the other must die if either has to live, and yet, he did not think that the end of racial tension was in sight. He predicted that 'both races will live here permanently' as 'Providence has decreed that the European and the African shall live together in South Africa' but that 'for a long time, the European will be ruler or "baas", even when 'in the near future', South Africa would be 'a republic, run and ordered largely by the Dutch Afrikaner'.

He predicted, in fact accurately foresaw, that under that scenario the African would have 'futile Local Councils on ethnic affiliations in various tribal areas', while the government 'confines his interests and aspirations to tribal, rather than to national African matter', such that 'the doctrine of "Apartheid" will be realised'. His mistake was thinking it would not last 'more than twenty years'. The end, he continued, would come not by revolution but by evolution. There would be a painful process by which the government tries one dispensation of reform after another due to Africans' resistance. Each new mode of domination would end in failure, forcing the government to offer one concession after another, 'in despair', but find itself unable to sustain its grip on power, and then, ultimately, the dam would burst, and 'the rulers are forced back along the beaten tracks'. It was, in his reading, how Thomas Carlyle understood the French Revolution. Though that revolution had been a single instance of revolt, it had been preceded by generations of rot at the foundations of society, until eventually the house collapsed when the rulers could no longer offer some concession here, some compromise there, to keep the walls standing. That was the meaning of 'evolution'. The people would not once suddenly storm the gates of a powerful and strong state. Rather, their persisting rebellion would in the final instance bring the state to its knees because the state would have then weakened itself, having emaciated itself through 'indolence and inertia', clasping on to the 'rotten' and 'old ways'.

He thought the European in South Africa ought to learn from that historical example to save himself. The social world was not a jungle. They erred who imagined they could survive as the fittest at the peril of the other. He accurately predicted that in South Africa, the African and the European would have to meet at the table of negotiation.

> There are really only two ways or settling differences, the one is the jungle way, by ruthless extermination of the weaker, and the other is the moral

way by association and equal collaboration. The way of human progress is not simply the transference to the human sphere of the Laws of the vegetable and animal evolution.[282]

That June, the apartheid government proclaimed the Bantu Authorities Act, No. 68 of 1951. This legislation made provision 'for the establishment of certain Bantu authorities and to define their functions', as well as 'to abolish the Natives Representation Council' that Hertzog's government had legislated in 1936.[283] Instead, every 'native tribe or community' would belong to a 'Bantu tribal authority'. This consisted of 'the chief or headman of the tribe or community in question and so many councilors as may be determined by the Governor-General'. Two or more such 'tribal authorities' would constitute a 'Bantu regional authority'. This would consist of a 'chairman and the members' who could be 'elected or selected' according to the regulations of the tribal authorities. Two or more of the 'regional authorities' would make up a 'Bantu Territorial Authority', whose 'chairman and members' could be 'elected or selected' according to the regulations of the 'regional authorities'. Nevertheless, the government reserved the right to remove or not recognise appointed persons. It might also appoint a 'public officer' as an overseer, free to attend meetings but without the right to vote. These would be jurisdictions of 'native law and custom'.

The 'tribal authority' would 'generally administer the affairs of the tribes and communities' and offer the chief or headman advice or support 'with the performance of his functions and duties, including any of the powers, functions or duties conferred or imposed upon its chief or headman'. It also had the responsibility to 'advise and assist the Government' and the higher regional and territorial authorities about 'matters relating to the material, moral and social well-being of natives resident in that area, including the development and improvement of any land within that area'. These 'tribal authorities' would also exercise all the powers and duties that the government considered to be 'within the sphere of tribal administration'. The 'regional authorities' could have a major influence on government policy because they could advise the Minister about the development of educational facilities, infrastructure such as roads, dams, sanitation, agrarian production and health care services. In effect these regional authorities handled 'all such matters as in the opinion of the Governor-General are within the sphere of regional administration', including making by-laws and collecting taxes and fines towards a regional treasury.

Although historians have interpreted this Bantu Authorities Act of

1951 as a continuation of the Native Administration Act of 1927, the two policies put in place very different structures of 'native administration' in the reserves. The Native Administration Act of 1927 placed the weight of judicial responsibility and of the distribution of land primarily on white Civil and Native Commissioners that relied on customary law – not mainly on chiefs in the reserves. The white Native Commissioner was the 'Supreme chief' of the reserve. Particularly in the large territories of Bechuanaland, the colonial government *directly* ruled the African population. On the other hand, the Bantu Authorities Act of 1951 eradicated this white, mainly English- speaking, overburdened bureaucracy and transferred all its duties to a black administration with full judicial jurisdiction and control over the land. Africans would now be ruling themselves directly in their own jurisdictions of law and custom, which in the government's view, would abolish the need for their representation in the parliamentary system of a white South Africa. In practice, the land would once again belong to the 'tribes' and their chiefs. These chiefs' judicial powers would return to them without routes of appeal, subject only to the advice of the 'tribal authority' whose members chiefs could of course influence. Chiefly bureaucracies would be the twentieth century home of every black person.

At first glance, the Bantu Authorities Act of 1951 seems to more than satisfy the early twentieth-century political vision of the fathers. They had attempted to establish self-directing chiefly domains within the British Empire. Now the mid-twentieth-century legislation was presenting chiefs with a situation of relative autonomy in the Union of South Africa and therefore within the British Commonwealth. However, the Bantu Authorities Act was creating quite a different world from that of the fathers' aspirations. In the first place, the legislation was establishing territories segregated according to a conception of who belongs to a primordial 'tribe' and not according to the ethical constellation of the *morafe* through continuing moral negotiations of placement on the land. Secondly, Silas Molema and his generation held an openness about skin colour with regard to the *morafe*. The mores of the countryside, language and the intimate hierarchies of everyday life mattered more than pigmentation. Thirdly, the Barolong chieftaincies of the fathers had wanted to answer only to Britain, and not at all to a settler government. As such, the reserves were countries in themselves – in direct communication with the Colonial Office and not subsidiaries of a settler government.

Yet for living chiefs whose powers the Natives Land Act of 1913 and its more effective extension, the Native Administration Act of 1927, had attenuated to little beyond symbolic pomp, the Bantu Authorities Act of 1951 had clear benefits. The Bantu Administrative Act was installing chiefs and senior patriarchs as the main facilitators of aspiration in the reserves because they would be in charge of the money the government had available to use in the reserves, which it mainly raised through taxation. Modiri Molema would have immediately recognised some striking similarities between the Bantu Authorities Act of 1951 and Charles Rey's two proclamations of 'native administration' in the Bechuanaland Protectorate. For instance, Rey's system of tribunals that decentralised and limited chiefly powers had their counterparts in the body of the 'tribal authorities' in the Union reserves. Furthermore, the 'regional authorities' also had a role akin to the Native Advisory Council of the Bechuanaland Protectorate because it was a forum where chiefs met with the government to discuss policy.

However, the Bantu Authorities Act of 1951 offered chiefs significantly more than the Protectorates' proclamations, which had allowed the government more direct intervention in the lives of the populations of the reserves. Protectorate chiefs had had to fight to turn the proclamations into a framework that also supported the everyday institutions of chiefly and patriarchal power in the reserves. Even though Protectorate chiefs' powers were significantly undermined, 'native administration' in their reserves left the control of land in their hands and, significantly, it ameliorated their capacities in the fight against *Sekhoa*. The Bantu Authorities Act was handing the land and the people of the reserves fully into the hands of chiefs. In Bechuanaland particularly, this would be a new colonial dispensation of *indirect* rule, returning chiefs to power after an absence of thirty years. The government would be so far removed from the everyday structures of rule that chiefs and seniors could successfully impose their interpretation of *Sechuana* on women and their children. The new legislation would provide money to fund aspiration, including landholding and education, in line with the hierarchy of gender and generation in 'Bantu areas'.

The attractions were clear, more so when the books on the question of segregation remained opened in the Congress. The fact that the idea would have strong merit to chiefs and senior men, even those in the cities, explains the tone and caution of a report an unknown author, or another committee of Congress, compiled in response to the Bantu Administration Act.[284] The writer noted that he 'can say without prejudice that part of the broad underlying principle of the Act is to modernize and reform on democratic lines the African tribal system of administration'. He continued that 'we view this as useful training of Africans in the rudiments of self-government and as preparation for their eventual participation in full citizen duties and rights'.

The report acknowledged that there was support for the legislation not only 'in Government circles' but also 'by many outside'. Yet, the author warned, the legislation was a 'sop to Cerberus'.

> It is a policy of creating what have been euphemistically called 'parallel institutions' alongside the Central government, being institutions in which all legislative and administrative problems affecting Africans will be discussed, and thus defer, if not forever make it impossible for Africans to claim or obtain political equality with Europeans. We know that it is the declared policy of the present Nationalist Government to create such a gulf of separation between Europeans and non-Europeans in all matters social, educational, political, industrial and residential.[285]

The author rejected the Bantu Authorities Act of 1951 with extreme caution. He was not willing to risk alienating support for Congress, just at the time when chiefs, as Msimang had observed, were now 'awakening' into their role in the political struggle.

Moreover, as the author clearly recognised, the executive committee and the Youth Leagues were implementing a resolution that was still not popular within the Congress and in fact, was unpalatable to some important leaders of Congress. Moreover, not only Congress, but also families and households in general were at the height of a strife between generations over morality and authority that had been raging for decades, with strongly gendered dynamics. The older generation had come to the cities, like James Molebaloa, Solomon Plaatje and Pixley Seme, and yet they had never abandoned the countryside, its hierarchies and ideals. Hence, the author trod cautiously, cognisant of a reality that the world that the National Party was proclaiming through the Bantu Authorities Act of 1951 was one that many would have found desirable and satisfactory and would therefore agree at least to experiment with it and not reject it untested. They would of course need certain assurances, such as making sure that the terms of segregation were equitable so as to guarantee the black population more land. The proposed legislation gave these people, whom racial discrimination had reduced into roaming, landless masses with no land of their own, a place to live under their own authority. If there was scope for negotiation with the government, the legislation lent some hope of homecoming.

> We realise that parallel institutions may, to a point, be useful or even better than mixed representation, but we believe that they can only be

justifiable if envisaged as a phase in the training, a stage in the evolution of the African, which they of necessity must be, and not as permanently subordinate political organisation, which they can never be, either by intention or design. The only alternative to this view is that the parallelism of Black and White institutions should be complete and carried to its logical conclusion. Each act of institutions should be fully autonomous and completely independent of the other. The gulf should be unbridged. [sic] And the separation must of course be equitable.[286]

This was the restrained middle statement of the report, which then proceeded into the more technical questions of due process, arguing that the government ought to have consulted the black population before proceeding with legislation. Nevertheless, the author concluded with the observation that the cultural divide between European and African was narrowing so rapidly that 'the government's native policies should aim at adaptation and assimilation rather than separation and apartheid'. 'In any case,' the author continued, 'so many Africans have assimilated European culture and standards of living that it is unrealistic to speak of thrusting them back into the seclusion of tribalism.' The report was likely the joint consensus of the executive committee, although the language of 'assimilation' and 'adaptation' sounds very much like that of Modiri Molema.

In the meantime, Modiri Molema continued to correspond with disappointed Congress leaders who were keenly sensitive to the 'tribal' constitution of Congress' national executive and concerned about the lack of activity and factional fights that had emerged on the ground. He worked hard to diffuse the anger of the discontented. Moses Kotane wrote to him in 'excellent Setswana', but Molema was 'answering in English because my typist is an Englishman from London West'.[287] He agreed with Kotane that 'Congress needs overhauling' and was aware, as Kotane had written, that 'the Xhosa-Zulu group will look upon this dormancy with an amused concern because it is the first time that the principal leaders have been of Tswana stock'. Kotane had raised the leadership dispute in the Transvaal Congress, where there were 'three Presidents – Marks, Ramohanoe and Thema' competing for power. Modiri assured him that Moroka would travel to Johannesburg, make the decision and 'put the final official stamp on the Presidency'. Further, he urged Kotane not to focus on squabbles but on the critical Congress matters at hand. Modiri's most serious concern was the finances of the organisation that continued to be 'in a bad way'. He wanted every member of Congress to 'bind himself' to pledge money to the Congress every year. 'I feel that if the members are at all conscientious, we should be able to pay our way comfortably'. His fellow members, in his opinion, were not willing to pay the price of freedom. Money was a sacrifice without which 'Africanism' would remain a pipedream.

> Finally, I am conscious of the fact, which has become an obsession with me that the African character has not got the same sacrificial spirit as the Asiatic. We have yet to raise martyrs of the calibre of Ghandi, or even Dadoo. I fear that we are too concerned with our personal comforts, rather than with our national security. May the God who looks after the interests of Africa inspire all of us, sons of Africa with a nobler spirit of self-sacrifice for our fatherland.[288]

In December 1951 Congress assembled as usual in Bloemfontein. In his presidential address, James Moroka asserted that members had come to 'rededicate themselves' and to 'baptise your sons and daughters into the cause of African Nationalism'.[289] He urged members to 'realise that whilst other people can help you in your direction towards your Nationalist ideals, upon you and you alone lies the ultimate salvation of your individual selves and of your nationhood'. Thereafter, the executive committee passed a resolution that Congress would proceed with a 'campaign of defiance and disobedience' the following year if the Nationalist government did not yield to the organisation's demands. These were that the government abolish all the laws that differentiated between Europeans and non-Europeans; that it extend the franchise to the latter on the same terms as it applied to Europeans, and that it abandon the project of separate development, including the Bantu Authourities Act of 1951.[290] The executive committee also outlined that it would embrace cooperation in its programme of action with other likeminded organisations amongst 'Indians', 'Whites', 'Coloureds' and 'Africans', especially the South African Indian Congress. The Prime Minister, Dr D.F. Malan refused to agree to any of Congress' demands and committed 'to make full use of all the machinery at its disposal' against any 'subversive activities'. There was as far as Malan was concerned, nothing to discuss.

At the end of January 1952, Modiri Molema gave the opening address at the twentieth conference of the South African Indian Congress in Johannesburg. 'The Congress meets today,' he said in his opening remarks, 'at the zero hour of our national life as the black and despised inhabitants of this sub-continent.'[291] At the end, he called for unity between this collective of 'black' experience that was not only the black African.

> Earnestly I call upon you, sons and daughters of Africa and India – Unite. Passionately I call upon you men and women of colour – Unite. Prayerfully, I call upon you Coloured, Africans and Indians – Unite.²⁹²

However, the house of the African National Congress was itself divided on this issue of unity and, in some places, on the question of going forward with a strategy of defiance. At least two of the most important stalwarts who had stood by Congress after the 1949 conference had set themselves to abandon Congress and go their own way, so strong was the dissent on cooperation with Indians, Coloureds and with 'Communists'. The first was Selope Thema, who in fact broke away with a defecting faction as soon as J.B. Marks won the presidential contest in the Transvaal. Thema founded the National Minded Bloc, which opposed the new militancy of Congress and what it understood as the influence of the Communist Party of South Africa on the Congress. Modiri Molema used the opportunity of travelling to Johannesburg where he would address the South African Indian Congress also to meet with Thema at his home, personally, to try to bring him back into the fold. He spent nearly two hours 'criticising his views and asking him to criticise mine'.²⁹³ He wrote to Selby Msimang that

> My criticism of him [Thema] was that he, a founder had led a secessionist movement and was now attacking the citadel he had built from without, and had even allowed the printing of separate cards. He half-admitted and said they were willing to pay into Congress the funds of a share of the funds they had collected. His criticism of Congress was that it was dominated by youthful extremism and Communistic thought and personnel, but as I told him that criticism loses its weight because of his defection. Now I want to say that we must build up a case for the inclusion of the Bloc, not actually a case for them as such, but rather open an avenue for their honourable retreat into the mother body, and although some of them may feel bitter, the older Congressites will be glad to avail themselves of such a gesture, and as I say, Thema, as a foundation member of this Structure must be got back to the honourable place he is entitled to.²⁹⁴

Selby Msimang had also notified Molema that he was abandoning Congress because the members of the executive had not heeded his appeal at the Bloemfontein conference that they solicit the firm support of provincial leaders before embarking on the Programme of Action on the terms they had established.²⁹⁵ The urgency of the political situation and his own support of the Programme of Action notwithstanding, Msimang could see no prospect of success in now launching a campaign of defiance and civil disobedience when the executive had not persuaded provincial leaders to the course beforehand, especially in Natal where, as he explained, Congress leaders would hear nothing of cooperation with Indians. 'Passive resistance is a spiritual weapon and cannot be sustained by emotionalism,' Msimang wrote. 'Natal recognised its peculiar position with regard to the Indian relations which are extremely delicate and explosive, and had sought an opportunity to make its attitude clear so that in any procedure adopted for the carving of the programme of action there might be elasticity.' Msimang recalled that Moroka and Sisulu had refused this consultation prior to conference 'where the field would have been prepared for launching the campaign'. The consequences, Msimang now feared, were disastrous.

> Upon the publication of the programme of action as adopted by the Conference there is brewing in this Province a movement seeking to create a rival Congress to be known as the Bantu National Congress, suspected to be Government inspired and having at its plank non-corporation with the Indians. Our Congress is being accused of having surrendered its leadership to the Indians. Only those who know Natal as well as we do can appreciate the volume of support such a movement will receive from the masses – the masses we must look to for the success of the implementation of our programme of action.[296]

Under the circumstances, Msimang felt that his capabilities would not square up to the responsibilities of being in the middle of and managing such a conflict and he was resigning as both Provincial Secretary and member of the Natal Provincial Executive. In 1949, Msimang reminded Molema that he, Msimang, had been a member of the committee that drafted the Programme of Action, 'which I fully support' and so did the present Natal Executive 'but the methods for its implementation are to me uncouth and frivolous – toying with an extremely important weapon'. The important weapon was the campaign of civil disobedience, but the insistence of the national executive that Indians and Africans work together across organisations, he felt, wasted Natal's role in the struggle. 'Leaders in Natal can enter into a working arrangement with the Indians without bringing them into their councils.' He understood that his stepping down would jeopardise the campaign in Natal. He had been making enormous sacrifices for the African National Congress over the years but could not continue to do so unless he believed that the risks required were for a plausible plan. Moreover, he thought it was a foolish strategy on the part of the executive committee to send 'an ultimatum' to Malan. 'We have warned him to prepare before we are prepared.' In reply, Molema pleaded with him to stay in the same terms he had used to try coax Thema back into the main fold of Congress politics.[297]

> There is however this very weighty, and in fact over-ruling proviso that whether you did or did not make a dissentient statement, and whether or not you have changed your views, the African National Congress of which you are one of the founders is not a party machine. It is an organisation, a one party organism which presents just one phalanx, and therefore, whose decisions are binding on each individual member by a majority vote, wherefore each member must, constitutionally march in step with the rest.... I also do not fear that my reminding you of the duties of a member of an organisation will suggest to you to withdraw from it like Thema did. An organisation is really an organism and who can conceive of one organ like the hand, the eye of the tongue withdrawing from an organism because its chief administrative centre, the brain, had decided, perhaps wrongly to act this or thus.[298]

Molema was unwilling to persuade Moroka not to meet with the Natalians. The way forward was everyone marching in line with the decision of the executive. Furthermore, 'you and Thema and myself, and I have no doubt a few others, are the oldest surviving members' amongst 'a lot of young bloods' who were at times 'emotional and extreme, as we also have been in our youth'. It was important that they, as elder men, not make the same 'emotional and extreme' decisions as the youth, like breaking away or resigning from a platform of leadership because of serious disagreements. From the 'elders, he expected, 'balance and discretion', which was not, he explained, the same thing as being 'a rank pacifist or a craven defeatist'.[299] Msimang nevertheless stepped down and became one of the founding members of the Liberal Party of South Africa in May 1953.

In the meantime, Modiri Molema's own commitment to Congress' collaboration with others across the colour line and to the Defiance Campaign of 1952 was unflinching. He was not following the dictates of the younger generation; he was himself provocateur, proposing and supporting a purpose he had been thinking about for years. This *morafe* had been his longing from his youth, fermenting in the experiences of placement in his family, in the households of the families with whom he sometimes stayed in Kimberley and in Cape Town, and during his time in Scotland. This *morafe* was the happy placement of his first love. He was not young, at sixty-one, not indefatigable, yet he threw himself unreservedly into the activities of the movement. It had been a lifelong mission to be midwife to this *morafe*, which by 1952 had gained concise conceptualisation during and after the Second World War.

Also, the role did not begin with political organisation but rather with his private struggles, the personal and difficult choices he had had to have the courage to make. It had cost him the approval of the fathers, which had mattered greatly to him but also now of his contemporaries and, as far as chiefs in the Protectorate were concerned, even of younger men like Bathoen who wanted to have a return to the constrained freedoms of the fathers' world. There was now emerging precise political blueprints that would support the solidarity of reputation to which he had long ago belonged. This was the nation state. Persisting in that struggle was in many ways also a proof of manhood. It involved painful events of cutting and cleaving, like in the rituals of initiation that separated a young boy from his mother's world, only it was not enough once to raze the hut of boyhood and leave the past behind. This rebirth had many beginnings, many rites of passage. In his early thirties, he would only have married an African woman, but he had walked a journey towards shifting the boundaries of blackness and, once again, had become entangled in love and desire beyond the point he once thought the *morafe* ended. He had married a so-called 'Coloured' woman. His embrace of the 'brown' people, the 'Coloureds' and the 'Indians' had become both as natural as breathing to him and stood as a moral example of the unity of black people. These private undertakings to become the *morafe* had preceded the formal platforms of his political involvement, of which Congress was the most recent.

He had been defending the freedoms that he now believed would be secure in the nation state from his very first meetings in the Native Advisory Council in Bechuanaland. The ANC in South Africa and the forum of the NAC in the Bechuanaland Protectorate were the places where he gave his ideas expression but also, in so doing, where he hoped to meet likeminded others who could further influence his thinking. His political flowering had preceded his involvement in these platforms and, indeed, he remained consistent in the views he had already formed in his early thirties when the work on the NAC began. These were the need for democratic institutions that would protect ordinary people from the arbitrary powers of both the state and chieftaincy, a centralised state that would eradicate the ethnic cleavages of the past and, a society that agreed on the futility and moral repugnance of racial segregation.

As far as the campaign of civil disobedience was concerned, he had already settled on the utility and moral justification of this method of struggle even before the Congress meeting of 1942. A few weeks after that meeting, he had written about his thinking that Congress should adopt Gandhi's strategy, meaning mass membership and strategies of passive resistance. This was a full five years before the 'young bloods' entered the ranks of the executive and the formation of the Transvaal Youth League.[300] When the campaign was underway, he wrote a statement in defence of the campaign, and said it would be a fatal blow to the European not because of its immediate effects, but its long-term outcomes.[301] Malan's unwillingness to negotiate was, in his view, 'narrow and short-sighted'. The danger to the European would be that in its militancy, the campaign was bound to be also anti-European, and to seek alliances, not only with the local anti-white groups, but also with other groups in Africa to 'form Pan-Africanism and its corollary Europhobia.' Therefore, he concluded, the 'proper method of making South Africa safe for the white man and the white man's civilisation is surely the direct opposite of that now being pursued by the white man.'

As far as the black population was concerned, such a campaign of passive resistance, would not break the system in one swift blow. In fact, such a single revolutionary blow was not the intention. He considered that the campaign was only the beginning; people were feeling the pangs of their own birth as Africans.

> Finally, many people are apt to judge the present campaign of Defiance of Unjust Laws by its immediate results and to solace their minds by prophesying that it will soon fizzle out. They completely overlook the prodigious and lasting effects it has upon African temper and morale. The Campaign is teaching them cooperation and discipline, union, and that invaluable thing called 'self-sacrifice'. The African is, as it were, trying his limbs and discovering his power. He is, as it were, undergoing practice for some colossal stake, something stupendous and vital in the very near future.[302]

The first big day of civil disobedience was 6 April where, according to Congress, more than 100,000 people demonstrated, including in the small Orange Free State town of Ladybrand where 2000 people held a meeting.[303] People took the pledge 'to carry on the relentless struggle for the repeal of Unjust Laws' through the African National Congress, accepting the support of the South African Indian Congress, the Coloured Organisation and 'the other freedom loving peoples'. The *Bantu World* carried a disparaging report of the events, as proof that the Congress 'is a Communistic Organisation' influenced by the doctrine of Karl Marx.³⁰⁴ Molema wrote a reply, asking 'Why not "Unity in Diversity"?' 'Listen', he wrote, quoting a New Testament scripture, 'And John said: "Master, we saw one casting out devils in thy name, and we forbade him because he followest not us. And the Master said: Forbid him not, for he that is not against us is for us".' The 'Congress Alliance' was gaining momentum and set 26 June as the official starting date of the Defiance Campaign. The government had also set itself to crush it.

Between June and December, the police arrested and jailed more than 8000 people, including Modiri Molema. He appeared before the Supreme Court in Kimberley on 10 August 1953 on charges that he and nine others, all members of the African National Congress encouraged acts of disturbance and disorder in that city between July and December of that year, influenced by Communism.³⁰⁵ A month later, the Department of Justice ordered him to resign from Congress and not to participate in 'any gathering' within the Union for a period of two years.³⁰⁶ In turn, the government would not pursue the charges for those who agreed and held their end of the bargain. Modiri Molema surrendered immediately to the official instruction to resign permanently from his position as office bearer and member of the African National Congress after his trial, but it was not clear to him whether the government was prohibiting his participation in all forms of gatherings, including funerals, church services, literary discussions, school committees, the Kgotla and professional forums.³⁰⁷ He wrote at least two letters to the Department of Justice to inquire, hoping he could 'still serve my people in ways which cannot be construed as inimical to the Government'.

Of the success of the Defiance Campaign, and more generally of the activism of the years 1949 to 1952, he had no doubt. Historically, his inspiration had not been only Gandhi's passive resistance in India, but also, as he wrote around this time, the struggle of the 'Boer' against the 'British' after the annexation of the Transvaal in 1877.³⁰⁸ In his understanding, when the new Prime Minister William Gladstone failed to fulfil a promise to secure the Transvaalers' independence, they took up 'Civil Disobedience and the Defiance of Unjust Laws, and accordingly refused to pay taxes'. That struggle ended in victory, and so did Gandhi's own. There was no reason, as he considered circumstances, why the same end was not in sight for the 'non-European Front' of the Union of South Africa, but it would take time.

After the state clamp down, Congress was largely in the hands of the new generation, who sought a new leader, Chief Albert Luthuli, as president. The Programme of Action had turned Congress into a mass movement under a brand of 'African nationalism', the aim of which was to bring about an independent and democratic nation state, but not because the Youth League had pushed its agenda against an elderly and unwilling vanguard. There were key personalities of the old guard, especially Modiri Molema, who had been nursing, for a lifetime, a moral ideal he later understood to be commensurate with the nation state.

XV

In 1942, Modiri Molema passed a first mortgage for the farm Vryhof in favour of the trader S. Kemp & Co to the value of £3000, in a matter that was 'urgent', and required that consent 'be obtained without delay'.[309] Due to the promulgation of the Natives Land Act of 1913, any market transactions that involved blacks outside the Schedule of Native Areas required approval from the Governor General. S. Kemp & Co was charging him interest at five and a half, rather than the eight per cent per annum he was already paying to the present lender. Hence, the Assistant Native Commissioner recommended the approval of the Governor General because 'the matter is purely one for the advantage of Dr Molema'.[310] After some further clarification, the Native Affairs Department issued a certificate of approval.[311] The mortgage may have been due to a burden of debt that Molema had inherited from his late father and remained saddled with as he educated his siblings, including Sefetogi, who followed him to Scotland also to study medicine. Alternatively, perhaps he needed the money for investment into his nursing home and the expansion of his medical practice. In 1945, he had cleared the debt when he entered into partnership with Abraham Holmes and Paul Eitner to establish and run a store on Vryhof. Eitner was responsible for the daily management of the store without a wage, as he had only contributed one fifth of the required capital, whilst the other two had each equally contributed towards the remaining costs. Once again, it was necessary to request permission of the Governor General to proceed. The trio's application for a general dealer's license was successful, but it had required clearance from the office of the prime minister.[312]

In April 1948, Molema once again wished to take out a mortgage over Vryhof, this time in favour of Standard Bank for £2000 'in respect of overdraft'[313] He was indebted to the bank in 'diverse sums of money'. He followed the same procedure. As usual, the Assistant Native Commissioner gave the application his strongest recommendation as did the Chief Native

Commissioner, because 'Dr Molema will be able to meet his commitments under the bond'. This time, however, the situation of the property outside the Schedule of Native Areas seems to have caused the senior officials of the Native Affairs Department great consternation because they were unsure whether to treat Molema as a black or white landholder. The Secretary for Native Affairs explained to his uncertain undersecretary that,

> As this bond is in the form usually employed by the bank, and it is intended inter alia to cover overdraughts [sic], I do not think it necessary to inquire about repayment at any time nor to insist that there may be no re-advances without the Governor-General's consent. The interest at bank rates from time to time is in order. Finally as Dr Modiri Molema is well educated I don't think it at all necessary that we protect his interests in any way. Recommended that G.G's consent be sought as applied for.[314]

The Native Affairs Department would treat Molema as they would a white landowner. In other words, the department could dispense with the usual precautions that protected black landholders from unscrupulous lenders. It issued the required certificate approving the mortgage bond and Molema was free to proceed[315]

About a year and a half later, Molema once again needed to pass a mortgage bond, this time to the value of £2500 to Charles Slater Strickland and a further £500 to Spencer Percival Minchin in order to pay off the money owing to the bank. Again, the Native Commissioner in Mafeking was ready to 'recommend that the bond be granted as I am of opinion that Dr Molema will be able to meet his commitments under the bond'.[316] This time, there was no response forthcoming from the Chief Native Commissioner until over a month later. The Native Commissioner had had to press the higher office for a response by telegram as 'Dr Molema has to meet certain commitments by tomorrow'.[317] A response finally arrived from the Secretary of Native Affairs that there would be no response 'until sometime in January'.[318] At the beginning of January 1951, the Native Affairs Department held a meeting to consider nine similar applications by nine black and two white landowners. In the meantime, Molema was anxious, telephoning the Native Commissioner 'a number of times' to find out what had transpired.[319] The Chief Native Commissioner could only respond that the matter is 'still being considered by Head Office'.[320] The Department of Native Affairs finally issued a certificate of approval at the beginning of February, but it was too late and 'the arrangement made unfortunately fell through'.[321] Molema had to find a new lender, Ernest Higgs, who was 'a farmer and business man in the district'.[322] He now required a new certificate of approval, and this time, his attorneys made application directly to the Secretary of Native Affairs.

The delay was due to a change in the face and policy of the Native Affairs Department under a new minister, Hendrik Verwoerd. The approval of such applications was no longer a matter of the Secretary of Native Affairs' discretion on a case-by-case basis, but subject to the minister's tighter, more systemised oversight with the political intent at last to segregate white areas, as the case of Vryhof suggests. For half a century, the government had not intervened in these areas. On the contrary, the department seemed, at worst, to protect and support black landholding in such areas or, at best, to be negligent or turning a blind eye. In the Transvaal, blacks bought more than 3200 farms and smaller portions outside the Schedule of Native Areas between 1913 and 1936. The government approved purchase through an exception clause in the Natives Land Act.[323] Indeed, the primary motivation of that legislation was to delineate 'natives' lands' and afford the then new Union government ownership and jurisdiction over them as domains of 'native administration'. The Natives Land Act was not primarily a mechanism to intervene in relationships of landholding and settlement in white areas, although it had given white landowners the upper hand over black sharecroppers.

The Native Affairs Department approved Molema's bond application, but under a new framework, both of legislation and of political motivation.

> ... in terms of the provisions of the Group Areas Act, 1950 (Act No, 41 of 1950) it would appear that no approval is necessary, in respect of bonds by Natives in favour of Non-Natives over properties situate outside the Scheduled Areas in the Cape Province, Natal and Transvaal.[324]

The present administration was now making possible a process that the Native Affairs Department had long been attempting to hinder, that of black landowners losing their properties to indebtedness, as long as the lender was white. By August 1960 Modiri Molema had decided to sell Vryhof. It was going to be a nightmare to manage a property where every decision involving credit was subject to the approval of the minister. The prospective buyer, W.J.J. Hartzenberg wrote to the then renamed Department of Bantu Affairs for permission to purchase Vryhof at £27-10-0 per morgen.[325] The Deputy Secretary of Bantu Areas and Development had a concern that although the department supported the sale of the land because if would eradicate a 'black spot', meaning a portion of black landholding in an overall white area, the transaction should not be handled as such because that would force the government to offer replacement land for Molema. The department replied to Hartzenberg that it had no objection to the sale, and he could apply for a permit from the relevant Group Areas Board.[326] Molema sold Vryhof, not to Hartzenberg, but to Francois Jacobus Prins in March 1961.[327]

The Department of Bantu Administration and Development had supported the sale because it had eradicated a 'black spot', but this was only on paper. On the ground, the problem of a resident population of black householders on the farm persisted.

> The removal of the Bantu currently living on the above-mentioned farm is currently receiving the attention of this department. Difficulty is being experienced with determining ownership and it will be appreciated if you would provide the full details with regard to the following: (a) stand number and size of each subdivision (b) the name of the owner of every subdivision (c) the name and dates on title deed.[328]

Vryhof had been a 'private location' since the 1880s. There were dozens of placement holders on the farm. Silas Molema's 1003 morgen, which his son had inherited, was only one portion of the larger farm, which was 6018 morgen. Prins had already been an owner of likely an adjoining portion to Molema's before the purchase. Helena Britz, Theuns Pollard and Petrus van Biljon were the three other owners of Vryhof's subdivisions. Like Prins, they had all purchased their portion between 1903 and 1914.[329] The black residents on the white-owned farms were most certainly sharecroppers. Molema's portion presented a larger density of resident householders because that property had been a chiefly jurisdiction alongside other arrangements of tenancy, including at least three generations of white tenants. Vryhof was not the only farm in the district that presented this problem. Black peoples on the land had to go. The apartheid dispensation of 'forced removals' in the areas of 'white' designation in the South African countryside had begun.

XVI

Sebopioa and Modiri Molema, along with four other senior chiefs of the Barolong approached the District Commissioner of Lobatse to discuss the legal status of the Barolong Farms.[330] It was in the wake of Lotlamoreng

Montsioa's death five months before in February 1954.[331] Tiego Tawana, also in attendance, was the acting paramount chief of the Barolong in the Union, but the Bechuanaland Protectorate government was still uncertain about how to proceed on Barolong Farms.[332] The delegation made a written presentation that the Barolong and the government were at 'cross purpose' about the legal status of the Barolong Farms.[333] It was aware that the late paramount chief, 'under some mysterious purpose'

> vacillated between two extremes, now wishing to nullify the rights of registered owners or their successors by attempting to have the farms converted into an ordinary tribal area, and now favouring the intention of the status quo. We know that a small section of the residents of these farms, presumably swayed by this attitude of the Chief, and perhaps also manipulated from this background, or prompted by some vague considerations have been secretly plotting to stimulate a wave of popular feeling to have the Barolong Farms converted into a Native Reserve.[334]

The delegation thought that the Bechuanaland Protectorate administration was not confirming the appointment of Tiego Tawana as acting chief on the Barolong Farms because it supported the late paramount chief's 'representative' on his farm Good Hope, who, it claimed, was disregarding Tawana in Mafikeng. This man was apparently nursing hopes that the Barolong Farms 'may somehow be alienated from their registered occupants and successors' so that he could become paramount chief over the territory.

The occupants and their successors were no longer pressing for private titling, only a continuation of the status quo that the Barolong chiefs had negotiated at the time of British annexation. The Protectorate government, in an attempt to stir popular opinion against the holders of the farms had decided to withhold some of the improvements that the other reserves with representation on the Native Advisory Council were receiving, including developments for water. The delegation presented that they were 'determined to abide by the conditions of our father Montsioa as contained in the Certificates of Occupation, and shall resist any attempt to diminish the occupation rights which have developed upon us as natural laws of inheritance and succession'. It gave the government assurance that the farms' occupants were not seeking private title deeds, but neither were they proposing that the Barolong Farms should become a reserve.

The petition continued that 'we believe that the Certificates of Occupation while not vesting absolute title of ownership in the occupants are nevertheless a collateral security against alienation, which though unlikely is always possible by government in the case of tribal lands or reserves'. The Divisional Commissioner of the Southern Protectorate interpreted the petition accurately. He noted that the 'Certificate Owners led by Dr Molema' had been the force opposing the late Lotlamoreng Montsioa's 'attempts to treat all these farms as tribal lands'.[335] In reasserting the validity of and the rights that the certificates conferred, he noted that the same cohort were insisting on a 'clear understanding that these Barolong Farms are not tribal land in the ordinary sense of the word'.

At the same time, the Native Commissioner of the District of Mafeking in the Union wrote to the Resident Commissioner of the Bechuanaland Protectorate.[336] His was a word of warning about matters that could undermine the Protectorate's administration on Barolong Farms, where the government had not yet recognised a successor, given the state of affairs he observed unfolding in Mafikeng. His concern was that Modiri Molema had become the 'virtual head of the Tribe' there. He did not trust the doctor 'who is known as one of the leaders of the African National Congress' and believed the report of the late paramount chief's son, Kebalepile Montsioa, that Sebopioa and Modiri Molema were plotting with Tawana to use the duration of his minority to usurp the chieftaincy. The official reported that Modiri Molema had taken the leading part during the late chief's funeral proceedings and, as far as the Native Commissioner had confirmed, 'is now in the Chair when tribal matters are discussed, frequently behind closed doors in the evening'.

Kebalepile had approached the Native Commissioner with reports of the 'secret meetings', with the feeling that 'the African National Congress is trying to take over the position that is his by birth, by nomination, and in accordance with a Notarial agreement'. Kebalepile was convinced that the only reason Modiri Molema was encouraging him to continue with his education was to 'estrange him from his people'. Hence, Kebalepile and 'the councilors of the late chief's regime' were of the opinion that the minor should not proceed with his education beyond his matriculation at the end of the following year. The Native Commissioner himself was suspicious of Modiri Molema's intentions.

> Dr Molema has always tried to create the impression that he strongly supports me in my effort to have a Tribal Authority established under the provisions of the Bantu Authorities Act. At a meeting which I held in this connection recently, the questions he asked indicated the views of the African National Congress, i.e. opposition to the scheme.[337]

The Divisional Commissioner of the Southern Protectorate 'held back' the Government Gazette that would have appointed Tawana as acting chief on Barolong Farms, but the District Commissioner at Lobatse, probably tired of a situation where the territory had had no chief for almost six months, insisted that 'there would be no good purpose' in not making the appointment.[338] The Deputy High Commissioner reluctantly approved the appointment, highlighting that 'Tiego Tawana is not a strong personality and there was some evidence that he was being misled by Dr Molema and other members of the African National Congress'.[339] In the meantime, Kebalepile Montsioa 'was very worried about his position'.

In March 1955, the Resident Commissioner received the office of the High Commissioner's reply to the representation the Barolong delegation had made about the legal status of the Barolong Farms.[340] The Attorney General had explained that the 'Certificates of Occupation' were only a written description of the ordinary routines of landholding in African societies. 'But the method of allocation amongst the Barolong', he explained to the Deputy High Commissioner, 'differs fundamentally from the method adopted by other Bantu tribes throughout southern Africa'. His observation was that here as elsewhere the 'tribe' owned the land, but its control and allocation of holding rested solely in the hands of the chief. The difference was that elsewhere the allocation was verbal, and no written record existed, such as a 'certificate of occupation' registered in a lands registry. The advantage to the occupants was that the 'certificate makes them tenants for life on certain conditions', but even that was congruent with what he understood of landholding practices in such societies.

Rather than create an exception, in fact all that the Land Commission had done on the Barolong Farms, he argued, had been to put an official stamp on custom. For that reason, 'there can be no question but that the Government recognises the rights of holders thereof, if the holders comply with the conditions'. He could see absolutely no reason for consternation, as the 'certificates of occupation' were the very proof that the government needed that the Barolong Farms were not an exception to 'custom', but a written testament thereof. 'In my opinion, the Barolong Farms are tribal land, owned by the tribe but demarcated and leased in 'a manner unique in the Territory and elsewhere'. With that memo, the dilemma that had persisted for decades without resolution had instantly disappeared, to the relief and new confidence of the Resident Commissioner.

The colonial government decided that in fact it had never had a problem, other than lacking expertise on custom, which now that it had acquired it, illuminated and dispelled the problem. This is despite the fact that over a decade before, the administration had as eagerly accepted Isaac Schapera's contrary position that the Barolong Farms were an anomaly in such societies because individuals were collecting rents on the farms as though they were private property. Nevertheless, across these two positions, the common understanding was that there was no 'individual tenure' in African society and that the land belongs to the 'tribe'. Moreover, the paramount chief was landlord, but not in his own private capacity, only as the head of, and inseparable from the 'tribe', such that all rents that accrued did not belong to him but to the tribe. Now confident, the office of the Resident Commissioner dispatched notice to the Divisional Commissioner of the Southern Protectorate that the government has a strong position, strong enough in fact that he would be willing to take the matter to court.[341]

> The 'leases' granted by the certificates of occupation originally can be considered no more than paper confirmations of the normal customary allocations made by Tswana chiefs towards headmen and individuals. As such their issue was an interesting historical accident but they have no intrinsic value other than that of customary allocation ... They [certificate holders] should be told that the government recognises no rights as being granted by the certificates other than the normal customary rights ... Rights of sub-leasing, or of charging rentals to their own people for grazing do not exist and will not be recognised. Leases of any part of tribal land ... will only be so permitted on the basis that the tribe is the lessor, and that the rental will go to the Tribal Treasury.[342]

In fact, as the Government Secretary explained, the government was prepared and actually preferred to force the matter to reach the courts. It had a plan. The white Europeans on the farms, though there were not many left, were the bait that would lure the occupants to litigation. First, the government would invite occupants to make claims towards private title for those who wished to claim exemption from rules otherwise applying to a reserve. The government would then insist that 'any individual attempting to assert other rights must ask the Registrar to register transfer to himself in order that normal legal processes governing normal European land usage may be followed'. The next step was that the Registrar then iterate the interpretation that the certificates are merely a written version of customary practice and cannot apply to Europeans and refuse such transfer. 'The individual's only remedy will then be to sue the Registrar.' All that was necessary was a 'test case' which 'conveniently had presented itself' only two months after the plan.

The original occupant of the farm Klipputs had recently died, and the government had instructed that all 'arrears and future rentals' go into the Barolong Tribal Revenue, and if the 'rightful heir desires to dispute this disposal, he should do so through the courts'. The government would also investigate other leases and handle them similarly. Two of them were on Mabete – that of Phoebus Marie Fincham, which seemed to have expired after its renewal for five years in 1947, and that of J. Gouws who no longer seemed to have a lease. D. Immelman had agreed to pay into the Tribal Authority after renewing his lease on Korwe, while on Ramah, the tenants P.J. Fincham and the Native Recruiting Corporation were already paying their rents into Tribal Treasury. P.J. Lemmer had vacated his portion of Korwe 'in accordance with instructions'.

The Divisional Commissioner of the Southern Protectorate discussed the matter with Kebalepile Montsioa.[343] Although Tiego Tawana was acting paramount chief on the Barolong Farms, the Protectorate government had made it very clear this was not a regency during Kebalepile's minority. The government would only make a decision when Tawana's tenure ended. The Divisional Commissioner had suggested to his superiors in Mafeking that 'it would be more advisable not to mention him [Kebalepile] by name in any notice of appointment'.[344] That situation, added to which was Kebalepile's paranoia that Sebopioa and Modiri Molema meant to alienate him from his position as paramount chief through the person of Tiego Tawana, allowed the Divisional Commissioner more than enough room to have his way.

He relayed to Kebalepile that the government would recognise him as the paramount chief on Barolong Farms on the understanding that the territory becomes an ordinary reserve. Kebalepile committed that as soon as he had been appointed, he would recall all the certificates 'for examination' after which if he does reissue them, it would be 'on the clear understanding that they convey no title whatsoever'.[345] The official was already referring to him as the 'young Barolong Chief'. Kebalepile was very young, twenty-four years old, fresh out of boarding school. Understandably, he sought experienced Protectorate chiefs for support and council. He found one at least, or perhaps the older chief, Bathoen, had sought him, happy to be friend and guide to a novice wet behind the ears. The young man, Kebalepile was terrified of the man that he, Bathoen, himself had despised since their frictions in the Native Advisory Council. Their mutual enemy was Modiri Molema.

XVII

Sebopioa Molema's new understanding of his purpose in life connected him to the pioneering spirit of his grandfather, Isaac, as an evangelist and teacher. Nevertheless, he had a different message, one of the revelation of the Kingdom of rest and wholeness to which the Adventists daily 'reawakening'. Church life, the rhythms of living on the land, and being with Emang occupied his time. He had no real interest in chiefly politics any more. If anything, he wished to be left alone, preferably under the jurisdiction of the Native Commissioner, as he had requested in 1936.[346] He felt harassed by the paramount chief's 'cruel, arbitrary and autocratic treatment towards my person'. He rarely contributed to the meetings of the Native Advisory Council although he duly attended. He remained at Signal Hill, not in the bustle of Mafikeng. Money was very short, but during war years scarcity applied to everyone. He was the only Molema man among the women – Emang Molema, Anna Molema, Hellen Molema and Ella Khama – who saw Adventist evangelism not merely as a personal work of salvation, but as the redeeming path of the *morafe*.

He made no further applications for work until eventually work with fulltime pay found him.[347] The appointment followed the death of Tiego Tawana. Sebopioa would occupy that position during the 'minority of the heir'. The Assistant Native Commissioner recommended him to the Secretary of Native Affairs as a 'suitable person for the appointment' and 'known to me personally'. He started work on 1 July 1941.[348] He wrote very infrequently to the colonial administration, once in 1944 to request permission to purchase ammunition.[349] For five years, the government had prohibited such purchase because of the war. Sebopioa complained that 'vermin and strange dogs which run loose in the Native Reserve are killing livestock'. His next correspondence to the government was in July 1948.[350] He requested three weeks of medical leave so he could proceed to Johannesburg for treatment. In the meantime, his son, Matlho, had returned home. He had not proceeded to Fort Hare and had become a very keen farmer and cultivator. In 1949, Matlho made a bulk order for seedlings of a wide range of fruit.[351] He ordered no less than thirteen varieties of peach, two of naartjies and four of orange. In his grandfather's time, cultivating orchards had been the responsibility of white tenant farmers. Father and son, both devoted Adventists, now lived off the land and worked it with their own hands.

In her old age, Matlho Molema's wife, Mmaditshepe Mercy Molema, still remembered her father-in-law, Sebopioa, particularly the spiritual stature of the man who left her an inheritance of Seventh Day Adventism to which she remained devoted until her death in 2017.[352] His photograph, the fixed questioning eyes under the Wilberforce cap hung in her living room. She remembered his trumpet. She remembered Emang, her mother-in-law, but otherwise the memory of Sebopioa Molema was faint and fragmented, apart from the single story that has remained in the family's oral rendition of its past and ancestry. On the evening of 26 June 1952, Sebopioa Molema led a group of men from the reserve into the town of Mafeking. Black people could not lawfully be in the city at night. He was an elderly man by then, seventy-two years old, of very fragile health, taking part in the Defiance Campaign of 1952. No newspaper reports of the event have survived, but apparently, the men remained in the town until morning.

In February of 1953, Sebopioa Molema had once again to apply for medical leave, this time to travel to a hospital at Kanye in the Bechuanaland Protectorate.[353] The face and language of the colonial administration had changed. Some of the government bureaucrats wrote their memoranda and reports in Afrikaans.[354] Sebopioa was at that point earning £24 and received an increase to £30 a year.[355] He had very little, if any, of the administrative enthusiasm and vision of his youth. He was merely earning a salary, carrying on with life. At the beginning of 1955, his health was still declining and he had to proceed to Johannesburg for hospitalisation.[356] He died on 25 February 1955.[357] Other Molemas' graves are in Mafikeng, but his and his household's are at Signal Hill, the dry, rocky place where he had made his home.

XVIII

As soon as Kebalepile Montsioa became the paramount chief on the Barolong Farms and the paramount ruler across the border in Mafikeng, the Protectorate government hurried to settle the matter of the farms. At the beginning of 1956, the government investigated all the leasing agreements on the farms, making sure that either all the rents went to the Tribal Treasury or all such arrangements be in abeyance until the final resolution of the matter.[358] The Divisional Commissioner of the Southern Protectorate had also been discussing the matter with Bathoen to gauge whether 'it would not be better to delay action until such time as Kebalepile was more firmly in the saddle', but he found that Bathoen had already settled the matter with the young chief.[359] Bathoen had already warned and convinced the younger man that the issue of Barolong Farms was the 'first major problem which he would have to deal with as Chief', and further that he should take 'immediate action', which would guarantee the support from 'the mass of his people'. Bathoen had also prepared Kebalepile for the opposition that would certainly come from Modiri Molema 'and one or two others'. 'In addition,' Bathoen had warned him, 'the people looked to the Chief for a decision in this matter and if he hesitated to seize the nettle now he would lose prestige with the common people.' Kebalepile, Bathoen and the Commissioner agreed that the government would take no part in these 'preliminary moves'.[360]

Bathoen had invited Kebalepile to spend some months at Kanye 'during the period of his tutorship'. In the sixth month of his office, both men approached the Divisional Commissioner, who was pleased that Bathoen had suggested a plan of action.[361] 'The young chief has taken his advice.' According to the plan, all that would be 'natural' and necessary to do would be for Kebalepile to assemble a Kgotla on the Barolong Farms. He would then vocalise 'the thought that the delay in the development programme for the Barolong Farms was due to the uncertainty regarding the present tenure of these farms and that it was clear that Government was loath to start a development plan on what might be private farms'. This would provide a sure opening for a discussion on the Certificates of Occupation at the Kgotla. Thereafter he would recall all the certificates and cancel them 'because they obviously create confusion in the minds of the people who possess them by encouraging them to believe that they give a form of title on the land'. Kebalepile's only serious concern was that Modiri Molema would oppose him, not only contesting that the chief could recall the certificates, but that Molema would wish to take the matter all the way to court. Other than that, the young chief was confident, having no doubt that 'the mass of the people will side with him'.

The Kgotla assembled about three weeks later in the winter of 1955, with about seventy Barolong present as well as Bathoen.[362] Kebalepile then proceeded to provide a history of how the land acquired the name 'farm'. He said his grandfather had 'distributed lands to his children' and gave them 'right to plough, breed cattle and build houses on these lands'. He had also divided the country up so that 'certain people would be responsible for these divisions and from these divisions the word "farms" arose'. Beyond that, he said, the word was meaningless, but allowed some people, the occupants, to carry on 'selling timber, thatching grass and other things for which the tribe received nothing' and, worse, to cause a state of confusion that prohibited the government from bringing development to the farms.

One Phetogare Motshegare raised a point that, if an objection, was a muted one. He thought certificates of occupation were already in existence and that attempting to reverse the status quo would be effectively an act of dispossession, 'to take fat from a person'. Moreover, the chief's grandfather 'did not make use of the people who did not get certificates'. In other words, in his understanding, the allocation of farms was remuneration for service in the chiefly bureaucracy. Some agreed with the chief, wishing to see the kinds of development on the farms that the government was facilitating in the surrounding reserves. 'The country should now progress' was one resident's words. Others thought the matter was a tired affair, 'old talk' that had been going on for years. 'Some people say it is their country. Others say it is the country of the Chief and it must be ruled only by the Chief.' Bathoen argued that there was nothing extraordinary in what the chief's grandfather had done, only that the words 'farms' and 'rent' were causing unnecessary confusion.

> This name 'farm' was probably meant to show the white people that the land was owned by certain people. The rent of these farms should have been regarded as a 'tribute' to the Chief. This is an old custom whereby the chest of an animal killed must go to the Chief. Even when berries were collected some of them had to go to the Chief. The Chiefs have always received things of this sort and they have shared them with the Tribe.[363]

Modiri Molema, as the colonial official in attendance noted, sat 'with the rest of his tribesmen', saying nothing, but taking 'voluminous notes of everything'. When he did stand up to speak, the young paramount chief, 'in quiet voice', ordered the elderly doctor to remove his hat. Molema 'did so hurriedly' before stating that he did not agree, but that 'he would not say anything further'. 'The Kgotla noted his objection to the otherwise 'unanimous' agreement that 'the country belonged to the Tribe and that it was for all of them to let the Government know that this country is for all the people and not for one or two people'.

Soon afterwards at the end of the year, to stamp his victory in legal writ, Kebalepile Montsioa drew up a contract between himself, as paramount chief, and the Finchams who were trading as P.M. Fincham and Sons on Mabete.[364] The leasing agreement clearly stated that the lessees had rented the property since 1911 from 'the late Silas Tau Molema and on his death from his successor, Modiri Molema'. The agreement stated that the property was now under 'Tribal Authority'. P.M. Fincham and Sons could only let ten morgen from 1 January 1957 at £18-15-0 per month and must carry out 'repairs required to put the property leased into a good state or repair' to the value of £150. Modiri Molema objected to the leasing agreement, arguing that 'he had the sole right to the land in question'. The Government Secretary in Mafeking anticipated that 'Molema will certainly bring action in the Courts to attempt to substantiate his claims to the ground either by way of ejectment [sic] of Fincham of by some other means'. On another farm, Ramah where Fincham and Sons also operated a store, it had not been possible to renew the agreement when it expired in 1946. Lotlamoreng Montsioa had 'cancelled' the 'certificate of occupation' because the lawyer, George Montsioa, had failed both to pay the 'perpetual life rent' and had been absent from the farm for a period of three years without placing a representative who had a chief's approval on the farm. The Finchams had been paying the rent to the 'Tribal Administration'. Kebalepile was 'anxious' to achieve the same result with the Finchams on Mabete. In the meantime, Modiri Molema was pressing for approval of a fresh lease between himself and Fincham and Sons.

However, the Attorney General was not at all keen to recommend the approval of the new leasing agreement between Kebalepile Montsioa and P.M. Fincham and Sons on Mabete. He thought that Modiri Molema's existing leasing agreements were not a contravention of customary law and were therefore valid if the occupant had not breached any of the clauses.[365] Silas Molema, whose name still appeared on the certificate, had not breached any of the clauses. However, there had also been no record of transfer of the rights of occupation from father to son and therefore, 'if such approval is absent, or any rate not demonstrable, how can Dr Molema claim any right under this Certificate of Occupation'. The administration had also suggested, as an alternative, that Kebalepile Montsioa write to 'all present holders of certificates' and inform them that he was cancelling and withdrawing such certificates.[366] After that notification, the new leasing agreement between himself and Fincham and Sons would be valid. In this case, the Attorney General had 'difficulty in justifying wholesale cancellation of existing valid certificates, in cases where there had been no breach of conditions'.[367] It would be 'a unilateral act' on the part of the paramount chief, indefensible in law'. The only way to intervene in the practice of landholding, he advised, was through legislation. The Protectorate Government, he argued, could simply issue 'a Proclamation cancelling all existing certificates, but protecting the right of those in occupation under such certificates'.[368]

Modiri Molema was familiar with this computation of variables. He could have pursued litigation, expensive as that route would have been, to defend the independent status of the Barolong Farms. Not only had this been the route his fathers had undertaken, but he had been deeply involved in Tshekedi Khama's preparations for his court battle against Charles Rey's proclamations. If he went ahead and approached the courts, it would be an exacting and expensive process. However, his own motivations would be quite different from these earlier court battles. Modiri Molema had no interest in strengthening a 'tribal' Barolong enclave in the Bechuanaland Protectorate. If he were to proceed to the courts, his strategy would not be to argue that Barolong Farms was an independent chiefly jurisdiction. Rather he would defend his claim to Mabete by arguing that customary law guaranteed 'security of tenure', as he had stated to Isaac Schapera. His conviction was that 'security of tenure' gave him and his heirs rights and entitlements to Mabete as though he held an actual title deed. He wanted private title, not an independent reserve.

He was during that time pushing hard for the administration to establish a legislative council out of the then Joint Advisory Council, which was constituted by representatives from both the old European and Native Advisory Councils. This legislative council could then inherit the independent status from the British administration and facilitate a parliamentary system, rule by the people themselves. He could not, and would not, support a separatist agenda. He had always worried about how easily chieftaincy overreached into individuals' personal freedoms, which was precisely what was happening to him on Mabete. He had often broken ranks with the chiefs in the Council over this question, which is how he earned the reproach of the Protectorate paramount chiefs, especially Bathoen, who was now leading the strategy to dispossess him of his family farm.

The government did not know which route he would pursue, but it stood waiting for him to act, but Kebalepile Montsioa acted quickly to force a solution before Molema could take any further action. He managed a 'transfer' of the Barolong Farms from the occupants to the 'tribe', that is, as the Government Secretary commented, 'if that word [transfer] can be correctly used'.[369] As the paramount chief, he had carried out the transaction 'on tacit reallocation [of the land] by the Chief on the death of the father'. As far as the query of the Attorney General against such a unilateral act was concerned, the Government Secretary replied that

> We think that your opinion conveyed [to the] Deputy High Commissioner 'the Barolong Farms are tribal land, owned by the tribe, but demarcated and leased in a manner unique in the territory and elsewhere' correctly

sums up the position .... The wholesale cancellation of the existing certificates may be a unilateral act but it is considered [that] such an act is defensible since the certificates do not grant any rights other than those held under normal tribal law and moreover there is no intention to deprive the holders of their rights or to displace them. The object is to clarify the occupants' conditions of occupancy.[370]

At the same time, the government was not in favour of the Attorney General's suggestion of issuing a proclamation because it would open itself up to precisely the scenario of intervening in a territory where it had not firmly established its jurisdiction. 'Would it not be to open to criticism as arbitrary Government action to extinguish what are regarded as rights without it being made clear by ordinary process that such rights do not exist?'[371] For that reason, the administration thought the Government should as far as possible be kept out of this matter and that if the issue is to be questioned, the decision should be reached if necessary by recourse to the Courts'. The colonial government did not wish to issue a proclamation on this territory, as the Cape government had done from 1902 on the Barolong territories across the border. That course had failed repeatedly, as the courts found the colonial government to be acting *ultra vires*, beyond its powers in intervening in the territories. This Protectorate administration did not want to make the same mistake.

The Attorney General understood, but was not entirely satisfied. He wanted a decision that had a firm legal basis even if there had been no litigation. The Barolong Farms were under the then renamed African Administration Proclamation because, partly in an attempt to retain the peculiar legal status of the territory, Lotlamoreng Montsioa, Modiri Molema and others had reached a compromise with Charles Rey and agreed to the proclamation. Now the Attorney General was suggesting that according to the proclamation, and in line with Isaac Schapera's description of customary law, the chief had power 'to regulate the law of occupation'.[372] 'This is one of the matters therefore on which the chief could lawfully issue orders.' Moreover, he thought it was possible to legalise the 'transfer' through a clause in the Certificates of Occupation that made the occupation 'subject to the laws, regulations and conditions that at the present or at any future time may be enforced in the Territory by me or my successor ... with reference to leases or grants of law'. The Attorney General thought that it might be acting *ultra vires* for the government to do this but at the same time 'be *intra vires* for the Chief to make regulations and conditions regarding these farms' through

381

the Kgotla'. The Government Secretary agreed.[373]

The next step was for Kebalepile to assemble the Kgotla. He did so in August 1957.[374] There were between 100 and 150 men, including twenty-five occupants one of whom was the paramount chief himself. Modiri Molema did not attend. According to the minutes, the 'Chief made clear that Barolong Farms were Barolong territory regardless of whether occupants surrendered their occupation certificates or not, including his five farms'. He explained that from then on Fincham and Sons would pay their rent into the Tribal Treasury, as some of the tenants elsewhere on the farms were already doing. However, he stated that the 'tribe' would reimburse Modiri Molema for any 'improvements' that Fincham had made on Mabete. He explained further that the only reason why his grandfather had divided the land in the manner he had done was that he had learnt from Europeans that this was the only way to protect the land from European conquest.

This time, there were some strong objections from some of the men gathered, although they were not occupants themselves. One said that the old Montsioa 'had acted very wisely' to cut up the land for 'his Headmen to look after'. He could not understand why anything had to change just because 'one or two "occupiers" had been selling thatching grass and firewood' when the chiefs could simply punish the acts 'without changing things'. He could see no reason to cancel the certificates. 'The land,' he said, 'belongs to the Chief and Tribe.' He did not consider individual certificates of occupation to suggest that the land no longer belonged to the 'tribe'. Kebalepile's short reply was that 'if people wanted to follow Montsioa's customs then they should do so properly, but he would remind them that Montsioa had powers of life and death'.

> The 24 'occupiers' present were then told to stand up. The Chief addressed them saying that he now ordered that they were not private owners of land and that the land belongs to the Tribe. He then told them that those who disagreed with this order should remain standing. The promptness of all them in sitting down was remarkable ... At the request of the Chief, the Tribe gave him authority to call in all certificates; to declare all of them to have no further legal force or effect; and to charge any person who failed on demand to surrender his certificate.[375]

Almost a month later, Kebalepile Montsioa wrote to the administration. 'The tribe agrees to all I said, and in the very near future I shall write to all the certificate holders directing them to hand over their certificates of occupation.'[376] The administration agreed that he should issue such an order under the terms of the African Administration Proclamation, as the Attorney General had advised.[377] All the rents accruing to the properties would go to the Tribal Treasury. However, Kebalepile would have to submit his cancellation notice to the administration for approval. 'The reason for the proviso which the chief may wish to know is presumably that it is desired that the order is so legally correct that no possible loopholes for intended disobedience may be left.'[378] Now all of the Barolong territory on both sides of the Molopo River, the land and the people were under the jurisdiction of the colonial government.

Once again, the colonial government had not managed to usurp the territory and bring it under its own control even when a system of 'native administration' applied on the land and the people. As had happened in the Molopo Reserve across the border, the colonial government was assisted to this end by the contestations unfolding on the ground. The eventual conquest of Barolong Farms was in part the final episode in the family feud between the Molemas and the Montsioas that very often created tension, distrust and always some degree of instability within the Ratshidi ruling class. Bathoen could easily exploit this fragility but it was more difficult to stir popular feeling against the chiefly landlords to whom many householders owed their placement. Kebalepile and Bathoen had to go to the people and persuade them that their interests were best secured by a 'tribal' system, and not the *Sekhoa* implicit in a system of tenure that protected private entitlements. There were certainly complaints about the increase in the rents and levies owed to chiefs, and anxiety that unless the status of the Barolong Farms was clarified, government improvements on the farms may not continue. Yet there was always some strong dissenting opinion against the argument that private entitlements and rents were not *Sechuana* and that they did not have roots in Barolong's history of placement.

In fact, ordinary people's rage, especially in the 1920s, had been directed at the white tenants who were fencing off pasture, water and other natural resources, and not chiefs who owned the land. Those increasingly aggressive confrontations with white farmers, the incapacity of the Protectorate government to intervene decisively in the difficult conditions of white farming enterprises in the territory and, most importantly, the system of white privilege that was emerging across the border and white settlers' failure to have the Protectorate incorporated into South Africa, were some of the reasons why there were not many white tenants left on the farms. Land, labour and capital were available for white landless men across the border in the Union of South Africa. These peasant populations on Barolong Farms had been beyond the control of the colonial government for more than seventy years. These people had been left almost entirely alone to manage their own affairs by chiefly landlords like the Molemas, but Kebalepile Montsioa had no intention to rule from afar.

XIX

In 2012, nobody in the Molema family or other relations knew anything of the struggle against Dog Tax, or of the litigation that consumed almost two decades of their great-grandfathers' and grandfathers' generations. Batho Molema said there was much that their elders had not told them, as though the past were a moment they wanted to throw away and forget about.[379] His father was Silas Molema's son, Morara Molema. His mother was Solomon Plaatje's daughter, the musical prodigy, Violet Plaatje. He remembered that many in his father's generation lived like broken men, given to drink, while their mothers looked on indifferently, pious and exhausted. He felt he had nothing to give to historians about his family – no letters, none of the gramophone records where Solomon Plaatje sang, and none of the photographs of his mother playing the piano or dancing and teaching ballet.

The transmission of the things that mattered, parents to children, children to grandchildren, had suffered an interruption that he could not explain. Every generation let the sacred things of history and memory slip through the next generation's fingers. He grew up playing with the photographs of his mother's ballet studio and the musical records with his grandfather's voice. The adults had looked on whilst the children played with family treasure. Now he felt he knew nothing of the family's history, apart from this, that 'the Molemas are a great river, whose tributaries have run dry'. Yet, perhaps – indeed more likely, both inheritance and memory disappeared under the many currents of generational conflict. The names of 'fathers' were forgotten when 'sons' were 'cutting themselves away' from the old courses of the 'fathers'.

In 1970, Nelson Mandela had spent eight years serving his life sentence on Robben Island. He had not forgotten Modiri Molema. He was thinking about him affectionately and respectfully called him 'father'.[380] He regretted that '*Ra*' had died four years before, just at the time when the struggle of apartheid was intensifying. 'The sixties were for us a decade of significant progress & achievement but they were also years of heavy reverses in which we lost, all in a row, men of eminent qualities at the very hour we needed them the most – '*Ra*, Letele, Luthuli and Prof Matthews, four hardboiled veterans who brought us countless victories and much honour.' Nevertheless, when Mandela makes mention of this older generation in his biography *Long Walk to Freedom*, first published in 1994, he does so only in harshly critical terms.[381] His recollection there is that the Transvaal Congress had carried out a coup at the 1949 conference entirely unaided, and unsupported by any of the older vanguard. He makes no mention of Modiri Molema, implicitly including him in the circle of an unhelpful, compromised and conservative old guard.

In his private archive, as a younger man, writing to Lucretia Molema, Mandela paid his due homage. In fact, his thoughts in this letter convey that he was one of the readers who had understood the message that the writer and ethnographer, Modiri Molema, had already conceptualised and narrated by 1920 in the *Bantu Past and Present*. Mandela wrote to Modiri Molema's widow that '*Ra*'s later works deal with aspects of Tswana history, but his *Bantu Past and Present* … reveals him as one who was free of ethnic limitations and very much preoccupied with national affairs'.[382] Modiri had written that first book for the fathers, who barely responded, but a much younger generation, indeed the same radical Congress from the Transvaal, had read him and understood him.

Modiri Molema had played his role as their patron in the Congress and had manoeuvred to facilitate their political success. He had waited for almost thirty years for the Congress to acquire a critical mass of likeminded men, like the Youth League, before he stepped into a political role in the executive that a man of his education and social standing would ordinarily have embraced much earlier. The Youth League had called him '*Ra*', that is to say, 'father'. Appropriately so, for they had depended to a great extent on his practices of virtue in their struggle to become men. It was not long after Mandela penned this letter that he had to confront the '1976 generation' who came to Robben Island and challenged him and his generation in the Congress. The youth considered him not to be sufficiently militant against the white regime. Indeed, the place of 'civilising heroes' in the memories of a new generation is never guaranteed as one of honour.

In fact, Modiri Molema's 'later works' are essentially not very different from the earlier *Bantu Past and Present*, which is followed by at least four biographies. The first two are of Barolong chiefs – Montsioa and Moroka, under whose reign literacy and Christianity fashioned families like the Molemas. These chiefs provided the routes of assembling the otherwise mixed, displaced frontier populations in the interior into a people who came to understand themselves as the 'Barolong'. Next, he wrote a biography of Solomon Plaatje and significantly, that of the Old Testament figure, Moses. He understood Moses as a historical figure that has inspired most of the *merafe* in the world today.[383] Moses is a prototype of the 'father'. He inspires homecoming across every corner of the Christian world. Moses accrues virtue through his difficult struggle to fashion a people. These works are not just historical texts. They also demonstrate to the reader that the efforts to make a *morafe* emerge from the labour (*tiro*) that one undertakes for the sake of another. *'Motho ke motho ka batho!'*/ 'A person is a person through other persons!' This remains a common saying in former Bechuanaland.

The contestations around *botho* are as vociferous today as they were in the past. Moreover, the everyday struggles for personhood are not a peculiarity of southern Africa or even of the continent. However, the urgency to assemble an infrastructure of connectedness to others that confers recognition, the desire for homecoming, is more desperate and palpable in the colonial world than elsewhere, and it has its own peculiarities. As historian John Iliffe observes, in African society political struggle turns on successive waves of generational conflict.[384] The colonial situation means every generation experiences a crisis of personhood more severe than the one before. Sons and daughters are likely to inherit a broken or collapsing infrastructure of personhood. Every generation's need for new repertoires of personhood, meaning new practices of making the *morafe*, locks it in contestation with the previous generation over 'tradition'. These include confrontations of blame and indignation over arrangements of placement – on the land, in families, in love and marriage, in sexuality and gender, in matters of language and everyday governance. One generation after another, the tributaries run dry where the *morafe* of the fathers implodes in the next generation 'reawakening'. The sea never settles; tides ebb and flow; castles of sand are made and remade.

Conclusion

THIS BOOK WOULD HAVE been impossible without the advantage of an astonishingly rich quotidian record created by two generations of a chiefly family whose everyday lives affected the lives of thousands of others around them. This archive allows a detailed reconstruction of everyday life: marriage, child rearing, education, piety, landholding, consumption, work and political office. The book relays the story as an entanglement of two generations, fathers and children, especially sons, in a colonial setting where institutions of chiefly and patriarchal power confronted unprecedented changes in everyday life. Innovations like waged labour and literacy could strengthen these institutions as easily as destabilise and cripple them. We met Silas Molema in the late 1880s, just after the chieftaincy became part of a British colony. Britain was relieved to find such educated, Protestant chiefs because it had acquired the territory by force of circumstance and had neither will nor money enough to rule Bechuanaland. It had taken up two giant territories, British Bechuanaland, which incorporated today's North West and Northern Cape provinces of South Africa, and the neighbouring Bechuanaland Protectorate, which is today's Botswana. The Molopo River separated the two British domains. Here were dozens of willing collaborators who wanted British protection but had a well-established infrastructure of governance to rule themselves. Britain agreed that the reserves of Bechuanaland on both sides of the Molopo would not be Crown Lands, but territory belonging to chiefs themselves. Britain would pay chiefs' salaries but would minimise interference in the reserves.

Having now come to the end of the story, what is clear is that of all the roles that Silas Molema relished – as did his sons later – none mattered more than being a father, but not in the sense of a family man. Silas Molema was a father in the sense that the anthropologists of Bechuanaland identify as a particular orientation to everyday practice. The introductory section of this book foregrounds the concept of personhood (*botho*) through the anthropological literature on Bechuanaland, but with the Molemas' story now told, it is useful both to revisit that literature and to highlight the significance this book brings to our understanding of personhood. In the 1920s, as the introductory and earlier chapters outlined, anthropologist J.T. Brown described how people of Bechuanaland spoke of all everyday practice, from tilling the ground to marriage, as *tiro*, meaning to work, even when there was no accumulation nor active exercise of labour.[1] In the 1970s, Hoyt Anderson encountered the same situation. People said they were working even when they were napping in the sun.[2] In the early 1990s, Jean and John Comaroff came across hardworking mineworkers earning a wage, but despairing that they have not worked at all.[3] The Comaroffs explain that this work, *tiro*, was not reducible to labour power but was the self-construction of the person in relation to others, a 'creative process'.[4] In this cosmology, 'an individual not only produces for himself, but actually produces his entitlement to be a social person'.[5] One yields value from this work partly in the form of things, but most importantly in the form of relationships, that is to say, connectedness to others. Where there has been no such work, there are no 'persons' or, in the vernacular, there are no *batho*. Brown describes people's understandings of social death as a situation where 'though the body lives and moves it is only a grave ... the essential "personhood" is dead'.[6]

However, the anthropological literature does little more than describe this peculiar orientation to work and how it differed from Europeans' understanding of labour. The significance of this book is in its analytical conceptualisation of the work of personhood. It reveals personhood as primarily a moral category in a setting where everyday practice is both an opportunity and a moral duty to transform another's body, consciousness and mental capacity into being a 'person' and, in so doing, confirm one's own position within the moral universe of personhood. In fact, without another's work, one cannot be a person. Without this reciprocal transaction, though one may be alive, one remains merely a living thing, an organism like dogs and birds, merely an extension of the natural environment. In the language of a painter, Gustav Klimt, to remain alive, indeed to *be*, is to be held securely by another in the colourful universe of connectedness.[7] To die is to fade away like a shadow receding in the background: solitary, undistinguished and unnoticed. At any moment, death threatens to encroach upon the social mechanisms of mutual recognition. This book foregrounds personhood as the 'measure' of this existential worth. Personhood is an existential capacity, a quality not related primarily to material interest nor to status.

The important question for the historian of the colonial frontier is this: in a context of continuous cultural change, what are those routines, those everyday practices, that yield a reciprocal exchange of existential weight? I am proposing that one of these practices was 'fatherhood', leading us back to Silas Molema's understanding of himself. He saw himself as the father of 'the House' in Jan Vansina's sense of the concept, which means the solidarity that emerges from strategies of accumulating people into the homestead.[8] Biological children count but are far from enough. Molema's role as a father was the work, or *tiro*, of making persons. I have described the negotiations of intimacy and dependence that emerged along this colonial frontier where men of different skin colour shared the land through complicated arrangements of tenancy and kinship, landlordism and fathering, private entitlements and communal claims. Human beings' apprehension and experience of time matters here. A son who accepts placement on his father's lands today can tomorrow claim to have been merely a tenant whose lifetime of working the same land had been the down payment that made him an independent landowner. The key frame of reference here is the relationship between time, being and narrative.

The intimacies of family, friendship, Christian 'brotherhood' and chiefly patronage all mediate and are themselves sustained by the motivation to stand out as a man. In the relationship between Phoebus Fincham and Silas Molema for instance, these ambiguous entanglements both suspended race but also revealed the prejudices of skin colour when tensions around morality and common decency erupted. Molema's 'House' had an intricate, not often consistent, system of subscription where intimacy involved various kinds of rents and expectation. Not only tenancy and other relationships on the land, but also marriage, reflected how the negotiations of intimacy in everyday practice staged and mediated people's imperative to make personhood. Every new marriage posed a threat to the established routines of personhood because the rearing of children was women's work and gave them the power to influence children's disposition and mores. The fathers arranged marriages to ensure that sons brought in women who shared the moral sensibility of 'the House' and who would consolidate it by reproducing members that would bolster its esteem. There was too much at stake, not least fathers' own personal esteem as men, to risk an inappropriate match. Fathers never anticipated that young people could consider love and intimate partnership to be a more enabling context of personhood. They could not conceive of how romantic pairing can mediate honour, personal esteem and purpose beyond the couple's own homestead.

The family, in its intimate hierarchies, extends as a negotiation from the homestead into the world beyond. Time and circumstance, not biological or social proximity, form the homestead. The Africanist scholarship on this incorporationist tradition has grown, from John Iliffe who stresses the demographic imperatives of this tradition for state formation and political identity, especially in situations of land shortage to Jane Guyer and others' emphasis on people as depositories of multiple capacities, including knowledge and social status.[9] James Ferguson and Paul Landau both highlight the political significance of this incorporationist tradition in the making of precolonial and colonial political identities and the possibilities that this tradition present to postcolonial states to address the injustices of the past, especially landlessness, poverty and inequality.[10] However, whilst foregrounding the continent's key orientation of 'wealth in people', this literature does not consider these essentially moral processes of incorporation as fundamental to how we, human beings everywhere, daily grapple with the dilemmas of existence.

The literature's conception of 'wealth' remains within the already widely theorised categories of material accumulation, knowledge, status and other 'symbolic' wealth. We have not yet considered, much less theorised, the place of a different yet fundamental social currency, which is the capacity of existence, the very capacity for one to *be*.[11] It is a capacity that, as I shall again highlight below, resides in-between the sociology of practice and the phenomenology of being. It brings Durkheim to Heidegger, making the analysis of the 'social' inseparable from the understanding of the singular entity we call 'self'. When we take into account that the imperative of the incorporationist tradition, making persons, is a moral negotiation, then we can understand that there are moral limits and considerations to this incorporationist tradition. Making a dozen proper persons is more important and better than accumulating hundreds of individuals of doubtful personhood. In fact, a rapidly growing population of individuals that are of compromised or inadequate personhood (at least in the assessment of one or more strata of society) makes for a grim prognosis of social stability. It is a perfect recipe for splits and cleavages. In view of personhood as an existential capacity, I have considered in this book what it takes to assemble the existential weight of 'the House' through incorporation and other means. I suggest that such accumulation of existential weight or existential 'wealth' depends on at least three related orientations of *being in time*.

Firstly, 'moreness' speaks to the audacious agency of an individual standing alone yet being made 'more', being injected with a capacity beyond himself or herself, amplified by the substance of personhood that can only come by the recognition of another through moral routines of practice. Secondly, 'placement' is the experience of simultaneous dependence and autonomy available to the members of 'the House'. One's experience of freedom paradoxically articulates in a situation of care for and dependence on others. Lastly, 'homecoming' speaks to human beings' inclination to forge coherence and continuity out of a disjointed lifetime of practice in an attempt to remember the past in ways that preserve our location in 'the House' despite actual events of distance and dislocation. Homecoming inhabits the amorphous terrain of memory and imagination. Thus, a younger generation can lend their new practices a moral hue by relaying them as a legacy of an older generation. At the same time, homecoming captures the mind's tendency to sift through the present to find ideas and practices that can redeem the outcome of past events and 'make them right'. In memory, the past also presents fertile potentialities for what the future might yet become. Homecoming is the element of personhood that speaks most directly to the narrative dimensions of 'reawakening'. These three elements, in my conception, shape one's experience of 'the House' along a continuum of 'fullness' to 'lightness'. The 'mood' through which one apprehends oneself is along the continuum between the 'nothingness' we experience in anxiety and the 'abundance' of happiness or feelings of achievement or fulfilment.

The crisis of personhood and practices of nationalism

In Bechuanaland, the name *morafe* stood for the solidary of personhood, referring to all those who belong in 'the House'. The Molemas' historical significance emerges from how they saw their family as holding a divine revelation about which repertoires of everyday practice made persons. They considered it a calling to answer the following question: how does one know that he or she is living amongst persons and is therefore himself a person? We can say they led a life of 'proclamation', like Old Testament prophets, daily announcing a revelation of the true *morafe*'s moral repertoires that yielded a substantial weight of personhood. They sought to admonish those whose way of life diminished the *morafe*. This is what the twin vernacular concepts in colonial Bechuanaland, *Sekhoa* and *Sechuana*, referred to. Those repertoires of practice that did not yield much in the existential currency of personhood were *Sekhoa*. In the currency of existential worth, they were impoverishing, even though they could enhance one's capacity to become materially rich or help one's professional aspirations. On the other hand, *Sechuana* was how people referred to 'tradition', those repertoires of practice that people utilised to confer and amplify existential worth and recognition on one another. *Sechuana* built the existential weight of 'the House'. Its 'fullness' depended on *Sechuana* but *Sekhoa* crippled and diminished the *morafe*. *Sekhoa* precipitated the event of existential death. Molemas considered 'reawakening' the *morafe* into traditions of personhood as a divine vocation, which they carried out in typical Protestant piety as a sacrifice, a duty whose reward was a personal revelation of God.

Over the seventy years covered in this book, we see that at any given time there was always more than one such charismatic leader, more than one set of followers, and therefore, the *morafe* always existed in overlapping multiples, sometimes in plural harmony, at other times in ferocious competition for moral supremacy. We also see a correlation between moments of anxiety over thinning or diminishing personhood and the everyday narrative of 'reawakening' to the *morafe*'s 'origins'. Land shortages, the influence of paid work and education on gender roles, and a sense of accelerated social change often created anxiety over manhood. Those affected debated and introduced new ideas of what would make the *morafe* great again, of who was in and who was out, and how they should live with reference to an idea of a perfect antiquity.

The dearth of personhood was a fertile moment for charismatic leaders to emerge and mobilise others to 'reawaken' to their 'origin'. These leaders both pronounced and modelled new moral repertoires for making persons, whilst also competing for power. These leaders were not necessarily people of gravitas who mobilised others by speaking and preaching. Rather, they *lived* the redemptive repertoires of personhood through their works of everyday life, similar to how early Protestants first institutionalised the disciplines that forged capitalist accumulation within everyday worlds of virtue. It is the same discipline of the Pauline epistles, 'working out your salvation in fear and trembling'.[12] Their followers 'recognised' these leaders as the latter continuously proved themselves by demonstrating the discipline that leads to personal esteem.[13] Solomon Plaatje identified Silas Molema. He initiated a reciprocal transaction of recognition and esteem that drew other educated men around the virtues of formal schooling in the pages of *Koranta ea Becoana* during the crisis of personhood that such men confronted in the early twentieth century.

Historians associate the narrative of 'reawakening' with a unique 'origin' as indicative of a peculiar sensibility – that of the 'nation', but I have been very cautious throughout this book not to couple the analytical category 'nation', with the vernacular concept '*morafe*'. I do not consider them to be the same even though, as often happens in the archive, people many times translated the Sechuana word '*morafe*' into the English word 'nation'. In exploring the shifting meanings of the *morafe* over time, I observed that the idea of 'reawakening' emerged in discourses about the *morafe* only at certain points in time, which is when one or other stratum of society was experiencing a dearth of personhood. It was during such moments of 'reawakening' that the vernacular, existential category *morafe* became commensurate with the analytical category 'nation'. This implies that the nation is a moment in time *within* the *morafe*, that is to say, the nation is one distinctive and potent instance within this already existing solidarity of personhood. This is when people announce new routines of practice that manufacture personhood or innovate upon existing ones in an attempt to rehabilitate a thinning experience of the same. The experience of 'reawakening' allows novelty and innovation in the sphere of moral practice but in a manner that preserves individuals' place in the *morafe* as a continuing, ethical universe. People can access the capacity to live in new ways, and yet remain the persons they have always been from 'long ago'. The 'origin' lies, not behind them, but ahead of them like an invitation to destiny. Narrative is how human beings manipulate time, shortening and lengthening duration, altering the sequence of events. In the moment of 'reawakening', the anxiety of thinning personhood coincides with the capacity to amplify this existential currency.

The book has identified the narrative of 'reawakening' to the *morafe*'s origins to occur during the anxieties of a dearth of personhood. If anxiety is the apprehension of self in 'nothingness', as the introductory chapter describes, then such a dearth of personhood is the event for the dislocating, nullifying 'lightness of being' in 'the House' or the *morafe*. Thus, in the anxieties of the dearth of personhood, we enter the terrain of 'self', or at least, one key 'mood' of its apprehension. The power of the nation as a plural affinity is the hallmark of Benedict Anderson's work, as he interrogates why the national sensibility has such strong affinities that people have gone to war for their nation, surrendering their own lives for a perfect stranger. This book suggests that this is because a connectedness to another is critical, in fact necessary, for the apprehension of oneself. That the capacity to be oneself relies profoundly on a connectedness to another, is in part the answer to Anderson's question. How this work of personhood is achieved is precisely the heart of the contestations around personhood and the boundaries of its moral communities.

This point is worth repeating as it has theoretical implications. It is a subtle but critical paradox that the everyday works necessary for the apprehension of self, or *tiro* in the language of Bechuanaland, are wholly social and reciprocal. They require 'another'. This is contrary to the phenomenologist's stipulation that that the place of 'self' is outside, even opposed to, the anonymity of the social. The introductory chapter, for this reason, highlighted the writings of Siri Hustvedt, who maintains that the prevailing philosophical paradigms that theorise 'self' outside of 'another' require revision. At the same time, these processes of personhood suggest that the sociologies of practice must come to grips with 'self' as a *real* analytical category, which is not to say that it is a stable, consistent capacity. It cannot be so because we are beings in *time*, through whichever orientation of practice at our disposal, including language. Thinking about personhood places the conceptualisation of nationalism not primarily 'out there' in the sphere of public, political mobilisation, but 'in here', in the very intimate spaces between us.

In recent years, as a colloquial term, personhood has acquired warm, imprecise feelings of community and mutual support, but actually, personhood is a capacity that we work, struggle and compete to make every day. During these struggles in colonial Bechuanaland, charismatic leaders and their followers did not stop at gathering numbers to grow their solidarity of personhood as they 'reawakened' to a new *morafe*. They also sought to transform the infrastructure of practice permanently. Political power is required to provide the material and ideological infrastructure needed to change the present and support new interpretations of personhood, and then to recalibrate the sphere of everyday relationships in ways that confirm and entrench these new practices and conceptions of personhood. Hence, charismatic leaders and their followers court state or state-like institutions because these have the judicial and legislative powers, as well as other coercive measures to intervene in everyday relationships. Not only can these institutions disallow or hinder practices that do not conform to the new or recalibrated repertoires of a moral life, but they can also enforce the new boundaries of emerging solidarities of personhood. They can help coin and enforce classifications like 'black' and 'white' for instance and map their territories. These political means refurbish or replace those everyday institutions that no longer support personhood and quash alternative moral outlooks whose supporters are also working to institutionalise them.

As we see in colonial Bechuanaland, these moral struggles pitted men against women, sons against fathers, age against youth, because whilst some were pressing for institutional change, others of course were succeeding in making personhood through these same institutions. These were protracted struggles taking place along many fronts, as new permutations of 'the House' attempted to establish themselves when others remained standing or were in the making. The arena of these intimate battles includes class relations. As John Lonsdale puts it, '[t]he real class issue is how within the most pressing community of reputation . . . one may gain or retain the status of moral agent, neither an anti-social swindler on the make nor slavish instrument of stronger men's wills'.[14] In John Iliffe's conceptualisation, in these everyday struggles we are dealing with the making or unravelling of 'honour'.[15] The way to win is not only to forge alliances with powerful institutions, including the British Empire in this instance, but also to transform these existing institutions. Moreover, for those who win the battle, political power also supports the cultural and other tools that can establish the new moral worlds as 'natural'. In lobbying political power to intervene in struggles for personhood, as Solomon Plaatje did superbly, people were also putting across their own political ideologies and imaginations to shape and transform these political institutions. We see that Plaatje was not only lobbying the British Empire. He was also attempting to influence how Britain and especially ordinary British people in the metropolis understood the moral responsibilities of their government and empire. Like Plaatje's attempts, many of these struggles are undertakings that do not succeed. Many do not gain momentum beyond their regional geographies and they later dissipate. They would remain unknown to us were it not for archives like the Molemas' remarkable records. These failed experiments never acquire the institutional political muscle to create an 'official' archive.

I coin the term 'practices of nationalism' to refer both to the many private everyday routines of charismatic leadership that aim to reinterpret and remodel the infrastructure of virtue and also to the public strategies of lobbying state institutions to intervene in the crisis of personhood by institutionalising new and recalibrated repertoires of virtue. At least three distinct practices of nationalism appear in this book, each affecting the next in intricate and unexpected ways. All these practices of nationalism emerged in a situation of intensifying generational conflict, worsening land shortages and the dry, hard conditions of living along the fringes of the Kalahari. This was also a time when the white settler demographic was stratifying. Many of those who were embracing the identity of 'whites' had plunged into poverty just as the consciousness of race as skin colour was emerging from the late nineteenth century along the frontier.

Practices of nationalism in Bechuanaland: Making of Botswana and South Africa

In the first part of the book, 'Fathers/Moreness', *Koranta ea Bechuana* captured educated patriarchs' practices of nationalism. This is the first distinct practice of nationalism described in the book. The newspaper was both a moral practice and a political manoeuvre to court both chieftaincies and the British Empire as allies in educated men's efforts to remake manhood. At the beginning of the twentieth century, the educated generation of 'the fathers' understood formal schooling as a moral practice, like a circumcision of the soul, that would turn the sensibility of women and youth away from lifestyles and choices that privileged individual aspiration at the cost of thinning men's experience of personhood. Formal schooling would encourage submission to chiefly and patriarchal authority, and teach Sechuana, a literary vernacular by which frontier people would identify as the 'Bechuana' – that is if they would 'reawaken' to the announcement of those like the Molemas who had the divine revelation of the *morafe* and revealed it through their everyday works of personhood (*tiro*).

Although this practice of nationalism was ultimately unsuccessful, Solomon Plaatje's political disposition and writings on race and empire at the time is a sterling example of how some Africans have lobbied and aimed to transform the British Empire in the struggle to preserve and bolster personhood. There was a diminishing expectation of white collar-work, which meant that educated men had few means to support their own and their dependants' aspirations. They could neither establish nor grow their own 'house'. In a word, they could not become fathers. *Koranta* proclaimed that property in the countryside and a profitable livelihood working the land were precisely the ways of personhood from 'long ago' that formal schooling, appropriately, should inculcate. Britain could intervene in the crisis of manhood by freeing the agrarian market economy of racial bias and upholding independent chiefly institutions that both facilitated access to land and kept women and youth in tow and submissive to patriarchal authority. The empire could thus help to rehabilitate and sustain manhood.

The 'South Africa' that Solomon Plaatje envisioned was by no means the 'South Africa' we have today, or even that of the early Congress at this time. Then the border between present-day South Africa and Botswana had some implication for the movement of animals, but less for that of people, nor did it break up colonial Bechuanaland into separate political geographies. Solomon Plaatje's vision was of autonomous chiefly jurisdictions both woven into a liberal parliamentary system and welded onto a global imperial federation of 'progress' under British rule. This convoluted conception of political authority was not a political idea he was borrowing from elsewhere; it is how he lived, as a progressive 'Mochuana' loyal to his chief, a voter in the Cape's liberal franchise, an ambitious internationalist, and a proud British subject. Each of these practical locations of his lived experience facilitated and strengthened the other. He was attempting to make permanent an existing reality within imperial governance that could safeguard the landscape of virtue that Silas Molema, as a charismatic leader, was modelling to his followers every day. Plaatje's ideas fit into a larger story. As Frederick Cooper observes, it is important for historians to explore the contingency of the nation state on the continent and thereby discover the failed experiments of how Africans positioned themselves in relation to European empire.[16]

The second distinct practice of nationalism appears in the second part of the book, 'Family/Placement'. After the South African War (1899–1902) a new settler government wished to take control of the reserves of Bechuanaland south of the Molopo River – that is to say, former British Bechuanaland, as part of the Union of South Africa. During the late nineteenth century chiefly power in Bechuanaland had remained valuable to British imperial and colonial rule, but less so to the new settler Union government established in 1910. The settler government found that chiefly power remained strong and difficult to break where a mixed population of black, white, brown, yellow and *métis* had made a home on the land. The cornerstone segregationist legislation in what would become South Africa, the Natives Land Act of 1913, conquered the reserves of Bechuanaland, and designated all the reserves south of the Molopo River as territories for a population it classified as 'black'. However, powerful chiefs continued both to resist the conquest of their lands, but also to fight among themselves for the control of the lands and people of colonial Bechuanaland. In the Molopo Reserve the government was unable to break the stalemate at Rietfontein where chiefs were fighting for power and territory.

The colonial government was looking for a mechanism to crush the power of chiefs and ultimately take control of the land and the people. For at least two decades, the government remained a frustrated onlooker as the contest between chiefs raged on. The colonial government could neither subdue the war amongst chiefs for land nor maintain law and order in the reserve it then owned. However, from the 1920s, ordinary people's moral contestations around personhood at Rietfontein proved critical to the success of the settler government and to the legitimacy of segregation and racial ordering from below. The colonial government became many landless people's ally against chieftaincy and the property dispensation it mediated. Landless people knocked on the door of the local state, seeking free access to land in the reserve, and wishing to do away with rents and other moral requirements of chiefly placement there. People said they were 'reawakening' to the practice of chieftaincy from 'long ago', where chiefs had no control over land and people unless an individual gave a chief such personal jurisdiction.

Newspapers had no role in these practices of nationalism from below, only the disciplined works of everyday life as demonstrated by the leading charismatic instigators. These leaders ploughed the ground and raised their mealies without yielding their rents, tributes and 'subscriptions' to chiefs in Mafikeng. They relied on oral repertoires of history telling in communal gatherings to announce their 'reawakening' to the ways of being on the land from 'long ago'. They attempted to announce their 'reawakening' also through the hard labour of building an Anglican church, which was an attempt both to lobby a powerful institution that could intervene in the struggle for personhood and to create a distinguishing religious marker for their unique *morafe*. Men's motivation in these struggles was the desire to establish and maintain an independent home of one's own. For each to possess their own 'house' necessitated a recalibration of the ways and the boundaries of 'the House'. This moment was critical to the evolution and successful implementation of segregationist policy in South Africa just at a time when the stalemate at Rietfontein was demonstrating the severe limits of colonial rule on the ground. The colonial government proved to have very little capacity to act despite the promulgation of the Natives Land Act which had given the Union government complete ownership and control of the reserves of Bechuanaland.

The 'reawakening' from below fashioned a peculiar bureaucracy of native administration from the 1920s in Bechuanaland. After the Supreme Court ruled that chiefs' jurisdiction was 'personal' and not 'territorial', chiefs kept their salaries but had increasingly limited functions south of the Molopo. Ordinary people streamed instead to the offices of Native Commissioners. Overworked white colonial administrators used customary law to regulate diverse spheres of practice, from marriage to property. They adjudicated an increasing number of cases and maintained law and order. The result was, in a sense, not only an assertion of a central settler government but a whitening of chieftaincy from below, under Anglophone rule, in which white officials governed thousands of black people *directly* through customary law. The government promulgated the Native Administration Act of 1927 guided and emboldened by this rearrangement of colonial rule in the reserves of Bechuanaland. That legislation finally brought the old arrangement of chieftaincy in former British Bechuanaland, and its control over the land, to its knees.

As we turn to the third part of the book, 'Sons/Homecoming', there emerged a dispensation of empire south of the Molopo River that differed significantly from that across the river in the Bechuanaland Protectorate. Even before the victory of Afrikaner power in 1948, educated chiefs in the Protectorate understood that the border running through colonial Bechuanaland now had serious political implications. There was a 'South Africa' in the making, and they set themselves on a course determined never to experience anything like it. The formation of the Native Advisory Council in the Protectorate from the early 1920s was fortuitous in that, whilst the colonial administration intended to use it primarily to help generate funds through taxation, the Council assembled senior chiefs from across the Protectorate together. Even though some British administrators sought to weaken the powers of chiefs, the Council nevertheless created a forum of collaboration and bargaining with government officials. Indeed, at the heart of chiefs' own debates and disagreements about *Sechuana* and *Sekhoa* was a shared alarm that 'native administration' could blow them away like a wind from across the Molopo River and establish in the Protectorate the same template of race and segregation that was solidifying in the Union. Despite their quarrels over *Sechuana*, their mistrust of one another and the backroom dealing that sometimes took place behind one another's backs, chiefs all nevertheless agreed that '*Bochuana*', the state of being in *Sechuana*, required a permanent, secure border with the Union of South Africa.

Moreover, chiefs were willing to hold hands with the empire through the Council in order to avoid precisely the crisis of personhood on the land that had turned ordinary people determinedly against chiefs south of the Molopo River. Through this collaboration, chiefs had a say in how the money collected through taxation could support the reserves. They had the means to sponsor the agrarian aspirations of their people. They could become fathers and grow 'the House' of the *morafe* whose repertoires of personhood they were, at the same time, asserting, innovating upon, and vociferously debating. They kick-started impressive agrarian developments that alleviated cattle disease and provided irrigation to increase food yields. They built schools and paid salaries to teachers and a stratum of civil servants in chiefly bureaucracies. They prevented contestations around landholding and chiefly power by participating in legislation on land tenure in ways that firmly entrenched their place in the control of the land. At first, chiefs feared and abhorred the thought of 'native administration'. Tshekedi Khama resisted it fiercely, but in time, even he saw opportunities to turn the new legislation to advantage. Chiefs welcomed 'progress' but made sure such progressive ideas were of their own making, protective of chiefly and patriarchal power. They remained suspicious of 'educated' youth who, in their view, enjoyed so much 'freedom' in South Africa that they would infect the reserves with *Sekhoa*.

Chiefs' practice of nationalism, as they were 'reawakening' into *Sechuana*'s way of personhood, *Bochuana*, captured much of *Koranta*'s earlier vision but was ultimately more successful in shaping the empire as an instrument to uphold chiefly and patriarchal power. It is the third distinct practice of nationalism in this book. The word *Bochuana* would become *Botswana* in the new late-twentieth-century orthography. As the configuration of the nation state became more popular in political discourse after the Second World War, the Native Advisory Council was an important forum where chiefs embraced the nation state as the appropriate political arrangement of the solidarity of personhood they had been institutionalising through the Council for over two decades. The later transformation of the Native Advisory Council into a legislative body, shaped in part by the growing appeal of the nation state as the moral articulation of the *morafe*, ensured that chiefs took the leading role in the evolution of democratic state institutions in what would become Botswana. Chiefly power and democratic state institutions would continue to reinforce each other in this country many decades into the dispensation of self-rule in Botswana.

Modiri Molema's intense longing for personal freedom as paramount to a weight of being and his fierce distrust of unmitigated chiefly power, were to a significant degree also about the pain he suffered having had to choose between obedience to his father and love for his intended wife. It was a private loss he probably never shared with anyone. Especially in the aftermath of this personal pain, he determined to give political shape to that *morafe* of his personal esteem, one where mutual recognition did not depend on the sacrifice of desire. One could love one's father without surrendering one's own freedoms of movement, association and imagination. These conceptions of placement, of how to live freely and yet remain in the care of others, differed from the expectations of virtue in his father's 'House'. He searched for concepts, words, models and theories that could give name to the political infrastructure that would legitimate and support the alternative solidarity of personhood in which he already lived. He had a long journey of homecoming.

Conclusion

From his time at Kimberley and Glasgow, he had settled on the ideological matrix of 'blackness' as a unifying frame that connected him to his first love and made honourable what would otherwise have been an illicit association. At the same time, the marriage would have facilitated his own charismatic role of 'proclamation'. His marriage would have been an ordinary, mundane work of everyday life, *tiro*, which revealed to others the essential truth of the *morafe*'s ethical boundaries. The *morafe*'s boundaries were the breath of the African continent and its diaspora. It was black people, *Bancho*, and not the regionalist 'little people', *dichabanyana*, of the fathers. His marriage would demonstrate the fertility and enlarged capacities of this ethical universe. For instance, the couple had had in mind to create the first black-owned hospital in southern Africa. Their union would serve as a prophetic occurrence, proving fruitful in not merely birthing children, but also in growing 'the House' as it brought black people together in this and other works of 'progress'. The pair would model to others what was possible when a solidarity of blackness came together. For him, love was an encounter with truth where being two, a couple, facilitates the apprehension of being oneself in 'fullness', abundance, moreness.[17] Love was not a sacrifice, not an emptying, but a fertile event that revealed a new truth and thereby achieved a shift in the understanding of virtue, of the world and its possibilities. When the marriage was dashed, seven years later in 1919, Modiri Molema's displacement from this deeply intimate encounter of mutual recognition sealed his conviction that the world he desired was indeed moral and just, and propelled him deeper into the 'reawakening' into his *morafe*, a 'House' that preserved the intimate freedoms of his soul. In Alain Badiou's language, Modiri Molema remained faithful to that 'Event' for the rest of his life.[18] This is how he too became a father of his own 'House'.

The appellations 'nation', 'nationalism' and, especially, 'national' had been around throughout Modiri Molema's life, but it was only in the 1940s that the political crisis and discourses of the Second World War attached these words to a precise model of statehood – the nation state. What mattered most, at least for him, was that the model allowed for the kinds of freedoms he valued in his intimate associations. People had a say through the ballot and were therefore not subject to the arbitrary dictates of rulers, including chiefs and fathers. In fact, the nation state, in his mind, subjugated these regionalist identities and countered the segregationist design of the colonial government on the land. By the time he had settled on the meaning that the word 'nation' held in the political discourse of the 1940s, he had already been embracing the strategies, boundaries and possibilities of this unique

'House' but it had been as a constellation of freedoms that did not have an actual, substantive model.

However, his everyday orientation to others also greatly complicated the place of skin colour in the incorporationist tradition of his *morafe*. Like his father, he was a Christian and a man of the frontier. He disavowed racial segregation. The fraternity of Christendom to which he remained attached was an inheritance from the fathers, a robe of many colours, as were his relationships with his tenants, friends and workers across the colour bar. He was also an internationalist. Even in the Congress, he worked looking outward to the world beyond Africa's shores, observing global trends, looking for partnerships in other parts of the world, and seeing the democratisation of southern Africa as part of a progressive and global movement. He held both a firm embrace of 'blackness' and a trenchant disavowal of racial segregation. The nation state as a lived experience, or at least as a moral negotiation, had the potential to satisfy this ambiguity. Otherwise he certainly would have rejected it.

Thus, Modiri Molema found the *morafe* of his esteem in the moment of the nation state. That was the final episode of his homecoming, and with very significant implications for the African National Congress, which he finally joined in the late 1940s. There he betrayed his generational peers and found likeminded allies in the radical youth. The firebrands of Congress were having their own discourse on 'nationalism' and what it meant. Their moment of 'reawakening', as we see in the *Lodestar*, had its own Africanist and other influences. This moment would have been the fourth distinct practice of nationalism discussed in this book had I also fully explored the moral repertoires of everyday life that its proponents embraced, and how they imagined the future independent nation state would enforce and support these moral worlds. What was important in this biographical inquiry was only how Modiri Molema's homecoming, which started more than two decades earlier, directly facilitated the Congress Youth League's political victory in 1949. The mass nationalism that began definitively with the Defiance Campaign of 1952 and its insistence on self-rule, were significantly shaped by biographical elements at the centre of Modiri Molema's political outlook. These same biographical elements had a critical role in the evolution of the Native Advisory Council in the Bechuanaland Protectorate into a legislation council. He had had that intention from the earliest meetings of the NAC. The NAC's transformation into a legislative council helped chiefs to position themselves as ordinary people's choice in a democratic dispensation when the territory became independent Botswana in 1966.

Conclusion

Yet Modiri Molema also admired the world and disposition of the fathers. Through narrative, and therefore through the lever of time, he walked back into the father's 'House'. In later years, he wrote affectionately of Silas Molema and his peers as founding members of Congress, praising their strength of organisation, their discipline and ambition as his inspiration as a Congress leader. Indeed, he became a member of the Congress executive with the intention of resuscitating the glory days of the organisation when the fathers were in charge. He later wrote biographies of Bechuana chiefs. It is not that he had forgotten the hurts and discontents of the past, but somehow, the wound healed, and he returned to the father's 'House', albeit on his own terms. It is one of the many graces of time that there can be a moment when all win, the living and the dead. In his displacement from the father's 'House' but also in his returning to it, we see that his father was probably the most intimate 'other' in Modiri Molema's apprehension of 'self'. Silas Molema was the primary entanglement in his children's making of personhood. He was essential to the everyday intimacies that created and reflected a son's or daughter's substance of being, as in a mirror, either magnified in confidence or crippled in shame.

These private hopes, disappointments and emotional entanglements that are, as it were, the factory floor of personhood, also shaped South Africa's history of segregation, given Sebopioa Molema's role in the litigation that directly impinged on the making of the Natives Land Act of 1913. We saw how the fathers' eldest son found courage and the will to return home without his full qualification, and without opportunity to say goodbye to the work and intimacies he had found in America, when duty called him back to Mafikeng. He braced himself for the task by 'reawakening' again to the world of the fathers, counting a risky venture as an honour befitting a man of his reputation. The encounter happened in solitude, shaped by years of continued silence and an emotional distance from a father he desperately longed for. His initial induction into this *morafe* started when he was growing up in Mafikeng, more so when he was reading, writing to and belonging to the family of *Koranta*. However, this *morafe* of the fathers never found imperial allies in the Union and never thrived, and the possibility of the esteemed life that he could have achieved within it as a chief and educated man collapsed almost entirely with that broken dream.

He was a resilient man but, as we saw, the typical signs of disappointment, prolonged penury and lethargy developed, but only until another 'reawakening' that replenished a life thinned by loss, unending sacrifice and some compromises of his personal values. In the 1930s, he was 'born again' into a Protestantism that turned the mundane routines of everyday life into the practical instalments of personhood: resting, growing food, spending time in nature, reading the scriptures, following a diet of grains, fruit and vegetables. In fact, to a large measure, these routines of everyday life were the only available ways of living he had left. He no longer had the opportunity enjoyed by the fathers of being a chief and landlord. The story of how the Molemas lost their massive landholdings on both sides of the Molopo River relates the events both of territorial segregation, including 'forced removals', and the centralisation of land under new kinds of chiefly institutions in the making of South Africa and Botswana. Sebopioa had to work the land with his own hands. It would have been shameful if he had not had a 'reawakening' to a higher truth. Seventh Day Adventism made a virtue out of the circumstance of his family's genteel poverty and loss of power. He made a new life as a devoted family man, a keen farmer, a trumpeter and a writer of religious texts. Adventism made a virtue out of the tools he had in hand. Life had come together at last. There were no longer loose pieces of uncertainty, shame and anxiety.

The question is whether Sebopioa Molema was making a *morafe* through these religious practices. Indeed so, but one whose boundaries extended beyond the constraints of culture and geography. Firstly, we can say, he was assembling all the resources of a 'Kingdom' he believed to be greater than any on earth, so that it would intervene in the state of the world, as it had done in his own crisis of manhood. The coincidence of the moment of his 'salvation' with the eye operation that saved him from near blindness made the 'reawakening' all the more powerful, involving his mind and body. Piety is in part how the believer lobbies the infrastructure of a supernatural kindred state to intervene and support personal struggles for mutual recognition, connectedness and moral esteem in this world. Religion is a strategy in the struggles of personhood.

Secondly, in Sebopioa Molema's religious 'reawakening,' we have an example of how Protestantism facilitates exchanges with 'Another' who is apprehended, as it were, through the 'eyes of the spirit'. To the extent that the Protestant believer locates himself in a personal relationship with this 'Another', this intimacy facilitates a new revelation of 'truth' in an eternal solidarity of reputation that does not necessarily have a geographical location. It imbues the believer with confidence to withdraw from public institutions, where he does not experience much recognition by and connectedness to others, into a private realm of virtue. Similarly, in Karel Schoeman's *Promised Land*, which finds reference in my introductory chapter, a small rural community has suffered a loss of power. It creates a secluded life in the ruins of their privileged past.[19] These families are poor, unseen and forgotten by their countrymen, but they remain alive with a sense of destiny through the routines that tie them together on the land and, most importantly, bestow honour. They exist on the margins of society like a religious sect.

As an Adventist, Sebopioa Molema could take upon himself the baton of the fathers as a charismatic authority, demonstrating to others how they too ought to live. Only he was not searching for an earthly political power that could support these repertoires of practice. More generally, nevertheless, this Protestant sensibility has historically shaped political futures. Adrian Hastings describes how Protestant piety provides believers with a model of statehood through the Old Testament model of a 'peculiar people' with a divine destiny and a claim to a specific territory.[20] Significantly, this 'peculiar people' share a linguistic and cultural heritage. The elderly Sebopioa Molema's motivations were not to establish a *morafe* with such territorial and political claims. He had come home to a very different 'Father'. Nevertheless, the Old Testament would have been in part what inspired the *morafe* of the fathers. Harriet Molema's devotion to the men in her life – her father, her brothers, her husband – was as strong as her submission to that Old Testament influence that Hastings describes. She considered herself to be serving a *morafe* of a peculiar people 'claiming special privileges in the British Empire', one which enjoyed sovereignty and clear territorial boundaries within the British Empire. She remained faithful to that *morafe*, indeed as faithful as she remained to her marriage, even when both were unravelling. As the men left the reserves, she thrived in the very roles that men were finding difficult to achieve and maintain. In their absence she was a breadwinner, a woman with a career, and a *de facto* recognised chief. She did not live long enough to become elderly. Perhaps she too, in time, would have come to new crossroads in the *morafe*.

Persisting vernacular categories of personhood and histories of nationalism

In conclusion, an analytical framework that explores the evolution of vernacular categories like the *morafe*, which all stand for solidarities of personhood, is critical for a theoretical understanding of the nation. Firstly, it allows for the conceptualisation of the national sensibility as a unique moment in time and in the orientation of being. This sensibility includes the nation state but also other configurations of the nation that do not conform to this political arrangement. The nation is a permutation of dynamic political configurations, each of them contingent on time and circumstance. People may continue in them but the nation is not a necessary orientation in time. We slip in and emerge out of an existing conception of the nation in varying degrees, plunging only as deep and as long as it preserves our standing in the ethical universe of personhood, whilst creating for ourselves many other solidarities of personhood that may have none of the political routines that make nationalism. A family, a church, a relationship, one or other place of connectedness – these are all our attempts to find partners in the reciprocal assembly of personhood. It is how one is in the world. The peculiarity of the nation is that it is the most common and powerful response to a crisis of personhood that affects one or more segments of society. It can take many forms. Thus, the nation emerges from the experiences of intimate, everyday lives before it finds political expression in public life.

Moreover, widening the conception of nationhood beyond the nation state may suggest a periodisation of the nation that is earlier than the now widely accepted nineteenth century, which is when the political theory of the nation state first emerged in Europe, or more accurately, in what had become 'the West'. Studies that both broaden the concept of the nation beyond the nation state and explore its periodisation before the nineteenth century would make it possible for the postcolonial world, especially Africa, to investigate its history of nationhood outside the frame of European empire, and therefore outside the theoretical frames of nationhood in the 'West'. We would appreciate Africans' attempts at nationhood as neither a recent event brought about by the encounter with Europe nor a mimicry of a world beyond their own shores. In the struggle to preserve their footing in personhood's moral universes, they incorporate vocabularies and ideas, like the language of 'nationalism', instrumentally and to their benefit. Like everyone else, Africans experiment on the hoof as they grapple with dilemmas of existence, and some strategies are more successful than others are.

Finally, many generations can live in one reasonably stable nation state and yet continue to belong to solidarities of personhood that are plural, and that have not acquired the momentum of practices of nationalism to the same degree. So far, in South Africa and Botswana, the nation state has accommodated these plural moral communities. Only when one or more of these solidarities become plunged into a crisis of personhood that requires serious political resolution, will the nation state confront the risk of destabilisation. Where the crisis of personhood on the African continent deepens, we can expect ordinary people to rely on practices of nationalism that destabilise and aim to transform structures of government, but for the most part, at least in former colonial Bechuanaland, people are lobbying the nation state as an ally in their struggles. Given for instance, the severe crisis of lack and landlessness in the former reserves of Bechuanaland in South Africa today, only time will tell whether, and for how long, these percolating struggles of personhood will remain commensurate with the political practices and boundaries of the nation state.[21]

Notes

Introduction

1. Kevin Grant, Philippa Levine and Frank Trentmann, 'Introduction', in *Beyond Sovereignty: Britain, Empire and Transnationalism, c. 1880–1950*, edited by Kevin Grant, Philippa Levine and Frank Trentmann (London, Palgrave Macmillan, 2007), pp. 6, 10.
2. The term 'ecclesiastical statehood' belongs to Paul Landau in *The Realm of the Word: Language, Gender, and Christianity in a Southern African Kingdom* (Cambridge, Cambridge University Press, 1995). On early state formation along this frontier, see Stephen Volz, *African Teachers on the Colonial Frontier: Tswana Evangelists and Their Communities during the Nineteenth Century* (New York, Peter Lang, 2011).
3. Daniel T. Rodgers, *Atlantic Crossings: Social Politics in a Progressive Age* (Cambridge, Massachusetts and London, The Belknap Press of Harvard University Press, 1998).
4. See Ann Stoler, 'Making Empire Respectable: The Politics of Race and Sexual Morality in Twentieth-Century Colonial Cultures', *Cultural Politics*, 11 (1997), pp. 344–373.
5. Jean Comaroff and John Comaroff, *Of Revelation and Revolution: Christianity, Colonialism and Consciousness in South Africa, Vol 1* (Chicago, Chicago University Press, 1991); *The Dialectics of Modernity on a South African Frontier, Vol 2* (Chicago, Chicago University Press, 1997).
6. Jane Starfield, 'Dr S. Modiri Molema (1891–1965): The Making of an Historian' (PhD thesis, University of the Witwatersrand, 2008); 'A Dance with the Empire: Modiri Molema's Glasgow Years, 1914–1921', *Journal of Southern African Studies*, 27, 3 (2001), pp. 479–503.
7. Brian Willan, *Sol Plaatje: South African Nationalist, 1876–1932* (London, Heinemann, 1984); *Sol Plaatje, A Life of Solomon Tshekisho Plaatje, 1876–1932* (Johannesburg, Jacana Media, 2018).
8. John Gallagher and Ronald Robinson, 'The Imperialism of Free Trade', *The Economic History Review*, 6, 1 (1953), pp. 1–15; Ronald Robinson and John Gallagher with Alice Denny, *Africa and the Victorians: The Official Mind of Imperialism* (London, Macmillan, 1984), pp. 25, 201–253. For alternative accounts of the colonisation

	of Bechuanaland see, Anthony Atmore and Shula Marks, 'The Imperial Factor in South Africa in the Nineteenth Century: Towards a Reassessment', *The Journal of Imperial and Commonwealth History*, 3, 1 (1974), pp. 105–139.
9	John Darwin, *Unfinished Empire: The Global Expansion of Britain* (London, Bloomsbury Publishing, 2012).
10	See for example, Atmore and Marks, 'The Imperial Factor in South Africa'; Kevin Shillington, *The Colonisation of the Southern Tswana, 1870–1900* (Braamfontein, Ravan Press, 1985).
11	Kevin Shillington, *Luka Jantjie: Resistance Hero of the South African Frontier* (New York, Palgrave Macmillan, 2011).
12	Shillington, *Luka Jantjie*.
13	John Iliffe, *Africans: The History of a Continent*, second edition, orig. 1995 (Cambridge, Cambridge University Press, 2017).
14	Rosalind Edwards, Jane McCarthy and Val Gilles, 'The Politics of Concepts: Family and its (Putative) Replacements', *The British Journal of Sociology*, 63, 4 (2012), pp. 731–746.
15	Pierre Bourdieu, *The Logic of Practice*, translated by Richard Nice (Stanford, Stanford University Press, 1990), p. 5.
16	Pierre Lamaison: Pierre Bourdieu, 'From Rules to Strategies: An Interview with Pierre Bourdieu', *Cultural Anthropology*, 1, 1 (Feb 1986), p. 115.
17	*Ibid.*
18	Pierre Bourdieu, *Distinction: A Social Critique of the Judgement of Taste*, translated by Richard Nice (London and New York, Routledge, 2010), p. 309.
19	Martin Heidegger, 'Being and Time', in *Basic Writing, From Being and Time (1927) to The Task of Thinking (1964)*, edited by David Farrell Krell (London and New York, Routledge, 1993), p. 20.
20	*Ibid.*
21	Siri Hustvedt, 'Suicide and the Drama of Consciousness', in *A Woman Looking at Men Looking at Women: Essays on Art, Sex and the Mind* (London, Sceptre, 2016), p. 433.
22	David Farrell Krell, 'General Introduction: The Question of Being', in Martin Heidegger, *Basic Writings, From Being and Time (1927) to the Task of Thinking (1964)*, edited by David Farrell Krell (London and New York, Routledge, 1993), p. xxx
23	Barbara Taylor, 'Separations of Soul: Solitude, Biography, History', *The American Historical Review*, 114, 3 (2009), pp. 641 and 642.
24	Pierre Bourdieu, 'The Biographical Illusion' in *Identity: A reader*, edited by Paul du Gay, Jessica Evans and Peter Redman (London, SAGE, 2000) pp. 297–303.
25	Siri Hustvedt, *The Blazing World* (London, Sceptre, 2014), pp. 339–340.
26	Karel Schoeman, *Promised Land* (Johannesburg, Jonathan Ball Paperbacks, 1979), p. 125.
27	*Ibid*, p. 125.
28	Hustvedt, *Blazing World*, p. 340; 'Suicide and the Drama of Consciousness', p. 433.
29	William James, *The Principles of Psychology*, cited in Hustvedt, 'Suicide and the Drama of Self-Consciousness', p. 422.
30	John Lonsdale, 'The Moral Economy of the Mau Mau: Wealth, Poverty and Civic Virtue', in Bruce Berman and John Lonsdale, *Unhappy Valley: Conflict in Kenya and Africa, 2* (London, James Currey, 1992), pp. 315–504.
31	*Ibid.*, p. 360.
32	Bernard Magubane, 'A Critical Look at the Indices Used in the Study of Social

Change in Colonial Africa', *Current Anthropology*, 12, 4/5 (1971), pp. 419–445.
33 Comaroff and Comaroff, *Of Revelation and Revolution, Vol 2*, pp. 43 and 45.
34 *Ibid.*, pp. 240 and 261.
35 A seminal early contribution in this regard is Paul Ricoeur, 'The Human Experience of Time and Narrative', *Research in Phenomenology*, 9 (1979), pp. 17–34.
36 Jan Vansina, *Paths in the Rainforests: Towards a History of Political Tradition in Equatorial Africa* (Madison, Wisconsin, University of Wisconsin Press, 1990), p. 8.
37 *Ibid.*, p. 247.
38 *Ibid.*
39 *Ibid.*
40 *Ibid.*
41 Nancy Rose Hunt, *A Nervous State: Violence, Remedies and Reverie in Colonial Congo* (Durham, Duke University Press, 2015).
42 Chinua Achebe, *Things Fall Apart* (New York, Fawcett Crest, 1959).
43 Jacob Dlamini, *Native Nostalgia* (Johannesburg, Jacana Media, 2009).
44 Terence Ranger, 'The Invention of Tradition Revisited: The Case for Colonial Africa', in *Legitimacy and the State in Twentieth Century Africa, Essays in Honour of A.H.M. Kirk-Greene*, edited by Terence Ranger and Olufemi Vaughan (New York, Springer, 1993), p. 84.
45 Eric Hobsbawm and Terence Ranger, eds, *Invention of Tradition* (Cambridge, Cambridge University Press, 1983).
46 Terence Ranger, 'Connections between "Primary Resistance" Movements and Modern Mass Nationalism in East and Central Africa: I & II', *Journal of African History*, 9, 3 & 4 (1968), pp. 631–641.
47 *Ibid.*, p. 641.
48 Max Weber, 'The Sociology of Charismatic Authority', in *From Max Weber: Essays in Sociology*, translated and edited by Hans H. Gerth and C. Wright Mills (New York, Oxford University Press, 1958), p. 246.
49 Emile Durkheim, *The Elementary Forms of Religious Life*, translated by Karen E. Fields (New York, Free Press, 1995).
50 Taylor Carman, 'Foreword', in Martin Heidegger, *Basic Writing, From Being and Time (1927) to The Task of Thinking (1964)*, edited by David Farrell Krell (London and New York, Routledge, 1993), p. xi.
51 The phrase is from Milan Kundera, *Unbearable Lightness of Being* (London, Faber and Faber, 2020).
52 Benedict Anderson, *Imagined Communities: Reflections on the Origin and Spread of Nationalism*, second edition, orig. 1983 (London, New York, Verso Book, 2006).
53 George Mosse, *Nationalism and Sexuality: Respectability and Abnormal Sexuality in Modern Europe* (New York, Howard Fertig, 1997).
54 Durkheim, *The Elementary Forms of Religious Life*.
55 Vansina, *Paths in the Rainforests*.
56 Iliffe, *The Africans*.
57 Edward P. Thompson, 'Custom, Law and Common Right', in E.P. Thompson, *Customs in Common: Studies in Traditional Popular Culture* (London, The New Press, 1991), p. 178.
58 *Ibid.*, p. 164.
59 *Ibid.*, p. 135.
60 Ricoeur, 'The Human Experience of Time', p. 25.
61 Lamaison: Bourdieu, 'From Rules to Strategies', p. 115.
62 Mahmood Mamdani, *Citizen and Subject: Contemporary Africa and the Legacy of*

Late Colonialism (Princeton, Princeton University Press, 1996), p. 23.
63 Arabella Kurtz and J.M. Coetzee, *The Good Story: Exchanges on Truth, Fiction and Psychoanalytic Psychotherapy* (London, Vintage, 2016), p. 11.

Fathers/Moreness

1   Igor Kopytoff, 'Permutations in Patrimonialism and Populism: The Afgem Chiefdoms of Western Cameroon' in *Beyond Chiefdoms, Pathways to Complexity in Africa*, edited by Susan Keech McIntosh (Cambridge, Cambridge University Press, 1999), p. 89.
2   *Ibid.*
3   Hoyt Alverson, cited in John L. Comaroff and Jean Comaroff, *Ethnography and the Historical Imagination* (Boulder, West View Press, 1992), p. 163.
4   *Ibid.*, pp. 164–165.
5   Tom Brown, cited in John L. Comaroff and Jean Comaroff, *Ethnography and the Historical Imagination* (Boulder, West View Press, 1992), p. 165.
6   *Ibid.*
7   Jean Comaroff and John L. Comaroff, *Of Revelation and Revolution, Vol 1, Christianity, Colonisation and Consciousness in South Africa* (Chicago, Chicago University Press, 1991), p. 11.
8   Martin Legassick, *Hidden Histories of Gordonia: Land Dispossession and Resistance in the Northern Cape, 1800–1990* (Johannesburg, Wits University Press, 2016), pp. 1–2; *The Politics of a South African Frontier: The Griqua, the Sotho-Tswana and the Missionaries, 1780–1840* (Basel, Basler Afrika Bibliographien, 2010); 'The Frontier Tradition in South African Historiography', in *Economy and Society in Pre-Industrial South Africa*, edited by Shula Marks and Anthony Atmore (London, Longman,1980), pp. 44–80.
9   John Iliffe, *Africans: The History of a Continent*, 2nd edition (Cambridge, Cambridge University Press, 2017, orig. published 1995).
10 Khumisho Moguerane, 'A Home of One's Own: Women and Home Ownership in the Borderlands of Post-Apartheid South Africa and Lesotho', *Canadian Journal of African Studies*, 52, 2 (2018), pp. 139–157.
11 Jan Vansina, *Paths in the Rain Forests: Towards a History of Political Tradition in Equatorial Africa* (Wisconsin, University of Wisconsin, 1990).
12 Paul Landau, *Popular Politics in the History of South Africa, 1400–1948* (Cambridge, Cambridge University Press, 2010), p. 8.
13 *Ibid.*
14 *Ibid.*, p.8.
15 *Ibid.*, p. 9.
16 For a different interpretation of these binary concepts, see Comaroff and Comaroff, *Revelation and Revolution, Vol 1*. For a critical evaluation of that position, see Khumisho Moguerane, 'A History of the Molemas: African Notables in South Africa, 1880s to 1920s', DPhil thesis, University of Oxford, 2014.
17 Stephen Volz, *African Teachers on the Colonial Frontier: Tswana Evangelists and Their Communities During the Nineteenth Century* (New York, Peter Lang, 2011), p. 103.
18 *Ibid.*
19 Adrian Hastings, *The Construction of Nationhood: Ethnicity, Religion and Nationalism* (Cambridge, Cambridge University Press, 1997).

20 Paul Landau, *The Realm of the Word: Language, Gender, and Christianity in a Southern African Kingdom* (Cambridge, Cambridge University Press, 1995).
21 Comaroff and Comaroff, *Revelation and Revolution, Vol 1*, p. 263.
22 Emile Durkheim, *Suicide: A Study in Sociology*, translated by John A. Spaulding (London, Routledge, 2005).
23 This section relies on University of South Africa (UNISA), Pretoria, Fort Hare Papers, ZKM_A2_42_ Part, Z.K. Matthews, Barolong Research, 'A Short History of the Tshidi Barolong, June 1945, p. 22.
24 Kevin Shillington, *Luka Jantije: Resistance Hero of the South African Frontier* (London, Aldridge, 2011); Kevin Shillington, *The Colonisation of the Southern Tswana, 1870–1900* (Johannesburg, Ravan Press, 1985).
25 Anthony Dachs, 'Missionary Imperialism – The Case of Bechuanaland', *Journal of African History*, 13, 4 (1972), pp. 647–658.
26 University of the Witwatersrand Historical Papers (UWHP), Silas T. Molema and Solomon T. Plaatje Papers (Molema Papers) (1874–1932), A979Ba7, Montsioa to Captain H. Nourse, 2 November 1881.
27 Shillington, *The Colonisation of the Southern Tswana*, pp. 133–143.
28 *Ibid.*
29 Comaroff and *Comaroff, Revelation and Revolution, Vol 1*, p. 264.
30 Ronald Robinson and John Gallagher with Alice Denny, *Africa and the Victorians: The Official Mind of Imperialism* (London, MacMillan, 1981).
31 UWHP, Molema Papers A979Bc3.2, R.C. Lloyd to the Secretary of Native Affairs, 23 July 1913.
32 Shillington, *The Colonisation of the Southern Tswana*, pp. 93, 177.
33 UWHP, Molema Papers, A979Ba29, S. Shippard to Montsioa, 29 August 1895.
34 Shillington, *The Colonisation of the Southern Tswana*, p. 203.
35 UWHP, Molema Papers, A979Bc3.2, R.C. Lloyd to the Secretary of Native Affairs, 23 July 1913.
36 John Comaroff, 'Class and Culture in a Peasant Economy: The Transformation of Land Tenure in Barolong', *Journal of African Law*, 24, 1 (1980), pp. 85–113.
37 UWHP, Molema Papers, A 979Ba, Montsioa to Victoria, c. 1894–85.
38 Stephen C. Volz, 'They Who Kill the Body: Christian Ideals and Political Realities in the Interior of Southern Africa during the 1850s', *Journal of Southern African Studies*, 36, 1 (2010), p. 46.
39 Comaroff and Comaroff, *Revelation and Revolution, Vol 1*, p. 263.
40 I am grateful to Dr Leloba Molema for showing me this photograph.
41 UWHP, Molema Papers, A979Aa3.2, account statement for Whiteley, Walker & Co., 31 October 1900.
42 UWHP, Molema Papers, A979Aa3.3, account statement for Musson Bros invoice, 18 September 1890; and others, 10 August 1891.
43 Pim de Zwart, 'South African Living Standards in Global Perspective, 1835–1910', *Economic History of Developing Regions* 26, 1 (2011), pp. 49–74.
44 See for example, UWHP, Molema Papers, A979Aa3.2, N. Howse & Co invoice 14 January 1888.
45 Modiri Molema, *Lover of His People: A Biography of Sol Plaatje*, translated and edited by D.S. Matjila and Karen Haire (Johannesburg, Wits University Press, 2012), p. 5.
46 *Ibid.*
47 *Ibid.*
48 *Ibid.*, p.3.

49 UWHP, Molema Papers, A979Aa3.3, Musson Bros invoice, 18 September 1890 and 10 August 1891.
50 UWHP, Molema Papers, A979Aa3.3, Invoice Whiteley, Walker & Co, 3 January 1891; 17 September 1891; 4 January 1892; Invoice N. House & Co, 27 September 1892.
51 UWHP, Molema Papers, A979Aa3.3, Whiteley, Walker & Co receipt, 27 October 1892.
52 UWHP, Molema Papers, A979Aa3.3; Credit statement, Whiteley, Walker & Co, 24 March 1893, Unspecified credit 15 March 1893, 8 November 1893 and 28 May 1894; A979Aa3.4, Promissory Note, Whiteley, Walker & Co, 15 June 1894.
53 Shillington, *Luka Jantjie*, p. 180.
54 UWHP, Molema Papers, A979Aa3.2, Whiteley, Walker & Co statement, 21 September 1895.
55 UWHP, Molema Papers, A979Cb2.2. Testimony of Paul Sebaetse, Case 34, Kgotla, 9 April 1901.
56 UWHP, Molema Papers, A979Aa3, Musson Bros to S.T. Molema, 5 August 1895.
57 UWHP, Molema Papers, A979Ba16, Montsioa to Victoria, undated c. 1895.
58 Shillington, *Luka Jantjie*, p. 194; Charles van Onselen, 'Reactions to Rinderpest in South Africa, 1896–97', *Journal of African History*, 13, 3 (1972), pp. 473–488.
59 UWHP, Molema Papers, A979Aa3, Credit note from Whiteley, Walker & Co statement, 19 December 1896.
60 UWHP, Molema Papers, A979Aa3.2, Account statement from Whiteley, Walker & Co statement, 31 July 1897.
61 UWHP, Molema Papers, A979Aa3, Promissory note, C. de Clarke, 18 February 1897.
62 Munashe Chideya, compilation of 'List of salaries of civil servants in Mafeking, 1897–1902'. I am grateful to Johan Fourie who referred me to this material.
63 UWHP, Molema Papers, A979Aa3.2, Account statement, Whiteley, Walker & Co, 16 November 1897.
64 *Ibid*.
65 UWHP, Molema Papers, A979Aa3.3, Receipt, September 1897 (undated).
66 Shillington, *Luka Jantjie*, pp. 174, 177.
67 Colin Bundy, 'Vagabond Hollanders and Runaway Englishmen: White Poverty in the Cape before Poor Whiteism', in *Putting a Plough to the Ground: Accumulation and Dispossession in Rural South Africa 1850–1930*, edited by William Beinart, Peter Delius and Stanley Trapido (Braamfontein, Raven Press, 1986), pp. 101–128.
68 Gordon Pirie, 'Slaughter by Steam: Railway Subjugation of Ox-Wagon Transport in the Eastern Cape and Transkei, 1886–1910', *The International Journal of African Historical Studies*, 26, 2 (1993), pp. 319–343.
69 UWHP, Molema Papers, A979Aa3.2, Account statement, Loosely & McLaren General Merchants, 19 December 1898.
70 UWHP, Molema Papers, A979Aa3.3, Fee Statement, Lovedale Missionary Institute, 9 February, 18 June and 12 September 1898; A979Aa3, Fee Statement, Lovedale, 2 April 1898.
71 For example, UWHP, Molema Papers, A979Ca4, Receipt for A. Transfeldt, 9 November 1898.
72 UWHP, Molema Papers, A979Aa3, Lovedale Missionary Institute to S.T. Molema, 16 September 1898.
73 UWHP, Molema Papers, A979Aa3.2, Account statement, Loosely & McLaren, 2 May 1898, 4 October 1898 and 19 December 1898.
74 UWHP, Molema Papers, A979Aa3.2, S. Minchin to S.T. Molema, 9 November 1898.

75 UWHP, Molema Papers, A979Aa3.2, Account statement, Whiteley, Walker & Co, 19 December 1898.
76 UWHP, Molema Papers, A979Aa3, J.W. de Kock to S.T. Molema, 5 January 1899.
77 UWHP, Molema Papers, A979Aa3.3, Fee statements Lovedale Missionary Institute, 4 and 13 February, 6 March, 5 April 1899.
78 UWHP, Molema Papers, A979Aa3, De Kock to S.T. Molema, 7 April 1899.
79 UWHP, Molema Papers, A979Aa3.2, Account statement, Loosely & McLaren Co, 31 May 1899.
80 UWHP, Molema Papers, A979Cc2, G.H. Bell to S.T. Molema and Molema's copy of response, 29 July 1900.
81 UWHP, Molema Papers, A979Aa3.3, Lovedale Missionary Institute to S.T. Molema, 18 July and 4 October 1900.
82 UWHP, Molema Papers, A979Ca4, Receipt of (private) transaction, 27 February 1900; A979Aa3.2, Rent from J. Dall, 9 May 1900, A979Ca4, Rent from J. Kay, 1 September 1900; A979Aa3.3, Payment to Whiteley, Walker & Co, 1 September 1900.
83 UWHP, Molema Papers, A979Bb2, J.M. Moffat to S.T. Molema or W. Montsioa, undated.
84 UWHP, Molema Papers, A979Aa3.2, Receipt from E. Platnauer Auctioneers, 20 and 27 October 1900; Receipt from Dennison & Cranswick Auctioneers, 27 October 1900.
85 UWHP, Molema Papers, A979Aa3.2, Receipt from E. Platnauer, 20 October 1900; Receipt from Dennison & Cranswick, 15 September 1900, 1 December 1900, 22 December 1900, 29 December 1900; account for Whiteley, Walker & Co, 31 October 1900.
86 UWHP, Molema Papers, A979Aa3, Lovedale Missionary Institute to S.T. Molema, 4 October 1900, A979Aa3.3, 17 November 1900.
87 UWHP, Molema Papers, A979Aa3, Lovedale Missionary Institute Memorandum, November 1900, undated.
88 UWHP, Molema Papers, A979Aa3.2, Standard Bank to S.T. Molema, 31 December 1900.
89 UWHP, Molema Papers, A979Aa3.2, Receipt from Dennison & Cranswick, 9 and 15 January 1901.
90 UWHP, Molema Papers, A979Aa3.3, Account statement, Whiteley, Walker & Co, 26 January 1901.
91 UWHP, Molema Papers, A979Aa3, Account statement, Whiteley, Walker & Co, 28 February 1901.
92 UWHP, Molema Papers, A979Aa3, Lovedale Missionary Institute to S.T. Molema, 21 March 1901.
93 *Mafeking Mai*, 8 December 1900.
94 UWHP, Molema Papers, A979Aa3.2, Receipt from Lovedale Missionary Institute, 13 May 1901. A979Aa3, Account statement Whiteley, Walker & Co, 3 August 1901.
95 UWHP, Molema Papers, A979Aa3.2, Receipt from Dennison & Cranswick, 28 September 1901; Account statement from Dr W.S. Keurs, 31 December 1901.
96 Chidaye, 'List of salaries of civil servants in Mafeking, 1897–1902.'
97 An interpretation of initiation ceremonies from Emile Durkheim, *The Elementary Forms of Religious Life*, translated by Karen E. Fields (New York, The Free Press, 1995), p. 37.
98 *Ibid*.

99   *Ibid.*, p. 268.
100 *Ibid.*, p. 213.
101 For such an interpretation of 'moreness' or of how being oneself is impossible without connectedness to another, see Homer, *The Odyssey*, translated by Robert Fitzgerald (London, Vintage Books, 2007), p. 151.
102 *Ibid.*, p. 148.
103 See *Words of Batswana: Letters to Mahoko a Becwana, 1883–1896*, translated and edited by Part T. Mgadla and Stephen C. Volz (Cape Town, Van Riebeeck Society for the Publication of South African Historical Documents, 2006), p. 203.
104 Hlonipha Mokoena, 'An Assembly of Readers: Magema Fuze and *His Ilanga Lase Natal* Readers', *Journal of Southern African Studies*, 35, 3 (2009), pp. 595–607.
105 Michael Tshabadira Moroka, letter to *Mahoko a Becwana*, June 1891 in *Words of Batswana*, translated and edited by Mgadla and Volz, p. 203.
106 UWHP, Molema Papers, A979Aa2.21, S. Sechele to S.T. Molema, 20 July 1904, Sechuana [i.e. translated from Sechuana], including quotation below.
107 *Ibid.*
108 *Ibid.*
109 UWHP, Molema Papers, A979Aa2.21, S. Sechele to S.T. Molema, 20 July 1904, Sechuana [i.e. translated from Sechuana], including quotation below.
110 UWHP, Molema Papers, A979Cb2.2, transcript of case only referenced as Case 34, Paul Motsoamolimo Sebaetse and son Paul Sebaetse, 9 April 1901.
111 *Ibid.*
112 Solomon T. Plaatje, *The Mafeking Diary of Sol T. Plaatje*, edited by John Comaroff and Brian Willan with Solomon Molema and Andrew Reed (Cape Town, David Phillip, 1999), p. 126.
113 UWHP, Molema Papers, A979Bc1, B. Montsioa to W. Major, 14 January 1904.
114 Tim Couzens, 'History of the Black Press in South Africa, 1836–1960', Additional Seminar Paper, No A15, University of the Witwatersrand, Institute for Advanced Social Research, undated, p. 4.
115 UWHP, Molema Papers, A979Cc9, T. Jabavu to S.T. Molema, 5 February 1910.
116 *Koranta*, 27 April 1901, Sechuana.
117 See *Koranta*, 31 August 1901, Sechuana.
118 *Koranta*, 31 August 1901, Sechuana.
119 *Koranta*, 8 October 1903, Sechuana.
120 *Koranta*, 4 October 1902, Sechuana.
121 *Koranta*, 10 January 1903, Sechuana.
122 See for example *Koranta*, 1 November 1902.
123 Durkheim, *The Elementary Forms of Religious Life*, p. 273.
124 *Ibid.*
125 *Koranta*, 8 October 1903, Sechuana.
126 Friedrich Hölderlin, cited in Nicolai Krejberg Knudsen, 'Depopulation: On the Logic of Heidegger's *Volk*', *Research in Phenomenology*, 47 (2017), p. 307.
127 *Koranta*, 25 October 1902.
128 *Koranta*, 28 February 1903.
129 *Koranta*, 25 October 1902.
130 *Koranta*, 7 March 1903, Sechuana.
131 *Koranta*, 10 November 1903.
132 Timothy Keegan, 'Crisis and Catharsis in the Development of Capitalism in South African Agriculture', *African Affairs*, 84, 336 (1985), p. 372.
133 *Koranta*, 13 September 1902 and 21 December 1904.

134 *Ibid.*
135 Plaatje, *The Mafeking Diary of Sol T. Plaatje*, p. 148.
136 *Ibid.*, pp. 122–123.
137 *Ibid.*, p. 123.
138 UWHP, Molema Papers, A979Aa3, Rent receipts from S. Abrams, 10 August 1905.
139 *Words of Batswana*, translated and edited by Mgadla and Volz, p. 51.
140 University of Cape Town Library, (UCTL), G. 682 A. POPU. 04. RESU. Cape of Good Hope Census Office, Results of a Census of the Cape Colony of the Cape of Good Hope, Cape Town, 1905.
141 *Koranta*, 1902 January 31, Sechuana.
142 UCTL. G. 682 A. POPU. 04. RESU. Results of a Census of the Cape Colony of the Cape of Good Hope.
143 Colin Bundy, *The Rise and Fall of the South African Peasantry* (California, University of California Press, 1979).
144 UWHP, Molema Papers, A979Aa1, J. Molema to S.T. Molema, 22 December 1899, Sechuana.
145 UWHP, Molema Papers, A979Aa2.9, L. Monnarora to S.T. Molema, 25 March 1921, Sechuana.
146 *Koranta*, 7 March 1903, Sechuana.
147 *Ibid,*
148 *Koranta*, 10 November 1903.
149 Molema, *Lover of His People*, pp. 19–20.
150 *Koranta*, 13 November 1902.
151 *Koranta*, 28 February 1903, Sechuana.
152 *Koranta*, 20 November 1902.
153 *Koranta*, 20 September 1903, Sechuana.
154 *Koranta*, 1902 October 1902, Sechuana.
155 *Koranta*, uncertain, 1902, Sechuana.
156 *Koranta*, 31 August 1901, Sechuana.
157 *Koranta* 2 and 8 May 1903, Sechuana.
158 *Ibid.*
159 *Koranta*, 9 May 1903, Sechuana.
160 *Koranta*, 29 November 1902, Sechuana.
161 *Ibid.*
162 *Koranta*, 28 February 1903, Sechuana.
163 *Ibid.*
164 Christopher Saunders, 'Pixley Seme and Abantu-Batho', in *The People's Paper: A Centenary History and Anthology of Abantu-Batho*, edited by Peter Limb (Johannesburg, Wits University Press, 2012), pp. 118.
165 Christopher Saunders, 'Pixley Seme: Towards a Biography', *South African Historical Journal*, 25, 1 (1991), pp. 196–217. For a complete biography of Seme, including his international networks, see Bongani Ngqulunga, *The Man who Founded the ANC: A Biography of Pixley ka Isaka Seme* (Cape Town, Penguin Random House South Africa, 2017).
166 Saunders, 'Pixley Seme and Abantu-Batho, pp. 117–118.
167 John Maxwell Coetzee, 'What is a Classic?', *Current Writing: Text and Reception in Southern Africa*, 5, (1993), pp. 7–24.
168 Plaatje, *The Mafeking Diary of Sol T. Plaatje*, p. 69.
169 *The Bechuanaland News*, 23 August 1902.

170 Frederick Cooper, 'Conflict and Connection: Rethinking Colonial African History', *The American Historical Review*, 99, 5 (1994), p. 1539.
171 *Koranta*, 4 April 1903.
172 *Koranta*, 31 December 1902, Sechuana.
173 UWHP, Molema Papers, A979Ac1, S.J. Molema to S.T. Molema, 18 December 1904.
174 James Campbell, *Songs of Zion: The African Methodist Episcopal Church in the United States and South Africa* (New York, Oxford University Press, 1995), pp. 255, 268.
175 UWHP, Molema Papers, A979Aa3.3, S.J. Account statement, Healdtown Institute, 7 June 1905.
176 *Koranta*, 15 November 1902, Sechuana.
177 UWHP, Molema Papers, A979Aa3.3, Receipt from Joseph Whiffer, 27 November 1902.
178 UWHP, Molema Papers, A979Ca4, Rent receipts from John Kay, 17 March 1902, 16 June 1902; J. Robinson 16 September 1902; A979Aa3.3, Promissory notes to De Kock 1 February 1902, A979Aa3.4, Promissory notes to M. Heffler 26 January 1902, Unknown 5 May 1902.
179 UWHP, Molema Papers, A979Aa3, S. Minchin to S.T. Molema, 14 November 1903; A979Aa2.3, S. Minchin to S.T. Molema, 10 December 1903.
180 UWHP, Molema Papers, A979Aa3.3. De Kock & De Kock statements to S.T. Molema, 14 September 1903, 16 October 1903.
181 UWHP, Molema Papers, A979Aa3.3, Receipt from E. Fincham to S.T. Molema, 18 September 1903; A979Aa2.3, Grant & Pennycook, 1 December 1903.
182 UWHP, Molema Papers, A979Aa3.3, S. Minchin to S.T. Molema, 15 July 1904; A979Aa3.3, Receipt from Peter Lekgatla 6 July 1904.
183 UWHP, Molema Papers, A970Aa2.20, Bathoen to S.T. Molema, 14 July 1904, Sechuana.
184 *Ibid.*
185 *Ibid.*
186 UWHP, Molema Papers, A979Aa3, S. Minchin to S.T. Molema, 30 June 1906; A979Aa3.6.2, S. Minchin to S. T. Molema, 26 November 1906.
187 UWHP, Molema Papers, A979Aa2.23, Bathoen to S.T. Molema, 23 November 1904, Sechuana.
188 UWHP, Molema Papers, A979Aa2.10, R. Sekhoma to S.T. Molema, 20 April 1898, A979Aa2.11, R. Sekhoma to S.T. Molema, 26 April 1898; A979Aa2.12, R. Sekhoma to S.T. Molema, 16 August 1898, Sechuana.
189 UWHP, Molema Papers, A979Aa2.16, Sekhoma to S.T. Molema, 20 November 1900, Sechuana.
190 UWHP, Molema Papers, A979Aa3.3, S. Minchin to S.T. Molema, 12 September 1904, Sechuana.
191 UWHP, Molema Papers, A979Aa3, Receipt for transport for B. May, 28 April 1904.
192 UWHP, Molema Papers, A979Aa3.3.6.1.4, Bond agreement, S.T Molema and C. Wenham, 15 July 1904.
193 UWHP, Molema Papers, A 979 Ca4, Receipt from Z.Z. Nko, 14 September 1904; A979Aa3.3, Lovedale statement, 20 October 1904.
194 UWHP, Molema Papers, A979Aa3.5.18, Bond agreement, S.T. Molema and C. Wenham, 1 October 1904.
195 UWHP, Molema Papers, A979Ca4, Rent receipts to Chaen Hong 30 April, 7 May,

Notes

1 July, 10 Oct 1904, Mr Leng, 1 August 1904, Mr Ly Wing, 10 October 1904.

196 UWHP, Molema Papers, A979Aa3.5.19, Acknowledgement of debt, S.T. Molema to S. Minchin, 10 April 1905.
197 UWHP, Molema Papers, A979Aa3, S. Minchin to S.T. Molema, 22 February 1905.
198 UWHP, Molema Papers, A979Aa3, S. Minchin to S.T. Molema, 10 April 1905.
199 UWHP, Molema Papers, A979Aa3.5.19, S. Acknowledgement of debt, 10 April 1905.
200 UWHP, Molema Papers, A979Aa1, J. Moses to S. Molema, 10 August 1905, Sechuana.
201 UWHP, Molema Papers, A979Aa3.2, Statement from Minchin to S.T. Molema, 15 July 1905.
202 UWHP, Molema Papers, A979Aa3, Rent receipts from S. Abrams, 10 August 1905; 16 January 1906; C.F. Herber, 29 January 1906.
203 UWHP, Molema Papers, A979Aa3.6.2, G. Whales to Minchin, 8 January 1906.
204 *Ibid.*
205 UWHP, Molema Papers, A979Aa3, S. Minchin to S.T. Molema, 15 October 1906.
206 UWHP, Molema Papers, A979Aa3, Denwon, Duncan and Brown to S.T. Molema, 21 August 1906.
207 UWHP, Molema Papers, A979Aa3, S. Minchin to S.T. Molema, 15 October 1906.
208 UWHP, Molema Papers, A979Aa3, S. Minchin to S.T. Molema, 25 October 1906.
209 *Ibid.*
210 UWHP, Molema Papers, A979Aa3, S. Minchin to S.T. Molema, 15 October 1906.
211 UWHP, Molema Papers, A979Aa3.6.2, S. Minchin to S.T. Molema, 26 November 1906.
212 UWHP, Molema Papers, A979Aae.6.2, S. Minchin to S.T. Molema, 17 January 1906.
213 UWHP, Molema Papers, A979Aa3, S. Minchin to S.T. Molema, 4 December 1906.
214 UWHP, Molema Papers, A979Aa3.6.2, S. Minchin to S.T. Molema, 7 January 1907.
215 UWHP, Molema Papers, A979Aa3, E.W. Joyce to S.T. Molema, 23 January 1907.
216 UWHP, Molema Papers, A979Aa3.6.2, S. Minchin to S.T. Molema, 29 January 1907.
217 UWHP, Molema Papers, A979Aa3.6.2, G. Whales to S.T. Molema, 19 February 1907.
218 UWHP, Molema Papers, A979Aa3.6.2, R. de Beers to S.T. Molema, c. 1907 December.
219 UWHP, Molema Papers, A979Aa3.6.2, S. Minchin to S.T. Molema, c. 1907 December.
220 UWHP, Molema Papers, A979Aa3.6.2, S. Minchin to S.T. Molema, 14 February 1908.
221 UWHP, Molema Papers, A979Aa3.6.2, S. Minchin to S.T. Molema, 13 March 1908.
222 Cape Town Archives (CTA), Government Papers, 1 MFK 15 N1/4/3 (13) 38, (1938–1959), Volume 18, R. Lekoko.

Family/Placement

1. John Comaroff, 'Class and Culture in a Peasant Economy: The Transformation of Land Tenure in Barolong', *Journal of African Law*, 24, 1 (1980), pp. 85–113.
2. See Michael Hubbard, *Agricultural Exports and Economic Growth: A Study of the Botswana Beef Industry* (London, Routledge, 1986).
3. Comaroff, 'Class and Culture in a Peasant Economy', p. 90.
4. University of the Witwatersrand Historical Papers (UWHP), Silas. T. Molema and Solomon. T. Plaatje Papers, (Molema Papers) (1874–1972), A979Aa3, R. Transfeldt to S.T. Molema, 15 January 1899.
5. UWHP, Molema Papers, A979Aa3, R. Transfeldt to S.T. Molema, 15 January 1899, 15 January 1899 and 21 January 1899.
6. UWHP, Molema Papers, A979Aa3, R. Transfeldt to S.T. Molema, 2 March 1899.
7. UWHP, Molema Papers, A979Aa3, R. Transfeldt to S.T. Molema, 17 September 1899.
8. See for example, Charles van Onselen, *The Seed is Mine: The Life of Kas Maine: A South African Sharecropper, 1894–1985* (Johannesburg, Jonathan Ball, 2019); 'Race and Class in the South African Countryside: Cultural Osmosis and Social Relations in the Sharecropping Economy of the South African Western Transvaal, 1900–1950', *The American Historical Review*, 95, 1 (1990), pp. 99–123; Timothy Keegan, 'The Sharecropping Economy on the South African Highveld in the Early Twentieth Century', *The Journal of Peasant Studies*, 10, 2/3 (1983), pp. 201–226.
9. Solomon Plaatje, *Native Life in South* Africa (Johannesburg, Picador Africa, 2007, first published 1916), pp. 83–91.
10. Karel Schoeman, *This Life*, translated from Afrikaans by Else Silke (Brooklyn, NY, Archipelago Books, 2015), p. 73.
11. For such an interpretation of 'placement' or of how being oneself is impossible without a dwelling place, see Homer, *Odyssey*, translated by Robert Fitzgerald (London, Vintage Books, 2007), pp. 129–130.
12. Colin Bundy, 'Vagabond Hollanders and Runaway Englishmen: White Poverty in the Cape before Poor Whiteism', in *Putting a Plough to the Ground: Accumulation and Dispossession in Rural South Africa, 1850–1930*, edited by William Beinart, Peter Delius and Stanley Trapido (Johannesburg, Ravan Press, 1986).
13. UWHP, Molema Papers, A979Aa3.5.2, Lease Agreement: P. Crause and S.T. Molema, 2 October 1891.
14. UWHP, Molema Papers, A979Aa3.5.8, Lease Agreement: H. Wright and S.T. Molema, 1 May 1901.
15. UWHP, Molema Papers, A979Aa3.5.11, Lease Agreement: E. Rowlands, R. Rowlands and S.T. Molema, 16 October 1905.
16. UWHP, Molema Papers, A970Aa, Anonymous tenant to S.T. Molema, undated.
17. UWHP, Molema Papers, A979Aa3.5.3, Lease Agreement: J.J. Panter and S.T. Molema, 1 January 1898.
18. UWHP, Molema Papers, A979Aa3.5.6, Lease Agreement: O. Nell and S.T. Molema, 7 September 1899.
19. UWHP, Molema Papers, A979Aa3.5.7, Lease Agreement: J. Kay and S.T. Molema, 23 April 1900.
20. UWHP, Molema Papers, A979Aa3.5.4, Lease Agreement: J.J. van Roeyen and S.T. Molema, undated May 1898.
21. UWHP, Molema Papers, A979Aa3.5.14, Lease Agreement: P.F. Meintjes and S.T. Molema, undated May 1912.

22   UWHP, Molema Papers, A979Aa3, Lease Agreement: 'Philip's son' and S.T. Molema, undated 1908.
23   UWHP, Molema Papers, A979Ca4, Receipts: S.T. Molema to Chaeng Hong, 27 March, 30 April, 7 May, 1 July, 10 October 1904; S.T. Molema To Yokehon, 12 November 1903; S.T. Molema to Ly Wing, 10 October 1904.
24   UWHP, Molema Papers, A979Aa3, Lease Agreement: S.T. Molema and J. Ludick, 1904 undated.
25   *Mafeking Mail*, 22 February 1910.
26   *Ibid*.
27   *Mafeking Mail*, 2 March 1910.
28   *Mafeking Mail*, 22 February 1910.
29   *Ibid*.
30   *Mafeking Mail*, 2 May 1910.
31   William Beinart, *The Rise of Conservation in South Africa* (Oxford, Oxford University Press, 2003), pp. 236–256.
32   *Mafeking Mail*, 17 March 1910.
33   *Mafeking Mail*, 5, 10 January 1910.
34   UWHP, Molema Papers, A979Bc1, B. Montsioa to W.J. Mahony, 15 January 1904.
35   UWHP, Molema Papers, A979Bb1, G. Boyes to R. Innes, 19 October 1896.
36   UWHP, Molema Papers, A979Bc3, G. Green to W.C. Cumming, 3 December 1903.
37   William Beinart, 'Settler Accumulation in East Griqualand from the Demise of the Griqua to the Natives Land Act', in *Putting a Plough to the Ground: Accumulation and Dispossession in Rural South Africa, 1850–1930*, edited by William Beinart, Peter Delius and Stanley Trapido (Johannesburg, Ravan Press, 1986), pp. 289–300; Jacob Tropp, 'Dogs, Poison and the Meaning of Colonial Intervention in the Transkei, South Africa', *The Journal of African History*, 43, 3 (2002), pp. 451–472. esp. p. 456.
38   The material for the legislation and legal status of the reserve is largely from Cape Town Archives, (CTA) Union of South Africa Illiquid Cases, (1910–1913) CSC 2/1/1/717 1913, Volume 21, 244–254, Badirile/Lekoko Montsioas, in his capacity as the Principal Chief of the Barolong (Plaintiff) vs Jan Smuts/Abraham Fischer representing Union of South Africa and the Divisional Council of Mafeking, 10 June 1913.
39   University of South Africa (UNISA), Pretoria, Fort Hare Papers, ZKM_A2_42_Part, Z.K. Matthews, Barolong Research, 'A Short History of the Tshidi Barolong, June 1945, p. 22.
40   UWHP, Molema Papers, A979Ba29, Sidney Shippard to Montsioa (Tawana), 29 August 1895.
41   CTA, Union of South Africa Illiquid Cases, (1910–1913) CSC 2/1/1/717 1913, Badirile/Lekoko vs Smuts/Fischer, Testimony of Silas Molema in Supreme Court, 10 June 1913.
42   UWHP, Molema Papers, A979Bc1, B. Montsioa to W.J. Mahony, 15 January 1904.
43   UWHP, Molema Papers, A979Bc1, B. Montsioa to Graham Green, 03 February 1904.
44   CTA, Union of South Africa Illiquid Cases, CSC 2/1/1/717 1913, Badirile/Lekoko vs Smuts/Fischer.
45   UWHP, Molema Papers, A979Bc1, B. Montsioa to Graham Green, 1905 March undated.
46   *Ibid*.
47   UWHP, Molema Papers, A979Bc1, Undated 'opinion' from anonymous official, copied to Badirile Montsioa.

48 Ibid.
49 CTA, Union of South Africa Illiquid Cases, CSC 2/1/1/717 1913, Badirile/Lekoko vs Smuts/Fischer.
50 CTA, Records of the Department of Justice, Badirile/Lekoko Montsioas, in his capacity as the Principal Chief of the Barolong (Plaintiff) vs Jan Smuts/Abraham Fischer in his capacity as Minister of Interior representing Union of South Africa and the Divisional Council of Mafeking, JUS 109 File 23079/10. Reference 2/323/10/13/B/Co, Reid & Nephew to Department of Justice, 30 May 1910.
51 CTA, Records of Department of Justice, JUS 109 File 23079/10. Reference 2/323/10/13/B/Co, Findlay & Tait to Reit & Nephew, 22 November 1910.
52 James Campbell, *Songs of Zion: The African Methodist Episcopal Church in the United States and South Africa* (New York, 1995), pp. 255 and 268.
53 *Ibid.*, p. 272.
54 *Koranta*, 5 November 1902, Sechuana.
55 James Campbell, 'The Seed You Sow in South Africa: South African Students in the United States', Additional seminar paper prepared for the University of the Witwatersrand's Institute for Social Research, undated.
56 Campbell, 'The Seed You Sow in South Africa'.
57 *Koranta*, May 1904 date unclear.
58 *Ibid.*
59 UWHP, Molema Papers, A979Aa2.22, L. Coppin to S.T. Molema, 6 July 1904.
60 UWHP, Molema Papers, A979Ca11, S.T. Molema to L. Coppin, (undated draft) c. 1903.
61 UWHP, Molema Papers, A979Aa3, Lovedale Missionary Institute to S. T Molema, 17 & 23 November 1900.
62 UWHP, Molema Papers, A979Aa2, S.J. Molema to S.T. Molema, November 1900, undated.
63 UWHP, Molema Papers, A979Ac1, S.J. Molema to S.T. Molema, 6 July 1904.
64 UWHP, Molema Papers, A979Ac1, S.J. Molema to S.T. Molema, 18 October 1904.
65 Campbell, 'The Seed You Sow in South Africa'.
66 Campbell, *Songs of Zion*, p. 268.
67 W.E.B Du Bois., 'The Future of Wilberforce', *The Journal of Negro Education*, 9, 4, (1940), pp. 553–70.
68 M. Little, 'The Extra-Curricular Activities of Black College Students, 1868–1940, *Journal of Negro History*, 65, 1 (1980) pp. 135–148.
69 Signal Hill Mafikeng Archives (SHMA), Sebopioa Molema Papers, Freemen's Aid Society to S.J. Molema, 29 October 1909.
70 SHMA, Sebopioa Molema Papers, Advertisement, 08 March 1910.
71 UWHP, Molema Papers, A979Ac1, S.J. Molema to S.T. Molema, 18 October 1910.
72 *Ibid.*
73 Willan, *Sol Plaatje South African Nationalist*, p. 35.
74 UWHP, Molema Papers, A979Ac1, S.J. Molema to S.T. Molema, 18 October 1910.
75 South African National Archives, Pretoria (SNA) Government Papers, SAB GG 1182, 28/1-28/28, E.C. Welsh to E. Dower, 27 July 1910: E. Dower to L. Botha 6 August 1910.
76 *Tsala ea Becoana*, 14 January 1911, Sechuana.
77 *Tsala ea Becoana*, 11 October 1911.

78 *Tsala ea Becoana*, 8 April 1911.
79 *Tsala ea Becoana*, 23 September 1911, Sechuana.
80 UWHP, Molema Papers, A979Da23, S. Plaatje to S.T. Molema, undated c. 1912.
81 UWHP, Molema Papers, A979Cc7, Memorandum, W. Wickham, A.A.G. Transport, 6 February 1902.
82 Bill Nasson, 'Moving Lord Kitchener: Black Military Transport and Supply Work in the South African War, 1899–1902, with particular reference to the Cape Colony', *Journal of Southern African Studies*, 11, 1 (1984) pp. 21–55.
83 SHMA, Sebopioa Molema Papers, E.C. Welsh to L. Marumoloa, 24 January 1910.
84 UWHP, Molema Papers, A979Bd1, S.J. Molema for L. Marumoloa to E.C. Welsh, 22 November 1911.
85 SHMA, Sebopioa Molema Papers, E.C. Welsh to L. Marumoloa, 27 December 1912.
86 SHMA, Sebopioa Molema Papers, S.J. Molema for L. Marumoloa to R. Lloyd, 30 April 1913.
87 SHMA, Sebopioa Molema Papers, Notes for a meeting, December 1913.
88 UWHP, Molema Papers, A979Ac1, S.J. Molema to S.T. Molema, 27 December 1913.
89 SHMA, Sebopioa Molema Papers, photograph with inscription from Nora to S.J. Molema, c. 1911. I am grateful to Galefele Molema for sharing the contents of the letter accompanying the photograph, which is no longer available.
90 UWHP, Molema Papers, A979Bd1, R. Hornabrook to L. Marumoloa, 9 April 1914 and reply, 28 April 1914.
91 UWHP, Molema Papers, A979Bd1, S.J. Molema for L. Marumoloa to G.B. Gaseitsewe, 17 May 1915; S.J. Molema to G. Weavind, 17 June 1915.
92 UWHP, Molema Papers, A979Cc9, T. Jabavu to S.T. Molema, 5 February 1910, Sechuana.
93 Willan, *Sol Plaatje, South African Nationalist*, p. 144.
94 Shula Marks, *Reluctant Rebellion: The 1906–8 Disturbances in Natal* (Oxford, Clarendon Press, 1970).
95 UWHP, Molema Papers, A979Cc9, Notice of meeting, 24 March 1924.
96 Hugh MacMillan, 'A Nation Divided? The Swazi in Swaziland and the Transvaal, 1865–1986', in *The Invention of Tribalism in Southern Africa*, edited by Leroy Vail (Berkeley, University of California Press, 1991), pp. 289–323, especially p. 295.
97 UWHP, Molema Papers, A979Aa3.6.2, J. Goronyane to S.T. Molema, 5 June 1911.
98 *Tsala ea Batho*, 14 March 1914. For advertisements of Pink Pills, see *Tsala ea Becoana*, 15 April 1911 as one example.
99 UWHP, Molema Papers, A979Da8, S. Plaatje to S.T. Molema, 17 January 1911, Sechuana.
100 UWHP, Molema Papers, A979Da14, S. Plaatje to S.T. Molema, c. January 1911, Sechuana.
101 *Ibid.*
102 *Ibid.*
103 UWHP, Molema Papers, A979Da9, S. Plaatje to S.T. Molema, 1 March 1911.
104 UWHP. Molema Papers, A979Da15, S.T. Plaatje to S.T. Molema, c. February 1911, Sechuana.
105 UWHP, Molema Papers, A979Da17, S.T. Plaatje to S.T. Molema, c. March 1911, Sechuana and English.
106 *Tsala ea Batho*, 13 January 1912, Sechuana.

107 *Ibid.*
108 *Tsala ea Batho*, 24 February 1912, Sechuana.
109 UWHP, Molema Papers, A979Cc9, J. Dube to L. Marumoloa, 13 April 1912.
110 UWHP, Molema Papers, A979 Da19, S.T. Plaatje to S.T. Molema, 14 August 1912, Sechuana.
111 *Ibid.*
112 *Ibid.*
113 *Ibid.*
114 *Ibid.*
115 *Ibid.*
116 UWHP, Molema Papers, A979Da20, S.T. Plaatje to S.T. Molema, (1)8 August 1912, mostly Sechuana.
117 *Ibid.*
118 *Ibid.*
119 UWHP, Molema Papers, A979Da21, S.T. Plaatje to S.T. Molema, 14 September 1912. Mostly Sechuana.
120 *Ibid.*
121 UWHP, Molema Papers, A979Da22 S.T. Plaatje to S.T. Molema, 12 December 1912. Mostly Sechuana.
122 *Ibid.*
123 *Ibid.*
124 UWHP, Molema Papers, A979Da26, S.T. Plaatje to S.T. Molema, 16 January 1913. Mostly Sechuana.
125 *Ibid.*
126 UWHP, Molema Papers, A979Da29, S.T. Plaatje to S.T. Molema, 17 April 1913. Mostly Sechuana.
127 UWHP, Molema Papers, A979Bc3.1, G. Green to De Kock & De Kock, 1 April 1910
128 *Ibid.*
129 UNISA, Fort Hare Papers, ZKM_A2_42_Part , Z. K. Matthews, Barolong Research, 'A Short History of the Tshidi Barolong, June 1945, p.22.
130 UWHP, Molema Papers, A979Da14, S. Plaatje to S.T. Molema, 2 April 1911.
131 UWHP, Molema Papers, A979Cc9, E. Dower to B. Montsioa, 2 February 1911.
132 *Tsala ea Batho*, 2 September 1912.
133 UWHP, Molema Papers, A979Bd1, L, Marumoloa to W.P. Schreiner, c. May 1911.
134 *Ibid.*
135 *Ibid.*
136 UWHP, Molema Papers, A979Bd1, E. Dower to L. Marumoloa, 14 June 1911, Sechuana.
137 SHMA, Sebopioa Molema Papers, S.J. Molema for L. Marumoloa to S. Plaatje, 29 May 1912.
138 UWHP, Molema Papers, A979Bd1, E. Dower to L. Marumoloa, 14 June 1911, Sechuana.
139 *Ibid.*
140 CTA, Records of Department of Justice, JUS 109 File 23079/10. Reference 2/323/10/13/B/Co, Reid & Nephew to Department of Native Affairs, 4 October 1911.
141 CTA, Records of Department of Justice, JUS 109 File 23079/10. Reference 2/323/10/13/B/Co, E. Dower to Reid & Nephew, 4 October 1911.
142 CTA, Records of Department of Justice, JUS 109 File 23079/10. Reference

2/323/10/13/B/Co, J. Roos (Secretary of Justice) to E. Dower, 31 October 1911.
143 CTA, Records of Department of Justice, JUS 109 File 23079/10. Reference 2/323/10/13/B/Co, E. Dower to J. Roos, 3 November 1911.
144 CTA, Records of Department of Justice, JUS 109 File 23079/10. Reference 2/323/10/13/B/Co, J. Roos to E. Dower, 19 December 1911.
145 CTA, Records of Department of Justice, JUS 109 File 23079/10. Reference 2/323/10/13/B/Co, E. Dower to J. Roos, 19 January 1912.
146 SHMA, Sebopioa Molema Papers, E.C. Welsh to L. Marumoloa, 12 June 1912.
147 SHMA, Sebopioa Molema Papers, E.C. Welsh to L. Marumoloa, 25 May 1912.
148 Harvey Feinberg, 'The 1913 Natives Land Act in South Africa: Politics, Race and Segregation in the Early 20th Century', *The International Journal of African Historical Studies*, 26, 1 (1993), p. 89.
149 SHMA, Sebopioa Molema Papers, S.T. Molema for L. Moramuloa to E.C. Welsh, 16 March 1912.
150 *Ibid.*
151 SHMA, Sebopioa Molema Papers, S.T. Molema for L. Marumoloa to E.C. Welsh, 07 February 1912.
152 *Ibid.*
153 UWHP, Molema Papers, A979Bd1, H. Frost to L. Marumoloa, 2 January 1913, Sechuana.
154 UWHP, Molema Papers, A979Bd1, H. Frost to L. Marumoloa, 1 January 1912.
155 UWHP, Molema Papers, A979Bd1, H. Frost to E. C. Welsh (quoting communication from E. Dower), 22 January 1912.
156 UWHP, Molema Papers, A979Cc9, J. Dube to L. Marumoloa, 13 April 1912.
157 SHMA, Sebopioa Molema Papers, E.C. Welsh to L. Marumoloa, 26 April 1912.
158 SHMA, Sebopioa Molema Papers, S.J. Molema for L. Marumoloa to E.C. Welsh, 1 May 1912.
159 SHMA, Sebopioa Molema Papers, S.J Molema for L. Marumoloa to H. Burton, 08 May 1912
160 SHMA, Sebopioa Molema Papers, S.J. Molema for L. Marumolar to E.C. Welsh, 12 June 1912.
161 Feinberg, 'The 1913 Natives Land Act in South Africa', p. 76.
162 SHMA, Sebopioa Molema, Reference to enclosed letters to Native Affairs Department and Department of Justice, 24 July 1912.
163 SHMA, Sebopioa Molema Papers, E.C. Welsh to L. Marumoloa, 12 August 1912.
164 UWHP, Molema Papers, A979Bd3.2, L, Marumuloa to W.P. Schreiner, 23 September 1912.
165 CTA, Records of Department of Justice, Union of South Africa Illiquid Cases, CSC 2/1/1/717 1913, Badirile/ Lekoko vs Smuts/Fischer.
166 UWHP, Molema Papers, A979Bd1, E. Barrett to E.C. Welsh, 14 October 1912.
167 UWHP, Molema Papers A979Bd1 H. Frost to E. C. Welsh, 25 November 1912.
168 UWHP, Molema Papers A979Bd1, Copy of article, *Tsala ea Batho*, November 1912, undated A979Bd1.
169 *Ibid.*
170 Feinberg, 'The 1913 Natives Land Act in South Africa', pp. 67, 71–73, 77–78.
171 SHMA, Sebopioa Molema Papers, S.J. Molema to E. Molema, 23 January 1913.
172 UWHP, Molema Papers, A979Aa4, L. Marumoloa to S.T. Molema, 24 January 1913, Sechuana.
173 UWHP, Molema Papers, A979Aa4, L. Marumoloa to S.T. Molema, 26 January 1913, Sechuana.

174 UWHP, Molema Papers, A979Aa3.1.1, P. Fincham to S.T. Molema, 1 March 1911.
175 *Mafeking Mail*, 7 March 1910.
176 See for example, *Mafeking Mail*, 4 January 1910.
177 See *Mafeking Mail*, 4 March 1910.
178 UWHP, Molema Papers, A979Aa3.1.1, P. Fincham to S.T. Molema, 1 March 1911.
179 Quill Hermans, 'Towards Budgetary Independence: A Review of Botswana's Financial History, 1900 to 1973', *Botswana Notes & Records*, 6 (1974), p. 91.
180 UWHP, Molema Papers, A979Aa3.1.1, P. Fincham to S.T. Molema, 18 May 1912.
181 UWHP, Molema Papers, A979Aa3.4, Invoice: L. Irving to S.T. Molema, 21 May 1912.
182 UWHP, Molema Papers, A979Aa3.1.1, Promissory note: Luk Long, late 1911; Loan invoice: A. van Jaarsveld, 26 November 1912.
183 UWHP, Molema Papers, A979Aa3.3, De Kock and De Kock to S.T. Molema, 21 June & 22 August 1912.
184 UWHP, Molema Papers, A979 Aa3.4, Promissory notes: 3 and 4 February, 11 September, 30 December 1911; 29 February and 7 March 1912; General bond agreement S. Gordon and S.T. Molema, 16 March 1912, Cape Town Archives, CTA (Illiquid Cases), 1912 to 1917, CSC 2/1/1/801 84. Silas Tawana Molema and Joshua Molema versus Sundel Gordon.
185 UWHP, Molema Papers, A979Aa1, J, Moshoela to S.T. Molema, 25 June 1912.
186 UWHP, Molema Papers, A979Aa1, J, Moshoela to S.T. Molema, 02 July 1912.
187 UWHP, Molema Papers, A979Aa1, J, Moshoela to S.T. Molema, 11 July 1912.
188 UWHP, Molema Papers, A979Aa1, J, Moshoela to S.T. Molema, 19 July 1912.
189 UWHP, Molema Papers, A979Aa1, J, Moshoela to S.T. Molema, 09 August 1912.
190 UWHP, Molema Papers, A979Aa1, J, Moshoela to S.T. Molema, 02 September 1912.
191 UWHP, Molema Papers, A979Aa1, J, Moshoela to S.T. Molema, 02 October 1912.
192 UWHP, Molema Papers, A979Aa3.1.1, P. Fincham to S.T. Molema, 18 May 1912.
193 UWHP, Molema Papers, A979Aa3.1.1, P. Fincham to S.T. Molema, 30 July 1912.
194 UWHP, Molema Papers, A979Aa3.1.1, P. Fincham to S.T. Molema, 17 September 1912.
195 UWHP, Molema Papers, A979Aa3.1.1, P. Fincham to S.T. Molema, 25 March 1913.
196 UWHP, Molema Papers, A979Aa3.1.1, P. Fincham to S.T. Molema, 25 April 1913.
197 UWHP, Molema Papers, A979Aa3.1.1, J. Higgs to S.T. Molema, 21 April 1913.
198 Isaac Schapera, 'The System of Land Tenure on the Barolong Farms (Bechuanaland Protectorate): Report and Recommendations submitted to the B.P. Administration', *Botswana Notes and Records*, 15 (1943), p. 21.
199 UWHP, Molema Papers, A979Aa3.1.1, P. Fincham to S.T. Molema, 21 May 1913.
200 UWHP, Molema Papers, A979Aa3.1.1, P. Fincham to S.T. Molema, 5 June 1913.
201 *Ibid.*
202 UWHP, Molema Papers, A979Aa3.1.1, P. Fincham to S.T. Molema, 25 July 1913.
203 UWHP, Molema Papers, A979Aa3.1.1, P. Fincham to S.T. Molema, 25 July 1913.
204 UWHP, Molema Papers, A979Aa3.1.1, P. Fincham to S.T. Molema, 30 July 1913.
205 SHMA, Sebopioa Molema Papers, S.J. Molema for L. Marumoloa to R. Llyod, 4 July 1913.
206 SHMA, Sebopioa Molema Papers, Superintendent of Natives to Chief Lekoko, 13 December 1913.

207 UWHP, Molema Papers, A979Ad1, S.M. Molema to S.T. Molema, 28 February 1910, 9 July 1911.
208 S.J. Ngqongqo, 'Mpilo Walter Benson Rubusana, 1858–1910: The Making of the New Elite in the Eastern Cape', MA thesis, University of Fort Hare, 1996.
209 UWHP, Molema Papers, A979Ad1, S.M. Molema to S.T. Molema, 21 July 1908.
210 UWHP, Molema Papers, A979Ad1, S.M. Molema to S.T. Molema, 28 February 1910.
211 UWHP, Molema Papers, A979Ad1, S.M. Molema to S.T. Molema, 18 October 1910.
212 UWHP, Molema Papers, A979Ad1, S.M. Molema to S.T. Molema, 27 September 1910.
213 UWHP, Molema Papers, A979Ad1, S.M. Molema to S.T. Molema, 28 February 1910.
214 UWHP, Molema Papers, A979Aa2.28, R. Moikangoa to S.T. Molema, 28 February 1910.
215 UWHP, Molema Papers, A979Ad1, S.M. Molema to S.T. Molema, undated, c. 1911.
216 UWHP, Molema Papers, A979Ad1, S.M. Molema to S.T. Molema, 11 July 1911.
217 UWHP, Molema Papers, A979Ad1, S.M. Molema to S.T. Molema, 9 July 1911.
218 UWHP, Molema Papers, A979Ad1, S.M. Molema to S.T. Molema, 7 January 1912.
219 UWHP, Molema Papers, A979Ad1, S.M. Molema to S.T. Molema, 26 March 1912.
220 UWHP, Molema Papers, A979Ad1, S.M. Molema to S.T. Molema, 22 October 1912.
221 UWHP, Molema Papers, A979Ad1, S.M. Molema to S.T. Molema, 27 October 1912.
222 UWHP, Molema Papers, A979Ad1, S.M. Molema to S.T. Molema, 24 November 1912.
223 UWHP, Molema Papers, A979Ad1, S.M. Molema to S.T. Molema, 14 December 1912.
224 UWHP, Molema Papers, A979Ad1, S.M. Molema to S.T. Molema, 30 December 1912.
225 *Ibid.*
226 *Ibid.*
227 UWHP, Molema Papers, A979Ad1, S.M. Molema to S.T. Molema, 16 March 1913.
228 *Ibid.*
229 UWHP, Molema Papers, A979Ad1, S.M. Molema to S.T. Molema, 20 April 1913.
230 UWHP, Molema Papers, A979Ad1, S.M. Molema to S.T. Molema, 30 April 1913.
231 UWHP, Molema Papers, A979Ad1, S.M. Molema to S.T. Molema, 27 August
232 UWHP, Molema Papers, A979Ad1, S.M. Molema to S.T. Molema, 4 July 1913.
233 Timothy Keegan, 'Crisis and Catharsis in the Development of Capitalism in South African Agriculture', Paper presented at University of the Witwatersrand, African Studies Institute, October 1984, p. 12.
234 Feinberg, 'The 1913 Natives Land Act in South Africa', p. 108.
235 *Ibid.*, p. 93.
236 *Ibid.*, p. 94.
237 *Ibid.*, p. 97.

238 SHMA, Sebopioa Molema Papers, E.J. Schultz to L. Moramoloa, 29 January 1913.
239 Ibid.
240 Feinberg, 'The 1913 Natives Land Act', p. 94.
241 Ibid.
242 These testimonies are in CTA, Union of South Africa Illiquid Cases, (1910–1913) CSC 2/1/1/717 1913, Badirile/Lekoko vs Smuts/Fischer, 10 June 1913.
243 Ibid.
244 William Beinart and Peter Delius, 'The Historical Context and Legacy of the Natives Land Act of 1913', *Journal of Southern African Studies*, 40, 4 (July 2014), p.669.
245 Andrew Roberts, 'The Sub-Imperialism of the Baganda', *The Journal of African History*, 3, 3 (1962), pp. 435–450.
246 CTA, Records of Department of Justice, JUS 109 File 23079/10. Reference 2/323/10/13/B/Co, Reid & Nephew to Department of Justice, 8 August 1913.
247 CTA, Records of Department of Justice, JUS 109 File 23079/10. Reference 2/323/10/13/B/Co, Reid & Nephew to Department of Justice, 13 and 24 January 1913.
248 SHMA, Sebopioa Molema Papers, S.T. Molema for L. Marumoloa to E.C. Welsh, 13 June 1913.
249 Ibid.
250 Keegan, 'Crisis and Catharsis in the Development of Capitalism in South African Agriculture', p. 26.
251 Ibid., p. 31.
252 Ibid., p. 21.
253 UWHP, Molema Papers, A979Aa3.5.1. J.W. Hall to S.T Molema, c. 1880s.
254 UWHP, Molema Papers, A979Aa3.5.1. J.W. Hall to S.T Molema, c. 1880s.
255 UWHP, Molema Papers, A979Ba9, Treaty between Paramount Chief Montsioa his sons and councillors and the Imperial Government, 22 May 1884.
256 UWHP, A979Ba12, E. Rowlands to Montsioa, 18 July 1894.
257 UWHP, Molema Papers, A979Aa3.5.11, Agreement between E. Rowlands and R. Rowland and S.T. Molema, 16 October 1905.
258 UWHP, Molema Papers, A979Cb1, Agreement between R. Rowland and S.T. Molema, 16 October 1901.
259 UWHP, Molema Papers, A979Aa3. C. Hall to S.T. Molema, 09 November 1911.
260 Ibid.
261 UWHP, Molema Papers, A979Aa3. E.C. Welsh to C. Hall, 2 February 1913.
262 UWHP, Molema Papers, A979Aa3. C. Hall to S.T. Molema, 14 March 1913.
263 UWHP, Molema Papers, A979Aa3. S.T. Molema to C. Hall, 15 May 1914.
264 UWHP, Molema Papers, A979Aa3. S.T. Molema to C. Hall, 5 January 1914.
265 UWHP, Molema Papers, A979Aa3. C. Hall to S.T. Molema, 22 May 1914.
266 UWHP, Molema Papers, A979Aa3. S.T. Molema to C. Hall, 13 April 1915.
267 Ibid.
268 These testimonies are in CTA, Union of South Africa Illiquid Cases, (1910–1913) CSC 2/1/1/717 1913, Badirile/Lekoko vs Smuts/Fischer, 10 June 1913.
269 UWHP, Molema Papers, A979Aa3. R. Rowland to S.T. Molema, 27 August 1913.
270 Ibid.
271 *Tsala ea Batho*, 1914 June 20, Sechuana.
272 *Tsala ea Batho*, 1914 September 12, Sechuana.
273 UWHP, Molema Papers, A979Da3. S.T. Plaatje to S.T. Molema, 12 May 1913.
274 Ibid.

275 *Ibid.*
276 UWHP, Molema Papers, A979Aa3. S. Minchin to S.T. Molema, 04 July 1914.
277 UWHP, Molema Papers, A979Da38. S.J. Molema to S.T. Molema, 11 May 1914.
278 *Ibid.*
279 Plaatje, *Native Life in South Africa*, p. 23.
280 *Ibid.*, p. 23.
281 *Ibid.*, p. 24.
282 *Ibid.*
283 UWHP, Molema Papers, A979Aa2.1, J. Molebaloa to S.T. Molema, 1 February 1913, Sechuana.
284 *Ibid.*
285 SHMA, Sebopioa Molema Papers, James Molebaloa, *The Barolong and Native Affairs Administration Bill, Native Affairs and Amacqumukwebe Tribe* (self-published, 1936).
286 UWHP, Molema Papers, A979Aa2.1, J. Molebaloa to S.T. Molema, 1 February 1913, Sechuana.
287 *Ibid.*
288 *Ibid.*
289 UWHP, Molema Papers, A979Aa2.1, J. Molebaloa to S.T. Molema, 7 February 1913, Sechuana.
290 *Ibid.*
291 For such 'charismatic' leadership, see Max Weber, 'The Sociology of Charismatic Authority' in *From Max Weber: Essays in Sociology*, translated and edited by Hans H. Gerth and C. Wright Mills (New York, Oxford University Press, 1958), p. 246.
292 Alain Badiou, *Infinite Thought: Truth and the Return of Philosophy*, translated and edited by Oliver Feltham and Justin Clemens (London, New York, Continuum, 2003).
293 UWHP, Molema Papers, A979Aa2.39, C. Maseloanyana to S.T. Molema, 15 August 1913, Sechuana.
294 *Ibid.*
295 UWHP, Molema Papers, A979Aa2.42, S.T. Molema to C. Maseloanyana, 15 August 1913, Sechuana.
296 UWHP, Molema Papers, A979Aa2.43, C. Maseloanyana to S.T. Molema, 15 August 1913, Sechuana.
297 UWHP, Molema Papers, A979Aa2.45, S.T. Molema to J.L. Masigo, 4 December 1913, Sechuana.
298 UWHP, Molema Papers, A979Aa2.46, J.L. Masigo to S.T. Molema, 12 December 1913, Sechuana.
299 UWHP, Molema Papers, A979Aa2.47, C. Maseloanyana to S.T. Molema, 1 January 1914, Sechuana.
300 UWHP, Molema Papers, A979Aa2.48, S.T. Molema to J.L. Mosiga, 19 January 1914, Sechuana.
301 UWHP, Molema Papers, A979Aa2.58, J.N.R. Mosaka to S.T. Molema, 14 August 1914, Sechuana.
302 *Ibid.*
303 UWHP, Molema Papers, A979Aa2.64, S.T. Molema to J.L. Mosiga, 04 April 1915, Sechuana.
304 *Ibid.*
305 UWHP, Molema Papers, A979Aa2, J. Goronyane to W. Letsapa, 18 July 1921, then to S.T. Molema, 13 September 1921, Sechuana.

306 *Ibid.*
307 UWHP, Molema Papers, A979Aa2.40, J. Moishumi to S.T. Molema, 14 February 1913, Sechuana.
308 Silas Molema, 'Modimo ke a go baka', Hymn 64, in *Buka ya Merapelo, Ditirelo le Difela* (Cape Town, Methodist Publishing House, 1953), p. 64.
309 Silas Molema, 'Rara le Morwa le Mowa', Hymn 248, in *Buka ya Merapelo, Ditirelo le Difela*, p. 203.
310 Silas Molema, 'Jesu, 'Tsatsi ja Tshiamo', Hymn 395, in *Buka ya Merapelo, Ditirelo le Difela*, p. 322.
311 *Tsala ea Batho*, 14 May 1914.
312 UWHP, Molema Papers, A979Aa2.9, S.T. Molema to J. Molebaloa, 1914 undated, Sechuana
313 UWHP, Molema Papers, A979Aa3, S.T. Molema to Amos, undated 1913.
314 UWHP, Molema Papers, A99Aa3, Invoices, c. 1913, records not clear.
315 *Ibid.*
316 UWHP, Molema Papers, A979Aa3.4, Promissory Note, 31 March 1913; A979Aa3.3, Payment note, 15 July 1913.
317 UWHP, Molema Papers, A979Aa3.1.1, P. Fincham to S.T. Molema, 22 October 1913.
318 UWHP, Molema Papers, A979Aa3.1.1, P. Fincham to S.T. Molema, 31 October 1913.
319 UWHP, Molema Papers, A979Aa3.1.1, P. Fincham to S.T. Molema, 7 December 1913.
320 UWHP, Molema Papers, A979Aa3.1.1, P. Fincham to S.T. Molema, 22 December1913.
321 UWHP, Molema Papers, A979Aa3.1.1, P. Fincham to S.T. Molema, 07 January 1914.
322 UWHP, Molema Papers, A979Aa3.1.1, P. Fincham to S.T. Molema, 23 February 1914, 27 February 1914.
323 UWHP, Molema Papers, A979Aa3.1.1, P. Fincham to S.T. Molema, 11 March 1914.
324 See for example, UWHP, Molema Papers, A979Aa3.1.1, Ruthenberg to S.T. Molema, 28 May 1914.
325 UWHP, Molema Papers, P. Fincham to S.T. Molema, A979Aa3.1.1, 3 May 1914.
326 UWHP, Molema Papers, A979Aa3.1.1, P. Fincham to S.T. Molema, 17 May 1914.
327 UWHP, Molema Papers, A979Aa3.1.1, S.T. Molema to P. Fincham, 26 June 1914.
328 UWHP, Molema Papers, A979Aa3.1.1, P. Fincham to S.T. Molema, 30 May 1914.
329 UWHP, Molema Papers, A979Aa3.1.1, S.T. Molema to G.F.J van Rensburg, 23 June 1913.
330 UWHP, Molema Papers, A979Aa3.1.1, P. Fincham to S.T. Molema, 29 June 1914.
331 *Ibid.*
332 *Ibid.*
333 UWHP, Molema Papers, A979Aa3.1.1, P. Fincham to S.T. Molema, 24 August 1914.
334 UWHP, Molema Papers, A979Aa3.1.1, J Higgs to S.T. Molema, 10 October 1914.
335 *Ibid.*
336 UWHP, Molema Papers, A979Aa3.1.1, T. Dickerson to S.T. Molema, 7 September 1914.
337 UWHP, Molema Papers, A979Aa3.1.1, P. Fincham to S.T. Molema, 2 September 1914.

338 UWHP, Molema Papers, A979Aa3.1.1, T. Dickerson to S. T. Molema, 7 September 1914.
339 UWHP, Molema Papers, A979Aa3.1.2, T. Dickerson to G. Beukes, 27 June 1915.
340 UWHP, Molema Papers, A979Aa3.1.1, Summons: S. Minchin to S.T. Molema, 24 December 1914.
341 UWHP, Molema Papers, A979Aa3.1.2, P. Fincham to S.T. Molema, 26 March 1915.
342 *Ibid.*
343 UWHP, Molema Papers, A979Aa3.1.1, P. Fincham to S.T. Molema, 30 November 1913.
344 UWHP, Molema Papers, A979Aa3.1.2, P. Fincham to S.T. Molema, 26 March 1915.
345 UWHP, Molema Papers, A979Aa3.1.2, S. Minchin to S.T. Molema, 26 March 1915.
346 UWHP, Molema Papers, A979Aa3.1.2, P. Fincham to S.T. Molema, 31 March 1915.
347 UWHP, Molema Papers, A979Aa3.1.2, P. Fincham to S.T. Molema, 7 June 1915.
348 UWHP, Molema Papers, A979Aa3.1.2, S.T. Molema to P. Fincham, 30 November 1916.
349 UWHP, Molema Papers, A979Aa3.1.2, P. Fincham to S.T. Molema, 7 June 1915.
350 UWHP, Molema Papers, A979Aa3.1.2, P. Fincham to S.T. Molema, 20 April 1915.
351 UWHP, Molema Papers, A979Aa3.1.2, P. Fincham to S.T. Molema, 23 April 1915.
352 UWHP, Molema Papers, A979Aa3.1.2, S.T. Molema to T. Dickerson, 20 April 1915.
353 UWHP, Molema Papers, A979Aa3.1.2, T. Dickerson to S.T. Molema, undated.
354 UWHP, Molema Papers, A979Aa3.1.2, Agreement: S.T. Molema and T. Dickerson, 1 June 1915.
355 UWHP, Molema Papers, A979Aa3.1.2, P. Fincham to S.T. Molema, 9 July 1915.
356 UWHP, Molema Papers, A979Aa3.1.2, P. Fincham to S.T. Molema, 20 July 1915.
357 UWHP, Molema Papers, A979Aa3.1.2, S. T. Molema to P. Fincham, 31 July 1915.
358 UWHP, Molema Papers, A979Aa3.1.2, P. Fincham to S.T. Molema, 2 August 1915.
359 UWHP, Molema Papers, A979Aa3.1.2 G. Beukes to S.T. Molema, 11 March 1916.
360 UWHP, Molema Papers, A979Aa3.1.2 P. Fincham to S.T. Molema, 23 May 1916.
361 UWHP, Molema Papers, A979Aa3.1.2, W. Hyde to P. Fincham, 20 June 1916.
362 UWHP, Molema Papers, A979Aa3.1.2, S.T. Molema to P. Fincham, 13 June 1916.
363 UWHP, Molema Papers, A979Aa3.1.2, P. Fincham to S.T. Molema, 23 June 1916.
364 UWHP, Molema Papers, A979Aa3.1.2, P. Fincham to S.T. Molema, 24 July 1916.
365 UWHP, Molema Papers, A979Aa3.1.2, P. Fincham to S.T. Molema, 26 October 1916.
366 UWHP, Molema Papers, A979Aa3.1.2, P. Fincham to S.T. Molema, 26 October 1916.
367 UWHP, Molema Papers, A979Aa3.1.2, P. Fincham to S.T. Molema, 15 October 1916.
368 UWHP, Molema Papers, A979Aa3.1.2, P. Fincham to S.T. Molema, 26 October 1916.
369 UWHP, Molema Papers, A979Aa3.1.2, S. Minchin to S.T. Molema, 27 October 1916.

370 UWHP, Molema Papers, A979Aa3.1.2, P. Fincham to S.T. Molema, 10 November 1916.
371 UWHP, Molema Papers, A979Aa3.1.2, P. Fincham to S.T. Molema, 10 November 1916.
372 UWHP, Molema Papers, A979Aa3.1.2, P. Fincham to S.T. Molema, 11 November 1916.
373 UWHP, Molema Papers, A979Aa3.1.2, P. Fincham to S.T. Molema, 22 November 1916.
374 UWHP, Molema Papers, A979Aa3.1.2, S.T. Molema to P. Fincham, 30 November 1916.
375 UWHP, Molema Papers, A979Aa3.1.2, S.T. Molema to P. Fincham, 30 November 1916.
376 UWHP, Molema Papers, A979Aa3.1.2, H.M. Beukes to S.T. Molema, 8 January 1917. Dutch.
377 UWHP, Molema Papers, A979Aa3.1.2, S.T. Molema to J. Van Rensburg, 10 March 1917.
378 UWHP, Molema Papers, A979Aa3.1.2, De Kock and De Kock, 13 March 1917.
379 UWHP, Molema Papers, A979Aa3.1.2, P. Fincham to S.T. Molema, 22 December 1916.
380 UWHP, Molema Papers, A979Aa3.1.2, S.T. Molema to P. Fincham, 4 January 1917.
381 UWHP, Molema Papers, A979Bd1, E.C. Welsh to L. Montsioa, 15 March 1913.
382 SHMA, Sebopioa Molema Papers, L. Montsioa to E.C. Welsh, 13 March 1913.
383 UWHP, Molema Papers, A979Bd1, H. Frost to L. Montsioa, 23 May 1913.
384 UWHP, Molema Papers, A070Bd1 R.C. Lloyd to E. Barrett, 23 July 1913.
385 *Ibid.*
386 *Ibid.*
387 *Ibid.*
388 *Ibid.*
389 *Ibid.*
390 UWHP, Molema Papers, A979Aa1, J. Molema to S.T. Molema, 1 June 1913.
391 UWHP, Molema Papers, A979Bc3.2 H. Frost to R. Lloyd, 2 July 1913.
392 *Ibid.*
393 UWHP, Molema Papers, A979Bc3.2, S. Molema for L. Montsioa to R. Lloyd, 2 July 1913.
394 UWHP, Molema Papers, A979Bc3.2, S. Molema for L. Montsioa to G. Weavind, 18 January 1914.
395 *Ibid.*
396 UWHP, Molema Papers, A979Bd1, S.J. Molema for L. Montsioa to G. Weavind, 8 January 1915.
397 *Ibid.*
398 UWHP, Molema Papers, A979Bd1, S.J. Molema for L. Montsioa to H. Frost, 12 April 1915.
399 UWHP, Molema Papers A979Bd1, S.J. Molema for L. Montsioa to H. Frost, 12 April 1915.
400 SHMA, Sebopioa Molema Papers, S.J. Molema for L. Montsioa to R. Lloyd, 13 October 1913.
401 SHMA, Sebopioa Molema Papers, S.J. Molema for L. Montsioa to E.C. Welsh, 10 March 1913.
402 SHMA, Sebopioa Molema Papers, S.J. Molema for L. Montsioa to E.C. Welsh, 13 October 1913.

403 UWHP, Molema Papers, A979Bd1, S.J. Molema for L. Montsioa to H. J Frost, 21 January 1915.
404 UWHP, Molema Papers, A979Be1, E. Barret to E.C. Welsh, 4 November 1915.
405 UWHP, Molema Papers, A979Ad1, S.M. Molema to S.T. Molema, 6 March 1914.
406 UWHP, Molema Papers, A979Ad1, S.M. Molema to S.T. Molema, 26 March 1914.
407 *Ibid.*
408 UWHP, Molema Papers, A979Ad1, S.T. Molema to S.M. Molema, 16 March 1914.
409 UWHP, Molema Papers, A979Ad1, S.M. Molema to S.T. Molema, 26 March 1914.
410 UWHP, Molema Papers, A979Ad1, S.M. Molema to S.T. Molema, 24 April 1914.
411 *Ibid.*
412 CTA, Records of Department of Justice, JUS 109 File 23079/10. Reference 2/323/10/13/B/Co, Finance Department, and R.C. Lloyd, 3 March 1914 to 19 March 1915.
413 *Tsala ea Batho*, 18 July 1914, Sechuana.
414 *Ibid.*
415 *Tsala ea Batho*, 27 June 1914, Sechuana.
416 *Ibid.*
417 UWHP, Molema Papers, A979Aa1, H. Molema to S.T. Molema, 4 March 1909.
418 UWHP, Molema Papers, A979 Da15, S. Plaatje to S.T. Molema, c. April 1911.
419 UWHP, Molema Papers, A979Ad1, S.M. Molema to S.T. Molema, 8 March 1911.
420 *Tsala ea Becoana*, 23 October 1911, 24 February 1912.
421 UWHP, Molema Papers, A979Da14, S. Plaatje to S.T. Molema, c. April 1911.
422 *Tsala ea Becoana*, 28 October 1911.
423 UWHP, Molema Papers, A979Ae1, School Board to H. Molema, 9 December 1912.
424 UWHP, Molema Papers, A979Ad1, S.M. Molema to S.T. Molema, 2 June 1912.
425 UWHP, Molema Papers, A979Bd1, G. Rolland to L. Marumoloa, 7 April 1913.
426 UWHP, Molema Papers, A979 Bd1, G. Rolland to Lekoko, 18 August 1913.
427 UWHP, Molema Papers, A979Aa3, S.T Molema to G. Rolland, 1 May 1914.
428 UWHP, Molema Papers, A979Bd2, Memorandum of Agreement, L. Marumoloa and G. Phoi, Barolong Educational and National Fund, 12 February 1915.
429 UWHP, Molema Papers, A979Cc5.1, List of contributions from men and headmen, 1 October 1914.
430 UWHP, Molema Papers, A979Bd1, S.J. Molema to Native Recruiting Cooperation, 30 June 1915.
431 UWHP, Molema Papers, A979Bd1, S.J Molema for L. Marumoloa to 'All Compound Managers in the Transvaal', 29 April 1914.
432 UWHP, Molema Papers, A979Cc5.1, List of contributions from men and headmen, 1 October 1914.
433 UWHP, Molema Papers, A979Aa1, J. Molebaloa to S.T. Molema, 7 February 1913, Sechuana.
434 UWHP, Molema Papers, A979Aa2, Superintendent of Natives to S.T. Molema, 12 August 1924.
435 Jane Starfield, 'Dr S. Modiri Molema (1891–1965): The Making of an Historian', PhD thesis, University of the Witwatersrand (2008).
436 John Comaroff, 'Rules and Rulers: Political Processes in a Tswana Chiefdom', *Man*, 13, 1 (1978), pp. 1-20.

437 UWHP, Molema Papers, A979 Be1, Unspecified person to J. Montsioa, 5 September 1917.
438 UWHP, Molema Papers, A979Be1, H. Molema, Petition to L. Botha, 5 July 1916.
439 Ibid.
440 UWHP, Molema Papers, A979 Be1, E. Barret to L. Lloyd, 15 February 1917.
441 UWHP, Molema Papers, A979Ae1, Medical Bills, H. Molema, c, June 1917.
442 UWHP, Molema Papers, A979Aa2.74, W. Letsapa to S.T. Molema, 23 June 1917.
443 Ibid.
444 UWHP, Molema Papers, A979Cc4.1, Notice from Barolong National Council, c. April 1918.
445 Ibid.
446 UWHP, Molema Papers, A979 Cc5.1, Barolong Educational and National Fund, 1920–1921.
447 433 UWHP, Molema Papers, A979 Cc5.1, Barolong Educational and National Fund, 1924–1926.
448 434 UWHP, Molema Papers, A979 Be1, Unspecified person to J. Montsioa, 5 September 1917.
449 CTA, Native Administration in Mafeking District, 1 MFK N1/1/2 2/4/2/27, R.C Lloyd to Secretary of Public Services Commission 1915 February 8.
450 UWHP, Molema Papers, A979Ac1, S.J. Molema to S.T. Molema, 9 August 1915.
451 UWHP, Molema Papers, A979Ac1, S.J. Molema to J. Molema, 12 March 16.
452 UWHP, Molema Papers, A979Ac1, S.J. Molema to S.T. Molema, 9 January 1916.
453 UWHP, Molema Papers, A979Ac1, S.J. Molema to S.T. Molema, 9 August 1915.
454 UWHP, Molema Papers, A979Ac1, S.J. Molema to S.T. Molema, 9 January 1916.
455 Ibid.
456 UWHP, Molema Papers, A979Ac1, S.J. Molema to S.T. Molema, 9 January 1916.
457 UWHP, Molema Papers, A979Ac1, S.J. Molema to K. Makhobi, 6 February 1917.
458 UWHP, Molema Papers, A979Ac1, S.J. Molema to S.T. Molema, 9 August 1915.
459 UWHP, Molema Papers, A979Ac1, S.J. Molema to S.T. Molema, 29 June 1916.
460 UWHP, Molema Papers, A979Ac1, S.J. Molema to J. Molema, 12 March 16.
461 Ibid.
462 UWHP, Molema Papers, A979Ac1, S.J. Molema to S.T. Molema, 16 April 1916.
463 UWHP, Molema Papers, A979Ac1, S.J. Molema to S.T. Molema, 29 June 1916.
464 Ibid.
465 UWHP, Molema Papers, A979Ac1, S.J. Molema to S.T. Molema, 29 June 1916.
466 Ibid.
467 UWHP, Molema Papers, A979Ac1, S.J. Molema to S.T. Molema, 2 September 1916.
468 Ibid.
469 UWHP, Molema Papers, A979Ac1, J. Molema to S.J. Molema, included in S.T. Molema to S.J. Molema, 1 October 1917.
470 UWHP, Molema Papers, A979Ac1, S.J. Molema to S.T. Molema, 16 November 1917.
471 Ibid.
472 Ibid.
473 UWHP, Molema Papers, A979Ac1, S.J. Molema to S.T. Molema, 2 September 1916.
474 UWHP, Molema Papers, A979Ac1, S.J. Molema to S.T. Molema, 26 April 1918.
475 UWHP, Molema Papers, A979Ac1, S.J. Molema to S.T. Molema, 2 September 1916.

476 UWHP, Molema Papers, A979Ac1, S.J. Molema to S.T. Molema, 4 January 1918.
477 UWHP, Molema Papers, A979Ac1, S.J. Molema to S.T. Molema, 26 April 1918.
478 UWHP, Molema Papers, A979Ac1, S.J. Molema to S.T. Molema, 5 August 1918.
479 UWHP, Molema Papers, A979Ac1, S.J. Molema to Assistant Resident Magistrate, 5 August 1918.
480 UWHP, Molema Papers, A979Ac1, S.J. Molema to S.T. Molema, 15 September 1918.
481 UWHP, Molema Papers, A979Ac1, S.J. Molema to S.T. Molema, 18 October 1918.
482 Ibid.
483 Ibid.
484 Ibid.
485 UWHP, Molema Papers, A979Ac1, S.J. Molema to S.T. Molema, 1 November 1918.
486 Ibid.
487 Shula Marks, 'The Ambiguities of Dependence: John L Dube of Natal', *Journal of African History*, 27, 1 (1975), p.162.
488 Heather Hughes, 'Dialectical Dance: Exploring John Dube's Public Life', *South African Historical Journal*, 64, 3 (2012), pp. 418–433. Marks, 'The Ambiguities of Dependence'.
489 Marks, 'The Ambiguities of Dependence'.
490 Heather Hughes, *First President: A Life of John L. Dube, Founding President of the ANC* (Johannesburg, Jacana Media, 2011).
491 Brian Willan, *Sol Plaatje: A Life of Solomon Tshekisho Plaatje, 1876–1932* (Johannesburg, Jacana Media, 2018), p. 274.
492 University of Johannesburg Archives, TEBA Papers, American Board of Missions (1937–1947), NRC 224, Pad 2, R. Phillips to W. Gemmill, 09 October 1937. I am grateful to Rethabile Headbush for this reference.
493 Helen Bradford, 'Mass Movements and the Petty Bourgeoisies: The Social Origins of ICU Leaders, 1924–1929', *Journal of African History*, 25, 3 (1984), pp. 295–310.
494 Willan, *Sol Plaatje: A Life of Solomon Tshekisho Plaatje, 1876–1932*, p. 333.
495 Ibid.
496 Ibid., p. 334.
497 Ibid.
498 Ibid., p. 331.
499 Ibid., p. 337.
500 UWHP, Molema Papers, Copy of advertisement, A979Da, undated.
501 Willan, *Sol Plaatje: A Life of Solomon Tshekisho Plaatje, 1876–1932*, p. 337.
502 UWHP, Molema Papers, A979Da47, S.T. Plaatje to S.T. Molema, 3 August 1918.
503 Ibid.
504 UWHP, Molema Papers, A979Da48, S.T. Plaatje to S.T. Molema, 10 August 1918.
505 UWHP, Molema Papers, A979Da52, S.T. Plaatje to S.T. Molema, 20 October 1918.
506 Willan, *Sol Plaatje: A Life of Solomon Tshekisho Plaatje, 1876–1932*, p. 328.
507 UWHP, Molema Papers, A979Da55, S.T. Plaatje to S.T. Molema, 14 March 1919, Sechuana.
508 Ibid.
509 Ibid.
510 UWHP, Molema Papers, A979Da55, S.T. Plaatje to S.T. Molema, 14 March 1919, Sechuana.

511 UWHP, Molema Papers, A979Cc9, S.T. Molema to W.Z. Fenyang, 15 March 1919, Sechuana.
512 UWHP, Molema Papers, A979Da58, S. Plaatje to S.T. Molema, 1919 June, date unknown, Sechuana.
513 UWHP, Molema Papers, A979Aa2.88, S.T. Molema to S. Motshegare, 21 July 1919, Sechuana.
514 *Ibid.*
515 UWHP, Molema Papers, A979Aa2.87, S.T. Molema to M. Mankuroane, 16 April 1919, Sechuana.
516 Willan, *Sol Plaatje: A Life of Solomon Tshekisho Plaatje, 1876–1932*, pp. 371–372.
517 *Ibid.*, p. 379.
518 UWHP, Molema Papers, A979Da62, S.T. Plaatje to S.M. Molema, 5 August 1920, Sechuana.
519 *Ibid*. Italics in English.
520 Starfield, 'Dr S. Modiri Molema', p. 146.
521 UWHP, Molema Papers, A979Aa3.5.15, Agreement: S.T. Molema with 'Fingoes and Xosas', 24 March 1919.
522 *Ibid.*
523 SHMA, Sebopioa Molema Papers, Molebaloa, James, *The Barolong and Native Affairs Administration Bill, Native Affairs and Amacqumukwebe Tribe* (self-published, 1936).
524 *Ibid.*
525 *Ibid.*
526 *Ibid.*
527 UWHP, Molema Papers, A979Be1, E. Barret to L. Lloyd, 15 February 1917.
528 UWHP, Molema Papers, A979Bc3.2, S.T. Molema to R. Lloyd, 20 April 1917.
529 UWHP, Molema Papers, A979 Be1, Unspecified person to J. Montsioa, 5 September 1917.
530 *Ibid.*
531 UWHP, Molema Papers, A979Bd1, S. Minchin to S.T. Molema, 24 October 1917; A979Aa3, Notice from the Supreme Court of South Africa, Griqualand West Local Division, Israel Matlaba & others & Arie Kgosi (plaintiffs) vs John Bakolopang Montsioa and Johannes Arnoleous Graff, Acting Minister for Native Affairs (defendants); A979Bd1, S.T. Molema and others to S. Minchin, 16 February 1918.
532 UWHP, Molema Papers, A979Be3, A. Wilmot to Chiefs and Headmen, 23 December 1920.
533 UWHP, Molema Papers, A070Bd1 R.C. Lloyd to E. Barrett, 23 July 1913.
534 Alain Badiou, *Infinite Thought: Truth and the Return of Philosophy*, translated and edited by Oliver Feltham and Justin Clemens (London, New York, Continuum, 2003), pp. 39–57.
535 Pierre Lamaison and Pierre Bourdieu, 'From Rules to Strategies: An Interview with Pierre Bourdieu', *Cultural Anthropology*, 1, 1 (1986), p. 117.
536 UWHP, Molema Papers, A979Ad1, S.M. Molema to M. Molema, 9 July 1915, Sechuana. S.M. Molema stands for Silas Modiri Molema.
537 *Ibid.*
538 UWHP, Molema Papers, A979Ad1, S.M. Molema to S. Molema, 22 March 1920, A979Ad2; S.M. Molema to M. Molema, 9 July 1915, Sechuana.
539 UWHP, Molema Papers, A979Ad1, S.M. Molema to S.T. Molema, 17 June 1916.
540 UWHP, Molema Papers, A979Ad1, S.M. Molema to S.T. Molema, 10 July 1917.
541 UWHP, Molema Papers, A979Ad3, S.T. Molema to H. Molema, 04 August 1917.

542 UWHP, Molema Papers, A979Ad3, S.M. Molema to H. Molema, 22 June 1919.
543 UWHP, Molema Papers, A979Ad3, S.M. Molema to H. Molema, 24 March 1918.
544 *Ibid.*
545 UWHP, Molema Papers, A979Ad3, S.T. Molema to H. Molema 24 March 1918.
546 UWHP, Molema Papers, A979Ad1, S.M. Molema to S.T. Molema, 12 May 1918.
547 Interview, Leloba Molema, 1912 August, Gaborone.
548 UWHP, Molema Papers, A979Ad3, S.M. Molema to H. Molema, 15 July 1918.
549 UWHP, Molema Papers, A979Ad3, S.M. Molema to S.T. Molema, 10 July 1918.
550 UWHP, Molema Papers, A979Ad3, S. M. Molema to S. T. Molema, 5 August 1918.
551 UWHP, Molema Papers, A979Ad3, S.M. Molema to H. Molema, 19 May 1919.
552 UWHP, Molema Papers, A979Ad3, S.M. Molema to H. Molema 28 July 1920.
553 UWHP, Molema Papers, A979Ad3, S.M. Molema to H. Molema, 4 August 1917.
554 UWHP, Molema Papers, A979Ad3, S.M. Molema to H. Molema, 4 August 1917.
555 *Ibid.*
556 UWHP, Molema Papers, A979Ad1, S.M. Molema to S.T. Molema, 12 May 1918.
557 *Ibid.*
558 UWHP, Molema Papers, A979Ad1, S.M. Molema to S.T. Molema, A979Ad3, S.M. Molema to H. Molema, 18 April 1919.
559 UWHP, Molema Papers, A979Ad1, S.M. Molema to S.T. Molema, A979Ad3, S.M. Molema to H. Molema, 22 June 1918.
560 *Ibid.*
561 UWHP, Molema Papers, A979Ad3, S.M. Molema to H. Molema, 18 April 1919.
562 UWHP, Molema Papers, A979Ad1, S.M. Molema to S.T. Molema, 1 September 1919.
563 *Ibid.*
564 *Ibid.*
565 *Ibid.*
566 UWHP, Molema Papers, A979Ad1, S.M. Molema to S.T. Molema, 27 April 1920.
567 UWHP, Molema Papers, A979Ad1, S.M. Molema to S.T. Molema, 27 April 1920.
568 *Ibid.*
569 UWHP, Molema Papers, A979Ad1, S.M. Molema to S.T. Molema, 16 May 1920.
570 *Ibid.*
571 *Ibid.*
572 UWHP, Molema Papers, A979Ad1, S.M. Molema to S.T. Molema, 16 May 1920.
573 UWHP, Molema Papers, A979Ad1, S.M. Molema to S.T. Molema, 18 July 1920.
574 UWHP, Molema Papers, A979Ad1, S.M. Molema to S.T. Molema, 10 October 1920, Sechuana.
575 *Ibid.*
576 *Ibid.*
577 Modiri Molema, *The Bantu Past and Present: An Ethnographical and Historical Study of the Native Races of South Africa* (Alpha Editions, Edinburgh, 1920).
578 UWHP, Molema Papers, A979Da61, S. Plaatje to S.M. Molema 11 July 1920.
579 UWHP, Molema Papers, A979Ad1, S.M. Molema to S.T Molema, 10 October 1920, Sechuana.
580 UWHP, Molema Papers, A979Ad1, S.M. Molema to S.T Molema, 10 October 1920, Sechuana.
581 UWHP, Molema Papers, A979Ad1, S.M. Molema to S.T Molema 15 December 1920.
582 UWHP, Molema Papers, A979Aa4, P. Seme to S.T. Molema, 1 February 1918.

583 Ibid.
584 Starfield, 'Dr S Modiri Molema', pp. 160–162.
585 UWHP, Molema Papers, A979Aa1, H. Molema to S.T. Molema, 26 April 1920.
586 UWHP, Molema Papers, A979Ad3, S.M. Molema to H. Molema, 20 July 1920.
587 UWHP, Molema Papers, A979Be1, J. Montsioa to S.T. Molema, 8 April 1920.
588 Starfield, 'Dr S Modiri Molema', p. 162.
589 UWHP, Molema Papers, A979Aa1, H. Molema to S.T. Molema, 1 July 1920.
590 UWHP, Molema Papers, A979Be1, Superintendent of Natives to S.T. Molema, 24–26 July 1920.
591 UWHP, Molema Papers, A979Ad3, S.M. Molema to H. Molema 28 July 1920.
592 UWHP, Molema Papers, A979Aa4, Superintendent of Natives to S.T. Molema, 11 May 1922.
593 UWHP, Molema Papers, A979Aa4, S.J. Molema to H. Bud-Mbelle, 29 September 1922.
594 UWHP, Molema Papers, A979Ae1, Draft, H. Molema, undated.
595 UWHP, Molema Papers, Chief John Legal Affairs, A979Be4, Undated document of Supreme Court, c.1925.
596 UWHP, Molema Papers, A979Aa2.111, G.B. Gaseitsioe to S.T. Molema, 26 March 1924.
597 UWHP, Molema Papers, A979Aa1, J. Moshoela to S.T. Molema, 29 May 1925, Sechuana.
598 UWHP, Molema Papers, A979Aa2.9, L. Monnarora to S.T. Molema, 25 March 1921, A979Aa2.9, Sechuana.
599 Botswana National Archives (BNA), Gaborone, Government Papers, S. 13/4, R.C. Macgregor to High Commissioner, 5 April 1921.
600 UWHP, Molema Papers, A979Ac1, S.J. Molema to S.T. Molema, 27 June 1922.
601 Ibid.
602 Woods, *The Extraordinary Khotso: Millionaire Medicine Man from Lusikisiki* (Johannesburg, Jacana Media, 2007).
603 UWHP, Molema Papers, A979Ac1, S.J. Molema to S.T. Molema, 27 June 1922.
604 UWHP, Molema Papers, A979Ac1, S.J. Molema to S.T. Molema, 8 July 1922.
605 UWHP, Molema Papers, A979Ac1, S.J. Molema to S.T. Molema, 2 May 1923.
606 SHMA, Sebopioa Molema Papers, S. J. Molema to Mitchell, 12 February 1934.
607 UWHP, Molema Papers, A979Ac1, S.J. Molema to S.T. Molema, 2 May 1923.
608 UWHP, Molema Papers, A979Ac1, S.J. Molema to S.T. Molema, 29 May 1925.
609 UWHP, Molema Papers, A979Ac2, Minutes of Barolong Kgotla, 7 July 1926.
610 UWHP, Molema Papers, A979Ac1, S.J. Molema to S.T. Molema, 19 March 1926.
611 UWHP, Molema Papers, A979Aa3.1.3, P. Fincham to S.T. Molema, 6 May 1918.
612 UWHP, Molema Papers, A979Aa3.1.3, P. Fincham to S.T. Molema 6 May 1918.
613 UWHP, Molema Papers, A979Aa3.1.3, S.T. Molema to P. Fincham, 13 July 1918.
614 UWHP, Molema Papers, A979Aa3.1.3, P. Fincham to S.T. Molema, 25 May 1918.
615 UWHP, Molema Papers, A979Aa3.1.3, P. Fincham to S.T. Molema, 3 October 1918.
616 UWHP, Molema Papers, A979Aa3.1.3, P. Fincham to S.T. Molema, 28 May 1919.
617 UWHP, Molema Papers, A979Aa3.1.3, Wolhuter to S.T. Molema, 23 September 1919.
618 UWHP, Molema Papers, A979Aa3.1.3, P. Fincham to S.T. Molema, 26 September 1919.
619 UWHP, Molema Papers, A979Aa3.1.3, P. Fincham to S.T. Molema, 24 October 1919.

Notes

620 UWHP, Molema Papers, A979Aa3.1.3, P. Fincham to S.T. Molema, 31 July 1919.
621 UWHP, Molema Papers, A979Aa3.1.3, P. Fincham to S.T. Molema, 24 October 1919.
622 *Ibid*.
623 UWHP, Molema Papers, A979Aa3.1.3, P. Fincham to S.T. Molema, 14 January 1920.
624 UWHP, Molema Papers, A979Aa3.1.3, S.T. Molema to P. Fincham, 2 February 1920.
625 *Ibid*.
626 UWHP, Molema Papers, A979Aa3.3, promissory notes 25 June 1918 for J. Goosent, 1 June 1918, 1 August 1918, 19 February 1919.
627 UWHP, Molema Papers, A979Aa3, The children of Daniel Mokaka to S.T. Molema, 12 August 1919.
628 UWHP, Molema Papers, A979Aa3, Benefits Limited contract, 20 July 1920.
629 UWHP, Molema Papers, A979Aa3.1.3, P. Fincham to S.T. Molema, 17 February 1921.
630 *Ibid*.
631 BNA, Government Papers, S.168/5, V.F. Ellenberger to the Agricultural Officer, Lobatse, Barolong Farms: Agro-Economic Survey, by F.O.A. Wande, 16 September 1949.
632 UWHP, Molema Papers, A979Aa3.1.3, P. Fincham to S.T. Molema, 31 March 1921.
633 UWHP, Molema Papers, A979Aa3.1.3, P. Fincham to S.T. Molema, 2 April 1921.
634 UWHP, Molema Papers, A979Aa3.1.3, Unnamed to S.T. Molema, 3 April 1921, Sechuana.
635 See, the following section, 'Sons', below.
636 UWHP, Molema Papers, A979Aa3.1.3, P. Fincham to S.T. Molema, 22 April 1921.
637 UWHP, Molema Papers, A979Aa3.1.4, P. Fincham to S.T. Molema, 16 May 1921.
638 UWHP, Molema Papers, A979Aa3.1.4, P. Fincham to S.T. Molema, 16 May; 10 August; 4 October 1921.
639 UWHP, Molema Papers, A979Aa3.1.4, P. Fincham to S.T. Molema, 4 October 1921.
640 UWHP, Molema Papers, A979Aa3.1.4, P. Fincham to S.T. Molema, 5 June 1922.
641 UWHP, Molema Papers, A979Aa3.1.4, P. Fincham to S.T. Molema, 1 March 1922.
642 UWHP, Molema Papers, A979Aa3. S. Minchin to S.T. Molema, 04 July 1914.
643 UWHP, Molema Papers, A979Aa3, S.T. Molema's private notes on debt owed to Van Jaarsveld, 1922.
644 UWHP, Molema Papers, A979Aa3, J. Oosthuizen to S.T. Molema, 22 October 1922.
645 UWHP, Molema Papers, A979Aa3.1.4, P. Fincham to S.T. Molema, 8 August 1922.
646 UWHP, Molema Papers, A979Aa3.1.4, P. Fincham to S.T. Molema, 8 August 1922.
647 UWHP, Molema Papers, A979Aa3.1.4, P. Fincham to S.T. Molema, 8 August 1922.
648 UWHP, Molema Papers, A979Aa3.1.4, P. Fincham to S.T. Molema, 8 April 1923.
649 UWHP, Molema Papers, A979Aa3.1.4, Spencer and Kelly to Molema, 19 April 1923.

650 UWHP, Molema Papers, A979Aa3.1.4, De Kock and De Kock to S.T. Molema, 7 June 1923.
651 UWHP, Molema Papers, A979Aa3.1.4, S.T. Molema to P. Fincham, 13 October 1923.
652 UWHP, Molema Papers, A979Aa3.1.4, P. Fincham to S.T. Molema, 15 October 1923.
653 UWHP, Molema Papers, A979Aa3.1.4, P. Fincham to S.T. Molema, 19 October 1923.
654 UWHP, Molema Papers, A979Aa3.1.4, S.T. Molema to P. Fincham, 24 October 1923.
655 UWHP, Molema Papers, A979Aa3.1.4, P. Fincham to S.T. Molema, 26 October 1923.
656 UWHP, Molema Papers, A979Aa3.1.4, P. Fincham to S.T. Molema, 19 January 1924.
657 UWHP, Molema Papers, A979Aa3, Mitchell to S.T. Molema, 25 April 1924.
658 UWHP, Molema Papers, A979Aa3, Department of Mines and Industries to S.T. Molema, 13 May 1924.
659 UWHP, Molema Papers, A979Aa3, R. Wright to S. T, Molema, 1 July 1924.
660 UWHP, Molema Papers, A979Aa3, R. Wright to S. T, Molema, 15 June 1924.
661 UWHP, Molema Papers, A979Aa3.1.4, P. Fincham to S.T. Molema, 5 February 1925.
662 UWHP, Molema Papers, A979Aa3.1.4, S. T. Molema to J. van Zyl, 7 February 1925.
663 UWHP, Molema Papers, A979Aa3.1.4, P. Fincham to S.T. Molema, 20 April 1925.
664 UWHP, Molema Papers, A979Aa3.1.4, P. Fincham to S.T. Molema, 28 January 1926.
665 UWHP, Molema Papers, A979Aa3.1.4, J. Fincham to P. Fincham, 2 August 1927.
666 *Ibid.*
667 UWHP, Molema Papers, A979Aa3, S.T. Molema to Divisional Council of Mafeking, 31 May 1927.
668 UWHP, Molema Papers, A979Aa3, J.N. Kieser to S.M. Molema, 18 July 1927.
669 See for example, *Tsala ea Becoana*, 10 September 1910.
670 Willan, *Sol Plaatje: A Life of Solomon Tshekiso Plaatje*, p. 439.
671 UWHP, Molema Papers, A979Cc9, S. Msimang to S.T. Molema, 25 September 1924.
672 Willan, *Sol Plaatje: A Life of Solomon Tshekiso Plaatje*, p. 419.
673 John Mancoe, *First Edition of the Bloemfontein Bantu and Coloured People's Directory* (Bloemfontein, 1934).
674 School of Oriental and African Studies (SOAS) Papers of Silas Modiri Molema (1941–1966), GB 102 MS 380268, 19 January 1925.
675 *Ibid.*
676 *Ibid.*
677 *Ibid.*
678 *Ibid.*
679 *Ibid.*
680 Anne Digby, 'From Mahlangeni to Gumede: The Second Generation of Black Doctors in South Africa, 1913–1930', *South African Medical Journal*, 7, 6 (2007), pp. 424–429.
681 UWHP, Molema Papers, A979Ad5, R. Rowland to S.M. Molema, 30 November 1926.

682 UWHP, Molema Papers, A979Ad5, A. Moshoela to S.M. Molema, 27 March 1926.
683 *Ibid.*
684 UWHP, Molema Papers, A979Ad1, J. Moshoela to S.M. Molema, 27 September 1927.
685 Saul Dubow, *Racial Segregation and the Origins of Apartheid in South Africa, 1919–36* (New York, Springer, 1989), p. 89.
686 *Ibid.*, p. 44.
687 CTA, Native Administration in Mafeking District, 1 MFK 9 File 2/6/2, Native Administration Act, No. 38 of 1927 (1923–1931), Representations to Native Affairs Commission.
688 *Ibid.*
689 *Ibid.*
690 Dubow, *Racial Segregation*, p. 89.
691 CTA, Native Administration in Mafeking District, 1 MFK 9, File 2/6/2, Native Administration Act, No. 38 of 1927 (1923–1931), C. Loram to A. Wilmot, 20 April 1923.
692 CTA, Native Administration in Mafeking District, 1 MFK 9, File 2/6/2, Native Administration Act, No. 38 of 1927 (1923–1931), A. Wilmot to C. Loram, 5 May 1923.
693 CTA, Native Administration in Mafeking District, 1 MFK 9, File 2/6/2, Native Administration Act, No. 38 of 1927 (1923–1931), A. Wilmot to C. Loram, 5 May 1923.
694 CTA, Native Administration in Mafeking District, 1 MFK 9, File 2/6/2, Native Administration Act, No. 38 of 1927 (1923–1931), Secretary for Native Affairs to A. Wilmot, 22 May 1923.
695 CTA, Native Administration in Mafeking District, 1/MFK 9 N1/1/2 2/4/2/27, A. Wilmot to Secretary of Native Affairs, 10 March 1927.
696 *Ibid.*
697 *Ibid.*
698 Dubow, *Racial Segregation and the Origins of Apartheid*, p. 89.
699 SHMA, Sebopioa Molema Papers, Molebaloa, James, *The Barolong and Native Affairs Administration Bill, Native Affairs and Amacqumukwebe Tribe* (self-published, 1936).
700 UWHP, Molema Papers, A979Aa1, S. Molema to S.T. Molema, 3 March 1924.
701 UWHP, Molema Papers, A979Aa1, M. Molema to S.T. Molema, 24 April 1924.
702 *Ibid.*
703 UWHP, Molema Papers, A979Ad1, S.M. Molema to S.T. Molema, 27 April 1920.
704 UWHP, Molema Papers, A979Da62, S. Plaatje to S.T. Molema, 25 August 1920, Sechuana.
705 Colin Murray, *Black Mountain: Land, Class and Power in the Eastern Orange Free State, 1880s to 1980s* (Edinburgh, Edinburgh University Press, 1992). Colin Murray, *Black Mountain: Land, Class and Power in the Eastern Orange Free State, 1880s to 1980s* (Edinburgh, Edinburgh University Press, 1992).
706 UWHP, Molema Papers, A979Cb1.16, Agreement, C.R. Hulme and E. Molema, 15 May 1923.
707 UWHP, Molema Papers, A979Aa2.129, D. Marumoloa to S.T. Molema, 1 June 1927.
708 UWHP, Molema Papers, A979Cc11.1, Leteane to T. Leteane, 24 June 1924.
709 UWHP, Molema Papers A979Ad2, S.M. Molema to S. Molema 26 May 1921.
710 Willan, *Sol Plaatje, A Life of Solomon Tshekiso Plaatje*, p. 462.

Sons/Homecoming

1 Kenneth R.D. Manungo, 'The Role of the Native Advisory Council in the Bechuanaland Protectorate, 1991–1969', *Pula: Botswana Journal of African Studies*, 13, 1 & 2 (1999), p. 25.
2 *Ibid.*, p. 24.
3 University of the Witwatersrand Historical Papers (UWHP), Silas T. Molema and Solomon T. Plaatje Papers (Molema Papers), A979Ba1, Chief Montsioa to Queen Victoria, c. 1895.
4 Botswana National Archives (BNA), Gaborone, Government Papers, S. 13/4, J.C. Macgregor to S. Buxton, 19 December 1918.
5 *Ibid.*
6 BNA, Government Papers, S. 13/4, J.C. Macgregor to S. Buxton, 9 November 1919, Buxton to J.C. Macgregor, 15 December 1919, J. Ellenberger to S. Buxton, 26 January 1920; T. Sebosa to J. Ellenberger, 30 October 1920.
7 BNA, Government Papers, S. 13/4, J.C. MacGregor to S. Buxton, 2 November 1920; Manungo, 'The Role of the Native Advisory Council in the Bechuanaland Protectorate, pp. 42–43.
8 Michael Crowder, 'Tshekedi Khama and Opposition to the British Administration of the Bechuanaland Protectorate, 1926–1936', *Journal of African History*, 26 (1985), pp. 193–214.
9 *Ibid.*, p. 28.
10 Manungo, 'The Role of the Native Advisory Council in the Bechuanaland Protectorate', p. 28.
11 BNA, Government Papers, S. 13/4, Government Secretary to L. Montsioa, 4 March 1921.
12 BNA, Government Papers, S. 13/4, Government Secretary to L. Montsioa, 7 January 1922.
13 BNA, Government Papers, S. 13/4, J. C. Macgregor to A. Frederick, 27 May 1921.
14 John Comaroff, 'Class and Culture in a Peasant Economy: The Transformation of Land Tenure in Barolong', *Journal of African Law* 24, 1 (1980), pp. 85–113.
15 BNA, Government Papers, S. 13/4, G. Ellettelton to Government Secretary, 17 November 1920.
16 BNA, Government Papers, S. 13/4, L. Montsioa to Government Secretary, 30 January 1922.
17 BNA, Government Papers, S. 13/4, G. Ellettelton to Government Secretary, 11 January 1924.
18 BNA, Government Papers, S. 13/4, Government Secretary to G. Ellettelton, 23 March 1924.
19 BNA, Government Papers, S. 13/4, G. Ellettelton to Government Secretary, 15 January 1925.
20 BNA, Government Papers, S. 13/4, E. Ellenberger to A. Frederick, 8 February 1924.
21 BNA, Government Papers, BNB 235, Minutes of Advisory Council, 18 March 1924.
22 Manungo, 'The Role of the Native Advisory Council in the Bechuanaland Protectorate', pp. 29–30.
23 *Ibid.*
24 BNA, Government Papers, BNB 239, Minutes of Native Advisory Council, 26 and 27 April 1928.

Notes

25 BNA, Government Papers, S. 16/1, A. Frederick to R. Daniel, 22 August 1928.
26 BNA, Government Papers, BNB 240, Minutes of Native Advisory Council, 12 and 13 March 1929.
27 Ibid.
28 Ibid.
29 Ibid.
30 BNA, Government Papers, BNB 237, Minutes of Native Advisory Council, 22 and 23 March 1926.
31 Manungo, 'The Role of the Native Advisory Council in the Bechuanaland Protectorate, p. 34.
32 Cape Town Archives (CTA), Native Administration in Mafeking District, 12 N1/1/5 (1936–1939), 'Complaint against Chief Lotlamoreng', S.J. Molema to Secretary of Native Affairs, 25 August 1936.
33 Ibid.
34 Ibid.
35 Signal Hill Mafikeng Archives (SHMA), Sebopioa Molema Papers, Adventists pamphlets, undated. c. 1930s.
36 SHMA, Sebopioa Molema Papers, E. Molema to Rev. J.J. Mohau, 21 September 1933.
37 SHMA, Sebopioa Molema Papers, S. J. Molema to E. Molema, 15 October 1933.
38 CTA, Native Administration in Mafeking District, Native Administration in Mafeking District, 12 N1/1/2 2/4/4/27, L. Montsioa to Superintendend of Natives, 5 June 1933.
39 CTA, Native Administration in Mafeking District, 1/MFK 9 N1/1/2 2/4/2/27, S. Molema to Native Commissioner, 7 June 1933.
40 Ibid.
41 Ibid.
42 Ibid.
43 Ibid.
44 CTA, Native Administration in Mafeking District, 1/MFK 9 N1/1/2 2/4/2/27, transcript of hearing, 21 July 1933.
45 Ibid.
46 CTA, Native Administration in Mafeking District, 1/MFK 9 N1/1/2 2/4/2/27, Native Commissioner to Secretary of Native Affairs, 22 August 1933.
47 SHMA, Sebopioa Molema Papers, S.J. Molema to J. Ratshosa, 08 December 1933.
48 Ibid.
49 SHMA, Sebopioa Molema Papers, S.J. Molema to J. Kgosa, 7 September 1933.
50 SHMA, Sebopioa Molema Papers, S.J. Molema to A. N. Tonge, 11 September 1933.
51 SHMA, Sebopioa Molema Papers, S.J. Molema to E. Khumalo, 18 September 1933.
52 SHMA, Sebopioa Molema Papers, S.J. Molema to E. Molema, 23 September 1933.
53 SHMA, Sebopioa Molema Papers, S.J. Molema to E. Molema, 1 October 1933.
54 SHMA, Sebopioa Molema Papers, S.J. Molema to E. Molema, 15 October 1933.
55 Ibid.
56 School of Oriental and African Studies (SOAS) Papers of Silas Modiri Molema (1941–1966), GB 102 MS 380268S, Stockbook, c. (1932–1933).
57 BNB 246, Government Papers, 15th Meeting of Native Advisory Council, November 1932.
58 SOAS, Papers of Silas Modiri Molema, GB 102 MS 380268S, Stockbook, c. 1932–1933.

59 Ibid.
60 CTA, Native Administration in Mafeking District, 1 MFK 9, File 2/6/2, Native Administration Act, No. 38 of 1927 (1923–1931), Native Commissioner to Native Affairs Department, 21 October 1931.
61 CTA, Native Administration in Mafeking District, 1/MFK 15 N/1/5/18 Vol 2, S. Motshegare, M. Motshegare, L. Motshegare, M. Motshegare and M. Motshegare to Assistance Native Commissioner, 28 August 1936; L. Montsioa to Native Commissioner, 20 October 1936.
62 Ibid.
63 CTA, Native Administration in Mafeking District, 1/MFK 15 N/1/5/18 Vol 2, Resident Magistrate and Native Commissioner to Civil Native Commissioner, 15 December 1936.
64 SOAS, Papers of Silas Modiri Molema, GB 102 MS 380268S, Notes on cases of the Kgotla in Stockbook, c 1930s
65 Jane Starfield, 'Dr S. Modiri Molema (1891–1965): The Making of an Historian', PhD thesis, University of the Witwatersrand (2008), p. 148.
66 Michael Crowder, *The Flogging of Phineas McIntosh: A Tale of Colonial Folly and Injustice, Bechuanaland, 1933* (New Haven, Yale University Press, 1988).
67 SHMA, Sebopioa Molema Papers, S.J. Molema to J. Ratshosa, 14 September 1933.
68 Michael Crowder, 'Tshekedi Khama and Opposition to the British Administration of the Bechuanaland Protectorate, 1926–1936', *Journal of African History*, 26 (1985), p. 202.
69 Ibid., p. 212.
70 BNA, Government Papers, BNB 245, 14th meeting of Native Advisory Council, 18 November 1932.
71 Crowder, 'Tshekedi Khama and Opposition to the British Administration', p. 202.
72 Ibid., p. 206.
73 BNA, Government Papers, BNB 246, 14th meeting of Native Advisory Council, 10 July 1933, and Crowder, 'Tshekedi Khama and Opposition to the British Administration', p. 207.
74 SHMA, Sebopioa Molema Papers, S.J. Molema to J. Raphosa, 8 December 1933.
75 SHMA, Sebopioa Molema Papers, S.J. Molema to J. Raphosa, 1 January 1934.
76 SHMA, Sebopioa Molema Papers, S.J. Molema to J. Raphosa, 24 February 1934.
77 Crowder, 'Tshekedi Khama and Opposition to the British Administration of the Bechuanaland Protectorate', p. 209.
78 SHMA, Sebopioa Molema Papers, S.J. Molema to J. Raphosa, 1 March 1934.
79 For Tshekedi Khama's resistance and litigation against the proclamations of Natives Administration in the Bechuanaland, I rely again on Crowder, 'Tshekedi Khama and Opposition to the British Administration', pp. 206–211.
80 Crowder, 'Tshekedi Khama and Opposition to the British Administration', p. 211.
81 Compare Crowder. 'Tshekedi Khama and Opposition to the British Administration', p. 207 to BNB 245, 14th meeting of Native Advisory Council, 18 November 1932.
82 Crowder, Tshekedi Khama and Opposition to the British Administration', pp. 208 and 210.
83 BNA, Government Papers, S.426/9, 'Notes on Interview with Dr Molema', 27 February 1935.
84 Crowder, 'Tshekedi Khama and Opposition to the British Administration', p. 209.
85 BNA, Government Papers, BNB 241, 10th Meeting of Native Advisory Council, 15 April 1930.
86 Ibid.

87	BNA, Government Papers, BNB 242, 11th Meeting of Natives Advisory Council, 19 May 1931.
88	*Ibid.*
89	*Ibid.*
90	BNA, Government Papers, S. 429/8, E.C.F. Garraway to S. Buxton, 4 October 1916.
91	*Ibid.*
92	BNA, Government Papers, S. 429/8, J. Ellenberger to L. Montsioa, 16 April 1925.
93	BNA, Government Papers, S.429/8, J. Ellenberger to A. Cambridge, 21 January 1927.
94	*Ibid.*
95	BNA, Government Papers, S. 429/8, R. Daniel to L. Montsioa, 9 August 1928.
96	BNA, Government Papers, S. 429/8, Registrar of Deeds to L. Montsioa, 20 August 1928.
97	BNA, Government Papers, S. 429/9, C. Rey to H.J. Stanley, 9 December 1931.
98	BNA, Government Papers, S. 429/9, J. Stanley to C. Rey, 24 December 1931.
99	BNA, Government Papers, S. 429/9, L. Montsioa to 'the Government Office', 1 April 1933.
100	BNA, Government Papers, S. 429/9, A.H. Barnett to L. Montsioa, 22 April 1933.
101	BNA, Government Papers, S. 429/9, L. Montsioa to A.H. Barnatt, 1 May 1933.
102	BNA, Government Papers, S. 429/9, A.H. Barnett to L. Montsioa, 1 May 1933.
103	BNA, Government Papers, S. 429/9, L. Montsioa to Charles Rey, 10 April 1935.
104	BNA, Government Papers, S. 429.9, Report of C. Rey, undated.
105	BNA, Government Papers, S. 429.9, R. Reilly to C. Rey, undated.
106	BNA, Government Papers, S. 429, 9, J.H. Thomas to W. Clark, 27 August 1935.
107	*Ibid.*
108	BNA, Government Papers, S. 429/9, C. Rey to High Commissioner, 27 August 1935.
109	Richard Steyn, *Jan Smuts: Unafraid of Greatness* (Johannesburg and Cape Town, Jonathan Ball Publisher, 2015), p. 113. I mainly rely on Steyn where I wish to offer summaries of some of the key political events in the Union of South Africa after Unification in 1910, especially in the dominion's settler politics.
110	*Ibid.*, pp. 116–117.
111	*Ibid.*, p. 117.
112	*Ibid.*, p. 118.
113	Charles Feinstein, *An Economic History of South Africa* (Cambridge, Cambridge University Press, 2005), pp. 120–122.
114	Brian Willan, *Sol Plaatje: A Life of Solomon Tshekisho Plaatje, 1876–1932*, (Johannesburg, Jacana Media, 2018), pp. 507–514.
115	*Ibid.*, p. 556.
116	*Ibid.*, p. 557.
117	*Ibid.*
118	This is from an appendix of Plaatje's speeches in Modiri Molema, *Lover of His People: A Biography of Sol Plaatje*, translated and edited by D.S. Matjila and Karen Haire (Johannesburg, Wits University Press, 2012), pp. 105–106.
119	Molema, *Lover of His People*, p.96.
120	*Ibid.*, pp. 96–97.
121	For such an interpretation of 'homecoming', or of how being oneself is facilitated by narrative frames of remembering, forgetting and imagining, see Virgil, *The Aeneid*, translated by C. Day Lewis (Oxford, Oxford University Press, 1998), pp. 3–4.

122 Molema, *Lover of His People*, p. 97.
123 *Ibid.*
124 *Ibid.*
125 Steyn, *Jan Smuts*, pp. 121–128.
126 *Ibid.*
127 Molema, *Lover of His People*, p. 90.
128 *Ibid.*, p. 88.
129 The reference to Harriet Molema's death is in copies of Robert Setlogelo's papers, in Colin Murray's private archive for his book *Black Mountain: Land, Class and Power in the Eastern Orange Free State, 1880s to 1980s* (Edinburgh, Edinburgh University Press, 1992).
130 Emile Durkheim, *The Elementary Forms of Religious Life*, translated by Karen Fields (New York, The Free Press, 1995), p. 294.
131 *Ibid.*, p. 295.
132 *Ibid.*, p. 294.
133 Modiri Molema, *Mose: Mogogi le Moruti was Baisraele* (Johannesburg, Bona Press, 1961).
134 Molema, *Lover of His People*, p. 107.
135 *Ibid.*, p. 90.
136 *Ibid.*, p. 88.
137 SHMA, Sebopioa Molema Papers, S.J. Molema to E. Molema. 23 October 1933.
138 SHMA, Sebopioa Molema Papers, S.J. Molema to L. Mokolobala, 25 October 1933; S. Molema to Secretary of Mafeking Local Council, 13 November 1933.
139 SHMA, Sebopioa Molema Papers, S.J. Molema to Mrs. Gaisitsioe, 8 December 1933.
140 SHMA, Sebopioa Molema Papers, S.J. Molema to J. Ratshosa, 8 December 1933.
141 *Ibid.*
142 SHMA, Sebopioa Molema Papers, S.J. Molema to Assegain Tobacco, 8 December 1933.
143 SHMA, Sebopioa Molema Papers, S.J. Molema to M. Molema, 8 December 1933.
144 *Ibid.*
145 SHMA, Sebopioa Molema Papers, S.J. Molema to J. Ratshosa, 31 January 1934.
146 *Ibid.*
147 SHMA, Sebopioa Molema Papers, S.J. Molema to K. Makgothi, 2 February 1934.
148 SHMA, Sebopioa Molema Papers, S.J. Molema to M. Molema, 6 February 1934.
149 SHMA, Sebopioa Molema Papers, S.J. Molema to 'Mitchell of Western Exploration', 12 February 1934.
150 SHMA, Sebopioa Molema Papers, S.J. Molema to J. Ratshosa, 21 February 1934.
151 *Ibid.*
152 SHMA, Sebopioa Molema Papers, S.J. Molema to J. Ratshosa, 21 February 1934.
153 SHMA, Sebopioa Molema Papers, S.J. Molema to J. Ratshosa, I March 1934.
154 SHMA, Sebopioa Molema Papers, S.J. Molema to K. Mokgobi, 12 April 1934.
155 SHMA, Sebopioa Molema Papers, S.J. Molema to K. Mokgobi, 26 May 1934.
156 SHMA, Sebopioa Molema Papers, S.J. Molema to M. Molema, 27 August 1934.
157 SHMA, Sebopioa Molema Papers, S.J. Molema to M. Molema, 9 June 1934.
158 SHMA, Sebopioa Molema Papers, S.J. Molema to M. Molema, 27 August 1934.
159 SHMA, Sebopioa Molema Papers, S.J. Molema to Civil and Native Commissioner, 15 October 1934.
160 *Ibid.*
161 SHMA, Sebopioa Molema Papers, Office of Native Commissioner to S. Molema, 23 October 1934; S. Molema to Office of Native Commissioner, 8 November 1934.

162 SHMA, Sebopioa Molema Papers, S.J. Molema to M.L. Molefe, 6 November 1934.
163 SHMA, Sebopioa Molema Papers, S.J. Molema to Assegai Tobacco, 1 January 1935.
164 SHMA, Sebopioa Molema Papers, St. Mary's Mission to S. Molema, 26 March 1935.
165 SHMA, Sebopioa Molema Papers, Sentinel Publishing to S.J. Molema, 1935 March, undated.
166 SHMA, Sebopioa Molema Papers, S.J. Molema to J. Molebaloa, 3 May 1934.
167 *Ibid.*
168 BNA, Government Papers, BNB 252, 21st Meeting of Native Advisory Council, 26 March to 1 April 1940.
169 *Ibid.*
170 *Ibid.*
171 *Ibid.*
172 *Ibid.*
173 *Ibid.*
174 *Ibid.*
175 *Ibid.*
176 *Ibid.*
177 Steyn, *Jan Smuts*, p. 129.
178 *Ibid.*, p. 132.
179 *Ibid.*, p. 137.
180 Ellen Kuzwayo, *Call Me Woman* (Johannesburg, Ravan Press, 2017).
181 Saul Dubow, *The African National Congress* (Johannesburg, Jonathan Ball Publishers, 2000), p. 22.
182 *Ibid.*, p. 20.
183 Rhodes House Collection, University of Oxford (RHO) Collection of ephemera related to the African National Congress and Dr. S.M. Molema, Microform [19-], Micro. Afr. 551 (1 reel), 'Thoughts and Reflections on the African National Congress', 28 January 1943.
184 Alain Badiou, *Infinite Thought: Truth and the Return of Philosophy*, translated and edited by Oliver Feltham and Justin Clemens (London, New York, Continuum, 2003).
185 Interview with Ms Warada Molema, 2011, Mafikeng. The trip to Israel finds mention in Molema, *Mose*, p. 88.
186 Nelson Mandela Foundation (NMF), Letters of Nelson Mandela, N. Mandela to L. Molema, 31 August 1970. I am grateful to Galefele Molema for forwarding this letter to me, with permission from the Nelson Mandela Foundation. Interview with Ms Warada Molema, 2011, Mafikeng.
187 RHO, Modiri Molema, Micro, Afr. 551, 'Thoughts and Reflections on the African National Congress', 28 January 1943.
188 *Ibid.*
189 *Ibid.*
190 *Ibid.*
191 *Ibid.*
192 *Ibid.*
193 *Ibid.*
194 *Ibid.*
195 Derek Charles Catsak, 'Marching in the "Dark City": Bus Boycotts in South Africa

in the 1940s and the Limits and Promise of Comparative History', *Safundi: The Journal of South African and American Studies*, 8 (3) (2007), pp. 315-325.
196 Dubow, *The African National Congress*, p. 28.
197 RHO, Modiri Molema, 'African National Congress: A Critical Review', Micro, Afr. 551, December 1947.
198 Steyn, *Jan Smuts*, p. 147.
199 RHO, Modiri Molema Papers, Micro, Afr. 551, African National Congree Report, February 1946.
200 RHO, Modiri Molema Papers, Micro, Afr. 551, Minutes of meeting of African National Congress and Indian National Congress, 9 March 1947.
201 *Ibid.*
202 Steyn, *Jan Smuts*, p. 155.
203 RHO, Modiri Molema Papers, Martha Motlhakoana, Report ANC, Orange Free State Province, Micro, Afr. 551, December 1947.
204 RHO, Minutes of 36th annual conference of ANC, Bloemfontein, Micro, Afr. 551, December 1948.
205 *Ibid.*
206 WUHP, Molema Papers, A979Cc9, S. Msimang to S.T. Molema, 25 September 1924.
207 Minutes of 36th annual conference of ANC, Bloemfontein, RHO, Micro, Afr. 551, December 1948.
208 For this conception of regional identities, see Adrian Hastings, *The Construction of Nationhood: Ethnicity, Religion and Nationalism* (Cambridge, Cambridge University Press, 1997).
209 Minutes of 36th annual conference of ANC, Bloemfontein, RHO, Micro, Afr. 551, December 1948.
210 *Ibid.*
211 RHO, Modiri Molema, 'African National Congress: A Short Review', RHO, Micro, Afr. 551, December 1948.
212 *Ibid.*
213 BNA, Government Papers, BNB 252, 21st Meeting of Native Advisory Council, 26 March to 1 April 1940.
214 BNA, Government Papers, BNB 253, 22nd Meeting of Native Advisory Council, 21 April to 26 April 1941.
215 BNA, Government Papers, BNB 254, 23rd Meeting of Native Advisory Council, 13 April to 18 April 1942.
216 *Ibid.*
217 BNA, Government Papers, BNB 255, 24th Meeting of Native Advisory Council, 3 to 14 May 1943.
218 *Ibid.*
219 *Ibid.*
220 *Ibid.*
221 *Ibid.*
222 *Ibid.*
223 *Ibid.*
224 BNA, Government Papers, BNB 256, 25th Meeting of Native Advisory Council, 19 to 24 April 1944.
225 *Ibid.*
226 Atlantic Charter of 1941, FDR Library: http://www.fdrlibrary.org (accessed 2 October 2020).

227 BNA, Government Papers, BNB 256, 25th Meeting of Native Advisory Council, 24-19 April 1944.
228 *Ibid.*
229 *Ibid.*
230 *Ibid.*
231 *Ibid.*
232 SOAS, Papers of Silas Modiri Molema, GB 102 MS 380268S, Stockbook, Notes on Cases at Kgotla, c. 1932–1933.
233 *Ibid.*
234 Isaac Schapera, 'The System of Land Tenure on the Barolong Farms (Bechuanaland Protectorate): Report and Recommendtions submitted to the B.P. Administration, June 1943', *Botswana Notes and Records*, 15, pp. 33, 34, 35.
235 *Ibid.*, pp. 34–35.
236 *Ibid.*, p. 35.
237 BNA, S. 543/10, Barolong Tribal Affairs (General), RC Ellenburger to W.F. MacKenzie, 21 January 1947.
238 *Ibid.*
239 BNA, Government Papers, S. 543/10, Barolong Tribal Affairs, G. Ellettelton to W.F. MacKenzie, 22 February 1947.
240 BNA, Government Papers, S. 543/10, Barolong Tribal Affairs (General), District Commissioner to G.E. Nettleton, 2 June 1947.
241 BNA, Government Papers, S. 543/10, Barolong Tribal Affairs (General), L. Montsioa to District Commissioner, 1 September 1947; T. Tawana to Resident Commissioner, 25 February 1954.
242 RHO, Modiri Molema Papers, Micro, Afr. 551, Minutes of 37th annual conference of ANC, Bloemfontein, 15–19 December 1949.
243 See for example, Dubow, *The African National Congress*, p. 31.
244 RHO, Modiri Molema Papers, Micro, Afr. 551, Minutes of 37th annual conference of ANC, Bloemfontein, 15–19 December 1949.
245 RHO, Modiri Molema Papers, Micro, Afr. 551, See for example W. Sisulu's notice of a meeting of the executive, 1951 (otherwise undated).
246 RHO, Modiri Molema Papers, Micro, Afr. 551, Minutes of 37th annual conference of ANC, Bloemfontein, 15–19 December 1949.
247 RHO, Modiri Molema Papers, Micro, Afr. 551, W. Sisulu to ANC National Executive, 4 January 1950.
248 RHO, Modiri Molema Papers, Micro, Afr. 551, A.M. Kathrada to M. Molema, 28 February 1950.
249 RHO, Modiri Molema Papers, Micro, Afr. 551, Defend Free Speech Convention to M. Molema, 3 April 1950.
250 RHO, Modiri Molema Papers, Micro, Afr. 551, W. Sisulu to M. Molema, 2 April 1950.
251 RHO, Modiri Molema Papers, Micro, Afr. 551, W. Sisulu, V. V. T. Mbombo, D. Tloome, R. G. Baloyi, G.M. Pitjie and G. Radebe to J. Moroka, 9 April 1950.
252 RHO, Modiri Molema Papers, Micro, Afr. 551, W. Sisulu to M. Molema, 11 April 1950.
253 RHO, Modiri Molema Papers, Micro, Afr. 551, J. Moroka to ANC, National Executive, 12 May 1950.
254 RHO, Modiri Molema Papers, Micro, Afr. 551, Response of ANCYL, 31 May 1950.
255 *Ibid.*

256   RHO, Modiri Molema Papers, Micro, Afr. 551, *Lodestar*, Vol 1, No.1, May 1950.
257   RHO, Modiri Molema Papers, Micro, Afr. 551, W. Sisulu, Circular to National Executive, 22 May 1950.
258   RHO, Modiri Molema Papers, Micro, Afr. 551, M. Molema to J. C. Mavimbela, 25 May 1950.
259   RHO, Modiri Molema Papers, Micro, Afr. 551, W. Sisulu, Circular to National Executive, 02 June 1950.
260   RHO, Modiri Molema Papers, Micro, Afr. 551, W. Sisulu, Report on National Day of Mourning and Protest, 26 July 1950.
261   RHO, Modiri Molema Papers, Micro, Afr. 551, W. Sisulu to ANC, National Executive, 26 July 1960.
262   RHO, Modiri Molema Papers, Micro, Afr. 551, Report of Joint Committee, author unknown, undated.
263   *Ibid*.
264   RHO, Modiri Molema Papers, Micro, Afr. 551, Announcement (or report?) of Freedom Rally, undated
265   RHO, Modiri Molema Papers, Micro, Afr. 551, M. Modiri, fundraising letter, 4 July 1950.
266   *Ibid*.
267   RHO, Modiri Molema Papers, Micro, Afr. 551, A.W.G. Champion to M. Molema, 11 August 1950.
268   RHO, Modiri Molema Papers, Micro, Afr. 551, C.D. Modiakgotla to M. Molema, 1 February 1950.
269   RHO, Modiri Molema Papers, Micro, Afr. 551, C.D. Modiakgotla to M. Molema, 18 April 1950.
270   *Ibid*.
271   RHO, Modiri Molema Papers, Micro, Afr. 551, S. Msimang to M. Molema, 10 August 1950.
272   *Ibid*.
273   RHO, Modiri Molema Papers, Micro, Afr. 551, A.W.G. Champion to M. Molema, 11 August 1950.
274   *Ibid*.
275   RHO, Modiri Molema Papers, Micro, Afr. 551, S. Msimang to M. Molema, 10 August 1950.
276   RHO, Modiri Molema Papers, Micro, Afr. 551, Report of the National Executive Committee of the African National Congress, 38th Annual Conference to be held in Bloemfontein on the 15–17, December 1950.
277   *Ibid*.
278   *Ibid*.
279   RHO, Modiri Molema Papers, Micro, Afr. 551, M. Molema, General Pledge, 6 February 1951.
280   RHO, Modiri Molema Papers, Micro, Afr. 551, M. Molema to D. Twala, 15 May 1951.
281   RHO, Modiri Molema Papers, Micro, Afr. 551, M. Molema, Address to South African Institute of Race Relations, undated c. 1951.
282   *Ibid*.
283   Bantu Authorities Act, Act No 68 of 1951, Digital Innovation South Africa 2020, accessed 2 October 2020, http://disa.ukzn.ac.za.
284   RHO, Modiri Molema Papers, Micro, Afr. 551, Response to the Bantu Administration Act of 1951, anonymous.

285 *Ibid.*
286 *Ibid.*
287 RHO, Modiri Molema Papers, Micro, Afr. 551, M. Molema to M. Kotane, 5 March 1951.
288 *Ibid.*
289 RHO, Modiri Molema Papers, Micro, Afr. 551, J. Moroka, Presidential Address, 38th Annual Conference of the African National Congress, 15-17 December 1951.
290 RHO, Modiri Molema Papers, Micro, Afr. 551, M. Aucamp to W. Sisulu, 29 January 1952.
291 RHO, Modiri Molema Papers, Micro, Afr. 551, M. Molema, Opening of 20th Annual Congress of the SAIC, 25 January 1952.
292 *Ibid.*
293 RHO, Modiri Molema Papers, Micro, Afr. 551, M. Molema to S. Msimang, c. February 1952.
294 *Ibid.*
295 RHO, Modiri Molema Papers, Micro, Afr. 551, S. Msimang M. Molema, 13 February 1952.
296 *Ibid.*
297 RHO, Modiri Molema Papers, Micro, Afr. 551, M. Molema to S. Msimang, c. February 1952.
298 *Ibid.*
299 *Ibid.*
300 RHO, Modiri Molema, 'Thoughts and Reflections on the African National Congress', 28 January 1943.
301 RHO, Modiri Molema Papers, Micro, Afr. 551, M. Molema, 'The defiance of unjust laws: A historical parallel and warning', undated, c. 1952.
302 *Ibid.*
303 RHO, Modiri Molema Papers, Micro, Afr. 551, 'Demonstration throughout South Africa' 6, ANC, Bulletin No. 1, 6 April 1952.
304 RHO, Modiri Molema Papers, Micro, Afr. 551, M. Molema, letter to the editor, *Bantu World*, 19 April 1954.
305 RHO, Modiri Molema Papers, Micro, Afr. 551, Indictment in the Supreme Court of South Africa, Griqualand West Local Division, against Modiri Molema and ten others, 6 July 1953.
306 RHO, Modiri Molema Papers, Micro, Afr. 551, Notice in Terms of Section Nine of the Suppression of Communism Act, C. R. Swart to M. Molema, 11 September 1953.
307 RHO, Modiri Molema Papers, Micro, Afr. 551, M. Molema to S.C.R. Swart, c. 1953.
308 RHO, Modiri Molema Papers, Micro, Afr. 551, M. Molema, 'The Defiance of Unjust Laws: A Historical Parallel and Warning', undated, c. 1952.
309 South African National Archives, Pretoria, NTS 3097 1280/305, Hill & Fraenel Attorneys to Assistant Native Commissioner, 17 July 1942.
310 SAN, South African National Archive, Government Papers, SAB URU 2262, Assistant Native Commissioner to Secretary for Native Affairs (Pretoria), 17 July 1942.
311 SAN, Government Papers, NTS 3097 1280/305, Certificate issued by Department of Native Affairs, 3 September 1942.
312 SAN, Government Papers, NTS 3097 1280/305, Assistant Native Commissioner to Secretary of Native Affairs, 26 April 1945, 'Vryhof' 74, Mafeking. See also, SAB URU 2262, Office of the Prime Minister, Minute Number 2260, Leasing by Modiri Molema, AJE Holmes and PJ Eitner.

313 SAN, Government Papers, NTS 3097 1280/305, Minchin and Kelly Attorneys to Native Commissioner, 15 April 1948.
314 SAN, Government Papers, NTS 3097 1280/305, Secretary of Native Affairs to under-secretary, 7 May 1948.
315 SAN, Government Papers, NTS 3097 1280/305, Certificate issued by Department of Native Affairs, 21 June 1948.
316 SAN, Government Papers, NTS 3097 1280/305, Native Commissioner to Chief Native Commissioner of Western Areas, 10 November 1950.
317 SAN, Government Papers, NTS 3097 1280/305, Native Commissioner, Mafeking, to Chief Native Commissioner, Western Areas, 12 December 1950.
318 SAN, Government Papers, NTS 3097 1280/305, Secretary of Native Affairs to Chief Native Commissioner, 14 December 1950.
319 SAN, Government Papers, NTS 3097 1280/305, Native Commissioner to Chief Native Commissioner, 2 February 1951.
320 SAN, Government Papers, NTS 3097 1280/305, Chief Native. Commissioner to Native Commissioner, 6 February 1951.
321 SAN, Government Papers, NTS 3097 1280/305, Certificate issued by Department of Native Affairs, 6 February 1951.
322 SAN, Government Papers, NTS 3097 1280/30, Fraenkel & Gericke to the Secretary for Native Affairs, 6 April 1951.
323 Harvey Feinberg and Andre Horn, 'South African Territorial Segregation: New Data on African Farm Purchases, 1913–1936', *Journal of African History*, 50, 1 (2009), pp. 41–60.
324 SAN, Government Papers, NTS 3097 1280/305, Secretary for Native Affairs (W. O. H. Menge) to Fraenkel & Gericke, 5 May 1951; Reply by firm, 8 May 1951.
325 SAN, Government Papers, NTS 3097 1280/305, W.J.J. Hartzenberg to Minister of Bantu Affairs, 1 August 1960.
326 SAN, Government Papers, NTS 3097 1280/305, Secretary of the Minister of Bantu Affairs to W. J.J. Hartzenberg, 1 September 1960.
327 SAN, Government Papers, BAO 1/2438/D188/1401/53, Memorandum Department of Bantu Administration and Development, 9 June 1961.
328 SAN, Government Papers, BAO 1/2438/D188/1401/53, Secretary of the Department of Bantu Administration and Development, to the Registrar of Deeds, 16 June 1961.
329 SAN, Government Papers, BAO 1/2438/D188/1401/53, Registrar of Deeds to Secretary of the Department of Bantu Administration and Development, 27 June 1961.
330 BNA, Government Papers, S. 166/5/3, 'Barolong Farms: Leases of, General', Representation, Tiego Tawana and other, 26 July 1954.
331 BNA, Government Papers, S. 176/10/1, 'Tiego Tawana to Resident Commissioner, 25 February 1954.
332 BNA, Government Papers, S. 176/10/1, W. William (Divisional Commissioner Southern Protectorate) to Government Secretary, Mafeking, 16 June 1954.
333 BNA, Government Papers, S. 176/10/1, Representation, Tiego Tawana and others, 26 July 1954.
334 *Ibid.*
335 BNA, Government Papers, S. 166/5/3, Barolong Farms: Leases of, General', Divisional Commissioner Southern Protectorate to General Secretary, Mafeking, 31 July 1954.
336 BNA, Government Papers, S. 176/10/1, Native Commissioner, Union to Resident Commissioner, Bechuanaland Protectorate, 11 August 1954.

337 *Ibid.*
338 BNA, Government Papers, S. 176/10/1, J.D. A. Germond, Divisional Commissioner to Southern Protectorate to Native Commissioner in Mafeking, 13 August 1954, and Germond to S.V. Lawrenson, Government Secretary, 16 August 1954; Deputy High Commission to Resident Commissioner, Mafeking, 3 September 1954.
339 BNA, Government Papers, S. 176/10/1, Native Commissioner, Union to Resident Commissioner, BP, 11 August 1954.
340 BNA, Government Papers, S. 166/5/3 Barolong Farms: Leases of, General. Acting Deputy High Commissioner to Resident Commissioner, Mafeking, 4 March 1955.
341 BNA, Government Papers, S. 166/5/3, 'Barolong Farms: Leases of, General', Government Secretary, Mafeking to Divisional Commissioner Southern Protectorate, 25 May 1955.
342 *Ibid.*
343 BNA, Government Papers, S. 166/5/3, 'Barolong Farms: Leases of, General', Divisional Commissioner Southern Protectorate to Government Secretary, Mafeking, 18 June 1955.
344 BNA, Government Papers, S. 176/10/1, W. William (Divisional Commissioner Southern Protectorate) to Government Secretary, Mafeking, 1954 June 16, National Archive of Botswana, Gaborone,
345 BNA, Government Papers, S. 166/5/3 Barolong Farms: Leases of, General', 18 June 1955.
346 CTA, Native Administration in Mafeking District, 1/MFK 15 N/1/5/18, Vol 2, L. Montsioa to Native Commissioner, 25 August 1936.
347 CTA, 1/MFK 15 N/1/5, Vol 3, Assistant Native Commissioner to the Secretary of Native Affairs, 18 June 1941.
348 CTA, Native Administration in Mafeking District, 1/MFK 15 N/1/5, Vol 3, L. Montsioa to Assistant Native Commissioner, 27 July 1941.
349 CTA, Native Administration in Mafeking District, 1/MFK 15 N/1/5 Vol 3, S.J. Molema to South African Police, 11 May 1944.
350 CTA, Native Administration in Mafeking District, 1/MFK 15 N/1/5 Vol 3, S.J. Molema to Native Commissioner, 2 July 1948.
351 CTA, Native Administration in Mafeking District, 1/MFK 15 N/1/5 Vol 3, M. Molema to Marico Nurseries, 9 July 1949.
352 Interview with Ms Mercy Molema, 2011, Mafikeng, South Africa.
353 CTA, Native Administration in Mafeking District, 1/MFK 15 N/1/5 Vol 3, S.J. Molema to Native Commissioner, 9 February 1953.
354 See for example, CTA, Native Administration in Mafeking District, 1/MFK 15 N/1/5 Vol 3, 15 September 1953.
355 CTA, Native Administration in Mafeking District, 1/MFK 15 N/1/5 Vol 18, Native Commissioner's notification, 'Pay Raises for chiefs and headmen', 19 October 1953.
356 CTA, Native Administration in Mafeking District, 1/MFK 15 N/1/5 Vol 18, S.J. Molema to Native Commissioner, 24 January 1955.
357 CTA, Native Administration in Mafeking District, 1/MFK 15 N/1/5 Vol 18, T. Tawana to Native Commissioner, 24 January 1955.
358 BNA, Government Papers, S. 166/5/3, 'Barolong Farms: Leases of, General', Divisional Commissioner Southern Protectorate to Government Secretary, 31 January 1956.
359 BNA, Government Papers, S. 166/5/3, 'Barolong Farms: Leases of, General',

Divisional Commissioner Southern Protectorate to Government Secretary, Mafeking, 13 February 1956.
360 *Ibid.*
361 BNA, Government Papers, S. 166/5/3, 'Barolong Farms: Leases of, General', Divisional Commissioner Southern Protectorate to Government Secretary, Mafeking, 19 June 1956.
362 BNA, Government Papers, S. 166/5/3, 'Barolong Farms: Leases of, General', Minutes of Meeting on Good Hope, 29 June 1955.
363 *Ibid.*
364 BNA, Government Papers, S. 166/5/3, 'Barolong Farms: Leases of, General', Government Secretary, S. V. Lawrenson to (Deputy?) Attorney General, A.C. Thompson, 24 December 1956.
365 BNA, Government Papers, S. 166/5/3, 'Barolong Farms: Leases of, General', Attorney General to Government Secretary, S.V. Lawrence, 5 February 1957.
366 BNA, Government Papers, S. 166/5/3, 'Barolong Farms: Leases of, General', Government Secretary, S.V. Lawrenson to Attorney General, A.C. Thompson, 31 January 1957.
367 BNA, Government Papers, S. 166/5/3, 'Barolong Farms: Leases of, General', Attorney General, A.C. Thompson to Government Secretary, S.V. Lawrence, 5 February 1957.
368 *Ibid.*
369 BNA, Government Papers, S. 166/5/3, 'Barolong Farms: Leases of, General', Government Secretary, S.V. Lawrenson to Attorney General, A.C. Thompson, 12 March 1957.
370 *Ibid.*
371 *Ibid.*
372 BNA, Government Papers, S. 166/5/3, 'Barolong Farms: Leases of, General', Attorney General, A.C. Thompson to Government Secretary, S.V. Lawrenson, 21 June 1957.
373 BNA, Government Papers, S. 166/5/3, 'Barolong Farms: Leases of, General', Government Secretary, S. V. Lawrenson to Attorney General, A.C. Thompson, 18 July 1957.
374 BNA, Government Papers, S. 166/5/3, 'Barolong Farms: Leases of, General', Minutes of the Kgotla, 22 August 1957.
375 *Ibid.*
376 BNA, Government Papers, S. 166/5/3, 'Barolong Farms: Leases of, General', Kebalepile Montsioa to Divisional Commissioner of Southern Protectorate, 19 September 1957.
377 BNA, Government Papers, S. 166/5/3, 'Barolong Farms: Leases of, General', Resident Commissioner to Deputy High Commissioner, 21 November 1957.
378 BNA, Government Papers, Government Papers, S. 166/5/3, 'Barolong Farms: Leases of, General', J.A. Allison (Secretariat) to J.D.A. Germond.
379 Interview with Mr Batho Molema, 2011, Gaborone, Botswana.
380 NMF, Letters of Nelson Mandela, N. Mandela to L. Molema, 31 August 1970.
381 Nelson Mandela, *Long Walk to Freedom* (Boston, Little Brown and Company, 1994).
382 NMF, Letters of Nelson Mandela, Mandela to L. Molema, 31 August 1970.
383 Modiri Molema, *Mose: Mogogi le Moruti wa Baisraele* (Johannesburg, Bona Press, 1961).
384 John Iliffe, *The Africans: The History of a Continent* (Cambridge, Cambridge University Press, 2017).

Conclusion

1. Tom Brown, cited in John L. Comaroff and Jean Comaroff, *Ethnography and the Historical Imagination* (Boulder, West View Press, 1992) p. 165.
2. Hoyt Alverson cited in Comaroff and Comaroff, *Ethnography and the Historical Imagination*, p. 163.
3. Comaroff and Comaroff, *Ethnography and the Historical Imagination*, pp. 155–180.
4. *Ibid.*
5. *Ibid.*
6. Brown in Comaroff and Comaroff, *Ethnography and the Historical Imagination*, p. 165.
7. Gustav Klimt, *Death and Life* (Vienna, Leopold Museum, 1915).
8. Jan Vansina, *Paths in the Rainforests: Towards a History of Political Tradition in Equatorial Africa* (Madison, University of Wisconsin Press, 1990).
9. John Iliffe, *Africans: The History of a Continent* (Cambridge, Cambridge University Press, 2017); Jane Guyer, 'Wealth in People, Wealth in Things – Introduction', *The Journal of African History*, 31, 1 (1995), pp. 83–90.
10. James Ferguson, 'Declarations of Dependence: Labour, Personhood and Welfare in South Africa', *Journal of the Royal Anthropological Institute*, 19, 2 (2013) pp. 223–242; Paul Landau, *Popular Politics in the History of South Africa, 1400–1948* (Cambridge, Cambridge University Press, 2010); 'Land and Community in South Africa', *New Frame*, 17 September 2018.
11. See for instance Clifford Geertz, 'Deep Play: Notes on the Balinese Cockfight', *Daedalus*, 134, 4 (2005), pp. 56–86.
12. King James Bible, St Paul's letter to the Philippians 2: 12.
13. Max Weber, 'The Sociology of Charismatic Authority' in *From Max Weber: Essays in Sociology*, translated and edited by Hans H. Gerth and C. Wright Mills (New York, Oxford University Press, 1958), p. 246.
14. John Lonsdale, 'The Moral Economy of the Mau Mau: Wealth, Poverty and Civic Virtue in Kikuyu Political Thought' in *Unhappy Valley: Conflict in Kenya and Africa Book 2*, edited by Bruce Berman and John Lonsdale (Portsmouth, NH, Heinemann, 1992), p. 352.
15. John Iliffe, *Honour in African History* (Cambridge, Cambridge University Press, 2005).
16. Frederick Cooper, 'Reconstructing Empire in British and French Africa', *Past and Present*, 6 (2011) pp. 196–210.
17. Alain Badiou, with Nicolas Truong, *In Praise of Love*, translated by Peter Bush (London, Profile Books, 2012).
18. Alain Badiou, *Being and Event*, translated by Oliver Feltham (London, Continuum, 2005).
19. Karel Schoeman, *Promised Land* (Johannesburg, Jonathan Ball Paperbacks, 1979).
20. Adrian Hastings, *The Construction of Nationhood: Ethnicity, Religion and Nationalism* (Cambridge, Cambridge University Press, 1997).
21. On the theme of land in these former reserves see for example, *Land, Law and Chiefs in Rural South Africa: Contested Histories and Current Struggle*, edited by William Beinart, Rosalie Kingwill and Gavin Capps (Johannesburg, Wits University Press, 2021).

Index

A

Abantu-Batho 121, 122, 193, 218
Abdurahman, Abdullah 189
Aborigines' Protection Society 164
Abrams, *Sergeant* 74–75
African Administration Proclamation (Bechuanaland Protectorate) 383
African Holy Catholic Church 169
African Methodist Episcopal Church 108, 110
African National Congress (ANC)
    and Bantu Authorities Act (1951) 356–358
    delegations to Britain 164, 215–218, 219, 251
    early leaders 250–251
    and generational conflict 38, 39
    and non-racism 358–359
    post World War II 325–327, 341–342
    Programme of Action 325, 326, 342, 343, 344–345, 346, 348, 351, 352, 360–361, 365–366
    as SANNC 2, 4, 34, 37, 113–114, 118, 133
    in World War II 317–321, 322, 323
    Youth League (ANCYL) 322–323, 325, 342, 343, 345–346, 349, 351, 352, 357, 366, 385, 402

African People's Organisation (APO) 344, 348
African Races Association (ARA, Glasgow) 192
African Students Association (Glasgow) 228
Africanism 323, 346, 359
Afrikander mine (Klerksdorp) 240, 307
Afrikaners 213, 316
agriculture 101–102, 312–313, 332–333
alcohol 88, 238–239, 265, 271, 384
Alfred, Thomas 107
Amos, *Mr* 173
Anderson, Benedict 25, 393
Anderson, Hoyt 388
anxiety 24, 25, 392, 393
apartheid 38–39, 325, 353, 358
Appelby, *Reverend* 191
Arden-Clarke, Charles 310, 311, 313, 327–328, 338
Arthur of Connaught, *Prince* 271
Assembly Hall for Natives (Kimberley) 214
Atlantic Charter (1941) 333–334, 336
Austral Africa: Losing or Ruling It (John Mackenzie) 208
authenticity 22–23

B

Badiou, Alain 224, 401
Bahurutse people 46
Bakoena people 66
Bamalete people 298
Bamongoato people 298
Bangoaketse people 48, 270
Bantu Authorities Act (1951) 354–358, 359, 371
Bantu Mens' Social Centre (Johannesburg) 211
Bantu Methodist Church of South Africa 309
Bantu National Congress 361
The Bantu Past and Present (Modiri Molema) 230, 233, 235, 250, 252–253, 262, 385
Bantu-speaking people 29, 31, 43, 45, 46, 96, 192
Barolong Educational and National Council 201
Barolong Educational and National Fund 201, 217, 220
Barolong Farms 55, 91, 92, 138, 162, 217–218, 244, 245, 264, 269–270, 271, 272, 295–296, 297–299, 338–339, 340, 341, 369–371, 372–374, 376–383, 384
Barolong kingdom 45–46, 48, 52
Barolong people
  identity 386
  legal status 200, 298, 337
    Rapulana 59, 53, 126, 127, 132, 134, 184, 185, 186, 187–188, 223, 224, 231, 237, 241
    Ratloa 53, 126, 200
    Ratshidi 3, 53, 54, 91, 126, 127, 132, 133, 134, 185, 223, 224, 231, 237, 276, 383
Barolong reserves 8, 33, 34, 38, 53–54, 62, 82, 96, 99, 121, 127–136, 151–152, 154, 155–156, 158, 161, 162, 200–201, 216, 220, 222, 223–224, 260
Barrett, Edward 134, 221, 223
Bathoen, Chief 67, 79, 84–85, 275, 278, 287, 288, 293, 311, 314, 329, 335–336, 337, 363, 374, 376–377, 378, 380, 383

Batlhaping people 7, 48, 167, 239
Batlokoa people 298
Bechuana
  and Britain 3–4, 5–8, 17, 26, 27, 80–81, 82, 97, 116, 301, 302, 396–397, 399
  economic relationships 29, 30–31, 32–33
  and *morafe* 47, 65
  see also: Sechuana orthography
Bechuanaland News 81
Bechuanaland Protectorate
  annexation of 2, 53, 289, 297–298, 387
  and British South Africa Company 55, 56, 92, 269
  chiefs 4, 38, 97, 203, 269, 272, 332–333, 334–335, 336–337, 400
  land 338–340
  and South Africa 138, 272, 273–274, 336–337
  white settlers 250, 272, 338–339
  and World War II 327, 333, 335
  see also Barolong Farms; Native Advisory Council
Bechuanaland Protectorate Native Administration Proclamation 287, 289, 290, 291, 296–297, 307
Bechuanaland Protectorate Natives Tribunals Constitution and Jurisdiction Proclamation 287, 288, 289, 290, 291, 296–297, 307, 313
Bell, Charles 63, 126, 133
Benefits Limited (pyramid scheme) 244
Beukes, G. 177, 178, 179, 180, 181, 183, 245
Bhambatha rebellion (Natal, 1906) 116
black farms 368–369
black middle class 116–117
blackness (*boncho*) 27
The Blazing World (Siri Hustvedt) 15
Bokwe, Roseberry 343, 349
Bopape, David 326
Borcherds, Petrus 47
Botha, Louis 135, 200, 213, 214
botho see personhood
Botswana *see* Bechuanaland Protectorate
Bourdieu, Pierre 10, 14, 224–225

boycotts 346, 349, 352
Boyes, G.J. 60, 103
British Bechuanaland 2, 8, 33–34, 53, 54, 55, 92, 97, 104–105, 387, 397
British imperialism 5–7
British South Africa Company (BSAC) 55, 56, 92, 269
Britz, Helena 369
Brotherhood movement 211, 212–213, 214, 218–219
Brown, J.T. 388
Buchman, H. 156–157
Bud-Mbelle, Isaiah 111, 218, 320
Burger, Ben 141, 174–175, 176, 177
Burnett, Amos 128
Burton, Henry 127, 130, 133, 134–135
Buxton, Sydney 214, 215, 217, 270, 295

C

Cachalia, Yusuf 347, 348, 352
Cape Corps 214
Cape franchise 56, 82, 264, 300, 303, 352, 397
Carlyle, Thomas 353
cattle 102, 217–218, 245, 270, 272, 273, 306, 313, 328, 332, 333, 399; *see also* foot and mouth disease
Cele, Elka 121
Chamber of Mines 218, 219
Champion, A.W. George 348, 350, 351
chiefs and chiefdom
    and ANC 357
    authority and prestige 54, 66, 67, 97, 98, 99, 104–105, 202, 204, 221–222, 223, 224, 239, 263, 274–275, 314–315, 333, 355–356, 397
    and Britain 6–7, 214, 215, 216, 269, 387, 396–397
    and education 77–78, 80, 82, 192–193, 265
    and land and property 29, 33, 34, 35, 36, 103, 154–155, 158, 163, 378, 380, 381–382
    and mines 197, 201, 240–241
    and native administration 131, 132, 133–134, 157, 195–196, 256–257, 258, 259, 260, 273, 283–284, 287, 290, 291, 293–294, 313, 326, 329, 331–332, 398–399, 400
    and Native Affairs Council (Bechuanaland Protectorate) 335, 336, 337, 399, 400
    as vocation 144
civil disobedience *see* Defiance Campaign
Cloverly (farm) 102
Cole, Fitzpatrick 248
colonial lives 20, 23, 25
Comaroff, Jean and John 5, 17, 18, 388
Communist Party of South Africa (CPSA) 344, 346–347, 360
Congress of Non-European Trade Unions 317
Cooper, Frederick 397
Coppin, L.J. 108
Crause, P. 99
Crosby, N.J. 140, 245
Crown Lands 54
cultural assimilation 43, 358

D

Daniel, Rowland 296
De Beers 213, 215, 320
De Clarke, C. 60
De Kock, J.W. 61, 84, 101, 120
De Kock & De Kock (law firm) 84, 124, 183, 247
death 388–389
Defiance Campaign (1952) 359, 360, 361, 363–365, 376, 402
Dennison & Cranswick (firm) 63
Diamond Fields 7, 52, 59
diamonds 244
Dickerson, T. 175, 177, 178, 179, 180
Dithakoaneng 167
Ditlharapeng 207
dog tax *see* taxes, dog
Dota (stock owner) 246
Dower, Edward 127, 128–129, 130, 132–133, 155, 157, 320
drought 8, 30, 85, 91, 93, 113, 114, 139, 159, 161, 271–272, 281, 307

Drought Commission (1923) 251
Du Bois, W.E.B. 27, 72, 109
Dube, John 80, 117–118, 121, 133, 210–211, 218, 250
Durkheim, Emile 24, 26, 304

E
economic freedom 347–348, 350–351
Elen, G.L. 295
Ellenberger, Jules 272, 295, 296
Emgwadi (school) 194
Endloveni (company) 240
European Advisory Board/Council (Bechuanaland Protectorate) 245, 272, 273, 274, 380

F
Fagan Commission 324
family 390
farm novels 95
fatherhood 389–390
Fenyang, W.Z. 217
Ferguson, James 390
Fincham, Edward 84
Fincham, Phoebus Marie 32, 137, 138–139, 140, 141–142, 174–176, 177–180, 181–184, 242–250, 295, 374, 389
Fincham, P.J. 374
Fincham & Co. General Dealers 246, 247, 248
Fincham & Sons 382
Fincham's Ironmongery Stores (Mafeking) 137
Fomatsohle, Piet 120
foot and mouth disease 282, 283, 305, 307
forced removal 369
Forsyth Thompson, A.D. 329, 334–335, 336
franchise 216, 303, 324, 359; *see also* Cape franchise
Freedmen's Aid Society (USA) 110
freedom 294–295
frontier society 10–11, 19, 20, 74
Frost, H.J. 134, 184, 187, 188

G
Gaboutloeloe, Theo 147, 198, 338
Gaboutloeloe family 97, 98, 119
Gaisitsioe, Chief 217
Gaisitsioe, *Mrs* 306
Gandhi, Mahatma 322, 347, 364, 365
Garraway, E.C. 295
gender 5, 25, 66
German South West Africa 53
Gladstone, William 52, 365
Glen Grey Act (1894) 295
gold 6, 244, 300
Good Hope (farm) 275, 284, 340, 370
Gordon, Sundel 139, 183
Goronyane, Joel D. 70–71, 118, 172
Goshen 52, 53, 126
Gouws, J. 374
Graham Remedies Co. 147, 167, 168
Grant & Pennycook General Merchants 84
Green, Graham 103, 105, 124–125
Green Point School (Kimberley) 238
Group Areas Act (1950) 345, 368
Guyer, Jane 390

H
Hall, Charles 158, 159–160
Hall, J.W. 158
Handbook of Tswana Law and Custom (Isaac Schapera) 310–311, 314
Harris, David 213
Hartzenberg, W.J.J. 368–369
Hastings, Adrian 405
Healdtown Missionary Institute 83, 143, 146, 148, 261
healthcare 250, 252
Heath, *Mr* 88
Heidegger, Martin 13, 24
Henderson, James 115, 145, 148
heroes 304
Hertzog, Barry (J.B.M.) 129–130, 133, 135, 150, 153, 216–217, 299, 300, 303, 315–316
Higgs, Ernest 368
Higgs, James 141, 177
Hlazo 285

Holdsworth, *Reverend* 225–226
Holmes, Abraham 366
homecoming 37, 294, 386, 391
Hon, Chaeng 100
Hornabrook, Richard 143, 145
horticulture 375
hospitals 334, 335
houses (concept) 29, 31, 32, 98
Hulme, C.R. 264
Hustvedt, Siri 15, 394
hut tax *see* taxes, hut

I
I.L. Purcell (law firm) 110, 111
Iliffe, John 390, 395
Immelman, Dirk 140–141, 142, 374
Imperial Conference (1930) 300
Imvo Zabantsundu 115, 118
Indaba 69–70
independent African churches 169, 171
Independent Order of True Templars 300
Indian community 324, 361
Industrial and Commercial Union (ICU) 211, 212
industrialisation 300
influx control 253, 324
initiation 64, 68, 71, 72, 76, 82–83, 271, 363
irrigation 311, 399
Irving, L. 139

J
Jabavu, Tengo 70, 115, 121
Jameson Raid (1895) 92
Jasper, Karl 13
Johannesburg 316–317, 322, 348
Joint Advisory Council (Bechuanaland Protectorate) 380
Jorissen, J.A. 150

K
Kanye 67, 79, 168, 203, 208, 209, 210, 217, 239, 270, 277, 280, 281, 306, 376, 377
Kathrada, A.M. 344
Kawa, Peter 76–77

Kay, John 84, 100
Kemp & Co. 84
Keyter, J.G. 157
Kgotla 65, 96–97, 129, 130–131, 132, 135, 173, 202, 259, 273, 278, 279, 283, 288, 293, 294, 332, 382
Khama, *Chief* 203
Khama, Davide 203, 207
Khama, Ella (née Moshoela) 307, 310, 375
Khama, Tshekedi 271, 274, 275, 278, 286, 287, 288–289, 290, 291, 310, 311, 314–315, 328, 330–331, 332, 334, 335, 336–337, 380, 400
Kikuyu people 17
Kilnerton 194
Klimt, Gustav 388
Klipputs (farm) 374
Koranta ea Becoana 26–27, 28, 63, 70, 71–72, 73–74, 75, 78, 79, 80, 81, 82, 83–85, 86, 87–88, 109, 116, 118, 119, 120, 140, 212, 219, 251, 330, 333, 392, 396, 400, 403
Korwe Pan (farm) 271, 374
Kotane, Moses 358
Kraaipan 230
Kromdraai (farm) 62, 92, 99, 158, 159, 160, 163, 281, 282
Kruger, Paul 53
Kunana 149
Kuzwayo, Ellen 317
Kwinana, V.M. 326

L
labour tax *see* taxes, labour
land
　as commons 28, 29, 35
　entitlement 33, 34, 43, 67–68, 98–99
　and settlers 95
　social aspects 73–74, 77, 122
Land Commission (1886) 104, 105, 126, 141, 185, 271, 313, 314
Landau, Paul 390
landless people 398
laws and customs *see* social rules
leadership 23–24

Lee, Edgar 93
Lefenya, Stephen 52, 56, 68, 152, 158, 295
Lekoko, *Chief* 123, 124
Lembede, Anton 322–323
Lemmer, P.J. 374
Lenchoe, *Chief* 217
Leteane family 264
Letsapa, Williams 200
levirate 50, 57, 200, 261
Liberal Party of South Africa 362
limit situations 13, 14, 16, 17, 19, 20
literacy 70–71, 75, 76, 81; *see also* schooling
Litner, Paul 366
Lloyd, R.C. 184–185, 186, 187, 202–203
Lobatse 91
locations *see* reserves
Locke, Alain 80
locusts 307–308
Lodestar 346, 402
London Missionary Society (LMS) 65
Lonsdale, John 395
Loosely & McLaren General Merchants 61
Loram, C.T. 256, 258
Lotlage (farm) 264
love 224–225, 401
Lovedale Missionary Institute 58, 60, 61, 62–63, 75, 79, 139, 144, 145, 146, 148, 342
Ludick, John 100
Luthuli, Albert 365, 385
Lyndhurst Road School (Kimberley) 147, 148, 194
Lyons, Richard 277, 280

M

Mabete (farm) 91, 92–93, 137, 138–139, 140, 141–142, 162, 175–181, 242–249, 374, 378, 379, 380, 382
MacDonald, Malcolm 291
MacGregor, J.C. 270, 271
Machabi, *Chief* 126
Mackenzie, John 6, 52, 208
Macvicar, Neil 145, 146
Madibespruit (farm) 57, 92, 163, 220, 224, 246
Maduo (Ncoa), *Chief* 162
Mafeking 62
Mafeking Mail 81, 102, 106, 128
Mafikeng 4, 49, 50, 52, 54–55, 58, 62, 92, 134–135
Mahoko a Becwana 65, 75
Mahony, W.J. 103
Malan, D.F. 299, 303, 316, 324, 359, 362, 364
Malan, F.S. 236, 258
Mamdani, Mahmood 36
Mancho, Setlhako 142, 179, 181, 183
Mancoe, John 252
Mandela, Nelson 316, 318, 347, 384–385
Mankuroane, Molaloe 218
Marks, J.B. 348, 358, 360
marriage 66–67, 197–198, 207–208, 261, 389–390, 401
Marumoloa, Anna *see* Molema, Anna
Marumoloa, Dichukudu Richard (Dick) 88, 115, 146, 228, 256, 264, 275, 288
Marumoloa, Emang *see* Molema, Emang
Marumoloa, Lekoko *see* Molema, Lekoko
Maseloanyana, Cornelius 169–170, 171
Masigo, J.D. 170
Matabele people 122
Matthews, Z.K. 348, 349, 385
Matusing (farm) 159
Maxeke, Charlotte 252
McIntosh, Phineas 286, 290
Mda, A.P. 326, 341–342, 343
Meintjies, P.F. 100
migrant labourers 196–197, 201, 292–293
Milner, Alfred 298
Minchin, Spencer Percival 28, 61, 63, 84, 85, 86, 87, 88, 93, 102, 124, 132, 177–178, 181, 195, 215, 247, 367
mines and mineworkers 196, 197, 201, 211, 240–241, 292, 333, 388
missionaries 7, 49
Mochosa Estate 318
Modiakgotla, Doyle 349, 350
Modise, Seiso 126, 134, 184, 186
Mogani, Mancoe 186
Moikangoa, R. 145
Moiloa, Israel 85, 217

Index

Mokaka, Daniel 244
Mokhehle, Ntsu 342
Molale, *Chief* 239
Molebaloa, James 135, 146, 147, 166–168, 198, 221, 222, 259, 260, 309, 357
Molema, Anna (née Marumuloa, previously Moshoela) 192, 226, 228, 256, 307, 317, 375
Molema, Batho 384
Molema, Emang (née Marumoloa also known as Emma) 68–69, 114, 205–206, 208, 228, 241, 265, 276, 277, 280, 281, 305, 307, 308, 310, 375, 376
Molema, Ephraim 162, 264
Molema, Harriet
    absence from the literature 5
    and administration 200
    aspirations 1, 405
    birth and death 60, 304
    marriages 198–199, 202, 228, 236, 237–238, 265
    and Modiri Molema 198–199, 202, 226, 227, 228, 237, 238
    and *morafe* 405
    schooling 143, 194
    and Silas Molema 5, 193–194, 195, 198, 199, 202, 238
    and Solomon Plaatje 124, 194
    as a teacher 193, 194, 195, 196, 238, 265
Molema, Hellen (née Moshoela) 307, 375
Molema, Isaac 4, 5, 48, 49, 51–52, 122, 199, 375
Molema, Israel 52, 61, 158
Molema, Joseph 75
Molema, Joshua 51, 52, 57, 60, 61, 79, 83, 88, 91, 108–109, 110, 111–112, 120, 158, 162, 186–187, 199, 203, 206, 207–208, 209, 320
Molema, Lesedi 318
Molema, Lucretia (née Hommel) 318, 385
Molema, Margaret 261
Molema, Matlho 276, 306–307, 308, 375
Molema, Mmaditshepe Mercy 375–376
Molema, Modiri
    and ANC 317–322, 323, 324, 325, 326–327, 341, 342, 343, 344, 345, 346, 348, 349, 350, 351, 358, 359–360, 361, 362–365, 384–385
    archive 12
    aspirations 1, 38, 211
    in Britain 189–191, 192, 225–226, 244
    in Cape Town 146, 147, 166
    childhood 63–64
    as a doctor 144, 145, 244, 252–253, 255–256, 261
    and Harriet Molema 198–199, 202, 226, 227, 228, 237, 238
    and land 281, 282, 283, 366–369
    marriage 192, 256
    and *morafe* 39, 191–192, 252–255, 294–295, 337–338, 400–403
    and native administration 293, 299, 311–314, 315, 328, 329–330, 331, 332, 335, 336, 356, 371, 374, 377–378, 379–380, 381, 382
    and Native Advisory Council (Bechuanaland Protectorate) 271, 272, 275, 288, 291, 292, 310, 363
    schooling 83, 109, 143–148
    and Silas Molema 5, 143–149, 189–190, 192, 226, 229–236, 256, 262, 321, 403
    and Solomon Plaatje 58–59, 124, 143, 147, 148, 219, 229, 233, 235, 262, 303–304, 305, 321
    and South African Institute of Race Relations (SAIRR) 352–354
    and Walter Rubusana 144
    and women 225
    as a writer 262–263, 265, 385–386
Molema, Molalanyane 56–57, 209, 227, 228–229
Molema, Morara 261–262, 384
Molema, Officer 61, 196–197
Molema, Palo 162
Molema, Sebopioa
    as administrator 113–114, 128, 132, 133, 134, 135, 152, 156, 162, 164, 184, 187, 188, 189, 197, 199, 202–203, 205, 241–242, 261, 265, 272, 273–274, 275, 288, 289–290,

463

292, 293–294, 332, 333, 338, 369, 374, 375, 403
and ANC 217, 218, 331, 376
archive 11–12
aspirations 1, 38, 111–112
as bandmaster 309
in Bechuanaland Protectorate 203, 207, 208–209, 286
birth and death 51, 376
dismissal as administrator 277–280
and fathers (Joshua and Silas Molema) 5, 57–58, 108–109, 110, 111–112, 202, 203, 204, 205, 206–207, 208, 209, 210
health 280–281, 305–306
and land 241–242, 306, 307–309, 375
marriage 114–115, 228
in Natal and Transvaal 239–241
and Nora 110, 111, 115, 205
overseas and return to Mafikeng 109–110, 112–113
and religion 276–277, 280, 282, 306, 309, 375–376, 403–404, 405
as salesman 309
schooling 60, 61, 79, 83, 108, 143, 147
and Solomon Plaatje 217–218
as translator 309
Molema, Sefetogi 261, 307, 366
Molema, Seleje 57, 61, 109, 110, 143, 262
Molema, Silas Tawana
aspirations for family 1, 8–9
business and financial dealings 59–60, 61–63, 83–86, 88, 119, 123, 139–140, 146, 148, 173–174, 178, 227, 244, 246, 248, 250, 261
as chief, father and leader 30, 34, 56, 68, 133, 135, 136, 144, 214, 215, 217, 261, 387–388, 389, 392, 397
death 265, 304
and Harriet Molema 5, 193–194, 195, 198, 199, 202, 238
and James Molebaloa 166, 167–169
and John Montsioa 204, 236, 237–239
and land and labour 28, 29, 91, 92, 93, 97, 98, 99–100, 105, 137, 138–139, 140–142, 143, 152, 158, 159,

160–161, 163–164, 175, 176, 177, 179–184, 219–220, 221, 222, 224, 239, 242, 244–247, 263, 379
and legal cases 172, 173, 174
and Modiri Molema 5, 143, 144, 145, 146–149, 189–190, 192, 226, 229–236, 256, 262, 321, 403
and *morafe* 355
and newspapers 70, 72, 81, 83
and Phoebus Fincham 181–184, 242–249, 389
and religion 171, 172
and Sebopioa Molema 5, 57–58, 108–109, 110, 111–112, 202, 203, 204, 205, 206–207, 208, 209, 210
and *Sechuana* 26, 79
and Solomon Plaatje 5, 214–215, 65, 392
and South African Native Convention 117
Molema, Stella 261
Molema, Violet (née Plaatje) 384
Molema, Warada 318
Molema family
and anxiety 24–25
archive 11–12, 395
history 3, 4, 5, 6, 9, 12, 14, 18, 384, 387
house and land 4, 36
and local government 112, 131
and Montsioas 277–278
and *morafe* 2, 23–24, 27, 98, 391–392, 396
and Solomon Plaatje 1, 24
Molema Square (Mafikeng) 57
Moletsane, A. 78
Molopo diggings 248
Molopo reserve 54–55, 56, 92, 97–98, 100, 103, 104, 105, 106, 107–108, 111, 112, 113, 124, 126, 127, 128, 135–136, 137, 151, 153, 155, 156, 162, 185–186, 188, 202, 207, 220, 223, 224, 231, 241, 257, 258, 285, 332, 383, 397
Monnarora, L. 239
Montsioa, *Chief* 3, 49–50, 51–52, 54, 55–56, 63, 105, 126, 158, 185, 269,

272, 276, 278, 382, 385
Montsioa, Badirile 69, 79, 87, 88, 105–106, 107–108, 113, 125, 127, 132, 261
Montsioa, George 108, 112, 223, 379
Montsioa, John 188, 198–199, 200, 201–202, 203, 204, 207, 214–215, 223, 236–237, 238, 317
Montsioa, Kebalepile 340–341, 371, 372, 374, 376–377, 378, 379, 380, 382–383
Montsioa, Lekoko (formerly Marumoloa) 113, 115, 125–126, 128, 130, 132, 133, 134–135, 136–137, 140, 141, 142, 152, 153, 162, 184, 185, 187, 188, 195, 199, 208, 222
Montsioa, Lotlamoreng K. 199–200, 204, 236, 237, 241, 256, 258, 264, 270, 271, 272, 275, 276, 277–279, 280, 284, 285–286, 288, 293, 295, 296, 297, 332, 339–341, 369–370, 371, 379, 381
Montsioa, Paul 132, 133, 134, 184, 186, 223
Montsioa, Wessels 63, 78–79, 103, 276
Montsioa family 3, 97, 98
Monyatsi, J. 70
morafe (nation; as concept) 2, 12, 21–22, 44, 47, 70, 76, 192, 253, 386, 391, 392–393
Moroka, *Chief* 78, 361, 362, 385
Moroka, James 228, 250, 317, 342, 343–344, 345, 346, 348, 349, 350, 358, 359
Mosaka, J.N.R. 170–171
Mosekare, Ramathiledi 186
Moses (biblical figure) 386
Moses, Jacob 86
Moshoela, Anna *see* Molema, Anna
Moshoela, Joshua 139–140, 228, 238–239
Moshoela, Molema 88
Mosiba reserve 153
Mosibi, John 136
Mosigo, *Reverend* 170, 171
Mothibi, Sejesho 188, 223
Motlaba, Monchosi 187
Motlhakoana, Martha 325
Motlhokaditse 230

Motshegare, Phetogare 378
Motshegare, Phillip 197
Motshegare, Tantinyane 172–173
Motshegare family 98, 284
Motshumi, J. 147, 148
Motuba, George 134, 184, 186
Mpotokoane, Moutloatsi 330
Msimang, Selby 251, 252, 325, 341, 348, 350–351, 357, 360–362
Murman, Nills Frederick 102
Murray, *Mrs* 86, 87

N
Natal 239–240
nation (as concept) *see morafe*
National Minded Bloc 360
nationhood and nationalism 14–15, 20–21, 23, 25, 38, 39, 211, 321–322, 337, 395, 396, 397, 400, 401–402, 405–407
native administration 130–132, 155, 157, 221, 258, 260–261, 273, 283–285, 288, 294, 303, 329–330, 331, 332, 333, 398, 399, 400
Native Administration Act (1927) 35, 258–259, 260, 264, 279, 283, 355, 398–399
Native Advisory Council (Bechuanaland Protectorate) 37, 38, 270–271, 272–273, 274–275, 296, 310, 315, 332, 335, 336, 356, 363
Native Affairs Act (1920) 251, 256
Native Affairs Administration Bill (1917) 221, 222, 260
Native Affairs Commission (1920) 251, 256, 258
native commissioners 36, 38–39, 130–132, 135, 137, 155, 221, 222, 224, 241, 259–260, 355, 398
Native Fund (Bechuanaland Protectorate) 332
Native Life in South Africa (Solomon Plaatje) 164–165, 220–221
Native Locations Act (1884) 54, 105, 106, 107, 125
Native Races Committee 164
Native Recruiting Corporation (NRC)

218, 354, 374
Native Trust and Land Act (1937) 303
Natives Land Act (1913) 34–35, 153, 155, 156, 157, 160–161, 162, 163, 164, 165, 171–172, 192–193, 203, 212, 218, 219, 220, 221, 252, 254, 257, 260, 263, 264, 355, 368, 397, 398, 403
Natives Land Commission (Beaumont, 1916) 219–220
Nell, O. 100
Njongwe, James 342, 343, 344
Nora (friend of Sebopioa Molema) 110, 111, 115, 205
Northerners *see* white settlers
Nourse, Henry 52
Nourse mine 197

O

Ohlange Institute 80, 117–118
Oosthuizen, J. 246
Oppenheimer, E. 320
Orbell (Phoebus Fincham's son-in-law) 246–247, 248
Our Heritage 300–301

P

Padmore, George 269
Papename (quarry headman) 242
passive resistance *see* Defiance Campaign
patent medicine 118
patriarchy 65, 67–68
Paynter, J.J. 100
peasantry 26–27, 75, 76, 77, 114
personhood (*botho*) 2, 12, 14, 15, 16, 17, 20–21, 23, 24, 27, 35, 43, 44, 64–65, 222, 386, 388, 389, 390–392, 393–395, 403, 406–407
Phetu, Richard 197
Phillips, Ray 211
Phoi, G. 124
Phokoanyane, Hermanus 186
Pienaar, Charles 134
Pilane, Isaac 292
Pilane, Isang 270–271, 273, 275, 293
Pitsane Photlokwe (farm) 140
Pitsane siding 91, 138, 245

Plaatje, Elizabeth (née Mbelle) 122
Plaatje, Monnapula 119, 162
Plaatje, Solomon
  and ANC 118, 121, 133, 212, 215–216, 218, 250, 320, 344
  biography of 386
  and Brotherhood 211, 212–213, 214, 219
  death of 303–304, 305
  early life and education 76, 77–78
  family and home 118–119, 239
  finances 119–120, 211, 219
  and Harriet Molema 124, 194
  and identity 301–303, 396–397
  as an intellectual 58–59, 80, 304–305, 395
  as a journalist 72, 78, 82, 83–84, 86, 88, 115, 116, 117, 118, 120, 121, 123–124, 218–219, 300–301
  and land 73–74, 135, 163, 164, 210, 212, 220, 222, 251–252, 259, 357
  marriage 122, 123, 124
  and Modiri Molema 58–59, 124, 143, 147, 148, 219, 229, 233, 235, 262, 303–304, 305, 321
  and Molema family 1, 24
  and *morafe* 27–28, 396–397
  and religion 108, 214
  and Sebopioa Molema 217–218
  and *Sechuana* 26, 333
  and Silas Molema 5, 214–215, 265, 392
  as singer 384
  as writer 81, 128
  and the young 68
placement (*peo*) 28–29, 30, 31, 32, 34, 95, 96, 98–99, 154, 155, 161, 312–313
P.M. Fincham & Sons 378–379
Pollard, Theuns 369
poor whites 300, 303
Pound, Ezra 80
Pretorius, Gert 243
Prins, Francois Jacobus 369
private farms 54, 163, 185, 263, 264, 338–339, 377
private property 30–32, 33, 35, 55, 68, 163, 164, 373

Programme of Action *see* African National Congress, Programme of Action
Promised Land (Karel Schoeman) 15–16, 404–405
Protectorate Emergency and Development Fund 270, 272, 273, 275
Protestantism 48–50
Pueng (niece of Tantinyane Motshegare) 172–173

R

race classification 4–5, 8, 33, 169, 191–192, 265
Radebe, Gaur 341
railways 101, 102
Ramah (farm) 295, 374, 379
Ramohanoe, C.S. 358
Ranger, Terence 22, 23
Rapulana Barolong *see* Barolong people, Rapulana
Ratloa Baralong *see* Barolong people, Ratlou
Ratshidi Barolong *see* Barolong people, Ratshidi
Ratshosa, John 280, 286, 287, 305
regionalism 325–326
Reilly, R. 297
Representation of Natives Act (1936) 303
reserves 34, 35, 97, 104–105, 107, 165, 220–221, 251, 257, 325, 398; *see also* specific names
revolution and evolution 353–354
Rey, Charles 286, 287, 290, 291, 293, 294, 296–297, 299, 313, 339, 340, 356, 380, 381
Rhodes, Cecil John 55
Riceour, Paul 18
Rietfontein (Lotlhokane) 48, 49, 50, 51, 55, 125, 126–127, 132, 134, 136–137, 158, 184–188, 189, 199, 223, 224, 231, 236, 257, 397, 398
rinderpest 59, 60, 282
Robben Island 167
Robinson, George 188
Robinson, J. 84
Rolland, George 119, 194–195
Roos, J 133
Rosenberg (debtor of Solomon Plaatje) 119
Rowland, Edgar 152, 161
Rowland, Edward 158–159
Rowland, Richard 158–159, 161, 173, 256
Rubusana, Walter 144, 250, 320

S

S. Kemp & Co. 366
San people 45, 47
Sanger family 179
Sarra Kop (farm) 141, 142
Sauer, Jacobus W. 135, 136, 150–151, 152, 159, 162
Schapera, Isaac 38, 286, 310, 311, 315, 331, 332, 338, 341, 373, 380, 381
schooling 26, 27, 50, 65, 69, 72, 73, 75–77, 78, 79–80, 83, 194–196, 200, 330–331, 332, 396
Schreiner, W.P. 128, 134, 135, 151, 152, 289
Seabetse, Paul 67–68
Sechele, Macholohelo 66, 67
Sechele, Sebele 66–67
Sechuana and *Sekoa* 18, 21, 26, 27, 36, 37, 38, 47, 51, 65, 69, 72, 73, 78–79, 82, 291–292, 391, 399
Sechuana orthography 47, 300, 301, 310, 311, 333, 400
Segaloe, Mika 71
segregation 33, 153–154, 164, 169, 252–255, 402, 403
Sekhoma, R. 85
Selborne, *Lord* 138
self (concept) 13–14
self-reflexive consciousness 13
Seme, Pixley ka Isaka 80, 112, 113, 118, 121–122, 182, 189, 190, 212, 236, 252, 320, 357
Sethuntsa, Khotso 240
Setlagodi reserve 124, 153
settlements *see* economic freedom
Setumo (pseudonym) 192–193, 195
Seventh Day Adventist Church 276–277, 280, 281, 306, 307, 309, 375, 403

sharecropping 73, 94, 149–150, 153, 154, 157–158, 163, 166, 171, 222, 259–260, 368
Sharp, *Reverend* 191
Shippard, Sidney 53–54, 56, 97, 103, 105, 106, 116, 152, 153, 185, 187, 200, 203, 223, 224, 269–270, 289
Signal Hill 114–115, 205, 241, 265, 305, 306, 307, 309, 376
Sisulu, Walter 325, 326, 342, 343, 344–345, 346, 347, 361
Skota, T.D. Mweli and family 192, 225
Smuts, Jan 213, 303, 315, 316, 322, 323, 324
Sobukwe, Robert 341
social rules 10–11, 20
Soga, Tiyo 69, 70
South African Indian Congress (SAIC) 324, 346–347, 348, 359–360
South African Institute of Race Relations (SAIRR) 352–353
South African National Native Congress (SANNC) *see* African National Congress as SANNC
South African National Union (SANU) 101
South African Native Affairs Commission (1904) 116–117
South African Native Convention 117
South African Native Labour Contingent 213, 214, 215
South African Railways 245
South African War (1899–1902) 8
Spanish flu (1918) 209–210
squatters 130, 135, 150, 151, 160, 317, 322, 338
St Mary's Mission (Mafeking) 309
S.T. Molema General Dealer 250
Stanley, Herbert J. 287–288, 296
Stellaland 53
Strickland, Charles Slater 367
Suppression of Communism Act (1950) 345

T
Taberer, Henry 219
Tambo, Oliver 325, 343
Tantinyane (farm) 92, 100
Taoana, R. 162
Tawana, Joseph 162
Tawana, Tiego 197, 217, 275, 338, 341, 370, 371, 372, 374, 375
taxes
  dog 103–104, 105–106, 107, 132, 133, 137, 152, 193, 200, 384
  hut 92, 106–107, 142, 186, 195, 196, 207, 220, 260, 269, 270, 273, 274, 292, 298, 339
  labour 114
  native fund 298, 327–328
  war levy 328
Tebogo, Frank 72
tenants 93–94, 99–100, 102–103, 139, 159, 175, 339, 382, 383
tenure 311–315, 338, 340
Thaba Nchu 48, 123, 216
Thari, Phola 241
Thema, Richard Selope 251, 342, 358, 360, 362
Things Fall Apart (Chinua Achebe) 19–20
Thomas, J.H. 298
Tiger Kloof Native Institution 147
tiro (labour) 44, 46, 47, 50, 73, 388
Tiro-ea-Modimo (sub-chief) 285
Thompson, E.P. 30, 31
time (concept) 18–19, 20
Todd, A.H. 240
Tolstoy, Leo 347
Tonge, A.N. 277, 280
trading 92–93, 242–243, 247
tradition 19
Transfeldt, R. 92–93, 99
transport business 59–60, 142
Transvaal 97
Transvaal Indian Congress (TIC) 344
Tsala ea Batho 192–193, 195, 215, 216, 219
Tsala ea Becoana 112, 115, 118, 119, 120, 121, 123–124, 250
Tshongwana, E. 120
Tuskegee Institute 118, 251
Twala, D. 352

U

Uganda 155
Umteteli wa Bantu 218, 219
Union of South Africa
    and Bechuanaland Protectorate 138, 272, 273–274, 336–337
    flag 299
    and reserves 33–34, 104
    and settler state sovereignty 82, 216–217, 218, 300
    in World War I 213
    in World War II 315–316, 317, 322
United Nations Charter 323–324, 346
United Party 303, 322
University of Glasgow 226
Urban Areas Act (1923) 252

V

Van Biljon, Petrus 369
Van Jaarsveld, Stephanus 163, 246
Van Rensburg, G.F.J. 176, 177, 180, 183, 242
Van Rooyen, J.J. 100
Van Wyk (farmer) 180, 249
Van Zyl, J. 247
Vansina, Jan 19, 29, 389
vernacular newspapers 69–72, 115–116, 121–122, 193, 310, 305; *see also* individual titles
Verwoerd, Hendrik 368
Victoria Hospital (Mafeking) 255
violence 302
Vryhof (farm) 84, 92, 163, 246, 263, 281–283, 366–367, 368–369

W

Wallis, W.H. 245
Warren, Charles 289
Washington, Booker T. 27, 80, 117–118
Watkins, Owen 190
Weavind, George 128, 152, 188
Weber, Max 24

Welsh, E.C. 112, 114, 125, 127, 132, 133, 135, 160
Wenham, Charles 85, 86, 87
Wesleyan Methodist Mission School (Mafeking) 194–195
Wesleyan Methodist Missionary Society (WMMS) 48, 164, 166–167, 169, 170
Wessels, Daniel 127, 128
Western Native Township (Johannesburg) 316–317
Whales, George 86, 87–88
white farms 165, 167, 171
white settlers 6, 7, 8, 29–30, 31, 32, 45, 47, 52–53, 61, 74, 81–82, 94–96, 99–102, 103, 127, 128, 135–136, 137, 138, 153–154, 159, 167–168, 249–250, 272, 338–339, 373–374, 383–384, 395
Whiteley, Walker & Co. 57, 60, 61, 62, 63
Wilberforce University (USA) 83, 108, 109–110
Wilmot, A. 223, 258, 259
Wing, Ly 100
Wolhuter (farmer) 242–243, 244, 245, 247
women 65–66, 68–69, 70, 77, 78, 99, 101, 165, 193–194, 197, 225, 299–300, 317
Wright, Harry Roland 99
Wright, Richard 248

X

Xuma, Alfred 317, 318, 319, 321, 322, 324, 325, 326, 341, 342, 343

Y

Yokehon, *Mr* 100
Young Men's Christian Association (YMCA) 262

Z

Zion Gospel African Church 170, 171
Zonnebloem College (Cape Town) 109